ADHYATMA RAMAYANA

The Spiritual Version of the Rama Saga

Original Sanskrit with English Translation

BY

SWAMI TAPASYANANDA

SRI RAMAKRISHNA MATH
16, RAMAKRISHNA MATH ROAD,
MYLAPORE, MADRAS-600 004

Published by
Adhyaksha
Sri Ramakrishna Math
Mylapore, Chennai-4

**Total number of copies
printed before: 16,700**

VIII-2M 3C-12-2013
ISBN 81-7823-406-8

Printed in India at
Sri Ramakrishna Math Printing Press
Mylapore, Chennai-4

INTRODUCTION

THE personalities of Rama and Sita have become so deeply embedded in the minds of the Indian people that their story has found expression in the form of several Ramayanas. Some of these are: Valmiki's Ramayana, Adhyatma Ramayana, Vasishtha Ramayana, Ananda Ramayana and Agastya Ramayana in Sanskrit and Kamba Ramayana in Tamil, Tulsidas Ramayana in Hindi, Kirtivasa Ramayana in Bengali and Ezuthachan's Adhyatma Ramayana in Malayalam. For all these works on the Rama Saga, Valmiki's famous epic on that theme is the basis. But according to the fundamental objects, which the poet-devotees who composed the other Ramayanas had in mind, they have introduced many changes from Valmiki's composition. But all of them directly or indirectly pay obeisance to Valmiki's grand epic, which is called the Adhikavya (the primeval poem) in Sanskrit, and its author the Adikavi (the first of poets).

In an Introduction to the Adhyatma Ramayana, we have necessarily got to make a study in brief of the main difference between this text and Valmiki's epic. Valmiki's object seems to have been to describe an ideal human character, namely that of Rama, though he accepts Rama also as an Incarnation of Mahavishnu. But the divinity of Rama is kept in the background, although all through the narrative there is an attempt made to refer to that also symbolically as explicated by many interpreters of Valmiki Ramayana. The direct object of Valmiki's epic is made plain at the very beginning of that text in verses 1 to 18 of Chapter I of the Bala Kanda. It reads as follows: (1) "Once in all humility the austere sage Valmiki asked sage Narada, who was ever engaged in Tapas and Vedic study and who was the most noted among the knowers of the Vedas, the following question: (2) 'Who in the world today is a great personage endowed with all virtues, who is courageous, who knows the secret of Dharma, who is grateful, who is ever truthful and who is established in sacred observances; (3) Who has great family traditions, who has got sympathy for all creatues, who is most learned, who is skilful and whose outlook is ever kindly; (4) Who is courageous, who has subdued anger, who is endowed with splendour, who is free from jealousy, who when angry in the field of battle is a terror even to the Devas. (5) I am interested to know about this. My desire to know is intense. O sage! You have the capacity to know the real worth of a man.'

(6) "Being greatly pleased at these words of Valmiki, Narada the sage with the knowledge of the past, present and future, said, 'Listen', and began to give his reply as follows: (7) 'O great sage! The virtues that you have pointed out are many and very rare to be found in people. So I shall be giving you my reply after due deliberation. You now hear from me who that person is who is endowed with the qualifications mentioned by you. In the line of Ikshvakus, there was a prince named Rama who was very famous among men. He was possessed of self-control; he was powerful; he was endowed with splendour; he was firm in his resolve; he had the capacity to bring all under himself and govern. (9) He was highly intelligent and just; he was an accomplished speaker and possessor of all wealth. He was the dread of his enemies; he had sumptuous shoulders, long arms, conch-like neck and fleshy cheeks. (10) His chest was broad and collar bones invisible. He was the most noted of archers and a queller of all his foes. With arms extending upto the knees, his head and gaze were extremely charming. (11) His

height and attractive limbs were all proportionate to one another. All the limbs of his body were flawless; his complexion was shining; he was regal in his appearance, broad-chested and broad-eyed; he was endowed with beauty and all auspicious traits. (12) Established in Dharma and ever true to his words, he had the good of all creatures in mind. Far-famed, learned and pure, he was ever vigilant. He protected those who sought shelter under him—nay, he even subordinated his own interests to those of persons who thus sought refuge under him. Possessed of all auspicious traits, he was equal to Brahma himself. He ever protected his subjects and subdued his enemies. (13) A shelter to all living beings, he was the defender of Dharma and was ever devoted to his duties, always promoting the interests of his people. (14) He was interested in the truth of all the Vedas and their auxiliary subjects. He was not only versed in the science of arms, but had also the mastery of all the arts and sciences. His memory was most powerful and he had great powers of elucidating and explaining any subject. (15) Dear to all people, he was what a good man should be. He was given to both deep thought and to skilful action. As the ocean is ever accessible to all the rivers, so was he to all good men. (16) The worshipful personality that he was, he at the same time maintained a sense of equality with all, and was endowed with an outlook that cared for the interests of others. That dear son of Kausalya was endowed with every conceivable good quality. (17) In the gravity and depth of personality, he was like the ocean. In his capacity to bear heavy responsibilities, he was like the Himalayas. In valour and war-like qualities he was like Vishnu. In the mellowness of his personality he was like the moon. When his anger was roused, he was like the fire at the time of the world's dissolution. In patience, he was equal to the earth. In generosity he was a match to Kubera. In truthfulness, he was verily another Brahmadeva."

The object of an epic which begins with such a description of its hero is obviously to give us a picture of human perfection. This is not, however, to say that Valmiki does not recognise the divinity of Rama. When a personage is directly described as a Deity, he fails to be a model for human beings to imitate. Man's tendency with regard to such a personality is mainly to worship him. It was perhaps the recognition of this that made Valmiki propound the divinity of Rama only in subdued tones and paint him prominently as a great man. To make him human, the poet has even attributed to him some of the human weaknesses. But he takes care to see that Rama transcends them all, and teaches symbolically the great spiritual dictum of Saranagati, or resignation to the mercy of God. Vaishnava interpreters of the Ramayana have elaborately illustrated this teaching from various episodes in the life and doings of Rama. The most famous of those contexts is the episode in the Yuddha Kanda, where Vibheeshana takes shelter at the feet of Rama. Valmiki presents this teaching in his famous verse!

sakṛudeva prapannāya tavāsmīti ca yācate |
Abhayam sarvabhūtebhyo dadāmyetat vratam mama ||

It means. "It is my vow to grant protection to all who take refuge in me saying, 'I am thine', even if it be by an enemy in battle." Thus while describing Rama as an ideal human personality, Valmiki has not, however, forgotten to remind his readers that Rama is a divine incarnation and all his doings are by way of illustration of the great teachings of Vedanta. Exponents of Valmiki-Ramayana have discussed this elaborately in their writings and thus shown that while it is a great piece of literature, it is as holy and profound as the Vedas and that its study with devotion leads to man's spiritual and material welfare.

Coming to the Adhyatma Ramayana, its very name suggests the trend of its contents. While Valmiki's great epic is mainly a Rama Saga in respect of its direct meaning, Adhyatma Ramayana is a direct elaboration of its spiritual implications. While in the former Rama is a great hero, no doubt an incarnation of Vishnu, in the latter he is a Deity—Mahavishnu, in a thinly assumed mask of a man, held before all for worship. This is made plain in the very first chapter of the text. The whole text is in the form of a report of a conversation between the Lord Mahadeva and the Goddess Parvati occuring as a part of the Brahmanda Purana, whereas Valimiki Ramayana is recited by Lava and Kusa as instructed by sage Valmiki. The Adhyatma begins this way: (6) Once seated in a pavilion in the heaven of Kailasa on a diamond throne, luminous like a hundred suns, the three-eyed Deity Siva—who is the Supreme Lord, the bestower of refuge, the adored of the Siddhas and the abode of Bliss—was addressed with devotion by Parvati Devi, his consort, and the daughter of the mountains, in the following sin-effacing words. Parvati said: (7) ....(10) O lotus-eyed one! I have yet another question to ask about a supremely esoteric matter. Please reply first to me about that. It is a well-known fact that devotion to Rama, the Essence of all existence, is a secure ship for man to cross the ocean of Samsara. It is a well-known teaching that devotion to the Supreme Being is a royal road to liberation and that no means other than that is so secure for its attainment. Yet I have some doubts in respect of this......(12) Rama is said to be the Original Being transcending all the manifestations of the Gunas of Prakriti and unaffected by them. Accepting Him to be such, men devote themselves day and night without any laxity to his adoration and thereby they attain to the Supreme State. (13) Some people, however, say that in spite of being the Supreme One, Rama could not know himself to be the Supreme Self (Brahman) owing to the sway of the power of his own ignorance. When instructed by another (that is, by Brahma, as stated in Valmiki's Ramayana), he came to know the truth about the Transcendent Self. (14) If he had known the truth about himself earlier, how could he, the Supreme Being, be stricken with grief by the loss of Sita and bemoan his fate? If he was thus without the knowledge of the Self, how can he be a fit object of adoration, being on a par with all ignorant creatures? (15) Whatever explanation you may have got for this difficulty, deign to inform me of it and remove my doubt."

Mahadeva said: (16) "Never before have I been questioned by anyone on the truth concerning Rama, which is an esoteric doctrine, extremely profound and subtle. (17) I, who have been devotedly questioned and thus propitiated by you today, shall reply to your question after making due salutations to that noblest one of Raghu's line. Rama is the Supreme Self distinct from Prakriti. He is the one All-comprehending Being who is pure Bliss itself and the Spirit, supreme over all entities. Having projected all this universe by His power Maya-sakti, He dwells within and without the universe like the element sky. Though He is thus the resident within all beings, He is completely hidden from their vision, as He is their innermost self. He is the ultimate Seer and Witness of all this universe of His Maya's creation. (19) Before Him, the whole universe whirls as iron filings round a magnet. The unintelligent, with their minds covered by the power of ignorance (Avidya), know this not. On Him, Rama the Supreme Self, who is of the nature of Pure Consciousness, unaffected by Maya, ignorant Jivas superimpose their own ignorance and see Him as involved in worldly entanglements like themselves. Attached as they are to their own relatives and worldly assets, and involved in multifarious activities, they fail to perceive Rama dwelling within their hearts, just as they fail to recognise the presence of the golden necklaces adorning their necks. (21) In the sun, whose nature is luminosity, there can be no darkness. Even so, how can ignorance subsist in Rama, who is the condensation of Pure Consciousness and who is the transcendent and Supreme Self? A man of defective eye sight. whose vision is whirling, sees houses and other objects too as whirling. (The whirling movements of objects outside is only an attribution of his own whirling vision on them. So also men are deluded by superimposing on the Supreme Self egoistic actions of their own I-sense (Ahamkara), which in combination with the body and the senses assumes the role of the doer.) (23) In the sun, who is of the nature of unobstructible and changeless luminosity, there can be no day and night at any time. In the same way, in Rama, who is the Supreme Being Hari, who is the condensation of Pure Consciousness—how can there be knowledge and ignorance, the two changing states observed in limited centres of consciousness? (24) Rama, the noblest of the Raghus, is of the nature of Pure Bliss and Pure Consciousness that has no rise and fall. That lotus-eyed Lord is the witness of Ajnana (ignorance) and not a victim of it. Maya, the power of ignorance, is dependent on Him and therefore can never cause Him infatuation and ignorance."

A few verses after this we get a pointed statement of the above ideas in the following verse addressed by Sita to Hanuman. Sita says: (32) "Know Rama to be the Supreme Brahman, the Existence-Knowledge-Bliss Absolute and the One without a second. He is Pure Existence devoid of all adjuncts, whom the senses cannot perceive as their object. (33) Know Rama as Pure Bliss, as devoid of all impurities, as peace, as changeless substance, as free from the stain of ignorance, as all-pervading Spirit, as devoid of all disvalues and as the revealing Consciousness. (34) Know me to be the primeval Prakriti, the material and instrumental cause of the creation, sustentation and dissolution of the universe. In the mere presence of Rama, the Supreme Brahman, I, His Prakriti or Power, create the universe unwearied. (35) What I create in His mere presence, the ignorant superimpose on Him." She then explains what it is that is thus superimposed, and in doing so narrates in brief the incidents of Rama's life and concludes, saying: (44) "Rama walks not; He sits not; He sorrows not; He desires not, He abandons not; there is no trace of any activity in Him. Being pure Bliss itself, there is no movement, no transformation in Him. As He is the substratum of Maya, the changeful Nature of His, He underlies all these transformations of the constituents of Maya, and for those who cannot distinguish the substratum from the constituents of Maya, He seems to get transformed, whereas it is only the constitutents of Maya that undergo transformation."

Now this elaborate quotation makes plain that the object of Adhyatma Ramayana or the 'spiritual version of the Rama Saga' is to project Rama directly as the Supreme Self. But while doing so, the text takes care to see that He, who is the non-dual and uninvolved Self, is also the Personal Deity, the Supreme Isvara, who is to be adored and prayed to by all those who seek the knowledge of Non-duality described above. Bhakti of the most intense type is therefore taught, and it is also stressed that through devotion to Rama alone the saving knowledge would dawn in the Jiva. It pointedly says in verses 45 to 57 of the first chapter of Balakanda, well known as *Sri-Rāmahṛdaya*, "A devotee of Mine who understands the Supreme Truth is fit for My Status. On the other hand, one who ignorantly engrosses himself in the search for this knowledge in the pit of scriptural texts without any devotion to Me, never attains this knowledge of My nature. They will not have liberation too even in a hundred life spans." And further it is said, "This knowledge, which is superior even to the attainment of the heaven of Indra, should not be imparted by you to any conceited man who has no devotion to Me." (Ch. v. 53). Thus the teaching of the Adhyatma-Ramayana is only an elaboration of the declaration of the Svetasvatara Upanishad, "It is only in one who has supreme devotion to God and to his spiritual teacher that this Truth (knowledge of the non-dual Self), when taught, will shine." Sri Ramakrishna also emphasises this aspect of spiritual life in a beautiful parable. "Suppose a noble man has a big garden which he places under the care of a gardener. The gardener works hard and produces excellent fruits and vegetables all the year round. The master at last, in course of time, gets so highly pleased with him that he keeps him on his own seat and tells him that he is his own self. In place of seeking that place by the master's side by pleasing him through devotion, if he were to sit on that seat out of pride and greed, he will only be pushed away from it. Thus through devotion alone this Supreme knowledge is obtained." The Gita also declares: "Being gracious to those who are thus firmly devoted to Me, I destroy the darkness of ignorance in them, lighting the lamp of wisdom in them by My presence as their very self." (X-11).

Thus to establish Rama's divine status as an object of worship and devotion and to teach that Bhakti and Jnana are not only reconcilable but always go together—is the prime object of this great text. In order to achieve this objective, the Adhyatma Ramayana, while sticking to the main trends and incidents of the Rama Saga described in Valmiki's epic, makes various deviations here and there in the course of its extensive narration. To cite a few such examples: In the Adhyatama Ramayana, Rama at his very birth, reveals himself as the four-handed Mahavishnu. Rama's departure to the forest is only of his own making , and the intrigues of Kaikeyi and Manthara are only external pretexts brought about by his Maya.. The Sita who is abducted by Ravana is not the real Sita but an illusory double of hers. The real Sita is hidden by the Fire-deity. And finally at the end of the Yuddha Kanda Sita's entry into fire is only a ruse to take back the real Sita from the hands of the Fire-deity. Ravana, Kumbhakarna etc., know the spiritual identity of Rama, and are only seeking death at his hand, as a means for salvation. They know that 'devotion through confrontation' is a quicker path than that of Bhakti of the ordinary type. These are only a few striking deviations: there are many more of this type scattered all through the text. All these deviations are meant for preserving the Supreme status of Rama in the eyes of the devotees. More of such deviations are listed in the Appendix.

Another feature which distinguishes the Adhyatama-Ramayana is the large number of hymns sung by the various personages entering into the narrative as also the many philosophical discourses that are spread in various parts of the text. Besides teaching fervent devotion, these give a very simple and non-technical but profound exposition of the doctrine of non-dualism. This is a deviations from Valmiki's epic which contains no such hymns and discourses.

On the whole the general scheme of the text seems to follow the pattern set by the Bhagavata Purana in dealing with the life of Sri Krishna in its 10th Skandha. The aim of the Bhagavata Purana is declared in its dictum—*Kṛṣṇastu bhagavān svayam*—Krishna is really the Bhagavan Himself. The Adhyatma Ramayana seeks to provide the followers of the Rama cult with such an incarnation that is not merely a manifestation but is identical with the Deity Himself. This is achieved by Rama revealing himself as the four-handed Mahavishnu at his very birth, a feature that is not seen in Valmiki. It is for the achievement of this that many of the deviations from Valmiki are made. In most of the deviations, either whatever human imperfections there might be in Rama are explaind away or are made to be adopted with his previous knowledge in order to hide his divinity from unregenerate men. For example, the events leading to Rama's exile were superhumanly stage-managed by him, and Kaikeyi and Manthara were merely instruments he used to give the events the form of a court intrigue. The Sita who was abducted by Ravana was only a double and not the real Sita. Rama's weeping for Sita is expressly declared to be a mere assumption to look human in the eyes of men. The same object of deification of Rama is achieved by the numerous hymns addressed to him by the sages like Vasishtha, Parasurama, Bharadwaja, Agastya, Atri, Swayamprabha and others. The example of the Bhagavata Purana is very closely followed in respect of these hymns. They are couched in highly devotional language and all the attributes of the Supreme Deity are used for adressing Rama. Many of them are Advaitic in their philosophic content while their tone is intensely devotional. They again and again establish the doctrine that non-duality is the Supreme Truth but the way to its realisation is through devotion and divine grace. Without these, mere intellectualism will never bring spiritual illumination. Thus this great text seeks to reconcile Jnana and Bhakti as the obverse and reverse of an identical spiritual discipline, and being a text of the Rama cult, Rama is held forth as the Deity to be adored by those who seek salvation.

The Adhyatma Ramayana must have powerfully influenced the Ramayanas that came afterwards in regional languages. Though they all took Valmiki's great epic as the main source, the spiritual turn given to it by Adhyatma-Ramayana is reflected very strongly in the Ramayana of Tulsidas. While it is very doubtful whether it influenced Kamban's well-known Ramayana in Tamil, Ezuthachan's Ramayana, considered one of the greatest literary works in Malayalam, is a close translation of it, with its poetical and devotional excellence enhanced by that great literary man and Bhakta, giving to it the freshness of an original, inspired work.

A word in conclusion about the literary side of the text will not be out of place. Its poetry does not come anywhere near the epic grandeur of Valmiki but yet it is a text with considerable literary beauty and is couched in easy yet lucid Sanskrit with a highly devotional tone. Its authorship and date are unknown. It is purposeless to enter into the pure guess-work that modern scholars indulge in regarding these matters. However relevant it may be for scholarly purposes, it is of no use for those who approach the text from the devotional point of view,—just as counting the number of leaves on a mango tree is for one going to an orchad for eating mangoes. Valmiki's Ramayana was composed by that sage himself on the advice of Brahma. Thus advised, the sage through meditation recovered the whole history of Rama, composed a great epic on it in the Sloka form that he himself had devised, taught Lava and Kusa to recite it in a musical manner, and thus publicised it in the world. The traditional origin of Adhyatma Ramayana is quite different from this. It is a part of the Brahmanda Purana beginning from the 61st Adhyaya (chapter) of the first part of that text. Of all the Puranas, Veda Vyasa is the traditional author, and we can therefore attribute the Adhyatama Ramayana to him. There are, however, some modern scholars who guess saint Ramananda of the 14th century to be its author. Excluding the Uttara Kanda, it consists of six Kandas with 56 Sargas (chapters) comprising about 3643 verses. We have translated only these six Kandas, excluding the seventh chapter called Uttara Kanda, as it seems to be extraneous to Ramayana proper. The text is in the form of a conversation between Siva and Parvati, which is reported by Brahma to Narada. Though thus the traditional origins of these two Ramayanas are different, and though there are differences in the treatment of the subject, it should not be supposed that there is any contradiction between these. Both of them deal with the same history of Rama, and what Adhyatma Ramayana has done is only to make explicit what Valmiki has taught implicitly and indirectly in his great epic. As a much smaller text than that of Valmiki and complete in itself, it offers the devotees of Rama a smaller and directly devotional exposition of Rama's greatness which they can use in their daily practice of devotion. In conclusion it may be pointed out that Bhagavan SriRamakrishna refers often to Adhyatma Ramayana in his talks, thus drawing people's attention to the devotional importance of this text.

CONTENTS

ARANYA KANDAM

KISHKINDHA KANDAM

SUNDARA KANDAM

YUDDHA KANDAM

ADHYATMA RAMAYANA

THE SPIRITUAL VERSION OF THE RAMA SAGA

ॐ

अध्यात्मरामायणम्

बालकाण्डम्

प्रथमः सर्गः

रामहृदयम्

यः पृथिवीभरवारणाय दिविजैः संप्रार्थितश्चिन्मयः संजातः पृथिवीतले रविकुले मायामनुष्योऽव्ययः ।
निश्चक्रं हतराक्षसः पुनरगाद् ब्रह्मत्वमाद्यं स्थिरां कीर्तिं पापहरां विधाय जगतां तं जानकीशं भजे ॥ 1

विश्वोद्भवस्थितिलयादिषु हेतुमेकं मायाश्रयं विगतमायमचिन्त्यमूर्तिम् ।
आनन्दसान्द्रममलं निजबोधरूपं सीतापतिं विदिततत्त्वमहं नमामि ॥ 2

पठन्ति ये नित्यमनन्यचेतसः शृण्वन्ति चाध्यात्मिकसंज्ञितं शुभम् ।
रामायणं सर्वपुराणसंमतं निर्धूतपापा हरिमेव यान्ति ते ॥ 3

अध्यात्मरामायणमेव नित्यं पठेद्यदीच्छेद्भवबन्धमुक्तिम् ।
गवां सहस्रायुतकोटिदानात् फलं लभेद्यः शृणुयात्स नित्यम् ॥ 4

BALA KANDAM

Chapter 1

THE TRUTH ABOUT RAMA

Salutations to Rama (1-5)

1. He—the Light of Consciousness, the Undecaying One—who, being beseeched by the Devas, was born on earth in an assumed human form as a scion of the Solar Dynasty; who, after having effaced the tribe of the Rakshasas and established His eternal and sin-destroying holy fame all the world over, assumed again His own original form as Primeval Brahman—Him, the Lord of Janaka's daughter, I adore. **2.** He who is the sole cause of the origin, the sustentation and dissolution of the world-systems; who is the support of the manifesting power known as Maya but is at the same time free from all its effects; whose form transcends all mental conceptions; who is a condensation of Bliss and Pure Consciousness—Him, the Lord of Sita and the knower of Truth, I adore. **3.** Those who study or hear with whole-hearted attention this Text called the Adhyatma-Ramayana, which has the approval of all the Puranas, are freed from all sins, and they attain to Sri Hari. **4.** One who aspires for Mukti should verily study the Adhyatma-Ramayana. He

पुरारिगिरिसंभूता श्रीरामार्णवसङ्गता । अध्यात्मरामगङ्गेयं पुनाति भुवनत्रयम् ॥ 5

कैलासाग्रे कदाचिद्रविशतविमले मन्दिरे रत्नपीठे संविष्टं ध्याननिष्ठं त्रिनयनमभयं सेवितं सिद्धसंघैः।
देवी वामाङ्कसंस्था गिरिवरतनया पार्वती भक्तिनम्रा प्राहेदं देवमीशं सकलमलहरं
वाक्यमानन्दकन्दम् ॥ 6

पार्वत्युवाच—

नमोऽस्तु ते देव जगन्निवास सर्वात्मदृक् त्वं परमेश्वरोऽसि ।
पृच्छामि तत्त्वं पुरुषोत्तमस्य सनातनं त्वं च सनातनोऽसि ॥ 7

गोप्यं यदत्यन्तमनन्यवाच्यं वदन्ति भक्तेषु महानुभावाः ।
तदप्यहोऽहं तव देव भक्ता प्रियोऽसि मे त्वं वद यत्तु पृष्टम् ॥ 8

ज्ञानं सविज्ञानमथानुभक्तिवैराग्ययुक्तं च मितं विभास्वत् ।
जानाम्यहं योषिदपि त्वदुक्तं यथा तथा ब्रूहि तरन्ति येन ॥ 9

पृच्छामि चान्यच्च परं रहस्यं तदेव चाग्रे वद वारिजाक्ष ।
श्रीरामचन्द्रेऽखिललोकसारे भक्तिर्दृढा नौर्भवति प्रसिद्धा ॥ 10

who hears its recital every day derives merit equal to that gained by making a gift of several crores of cows. **5.** This Ganga of Adhyatma-Ramayana, which originates from the mountain of Siva, and has its estuary in the ocean of Rama, purifies all the three worlds.

Question of Parvati: Was Rama engrossed in worldliness? (6-15)

6. Once seated in a pavilion in the heaven of Kailasa, on a diamond throne luminous like a hundred suns, the three-eyed Deity Siva—who is the Supreme Lord, the bestower of refuge, the adored of the Siddhas, and the Abode of Bliss—was addressed with devotion by Parvati Devi his Consort, the Daughter of the Mountain, in the following sin-effacing words:

Parvati said: **7.** Salutations to Thee, the Shining One and the Abode of the world systems! Thou art the Ultimate Seer to whom all Jivas are objects! Thou art also the Supreme Lord over all beings. May Thou, who art the Eternal One too, be pleased to impart to me the truth about Purushottama, the supreme spiritual Substance. **8.** Lo! Great ones impart to devotees even important spiritual secrets which should not in the ordinary course be communicated to others. I am Thy devotee and Thou art my dear one. So, O Lord, be pleased to answer my question. **9.** Impart in brief and simple words, which could be grasped even by me, an ignorant woman, that knowledge which produces spiritual experience, followed by supreme devotion and non-attachment to worldly values.

10. O Lotus-Eyed One! I have yet another question to ask about a supremely esoteric matter. Please tell (reply) me first about that. It is a well-known fact that devotion to Rama, the Essence of all existence, is a well-built ship for man to

भक्तिः प्रसिद्धा भवमोक्षणाय नान्यत्ततः साधनमस्ति किञ्चित् ।
तथापि हृत्संशयबन्धनं मे विभेत्तुमर्हस्यमलोक्तिभिस्त्वम् ॥ 11

वदन्ति रामं परमेकमाद्यं निरस्तमायागुणसप्रवाहम् ।
भजन्ति चाहर्निशमप्रमत्ताः परं पदं यान्ति तथैव सिद्धाः ॥ 12

वदन्ति केचित्परमोऽपि रामः स्वाविद्यया संवृतमात्मसंज्ञम् ।
जानाति नात्मानमतः परेण सम्बोधितो वेद परात्मतत्त्वम् ॥ 13

यदि स्म जानाति कुतो विलापः सीताकृतेऽनेन कृतः परेण ।
जानाति नैवं यदि केन सेव्यः समो हि सर्वैरपि जीवजातैः ॥ 14

अत्रोत्तरं किं विदितं भवद्भिस्तद् ब्रूत मे संशयभेदि वाक्यम् ॥ 15

श्रीमहादेव उवाच—

धन्यासि भक्तासि परात्मनस्त्वं यज्ज्ञातुमिच्छा तव रामतत्त्वम् ।
पुरा न केनाप्यभिचोदितोऽहं वक्तुं रहस्यं परमं निगूढम् ॥ 16

cross the ocean of Samsara. **11.** It is a well-known teaching that devotion (Bhakti) to the Supreme Being is the royal road to liberation (Moksha), and that no means other than that is required for its attainment. Yet I have some doubts in respect of this. It behoves Thee to dispel such doubts from my mind by Thy clear exposition. **12.** Rama is said to be the Original Being transcending all the manifestations of the Gunas of Prakriti and is unaffected by them. Accepting him to be so, men devote themselves day and night without any reservation to his adoration and thereby they attain to the Supreme State. **13.** Some people, however, say that in spite of being the Supreme One, Rama could not know himself as the Spiritual Self (Brahman) owing to his own Power of Ignorance. When instructed by another (i.e. by Brahma as stated in Valmiki's Ramayana), he came to know the truth about the Transcendent Self. **14.** If he had known the truth about himself earlier, how could he, the Supreme Being, be stricken with grief by the loss of Sita and bemoan his fate? But if he was without knowledge of the Self, how can he be a fit object for adoration, being only on a par with all the ignorant living creatures? **15.** Whatever explanation you have for this conundrum, deign to inform me of it and remove my doubt.

Mahadeva On the Truth about Rama (16-24)

16. *Sri Mahadeva said:* You are indeed fortunate in having got this desire to know the truth concerning the Supreme Self. You are a devotee. Never before this have I been questioned by any one on the truth concerning Rama, which is an esoteric doctrine, extremely profound and subtle.

त्वयाद्य भक्त्या परिनोदितोऽहं वक्ष्ये नमस्कृत्य रघूत्तमं ते ।
रामः परात्मा प्रकृतेरनादिरानन्द एकः पुरुषोत्तमो हि ॥ 17
स्वमायया कृत्स्नमिदं हि सृष्ट्वा नभोवदन्तर्बहिरास्थितो यः ।
सर्वान्तरस्थोऽपि निगूढ आत्मा स्वमायया सृष्टमिदं विचष्टे ॥ 18
जगन्ति नित्यं परितो भ्रमन्ति यत्सन्निधौ चुम्बकलोहवद्धि ।
एतन्न जानन्ति विमूढचित्ताः स्वाविद्यया संवृतमानसा ये ॥ 19
स्वाज्ञानमप्यात्मनि शुद्धबुद्धे स्वारोपयन्तीह निरस्तमाये ।
संसारमेवानुसरन्ति ते वै पुत्रादिसक्ताः पुरुकर्मयुक्ताः ।
जानन्ति नैवं हृदये स्थितं वै चामीकरं कण्ठगतं यथाज्ञाः ॥ 20
यथाप्रकाशो न तु विद्यते रवौ ज्योतिःस्वभावे परमेश्वरे तथा ।
विशुद्धविज्ञानघने रघूत्तमेऽविद्या कथं स्यात्परतः परात्मनि ॥ 21
यथा हि चाक्ष्णा भ्रमता गृहादिकं विनष्टदृष्टेर्भ्रमतीव दृश्यते ।
तथैव देहेन्द्रियकर्तुरात्मनः कृते परेऽध्यस्य जनो विमुह्यति ॥ 22

17. I, who have been devotedly questioned and thus prompted by you today, shall reply to your question after making due salutations to that noblest one of Raghu's line. Rama is the Supreme Self, distinct from Prakriti. He is the one all-comprehending Being, who is pure Bliss itself and the Spirit Supreme over all entities. **18.** Having projected this entire universe by His Power, Maya-sakti, He dwells within and without the universe like the element ether. Though He is thus the resident within all beings, He is completely hidden from their vision, as He is their innermost Self. He is the ultimate Seer and Witness of all this universe of His Maya's creation. **19.** Before Him the whole universe whirls as iron filings round a magnet. The unintelligent, with their minds covered by the power of Ignorance (Avidya), know this not. **20.** On Him, Rama—the Supreme Self, the Pure Consciousness unaffected by Maya—ignorant Jivas superimpose their own ignorance and see Him as involved in worldly entanglements like themselves. Attached as they are to their own relatives and worldly assets, and involved in multifarious activities, they fail to perceive Rama dwelling within their hearts, just as they fail to recognise the presence of their golden necklaces adorning their own necks. **21.** In the sun whose nature is luminosity, there can be no darkness. Even so how can ignorance subsist in Rama who is the condensation of Pure Consciousness, and who is the transcendent and Supreme Self? **22.** A man of defective eye-sight, whose vision is whirling, sees the houses and other objects too as whirling. (The whirling movements of the objects outside is only an attribution on them of one's own whirling vision). So also men are deluded by superimposing on the

नाहो न रात्रिः सवितुर्यथा भवेत् प्रकाशरूपाव्यभिचारतः क्वचित् ।
ज्ञानं तथाज्ञानमिदं द्वयं हरौ रामे कथं स्थास्यति शुद्धचिद्घने ॥ 23

तस्मात्परानन्दमये रघूत्तमे विज्ञानरूपे हि न विद्यते तमः ।
अज्ञानसाक्षिण्यरविन्दलोचने मायाश्रयत्वान्न हि मोहकारणम् ॥ 24

अत्र ते कथयिष्यामि रहस्यमपि दुर्लभम् । सीताराममरुत्सूनुसंवादं मोक्षसाधनम् ॥ 25

पुरा रामायणे रामो रावणं देवकण्टकम् । हत्वा रणे रणश्लाघी सपुत्रबलवाहनम् ॥ 26

सीतया सह सुग्रीवलक्ष्मणाभ्यां समन्वितः । अयोध्यामगमद्रामो हनूमत्प्रमुखैर्वृतः ॥ 27

अभिषिक्तः परिवृतो वसिष्ठाद्यैर्महात्मभिः । सिंहासने समासीनः कोटिसूर्यसमप्रभः ॥ 28

दृष्ट्वा तदा हनूमन्तं प्राञ्जलिं पुरतः स्थितम् । कृतकार्यं निराकाङ्क्षं ज्ञानापेक्षं महामतिम् ॥ 29

रामः सीतामुवाचेदं ब्रूहि तत्त्वं हनूमते । निष्कल्मषोऽयं ज्ञानस्यपात्रं नो नित्यभक्तिमान् 30

Supreme Self egoistic actions of their own I-sense (Ahankara) which in combination with the body and the senses, assumes the role of the doer. **23.** In the sun who is of the nature of unobstructible and changeless luminosity, there can be no day and night at any time. In the same way, in Rama, the Supreme Being Hari, who is the condensation of Pure Consciousness, how can there be knowledge and ignorance, the two changing states observed in limited centres of consciousness? **24.** Rama, the noblest of the Raghus, is of the nature of Pure Bliss-Consciousness that has no rise and fall. That lotus-eyed Lord is the witness of Ajnana (ignorance) and not a victim of it. Maya, the power of ignorance, is dependent on Him, and can therefore never cause Him infatuation and ignorance.

Sita instructs Hanuman (25-31)

25. In further elaboration of this I shall narrate to you a conversation that took place between Sita, Rama and Hanuman. It is concerned with the means for the attainment of Moksha—a closely guarded, inaccessible secret. **(26-27).** In days of old when the events related in the Ramayana took place, Rama the heroic warrior, after destroying Ravana, the enemy of the Devas, along with all his sons, army and vehicles, returned to Ayodhya with Sita, accompanied by Lakshmana and Sugriva, and attended by the monkey leaders headed by Hanuman. **28.** Anointed king, Rama, who was luminous like numerous suns, sat on the royal throne surrounded by great men like the sage Vasishtha. **(29-30).** There Rama saw Hanuman, who had fulfilled all his duties, who was desireless, who was an aspirant for Knowledge, and who was high-minded, standing before him with hands held in salutation. Seeing him so standing, Rama said to Sita, "Impart to Hanuman the Knowledge of the Supreme Truth. He is without any impurity, and he is ever devoted to us. He is a fit recipient for

तथेति जानकी प्राह तत्त्वं रामस्य निश्चितम् । हनूमते प्रपन्नाय सीता लोकविमोहिनी ॥ 31

सीतोवाच—

रामं विद्धि परं ब्रह्म सच्चिदानन्दमद्वयम् । सर्वोपाधिविनिर्मुक्तं सत्तामात्रमगोचरम् ॥ 32

आनन्दं निर्मलं शान्तं निर्विकारं निरञ्जनम् । सर्वव्यापिनमात्मानं स्वप्रकाशमकल्मषम् ॥ 33

मां विद्धि मूलप्रकृतिं सर्गस्थित्यन्तकारिणीम् । तस्य सन्निधिमात्रेण सृजामीदमतन्द्रिता ॥ 34

तत्सान्निध्यान्मया सृष्टं तस्मिन्नारोप्यतेऽबुधैः । अयोध्यानगरे जन्म रघुवंशेऽतिनिर्मले ॥ 35

विश्वामित्रसहायत्वं मखसंरक्षणं ततः । अहल्याशापशमनं चापभङ्गो महेशितुः ॥ 36

मत्पाणिग्रहणं पश्चाद्भार्गवस्य मदक्षयः । अयोध्यानगरे वासो मया द्वादशवार्षिकः ॥ 37

दण्डकारण्यगमनं विराधवध एव च । मायामारीचमरणं मायासीताहृतिस्तथा ॥ 38

जटायुषो मोक्षलाभः कबन्धस्य तथैव च । शबर्याः पूजनं पश्चात्सुग्रीवेण समागमः ॥ 39

spiritual illumination." **31.** Sita, who is the Lord's Power infatuating the whole world with confusion about the true spiritual Self, agreed to do so, and imparted to Hanuman, who was a true spiritual refugee at the Lord's feet, the Truth about Rama in a convincing way.

Sita on the real nature of Rama (32-43)

Sita said: **32.** Know Rama to be the Supreme Brahman—the Existence-Knowledge-Bliss Absolute, the One without a second. He is Pure Existence devoid of all adjuncts, whom the senses cannot perceive as their object. **33.** Know Rama as pure Bliss, as devoid of all impurity, as peace, as changeless Substance, as free from the stain of ignorance, as all-pervading Spirit, as devoid of all disvalues, and as self-revealing Consciousness. **34.** Know me to be the Primeval Prakriti, the material and instrumental cause of the creation, sustentation and dissolution of the universe. In the mere presence of Rama the Supreme Brahman, I, His Prakriti (Power), create the universe unwearied.

35. What I create in His mere presence, the ignorant super-impose on Him. (Now hear about what is thus super-imposed). He was born in the city of Ayodhya in the very pure line of the Raghus. **36.** He helped Visvamitra to conduct the sacrificial rites safe from the obstruction of Rakshasas. He then terminated the effects of the curse that was on Ahalya. Next he broke asunder the great bow of Mahesvara at the court of Janaka, my father. **37.** Thereupon he solemnised his marriage with me, humbled the pride of Bhargava Rama on his way to Ayodhya after the marriage, and lived with me in Ayodhya for twelve years. **38.** Then took place his exile to Dandakaranya, followed by the destruction of Viradha, the slaughter of the demon Maricha who came to deceive us in the form of a deer, and the abduction of Maya-Sita by Ravana. **39.** Next he gave salvation to Jatayu and Kabandha, accepted the worshipful adoration of the ascetic woman Sabari, and

वालिनश्च वधः पश्चात्सीतान्वेषणमेव च। सेतुबन्धश्च जलधौ लङ्कायाश्च निरोधनम् ॥ 40
रावणस्य वधो युद्धे सपुत्रस्य दुरात्मनः। विभीषणे राज्यदानं पुष्पकेण मया सह ॥ 41
अयोध्यागमनं पश्चाद्राज्ये रामाभिषेचनम्। एवमादीनि कर्माणि मयैवाचरितान्यपि।
आरोपयन्ति रामेऽस्मिन्निर्विकारेऽखिलात्मनि ॥ 42
रामो न गच्छति न तिष्ठति नानुशोचत्याकाङ्क्षते त्यजति नो न करोति किञ्चित्।
आनन्दमूर्तिरचलः परिणामहीनो मायागुणाननुगतो हि तथा विभाति ॥ 43
ततो रामः स्वयं प्राह हनूमन्तमुपस्थितम्। शृणुतत्त्वं प्रवक्ष्यामि ह्यात्मानात्मपरात्मनाम् ॥ 44
आकाशस्य यथा भेदस्त्रिविधो दृश्यते महान्। जलाशये महाकाशस्तदवच्छिन्न एव हि।
प्रतिबिम्बाख्यमपरं दृश्यते त्रिविधं नभः ॥ 45
बुद्ध्यवच्छिन्नचैतन्यमेकं पूर्णमथापरम्। आभासस्त्वपरं बिम्बभूतमेवं त्रिधा चितिः ॥ 46

entered into a treaty with Sugreeva. **40.** Afterwards took place the destruction of Vali, the search for Sita, the spanning of the ocean with a bridge of rocks, and the siege of Lanka. **(41-42).** Next took place the destruction of the evil-minded Ravana with all his progeny, the gift of the Kingdom of Lanka to Vibhishana, the departure with me to Ayodhya in the aerial vehicle called Pushpaka, and finally the crowning of Rama as the King of Ayodhya. All these achievements, though accomplished by me (Prakriti), are superimposed on Rama, who is really changeless in Himself and is the soul of all beings. **43.** Rama walks not, He sits not; He sorrows not; He desires not; He abandons not; there is no trace of any activity in Him. Being Pure Bliss itself, there is no movement, no transformation in Him. As He is the substratum of Maya, the changeful Nature of His, He underlies all these transformations of the constituents of Maya, as their substratum; and for those who cannot distinguish the substratum from the changeful constituents of Maya, He seems to get transformed, whereas in fact it is only the constituents of Maya that undergo transformation.

Srirama-hridayam (44-56)

Sri Mahadeva said: **44.** Next Rama himself said to Hanuman who was standing near: I shall tell you the truth about Atma, Anatma (non-Atma) and Paramatma (transcendent Atma). **45.** The Akasa (sky) has three divisions. There is first of all the all-pervading sky. Then there is the Akasa or sky in association with (or pervading) the water receptacles like tanks, lakes, water pools etc. This sky cannot at all be called different from the universal sky in spite of its association with water receptacles. Apart from these, there is a third sky, namely, the reflection of the universal sky seen in the water of the vessel. **46.** In the same way Consciousness has three aspects First of all there is the all-pervading Pure Consciousness. Next there is the Consciousness that is associated with the Buddhi (intellect). Thirdly there is the Consciousness

साभासबुद्धेः कर्तृत्वमविच्छिन्नेऽविकारिणि । साक्षिण्यारोप्यते भ्रान्त्या जीवत्वं च तथा बुधैः ॥47
आभासस्तु मृषा बुद्धिरविद्याकार्यमुच्यते । अविच्छिन्नं तु तद्ब्रह्म विच्छेदस्तु विकल्पतः ॥ 48
अविच्छिन्नस्य पूर्णेन एकत्वं प्रतिपाद्यते । तत्त्वमस्यादिवाक्यैश्च साभासस्याहमस्तथा ॥ 49
ऐक्यज्ञानं यदोत्पन्नं महावाक्येन चात्मनोः । तदाविद्या स्वकार्यैश्च नश्यत्येव न संशयः ॥50
एतद्विज्ञाय मद्भक्तो मद्भावायोपपद्यते । मद्भक्तिविमुखानां हि शास्त्रगर्तेषु मुह्यताम् ।
न ज्ञानं न च मोक्षः स्यात्तेषां जन्मशतैरपि ॥ 51
इदं रहस्यं हृदयं ममात्मनो मयैव साक्षात्कथितं तवानघ ।
मद्भक्तिहीनाय शठाय न त्वया दातव्यमैन्द्रादपि राज्यतोऽधिकम् ॥ 52

श्रीमहादेव उवाच—

एतत्तेऽभिहितं देवि श्रीरामहृदयं मया । अतिगुह्यतमं हृद्यं पवित्रं पापशोधनम् ॥ 53

reflected in the Buddhi. **47.** Ignorant people with distorted understanding superimpose on the partless and unchanging Witness Consciousness the sense of agency of the Consciousness reflected in the Buddhi, whose movements and distortions are all assumed by the reflected Consciousness as its own. Along with that, the state of the Jiva is also assumed. (For, in order that the Pure Consciousness may be made into Witness Consciousness, there must be something outside to be witnessed, and this is provided by the emergence of the Jiva or Reflection of Consciousness in Buddhi simultaneously with the assumption of witnesshood in Pure Consciousness.) **48.** The Reflection (Jiva) is a false assumption: so also the Buddhi is a product of ignorance. Thus both the Jiva and the Buddhi are false. Brahman on the other hand is indivisible and therefore partless; divisibility in Him is due to adjuncts (which are unreal). **49.** The great Vedic doctrines like 'Thou Art That' assert the unity of this individual Reflection (Jiva), along with the Collective Reflection (*avichchinna*), with the Full i.e. Pure Consciousness devoid of the association of any adjuncts. **50.** When by hearing and meditating on the great Vedic Dicta like '*Tattvamasi*' the sense of the unity of the two Atmans (i.e. the Jivatman and the Paramatman) is recognised, then ignorance along with all its offshoots like the I-sense with regard to the body etc., will perish. There is no doubt about it.

51. A devotee of Mine, who understands this Supreme Truth, is fit for my Status. On the other hand one who ignorantly engrosses himself in the search for this Knowledge in the pit of scriptural Texts, without any devotion to Me, never attains to this Knowledge of My nature. He will not have liberation too, even in a hundred life-spans. **52.** O Sinless One! This esoteric Truth about Me known as '*Sri Rama-hridaya*' has been declared by Myself (the Divine Incarnate) to you. This Knowledge, which is superior even to the attainment of the heaven of Indra, should not be imparted by you to any conceited man who has no devotion to Me.

Sri Mahadeva said: **53.** O Devi! I have

साक्षाद्रामेण कथितं सर्ववेदान्तसंग्रहम् । यः पठेत्सततं भक्त्या स मुक्तो नात्र संशयः ॥54
ब्रह्महत्यादि पापानि बहुजन्मार्जितान्यपि । नश्यन्त्येव न सन्देहो रामस्य वचनं यथा ॥ 55
योऽतिभ्रष्टोऽतिपापी परधनपरदारेषु नित्योद्यतो वा ।
स्तेयी ब्रह्मघ्नमातापितृवधनिरतो योगिवृन्दापकारी
यः संपूज्याभिरामं पठति च हृदयं रामचन्द्रस्य भक्त्या
योगीन्द्रैरप्यलभ्यं पदमिह लभते सर्वदेवैः स पूज्यम् ॥ 56

इति श्रीमदध्यात्मरामायणे उमामहेश्वरसंवादे बालकाण्डे
श्रीरामहृदयं नाम प्रथमः सर्गः ॥ १ ॥

communicated to you this Knowledge known as *Sri Rama-hridayam* which I once imparted to Hanuman. It is a highly guarded secret, a panacea for all sins, holy and heart-delighting.

54. He who constantly studies with devotion this exposition given by Rama, the Lord Incarnate Himself, will surely attain to Moksha (liberation). **55.** The effect of heinous sins like Brahmahatya (murder of a holy man) committed in numerous lives past, will all be dissipated by the devout study of this—such is the unequivocal declaration of Rama Himself. **56.** A man may be an outcaste, a confirmed sinner—one ever given to the appropriation of other people's wealth and women, a thief, a murderer of holy men and one's parents, a persecutor of ascetics—, if even he worships Sri Rama and studies this *Sri Rama-hridayam* with true devotion, he attains in this very life to a status which is difficult of achievement even for great Yogis.

द्वितीयः सर्गः

पार्वत्युवाच—

धन्यास्म्यनुगृहीतास्मि कृतार्थास्मि जगत्प्रभो । विच्छिन्नो मेऽतिसन्देहग्रन्थिर्भवदनुग्रहात् ॥ 1
त्वन्मुखाद्गलितं रामतत्त्वामृतरसायनम् । पिबन्त्या मे मनो देव न तृप्यति भवापहम् ॥ 2

Chapter 2

ANNOUNCEMENT OF THE INCARNATION

The Vision of Brahma (1-13)

Parvati said: **1.** O Lord of the worlds! I am indeed fortunate and blessed, my hopes and expectations have been fulfilled by Thy grace. The knot of my complicated doubt has been cut asunder. **2.** O Lord! My mind has not yet reached the limits of satisfaction by imbibing Thy nectarine words concerning the Truth of Rama, which is capable of destroying one's worldly

श्रीरामस्य कथा त्वत्तः श्रुता संक्षेपतो मया। इदानीं श्रोतुमिच्छामि विस्तरेण स्फुटाक्षरम् ॥

श्रीमहादेव उवाच—

शृणु देवि प्रवक्ष्यामि गुह्याद्गुह्यतरं महत्। अध्यात्मरामचरितं रामेणोक्तं पुरा मम ॥
तदद्य कथयिष्यामि शृणु तापत्रयापहम्। यच्छ्रुत्वा मुच्यते जन्तुरज्ञानोत्थमहाभयात्।
प्राप्नोति परमामृद्धिं दीर्घायुः पुत्रसन्ततिम् ॥ 5

भूमिर्भारेण मग्ना दशवदनमुखाशेषरक्षोगणानां
धृत्वा गोरूपमादौ दिविजमुनिजनैः साकमब्जासनस्य।
गत्वा लोकं रुदन्ती व्यसनमुपगतं ब्रह्मणे प्राह सर्वं
ब्रह्मा ध्यात्वा मुहूर्तं सकलमपि हृदावेदशेषात्मकत्वात् ॥ 6

तस्मात्क्षीरसमुद्रतीरमगमद् ब्रह्माथ देवैर्वृतो
देव्या चाखिललोकहृत्स्थमजरं सर्वज्ञमीशं हरिम्।
अस्तौषीच्छ्रुतिसिद्धनिर्मलपदैः स्तोत्रैः पुराणोद्भवै-
र्भक्त्या गद्गदया गिरातिविमलैरानन्दबाष्पैर्वृतः ॥ 7

bondage. **3.** Having heard from Thee the life-story of Sri Rama in brief along with the metaphysical truth about him, there has arisen in my mind a desire to hear it in all detail and in a manner easy enough for me to grasp.

Sri Mahadeva said: **4.** O Devi! Listen to the story of Rama, the resident of the innermost soul of all—a supreme secret that I had heard in days of old from Rama himself. **5.** I shall narrate it to you now. Listen to this narrative which removes the threefold misery of man, which eradicates the great fear of death generated by ignorance, and which bestows prosperity, longevity and male progeny.

6. The Earth-deity, finding that the earth was about to sink due to the load of evil represented by the host of Rakshasas headed by Ravana, assumed the form of a cow, and along with all the great sages and celestials, resorted to the realm of Brahma, the Creator, and represented her tragic fate to him with tears in her eyes. Being the soul of all, Brahma, by a moment's reflection, grasped the situation mentally (without the help of any long narration). **7.** Next Brahma, the four-faced Creator, proceeded to the Milk Ocean, accompained by a large number of Devas and the Earth-deity. There, with voice trembling with the fervour of devotion and eyes brimming with tears of joy stimulated by the excess of Divine love, he began to invoke Hari, the omniscient, the unaging Resident of the hearts of all and the Lord of all, with a hymn couched in clear words of Vedic import and having the sanction of the ancient spiritual tradition.

ततः स्फुरत्सहस्रांशुसहस्रसदृशप्रभः । आविरासीद्धरिः प्राच्यां दिशां व्यपनयंस्तमः ॥ 8
कथंचिद्दृष्टवान्ब्रह्मा दुर्दर्शमकृतात्मनाम् । इन्द्रनीलप्रतीकाशं स्मितास्यं पद्मलोचनम् ॥ 9
किरीटहारकेयूरकुण्डलैः कटकादिभिः । विभ्राजमानं श्रीवत्सकौस्तुभप्रभयान्वितम् ॥ 10
स्तुवद्भिः सनकाद्यैश्च पार्षदैः परिवेष्टितम् । शङ्खचक्रगदापद्मवनमालाविराजितम् ॥ 11
स्वर्णयज्ञोपवीतेन स्वर्णवर्णाम्बरेण च । श्रिया भूम्या च सहितं गरुडोपरि संस्थितम् ॥ 12
हर्षगद्गदया वाचा स्तोतुं समुपचक्रमे ॥ 13

ब्रह्मोवाच—

नतोऽस्मि ते पदं देव प्राण-बुद्धीन्द्रियात्मभिः । यच्चिन्त्यते कर्मपाशाद्धृदि नित्यं मुमुक्षुभिः ॥ 14
मायया गुणमय्या त्वं सृजस्यवसि लुम्पसि । जगत्तेन न ते लेप आनन्दानुभवात्मनः ॥ 15
तथा शुद्धिर्न दुष्टानां दानाध्ययनकर्मभिः । शुद्धात्मता ते यशसि सदा भक्तिमतां यथा ॥16
अतस्तवाङ्घ्रिर्मे दृष्टश्चित्तदोषापनुत्तये । सद्योऽन्तर्हृदये नित्यं मुनिभिः सात्वतैर्वृतः ॥ 17
ब्रह्माद्यैः स्वार्थसिद्ध्यर्थमस्माभिः पूर्वसेवितः । अपरोक्षानुभूत्यर्थं ज्ञानिभिर्हृदि भावितः ॥ 18

8. Then did Hari manifest in the eastern quarter, luminous and brilliant like a thousand suns, dispelling the darkness everywhere. (**9-13**). After earnest supplications, Brahma now got the vision of Hari, which people without purity of mind can never have. The Lord, as He appeared in the Vision, was luminous like the Indranila gem (lapis lazuli); having a smiling face with a pair of lotus-like eyes; adorned with a crown, pearl necklaces and ear-pendants; shining with the lustre of Srivatsa mark, Kaustubha jewel etc.; hymned by sages like Sanaka and others; surrounded by His attendants; sporting the conch, discus, mace, and play-lotus in His hands; beautified by a garland of wild flowers; wearing a Yajnopavita of gold and a cloth of golden yellow; accompanied by His consorts Sri and Bhu; and seated on His mount Garuda. Seeing this glorious vision of the Lord Brahma began to praise Him in words couched in a voice that was choked with joyous emotion.

2. The Hymn of Brahma (14-21)

Brahma said: **14.** O Lord! Adoration to Thy lotus feet with my entire being—the body, vital forces, intellect, senses and mind—, to Thy lotus feet which are meditated upon constantly by those who yearn for liberation from the bonds of Karma. **15.** By virtue of Thy mysterious power Maya, constituted of the three Gunas, Thou createst, sustainest and destroyest the universe. But by these actions Thy nature as the Supreme Bliss-Consciousness is not in the least affected. **16.** The sinful mind of men is never purified as efficiently by good deeds like charity and scriptural study, as happens in the case of those who practise constant devotion to Thy holy fame. **17.** May Thy holy feet, a glimpse of which I have had in my heart all of a sudden, and which devoted sages choose to adore, eradicate all the evil traits of my mind. **18.** Thy feet which persons like me, the Creator, worship at the outset for the achievement of our purposes —say, in my

तवाङ्घ्रिपूजानिर्माल्यतुलसीमालया विभो । स्पर्धते वक्षसि पदं लब्ध्वापि श्रीः सपत्निवत् ॥19
अतस्त्वत्पादभक्तेषु तव भक्तिः श्रियोऽधिका । भक्तिमेवाभिवाञ्छन्ति त्वद्भक्ताः सारवेदिनः॥ 20
अतस्त्वत्पादकमले भक्तिरेव सदास्तु मे । संसारामयतप्तानां भेषजं भक्तिरेव ते ॥ 21
इति ब्रुवन्तं ब्रह्माणं बभाषे भगवान् हरिः । किं करोमीति तं वेधाः प्रत्युवाचातिहर्षितः ॥ 22
भगवन् रावणो नाम पौलस्त्यतनयो महान् । राक्षसानामधिपतिर्मद्दत्तवरदर्पितः ॥ 23
त्रिलोकीं लोकपालांश्च बाधते विश्वबाधकः । मानुषेण मृतिस्तस्य मया कल्याण कल्पिता ॥ 24
अतस्त्वं मानुषो भूत्वा जहि देवरिपुं प्रभो । 25

श्रीभगवानुवाच—

कश्यपस्य वरो दत्तस्तपसा तोषितेन मे । याचितः पुत्रभावाय तथेत्यङ्गीकृतं मया ।
स इदानीं दशरथो भूत्वा तिष्ठति भूतले ॥ 26
तस्याहं पुत्रतामेत्य कौसल्यायां शुभे दिने । चतुर्धात्मानमेवाहं सृजामीतरयोः पृथक् ॥ 27

case, for gaining the power of creation—, are contemplated in their hearts by knowing ones endowed with renunciation for gaining the direct experience of Thyself. **19.** Sri Devi, Thy Consort and Goddess of Prosperity, though having her residence on Thy chest, is jealous, like a co-wife, of the holy Tulasi wreaths offered by devotees and occupying Thy feet. (For she fears that, being offered by Thy devotees, Thou art more fond of that humble Tulasi than of herself in spite of her being the Deity of all beauty, prosperity and all other glorious features.) **20.** Therefore, Thy devotees of mature wisdom, knowing, as they thus do, that Thou art more fond of the genuine devotees than of Sri Devi, ever desire only for Bhakti, the highest form of devotion (in order that the Lord's choice may fall on them) **21.** May I therefore be blessed with devotion to Thy lotus feet ever more. For to one stricken with the fever of transmigratory existence, nothing is as effective a medicament as Bhakti.

The Lord Condescends to Incarnate (22-32)

(22-25). To Brahma who was thus hymning, the Supreme Being Hari spoke, enquiring what He should do for him. Delighted at this response of the Lord, Brahma said: "O Supreme Lord! A powerful Rakshasa named Ravana, who is the son of Visravas of the house of Pulastya, getting proud and audacious on account of certain boons I had given him, has now become a menace to the world at large, and is subjecting the three worlds and the celestials protecting them to terrible oppression. O Auspicious One! I had decreed that his death could be accomplished by a human being only. So, O Lord, deign to take a human embodiment and destroy this enemy of the celestials."

The Supreme Lord said: **26.** The Prajapati Kasyapa once propitiated Me by his austerities. As requested by him, I have agreed to be born as his son. That Kasyapa is now born on earth as King Dasaratha. **27.** I shall take a human embodi-

योगमायापि सीतेति जनकस्य गृहे तदा । उत्पत्स्यते तया सार्धं सर्वं सम्पादयाम्यहम् ।
इत्युक्त्वान्तर्दधे विष्णुर्ब्रह्मा देवानथाब्रवीत् ॥ 28

ब्रह्मोवाच—

विष्णुर्मानुषरूपेण भविष्यति रघोः कुले ॥ 29

यूयं सृजध्वं सर्वेऽपि वानरेष्वंशसम्भवान् । विष्णोः सहायं कुरुत यावत्स्थास्यति भूतले ॥ 30

इति देवान्समादिश्य समाश्वास्य च मेदिनीम् । ययौ ब्रह्मा स्वभवनं विज्वरः सुखमास्थितः ॥ 31

देवाश्च सर्वे हरिरूपधारिणः स्थिताः सहायार्थमितस्ततो हरेः ।
महाबलाः पर्वतवृक्षयोधिनः प्रतीक्षमाणा भगवन्तमीश्वरम् ॥ 32

इति श्रीमदध्यात्मरामायणे उमामहेश्वरसंवादे
बालकाण्डे द्वितीयः सर्गः ॥ 2 ॥

ment as his son by his wife Kausalya. In his two other wives My Essence itself will take birth as three issue (two in one and one in the other). **28.** When I incarnate, My Yoga-maya (Spiritual Power) will be born as Sita, the daughter of Janaka. In association with Her, I shall accomplish all your purposes. Saying so, the Lord Mahavishnu disappeared from the sight of all. Then Brahma said to the Devas as follows. **29.** "Mahavishnu will incarnate Himself in a human form in the royal house of Raghu. **30.** All of you take birth among the tribe of Vanaras (apes) by fractions of yourselves, and be the helpers of the Lord Vishnu as long as He is on earth for the accomplishment of His mission." **31.** Addressing the Devas thus and comforting Mother-earth, Brahma returned with a peaceful heart to his spiritual abode known as Satyaloka. **32.** And the Devas, expecting the advent of Hari and the chances of becoming His helpers in this divine mission, got embodied in different places in the form of apes capable of fighting with mountains and trees as their weapons.

तृतीयः सर्गः

श्रीमहादेव उवाच—

अथ राजा दशरथः श्रीमान्सत्यपरायणः । अयोध्याधिपतिर्वीरः सर्वलोकेषु विश्रुतः ॥ 1

सोऽनपत्यत्वदुःखेन पीडितो गुरुमेकदा । वसिष्ठं स्वकुलाचार्यमभिवाद्येदमब्रवीत् ॥ 2

Chapter 3

THE INCARNATION OF RAMA

Dasaratha's sacrifice for the Sake of Issue (1-9)

Sri Mahadeva said: **(1-2)**. There was in Ayodhya a king named Dasaratha supremely devoted to truth, heroic and renowned all the world over. Being worried that he

स्वामिन्पुत्रा कथं मे स्युः सर्वलक्षणलक्षिताः । पुत्रहीनस्य मे राज्यं सर्वं दुःखाय कल्पते ॥ 3
ततोऽब्रवीद्वसिष्ठस्तं भविष्यन्ति सुतास्तव । चत्वारः सत्त्वसम्पन्ना लोकपाला इवापराः ॥ 4
शान्ताभर्तारमानीय ऋष्यशृङ्गं तपोधनम् । अस्माभिः संहितः पुत्रकामेष्टिं शीघ्रमाचर ॥ 5
तथेति मुनिमानीय मन्त्रिभिः सहितः शुचिः । यज्ञकर्म समारेभे मुनिभिर्वीतकल्मषैः ॥ 6
श्रद्धया हूयमानेऽग्नौ तप्तजाम्बूनदप्रभः । पायसं स्वर्णपात्रस्थं गृहीत्वोवाच हव्यवाट् ॥ 7
गृहाण पायसं दिव्यं पुत्रीयं देवनिर्मितम् । लप्स्यसे परमात्मानं पुत्रत्वेन न संशयः ॥ 8
इत्युक्त्वा पायसं दत्त्वा राज्ञे सोऽन्तर्दधेऽनलः । ववन्दे मुनिशार्दूलौ राजा लब्धमनोरथः ॥ 9
वसिष्ठऋष्यशृङ्गाभ्यामनुज्ञातो ददौ हविः । कौसल्यायै सकैकेय्यै अर्धमर्धं प्रयत्नतः ॥ 10
ततः सुमित्रा संप्राप्ता जगृध्नुः पौत्रिकं चरुम् । कौसल्या तु स्वभागार्धं ददौ तस्यै मुदान्विता ॥11
कैकेयी च स्वभागार्धं ददौ प्रीतिसमन्विता । उपभुज्य च रुं सर्वाः स्त्रियो गर्भसमन्विताः ॥12

was issueless, he one day addressed his family preceptor Vasishtha, after making obeisance to him in due form. **3.** He said: "O Master! How can I have worthy sons with all auspicious features? My whole kingdom is only a cause of sorrow to me, as I have no issue to succeed me. **4.** Thereupon the sage Vasishtha said to him: "You shall have four worthy sons who will be equal to the guardian deities of the quarters. **5.** Without loss of time manage to get here the austere sage Rishyasringa, the husband of Santa, and perform Putra-kameshti, a sacrifice to be performed by one desiring issue, with him, Rishyasringa, as chief priest. He will be assisted by us, your family priests."

6. Complying with this instruction, King Dasaratha invited the sage Rishyasringa, and with due observance of preliminary sacrificial disciplines, commenced the performance of the sacrifice assisted by his ministers and sages like Vasishtha. **7.** When holy offerings were made in the sacrificial fire, with great faith, the Fire-deity possessing the luminosity of gold purified by heating, emerged from the sacrificial pit, holding forth a golden vessel containing Payasa (milk pudding). **8.** "Receive this divine Payasa made by the Devas, which is productive of issue. It will undoubtedly help you to obtain Mahavishnu Himself as son." **9.** Saying so, that Fire-deity gave the Payasa to the king and disappeared from sight. And the king, having achieved his object, made obeisance to both the sages, Vasishtha and Rishyasringa.

Rama Incarnates (10-18)

10. Permitted by the sages Vasishtha and Rishyasringa, the king gave half the quantity of that Payasa to Queen Kausalya, and the other half to Kaikeyi. **11.** Thereupon Sumitra, the third consort of the King, who too was extremely desirous of consuming that issue-conferring Payasa, came forward. Kausalya joyfully gave her one half from her own share. **12.** Kaikeyi too gave her (Sumitra) one half of her share of the Payasa. All these women who consumed the Payasa became big with child.

देवता इव रेजुस्ताः स्वभासा राजमन्दिरे । दशमे मासि कौसल्या सुषुवे पुत्रमद्भुतम् । 13
मधुमासे सिते पक्षे नवम्यां कर्कटे शुभे । पुनर्वस्वृक्षसहिते उच्चस्थे ग्रहपञ्चके ॥ 14
मेषं पूषणि संप्राप्ते पुष्पवृष्टिसमाकुले । आविरासीज्जगन्नाथः परमात्मा सनातनः ॥ 15
नीलोत्पलदलश्यामः पीतवासाश्चतुर्भुजः । जलजारुणनेत्रान्तः स्फुरत्कुण्डलमण्डितः ॥ 16
सहस्रार्कप्रतीकाशः किरीटी कुञ्चितालकः । शङ्खचक्रगदापद्मवनमालाविराजितः ॥ 17
अनुग्रहाख्यहृत्स्थेन्दुसूचकस्मितचन्द्रिकः । करुणारससम्पूर्णविशालोत्पललोचनः ।
श्रीवत्सहारकेयूरनूपुरादिविभूषणः ॥ 18
दृष्ट्वा तं परमात्मानं कौसल्या विस्मयाकुला । हर्षाश्रुपूर्णनयना नत्वा प्राञ्जलिरब्रवीत् ॥ 19

कौसल्योवाच—

देवदेव नमस्तेऽस्तु शङ्खचक्रगदाधर । परमात्माच्युतोऽनन्तः पूर्णस्त्वं पुरुषोत्तमः ॥ 20
वदन्त्यगोचरं वाचां बुद्ध्यादीनामतीन्द्रियम् । त्वां वेदवादिनः सत्तामात्रं ज्ञानैकविग्रहम् ॥ 21

13. In their quarters in the palace, these queens now shone like celestials, and in the tenth month Kausalya gave birth to a unique infant. **14-15.** The Supreme Spirit, the Eternal Being and the Lord of all, incarnated in the month of Chaitra (Madhumasa) amidst a shower of flowers, on the ninth day of the bright fortnight, under the constellation of Punarvasu in the auspicious zodiacal sign of Cancer when the five planets (the Sun, Mars, Saturn, Jupiter and Venus) were in the ascendant, and the sun was at the sign of the Ram (Mesha). **(16-18).** Blue in complexion like the petals of a blue lily; draped with a yellow wearing cloth; sporting four arms; with the corner of the eyes tinged lotus-red; wearing a pair of shining ear-pendants; luminous like a hundred suns; crowned with a diadem over His head of curly locks; resplendent with conch, discus, mace and lotus in His four arms and a wreath of wild flowers on the chest; with His face illumined by the lunar light of his smile indicative of the presence of the moon of grace in His heart; possessing lotus-like eyes overflowing with the sentiment of universal love; and adorned with the Srivatsa, necklace, armlets, anklets and other ornaments—such was the form of the Lord when He incarnated Himself as the son of Kausalya.

Kausalya's Hymn and the Lord's Response (19-34)

19. Wonderstruck at the sight of the Divine form of the Lord, Kausalya addressed Him with her hands held in salutation and eyes brimming with tears of joy.

Kausalya said: **20.** Salutations to Thee, the Lord over all divinities and the wearer of divine insignia like conch, discus and mace! Thou, O Lord, art the Supreme Spirit, the Highest of all beings, eternal, all-pervading and limitless. **21.** The knowers of the Vedas declare Thee to be indescribable by words, and ungraspable by the conceptual process of the intellect. Transcending the purview of the senses, Thou

त्वमेव मायया विश्वं सृजस्यवसि हंसि च । सत्त्वादिगुणसंयुक्तस्तुर्य एवामलः सदा ॥ 22
करोषीव न कर्ता त्वं गच्छसीव न गच्छसि । श्रृणोषि न श्रृणोषीव पश्यसीव न पश्यसि ॥ 23
अप्राणो ह्यमनाः शुद्ध इत्यादि श्रुतिरब्रवीत् । समः सर्वेषु भूतेषु तिष्ठन्नपि न लक्ष्यसे ॥ 24
अज्ञानध्वान्तचित्तानां व्यक्त एव सुमेधसाम् । जठरे तव दृश्यन्ते ब्रह्माण्डाः परमाणवः ॥ 25
त्वं ममोदरसम्भूत इति लोकान्विडम्बसे । भक्तेषु पारवश्यं ते दृष्टं मेऽद्य रघूत्तम ॥ 26
संसारसागरे मग्ना पतिपुत्रधनादिषु । भ्रमामि मायया तेऽद्य पादमूलमुपागता ॥ 27
देव त्वद्रूपमेतन्मे सदा तिष्ठतु मानसे । आवृणोतु न मां माया तव विश्वविमोहिनी ॥ 28
उपसंहर विश्वात्मन्नदो रूपमलौकिकम् । दर्शयस्व महानन्दबालभावं सुकोमलम् ।
ललितालिङ्गनालापैस्तरिष्याम्युत्कटं तमः ॥ 29

श्रीभगवानुवाच—
यद्यदिष्टं तवास्त्यम्ब तत्तद्भवतु नान्यथा ॥ 30

art the Essence of all beings as pure Existence, and Thy form is of Pure Consciousness. **22.** By Thy Power known as Maya Thou, in association with the Gunas of Rajas, Sattva and Tamas, createst, sustainest and destroyest the universe. But (unaffected by all this creative activity) Thou art ever the Pure Being, the Fourth transcending the three states of waking, dream and sleep. **23.** Though Thou appearest to be doing, Thou art no doer; though Thou appearest to be moving, Thou art not moving; though Thou appearest to be hearing, Thou art not hearing; and though Thou appearest to be seeing, Thou art not seeing. **24.** Without Prana, without mind, untainted—such is the declaration of the Vedas about Thee. Though Thou abidest in all beings alike as unmodified Being, Thou art outside the ken of all. **25.** Though thus outside the range of persons whose mind is overcast with the darkness of ignorance, those endowed with a pure mind perceive Thee clearly. All the world systems included in the cosmos are but minute atoms in Thy abdomen. **26.** Following the ways of the world, Thou art born of my womb. O Thou, the noblest one of Raghu's line! Today, by this condescension of Thine, I have come to understand how Thou dost subject Thyself to Thy devotees. **27.** Today have I attained to Thy holy feet—I who am submerged in the ocean of Samsara, the transmigratory cycle, and who am by Thy illusory Power forced into an infatuating involvement with husband, children, wealth and other worldly concerns. **28.** O Lord! May this form of Thine remain ever impressed in my mind, and let not Thy Maya, the Power that infatuates the whole world, affect and overpower me. **29.** Soul of the universe! Deign to withdraw this suprahuman form of Thine, and reveal Thy charming form as an infant that confers bliss on all who see it. I shall overcome the formidable darkness of ignorance by lovingly embracing and talking with Thee as an infant.

30. *The Lord said*: "O mother! Let every thing take place as you wish. It will never be otherwise.

अहं तु ब्रह्मणा पूर्वं भूमेर्भारापनुत्तये । प्रार्थितो रावणं हन्तुं मानुषत्वमुपागतः ॥ 31
त्वया दशरथेनाहं तपसाराधितः पुरा । मत्पुत्रत्वाभिकाङ्क्षिण्या तथा कृतमनिन्दिते ॥ 32
रूपमेतत्त्वया दृष्टं प्राक्तनं तपसः फलम् । मद्दर्शनं विमोक्षाय कल्पते ह्यन्यदुर्लभम् ॥ 33
संवादमावयोर्यस्तु पठेद्वा शृणुयादपि । स याति मम सारूप्यं मरणे मत्स्मृतिं लभेत् ॥ 34
इत्युक्त्वा मातरं रामो बालो भूत्वा रुरोद ह । बालत्वेऽपीन्द्रनीलाभो विशालाक्षोऽतिसुन्दरः ॥ 35
बालारुणप्रतीकाशो लालिताखिललोकपः । अथ राजा दशरथः श्रुत्वा पुत्रोद्भवोत्सवम् ।
आनन्दार्णवमग्नोऽसावाययौ गुरुणा सह ॥ 36
रामं राजीवपत्राक्षं दृष्ट्वा हर्षाश्रुसंप्लुतः । गुरुणा जातकर्माणि कर्तव्यानि चकार सः ॥ 37
कैकेयी चाथ भरतमसूत कमलेक्षणा । सुमित्रायां यमौ जातौ पूर्णेन्दुसदृशाननौ ॥ 38
तदा ग्रामसहस्राणि ब्राह्मणेभ्यो मुदा ददौ । सुवर्णानि च रत्नानि वासांसि सुरभीः शुभाः ॥ 39
यस्मिन् रमन्ते मुनयो विद्यया ज्ञानविप्लवे । तं गुरुः प्राह रामेति रमणाद्राम इत्यपि ॥ 40

31. "I have been entreated in the past by Brahma to relieve the earth of its burdens by destroying Ravana. For this purpose I have now assumed a human form. **32.** Besides, O virtuous lady, you and Dasaratha had in days of old performed austerities, praying that you should get Me as your son. **33.** This form of Mine which you have seen is a vision vouchsafed to you as the fruit of the austerities you have performed before. It is impossible for any one to experience this form otherwise. For, My vision bestows liberation on those who get it. **34.** Those who study this dialogue between us or even hear it read, will have remembrance of Me at the time of death and attain Sarupya, liberation consisting in the attainment of My form.

Rama's Infancy and Childhood (35-59)

35. Saying so to the mother, Rama adopted the form of an infant and cried like a newly born babe. Even in that infant's form, he was extremely handsome, blue in complexion like the Indra-neela gem, and having very broad eyes. **36.** He shone like the early sun, and all the protecting divinities of the quarters rejoiced at his birth. On hearing the gladdening news of a son's birth, King Dasaratha came running in great delight to see the infant, accompanied by his family priest Vasishtha. **37.** With eyes brimming with tears of joy at the sight of the infant Rama, having eyes resembling lotus petals, Dasaratha performed all the birth ceremonies for him as directed by his preceptor. **38.** Afterwards handsome Kaikeyi gave birth to Bharata, and Sumitra to a set of twins with faces resembling the full moon.

39. Overflowing with delight, Dasaratha made gifts of numerous villages, auspicious cows and dresses, besides gold and precious gems, to holy men in honour of the birth of his sons. **40.** The preceptor Vasishtha gave the name of Rama to Kausalya's infant, meaning the one in whom the sages, whose ignorance has been dispelled by Vidya,

भरणाद्भरतो नाम लक्ष्मणं लक्षणान्वितम् । शत्रुघ्नं शत्रुहन्तारमेवं गुरुरभाषत ॥ 41
लक्ष्मणो रामचन्द्रेण शत्रुघ्नो भरतेन च । द्वन्द्वीभूय चरन्तौ तौ पायसांशानुसारतः ॥ 42
रामस्तु लक्ष्मणेनाथ विचरन्बाललीलया । रमयामास पितरौ चेष्टितैर्मुग्धभाषितैः ॥ 43
भाले स्वर्णमयाश्वत्थपर्णमुक्ताफलप्रभम् । कण्ठे रत्नमणिव्रातमध्यद्वीपिनखाञ्चितम् ॥ 44
कर्णयोः स्वर्णसम्पन्नरत्नार्जुनसटालुकम् । शिञ्जानमणिमञ्जीरकटिसूत्राङ्गदैर्वृतम् ॥ 45
स्मितवक्त्राल्पदशनमिन्द्रनीलमणिप्रभम् । अङ्गणे रिङ्गमाणं तं तर्णकाननु सर्वतः ।
दृष्ट्वा दशरथो राजा कौसल्या मुमुदे तदा ॥ 46
भोक्ष्यमाणो दशरथो राममेहीति चासकृत् । आह्वयत्यतिहर्षेण प्रेम्णा नायाति लीलया ॥ 47
आनयेतिच कौसल्यामाह सा सस्मिता सुतम् । धावत्यपि न शक्नोति स्प्रष्टुं योगिमनोगतिम् । 48
प्रहसन्स्वयमायाति कर्दमाङ्कितपाणिना । किञ्चिद्गृहीत्वा कवलं पुनरेव पलायते ॥ 49

take delight (*ramante*). Because he delights (*ramaṇāt*) all, he was called Rama—this also can be another meaning of the name. **41.** The other infants were named as follows by the Guru: Kaikeyi's infant was named Bharata, because he would come to have great administrative skill (*bharaṇāt*), and of Sumitra's two infants, one was named Lakshmana because he was endowed with all marks indicative of auspiciousness (*lakṣaṇānvitam*), and the other Satrughna, because he would be a destroyer of all enemies (*satruhantāram*).

42. In accordance with the parts of Pāyasa that Sumitra received from Kausalya and Kaikeyi, these infants moved about in pairs, Lakshmana with Rama, and Satrughna with Bharata. **43.** Rama and Lakshmana, playing childish pranks, delighted their parents by their gestures and artless prattle. **(44-46).** Bedecked on the forehead with a golden Tilaka shaped like a banyan leaf studded in the centre with a pearl spreading its sheen all over the forehead; comely with necklaces of precious gems having a leopard claw in the centre; with cheeks illumined by the rays coming from ear ornaments made of gold and studded with precious gems; wearing anklets of gold giving out a jingling sound, besides a golden girdle and bracelets; and revealing the just sprouting teeth in his mouth—Rama of the blue lustre of an Indra-neela gem delighted his parents, as they witnessed him sporting with the calves in the inner quadrangle of the palace.

(47-48) Dasaratha, at the time of taking food, would call Rama with great affection and joy several times to eat with him. Being absorbed in play he would refuse to respond. So the King, with a smile on his face, would ask Kausalya to fetch him; but even after much chasing, she could never get hold of him who could be grasped only by the mind of the Yogi. **49.** Afterwards with a smile on his lips, Rama would go to the father of his own accord, and receiving in his mud-smeared hand, a

कौसल्या जननी तस्य मासि मासि प्रकुर्वती । बायनानि विचित्राणि समलङ्कृत्य राघवम् ॥50
अपूपान्मोदकान्कृत्वा कर्णशष्कुलिकास्तथा । कर्णपूरांश्च विविधान् वर्षवृद्धौ च वायनम् ॥ 51
गृहकृत्यं तया त्यक्तं तस्य चापल्यकारणात् । एकदा रघुनाथोऽसौ गतो मातरमन्तिके ॥ 52
भोजनं देहि मे मातर्न श्रुतं कार्यसक्तया । ततः क्रोधेन भाण्डानि लगुडेनाहनत्तदा ॥ 53
शिक्यस्थं पातयामास गव्यं च नवनीतकम् । लक्ष्मणाय ददौ रामो भरताय यथाक्रमम् ॥ 54
शत्रुघ्नाय ददौ पश्चाद्दधि दुग्धं तथैव च । सूदेन कथिते मात्रे हास्यं कृत्वा प्रधावति ॥ 55
आगतां तां विलोक्याथ ततः सर्वैः पलायितम् । कौसल्या धावमानापि प्रस्खलन्ती पदे पदे ॥56
रघुनाथं करे धृत्वा किञ्चिन्नोवाच भामिनी । बालभावं समाश्रित्य मन्दं मन्दं रुरोद ह ॥ 57
ते सर्वे लालिता मात्रा गाढमालिङ्ग्य यत्नतः । एवमानन्दसन्दोहजगदानन्दकारकः ॥ 58
मायाबालवपुर्धृत्वा रमयामास दम्पती । अथ कालेन ते सर्वे कौमारं प्रतिपेदिरे ॥ 59
उपनीता वसिष्ठेन सर्वविद्याविशारदाः । धनुर्वेदे च निरताः सर्वशास्त्रार्थवेदिनः ॥ 60

ball of rice, run away to play, once again.

(50-51) Every month His mother Kausalya used to observe vows and offer worship for counteracting all evil influences on the child, whom she would decorate well. She would also make elaborate preparations of various sweets and other dainties as offerings. **(52-53)** On account of the prankish movements of Rama, she would often be required to abandon her household duties. One day the boy went to his mother's side and said, "Oh mother! I am very hungry. Give me something to eat." But being absorbed in her work, she did not hear it. Extremely angry at this, Rama took a stick and with that broke all the vessels. **54.** He broke the vessels in which milk and butter were hung in slings and distributed their contents between Lakshmana and Bharata. **55.** Afterwards he gave that curd and milk to Satrughna also. When the cook reported this to the mother, she came running and laughing, to catch hold of Rama. **(56-57)**. Seeing her approaching, all the brothers ran away, with Kausalya pursuing them in spite of her feet stumbling against obstructions. She at last caught hold of Rama, the Lord of the Raghus, and holding him in her hand, that noble lady could only keep on looking at his face without showing anything like anger or annoyance. But lo! Rama in his childish mood began to weep. **(58-59)** Embraced by the mother, all of them were fondled intensely by her. Thus did Rama, the embodiment of bliss and the source of joy for all the worlds, entertain Dasaratha and Kausalya with that assumed form of his as a child. In this way they passed from the stage of childhood to that of boyhood.

Training of the Brothers (60-66)

60. Now they were invested with the sacred thread by the family preceptor Vasishtha and were instructed and made proficient in arts and sciences, especially in archery and bowmanship. They were thus

बभूवुर्जगतां नाथा लीलया नररूपिणः। लक्ष्मणस्तु सदा राममनुगच्छति सादरम् ॥ 61
सेव्यसेवकभावेन शत्रुघ्नो भरतं तथा। रामश्चापधरो नित्यं तूणीबाणान्वितः प्रभुः ॥ 62
अश्वारूढो वनं याति मृगयायै सलक्ष्मणः। हत्वा दुष्टमृगान्सर्वान्पित्रे सर्वं न्यवेदयत् ॥ 63
प्रातरुत्थाय सुस्नातः पितरावभिवाद्य च। पौरकार्याणि सर्वाणि करोति विनयान्वितः ॥ 64
बन्धुभिः सहितो नित्यं भुक्त्वा मुनिभिरन्वहम्। धर्मशास्त्ररहस्यानि शृणोति व्याकरोति च ॥ 65
एवं परात्मा मनुजावतारो मनुष्यलोकाननुसृत्य सर्वम्।
चक्रेऽविकारी परिणामहीनो विचार्यमाणे न करोति किञ्चित् ॥ 66

इति श्रीमदध्यात्मरामायणे उमामहेश्वरसंवादे
बालकाण्डे तृतीयः सर्गः ॥ ३ ॥

made competent in the knowledge of all the Sastras. **61.** Though lords of the world, they, having assumed human forms in a sportive manner, had to undergo all the above training. Of the four brothers, Lakshmana was always in the habit of reverently following Rama. **(62-63).** In the attitude of a servant towards his master, Satrughna always followed Bharata. Daily, Rama, equipped with bow and arrows, would go to the forest on horseback along with Lakshmana to hunt wild animals, and he would bring all the game and present them before his father.

64. Getting up early in the morning and finishing his ablutions and daily rites, he would salute his father and mother in all humility, and then attend to all the affairs of State. **65.** Every day he would take his food along with all his kith and kin. Then he would engage himself in hearing expositions of scriptural and administrative texts by learned men and offer his own explanations. **66.** In this way, incarnated in a human body, the Supreme Being, who is immutable and free from all transformations, did everything following the habits and customs of men. But when the truth about him is investigated it would be seen he was always unaffected by any change.

चतुर्थः सर्गः

श्रीमहादेव उवाच—

कदाचित्कौशिकोऽभ्यागादयोध्यां ज्वलनप्रभः। द्रष्टुं रामं परात्मानं जातं ज्ञात्वा स्वमायया ॥ 1

Chapter 4

RAMA'S ADOLESCENCE

Visvamitra's Arrival, Seeking Rama (1-11)

Sri Mahadeva said: **1.** Once sage Visvamitra, possessed of a radiance like that of the fire, having understood that the Supreme Being had incarnated Himself as

दृष्ट्वा दशरथो राजा प्रत्युत्थायाचिरेण तु । वसिष्ठेन समागम्य पूजयित्वा यथाविधि ॥ 2
अभिवाद्य मुनिं राजा प्राञ्जलिर्भक्तिनम्रधीः । कृतार्थोऽस्मि मुनीन्द्राहं त्वदागमनकारणात् ॥ 3
त्वद्विधा यद्गृहं यान्ति तत्रैवायान्ति संपदः । यदर्थमागतोऽसि त्वं ब्रूहि सत्यं करोमि तत् ॥ 4
विश्वामित्रोऽपि तं प्रीतः प्रत्युवाच महीपतिः । अहं पर्वणि संप्राप्ते दृष्ट्वा यष्टुं सुरान्पितॄन् ॥ 5
यदारभे तदा दैत्या विघ्नं कुर्वन्ति नित्यशः । मारीचश्च सुबाहुश्चापरे चानुचरास्तयोः ॥ 6
अतस्तयोर्वधार्थाय ज्येष्ठं रामं प्रयच्छ मे । लक्ष्मणेन सह भ्राता तव श्रेयो भविष्यति ॥ 7
वसिष्ठेन सहामन्त्र्य दीयतां यदि रोचते । पप्रच्छ गुरुमेकान्ते राजा चिन्तापरायणः ॥ 8
किं करोमि गुरो रामं त्यक्तुं नोत्सहते मनः । बहुवर्षसहस्रान्ते कष्टेनोत्पादिताः सुताः ॥ 9
चत्वारोऽमरतुल्यास्ते तेषां रामोऽतिवल्लभः । रामस्त्वितो गच्छति चेन्न जीवामि कथञ्चन ॥ 10
प्रत्याख्यातो यदि मुनिः शापं दास्यत्यसंशयः । कथं श्रेयो भवेन्मह्यमसत्यं चापि न स्पृशेत् ॥ 11

वसिष्ठ उवाच—

शृणु राजन्देवगुह्यं गोपनीयं प्रयत्नतः । रामो न मानुषो जातः परमात्मा सनातनः ॥ 12

Rama by assuming His power of Maya, came to Ayodhya in order to see him. **2.** Seeing that Visvamitra had arrived, King Dasaratha went in haste along with Vasishtha to receive him and make the customary offerings. **3.** Bowing down to him in great devotion with his palms joined together in salutation, the Raja said to the sage very respectfully, "O, great sage! I have attained the object of my life by this visit of your holiness. **4.** Wherever sages like you go, those houses attain to great prosperity. Whatever might be the object with which you have come, I offer in truth to fulfil the same."

(5-6). Greatly pleased with the king's hospitality, the high-souled Visvamitra said in reply, "Whenever on the fourteenth day of the fortnight I offer special worship to Devas and Pitris, two Rakshasas named Maricha and Subahu along with their followers obstruct my rites. **7.** Therefore in order to destroy these Rakshasas, please send with me Rama, the eldest of the brothers, along with Lakshmana. This will bring great good to you. **8.** If this proposal is agreeable to you, please take counsel with Vasishtha and then send them with me." Thinking deeply over the proposal, King Dasaratha approached his preceptor Vasishtha in solitude and asked him: **(9-10).** "O teacher! What am I to do now? My mind is very reluctant to send away Rama. It was after several thousand years of my life that I got these four sons. They are equal to celestials. Among them Rama is the dearest to me. If Rama goes away from here, it is impossible for me to sustain my life any longer. **11.** But if I refuse to send him at Visvamitra's request, that sage is sure to curse me. What course shall I take in this situation, consistent with my good? It is also impossible for me to speak an untruth."

The true object of Visvamitra's mission (12-19)

Vasishtha thereupon said: **12.** "O King!

भूमेर्भारावताराय ब्रह्मणा प्रार्थितः पुरा । स एव जातो भवने कौसल्यायां तवानघ ॥ 13
त्वं तु प्रजापतिः पूर्वं कश्यपो ब्रह्मणः सुतः । कौसल्या चादितिर्देवमाता पूर्वं यशस्विनी ॥ 14
भवन्तौ तप उग्रं वै तेपाथे बहुवत्सरम् ।
अग्राम्यविषयौ विष्णुपूजाध्यानैकतत्परौ । तदा प्रसन्नो भगवान् वरदो भक्तवत्सलः ॥ 15
वृणीष्व वरमित्युक्ते त्वं मे पुत्रो भवामल । इति त्वया याचितोऽसौ भगवान्भूतभावनः ॥ 16
तथेत्युक्त्वाद्य पुत्रस्ते जातो रामः स एव हि । शेषस्तु लक्ष्मणो राजन् राममेवान्वपद्यत ॥ 17
जातौ भरतशत्रुघ्नौ शङ्खचक्रे गदाभृतः । योगमायापि सीतेति जाता जनकनन्दिनी ॥ 18
विश्वामित्रोऽपि रामाय तां योजयितुमागतः । एतद्गुह्यतमं राजन्न वक्तव्यं कदाचन ॥ 19
अतः प्रीतेन मनसा पूजयित्वाथ कौशिकम् । प्रेषयस्व रमानाथं राघवं सहलक्ष्मणम् ॥ 20
वसिष्ठेनैवमुक्तस्तु राजा दशरथस्तदा । कृतकृत्यमिवात्मानं मेने प्रमुदितान्तरः ॥ 21
आहूय रामरामेति लक्ष्मणेति च सादरम् । आलिङ्ग्य मूर्ध्न्यवघ्राय कौशिकाय समर्पयत् ॥ 22

Hear the esoteric truth about Rama. It is in every way to be guarded from publicity. Rama is not a human being. He is the Eternal and Supreme Spirit incarnated. **13.** In order to relieve the earth of its burdens, Brahma, the creator prayed to Him to be incarnated as man. O pious one! It is He, the Supreme Being, that has been born in your house to Kausalya as Rama. **14.** In your previous embodiment, you were Kasyapa Prajapati, the off-spring of Brahma. This renowned lady, Kausalya was Aditi, the mother of celestials. **15.** Observing continence, you two engaged yourselves in the worship of, and meditation on, Mahavishnu, and performed severe austerities. The Lord, who is noted as the lover of His devotees and bestower of boons on them, became pleased with you. **16.** The Lord appeared to you and asked you to choose any boon you wanted. Thereupon, O sinless one, you wanted Him, the protector of the world, to be born as your offspring. **17.** Having agreed to your request, He the Lord is now born as your son Rama. O King! Lakshmana who is none but Sesha would always be accompanying Rama. **18.** The conch and the discus of Mahavishnu, the wielder of the mace, are incarnated as Bharata and Satrughna. The Lord's Power, Yogamaya, has been born as Sita, the daughter of Janaka. **19.** To unite her with Rama is the real object of Visvamitra's arrival. This is a very closely guarded secret which you should not reveal to any one."

Rama Goes with Visvamitra (20-25)

20. Afterwards the king in a very happy mood resolved to send Rama, the consort of Lakshmi, along with Lakshmana under the care of Visvamitra, whom he duly worshipped and honoured. **21.** Hearing the words of Vasishtha, King Dasaratha was overjoyed and considered himself to have attained the greatest aim of his life. **22.**

ततोऽतिहृष्टो भगवान्विश्वामित्रः प्रतापवान् । आशीर्भिरभिनन्द्याथ आगतौ रामलक्ष्मणौ ।
गृहीत्वा चापतूणीरबाणखड्गधरौ ययौ । 23
किञ्चिद्देशमतिक्रम्य राममाहूय भक्तितः । ददौ बलां चातिबलां विद्ये द्वे देवनिर्मिते ॥ 24
ययोर्ग्रहणमात्रेण क्षुत्क्षामादि न जायते ॥ 25
तत उत्तीर्य गङ्गां ते ताटकावनमागमन् । विश्वामित्रस्तदा प्राह रामं सत्यपराक्रमम् ॥ 26
अत्रास्ति ताटका नाम राक्षसी कामरूपिणी । बाधते लोकमखिलं जहि तामविचारयन् ॥ 27
तथेति धनुरादाय सगुणं रघुनन्दनः । टङ्कारमकरोत्तेन शब्देनापूरयद्वनम् ॥ 28
तच्छ्रुत्वासहमाना सा ताटका घोररूपिणी । क्रोधसंमूर्च्छिता राममभिदुद्राव मेघवत् ॥ 29
तामेकेन शरेणाशु ताडयामास वक्षसि । पपात विपिने घोरा वमन्ती रुधिरं बहु ॥ 30
ततोऽतिसुन्दरी यक्षी सर्वाभरणभूषिता । शापात्पिशाचतां प्राप्ता मुक्ता रामप्रसादतः ॥ 31
नत्वा रामं परिक्रम्य गता रामाज्ञया दिवम् ॥ 32

Calling Rama and Lakshmana to his side and smelling the crown of their heads with affection and embracing them, he entrusted them to the care of Visvamitra. **23.** The powerful sage Visvamitra was immensely pleased at this and expressed his joy by bestowing his unreserved blessings on all. Then accompanied by Rama and Lakshmana, who approached him fully equipped with bow, quiver, sword etc, he started from Ayodhya. **(24-25).** After travelling some distance, he called Rama with great affection and imparted to him two Vidyas, *Bala* and *Atibala* which were of celestial origin. Those who know these two Vidyas will be free from hunger and exhaustion.

Destruction of Tataka (26-33)

26. Then, after crossing the Ganga, they entered the region called the forest of Tataka. Visvamitra thereupon said as follows to Rama, who was endowed with the true quality of heroism. **27.** He said, "O Rama! Here dwells a Rakshasa woman called Tataka who is capable of taking any form she likes. She is a curse to all creatures passing this way. Kill her without any hesitation." **28.** Agreeing to do so, Rama, the scion of Raghu's family, strung his bow and twanged it, filling the whole forest with that sound. **29.** Hearing that sound and disturbed beyond measure by it, the fierce-looking Tataka rushed at Rama in a fit of terrible anger, like a rain cloud with a torrent of rain. **30.** Being struck by Rama with a single arrow on the chest, that terrible creature fell down, vomiting a torrent of blood. **31.** Then came out from her the form of an extremely lovely Yakshi bedecked with all kinds of beautiful ornaments. By Rama's grace this Yakshi, who out of a curse had become this ogress, was thus liberated. **32.** Saluting Rama and circumambulating him, she, as ordered by Rama, went back to her divine abode.

ततोऽतिहृष्टः परिरभ्य रामं मूर्धन्यवघ्राय विचिन्त्य किञ्चित् ।
सर्वास्त्रजालं सरहस्यमन्त्रं प्रीत्याभिरामाय ददौ मुनीन्द्रः ॥ 33

इति श्रीमदध्यात्मरामायणे उमामहेश्वरसंवादे
बालकाण्डे चतुर्थः सर्गः ॥ ४ ॥

33. The Rishi Visvamitra was very much delighted at this and embraced Rama and smelt the crown of his head out of affection. Then thinking for a while, he imparted to him with immense pleasure all the great divine missiles along with the Mantras relating to them.

पञ्चमः सर्गः

श्रीमहादेव उवाच—

तत्र कामाश्रमे रम्ये कानने मुनिसङ्कुले । उषित्वा रजनीमेकां प्रभाते प्रस्थिताः शनैः ॥ 1
सिद्धाश्रमं गताः सर्वे सिद्धचारणसेवितम् । विश्वामित्रेण संदिष्टा मुनयस्तन्निवासिनः ॥ 2
पूजां च महतीं चक्रू रामलक्ष्मणयोर्द्रुतम् । श्रीरामः कौशिकं प्राह मुने दीक्षां प्रविश्यताम् ॥ 3
दर्शयस्व महाभाग कुतस्तौ राक्षसाधमौ । तथेत्युक्त्वा मुनिर्यष्टुमारेभे मुनिभिः सह ॥ 4
मध्याह्ने ददृशाते तौ राक्षसौ कामरूपिणौ । मारीचश्च सुबाहुश्च वर्षन्तौ रुधिरास्थिनी ॥ 5
रामोऽपि धनुरादाय द्वौ बाणौ सन्दधे सुधीः । आकर्णान्तं समाकृष्य विससर्ज तयोः पृथक् ॥ 6

Chapter 5

REDEMPTION OF AHALYA

Destruction of Subahu (1-9)

1. After spending one night in a forest Ashrama of that place known as Kamashram and inhabited by a large group of Rishis and providing a charming scenery, the party slowly proceeded on their journey in the early morning. **(2-3).** On their reaching Siddhashrama, a resort of Siddhas and Charanas, the ascetics living there gave a cordial reception to Rama and Lakshmana at the instance of Visvamitra. Afterwards Rama requested the sage Visvamitra, "O holy one! Be pleased to start the disciplines connected with your sacrificial rite. **4.** And show me the direction from which those heinous Rakshasas come to distress you." The sage Visvamitra agreed to do so and began the sacrificial rite along with the other ascetics of the place. **5.** Towards noon appeared those two Rakshasas, Maricha and Subahu, who were capable of taking any form they liked. Approaching the Ashrama, they sent down a rain of blood and bones. **6.** Thereupon Rama of mighty intellect,

तयोरेकस्तु मारीचं भ्रामयञ्छतयोजनम् । पातयामास जलधौ तदद्भुतमिवाभवत् ॥ 7
द्वितीयोऽग्निमयो बाणः सुबाहुमजयत्क्षणात् । अपरे लक्ष्मणेनाशु हतास्तदनुयायिनः ॥ 8
पुष्पौघैराकिरन्देवा राघवं सहलक्ष्मणम् । देवदुन्दुभयो नेदुस्तुष्टुवुः सिद्धचारणाः ॥ 9
विश्वामित्रस्तु संपूज्य पूजार्हं रघुनन्दनम् । अङ्के निवेश्य चालिङ्ग्य भक्त्या बाष्पाकुलेक्षणः 10
भोजयित्वा सह भ्रात्रा रामं पक्वफलादिभिः । पुराणवाक्यैर्मधुरैर्निनाय दिवसत्रयम् ॥ । 11
चतुर्थेऽहनि संप्राप्ते कौशिको राममब्रवीत् । राम राम महायज्ञं द्रष्टुं गच्छामहे वयम् ॥ 12
विदेहराजनगरे जनकस्य महात्मनः । तत्र माहेश्वरं चापमस्ति न्यस्तं पिनाकिना ॥ 13
द्रक्ष्यसि त्वं महासत्त्वं पूज्यसे जनकेन च । इत्युक्त्वा मुनिभिस्ताभ्यां ययौ गङ्गासमीपगम् ॥ 14
गौतमस्याश्रमं पुण्यं यत्राहल्यास्थिता तपः । दिव्यपुष्पफलोपेतपादपैः परिवेष्टितम् ॥ 15
मृगपक्षिगणैर्हीनं नानाजन्तुविवर्जितम् । दृष्ट्वोवाच मुनिं श्रीमान् रामो राजीवलोचनः ॥ 16
कस्यैतदाश्रमपदं भाति भास्वच्छुभं महत् । पत्रपुष्पफलैर्युक्तं जन्तुभिः परिवर्जितम् ॥ 17
आह्लादयति मे चेतो भगवन् ब्रूहि तत्त्वतः ॥ 18

drawing his bowstring to his ear, released two arrows at the Rakshasas. **7.** Wonder of wonders! One of those arrows, striking Maricha, hurled him away to a distance of a hundred Yojanas into the sea. **8.** The second arrow, which was a fiery missile, struck Subahu dead, while his Rakshasa following was all destroyed by Lakshmana. **9.** The Devas now showered a rain of flowers on Rama and Lakshmana. Their kettle drums began to sound, and the Siddhas and Charanas sang songs of praise.

Rama at the ashrama of Gautama (10-18)

(10-11). Viswamitra bestowed all honours on Rama, which he richly deserved. Moved by respect and love, he seated Rama on his lap, and with his eyes brimming with tears, embraced him. He kept Rama along with the brother Lakshmana in his Ashrama for three days, feeding them with ripe fruits and other edibles, and entertaining them with ancient stories and anecdotes. **12.** On the fourth day, the sage said to Rama: "O Rama! Let us go and see a great sacrifice that is about to take place. **13.** In the palace of the great king Janaka situated in the city of Videha, there is a divine bow deposited there by Maheswara. **(14-16).** You can have a look at that mighty bow. King Janaka too will welcome you with honours." Saying so, Viswamitra started with some other Munis as well as Rama and Lakshmana, and went towards the Ganga to reach the place where the holy Ashrama of Gautama stood and where the lady Ahalya was engaged in austerities. The place was full of trees laden with celestial flowers and fruits, but devoid of any birds or animals. Seeing the place so lifeless, the lotus-eyed Rama now asked the Muni as follows: **(17-18).** "Whose Ashrama is this? It looks like a very holy and extremely charming place. I find it full of trees with flowers and fruits, but without any

विश्वामित्र उवाच—

श्रृणु राम पुरा वृत्तं गौतमो लोकविश्रुतः । सर्वधर्मभृतां श्रेष्ठस्तपसाराधयन् हरिम् ॥ 19
तस्मै ब्रह्मा ददौ कन्यामहल्यां लोकसुन्दरीम् । ब्रह्मचर्येण सन्तुष्टः शुश्रूषणपरायणाम् ॥ 20
तया सार्धमिहावात्सीद्गौतमस्तपतां वरः । शक्रस्तु तां धर्षयितुमन्तरं प्रेप्सुरन्वहम् ॥ 21
कदाचिन्मुनिवेषेण गौतमे निर्गते गृहात् । धर्षयित्वाथ निरगात्त्वरितं मुनिरप्यगात् ॥ 22
दृष्ट्वा यान्तं स्वरूपेण मुनिः परमकोपनः । पप्रच्छ कस्त्वं दुष्टात्मन् मम रूपधरोऽधमः ॥23
सत्यं ब्रूहि न चेद्भस्म करिष्यामि न संशयः । सोऽब्रवीद्देवराजोऽहं पाहि मां कामकिङ्करम् ॥ 24
कृतं जुगुप्सितं कर्म मया कुत्सितचेतसा । गौतमः क्रोधताम्राक्षः शशाप दिविजाधिपम् ॥25
योनिलम्पट दुष्टात्मन्सहस्रभगवान्भव । शप्त्वा तं देवराजानं प्रविश्य स्वाश्रमं द्रुतम् ॥26
दृष्ट्वाहल्यां वेपमानां प्राञ्जलिं गौतमोऽब्रवीत् । दुष्टे त्वं तिष्ठ दुर्वृत्ते शिलायामाश्रमे मम ॥ 27

living creatures. It gives me great delight to be here. All these look wonderful. O great sage! Please tell me all the facts about this place and its peculiarities."

Curse on Ahalya & her Redemption (19-42)

Viswamitra said: **19.** "O Rama! Listen to what I say about the old traditions of this place. There was a great ascetic named Gautama, noblest among the observers of Dharma and famous all over the world. He adored Sri Hari with the austerities he was given to practising. **20.** Highly pleased with him for the very strict way in which he observed Brahmacharya, Brahma bestowed upon him his own daughter Ahalya, the most handsome girl of her times, noted also for her devotion to the discipline of service. **21.** That great ascetic Gautama was staying with Ahalya in this place. Now Indra developed a great passion for this girl Ahalya, and was on the look out for an opportunity to enjoy her by deception. **22.** An opportune moment came for him when the sage had gone out of the Ashrama for some time. Indra then approached Ahalya in the disguise of Gautama and after gratifying his passion was departing thence in haste when the sage Gautama returned. **23.** Seeing Indra going away disguised in his own (the sage's) form, Gautama was terribly angry, and he asked Indra, "Sirrah! You miscreant! Who are you that have assumed my form? **24.** Tell the truth. Otherwise I shall certainly reduce you to ashes by a curse!" Thereupon Indra replied: "I am Indra, the chief of the celestials. I have been a slave to Cupid, the god of love. I seek your pardon and protection. **25.** I have done a despicable act, the evil-natured fellow that I am." Thereupon Gautama, with eyes red with anger, pronounced a curse upon him. **(26-27).** Gautama cursed in great wrath: "O evil one! You who revel in the female genitals! I curse you to be deformed with a thousaud female genitals on your body." After thus cursing Indra, the chief of celestials, he entered his hermitage, and there saw Ahalya standing, trembling in fear and with palms joined in salutation. Gautama said to her: "O

निराहारा दिवारात्रं तपः परममास्थिता । आतपानिलवर्षादिसहिष्णुः परमेश्वरम् ॥ 28
ध्यायन्ती राममेकाग्रमनसा हृदि संस्थितम् । नानाजन्तुविहीनोऽयमाश्रमो मे भविष्यति ॥ 29
एवं वर्षसहस्रेषु ह्यनेकेषु गतेषु च । रामो दाशरथिः श्रीमानागमिष्यति सानुजः ॥ 30
यदा त्वदाश्रयशिलां पादाभ्यामाक्रमिष्यति । तदैव धूतपापा त्वं रामं संपूज्य भक्तितः ॥ 31
परिक्रम्य नमस्कृत्य स्तुत्वा शापाद्विमोक्ष्यसे । पूर्ववन्मम शुश्रूषां करिष्यसि यथासुखम् ॥ 32
इत्युक्त्वा गौतमः प्रागाद्धिमवन्तं नगोत्तमम् । तदाद्यहल्या भूतानामदृश्या स्वाश्रमे शुभे ॥ 33
तव पादरजःस्पर्शं काङ्क्षते पवनाशना । आस्तेऽद्यापि रघुश्रेष्ठ तपो दुष्करमास्थिता ॥ 34
पावयस्व मुनेर्भार्यामहल्यां ब्रह्मणः सुताम् । इत्युक्त्वा राघवं हस्ते गृहीत्वा मुनिपुङ्गवः ॥ 35
दर्शयामास चाहल्यामुग्रेण तपसा स्थिताम् । रामः शिलां पदा स्पृष्ट्वा तां चापश्यत्तपोधनाम् 36
ननाम राघवोऽहल्यां रामोऽहमिति चाब्रवीत् । ततो दृष्ट्वा रघुश्रेष्ठं पीतकौशेयवाससम् ॥ 37
चतुर्भुजं शङ्खचक्रगदापङ्कजधारिणम् । धनुर्बाणधरं रामं लक्ष्मणेन समन्वितम् ॥ 38
स्मितवक्त्रं पद्मनेत्रं श्रीवत्साङ्कितवक्षसम् । नीलमाणिक्यसङ्काशं द्योतयन्तं दिशो दश ॥ 39

degenerate one! You will be converted into a rock in this Ashrama. **(28-29).** Without any food and drink day and night, and subjected to all the inclemencies of weather like rain, sun, wind etc., you will be stationed here in the practice of severe austerity, meditating on the Supreme Being Rama dwelling in the hearts of all. This place, which has been my hermitage, will hereafter be without any living creature. **(30-32).** After you have spent several thousand years in this condition, Sri Rama, the son of Dasaratha, along with his brother Lakshmana will be coming to this place. When he places his feet on the rock, with which you will now gain identity by my curse, you will be freed from sin. You will then adore Rama with great devotion, circumambulating him and prostrating before him. Liberated from the effects of the curse, you will again have opportunity to serve me."

(33-36). Saying so, Gautama went away and took his residence on that greatest of mountains, the Himalayas. From that day, O Rama, unseen by any living being, Ahalya has been till this present moment observing severe penance eschewing all food, and ever awaiting the holy contact of the dust of your feet. Now deign to purify Ahalya, the daughter of Brahma and the wife of Gautama." Saying so, Viswamitra took Rama by the hand to the place where Ahalya was standing as a stone and observing the most rigorous penance. On Rama placing his feet on the stone, he saw Ahalya coming out of it and standing before him.

(37-39). Rama of Raghu's line thereupon saluted Ahalya, and announced himself to her. Then did Ahalya see Rama, the best of Raghu's line, along with Lakshmana, in his form as Mahavishnu—wearing a yellow silk, sporting in His four arms the conch, discus, mace and lotus; equipped with bow and arrows; revealing a face with lotus-like eyes and a comely smile playing on it; bearing the Srivatsa mark on His

दृष्ट्वा रामं रमानाथं हर्षविस्फारितेक्षणा । गौतमस्य वचः स्मृत्वा ज्ञात्वा नारायणं वरम् ॥ 40
संपूज्य विधिवद्राममर्घ्यादिभिरनिन्दिता । हर्षाश्रुजलनेत्रान्ता दण्डवत्प्रणिपत्य सा ॥ 41
उत्थाय च पुनर्दृष्ट्वा रामं राजीवलोचनम् । पुलकाङ्कितसर्वाङ्गा गिरा गद्गदयैलत ॥ 42

अहल्योवाच—

अहो कृतार्थास्मि जगन्निवास ते पादाब्जसंलग्नरजःकणादहम् ।
स्पृशामि यत्पद्मजशंकरादिभिर्विमृग्यते रन्धितमानसैः सदा ॥ 43
अहो विचित्रं तव राम चेष्टितं मनुष्यभावेन विमोहितं जगत् ।
चलस्यजस्रं चरणादिवर्जितः सम्पूर्ण आनन्दमयोऽतिमायिकः ॥ 44
यत्पादपङ्कजपरागपवित्रगात्रा भागीरथी भवविरिञ्चिमुखान्पुनाति ।
साक्षात्स एव मम दृग्विषयो यदास्ते किं वर्ण्यते मम पुराकृतभागधेयम् ॥ 45
मर्त्यावतारे मनुजाकृतिं हरिं रामाभिधेयं रमणीयदेहिनम् ।
धनुर्धरं पद्मविशाललोचनं भजामि नित्यं न परान्भजिष्ये ॥ 46

chest; and illumining the ten quarters with the lustre of his blue emerald-like splendour. Such was the form of Rama that Ahalya now saw. **(40-42).** Seeing Rama, the consort of Ramā, Ahalya shed tears of joy. Remembering the words of Gautama, she recognised Rama to be Narayana Himself. That holy lady, with her eyes brimming with tears, worshipped Rama in due form with Arghya and other ingredients. Then falling before him in full prostration and getting up, she saw the lotus-eyed Rama once again, and with horripilations all over her body, and voice choking with emotion, began to praise him with a hymn.

Ahalya's Hymn (43-65)

Ahalya said: **43.** O Thou Indweller of the whole universe! Blessed am I with the contact I have had with the particles of dust adhering to Thy lotus-feet—the feet which form only an object of quest for Brahma and Sankara with concentrated minds, but which I have now been fortunate to contact even with the physical body. **44.** Everything about Thee is wonderful indeed O Rama! Thy human form only deludes the world. For, Thou, the super-magician immersed in the plenitude of Bliss and infilling the whole universe with Thy presence, art without any particular form (having hands and feet; but yet as the Incarnate Thou art none the less moving about as a man with a particular form. **45.** He the dust of whose lotus-feet rendered the waters of the Ganga sacred enough to sanctify even great beings like Brahma, even He is now present here for my corporeal eyes to see. This indeed is a rare good fortune, indescribable by words, arising from some meritorious deeds of mine in the past. **46.** To none else is the adoration of my heart directed than to Sri Hari now embodied in a human form in His incarnation as Rama revealing a body of exquisite beauty, having broad eyes like lotus-petals and holding a bow in

यत्पादपङ्कजरजः श्रुतिभिर्विमृग्यं यन्नाभिपङ्कजभवः कमलासनश्च ।
यन्नामसाररसिको भगवान्पुरारिस्तं रामचन्द्रमनिशं हृदि भावयामि ॥ 47
यस्यावतारचरितानि विरिञ्चिलोके गायन्ति नारदमुखा भवपद्मजाद्याः ।
आनन्दजाश्रुपरिषिक्तकुचाग्रसीमा वागीश्वरी च तमहं शरणं प्रपद्ये ॥ 48
सोऽयं परात्मा पुरुषः पुराण एकः स्वयंज्योतिरनन्त आद्यः ।
मायातनुं लोकविमोहनीयां धत्ते परानुग्रह एष रामः ॥ 49
अयं हि विश्वोद्भवसंयमानामेकः स्वमायागुणबिम्बितो यः ।
विरिञ्चिविष्ण्वीश्वरनामभेदान् धत्ते स्वतन्त्रः परिपूर्ण आत्मा ॥ 50
नमोऽस्तु ते राम तवाङ्घ्रिपङ्कजं श्रिया धृतं वक्षसि लालितं प्रियात् ।
आक्रान्तमेकेन जगत्त्रयं पुरा ध्येयं मुनीन्द्रैरभिमानवर्जितैः ॥ 51
जगतामादिभूतस्त्वं जगत्त्वं जगदाश्रयः । सर्वभूतेष्वसंयुक्त एको भाति भवान्परः ॥ 52
ओंकारवाच्यस्त्वं राम वाचामविषयः पुमान् । वाच्यवाचकभेदेन भवानेव जगन्मयः ॥ 53

hand. **47.** He whose lotus-feet are always the object of quest for the Srutis, He whose navel-lotus is the birth place of Brahma the Creator; He whose holy name of Rama is the dearest among His thousand names to Lord Siva, the destroyer of cities—on that Sri Ramachandra I contemplate in my heart. **48.** He whose deeds in His incarnations are glorified in Brahma-loka by sages like Narada and Divinities like Bhava (Siva) and the lotus-born Brahma, as also by Saraswati the goddess of learning with outbursts of bliss-inspired streams of tears, wetting her breasts—in that Sri Rama I take refuge. **49.** Rama, the adorable, is the supreme Self; He is the eternal and all-pervading Being, the Self-luminous Consciousness by whom everything is revealed. He is the First Cause who is without an end. For the blessing of the world He has now assumed a form of heart-ravishing beauty. **50.** He is the One Being that forms the cause of the creation, sustentation and dissolution of the universe. The free and the perfect being that He is, He assumes the different names of Brahma, Vishnu and Maheswara when He reflects Himself in the three Gunas of His Maya, namely Rajas, Sattva and Tamas, respectively. **51.** Obeisance to Thee, O Rama! Thy Lotus feet are ever held by Sri on her breast and fondled. It was with a single one of those feet that Thou didst measure the three worlds in ancient times. Again those feet are holy enough to be contemplated upon by sages who have abandoned identification with the narrow self. **52.** Thou art the origin of all the worlds, nay, Thou art the world itself, in its totality, and the support of the worlds as well. Unrelated to any second existence, Thou art the transcendent and unitary Being. **53.** O Rama! Thou art denoted by the sound symbol Om, but Thou art also the all-pervading Being transcending the scope of any verbal description. Thou who dost comprehend the

कार्यकारणकर्तृत्वफलसाधनभेदतः । एको विभासि राम त्वं मायया बहुरूपया ॥ 54
त्वन्मायामोहितधियस्त्वां न जानन्ति तत्त्वतः । मानुषं त्वाभिमन्यन्ते मायिनं परमेश्वरम् ॥ 55
आकाशवत्त्वं सर्वत्र बहिरन्तर्गतोऽमलः । असङ्गो ह्यचलो नित्यः शुद्धो बुद्धः सदव्ययः ॥ 56
योषिन्मूढाहमज्ञा ते तत्त्वं जाने कथं विभो । तस्मात्ते शतशो राम नमस्कुर्यामनन्यधीः ॥ 57
देव मे यत्र कुत्रापि स्थिताया अपि सर्वदा । त्वत्पादकमले सक्ता भक्तिरेव सदास्तु मे ॥ 58
नमस्ते पुरुषाध्यक्ष नमस्ते भक्तवत्सल । नमस्तेऽस्तु हृषीकेश नारायण नमोऽस्तुते ॥ 59

भवभयहरमेकं भानुकोटिप्रकाशं करधृतशरचापं कालमेघावभासम् ।
कनकरुचिरवस्त्रं रत्नवत्कुण्डलाढ्यं कमलविशदनेत्रं सानुजं राममीडे ॥ 60

स्तुत्वैवं पुरुषं साक्षाद्राघवं पुरतः स्थितम् । परिक्रम्य प्रणम्याशु सानुज्ञाता ययौ पतिम् ॥ 61
अहल्यया कृतं स्तोत्रं यः पठेद्भक्तिसंयुतः । स मुच्यतेऽखिलैः पापैः परं ब्रह्माधिगच्छति ॥ 62

totality of existence in Thyself, art both the object and the idea. **54.** By Thy Power of Maya which is capable of projecting this multiplicity, Thou, the Unitary Being, seemest to be manifested as the all—Prakriti the Root Cause, its evolutes known as the categories, the worlds forming their products, sufferings and enjoyments forming the fruits of creative activity, and the various types of rites and deeds that yield such fruits. **55.** Those who are deluded by Thy Maya do not recognise Thy identity with the Supreme Lord of Maya, and consider Thee only to be a human being. **56.** Like the sky Thou art all-pervading, being both within and without and everywhere. Pure, unattached and unchanging, Thou art the eternal, immaculate, and Undecaying Being who can be described only as Pure Consciousness and Pure Existence. **57.** O All-pervading One! The senseless and ignorant woman that I am, how can I know Thee in truth and in reality? So, O Rama, I salute Thee a hundred times with wholehearted devotion. **58.** O Lord! Wherever I might be and at all times, may I have unobstructed devotion to Thy lotus feet. **59.** Salutations to Thee, the Supreme Spirit directing all! Salutations to Thee, the lover of all devotees! Salutations to Thee, the master of all the senses! Salutations to Thee, who dwellest in all Jivas. **60.** Adoration to Rama in the company of his brother Lakshmana—Rama who is the saviour of the Jivas from the cycle of births and deaths (Samsara), who is the One without a second, who is brilliant like a million suns, who sports a bow and an arrow in his hands, who has the lustre of a blue cloud, who is dressed in a cloth of bewitching golden colour, who bears earpendants studded with precious gems and who has eyes broad and beautiful like the petals of the lotus flower.

61. In this way praising, circumambulating and prostrating before Rama, the Eternal Being embodied as a scion of the Raghu's line, she stood before him; and on being permitted by him, she went away to join her husband, the sage Gautama. **62.** He who studies with devotion this hymn of Ahalya will be free from all sins. He will attain to

पुत्रार्थी पठेद्भक्त्या रामं हृदि निधाय च । संवत्सरेण लभते वन्ध्या अपि सुपुत्रकम् ॥ 63

सर्वान्कामानवाप्नोति रामचन्द्रप्रसादतः ॥ 64

ब्रह्मघ्नो गुरुतल्पगोऽपि पुरुषः स्तेयी सुरापोऽपि वा
मातृभ्रातृविहिंसकोऽपि सततं भोगैकबद्धातुरः ।
नित्यं स्तोत्रमिदं जपन् रघुपतिं भक्त्या हृदिस्थं स्मरन्
ध्यायन्मुक्तिमुपैति किं पुनरसौ स्वाचारयुक्तो नरः ॥ 65

इति श्रीमदध्यात्मरामायणे उमामहेश्वरसंवादे
बालकाण्डे अहल्योद्धरणं नाम पञ्चमः सर्गः ॥ ५ ॥

the Supreme Brahman. **63.** By studying this hymn with a mind concentrated on Rama, a woman, even if she be unfit for bearing children, will have an issue within one year. **64.** By the grace of Rama all one's desires will be fulfilled. **65.** Even a person who is guilty of various sinful acts like murder of holy men, indulgence in immorality, theft and drink, of cruel conduct towards parents and brothers, of indulgence in sensuous enjoyments always—even such a one will attain to liberation if he recites this hymn every day concentrating his mind on Rama, and meditating upon him with devotion. What then to speak of a man of good conduct!

षष्ठः सर्गः

विश्वामित्रोऽथ तं प्राह राघवं सहलक्ष्मणम् । गच्छामो वत्स मिथिलां जनकेनाभिपालिताम् । 1
दृष्ट्वा क्रतुवरं पश्चादयोध्यां गन्तुमर्हसि ।
इत्युक्त्वा प्रययौ गङ्गामुत्तर्तुं सहराघवः । तस्मिन्काले नाविकेन निषिद्धो रघुनन्दनः ॥ 2

नाविक उवाच—

क्षालयामि तव पादपङ्कजं नाथ दारुदृषदोः किमन्तरम् ।
मानुषीकरणचूर्णमस्ति ते पादयोरिति कथा प्रथीयसी ॥ 3

Chapter 6

RAMA'S MARRIAGE WITH SITA

Journey to Mithila (1-5)

1. Afterwards Viswamitra said to Rama and Lakshmana, "O Darlings! Let us now go to the country of Mithila governed by King Janaka. **2.** After witnessing the great sacrifice that is being performed there, we shall return to Ayodhya. Saying so, he, along with Rama and Lakshmana, set off for crossing the river Ganga. But the boatman there refused to take Rama into the boat. *The boatman said:* **3.** "O Lord! I would like

पादाम्बुजं ते विमलं हि कृत्वा पश्चात्परं तीरमहं नयामि ।
नोचेत्तरी सद्यु वती मलेन स्याच्चेद्विभो विद्धि कुटम्बहानिः ॥ 4

इत्युक्त्वा क्षालितौ पादौ परं तीरं ततो गताः । कौशिको रघुनाथेन सहितो मिथिलां ययौ ॥ 5
विदेहस्य पुरं प्रातर्ऋषिवाटं समाविशत् । प्राप्तं कौशिकमाकर्ण्य जनकोऽतिमुदान्वितः ॥ 6
पूजाद्रव्याणि संगृह्य सोपाध्यायः समाययौ । दण्डवत्प्रणिपत्याथ पजयामास कौशिकम् ॥ 7
पप्रच्छ राघवौ दृष्ट्वा सर्वलक्षणसंयुतौ । द्योतयन्तौ दिशः सर्वाश्चन्द्रसूर्याविवापरौ ॥ 8
कस्यैतौ नरशार्दूलौ पुत्रौ देवसुतोपमौ । मनःप्रीतिकरौ मेऽद्य नरनारायणाविव ॥ 9
प्रत्युवाच मुनिः प्रीतो हर्षयन् जनकं तदा । पुत्रौ दशरथस्यैतौ भ्रातरौ रामलक्ष्मणौ ॥ 10
मखसंरक्षणार्थाय मयानीतौ पितुः पुरात् । आगच्छन् राघवो मार्गे ताटकां विश्वघातिनीम् ॥ 11
शरेणैकेन हतवान्नोदितो मेऽतिविक्रमः । ततो ममाश्रमं गत्वा मम यज्ञविहिंसकान् ॥ 12
सुबाहुप्रमुखान्हत्वा मारीचं सागरेऽक्षिपत् । ततो गङ्गातटे पुण्ये गौतमस्याश्रमं शुभम् ॥ 13
गत्वा तत्र शिलारूपा गौतमस्य वधूः स्थिता । पादपङ्कजसंस्पर्शात्कृता मानुषरूपिणी ॥ 14

to wash and cleanse your feet first. What is the difference between a stone and wooden things? The news has spread that the dust of your feet can transform anything into a human being. (It happened with Ahalya.) **4.** Therefore I shall clean your feet of all the dust on it and then take you to the other shore. If this is not done, there is the danger of my boat being converted into a young woman. In that case, O Master, the livelihood of my family will be endangered." **5.** Saying so, he washed the feet of Rama and then took the party to the other side of the river. Then Viswamitra along with Rama, the leader of Raghu's line, proceeded to the kingdom of Mithila.

Breaking of Siva's Bow (6-27)

(6-7). By morning they reached Mithila—the Kingdom of Janaka-Videha. Viswamitra went to the quarters of the Rishis and took his station there. Hearing that Viswamitra had come to his city, King Janaka was rejoiced, and gathering all the necessary ingredients for worship, came along with his preceptor in great joy to the sage, prostrated before him and adored him in the proper way. **8.** Seeing the two princes of Raghu's line, illumining all the quarters by their brilliance like another sun and moon, and possessed of all auspicious marks on their body, Janaka asked: **9.** "Who are these two heroic boys resembling the children of celestials? Whose sons are they? My mind is filled with joy on seeing them, just like the experience one gets on seeing Nara and Narayana." **10.** Pleased at these words, the sage Viswamitra said to Janaka, delighting him, "These are two brothers—Rama and Lakshmana. They are sons of King Dasaratha.

(11-16). "In order to protect my Yajna (sacrificial rites) from the depredations of

दृष्ट्वाहल्यां नमस्कृत्य तया सम्यक्प्रपूजितः । इदानीं द्रष्टकामस्ते गृहे माहेश्वरं धनुः ॥ 15
पूजितं राजभिः सर्वैर्दृष्टमित्यनुशुश्रुवे ।
अतो दर्शय राजेन्द्र शैवं चापमनुत्तमम् । दृष्ट्वायोध्यां जिगमिषुः पितरं द्रष्टुमिच्छति ॥ 16
इत्युक्तो मुनिना राजा पूजार्हाविति पूजया । पूजयामास धर्मज्ञो विधिदृष्टेन कर्मणा ॥ 17

जनक उवाच—

ततः सम्प्रेषयामास मन्त्रिणं बुद्धिमत्तरम् । शीघ्रमानय विश्वेशचापं रामाय दर्शय ॥ 18
ततो गते मन्त्रिवरे राजा कौशिकमब्रवीत् । यदि रामो धनुर्धृत्वा कोटयामारोपयेद्‌गुणम् ॥ 19
तदा मयात्मजा सीता दीयते राघवाय हि । तथेति कौशिकोऽप्याह रामं संवीक्ष्य सस्मितम् ॥ 20
शीघ्रं दर्शय चापाग्र्यं रामायामिततेजसे । एवं ब्रुवति मौनीशे आगताश्चापवाहकाः ॥ 21
चापं गृहीत्वा बलिनः पञ्चसाहस्रसङ्ख्यकाः । घण्टाशतसमायुक्तं मणिवज्रादिभूषितम् ॥ 22
दर्शयामास रामाय मन्त्री मन्त्रयतां वरः । दृष्ट्वा रामः प्रहृष्टात्मा बद्ध्वा परिकरं दृढम् ॥ 23
गृहीत्वा वामहस्तेन लीलया तोलयन् धनुः । आरोपयामास गुणं पश्यत्स्वखिलराजसु ॥ 24

Rakshasas, I brought them from the palace of their father. On the way this heroic Rama of Raghu's line killed with a single arrow Tataka—the terror of the world. Afterwards, arriving at my Ashrama, he killed Subahu and other Rakshasas, who were obstructing the sacrificial rites there; and hurled away Maricha, their associate, into the sea. Reaching the banks of the holy river Ganga and the Ashrama of Gautama situated there, he by the touch of his feet redeemed Ahalya, the wife of Gautama, converted into a stone as the result of a curse. He restored her to her human form. After himself honouring Ahalya, he was adored by her. Now he has come over to your palace. He wants to see the great bow of Siva that is in your possession. It is well known that royalties from all places have been coming to see it. Therefore, O great king, be pleased to show him that bow. After seeing it, his idea is to go back to Ayodhya to join his father."

17. Hearing these words of the sage, King Janaka, who was a knower of Dharma, understood that these princes deserved all respectful reception. Therefore he extended to them honours with rites prescribed by the Sastras. **18.** Then the king sent for his highly accomplished minister and said to him, "Let the bow of Parameswara be brought here soon to be shown to Rama". **(19-20)** After the minister had departed, King Janaka said to Viswamitra, "If Rama is able to lift and string this bow, I shall certainly bestow my daughter Sita on him." At this, Viswamitra looking at Rama with a smile, said: **21.** "Let it be so. Without delay do please show this noble bow to Rama of unlimited prowess." While the sage was uttering these words, the bow was brought there by a set of carriers.

22. Five thousand men of strong build were carrying that bow studded with innumerable gems and diamonds and having on it numerous mini bells. **(23-24)** That highly

ईषदाकर्षयामास पाणिना दक्षिणेन सः । बभञ्जाखिलहृत्सारो दिशः शब्देन पूरयन् ॥ 25
दिशश्च विदिशश्चैव स्वर्गं मर्त्यं रसातलम् । तदद्भुतमभूत्तत्र देवानां दिवि पश्यताम् ॥ 26
आच्छादयन्तः कुसुमैर्देवाः स्तुतिभिरीडिरे । देवदुन्दुभयो नेदुर्ननृतुश्चाप्सरोगणाः ॥ 27
द्विधा भग्नं धनुर्दृष्ट्वा राजालिङ्गय रघूद्वहम् । विस्मयं लेभिरे सीतामातरोऽन्तःपुराजिरे ॥ 28
सीता स्वर्णमयीं मालां गृहीत्वा दक्षिणे करे । स्मितवक्त्रा स्वर्णवर्णा सर्वाभरणभूषिता ॥ 29
मुक्ताहारैः कर्णपत्रैः क्वणच्चरणनूपुरा । दुकूलपरिसंवीता वस्त्रान्तर्व्यञ्जितस्तनी ॥ 30
रामस्योपरि निक्षिप्य स्मयमाना मुदं ययौ । ततो मुमुदिरे सर्वे राजदाराः स्वलङ्कृतम् ॥ 31
गवाक्षजालरन्ध्रेभ्यो दृष्ट्वा लोकविमोहनम् । ततोऽब्रवीन्मुनिं राजा सर्वशास्त्रविशारदः ॥ 32
भो कौशिक मुनिश्रेष्ठ पत्रं प्रेषय सत्वरम् । राजा दशरथः शीघ्रमागच्छतु सपुत्रकः ॥ 33
विवाहार्थं कुमाराणां सदारः सहमन्त्रिभिः । तथेति प्रेषयामास दूतांस्त्वरितविक्रमान् ॥ 34

competent minister exhibited the bow before Rama. Glad on seeing it, Rama tightened his wearing cloth, and as in sport, lifted the bow with his left hand and, in the presence of all the assembled rulers, strung it. **25.** Holding the bow in his left hand and pulling the string by the right, Rama, who embodied in himself the energy of the whole universe, broke the bow producing a tremendous sound that resounded from all the quarters. **26.** That sound penetrated into all the worlds—those of celestials, of men, and of the Titans. With wonder, the celestials, stationing themselves in the sky, looked at the scene. **27.** They covered the earth with a rain of flowers, recited songs and panegyrics in praise of Rama and sounded their kettle-drums, while the celestial artistes danced in joy.

Sita's Choice of Rama (28-32)

28. Seeing the bow broken, King Janaka embraced Rama—the noblest of Raghu's line, while the womenfolk, stationing themselves in the courtyards of their quarters, looked on in great amazement. **29-32.** Then arrived Sita on the scene in all her natural splendour enhanced by her decorations. She was adorned with various kinds of ornaments like pearl necklaces and ear-pendants. On her feet she had anklets that produced a delightful tinkling sound. Dressed in a silken wearing-cloth and in a thin upper cloth that faintly revealed the contours of her breasts, the golden-hued Sita advanced towards Rama with a smiling face, and put on his neck a golden necklace which she held in her right hand. Her face, wreathed in smiles, revealed the supreme joy of her heart. Viewing through the windows of the galleries, the ladies of the royal household saw with great delight the forms of Rama and Sita whose exquisite beauty charmed the whole world. Now King Janaka, versed in all scriptures, said to sage Viswamitra as follows:

Arrangements for Marriage (33-44)

33. The King said, "O great sage Viswamitra! Send letters soon announcing this news to King Dasaratha, so that he may go over here soon with his sons. **34.** Let him

ते गत्वा राजशार्दूलं रामश्रेयो न्यवेदयन् । श्रुत्वा रामकृतं राजा हर्षेण महताप्लुतः ॥ 35
मिथिलागमनार्थाय त्वरयामास मन्त्रिणः । गच्छन्तु मिथिलां सर्वे गजाश्वरथपत्तयः ॥ 36
रथमानय मे शीघ्रं गच्छाम्यद्यैव मा चिरम् । वसिष्ठस्त्वग्रतो यातु सदार सहितोऽग्निभिः ॥ 37
राममातृः समादाय मुनिर्मे भगवान् गुरुः । एवं प्रस्थाप्य सकलं राजर्षिर्विपुलं रथम् ॥ 38
महत्या सेनया सार्धमारुह्य त्वरितो ययौ । आगतं राघवं श्रुत्वा राजा हर्षसमाकुलः ॥ 39
प्रत्युज्जगाम जनकः शतानन्दपुरोधसा । यथोक्तपूजया पूज्यं पूजयामास सत्कृतम् ॥ 40
रामस्तु लक्ष्मणेनाशु ववन्दे चरणौ पितुः । ततो हृष्टो दशरथो रामं वचनमब्रवीत् ॥ 41
दिष्ट्या पश्यामि ते राम मुखं फुल्लाम्बुजोपमम् । मुनेरनुग्रहात्सर्वं सम्पन्नं मम शोभनम् ॥ 42
इत्युक्त्वाघ्राय मूर्धानमालिङ्ग्य च पुनः पुनः । हर्षेण महताविष्टो ब्रह्मानन्दं गतो यथा ॥ 43
ततो जनकराजेन मन्दिरे सन्निवेशितः । शोभने सर्वभोगाढ्ये सदारः ससुतः सुखी ॥ 44

be pleased to come with his wives and ministers to attend the marriage ceremony of the princes." Accordingly speedy messengers were despatched immediately. **35.** Reaching Ayodhya quickly, they communicated the news of Rama's great success to the valiant King Dasaratha, who received the news with overwhelming joy. **(36-39).** He ordered his ministers to make quick preparations for going to Mithila. He said, "Let army divisions consisting of elephant regiments, cavalry and chariots be ordered to proceed to that city of Mithila in advance. Order my chariot to be made ready so that I may start even today. Let there be no delay on any account. Arrange for my preceptor Vasishtha to proceed in advance with his consort and his sacred fires. So also let the queens, the mothers of Rama, proceed in advance." Thus, after arranging for the journey of all others, Dasaratha got into his great chariot, and accompanied by a grand army proceeded to Mithila in all haste. The news of his arrival at Mithila reached the ears of King Janaka, filling the mind of that Rajarshi with great joy.

40. Accompanied by his preceptor Satananda, King Janaka hurried to receive the august guest, and arranged for a reception ceremony according to the programmes prescribed by custom and scriptural texts for such occasions. **41.** Then Rama and Lakshmana prostrated at the feet of their father in salutation. Dasaratha who was all joy, now spoke to Rama. **42.** He said, "O Rama! I am fortunate to see your lotus-like face again. Due to the grace of the sage Viswamitra, all circumstances have turned in our favour, bringing great good fortune to us." **43.** With these words he embraced Rama and smelt the crown of his head again and again, and thereby attained to the acme of joy like one enjoying the bliss of Brahman. **44.** Next. Dasaratha with his wives and sons was provided accommodation by Janaka in a spacious palace which had arrangements for every form of comfort and enjoyment.

ततः शुभे दिने लग्ने सुमुहूर्ते रघूत्तमम् । आनयामास धर्मज्ञो रामं सभ्रातृकं तदा ॥ 45
रत्नस्तम्भसुविस्तारे सुविताने सुतोरणे । मण्डपे सर्वशोभाढ्ये मुक्तापुष्पफलान्विते ॥ 46
वेदविद्भिः सुसम्बाधे ब्राह्मणैः स्वर्णभूषितैः । सुवासिनीभिः परितो निष्ककण्ठीभिरावृते ॥ 47
भेरीदुन्दुभिनिर्घोषैर्गीतनृत्यैः समाकुले । दिव्यरत्नाञ्चिते स्वर्णपीठे रामं न्यवेशयत् ॥ 48
वसिष्ठं कौशिकं चैव शतानन्दः पुरोहितः । यथाक्रमं पूजयित्वा रामस्योभयपार्श्वयोः ॥ 49
स्थापयित्वा स तत्राग्निं ज्वालयित्वा यथाविधि । सीतामानीय शोभाढ्यां नानारत्नविभूषिताम् ॥50
सभार्यो जनकः प्रायाद्रामं राजीवलोचनम् । पादौ प्रक्षाल्य विधिवत्तदपो मूर्ध्न्यधारयत् । 51
या धृता मूर्ध्नि शर्वेण ब्रह्मणा मुनिभिः सदा । ततः सीतां करे धृत्वा साक्षतोदकपूर्वकम् ॥ 52
रामाय प्रददौ प्रीत्या पाणिग्रहविधानतः । सीता कमलपत्राक्षी स्वर्णमुक्तादिभूषिता ॥ 53
दीयते मे सुता तुभ्यं प्रीतो भव रघूत्तम । इति प्रीतेन मनसा सीतां रामकरेऽर्पयन् ॥ 54
मुमोद जनको लक्ष्मीं क्षीराब्धिरिव विष्णवे । उर्मिलां चौरसीं कन्यां लक्ष्मणाय ददौ मुदा ॥55
तथैव श्रुतिकीर्तिं च माण्डवीं भ्रातृकन्यके । भरताय ददावेकां शत्रुघ्नायापरां ददौ ॥ 56

The Marriage Ceremony (45-57)

(45-48). Soon after, on an auspicious day at an auspicious hour, King Janaka, who was well acquainted with Dharma, led Rama and his brothers to a specially erected marriage pavilion, which was supported by columns studded with precious gems. The hall was spacious, splendorous, and well-decorated with festoons, flags and canopies and a profusion of pearl strings, fruits and flowers. Crowds of Brahmanas, learned in Vedas and wearing golden ornaments, were present there, while womenfolk, dressed in their best attire, and adorned with shining jewels, stood on all sides. Dancing, music and playing on percussion instruments added to the holiday atmosphere. Into such a splendid marriage pavilion Rama was brought and seated on a golden pedestal embellished with every kind of rare jewels. **(49-51)**. The preceptor Satananda now honoured the sages Vasishtha and Viswamitra with all due ceremony and seated them on either side of Rama. He then lighted the sacred fire before which the marriage ceremony was to be performed. Now Sita, resplendent with all jewellery and other decorations, was ushered into the marriage pavilion. Next, King Janaka with his consort went near Rama, washed his feet, and sprinkled that water on their own heads. **(52-56)**. That water from the feet of Rama the Incarnate is identical with the water with which Mahavishnu's feet were washed and which Brahma and Siva consider holy enough to bear on their heads. Next, holding Sita's hand Janaka gifted her to Rama along with offerings of water and Akshata (unbroken grains of rice), according to the rites of Panigrahana (marriage symbolised by the holding of the spouse's hand by the bridegroom). He said: "With this I am handing over to you my daughter Sita, lotus-eyed and bedecked with pearls

चत्वारो दारसम्पन्ना भ्रातरः शुभलक्षणाः । विरेजुः प्रजया सर्वे लोकपाला इवापरे ॥ 57
ततोऽब्रवीद्वसिष्ठाय विश्वामित्राय मैथिलः । जनकः स्वसुतोदन्तं नारदेनाभिभाषितम् ॥ 58
यज्ञभूमिविशुद्ध्यर्थं कर्षतो लाङ्गलेन मे । सीतामुखात्समुत्पन्ना कन्यका शुभलक्षणा ॥ 59
तामद्राक्षमहं प्रीत्या पुत्रिकाभावभाविताम् । अर्पिता प्रियभार्यायै शरच्चन्द्रनिभानना ॥ 60
एकदा नारदोऽभ्यागाद्विविक्ते मयि संस्थिते । रणयन्महतीं वीणां गायन्नारायणं विभुम् ॥ 61
पूजितः सुखमासीनो मामुवाच सुखान्वितः । श्रृणुष्व वचनं गुह्यं तवाभ्युदयकारणम् ॥ 62
परमात्मा हृषीकेशो भक्तानुग्रहकाम्यया । देवकार्यार्थसिद्ध्यर्थं रावणस्य वधाय च ॥ 63
जातो राम इति ख्यातो मायामानुषवेषधृक् । आस्ते दाशरथिर्भूत्वा चतुर्धा परमेश्वरः ॥ 64
योगमायापि सीतेति जाता वै तव वेश्मनि । अतस्त्वं राघवायैव देहि सीतां प्रयत्नतः ॥ 65
नान्येभ्यः पूर्वभार्यैषा रामस्य परमात्मनः । इत्युक्त्वा प्रययौ देवगतिं देवमुनिस्तदा ॥ 66

and gold. O Rama, the greatest of the Raghus! May you be pleased with this offering." Uttering these words, Janaka now placed the hand of Sita in Rama's to symbolise his having given her over to him with a heart over-flowing with joy, just like that of the deity of the milk-ocean when he gave away Lakshmi in marriage to Mahavishnu. On this occasion Janaka gave away his own daughter Urmila in marriage to Lakshmana, and his brother's daughters Srutikirti and Mandavi to Bharata and Satrughna respectively. **57.** United with their wives, the handsome princes shone resplendent like another set of Lokapalas (the celestial guardians of the quarters).

Janaka on the Antecedents of Sita (58-75)

58. Now that the marriage ceremony was over, Janaka narrated to the sages Vasishtha and Viswamitra, an account about Sita's past, which he happened to hear from Narada. **59.** Janaka said: "While I was once ploughing a field with the idea of making it into a holy site for a sacrifice, I got a beautiful female child from one of the furrows in the field (*Sīta-mukhāt*). **60.** Looking lovingly upon that moon-like infant as my own daughter, I handed her over to the care of my consort. **(61-62).** One day while I had withdrawn myself into solitude, there came sage Narada, singing to the accompaniment of his noted Vina, hymns in praise of the all-pervading Narayana. After he was duly honoured and seated on a comfortable seat, the sage Narada said to me: "Hear from me a secret that will lead to your welfare. **(63-64)**. For the blessing of devotees, for the destruction of Ravana and for the achievement of the purposes of the celestials, the Supreme Lord, the director and master of the senses, has incarnated Himself in a human body, which he has assumed by the power of His Maya. He is born as the son of King Dasaratha as the world-famous Sri Rama. In this incarnation the Lord has taken a fourfold form. **65.** His spiritual counterpart, Yoga-maya, has manifested Herself in your house. Strive in every way to give her in marriage to Rama and Rama alone. **66.** For, being

तदारभ्य मया सीता विष्णोर्लक्ष्मीर्विभाव्यते । कथं मया राघवाय दीयते जानकी शुभा ॥ 67
इति चिन्तासमाविष्टः कार्यमेकमचिन्तयम् । मत्पितामहगेहे तु न्यासभूतमिदं धनुः ॥ 68
ईश्वरेण पुरा क्षिप्तं पुरदाहादनन्तरम् । धनुरेतत्पणं कार्यमिति चिन्त्य कृतं तथा ॥ 69
सीतापाणिग्रहार्थाय सर्वेषां माननाशनम् । त्वत्प्रसादान्मुनिश्रेष्ठ रामो राजीवलोचनः ॥ 70
आगतोऽत्र धनुर्द्रष्टुं फलितो मे मनोरथः । अद्य मे सफलं जन्म राम त्वां सह सीतया ॥71
एकासनस्थं पश्यामि भ्राजमानं रविं यथा ॥ 72
त्वत्पादाम्बुधरो ब्रह्मा सृष्टिचक्रप्रवर्तकः । बलिस्त्वत्पादसलिलं धृत्वाभूद्दिविजाधिपः ॥ 73
त्वत्पादपांसुसंस्पर्शादहल्या भर्तृशापतः । सद्य एव विनिर्मुक्ता कोऽन्यस्त्वत्तोऽधिर क्षिता ॥74
यत्पादपङ्कजपरागसुरागयोगिवृन्दैर्जितं भवभयं जितकालचक्रैः ।
यन्नामकीर्तनपरा जितदुःखशोका देवास्तमेव शरणं सततं प्रपद्ये ॥ 75
इति स्तुत्वा नृपः प्रादाद्राघवाय महात्मने । दीनाराणां कोटिशतं रथानामयुतं तदा ॥ 76

Lakshmi, the eternal consort of Rama the Paramatman, she has never been the wife of anyone else before." Instructing me thus that celestial sage departed to his divine abode.

(67-72). "Ever since that time I have been looking upon Sita as Mahavishnu's consort Lakshmi, and planning how I could arrange to give her, my auspicious daughter, in marriage to Rama. In my ancestral palace there was in safe keeping this bow, which was deposited by Maheswara in times gone by after he destroyed the Tripuras. I resolved to make the stringing of this bow, which would humble the pride of any one attempting to do so, the wager for one aspiring to marry her. O great sage! By your grace Rama has come here to see this bow, and my long-standing desire has been fulfilled. Today, O Rama, I am fortunate to see Thee seated together with Sita on the same seat as husband and wife. Indeed the purpose of my life has thus been fulfilled.

(73-74). "Because he bears on his head the washings of Thy feet, Brahma the creator has gained the power to start and regulate the creative cycle. Bali, the king of the Asuras, became Indra, the king of the celestials, by sprinkling on himself the holy water of Thy feet. And today, O Supreme Saviour, the dust of Thy feet has liberated Ahalya from the effects of the curse of her husband. **75.** He, by intense devotion to the dust of whose lotus feet great Yogis overcome the wheel of Time and transcend the fear of transmigratory life, He, by absorption in the hymns and praises of whose sacred name the celestials overcome their woes and sorrows—in Him alone I seek refuge for ever more."

Rama's Departure to Ayodhya (76-82)

(76-78). After having praised Rama in this way, King Janaka gave valuable presents to that high-souled one of Raghu's line. He presented him with a hundred crores of gold coins (*dinara*), a thousand chariots,

अश्वानां नियुतं प्रादाद्गजानां षट्शतं तथा । पत्तीनां लक्षमेकं तु दासीनां त्रिशतं ददौ ॥ 77
दिव्याम्बराणि हारांश्च मुक्तारत्नमयोज्ज्वलान् । सीतायै जनकः प्रादात्प्रीत्या दुहितृवत्सलः ॥ 78
वसिष्ठादीन्सुसंपूज्य भरतं लक्ष्मणं तथा । पूजयित्वा यथान्यायं तथा दशरथं नृपम् ॥ 79
प्रस्थापयामास नृपो राजानं रघुसत्तमम् । सीतामालिङ्ग्य रुदतीं मातरः साश्रुलोचनाः ॥ 80
श्वश्रूशुश्रूषणपरा नित्यं राममनुव्रता । पातिव्रत्यमुपालम्ब्य तिष्ठ वत्से यथा सुखम् ॥81
प्रयाणकाले रघुनन्दनस्य भेरीमृदङ्गानकतूर्यघोषः ।
स्ववासिभेरीघनतूर्यशब्दैः संमूर्च्छतो भूतभयङ्करोऽभूत् ॥ 82

इति श्रीमदध्यात्मरामायणे उमामहेश्वरसंवादे
बालकाण्डे षष्ठः सर्गः ॥ ६ ॥

ten thousand horses, six hundred elephants, a lakh of foot-soldiers and three hundred female attendants. Besides he gave Sita, his dear daughter, valuable clothes and jewellery, resplendent with gems and pearls. **(79-80).** After honouring the sages like Vasishtha, the princes Bharata and Lakshmana, as also King Dasaratha according to protocol, King Janaka bade farewell to the Lord of the Raghus. Thereupon, with tears in their eyes the wives of the king embraced their weeping daughter Sita, and advised her: **81**. "O dear one, be devoted to the father and mother of your husband. Be with Rama wherever he is. Observing the duties of a chaste wife (*pativrata*), live in happiness."

82. Loud and awe-inspiring was the tumultuous sound produced by the orchestra of drums and other percussion instruments of men and celestials, signalling the departure of Rama from Mithila to Ayodhya.

सप्तमः सर्गः

अथ गच्छति श्रीरामे मैथिलाद्योजनत्रयम् । निमित्तान्यतिघोराणि ददर्श नृपसत्तमः ॥ 1
नत्वा वसिष्ठं पप्रच्छ किमिदं मुनिपुङ्गव । निमित्तानीह दृश्यन्ते विषमाणि समन्ततः ॥ 2

Chapter 7

THE DEFEAT OF BHARGAVA RAMA

Confrontation with Bhargava Rama (1-20)

1. When Rama and party had proceeded about three Yojanas from Mithila, King Dasaratha was taken aback to see various omens causing terror in the mind. **2.** Saluting the preceptor Vasishtha, he said to him, "Venerable Sir! How is it that portents foreboding evil are seen on

वसिष्ठस्तमथ प्राह भयमागामि सूच्यते । पुनरप्यभयं तेऽद्य शीघ्रमेव भविष्यति ॥ 3

मृगाः प्रदक्षिणं यान्ति पश्य त्वां शुभसूचकाः । इत्येवं वदतस्तस्य ववौ घोरतरोऽनिलः ॥ 4

मुष्णंश्चक्षूंषि सर्वेषां पांसुवृष्टिभिरर्दयन् । ततो व्रजन्ददर्शाग्रे तेजोराशिमुपस्थितम् ॥ 5

कोटिसूर्यप्रतीकाशं विद्युत्पुञ्जसमप्रभम् । तेजोराशिं ददर्शाथ जामदग्न्यं प्रतापवान् ॥ 6

नीलमेघनिभं प्रांशुं जटामण्डलमण्डितम् । धनुः परशुपाणिं च साक्षात्कालमिवान्तकम् ॥ 7

कार्तवीर्यान्तकं रामं दृप्तक्षत्रियमर्दनम् । प्राप्तं दशरथस्याग्रे कालमृत्युमिवापरम् ॥ 8

तं दृष्ट्वा भयसन्त्रस्तो राजा दशरथस्तदा । अर्घ्यादिपूजां विस्मृत्य त्राहि त्राहीति चाब्रवीत् ॥ 9

दण्डवत्प्रणिपत्याह पुत्रप्राणं प्रयच्छ मे । इति ब्रुवन्तं राजानमनादृत्य रघूत्तमम् ॥ 10

उवाच निष्ठुरं वाक्यं क्रोधात्प्रचलितेन्द्रियः । त्वं राम इति नाम्ना मे चरसि क्षत्रियाधम ॥ 11

द्वन्द्वयुद्धं प्रयच्छाशु यदि त्वं क्षत्रियोऽसि वै । पुराणं जर्जरं चापं भङ्क्त्वा त्वं कत्थसे मुधा ॥12

अस्मिंस्तु वैष्णवे चापे आरोपयसि चेद्गुणम् । तदा युद्धं त्वया सार्धं करोमि रघुवंशज ॥ 13

नो चेत्सर्वान्हनिष्यामि क्षत्रियान्तकरो ह्यहम् । इति ब्रुवति वै तस्मिंश्चचाल वसुधा भृशम् ॥ 14

all sides?" **(3-4)**. To him, Vasishtha replied:

"There are no doubt some indications showing that some terrible events are going to take place. But there are also simultaneous indications to the effect that their effects will be short-lived. Don't you see how auspicious animals are circumambulating you?" While they were thus conversing, a terrific wind began to blow. **(5-8)** It blinded the vision of all by raising clouds of dust. Proceeding a little further they came across a luminous mass, brilliant like numerous suns or an assemblage of flashing streaks of lightning. Closing nearer, Dasaratha saw therein the awe-inspiring form of Rama, the son of Jamadagni, the terror of Kshatriyas, and the destroyer of Karthavirya. Tall and blue like a rain-cloud in complexion, he with his matted locks and weapons consisting of a formidable bow and a battle axe, looked like the god of death embodied.

9. Confronted by him, King Dasaratha was in great fright and forgetting even to make the customary offerings at the reception of a great personage, he beseeched him, saying, "Save us, O mighty one! Save us! **(10-14)**. May you be pleased to spare the lives of my sons." With these words King Dasaratha made prostrations to him. But spurning him contemptuously, he (Jamadagni's son Rama) turned towards Sri Rama, and with body trembling in anger, said the following ominous words: "Sirrah, you, scum of the Kshatriya race! You have the temerity to go about the earth, bearing my name. If you are really a Kshatriya, take up my challenge for a duel. Breaking an old and flimsy bow, you go about boasting about your prowess. If you are able to string this bow of Vishnu that is in my possession, I shall consider you as one born in Raghu's line and therefore worthy of a fight. If you fail, I shall kill the whole lot of you. For, know me to be Jamadagni's

अन्धकारो बभूवाथ सर्वेषामपि चक्षुषाम् । रामो दाशरथिर्वीरो वीक्ष्य तं भार्गवं रुषा ॥ 15
धनुराच्छिद्य तद्धस्तादारोप्य गुणमञ्जसा । तूणीराद्बाणमादाय संधायाकृष्य वीर्यवान् ॥ 16
उवाच भार्गवं रामं शृणु ब्रह्मन्वचो मम । लक्ष्यं दर्शय बाणस्य ह्यमोघो मम सायकः ॥ 17
लोकान्पादयुगं वापि वद शीघ्रं ममाज्ञया । अयं लोकः परो वाथ त्वया गन्तुं न शक्यते ॥18
एवं त्वं हि प्रकर्तव्यं वद शीघ्रं ममाज्ञया । एवं वदति श्रीरामे भार्गवो विकृताननः ॥ 19
संस्मरन्पूर्ववृत्तान्तमिदं वचनमब्रवीत् । राम राम महाबाहो जाने त्वां परमेश्वरम् ॥ 20
पुराणपुरुषं विष्णुं जगत्सर्गलयोद्भवम् । बाल्येऽयं तपसा विष्णुमाराधयितुमञ्जसा ॥ 21
चक्रतीर्थं शुभं गत्वा तपसा विष्णुमन्वहम् । अतोषयं महात्मानं नारायणमनन्यधीः ॥ 22
ततः प्रसन्नो देवेशः शङ्खचक्रगदाधरः । उवाच मां रघुश्रेष्ठ प्रसन्नमुखपङ्कजः ॥ 23

श्रीभगवानुवाच

उत्तिष्ठ तपसो ब्रह्मन्फलितं ते तपो महत् । मच्चिदंशेन युक्तस्त्वं जहि हैहयपुङ्गवम् ॥ 24
कार्तवीर्यं पितृहणं यदर्थं तपसः श्रमः । ततस्त्रिःसप्तकृत्वस्त्वं हत्वा क्षत्रियमण्डलम् ॥ 25

son Rama, the destroyer of the whole tribe of Kshatriyas." As he spoke these violently threatening words, there arose severe tremors of the earth. **(15-17)**. A blinding darkness now came upon the eyes of all. Rama, the heroic son of Dasaratha, now looked angrily at Rama of Bhrigu's clan and snatched away the bow from the latter's hand. Possessed as he was of great prowess, he easily strung it, and fixing to it an arrow that he took from the quiver, addressed the scion of Bhrigu's clan thus: "O great Brahmana! Hark unto me. Show the target for my arrow. For an arrow shot by me shall never go in vain. **(18-20)**. Reply quickly to my command. Shall I with this arrow destroy all your prospects in the worlds to come, or those in this? Retribution so severe shall fall on you that you would have no place here or in the hereafter." When Sri Rama demanded in this way, the face of Rama of Bhrigu's line became distorted out of a sense of humiliation. Suddenly the memory of past incidents flashed in his mind, and he began to speak as follows :

The Hymn of Bhargava Rama (21-45)

(21-23). "O Rama, Thou great hero! I have now understood Thee to be the Supreme Lord Mahavishnu, who creates, preserves and dissolves the universe—the Eternal Being residing in the hearts of all. In my boyhood I sought to adore Mahavishnu through the practice of austerities at the holy spot known as Chakratirtha. Through austere living and unwavering concentration day after day, I propitiated the great Narayana, the indweller in all as their essence. Then, O great prince of Raghu's line, Mahavishnu, the Supreme Divinity of lotus-like face, appeared to me sporting the conch, discus, mace and other emblems in His hands, and said: **(24-29)**. 'O holy

कृत्स्नां भूमिं कश्यपाय दत्त्वा शान्तिमुपावह । त्रेतामुखे दाशरथिर्भूत्वा रामोऽहमव्ययः ॥ 26
उत्पत्स्ये परया शक्त्या तदा द्रक्ष्यसि मां ततः । मत्तेजः पुनरादास्ये त्वयि दत्तं मया पुरा ॥ 27
तदा तपश्चरंल्लोके तिष्ठ त्वं ब्रह्मणो दिनम् । इत्युक्त्वान्तर्दधे देवस्तथा सर्वं कृतं मया ॥ 28
स एव विष्णुस्त्वं राम जातोऽसि ब्रह्मणार्थितः । मयि स्थितं तु त्वत्तेजस्त्वयैव पुनराहृतम् ॥ 29
अद्य मे सफलं जन्म प्रतीतोऽसि मम प्रभो । ब्रह्मादिभिरलभ्यस्त्वं प्रकृतेः पारगो मतः ॥ 30
त्वयि जन्मादिषड्भावा न सन्त्यज्ञानसंभवाः । निर्विकारोऽसि पूर्णस्त्वं गमनादिविवर्जितः ॥ 31
यथा जले फेनजालं धूमो वह्नौ तथा त्वयि । त्वदाधारा त्वद्विषया माया कार्यं सृजत्यहो ॥ 32
यावन्मायावृता लोकास्तावत्त्वां न विजानते । अविचारितसिद्धैषाविद्या विद्याविरोधिनी ॥ 33
अविद्याकृतदेहादिसङ्घाते प्रतिबिम्बिता । चिच्छक्तिर्जीवलोकेऽस्मिन् जीव इत्यभिधीयते 34

one! Now stop your austere practices, for they have come to their fruition. You are endowed with a part of My divine power. By virtue of it, you will be able to destroy Kartavirya of Hehaya dynasty, the slayer of your father, and thus achieve the purpose for which you have been performing these austerities. After that you shall destroy the tribe of Kshatriyas in twenty-one campaigns, and then give as gift the whole of the earth you have conquered from them to Kasyapa. I, the eternal Being, will be incarnated on earth as Dasaratha's son in the Treta-yuga. You will meet me then, and on that occasion, you will remit to Me the power that I have endowed you with earlier. After that you will remain on earth till the end of Brahma's current day, performing austerities.' The Lord disappeared after commanding me thus. I have finished the mission entrusted to me. O Rama! Thou art verily that Mahavishnu. Implored by Brahma, Thou hast incarnated Thyself. Thou hast now taken back that divine power that Thou hadst endowed me with. **30.** My life has today become fruitful. I have now come within the purview of Thy remembrance. It is difficult for Brahma and other divinities to attain to Thee. The scriptures declare that Thou transcendest Prakriti, the matrix of this universe. **31.** The six states of ignorance like birth, growth, etc., are not in Thee. For Thou art ever the full and the changeless, devoid of all movements (which are characteristic only of adjuncts which ignorant beings attribute to Thee). **32.** Just as there is foam in water and smoke in fire, so the whole of the objective world is projected in Thee by Thy Maya (Power), who has her seat and support in Thee and who has no independent existence apart from being Thy object. **33.** As long as the Jivas are enshrouded in Maya, they do not know Thee. In the individual, Maya functions as Avidya, ignorance, obstructing Vidya or Enlightenment. This Avidya or Ignorance, experienced as a positive entity opposed to Vidya, is present in the absence of discriminative intelligence (*avicāritasiddha*). **34.** What is called Jiva is the reflection of the power of Pure Consciousness (*cicchakti*) in the complex aggregate of a body-mind generated by Ignorance

यावद्देहमनः प्राणबुद्ध्यादिष्वभिमानवान् । तावत्कर्तृत्वभोक्तृत्वसुखदुःखादिभाग्भवेत् ॥ 35
आत्मनःसंसृतिर्नास्ति बुद्धेर्ज्ञानं न जात्विति । अविवेकाद्द्वयं युङ्क्त्वा संसारीति प्रवर्तते ॥ 36
जडस्य चित्समायोगाच्चित्त्वं भूयाच्चितेस्तथा । जडसङ्गाज्जडत्वं हि जलाग्न्योर्मेलनं यथा ॥ 37
यावत्त्वत्पादभक्तानां सङ्गसौख्यं न विन्दति । तावत्संसारदुःखौघान्न निवर्तेन्नरः सदा ॥ 38
तत्सङ्गलब्धया भक्त्या यदा त्वां समुपासते । तदा माया शनैर्याति तानवं प्रतिपद्यते ॥ 39
ततस्त्वज्ज्ञानसम्पन्नः सद्गुरुस्तेन लभ्यते । वाक्यज्ञानं गुरोर्लब्ध्वा त्वत्प्रसादाद्विमुच्यते ॥ 40
तस्मात्त्वद्भक्तिहीनानां कल्पकोटिशतैरपि । न मुक्तिशङ्का विज्ञानशङ्का नैव सुखं तथा ॥ 41
अतस्त्वत्पादयुगले भक्तिर्मे जन्म जन्मनि । स्यात्त्वद्भक्तिमतां सङ्गोऽविद्या याभ्यां विनश्यति ॥
लोके त्वद्भक्तिनिरतास्त्वद्धर्मामृतवर्षिणः । पुनन्ति लोकमखिलं किं पुनः स्वकुलोद्भवान् ॥43

(Avidya). **35.** As long as one feels the 'I-sense' in relation to the complex aggregate of body-mind, Prana, Buddhi, etc., so long one is subject to the experience of agency and enjoyership, of happiness and misery. **36.** The Atman in himself has no transmigratory involvement. Nor has the Buddhi in itself consciousness or sentiency. When these two, the Atman and the Buddhi unite into one through imaginary identification arising from lack of discriminative reflection, then we get that complex entity called the Jiva (the individualised and embodied Atman). **37.** The insentient body-mind complex, by identification with the pure sentiency that is the Atman, assumes sentiency. So also the Atman, who is pure sentiency, assumes insentiency by identification with the insentient body-mind complex. It is just like the mutual superimposition of the properties of fire and water in the phenomenon of lightning in which water (cloud) and fire with opposite properties get a unified presentation as the brilliant and fiery lightning. **38.** Never shall man be free from that enormous body of miseries arising from involvement in transmigratory life brought about by the above-described state of Ignorance until he gets the good fortune of association with Thy ardent devotees. **39.** When man adores Thee with devotion fostered by association with holy men, then Maya (Ignorance) both recedes and gets attenuated. **40.** When this state of mental purity is attained, an aspirant will get an authentic teacher who is endowed with knowledge derived from the realisation of Thee. Gaining, through such a teacher, the knowledge of the true meaning of the scriptural dicta, he will attain liberation by Thy grace. **41.** Therefore for those who have no devotion to Thee, there is not the slightest chance, even in the course of a myriad cosmic cycles, of gaining enlightenment and liberation. Thus he will not have happiness even in life. **42.** Therefore bless me, so that in life after life I am born with devotion to Thee and with opportunities for association with Thy devotees; for, that is the only means for the dispelling of Ignorance. **43.** Men who have true devotion to Thee, and who by their life and words propagate the path of devotion, purify the whole

नमोऽस्तु जगतां नाथ नमस्ते भक्तिभावन । नमः कारुणिकानन्त रामचन्द्र नमोऽस्तु ते ॥ 44
देव यद्यत्कृतं पुण्यं मया लोकजिगीषया । तत्सर्वं तव बाणाय भूयाद्राम नमोऽस्तु ते ॥ 45
ततः प्रसन्नो भगवान् श्रीरामः करुणामयः । प्रसन्नोऽस्मि तव ब्रह्मन्यत्ते मनसि वर्तते ॥ 46
दास्ये तदखिलं कामं मा कुरुष्वात्र संशयम् । ततः प्रीतेन मनसा भार्गवो राममब्रवीत् ॥ 47
यदि मेऽनुग्रहो राम तवास्ति मधुसूदन । त्वद्भक्तसङ्गस्त्वत्पादे दृढा भक्तिः सदास्तु मे ॥48
स्तोत्रमेतत्पठेद्यस्तु भक्तिहीनोऽपि सर्वदा । त्वद्भक्तिस्तस्य विज्ञानं भूयादन्ते स्मृतिस्तव ॥ 49
तथेति राघवेणोक्तः परिक्रम्य प्रणम्य तम् । पूजितस्तदनुज्ञातो महेन्द्राचलमन्वगात् ॥ 50
राजा दशरथो हृष्टो रामं मृतमिवागतम् । आलिङ्ग्यालिङ्ग्य हर्षेण नेत्राभ्यां जलमुत्सृजत्॥51
ततः प्रीतेन मनसा स्वस्थचित्तः पुरं ययौ । रामलक्ष्मणशत्रुघ्नभरता देवसंमिताः ॥ 52
स्वां स्वां भार्यामुपादाय रेमिरे स्वस्वमन्दिरे ।
मातापितृभ्यां संहृष्टो रामः सीतासमन्वितः । रेमे वैकुण्ठभवने श्रिया सह यथा हरिः ॥ 53

world. What then to speak of the redeeming effect of their life on their own kith and kin, including their ancestors! **44.** Salutations to Thee, O Lord of the universe! Salutations to Thee, the generator and augmentator of devotion in aspirants! Salutation to Thee the embodiment of mercy and the Existence without end! To Thee, Ramachandra, my salutations! **45.** O Lord! Whatever meritorious deeds I have performed for the attainment of higher realms in the hereafter, may all those be the target for Thy arrow. With salutations, I dedicate them to Thee, O Rama!"

Rama Bestows his Grace on Bhargava Rama (46-50)

(46-48). Sri Rama, the embodiment of mercy, now graciously said to Rama of Bhrigu's line: "I am much pleased with you, O holy one. Whatever you desire, I shall grant without any hesitation." Then in a highly elated mood, that scion of Bhrigu's line said to Sri Rama: "O Rama! Thou the destroyer of the demon Madhu! If Thou art gracious to me, grant unto me communion with Thy devotees as also firm and constant devotion to Thee. **49.** May Thou be pleased to grant also that even a person without devotion, if he recites and studies this hymn regularly, comes to develop love and knowledge of Thee! And what is more. may he have the blessing of remembering Thee at the time of death!" **50.** Rama, the scion of Raghu's line, granted these prayers of his. Then Rama of Bhrigu's clan, adored Sri Rama, circumambulated him and, permitted by him, departed to Mount Mahendra.

Return to Ayodhya (51-57)

51. With his heart overflowing with joy King Dasaratha embraced Rama again and again, as if he had got him back from the jaws of death, and his surging delight welled up from his eyes as tears. **(52-53).** Then with a mind elated and peaceful, King Dasaratha resumed his journey to his city of Ayodhya. Reaching Ayodhya,

युधाजिन्नाम कैकेयीभ्राता भरतमातुलः । भरतं नेतुमागच्छत्स्वराज्यं प्रीतिसंयुतः ॥ 54

प्रेषयामास भरतं राजा स्नेहसमन्वितः । शत्रुघ्नं चापि संपूज्य युधाजितमरिन्दमः ॥ 55

कौसल्या शुशुभे देवी रामेण सह सीतया । देवमातेव पौलोम्या शच्या शक्रेण शोभना ॥56

साकेते लोकनाथप्रथितगुणगणो लोकसङ्गीतकीर्तिः
श्रीरामः सीतयास्तेऽखिलजननिकरानन्दसन्दोहमूर्तिः ।
नित्यश्रीर्निर्विकारो निरवधिविभवो नित्यमायानिरासो
मायाकार्यानुसारी मनुज इव सदा भाति देवोऽखिलेशः ॥ 57

इति श्रीमदध्यात्मरामायणे उमामहेश्वरसंवादे
बालकाण्डे सप्तमः सर्गः ॥ ७ ॥

Rama, Lakshmana, Bharata and Satrughna lived happily with their wives in their respective palaces. Rejoicing with his parents, Rama spent his days with Sita at Ayodhya in heavenly bliss like Mahavishnu with Sri Devi in Vaikuntha. **54.** At that time one day, the brother of Kaikeyi and uncle of Bharata named Yudhajit, came to Ayodhya in order to take Bharata on a visit to his kingdom. **55.** The loving and heroic King Dasaratha received Yudhajit with all honours, and permitted Bharata along with Satrughna to go with him. **56.** Kausalya in the company of Rama and Sita shone just as Aditi, the mother of the Devas, does in the company of her son Indra and his consort Indrani.

57. Rama is the most distinguished among the Divinities on account of his numerous excellences. His fame is sung about in all the spheres. He is, as it were, an embodiment of the totality of joy in the whole universe. His glory is eternal and his being undecaying. Devoid of the ignorance-generating film of Maya, He is the changeless One and the Lord of all. Yet, Sri Rama resided in Ayodhya with Sita, as if he were a human being following the ways of the life of Ignorance.

ॐ

अध्यात्मरामायणम्

अयोध्या काण्डः

प्रथमः सर्गः

एकदा सुखमासीनं रामं स्वान्तःपुराजिरे । सर्वाभरणसंपन्नं रत्नसिंहासने स्थितम् ॥ 1
नीलोत्पलदलश्यामं कौस्तुभामुक्तकन्धरम् । सीतया रत्नदण्डेन चामरेणाथ वीजितम् ॥ 2
विनोदयन्तं ताम्बूलचर्वणादिभिरादरात् । नारदोऽवतरद्द्रष्टुमम्बराद्यत्र राघवः ॥ 3
शुद्धस्फटिकसङ्काशः शरच्चन्द्र इवामलः । अतर्कितमुपायातो नारदो दिव्यदर्शनः ॥ 4
तं दृष्ट्वा सहसोत्थाय रामः प्रीत्या कृताञ्जलिः । ननाम शिरसा भूमौ सीतया सह भक्तिमान् ॥ 5
उवाच नारदं रामः प्रीत्या परमया युतः ।
संसारिणां मुनिश्रेष्ठ दुर्लभं तव दर्शनम् । अस्माकं विषयासक्तचेतसां नितरां मुने ॥ 6
अवाप्तं मे पूर्वजन्मकृतपुण्यमहोदयैः । संसारिणापि हि मुने लभ्यते सत्समागमः ॥ 7

AYODHYA KANDAM

Chapter 1

CONVERSATION BETWEEN RAMA AND NARADA

Hymn of Narada (1-31)

(1-3). One day Narada, the divine sage, descended from the skies to the presence of Rama, who was decorated with varieties of ornaments, who was seated on a gem-studded throne, who had the complexion resembling the colour of a blue lily, who was wearing on his neck the jewel called Kaustubha, who was being fanned with ornamental Chouries, and who was sitting at leisure chewing betels in the inner apartment of his palace. **4.** Shining like a white crystal and pure like the autumnal moon the divine-looking Narada presented himself all of a sudden before Rama. **5.** Seeing him, Rama got up from his seat immediately. With palms joined in salutation and moved by great devotion, he along with Sita prostrated himself before the sage. **6.** Highly gratified, Rama said to the sage: "O great sage! For one caught in the cycle of transmigratory life (Samsara), it is indeed a rare blessing to get your company. Much more is it so, O sage, for us who are immersed in worldliness. **7.** O holy one! The blessing

अतस्त्वद्दर्शनादेव कृतार्थोऽस्मि मुनीश्वर । किं कार्यं ते मया कार्यं ब्रूहि तत्करवाणि भोः ॥ 8
अथ तं नारदोऽप्याह राघवं भक्तवत्सलम् । किं मोहयसि मां राम वाक्यैर्लोकानुसारिभिः ॥ 9
संसार्यहमिति प्रोक्तं सत्यमेतत्त्वया विभो । जगतामादिभूता या सा माया गृहिणी तव ॥ 10
त्वत्सन्निकर्षाज्जायन्ते तस्यां ब्रह्मादयः प्रजाः । त्वदाश्रया सदा भाति माया या त्रिगुणात्मिका ॥ 11
सूतेऽजस्रं शुक्लकृष्णलोहिताः सर्वदा प्रजाः । लोकत्रयमहागेहे गृहस्थस्त्वमुदाहृतः ॥ 12
त्वं विष्णुर्जानकी लक्ष्मीः शिवस्त्वं जानकी शिवा । ब्रह्मा त्वं जानकी वाणी सूर्यस्त्वं जानकी प्रभा ॥13
भवान् शशाङ्कः सीता तु रोहिणी शुभलक्षणा । शक्रस्त्वमेव पौलोमी सीता स्वाहानलो भवान् ॥14
यमस्त्वं कालरूपश्च सीता संयमिनी प्रभो । निर्ऋतिस्त्वं जगन्नाथ तामसी जानकी शुभा ॥15
राम त्वमेव वरुणो भार्गवी जानकी शुभा । वायुस्त्वं राम सीता तु सदागतिरितीरिता ॥ 16
कुबेरस्त्वं राम सीता सर्वसंपत्प्रकीर्तिता । रुद्राणी जानकी प्रोक्ता रुद्रस्त्वं लोकनाशकृत् ॥17
लोके स्त्रीवाचकं यावत्तत्सर्वं जानकी शुभा । पुन्नामवाचकं यावत्तत्सर्वं त्वं हि राघव ॥ 18
तस्माल्लोकत्रये देव युवाभ्यां नास्ति किञ्चन ॥ 19

that I have now got must be the result of some very meritorious deeds I have done in the past; for, such meritorious deeds alone can help a worldly person to have the contact of a holy man. **8.** Therefore I have derived very great satisfaction by seeing you, O great sage! Is there anything that I can do for you? If so, tell me, what it is. And I shall try to accomplish it."

9. Thereupon Narada said to Rama, the lover of all devotees: "O Rama! Why art Thou trying to misguide me by such words, as if Thou wert just a worldly man? **10.** O All-pervading One! Thy statement that Thou art one involved in Samsara is true, indeed, in a way. For, is not Maya, the First Cause of the whole universe, Thy Consort? **11.** It is by Thy mere presence that she generates Brahma and the other offspring of hers. It is with Thee as her support that Maya, constituted of the three Gunas, subsists. **12.** It is by Thy support that she constantly gives birth to three types of beings—those that are Sattvika (Sukla or white), Rajasa (Lohita or red) and Tamasa (Krishna or black). In this huge household of these three worlds, Thou art truly the master-householder. **(13-19).** Thou art Vishnu; and Sita, Lakshmi Devi. Thou art Siva; and Sita, Parvati. Thou art Brahmā; and Sita, Saraswati. Thou art the Sun-deity; and Sita, Prabha (luminosity). Thou art the moon-deity; and Sita, auspicious Rohini. Thou art Indra; and Sita, Indrani. Thou art the Fire-Deity, and Sita, Svaha. Thou art Yama, the all-destroying Time (Kala); and Sita, his consort, Samyamini. Thou, O Lord of the worlds, art Nirriti; and Sita, his consort Tamasi. Thou art Varuna; and Sita, his consort Bhargavi. Thou art Vayu the wind-deity; and Sita, Sadagati. Thou art Kubera, O Rama; and Sita, prosperity. Thou art Rudra the destroyer; and Sita, Rudrani. To put it briefly, whatever female form is there in this universe, that the auspicious

त्वदाभासोदिताज्ञानमव्याकृतमितीर्यते । तस्मान्महांस्ततः सूत्रं लिङ्गं सर्वात्मकं ततः ॥ 20

अहङ्कारश्च बुद्धिश्च पञ्चप्राणेन्द्रियाणि च । लिङ्गमित्युच्यते प्राज्ञैर्जन्ममृत्युसुखादिमत् ॥ 21

स एव जीवसंज्ञश्च लोके भाति जगन्मयः । अवाच्यानाद्यविद्यैव कारणोपाधिरुच्यते ॥ 22

स्थूलं सूक्ष्मं कारणाख्यमुपाधित्रितयं चितेः । एतैर्विशिष्टो जीवः स्याद्वियुक्तः परमेश्वरः ॥ 23

जाग्रत्स्वप्नसुषुप्त्याख्या संसृतिर्या प्रवर्तते । तस्या विलक्षणः साक्षी चिन्मात्रस्त्वं रघूत्तम ॥ 24

त्वत्त एव जगज्जातं त्वयि सर्वं प्रतिष्ठितम् । त्वय्येव लीयते कृत्स्नं तस्मात्त्वं सर्वकारणम् ॥ 25

रज्जावहिमिवात्मानं जीवं ज्ञात्वा भयं भवेत् । परात्माहमिति ज्ञात्वा भयदुःखैर्विमुच्यते ॥ 26

चिन्मात्रज्योतिषा सर्वाः सर्वदेहेषु बुद्धयः । त्वया यस्मात्प्रकाश्यन्ते सर्वस्यात्मा ततो भवान् ॥27

अज्ञानान्न्यस्यते सर्वं त्वयि रज्जौ भुजङ्गवत् । त्वज्ज्ञानाल्लीयते सर्वं तस्माज्ज्ञानं सदाभ्यसेत् 28

Sita is. And whatever male form there is, that Thou art, O scion of the Raghu's line! Therefore in these three worlds, there is none but you two. **20.** What is called the Undifferentiated (*avyākrita*) is verily the category of Ignorance arising from Thy reflection. (*ābhāsoditam*). Out of it has come Mahat-tattva (the great element); from that the Sutratman (the cosmic I-sense); and from that, the cosmic subtle body (Linga). **21.** It is the complex constituted of I-sense, Buddhi (intellect), the five vital energies (Prana) and the five Indriyas (senses) that undergo birth, death, joy and sorrow. It is what learned men call the Linga -sarira (subtle body of the individual). **22.** Verily, it is He (the reflection of consciousness in the above-mentioned complex called Linga) that is called the Jiva. It is the same complex formation in the cosmic sense that manifests as Hiranyagarbha, having the universe as his body (*Jaganmaya*), while in the individual sense it is the Jiva with the individual physical body. The indescribable and beginningless Avidya (Maya) is what is called the causal Adjunct (*Kāraṇopādhi*), the medium in which Pure Consciousness reflects. **23.** Pure Consciousness has three adjuncts—gross, subtle and causal. When identified with these, Pure Consciousness is called Jiva, Cosmic or individual. Devoid of them He is the Supreme Lord. **24.** O the noblest of Raghu's line! Thou art the Pure Consciousness, the Witness—what is the opposite of the transmigratory life characterised by these three states of waking (Jagrat) dream (Svapna) and sleep (Sushupti). **25.** The whole universe has originated from Thee; it remains established in Thee; and it dissolves in Thee. Therefore Thou art verily the cause of all manifestations. **26.** By misunderstanding the Pure Consciousness (Atma) to be an individual Self (Jiva), fear arises, just as when a rope is mistaken for a snake. So knowing the 'I' (the Self in its true nature) to be the Supreme Self, one is rid of all fear and misery. **27.** Thou art the self of all, because Thou who art the light of Pure Consciousness illuminest the Buddhi associated with all bodies. **28.** Just as out of ignorance one superimposes a snake on a rope, so are all entities superimposed upon Thee. When Thou, the sub-

त्वत्पादभक्तियुक्तानां विज्ञानं भवति क्रमात् । तस्मात्त्वद्भक्तियुक्ता ये मुक्तिभाजस्त एव हि ॥29
अहं त्वद्भक्तभक्तानां तद्भक्तानां च किङ्करः । अतो मामनुगृह्णीष्व मोहयस्व न मां प्रभो ॥ 30
त्वन्नाभिकमलोत्पन्नो ब्रह्मा मे जनकः प्रभो । अतस्तवाहं पौत्रोऽस्मि भक्तं मां पाहि राघव ॥31
इत्युक्त्वा बहुशो नत्वा स्वानन्दाश्रुपरिप्लुतः । उवाच वचनं राम ब्रह्मणा नोदितोऽस्म्यहम् ॥32
रावणस्य वधार्थाय जातोऽसि रघुसत्तम । इदानीं राज्यरक्षार्थं पिता त्वामभिषेक्ष्यति ॥ 33
यदि राज्याभिसंसक्तो रावणं न हनिष्यसि । प्रतिज्ञा ते कृता राम भूभारहरणाय वै ॥ 34
तत्सत्यं कुरु राजेन्द्र सत्यसंधस्त्वमेव हि । श्रुत्वैतद्गदितं रामो नारदं प्राह सस्मितम् ॥ 35
शृणु नारद मे किञ्चिद्विद्यतेऽविदितं क्वचित् । प्रतिज्ञातं च यत्पूर्वं करिष्ये तन्न संशयः ॥ 36
किन्तु कालानुरोधेन तत्तत्प्रारब्धसंक्षयात् । हरिष्ये सर्वभूभारं क्रमेणासुरमण्डलम् ॥ 37
रावणस्य विनाशार्थं श्वो गन्ता दण्डकाननम् । चतुर्दश समास्तत्र ह्युषित्वा मुनिवेषधृक् ॥ 38
सीतामिषेण तं दुष्टं सकुलं नाशयाम्यहम् । एवं रामे प्रतिज्ञाते नारदः प्रमुमोद ह ॥ 39

stratum, art perceived, all these superimpositions dissolve in Thee. Therefore one should always practise this discipline of knowledge. **29.** In those who are endowed with true devotion to Thee this knowledge as an experience dawns by stages. Therefore it is only those who have devotion to Thee that attain to liberation (Mukti). **30.** I am the servant of Thy devotees and of those who are devoted to Thy devotees. Therefore, deign to bless me, O lord! and let not Thy Maya delude me. **31.** I am, O Lord! the offspring of Brahmā who was generated from Thy navel-lotus, and hence Thy grandchild. Therefore, O Rama! Deign to save me who am Thy devotee."

Narada's Departure (32-41)

(32-35). Saying so, Narada prostrated himself several times before Rama and with tears of joy flowing from his eyes, continued, "O Rama! I have been sent here by Brahmā. Thou, O the noblest one of Rahgu's clan, hast been born in this world for the destruction of Ravana. Now Thy father is going to install Thee as the ruler for the protection of the country. If Thou dost get busy with the affairs of State, the destruction of Ravana may not take place. But Thou hast taken the vow of relieving the world of its burdens. May Thou be pleased to fulfil that vow; for Thou art devoted to truth." Hearing these words, Rama said to Narada with a smile: **(36-39).** "O Narada! Listen to me. There is nothing that is not within my knowledge. What I had promised to do earlier, shall certainly be fulfilled. There need be no doubt about it. I shall be destroying the whole tribe of these Rakshasas and thus be relieving the earth of its burden. Only gradually, according as their Prarabdha (operating Karma), which takes effect only with the passage of time, would I be doing this. For the destruction of Ravana, I shall be starting for the forest of Dandakaranya tomorrow itself. I shall be staying

प्रदक्षिणत्रयं कृत्वा दण्डवत्प्रणिपत्य तम् । अनुज्ञातश्च रामेण ययौ देवगतिं मुनिः ॥ 40

संवादं पठति श्रृणोति संस्मरेद्वा यो नित्यं मुनिवररामयोः स भक्त्या ।
संप्राप्नोत्यमरसुदुर्लभं विमोक्षं कैवल्यं विरतिपुरःसरं क्रमेण ॥ 41

इति श्रीमदध्यात्मरामायणे उमामहेश्वरसंवादे
अयोध्याकाण्डे प्रथमः सर्गः ॥ १ ॥

there for fourteen years in the garb of a Muni (sage). Making the semblance of Sita the occasion, I shall destroy that evil fellow of a Ravana with all his kith and kin."

40. Thereupon the sage Narada, after circumambulating Rama three times and making a full prostration to him, departed with his permission, towards his divine abode. **41.** Whoever studies or hears or remembers this conversation between Rama and sage Narada with constant devotion every day, shall be blessed with renunciation followed by liberation, which is rarely obtained even by celestials.

द्वितीयः सर्गः

अथ राजा दशरथः कदाचिद्रहसि स्थितः । वसिष्ठं स्वकुलाचार्यमाहूयेदमभाषत ॥ 1

भगवन् राममखिलाः प्रशंसन्ति मुहुर्मुहुः । पौराश्च निगमा वृद्धा मन्त्रिणश्च विशेषतः ॥ 2

ततः सर्वगुणोपेतं रामं राजीवलोचनम् । ज्येष्ठं राज्येऽभिषेक्ष्यामि वृद्धोऽहं मुनिपुङ्गव ॥ 3

भरतो मातुलं द्रष्टुं गतः शत्रुघ्नसंयुतः । अभिषेक्ष्ये श्व एवाशु भवांस्तच्चानुमोदताम् ॥ 4

सम्भाराः सम्भ्रियन्तां च गच्छ मन्त्रय राघवम् । उच्छ्रीयन्तां पताकाश्च नानावर्णाः समन्ततः ॥ 5

Chapter 2

PROPOSAL OF INSTALLING RAMA AS YUVARAJA

Dasaratha's Decision to install Rama (1-16)

(1-2) One of those days, King Dasaratha called his preceptor Vasishtha to his side privately and said to him, "O great sage! Rama is receiving the repeated and unanimous praise of the citizens, learned men, the elders and above all the ministers. **3.** Therefore, O sage, I desire to install Rama, the lotus-eyed, who is endowed with all the great qualities and who is the eldest of my sons, as my successor. I am after all getting aged. **4.** Bharata and Satrughna have gone to their uncle's home. It is necessary that we should do this installation quickly tomorrow itself. Please give your permission for this with your full heart. **5.** And get together all the necessary ingredients for installation ceremony. Give information to Rama about this. Let banners and flags of various colours be

तोरणानि विचित्राणि स्वर्णमुक्तामयानि वै । आहूय मन्त्रिणं राजा सुमन्त्रं मन्त्रिसत्तमम् ॥ 6
आज्ञापयति यद्यत्त्वां मुनिस्तत्तत्समानय । यौवराज्येऽभिषेक्ष्यामि श्वोभूते रघुनन्दनम् ॥ 7
तथेति हर्षात्स मुनिं किं करोमीत्यभाषत । तमुवाच महातेजा वसिष्ठो ज्ञानिनां वरः ॥ 8
श्वः प्रभाते मध्यकक्षे कन्यकाः स्वर्णभूषिताः । तिष्ठन्तु षोडश गजाः स्वर्णरत्नादि भूषिताः ॥ 9
चतुर्दन्तः समायातु ऐरावतकुलोद्भवः । नानातीर्थोदकैः पूर्णाः स्वर्णकुम्भाः सहस्रशः ॥10
स्थाप्यन्तां नववैयाघ्रचर्माणि त्रीणि चानय । श्वेतच्छत्रं रत्नदण्डं मुक्तामणिविराजितम् ॥ 11
दिव्यमाल्यानि वस्त्राणि दिव्यान्याभरणानि च । मुनयः सत्कृतास्तत्र तिष्ठन्तु कुशपाणयः ॥ 12
नर्तक्यो वारमुख्याश्च गायका वेणुकास्तथा । नानावादित्रकुशला वादयन्तु नृपाङ्गणे ॥ 13
हस्त्यश्वरथपादाता बहिस्तिष्ठन्तु सायुधाः । नगरे यानि तिष्ठन्ति देवतायतनानि च ॥ 14
तेषु प्रवर्ततां पूजा नानाबलिभिरावृता । राजानः शीघ्रमायान्तु नानोपायनपाणयः ॥ 15
इत्यादिश्य मुनिः श्रीमान् सुमन्त्रं नृपमन्त्रिणम् । स्वयं जगाम भवनं राघवस्यातिशोभनम् ॥ 16
रथमारुह्य भगवान्वसिष्ठो मुनिसत्तमः । त्रीणि कक्षाण्यतिक्रम्य रथात्क्षितिमवातरत् ॥ 17

hoisted on all sides. **(6-7)**. Let canopies and other decorations inlaid with gold and pearls be put up." Then calling his chief minister Sumantra, he said to him, "Whatever the sage Vasishtha asks you to collect, gather them; for tomorrow I am going to install Rama as my successor."

8. In obedience to the King's command, Sumantra in great joy enquired of the sage Vasishtha what he should do in this connection. Thereupon Vasishtha, the greatest among men of knowledge, replied to him: **9.** "Tomorrow early morning, station at the main gate sixteen virgins adorned with ornaments of gold and an elephant also with decorations of gold studded with gems. **10.** A four-tusked elephant of the breed of Airavata has to be got for this, besides numerous golden pots filled with the waters of holy rivers. **11.** You must collect three fresh tiger skins. A ceremonial white umbrella with pearl pendants and a handle studded with gems is also required. **12.** There should be kept ready fragrant garlands, costly garments and exquisite jewellery. Let holy men, well-honoured and holding Kusa grass in hand, be stationed at the proper place. **13.** In the palace there must be assembled artistes of several kind, dancing girls, musicians, flutists, and experts in the use of various kinds of musical instruments. **(14-16).** Outside the palace regiments of elephants, horses and foot soldiers should stand attention with their arms. The Deities of all the temples in the city should be worshipped with ample offerings. Let vassal kings assemble with various articles of presentation." Having given these directions to the king's chief minister, Vasishtha himself went to the resplendent palace of Rama.

Vasishtha's Hymn (17-36)

17. Then proceeding to Rama's palace in a chariot, the great sage Vasishtha crossed three gates, and then got down from the

अन्तः प्रविश्य भवनं स्वाचार्यत्वादवारितः । गुरुमागतमाज्ञाय रामस्तूर्णं कृताञ्जलिः ॥ 18
प्रत्युद्गम्य नमस्कृत्य दण्डवद् भक्तिसंयुतः । स्वर्णपात्रेण पानीयमानिनायाशु जानकी ॥ 19
रत्नासने समावेश्य पादौ प्रक्षाल्य भक्तितः । तदपः शिरसा धृत्वा सीतया सह राघवः ॥ 20
धन्योऽस्मीत्यब्रवीद्रामस्तव पादाम्बुधारणात् । श्रीरामेणैवमुक्तस्तु प्रहसन्मुनिरब्रवीत् ॥ 21
त्वत्पादसलिलं धृत्वा धन्योऽभूद्गिरिजापतिः । ब्रह्मापि मत्पिता ते हि पादतीर्थहताशुभः ॥ 22
इदानीं भाषसे यत्त्वं लोकानामुपदेशकृत् । जानामि त्वां परात्मानं लक्ष्म्या संजातमीश्वरम् 23
देवकार्यार्थसिद्ध्यर्थं भक्तानां भक्तिसिद्धये । रावणस्य वधार्थाय जातं जानामि राघव ॥ 24
तथापि देवकार्यार्थं गुह्यं नोद्घाटयाम्यहम् । तथा त्वं मायया सर्वं करोषि रघुनन्दन ॥ 25
तथैवानुविधास्येऽहं शिष्यस्त्वं गुरुरप्यहम् । गुरुर्गुरूणां त्वं देव पितृणां त्वं पितामहः ॥ 26
अन्तर्यामी जगद्यात्रावाहकस्त्वमगोचरः । शुद्धसत्त्वमयं देहं धृत्वा स्वाधीनसम्भवम् ॥ 27
मनुष्य इव लोकेऽस्मिन् भासि त्वं योगमायया । पौरोहित्यमहं जाने विगर्ह्यं दूष्यजीवनम् ॥ 28
इक्ष्वाकूणां कुले रामः परमात्मा जनिष्यते । इति ज्ञातं मया पूर्वं ब्रह्मणा कथितं पुरा ॥ 29
ततोऽहमाशया राम तव सम्बन्धकाङ्क्षया । अकार्षं गर्हितमपि तवाचार्यत्वसिद्धये ॥ 30

chariot. (**18-21**). Being the family preceptor, he was allowed to enter the palace unobstructed. Seeing the preceptor coming, Rama immediately went to receive him with palms joined in salutation, and made a full prostration before him. Sita now brought water in a golden vessel, and seating Vasishtha on a bejewelled pedestal, washed his feet ceremonially. Then Rama, along with Sita, sprinkled that water on their heads, saying, "We are indeed blessed to bear your foot-washings on our head." To Rama who spoke thus the sage said smiling: **22.** "Bearing the Ganga, which is the water flowing from Thy feet, on his head, Parameswara became great. That same sacred water destroyed all the demerits of my father, Brahmā. **23.** What Thou hast said now about the washings of my feet purifying Thee, is only for the instruction of the world at large. For Thou, verily, art the Supreme Being and the Lord of all, incarnated on earth along with Thy consort Lakshmi. **24.** I know, O Rama, that Thou art born on earth for the achievement of certain purposes of the Devas, namely, the destruction of Ravana and for generating devotion in the minds of Thy votaries. (**25-26**). Though the facts are such, secrecy has to be maintained about the purpose of the Devas, so I am not revealing anything more prematurely. As Thou wishest to do things in Thy own mysterious way, let it happen in the fullness of time. I shall therefore continue to assume the pose of the preceptor, and Thou that of a disciple. But, O Lord, Thou art in truth the Teacher of all teachers, and the Progenitor of all fathers. (**27-30**). Though imperceptible to the senses, Thou art the inner pervader of all, and the One who regulates and sustains the progress of the world of Becoming. Thou who art born only out of Thy own accord, hast assumed a body of pure Sattva and hast

ततो मनोरथो मेऽद्य फलितो रघुनन्दन । त्वदधीना महामाया सर्वलोकैकमोहिनी ॥ 31
मां यथा मोहयेन्नैव तथा कुरु रघूद्वह । गुरुनिष्कृतिकामस्त्वं यदि देह्येतदेव मे ॥ 32
प्रसङ्गात्सर्वमप्युक्तं न वाच्यं कुत्रचिन्मया । राज्ञा दशरथेनाहं प्रेषितोऽस्मि रघूद्वह ॥ 33
त्वामामन्त्रयितुं राज्ये श्वोऽभिषेक्ष्यति राघव । अद्य त्वं सीतया सार्धमुपवासं यथाविधि ॥ 34
कृत्वा शुचिर्भूमिशायी भव राम जितेन्द्रियः । गच्छामि राजसान्निध्यं त्वं तु प्रातर्गमिष्यसि ॥ 35
इत्युक्त्वा रथमारुह्य ययौ राजगुरुर्द्रुतम् । रामोऽपि लक्ष्मणं दृष्ट्वा प्रहसन्निदमब्रवीत् ॥ 36
सौमित्रे यौवराज्ये मे श्वोऽभिषेको भविष्यति । निमित्तमात्रमेवाहं कर्ता भोक्ता त्वमेव हि ॥ 37
मम त्वं बहिः प्राणो नात्र कार्या विचारणा । ततो वसिष्ठेन यथा भाषितं तत्तथाकरोत् ॥ 38
वसिष्ठोऽपि नृपं गत्वा कृतं सर्वं न्यवेदयत् । वसिष्ठस्य पुरो राज्ञा ह्युक्तं रामाभिषेचनम् ॥ 39
यदा तदैव नगरे श्रुत्वा कश्चित्पुमान् जगौ । कौसल्यायै राममात्रे सुमित्रायै तथैव च ॥ 40

appeared as man in the world by virtue of Thy Yoga-maya. I know that the profession of priesthood is disreputable. But having known earlier from the words of Brahma that the Supreme Being will be born as Rama in the line of the Ikshvakus, I have, O Rama, accepted even this ignoble profession of priesthood in order that I may be related to Thee as Thy preceptor. **(31-32).** O Thou, the delight of Raghu's clan! My desire has now been fulfilled. I have now become Thy preceptor (Guru), and if Thou art inclined to pay back the debt that a disciple owes to the Guru, grant that Mahamaya, Thy Power, which is under Thy control and which deludes the whole world, may not delude me in that way. **33.** In this particular context I have revealed in Thy presence what I should not do anywhere else. Now coming to my present visit, I have come, sent by King Dasaratha. **(34-36).** O descendant of Raghus! Tomorrow you are going to be installed as the Yuvaraja. (the heir-apparent). I have come to inform you of this. You and Sita are required to fast and observe rules of purity and self-control and spend the night sleeping on the floor. I am now returning to the King. You are to come there tomorrow morning." After having communicated this, the royal preceptor Vasishtha got into his chariot and drove away in great haste. And Rama, now seeing Lakshmana near by, said as follows, smiling: **(37-38).** Rama said: "O son of Sumitra! Did you hear the news that I am going to be installed as the Yuva-raja tomorrow? In this matter I shall be only just like a proxy. You will be the real ruler and the enjoyer. For, you are verily my Prana externally manifested. It is undoubtedly so." Saying so, he proceeded to fulfil all the vows that Vasishtha had instructed him to observe.

Fears of Kausalya (39-43)

(39-40). Vasishtha on reaching Dasaratha, appraised him of all that had happened. Simultaneously with the King's announcement to Vasishtha about his intention to install Rama, the news was carried to Rama's mother Kausalya and to Sumitra, by some citizens who happened to hear

श्रुत्वा ते हर्षसम्पूर्णे ददतुर्हारमुत्तमम् । तस्मै ततः प्रीतमना कौसल्या पुत्रवत्सला ॥ 41
लक्ष्मीं पर्यचरद्देवीं रामस्यार्थप्रसिद्धये । सत्यवादी दशरथः करोत्येव प्रतिश्रुतम् ॥ 42
कैकेयीवशगः किन्तु कामुकः किं करिष्यति । इति व्याकुलचित्ता सा दुर्गां देवीमपूजयत् ॥ 43
एतस्मिन्नन्तरे देवा देवीं वाणीमचोदयन् । गच्छ देवि भुवो लोकमयोध्यायां प्रयत्नतः ॥44
रामाभिषेकविघ्नार्थं यतस्व ब्रह्मवाक्यतः । मन्थरां प्रविशस्वादौ कैकेयीं च ततः परम् ॥ 45
ततो विघ्ने समुत्पन्ने पुनरेहि दिवं शुभे । तथेत्युक्त्वा तथा चक्रे प्रविवेशाथ मन्थराम् ॥46
सापि कुब्जा त्रिवक्रा तु प्रासादाग्रमथारुहत् । नगरं परितो दृष्ट्वा सर्वतः समलंकृतम् ॥ 47
नानातोरणसम्बाधं पताकाभिरलंकृतम् । सर्वोत्सवसमायुक्तं विस्मिता पुनरागमत् ॥ 48
धात्रीं पप्रच्छ मातः किं नगरं समलंकृतम् । दानोत्सवसमायुक्ता कौसल्या चातिहर्षिता ॥ 49
ददाति विप्रमुख्येभ्यो वस्त्राणि विविधानि च । तामुवाच तदा धात्री रामचन्द्राभिषेचनम् ॥ 50
श्वो भविष्यति तेनाद्य सर्वतोऽलंकृतं पुरम् । तच्छ्रुत्वा त्वरितं गत्वा कैकेयीं वाक्यमब्रवीत् ॥51

about it. **(41-43)**. Both Kausalya and Sumitra were overjoyed to hear this good news and made presentation of a pearl necklace to the man who communicated the news to them. In a spirit of thanksgiving Kausalya, the loving mother, adored Lakshmi Devi with great joy. Yet an apprehension gripped her mind. She anxiously thought: "It is certain that King Dasaratha, who is devoted to truth, will stick to the word that he has given. But he is uxorious by nature and is under the control of Kaikeyi. I am therefore afraid about what he will do in the end." With such apprehensions in mind, she adored Durga for the removal of all obstacles.

Manthara Poisoning the Ears of Kaikeyi (44-84)

(44-46). In the meantime the Devas prompted Devi Saraswati, telling her "O Goddess of Speech! You must take the trouble of going to the earth, to the kingdom of Ayodhya. It is Brahma's command that you should strive to obstruct the installation of Rama. You have to possess Manthara first and then Kaikeyi and achieve this through them. After you have obstructed the coronation through them, you can return to your heavenly abode." Vani, the Goddess of Speech, did accordingly, and first entered into Manthara's heart and vocal organ.

(47-48). Now Manthara, who was a hunch-backed woman with three bents in the body, got on the terrace of a building in the morning, and was surprised to see the whole city decorated with flags and festoons and a holiday atmosphere prevailing everywhere. Astonished, she looked over the city, and then came down from the terrace. **(49-51)**. She then asked her foster-mother what it was all about. She enquired: "Mother, why is the city well decorated? I find Kausalya very joyous and enthusiastic, and she has been giving gifts of valuable cloth to many holy men. Why all this?"

पर्यङ्कस्थां विशालाक्षीमेकान्ते पर्यवस्थिताम् । किं शेषे दुर्भगे मूढे महद्भयमुपस्थितम् ॥ 52
न जानीषेऽतिसौन्दर्यमानिनी मत्तगामिनी ॥ 53
रामस्यानुग्रहाद्राज्ञः श्वोऽभिषेको भविष्यति । तत्श्रुत्वा सहसोत्थाय कैकेयी प्रियवादिनी ॥ 54
तस्यै दिव्यं ददौ स्वर्णनूपुरं रत्नभूषितम् । हर्षस्थाने किमिति मे कथ्यते भयमागतम् ॥ 55
भरतादधिको रामः प्रियकृन्मे प्रियंवदः । कौसल्यां मां समं पश्यन् सदा शुश्रूषते हि माम् 56
रामाद्भयं किमापन्नं तव मूढे वदस्व मे । तत्श्रुत्वा विषसादाथ कुब्जाकारणवैरिणी ॥ 57
श्रृणु मद्वचनं देवि यथार्थं ते महद्भयम् । त्वां तोषयन् सदा राजा प्रियवाक्यानि भाषते ॥ 58
कामुकोऽतथ्यवादी च त्वां वाचा परितोषयन् । कार्यं करोति तस्या वै राममातुः सुपुष्कलम् ॥ 59
मनस्येतन्निधायैव प्रेषयामास ते सुतम् । भरतं मातुलकुले प्रेषयामास सानुजम् ॥ 60
सुमित्रायाः समीचीनं भविष्यति न संशयः । लक्ष्मणो राममन्वेति राज्यं सोऽनुभविष्यति ॥ 61
भरतो राघवस्याग्रे किङ्करो वा भविष्यति । विवास्यते वा नगरात्प्राणैर्वा हायतेऽचिरात् ॥ 62

To these queries of hers, the foster-mother replied: "The installation of Rama as Yuva-raja is fixed for tomorrow. The city is decorated to celebrate that occasion." Hearing this, Manthara, the hunch-back, went to Kaikeyi and said to her as follows: **(52-57).** Addressing handsome Kaikeyi who was resting alone on a cot in a room, Manthara said: "You unfortunate and foolish woman! Why are you thus lying idle in this way when great danger is near at hand for you? You are going about proud of your beauty, but you are absolutely out of touch with the state of affairs round about you. By the King's gracious order, Rama's installation as the Yuvaraja will be taking place tomorrow." Hearing this news, Kaikeyi of sweet speech got up from the cot suddenly and gave to that hunch-back a golden waist-girdle as present, remarking, "How is it that you are saying that danger awaits me on an occasion like this, which is one of great joy for me? I hold Rama in greater esteem than my Bharata. He does and speaks what is dear to me. Looking upon me and Kausalya alike, he serves me in all respects. Foolish girl! What danger do you expect from Rama?" That hunch-backed woman, who had become antagonistic to Rama because of the prompting by Saraswati, was very sorry to hear these words of Kaikeyi. **(58-59).** She said to Kaikeyi: "O good lady! Hear my words. Truly there is great danger threatening you. King Dasaratha is supposed to be doing what is pleasing to you. But beware! He is only a sensual lover given to untruth. He is always pleasing you by words, but in action he is only doing what is wholly beneficial to Rama's mother, Kausalya. **60.** It is with this in mind that he has sent away your son Bharata from here under the pretext of sending him to his uncle's house along with his brother. **61.** Good will happen to Sumitra even if Rama's installation takes place. For, her son Lakshmana is devoted to Rama, and therefore he will enjoy royal favours when

त्वं तु दासीव कौसल्यां नित्यं परिचरिष्यसि । ततोऽपि मरणं श्रेयो यत्सपत्न्याः पराभवः ॥ 63
अतः शीघ्रं यतस्वाद्य भरतस्याभिषेचने । रामस्य वनवासार्थं वर्षाणि नव पञ्च च ॥ 64
ततो रूढोऽभये पुत्रस्तव राज्ञि भविष्यति । उपायं ते प्रवक्ष्यामि पूर्वमेव सुनिश्चितम् ॥ 65
पुरा देवासुरे युद्धे राजा दशरथः स्वयम् । इन्द्रेण याचितो धन्वी सहायार्थं महारथः ॥ 66
जगाम सेनया सार्धं त्वया सह शुभानने । युद्धं प्रकुर्वतस्तस्य राक्षसैः सह धन्विनः ॥ 67
तदाक्षकीलो न्यपतच्छिन्नस्तस्य न वेद सः । त्वं तु हस्तं समावेश्य कीलरन्ध्रेऽतिधैर्यतः ॥ 68
स्थितवत्यसितापाङ्गि पतिप्राणपरीप्सया । ततो हत्वासुरान्सर्वान् ददर्श त्वामरिन्दमः ॥ 69
आश्चर्यं परमं लेभे त्वामालिङ्ग्य मुदान्वितः । वृणीष्व यत्ते मनसि वाञ्छितं वरदोऽस्म्यहम् ॥70
वरद्वयं वृणीष्व त्वमेवं राजावदत्स्वयम् । त्वयोक्तो वरदो राजन्यदि दत्तं वरद्वयम् ॥ 71
त्वय्येव तिष्ठतु चिरं न्यासभूतं ममानघ । यदा मेऽवसरो भूयात्तदा देहि वरद्वयम् ॥ 72
तथेत्युक्त्वा स्वयं राजा मन्दिरं व्रज सुव्रते । त्वत्तः श्रुतं मया पूर्वमिदानीं स्मृतिमागतम् ॥ 73

Rama comes to power. **62.** One of these three alternatives will happen to Bharata if Rama comes to power. He may have to become a servant of Rama, or he may be expelled from the country, or he may be executed very soon. **63.** And as for you, you will have to serve Kausalya as her maid-servant all your life. Death is better for you than such humiliation at the hands of a co-wife. **64.** Therefore take steps at once to see that Bharata is installed and Rama is banished to the forest for fourteen years. **65.** O Queen! Then only can your son Bharata be free from all danger. There is a sure means for accomplishing this—a means for which past circumstances have paved the way. I shall now tell you what it is. **(66-69)**. In days of old, King Dasaratha was requested by Devas to help them in a battle with the Asuras. When Dasaratha went on this mission with his army, he had taken you also with him, O handsome one. While he was fighting with the Asuras bow in hand, the king-pin of his chariot axle broke! You, handsome lady, then kept the chariot on wheels by putting your hand in the hole of the broken king-pin with great heroism. Because of your anxiety to save your husband's life, you remained with your hand in that position till the end of the battle. It was only when the battle was over and he had destroyed all the Asuras, that King Dasaratha saw what you had done. **(70-73)**. Embracing you with great joy and wonder, he asked you to choose any two boons of your liking. 'I am pleased to grant you boons,' he said of his own accord, 'you ask of me for any two boons of your choice.' You replied: 'O royal husband! If you are pleased to bestow boons on me, let those boons rest with yourself to my credit for the time being. When I am in need of them, you can grant me the two boons.' 'Be it so, dear wife,' said the King in reply, 'let us now go to our camp.' This incident, which you had once narrated to me, has just now flashed in to my memory.

अतः शीघ्रं प्रविश्याद्य क्रोधागारं रुषान्विता । विमुच्य सर्वाभरणं सर्वतो विनिकीर्य च ॥ 74
भूमावेव शयाना त्वं तूष्णीमातिष्ठ भामिनि । यावत्सत्यं प्रतिज्ञाय राजाभीष्टं करोति ते ॥ 75
श्रुत्वा त्रिवक्रयोक्तं तत्तदा केकयनन्दिनी । तथ्यमेवाखिलं मेने दुःसङ्गाहितविभ्रमा । 76
तामाह कैकेयी दुष्टा कुतस्ते बुद्धिरीदृशी । एवं त्वां बुद्धिसम्पन्नां न जाने वक्रसुन्दरि ॥ 77
भरतो यदि राजा मे भविष्यति सुतः प्रियः । ग्रामान् शतं प्रदास्यामि मम त्वं प्राणवल्लभा ॥78
इत्युक्त्वा कोपभवनं प्रविश्य सहसा रुषा । विमुच्य सर्वाभरणं परिकीर्य समन्ततः ॥ 79
भूमौ शयाना मलिना मलिनाम्बरधारिणी । प्रोवाच शृणु मे कुब्जे यावद्रामो वनं व्रजेत् ॥ 80
प्राणांस्त्यक्ष्येऽथ वा वक्रे शयिष्ये तावदेव हि । निश्चयं कुरु कल्याणि कल्याणं ते भविष्यसि ॥81
इत्युक्त्वा प्रययौ कुब्जा गृहं सापि तथाकरोत् ॥ 82

धीरोऽत्यन्तदयान्वितोऽपि सगुणाचारान्वितो वाथवा
नीतिज्ञो विधिवाददेशिकपरो विद्याविवेकोऽथवा ।
दुष्टानामतिपापभावितधियां सङ्गं सदा चेद्भजे-
त्तद्बुद्ध्या परिभावितो व्रजति तत् साम्यं क्रमेण स्फुटम् ॥

(74-75). In pursuance of this, you now enter into the Chamber of Annoyance (*Krodhāgāram*) without delay. Scatter all your jewellery there and lie on the bare floor in order to express your anger. Until the King comes and promises to fulfil your demands, utter not a word."

76. Being thrown into a perverse way of thinking by the evil company of Manthara, the hunch-backed woman with three bents, Kaikeyi got convinced that the advice given to her by that woman was on right lines. **77.** And evil-minded Kaikeyi next said to her, "O you hunch-backed beauty! Where did you get this intelligence from? I never knew that you have such a resourceful mind. **78.** Dear as you are to my heart, I shall make you a gift of a hundred villages when my beloved son Bharata becomes the ruler." **(79-82).** With these words she quickly entered the 'chamber for angry protest' in a mood of violent temper, and scattering all her jewellery round about, stretched herself on the bare floor, with her body smeared with dirt and covered over only with a soiled piece of cloth. And she said to Manthara: "Hear me, O hunch-backed one! Until Rama is exiled to the forest, I shall certainly lie here in this condition. If he is not exiled, I am going to end my life here." "Stick to your resolution, O dear one. That will be for your good." Saying so, the hunch-backed woman went home, and Kaikeyi did exactly as she was advised by her.

83. However much a man be intelligent, kind by nature, virtuous in conduct, just, devoted to his moral instructor and endowed with learning and discrimination—if he always keeps the company of extremely wicked-minded people, he is sure to absorb

अत सङ्गः परित्याज्यो दुष्टानां सर्वदैव हि । दुःसङ्गी च्यवते स्वार्थाद्यथेयं राजकन्यका ॥ 84

इति श्रीमदध्यात्मरामायणे उमामहेश्वरसंवादे
अयोध्याकाण्डे द्वितीयः सर्गः ॥ २ ॥

the evil mentality of those associates. **84.** Therefore he should always be careful to avoid the association of wicked people. If he does not do so, he will lose all his goodness and become degenerate like Kaikeyi.

तृतीयः सर्गः

ततो दशरथो राजा रामाभ्युदयकारणात् । आदिश्य मन्त्रिप्रकृतीः सानन्दो गृहमाविशत् 1
तत्रादृष्ट्वा प्रियां राजा किमेतदिति विह्वलः । या पुरा मन्दिरं तस्याः प्रविष्टे मयि शोभना ॥ 2
हसन्ती मामुपायाति सा किं नैवाद्य दृश्यते । इत्यात्मन्येव संचिन्त्य मनसातिविदूयता ॥ 3
पप्रच्छ दासीनिकरं कुतो वः स्वामिनी शुभा । नायाति मां यथापूर्वं मत्प्रिया प्रियदर्शना ॥ 4
ता ऊचुः क्रोधभवनं प्रविष्टा नैव विद्महे । कारणं तत्र देव त्वं गत्वा निश्चेतुमर्हसि ॥ 5
इत्युक्तो भयसन्त्रस्तो राजा तस्याः समीपगः । उपविश्य शनैर्देहं स्पृशन्वै पाणिनाब्रवीत् ॥ 6
किं शेषे वसुधापृष्ठे पर्यङ्कादीन् विहाय च । मां त्वं खेदयसे भीरु यतो मां नावभाषसे ॥ 7

Chapter 3

OBSTRUCTION OF RAMA'S INSTALLATION

Kaikeyi in the 'Chamber of Angry Protest' (1-14)

1. King Dasaratha now called all his ministers and leading noble men and ordered them to make all arrangements for the installation of Rama as Yuvaraja. After that he went to his quarters in the palace. **(2-4).** On entering his quarters, he was shocked to notice the absence of his dear wife Kaikeyi and thought: "When I return to the palace, my handsome and dear wife usually approaches me smiling. Why is it that today I do not see her at all here?" Thinking like this within himself, he asked the group of attending maids there: "Why is it that your mistress, my most handsome and dear wife, has not come to receive me as usual?" **5.** They replied: "She has shut herself up in the 'chamber of angry protest!' We do not know why she has done so. It is better that Your Majesty is pleased to go in and ascertain the reason."

6. Stunned to hear this news, the King entered the room, and sitting by the side of Kaikeyi and stroking her body, said to her: **7.** "Dear one! Why is it that, abandoning cots and other furniture, you are lying on the bare floor? Why is it that you are not talking to me? I am extremely distressed by this conduct of yours, O timid one!

अलङ्कारं परित्यज्य भूमौ मलिनवाससा। किमर्थं ब्रूहि सकलं विधास्ये तव वाञ्छितम् ॥ 8
को वा तवाहितं कर्ता नारी वा पुरुषोऽपि वा। स मे दण्ड्यश्च वध्यश्च भविष्यति न संशयः ॥ 9
ब्रूहि देवि यथा प्रीतिस्तदवश्यं ममाग्रतः। तदिदानीं साधयिष्ये सुदुर्लभमपि क्षणात्। 10
जानासि त्वं मम स्वान्तं प्रियं मां स्ववशे स्थितम्। तथापि मां खेदयसे वृथा तव परिश्रमः ॥ 11
ब्रूहि कं धनिनं कुर्यां दरिद्रं ते प्रियङ्करम्। धनिनं क्षणमात्रेण निर्धनं च तवाहितम् ॥ 12
ब्रूहि कं वा वधिष्यामि वधार्हो वा विमोक्ष्यसे। किमत्र बहुनोक्तेन प्राणान्दास्यामि ते प्रिये ॥ 13
मम प्रणात्प्रियतरो रामो राजीवलोचनः। तस्योपरि शपे ब्रूहि त्वद्धितं तत्करोम्यहम् ॥ 14
इति ब्रुवाणं राजानं शपन्तं राघवोपरि। शनैर्विमृज्य नेत्रे सा राजानं प्रत्यभाषत ॥ 15
यदि सत्यप्रतिज्ञोऽसि शपथं कुरुषे यदि। याच्ञां मे सफलां कर्तुं शीघ्रमेव त्वमर्हसि ॥ 16
पूर्वं देवासुरे युद्धे मया त्वं परिरक्षितः। तदा वरद्वयं दत्तं त्वया मे तुष्टचेतसा ॥ 17
तद्द्वयं न्यासभूतं मे स्थापितं त्वयि सुव्रत। तत्रैकेन वरेणाशु भरतं मे प्रियं सुतम् ॥ 18
एभिः संभृतसंभारैर्यौवराज्येऽभिषेचय। अपरेण वरेणाशु रामो गच्छतु दण्डकान् ॥ 19

8. Abandoning all your jewellery, and wearing only a soiled cloth, why are you lying on this bare floor? Tell me what is the cause of your dissatisfaction, and I shall fulfil all your demands. **9.** Whoever it be that has caused you distress, whether it is man or woman, I am ready to inflict on that person punishment, including capital sentence. **10.** Dear one! Whatever it be that you are longing for, appraise me of it, and I shall accomplish it in no time, however difficult it might be. **11.** You know me to the core—that I am your dear husband completely under your control. When I am thus ever ready to fulfil your desires, it is needless for you to put yourself to all this trouble. **12.** If you want a person dear to you to be enriched, I am ready to enrich him. If you want one inimical to you to be impoverished, I am ready to accomplish that also in no time. **13.** Tell me whether you want any one to be executed. That shall certainly be done. Tell me whose sentence of execution you want to be revoked, that too shall be done. Why talk too much? O dear one! I am willing to offer even my life for your sake. **14.** I swear by the lotus-eyed Rama, who is dearer to me than my life itself, that I shall do whatever would give you satisfaction. Tell me what you want and I shall certainly accomplish it."

Kaikeyi's Request for Two Boons (15-22)

(15-17). To him who was speaking thus, swearing by Rama, Kaikeyi replied, after rubbing away the tears from her eyes. She said, "If you are truthful, if you are going to fulfil what you have sworn by, then you are bound to carry out my request immediately. In days of old, when you took part in a battle between the Devas and the Asuras, I happened to save your life in a critical situation. Being highly pleased with me for it, you offered me two boons. **(18-19).** O truthful one! Those two boons which you then

मुनिवेषधरः श्रीमान् जटावल्कलभूषणः । चतुर्दश समास्तत्र कन्दमूलफलाशनः ॥ 20
पुनरायातु तस्यान्ते वने वा तिष्ठतु स्वयम् । प्रभाते गच्छतु वनं रामो राजीवलोचनः ॥ 21
यदि किञ्चिद्विलम्बेत प्राणांस्त्यक्ष्ये तवाग्रतः । भव सत्यप्रतिज्ञस्त्वमेतदेव मम प्रियम् ॥ 22
श्रुत्वैतद्दारुणं वाक्यं कैकेय्या रोमहर्षणम् । निपपात महीपालो वज्राहत इवाचलः ॥ 23
शनैरुन्मील्य नयने विमृज्य परया भिया । दुःस्वप्नो वा मया दृष्टो ह्यथवा चित्तविभ्रमः ॥ 24
इत्यालोक्य पुरः पत्नीं व्याघ्रीमिव पुरः स्थिताम् । किमिदं भाषसे भद्रे मम प्राणहरं वचः ॥ 25
रामः कमपराधं ते कृतवान्कमलेक्षणः । ममाग्रे राघवगुणान्वर्णयस्यनिशं शुभान् ॥ 26
कौसल्यां मां समं पश्यन् शुश्रूषा कुरुते सदा । इति ब्रुवन्ती त्वं पूर्वमिदानीं भाषसेऽन्यथा ॥ 27
राज्यं गृहाण पुत्राय रामस्तिष्ठतु मन्दिरे । अनुगृह्णीष्व मां वामे रामान्नास्ति भयं तव ॥ 28
इत्युक्त्वाश्रुपरीताक्षः पादयोर्निपपात ह । कैकेयी प्रत्युवाचेदं सापि रक्तान्तलोचना ॥ 29

offered are still unfulfilled and are in your safe custody. Of those, one boon that I want now is that my dear son Bharata be immediately installed as Yuvaraja, utilising all these arrangements you have made for Rama's installation. The second boon I want is that Rama should be immediately sent into exile to the forest of Dandaka. **(20-21).** Let Sri Rama, dressed in an ascetic's garb of tree-bark, wearing matted locks, and devoid of all ornaments, live in the forest, subsisting on roots and fruits, for fourteen years. At the end of that period, let him return to the country or stay on in the forest itself if he prefers to do so. The lotus-eyed Rama should depart to the forest by the next sunrise. **22.** If there is any delay in carrying out my wish in these respects, I will put an end to my life in your very presence. Be true to your words. This is what I wish to be done."

King Dasaratha in Distress (23-32)

23. Hearing these shocking and frightening words of Kaikeyi, King Dasaratha fell on the floor, like a mountain struck by the thunderbolt weapon of Indra. **(24-25).** Slowly opening his eyes and rubbing them with his hands, Dasaratha, who was full of fear, felt confused. Was he experiencing an evil dream or had he lost his mind? Looking at his wife Kaikeyi, who was standing in front like a tigress, he said, "Dear one, how is it that you are speaking words that will virtually take my life away? **26.** What harm has the lotus-eyed Rama done to you? You have in the past been always speaking to me about the numerous virtues of Rama. **27.** You, who have said in the past that Rama looks on you and Kausalya alike, and that he is always serving you—how is it that you speak now in this strain against him? **28.** Let the kingdom go to your son, but let Rama stay on in the palace. Be pleased to favour me by accepting this proposal. What harm could you possibly have from Rama?" **29.** With these words and weeping, he fell at the feet of Kaikeyi; but she with her eyes red with anger said as follows in reply:

राजेन्द्र किं त्वं भ्रान्तोऽसि उक्तं तद्भाषसेऽन्यथा। मिथ्या करोषि चेत्स्वीयं भाषितं नरको भवेत् ॥ 30

वनं न गच्छेद्यदि रामचन्द्रः प्रभातकालेऽजिनचीरयुक्तः।
उद्बन्धनं वा विषभक्षणं वा कृत्वा मरिष्ये पुरतस्तवाहम् ॥ 31

सत्यप्रतिज्ञोऽहमितीह लोके विडम्बसे सर्वसभान्तरेषु।
रामोपरि त्वं शपथं च कृत्वा मिथ्याप्रतिज्ञो नरकं प्रयाहि ॥ 32

इत्युक्तः प्रियया दीनो मग्नो दुःखार्णवे नृपः। मूर्च्छितः पतितो भूमौ विसंज्ञो मृतको यथा ॥ 33
एवं रात्रिगता तस्य दुःखात्संवत्सरोपमा। अरुणोदयकाले तु वन्दिनो गायका जगुः ॥ 34
निवारयित्वा तान् सर्वान्कैकेयी रोषमास्थिता। ततः प्रभातसमये मध्यकक्षमुपस्थिताः ॥ 35
ब्राह्मणाः क्षत्रिया वैश्या ऋषयः कन्यकास्तथा। छत्रं च चामरं दिव्यं गजो वाजी तथैव च ॥ 36
अन्याश्च वारमुख्या याः पौरजानपदास्तथा। वसिष्ठेन यथाज्ञप्तं तत्सर्वं तत्र संस्थितम् ॥ 37
स्त्रियो बालाश्च वृद्धाश्च रात्रौ निद्रां न लेभिरे। कदा द्रक्ष्यामहे रामं पीतकौशेयवाससम् ॥ 38
सर्वाभरणसम्पन्नं किरीटकटकोज्ज्वलम्। कौस्तुभाभरणं श्यामं कन्दर्पशतसुन्दरम् ॥ 39
अभिषिक्तं समायातं गजारूढं सितानन्म्। श्वेतच्छत्रधरं तत्र लक्ष्मणं लक्षणान्वितम् ॥ 40
रामं कदा वा द्रक्ष्यामः प्रभातं वा कदा भवेत्। इत्युत्सुकधियः सर्वे बभूवुः पुरवासिनः ॥ 41

30. "O great King! Have you become mad? You are now speaking contrary to what you have spoken a moment before. If you prove false to your words, hell will be your fate. **31.** If Rama fails to go next morning to the forest, dressed in deer skin and tree-bark, I will be committing suicide in your very presence by hanging with a rope round my neck or by taking poison. **32.** In all assemblies in this world you are proclaimed as one true to your plighted words; and now after swearing in the name of Rama himself, if you fail to do according to your promise, you are sure to be consigned to hell."

Rama Summoned to Dasaratha's Presence (33-49)

33. Hearing these words of his wife, the hapless king, immersed in the ocean of sorrow, fell unconscious on the floor like one dead. **34.** On account of sorrow, he spent that night as if it were one year. When it was sunrise, the bards and the panegyrists began their recitals to the accompaniment of instrumental music to awaken the king. **(35-37).** But on Kaikeyi's order, these artistes had to stop their music and recitals. Kaikeyi stood there in a very angry mood. When it was daybreak, there assembled at the central gate all who had been ordered to do so by Vasishtha— citizens of the four classes, maidens, those holding superb ceremonial umbrellas and chowris, elephants and horses, dancing girls, and the general residents of the city and the villages. **(38-41)** All the citizens, men and women and children of the place, had no sleep that night. In great expectation, they were waiting for the morning when they could see, after the in-

नेदानीमुत्थितो राजा किमर्थं चेति चिन्तयन् । सुमन्त्रः शनकैः प्रायाद्यत्र राजावतिष्ठते ॥ 42
वर्धयन् जयशब्देन प्रणमन्शिरसा नृपम् । अतिखिन्नं नृपं दृष्ट्वा कैकेयीं समपृच्छत ॥ 43
देवि कैकेयि वर्धस्व किं राजा दृश्यतेऽन्यथा । तमाह कैकेयी राजा रात्रौ निद्रां न लब्धवान् ॥44
राम रामेति रामेति राममेवानुचिन्तयन् ।
प्रजागरेण वै राजा ह्यस्वस्थ इव लक्ष्यते । राममानय शीघ्रं त्वं राजा द्रष्टुमिहेच्छति ॥ 45
अश्रुत्वा राजवचनं कथं गच्छामि भामिनि । तत्श्रुत्वा मन्त्रिणो वाक्यं राजा मन्त्रिणमब्रवीत्॥46
सुमन्त्र रामं द्रक्ष्यामि शीघ्रमानय सुन्दरम् । इत्युक्तस्त्वरितं गत्वा सुमन्त्रो राममन्दिरम् ॥ 47
अवारितः प्रविष्टोऽयं त्वरितं राममब्रवीत् । शीघ्रमागच्छ भद्रं ते राम राजीवलोचन ॥ 48
पितुर्गेहं मया सार्धं राजा त्वां द्रष्टुमिच्छति । इत्युक्तो रथमारुह्य सम्भ्रमात्त्वरितो ययौ ॥ 49
रामः सारथिना सार्धं लक्ष्मणेन समन्वितः । मध्यकक्षे वसिष्ठादीन् पश्यन्नेव त्वरान्वितः ॥50
पितुः समीपं सङ्गम्य ननाम चरणौ पितुः । राममालिङ्गितुं राजा समुत्थाय ससम्भ्रमः ॥ 51
बाहू प्रसार्य रामेति दुःखान्मध्ये पपात ह । हाहेति रामस्तं शीघ्रमालिङ्ग्याङ्के न्यवेशयत् ॥52

stallation, the blue-complexioned and Cupid-like Rama dressed in yellow silk, decorated with jewellery, and adorned with a crown and shining armlets and the jewel Kaustubha, riding on an elephant along with Lakshmana under the cover of a ceremonial white umbrella. **42.** Seeing that the king had not yet awakened from sleep, the Minister Sumantra hurried to the palace where he was living. **43.** On greeting the king with good wishes and prostrations, Sumantra noticed him extremely grief-stricken. He addressed Kaikeyi as follows: **(44-45).** Sumantra said: "O honoured lady! May you be prosperous. How is it that I see the King with a sorrow-stricken face?" Kaikeyi replied, "The King had no sleep during the whole night. Uttering the name of Rama, he has been thinking of him alone. For want of sleep, you find him in this distressed condition. You bring Rama to this place quickly. The King desires to meet him."

(46-49). Sumantra said, "O lady! Without a word from the King, how can I to go and bring Rama?" Hearing these words of the Minister, King Dasaratha said to him, "O Sumantra! I wish to see Rama. Bring him here quickly." Being so commanded, Sumantra went to Rama's palace in great haste. Without being detained anywhere, he met Rama quickly and said, "O lotus-eyed Rama! Please come with me to your father's palace immediately. May good befall you!" Saying so, he ascended his chariot together with Rama and Lakshmana and departed immediately in an agitated mood.

Kaikeyi Demands Rama's Exile (50-66)

(50-52). Reaching the middle gate of the palace, along with Lakshmana and his charioteer, Rama saw there Vasishtha and all others assembled. In great haste, he proceeded to his father's presence and

राजानं मूर्च्छितं दृष्ट्वा चुक्रुशुः सर्वयोषितः । किमर्थं रोदनमिति वसिष्ठोऽपि समाविशत् ॥ 53
रामः पप्रच्छ किमिदं राज्ञो दुःखस्य कारणम् । एवं पृच्छति रामे सा कैकेयी राममब्रवीत् ॥ 54
त्वमेव कारणं ह्यत्र राज्ञो दुःखोपशान्तये । किञ्चित्कार्यं त्वया राम कर्तव्यं नृपतेर्हितम् ॥ 55
कुरु सत्यप्रतिज्ञस्त्वं राजानं सत्यवादिनम् । राज्ञा वरद्वयं दत्तं मम सन्तुष्टचेतसा ॥ 56
त्वदधीनं तु तत्सर्वं वक्तुं त्वां लज्जते नृपः । सत्यपाशेन सम्बद्धं पितरं त्रातुमर्हसि ॥ 57
पुत्रशब्देन चैतद्धि नरकात्त्रायते पिता । रामस्तयोदितं श्रुत्वा शूलेनाभिहतो यथा ॥ 58
व्यथितः कैकेयीं प्राह किं मामेवं प्रभाषसे । पित्रर्थे जीवितं दास्ये पिबेयं विषमुल्बणम् ॥ 59
सीतां त्यक्ष्येऽथ कौसल्यां राज्यं चापि त्यजाम्यहम् अनाज्ञप्तोऽपि कुरुते पितुः कार्यं स उत्तमः ॥ 60
उक्तः करोति यः पुत्रः स मध्यम उदाहृतः । उक्तोऽपि कुरुते नैव स पुत्रो मल उच्यते ॥ 61
अतः करोमि तत्सर्वं यन्मामाह पिता मम । सत्यं सत्यं करोम्येव रामो द्विर्नाभिभाषते ॥ 62
इति रामप्रतिज्ञां सा श्रुत्वा वक्तुं प्रचक्रमे । राम त्वदभिषेकार्थं संभाराः संभृताश्च ये ॥ 63

prostrated himself before him. The King then got up and with great affection proceeded to embrace Rama. But as he lifted his hand for the purpose, he fell down calling the name of Rama in an extremely distressed voice. Surprised at this, Rama immediately supported him, embraced him and stretched him in his own lap. **53.** Seeing the King unconscious, all the women there cried out in great agony. In order to ascertain the reason for these cries, sage Vasishtha also came into the palace.

54. Now Rama enquired of the persons present there, the cause of his father's sorrow. On his questioning thus, Kaikeyi said to him: **55.** "You alone, O Rama, can relieve the King of his sorrow. There is one thing which you have to do to bring him relief. **(56-57).** May you, who are yourself truthful, help the King to fulfil his plighted words. Once, highly pleased with me, the King had given me two boons. The fulfilment of these is in your hands. The King is hesitant to speak to you about it. Bound as he is by the cord of vow of truthfulness, he has to be saved from this difficult predicament by you. **(58-62).** For, the word son (*Putra*) means one who lifts his father from hell." Hearing her words, Rama felt agony like one struck with a trident and he said to Kaikeyi, "There is no need to speak to me in this strain. I am one who is ready to give up my very life for the sake of my father. If necessary, I am ready to give up Sita or Kausalya or the kingdom. The right type of son is the one who fulfils a father's desire even without being asked to do so. The middling type is the one who does so, when requested. And the degenerate one is the son who fails to do so even when asked. Such a son is designated as 'dirt'. So, whatever my father wants me to do, I am prepared to obey. I swear that I shall do accordingly. Rama never indulges in double-talk." **(63-66).** Hearing this vow of Rama, Kaikeyi began to tell him: "O Rama! Whatever preparations have been made for your installation, all that must

तैरेव भरतोऽवश्यमभिषेच्यः प्रियो मम । अपरेण वरेणाशु चीरवासा जटाधरः ॥ 64
वनं प्रयाहि शीघ्रं त्वमद्यैव पितुराज्ञया । चतुर्दश समास्तत्र वस मुन्यन्नभोजनः ॥ 65
एतदेव पितुस्तेऽद्य कार्यं त्वं कर्तुमर्हसि । राजा तु लज्जते वक्तुं त्वामेवं रघुनन्दन ॥ 66

श्रीराम उवाच

भरतस्यैव राज्यं स्यादहं गच्छामि दण्डकान् । किन्तु राजा न वक्तीह मां न जानेऽत्र कारणम् ॥67
श्रुत्वैतद्रामवचनं दृष्ट्वा रामं पुरः स्थितम् । प्राह राजा दशरथो दुःखितो दुःखितं वचः ॥ 68
स्त्रीजितं भ्रान्तहृदयमुन्मार्गपरिवर्तिनम् । निगृह्य मां गृहाणेदं राज्यं पापं न तद्भवेत् ॥ 69
एवं चेदनृतं नैव मां स्पृशेद्रघुनन्दन । इत्युक्त्वा दुःखसन्तप्तो विललाप नृपस्तदा ॥ 70
हा राम हा जगन्नाथ हा मम प्राणवल्लभ । मां विसृज्य कथं घोरं विपिनं गन्तुमर्हसि ॥ 71
इति रामं समालिङ्ग्य मुक्तकण्ठो रुरोद ह । विसृज्य नयने रामः पितुः सजलपाणिना ॥ 72
आश्वासयामास नृपं शनैः स नयकोविदः । किमत्र दुःखेन विभो राज्यं शास्तु मेऽनुजः ॥ 73
अहं प्रतिज्ञां निस्तीर्य पुनर्यास्यामि ते पुरम् । राज्यात्कोटिगुणं सौख्यं मम राजन्वने सतः ॥ 74

be utilised without fail for installing my dear son Bharata as the Yuvaraja. This is one of the boons that I have sought. The other is that at the command of your father, you should, wearing tree-bark and matted locks, go to the forest at once and live there for fourteen years subsisting on the diet of ascetics. These are what your father wants you to do. O scion of Raghu's line! The King is rather ashamed and hesitant to speak to you openly about it."

Rama's Reaction to the Demands of Kaikeyi (67-80)

67. Thus addressed, Rama said, "Let the kingdom go to Bharata and I shall go to the Dandaka forest. But I do not understand why the King is not so ordering me directly while I am standing in his presence." **68.** Hearing these words of Rama, standing in front of him, the sorrow-stricken King Dasaratha spoke very mournfully. **(69-70).** He said, "You take possession of this kingdom, killing or imprisoning me, who am treading the path of injustice, whose mind has lost its balance and who is under the domination of a woman. It will not be sinful of you to do so. If you do like that, O joy of the Raghus, I shall not be tainted with the stain of untruth." Saying so, the grief-stricken King began to cry aloud, exclaiming: **71.** "O Rama! O master of the world! O dearest object of my love! Abandoning me, how will it be possible for you to go to that dense forest!" **(72-74)**. With these words the King embraced Rama and began to weep without any restraint. And, alas! Rama taking some water in his hand from a pot, washed the King's eyes, and the adept in conciliation that he was, he began to console the King saying, "O wise one! Why should you be so down-hearted in this situation? Let my brother rule the kingdom, and as for myself, after fulfilling your plighted words, I shall come back to this city. O King! I shall

त्वत्सत्यपालनं देव कार्यं चापि भविष्यति । कैकेय्याश्च प्रियो राजन्वनवासो महागुणः ॥ 75

इदानीं गन्तुमिच्छामि व्येतु मातुश्च हृज्ज्वरः । सम्भारश्चोपह्रीयन्तामभिषेकार्थमाहृताः ॥ 76

मातरं च समाश्वास्य अनुनीय च जानकीम् । आगत्य पादौ वन्दित्वा तव यास्ये सुखं वनम् ॥ 77

इत्युक्त्वा तु परिक्रम्य मातरं द्रष्टुमाययौ । कौसल्यापि हरेः पूजां कुरुते रामकारणात् ॥ 78

होमं च कारयामास ब्राह्मणेभ्यो ददौ धनम् । ध्यायते विष्णुमेकाग्रमनसा मौनमास्थिता ॥ 79

अन्तःस्थमेकं घनचित्प्रकाशं निरस्तसर्वातिशयस्वरूपम् ।
विष्णुं सदानन्दमयं हृदब्जे सा भावयन्ती न ददर्श रामम् ॥ 80

इति श्रीमदध्यात्मरामायणे उमामहेश्वरसंवादे
अयोध्याकाण्डे तृतीयः सर्गः ॥ ३ ॥

be a hundred times more happy to live in the forest than to rule the kingdom. **75.** O great King! By this arrangement your promise will be fulfilled, and Kaikeyi too will be pleased. Thus my departure to the forest will prove highly beneficial. **76.** I would, therefore, go away now from here. May the pangs of mother Kaikeyi's heart be assuaged thereby! Let all the materials brought for the installation be abandoned. **77.** I shall now go and console my mother Kausalya and my wife Sita, the daughter of Janaka. After that I shall again come, do obeisance to you, and then depart to the forest with a peaceful mind."

(78-79). Saying so, Rama circumambulated his father and then went to see his mother Kausalya. At that time Kausalya, after having worshipped Hari for the welfare of Rama, had performed Homas and given gifts to holy men, and was observing silence and meditating in her palace with a concentrated mind. **80.** She did not notice Rama standing in front of her, as she was then intently meditating in her heart on Mahavishnu, the one Being who dwells in all, who is ever resplendent with the light of knowledge, who transcends all diversities and whose nature is constituted of Bliss.

चतुर्थः सर्गः

ततः सुमित्रा दृष्ट्वैनं रामं राज्ञींससम्भ्रमा । कौसल्यां बोधयामास रामोऽयं समुपस्थितः ॥ 1
श्रुत्वैव रामनामैषा बहिर्दृष्टिप्रवाहिता । रामं दृष्ट्वा विशालाक्षमालिङ्ग्याङ्के न्यवेशयत् 2
मूर्ध्न्यवघ्राय पस्पर्श गात्रं नीलोत्पलच्छवि । भुङ्क्ष्व पुत्रेति च प्राह मिष्टमन्नं क्षुधार्दितः । 3
रामः प्राह न मे मातर्भोजनावसरः कुतः । दण्डकागमने शीघ्रं मम कालोऽद्य निश्चितः । 4
कैकेयीवरदानेन सत्यसन्धः पिता मम । भरताय ददौ राज्यं ममाप्यारण्यमुत्तमम् ॥ 5
चतुर्दश समास्तत्र ह्युषित्वा मुनिवेषधृक् । आगमिष्ये पुनः शीघ्रं न चिन्तां कर्तुमर्हसि ॥ 6
तत्श्रुत्वा सहसोद्विग्ना मूर्च्छिता पुनरुत्थिता । आह रामं सुदुःखार्ता दुःखसागरसंप्लुता ॥ 7
यदि राम वनं सत्यं यासि चेन्नय मामपि । त्वद्विहीना क्षणार्द्धं वा जीवितं धारये कथम् ॥ 8
यथा गौर्बालकं वत्सं त्यक्त्वा तिष्ठेन्न कुत्रचित् । तथैव त्वां न शक्नोमि त्यक्तुं प्राणात्प्रियं सुतम् 9
भरताय प्रसन्नश्चेद्राज्यं राजा प्रयच्छतु । किमर्थं वनवासाय त्वामाज्ञापयति प्रियम् ॥ 10

Chapter 4

RAMA'S EXILE TO THE FOREST

Rama informing Kausalya of his Father's Order (1-13)

1. Seeing Rama thus standing without being noticed, Sumitra hurried to inform Queen Kausalya of Rama's presence before her. **2.** When the name of Rama was uttered, Kausalya opened her eyes, and she saw before her Rama of attractive eyes. She embraced him and seated him on her lap. **3.** Smelling the crown of his head and stroking his body resembling a blue lily, she said, "O child! You should take food to your satisfaction. You look like one starved." **4.** Rama said in reply, "There is no time for me to take food. I am to start immediately for the forest of Dandaka. **5.** My father, who ever sticks to truth, has given two boons to Kaikeyi, according to which he has assigned the kingdom to Bharata, and to me the glorious forest. **6.** After spending fourteen years there as an ascetic, I shall return without delay. Please be not worried on account of this."

7. Hearing these words, Kausalya fell down unconscious with a broken heart. Later, after coming to consciousness, she got up and, distressed by unbearable grief, nay, immersed in the ocean of sorrow, she said to Rama: **8.** "O Rama! If it is true that you are going to the forest, take me also with you. Without you, how can I live even for a moment? **9.** A cow cannot rest if its calf is taken away. Even like that, without you, my son, who is dearer to me than my life itself, how can I sustain my life? **10.** If the King is so pleased, let him give the

कैकेय्या वरदो राजा सर्वस्वं वा प्रयच्छतु। त्वया किमपराद्धं हि कैकेय्या वा नृपस्य वा ॥ 11
पिता गुरुर्यथा राम तवाहमधिका ततः। पित्राऽऽज्ञप्तो वनं गन्तुं वारयेयमहं सुतम् ॥ 12
यदि गच्छसि मद्वाक्यमुल्लङ्घ्य नृपवाक्यतः। तदा प्राणान्परित्यज्य गच्छामि यमसादनम् ॥ 13
लक्ष्मणोऽपि ततः श्रुत्वा कौसल्यावचनं रुषा। उवाच राघवं वीक्ष्य दहन्निव जगत्त्रयम् ॥ 14
उन्मत्तं भ्रान्तमनसं कैकेयीवशवर्तिनम्। बद्ध्वा निहन्मि भरतं तद्बन्धून्मातुलानपि ॥ 15
अद्य पश्यन्तु मे शौर्यं लोकान्प्रदहतः पुरा। राम त्वमभिषेकाय कुरु यत्नमरिन्दम ॥ 16
धनुष्पाणिरहं तत्र निहन्यां विघ्नकारिणः। इति ब्रुवन्तं सौमित्रिमालिङ्ग्य रघुनन्दनः ॥ 17
शूरोऽसि रघुशार्दूल ममात्यन्तहिते रतः। जानामि सर्वं ते सत्यं किन्तु तत्समयो न हि ॥ 18
यदिदं दृश्यते सर्वं राज्यं देहादिकं च यत्। यदि सत्यं भवेत्तत्र आयासः सफलश्च ते ॥ 19
भोगा मेघवितानस्थविद्युल्लेखेव चञ्चलाः। आयुरप्यग्निसन्तप्तलोहस्थजलबिन्दुवत् ॥ 20
यथा व्यालगलस्थोऽपि भेको दंशानपेक्षते। तथा कालाहिना ग्रस्तो लोको भोगानशाश्वतान् 21

kingdom to Bharata. Why should he order you, my dear son, to go to the forest ? **11.** Let the King, who has granted boons to Kaikeyi, give her all his possessions, but what harm have you done either to Kaikeyi or to the King to be expelled to the forest? **12.** O Rama! Just as your father is your respectable elder, much more so am I, your mother. If the father has ordered you to go to the forest, I, your mother, am prohibiting it. **13.** If, disobeying my words, you depart to the forest in obedience to the King's order, I shall abandon my life and attain the realm of Death."

Rama's Advice to Lakshmana (14-37)

14. Hearing Kausalya's words, Lakshmana who was burning with anger, as if he were going to burn the whole world, looked at Rama and said: **15.** "I shall put in fetters the King who is under infatuation, who is of unsteady mind, and who is entirely under the thumb of Kaikeyi. I shall then kill Bharata and his uncle and other relatives. **16.** Let Bharata and others now witness my prowess—the prowess by which I consume the whole universe in the fire of destruction. You should now, in every way, persist in this ceremony of installation. **17.** With bow in hand, I shall cause the destruction of all who dare to obstruct your installation." Embracing the son of Sumitra, who was speaking thus, Rama said: **18.** "O heroic scion of Raghu's line! You are indeed powerful and courageous. You are also well-intentioned towards me. I accept all this. But this is not the time for exhibiting your prowess. **19.** If this kingdom and all that we experience, including our bodies, were true in the ultimate sense, then it would have been proper for you to make an effort on the lines proposed by you. **20.** Enjoyments are momentary like streaks of lightning appearing in the clouds. So also is life—it is like a small drop of water sprinkled on a red hot piece of iron. **21.** For men in the grip of the serpent of Time, to long for these extremely temporary enjoyments

करोति दुःखेन हि कर्मतन्त्रं शरीरभोगार्थमहर्निशं नरः ।
देहस्तु भिन्नः पुरुषात्समीक्ष्यते को वात्र भोगः पुरुषेण भुज्यते ॥ 22

पितृमातृसुतभ्रातृदारबन्ध्वादिसंगमः । प्रपायामिव जन्तूनां नद्यां काष्ठौघवच्चलः ॥ 23

छायेव लक्ष्मीश्चपला प्रतीता तारुण्यमम्बूर्मिवदध्रुवं च ।
स्वप्नोपमं स्त्रीसुखमायुरल्पं तथापि जन्तोरभिमान एषः ॥ 24

संसृतिः स्वप्नसदृशी सदा रोगादिसङ्कुला । गन्धर्वनगरप्रख्या मूढस्तामनुवर्तते ॥ 25

आयुष्यं क्षीयते यस्मादादित्यस्य गतागतैः । दृष्ट्वान्येषां जरामृत्यू कथञ्चिन्नैव बुध्यते ॥ 26

स एव दिवसः सैव रात्रिरित्येव मूढधीः । भोगाननुपतत्येव कालवेगं न पश्यति ॥ 27

प्रतिक्षणं क्षरत्येतदायुरामघटाम्बुवत् । सपत्ना इव रोगौघाः शरीरं प्रहरन्त्यहो ॥ 28

जरा व्याघ्रीव पुरतस्तर्जयन्त्यवतिष्ठते । मृत्युः सहैव यात्येष समयं सम्प्रतीक्षते ॥ 29

देहेऽहंभावमापन्नो राजाहं लोकविश्रुतः । इत्यस्मिन्मनुते जन्तुः कृमिविड्भस्मसंज्ञिते ॥ 30

is like what it is for a frog to cry for food when it is already in the mouth of a serpent. **22.** Man struggles day and night in various kinds of work for securing objects of enjoyment for his body. But, the truth is that the body is different from the true Self. **23.** For all creatures, extremely temporary is the association with their kith and kin like father, mother, sons, brother, wife and others. It is only like the association that the traveller has in a way-side inn or even like pieces of wood floating down a river. **24.** Fortune is unstable like a shadow. So is youth, like a wave in a water receptacle. Sexual enjoyments are dream-like and unsubstantial. Life, after all, is of very short duration. Yet, strangely enough all living beings run after these values as the be-all and end-all of life.

25. This transmigratory life resembles a dream. It is full of sufferings arising from diseases. It is as evanescent as a castle in the air, but yet foolish man goes after it. **26.** Sunset and sunrise mark the ebbing away of life. We see all around others succumbing to old age and death. But still, man does not realise that this is his fate also. **27.** Without realising that every day and every night that he is now enjoying, mark the termination of those that have gone before, the foolish and unreflective man blindly runs after enjoyments. He does not realise the rapidity with which Time rolls on. **28.** The contents of our life-span are like water kept in an unbaked pot. It leaks out and is exhausted every moment. Like enemies, many kinds of diseases are ever ready to attack and destroy the body. **29.** Old age and disease are ever assailing the body, and in their wake death too is watching for the opportune moment to pounce upon man like a tigress. **30.** In this world you find that man thinks of his own body as 'I'—of this body which is only a synonym for worms, dirt and ashes. With reference to such a despicable thing

त्वगस्थिमांसविण्मूत्ररेतोरक्तादिसंयुतः । विकारी परिणामी च देह आत्मा कथं वद ॥ 31
यमास्थाय भवाँल्लोकं दग्धुमिच्छति लक्ष्मण । देहाभिमानिनः सर्वे दोषाः प्रादुर्भवन्ति हि ॥ 32
देहोऽहमिति यो बुद्धिरविद्या सा प्रकीर्तिता । नाहं देहश्चिदात्मेति बुद्धिर्विद्येति भण्यते ॥ 33
अविद्या संसृतेर्हेतुर्विद्या तस्या निवर्तिका ।
तस्माद्यत्नः सदा कार्यो विद्याभ्यासे मुमुक्षुभिः । कामक्रोधादयस्तत्र शत्रवः शत्रुसूदन ॥ 34
तत्रापि क्रोध एवालं मोक्षविघ्नाय सर्वदा । येनाविष्टः पुमान्हन्ति पितृभ्रातृसुहृत्सखीन् ॥ 35
क्रोधमूलो मनस्तापः क्रोधः संसारबन्धनम् । धर्मक्षयकरः क्रोधस्तस्मात्क्रोधं परित्यज ॥ 36
क्रोध एष महान् शत्रुस्तृष्णा वैतरणी नदी । सन्तोषो नन्दनवनं शान्तिरेव हि कामधुक् ॥ 37
तस्माच्छान्तिं भजस्वाद्य शत्रुरेवं भवेन्न ते । देहेन्द्रियमनःप्राणबुद्ध्यादिभ्यो विलक्षणः ॥ 38
आत्मा शुद्धः स्वयंज्योतिरविकारी निराकृतिः । यावद्देहेन्द्रियप्राणैर्भिन्नत्वं नात्मनो विदुः ॥ 39
तावत्संसारदुःखौघैः पीड्यन्ते मृत्युसंयुताः । तस्मात्त्वं सर्वदा भिन्नमात्मानं हृदि भावय ॥ 40
बुद्ध्यादिभ्यो बहिः सर्वमनुवर्तस्व मा खिदः । भुञ्जन्प्रारब्धमखिलं सुखं वा दुःखमेव वा ॥ 41

like this body, he feels that he is a world-renowned king. **31.** How can this body be the spirit (Atman)—this body which is nothing but a combination of skin, bones, excreta, semen, blood etc.? It is extremely changeful also. How can such a body be identified with the Atman? **32.** O Lakshmana! This body for the love of which you say you are going to destroy the world—this identification with the body is the cause of all evil. **33.** The conviction that 'I am the body' is what is called Avidya (ignorance). The conviction that 'I am not the body but the light of Consciousness,' is called Vidya (knowledge). **34.** Avidya is the cause of transmigratory life, and the eradication of it is accomplished by Vidya. Therefore, all who aspire for liberation should ever cultivate Vidya. In the cultivation of Vidya, the chief obstructing factors are passions like lust and anger. **35.** Of all these, anger is the greatest obstruction. For, overcome by anger, man murders even his father, brother, well-wishers and friends. **36.** From anger arises distress in mind. Anger keeps one tightly tied to the transmigratory life. Anger effaces a man's righteous tendencies. Therefore, anger is to be abandoned by all means. **37.** Anger is man's most terrible enemy. Desires and longings of the heart constitute the Vaitarani—the river of hell difficult to cross. Contentment is Nandanavana, the forest of Nandana—the garden of heaven. Peace at heart is verily Kamadhenu—the heavenly cow of plenty.

Control your Mind and be Calm (38-47)

(38-41). Therefore practise calmness of mind. Thereby you can avoid having enemies. The Atman is distinct from the senses, mind, Prana, Buddhi and other categories. Pure and changeless, the Atman is the universal self-conscious intelligence shining without the help of any other entity (*svayamjyoti*). As long as one does not

प्रवाहपतितं कार्यं कुर्वन्नपि न लिप्यसे । बाह्ये सर्वत्र कर्तृत्वमावहन्नपि राघव ॥ 42
अन्तःशुद्धस्वभावस्त्वं लिप्यसे न च कर्मभिः । एतन्मयोदितं कृत्स्नं हृदि भावय सर्वदा ॥ 43
संसारदुःखैरखिलैर्बाध्यसे न कदाचन । त्वमप्यम्ब ममाऽऽदिष्टं हृदि भावय नित्यदा ॥44
समागमं प्रतीक्षस्व न दुःखैः पीड्यसे चिरम् । न सदैकत्र संवासः कर्ममार्गानुवर्तिनाम् ॥ 45
यथा प्रवाहपतितप्लवानां सरितां तथा । चतुर्दशसमासङ्ख्या क्षणार्द्धमिव जायते ॥ 46
अनुमन्यस्व मामम्ब दुःखं सन्त्यज्य दूरतः । एवं चेत्सुखसंवासो भविष्यति वने मम ॥ 47
इत्युक्त्वा दण्डवन्मातुः पादयोरपतच्चिरम् । उत्थाप्याङ्के समावेश्य आशीर्भिरभ्यनन्दयत् ॥48
सर्वे देवाः सगन्धर्वा ब्रह्मविष्णुशिवादयः । रक्षन्तु त्वां सदा यान्तं तिष्ठन्तं निद्रयायुतम् ॥ 49
इति प्रस्थापयामास समालिङ्ग्य पुनः पुनः । लक्ष्मणोऽपि तदा रामं नत्वा हर्षाश्रुगद्गदः ॥ 50
आह राम ममान्तःस्थः संशयोऽयं त्वया हृतः । यास्यामि पृष्ठतो राम सेवां कर्तुं तदादिश ॥ 51

realise the distinctiveness of the Atman from the body, the senses and the Prana, so long will one be subject to the sufferings of transmigratory life, including death. Therefore, ever think of the Atman as residing in the heart in complete separation from the body-mind complex. While knowing the Atman thus, follow the ways of the world at the same time. Do not feel distressed. Enjoyments and sufferings befall man according to his operative Karma (*prarabdha*). **42.** Though coursing along the flow of worldly life and appearing to be the agent of various actions, one who knows the real Self is never bound by the good and evil fruits of actions. **43.** Being pure and unaffected within, one is not affected by Karmas. Always remember these instructions. **44.** Thus you will never fall a victim to the sufferings of Samsara; and you, too, O mother, keep in your mind all these truths that I have spoken to Lakshmana. **45.** You wait for my return. Your sorrows will not last very long. Living beings who are subject to their Karma cannot always live in the same situation, as different environments are required for the experience of the fruits of their Karmas. So it is not given to them to live always with the same people in the same place. They have to part according to the quanta of Karma coming to fruition. **46.** Men subject to Karma are like boats caught in a current of water. They go in different directions according to the speed and direction of the water. And, after all, fourteen years will pass away like a moment. **47.** O mother! Abandon grief and permit me to go. If you do so, I shall be able to live in the forest in peace."

Rama Reconciles Kausalya, Lakshmana and Sita to his Resolution (48-87)

48. Saying so, Rama lay flat at his mother's feet in prostration for a long time. Mother Kausalya lifted him up, seated him in her lap, and pronounced blessings on him. **(49-51).** After embracing him again and again, she permitted him to go with the following blessings: "May all the Devas along with Gandharvas—may the deities Brahma, Vishnu and Maheswara protect you wherever you go, wherever you

अनुगृह्णीष्व मां राम नोचेत्प्राणांस्त्यजाम्यहम् । तथेतिराघवोऽप्याहलक्ष्मणं याहि मा चिरम् ॥52

प्रतस्थे तां समाधातुं गतः सीतापतिर्विभुः । आगतं पतिमालोक्य सीता सुस्मितभाषिणी ॥ 53

स्वर्णपात्रस्थसलिलैः पादौ प्रक्षाल्य भक्तितः । पप्रच्छ पतिमालोक्य देव किं सेनया विना ॥ 54

आगतोऽसि गतः कुत्र श्वेतच्छत्रं च ते कुतः । वादित्राणि न वाद्यन्ते किरीटादिविवर्जितः ॥ 55

सामन्तराजसहितः सम्भ्रमान्नागतोऽसि किम् । इति सीतया पृष्टो रामः सस्मितमब्रवीत् ॥ 56

राज्ञा मे दण्डकारण्ये राज्यं दत्तं शुभेऽखिलम् । अतस्तत्पालनार्थाय शीघ्रं यास्यामि भामिनि ॥ 57

अद्यैव यास्यामि वनं त्वं तु श्वश्रूसमीपगा । शुश्रूषां कुरु मे मातुर्न मिथ्यावादिनो वयम् ॥58

इति ब्रुवन्तं श्रीरामं सीता भीताब्रवीद्वचः । किमर्थं वनराज्यं ते पित्रा दत्तं महात्मना ॥ 59

तामाह रामः कैकेय्यै राजा प्रीतो वरं ददौ । भरताय ददौ राज्यं वनवासं ममानघे ॥ 60

चतुर्दश समास्तत्र वासो मे किल याचितः । तया देव्या ददौ राजा सत्यवादो दयापरः ॥ 61

travel, wherever you stay and wherever you sleep!" Thereupon Lakshmana, saluting Rama, said with his throat choked with feelings: "O Rama! You have now cleared the doubt that was in my mind. Now may you be pleased to permit me to follow you and serve you. Be pleased to order so. **52.** O Rama! Bestow this blessing on me. If you do not, I shall give up my life." Rama, accepting Lakshmana's request, said to him, "Then be ready to start. Do not delay."

(53-56). Rama, who was none but the Lord of the universe, now went to console his wife Sita. Seeing her husband arrive, Sita received him with a smile and sweet words. She washed his feet with water kept in a golden vessel, and looking at him said, "O Lord, how is it that you have come without your body guard? Where have you been till now? Where is that ceremonial white umbrella that used to be held over you? How is it that musical instruments are not being played as you move about? Why is it that you have come without your crown and other royal insignia, and how is it again that you are not accompanied by any of the vassal princes?" Being thus questioned by Sita, Rama answered with a smile.

57. He said, "O handsome one! The King has assigned to me the kingdom of Dandakaranya. I am therefore proceeding quickly for ruling over it. **58.** I am starting for the forest even today. You therefore stay with my father and mother, serving the mother specially. I am not telling this in joke, but seriously." **59.** Overwhelmed by surprise and fear on hearing Sri Rama's words, Sita asked him why the noble-minded father had commanded him to go to the forest. **60.** Rama thereupon said to her: "Being highly pleased with Kaikeyi, the King had given her two boons. According to that he has assigned the kingdom to Bharata and the forest to me. **61.** Kaikeyi wanted that I should be an exile in the forest for fourteen years. The King, though really very kind to me, has yet, being a strict adherent of truth, assigned

अतः शीघ्रं गमिष्यामि मा विघ्नं कुरु भामिनि । श्रुत्वा तद्रामवचनं जानकी प्रीतिसंयुता ॥ 62

अहमग्रे गमिष्यामि वनं पश्चात्त्वमेष्यसि । इत्याह मां विना गन्तुं तव राघव नोचितम् ॥ 63

तामाह राघवः प्रीतः स्वप्रियां प्रियवादिनीम् । कथं वनं त्वां नेष्येऽहं बहुव्याघ्रमृगाकुलम् ॥ 64

राक्षसा घोररूपाश्च सन्ति मानुषभोजिनः । सिंहव्याघ्रवराहाश्च सञ्चरन्ति समन्ततः ॥ 65

कट्वम्लफलमूलानि भोजनार्थं सुमध्यमे । अपूपानि व्यञ्जनानि विद्यन्ते न कदाचन ॥ 66

काले काले फलं वापि विद्यते कुत्र सुन्दरि । मार्गो न दृश्यते क्वापि शर्कराकण्टकान्वितः ॥67

गुहागह्वरसम्बाधं झिल्लीदंशादिभिर्युतम् । एवं बहुविधं दोषं वनं दण्डकसंज्ञितम् ॥ 68

पादचारेण गन्तव्यं शीतवातातपादिमत् । राक्षसादीन्वने दृष्ट्वा जीवितं हास्यसेऽचिरात् ॥69

तस्माद्भद्रे गृहे तिष्ठ शीघ्रं द्रक्ष्यसि मां पुनः । रामस्य वचनं श्रुत्वा सीता दुःखसमन्विता ॥ 70

प्रत्युवाच स्फुरद्वक्त्रा किञ्चित्कोपसमन्विता । कथं मामिच्छसे त्यक्तुं धर्मपत्नीं पतिव्रताम् ॥71

त्वदनन्यामदोषां मां धर्मज्ञोऽसि दयापरः । त्वत्समीपे स्थितां राम को वा मां धर्षयेद्वने ॥72

फलमूलादिकं यद्यत्तव भुक्तावशेषितम् । तदेवामृततुल्यं मे तेन तुष्टा रमाम्यहम् ॥ 73

the forest to me. **(62-63).** I am therefore in a hurry to depart. O noble lady! Cause no obstructions to my plan." Hearing these words of Rama, Sita spoke to him with great joy. She said: "I will be the first to go to the forest. You shall only follow me. O scion of Raghu's line! It is not befitting that you go without me."

64. Though highly pleased with the attitude of his wife, Rama none the less said to her, "How can I take you. to the forest, which is full of tigers and other wild animals? **65.** The forest abounds also in terrible-looking Rakshasas who eat human beings. Everywhere, the forest is infested with wild animals like lions, tigers and wild boars. **66.** O handsome one! One will have to subsist there on roots and fruits that may be pungent and sour. Well prepared dishes and tasty edibles can never be had there. **67.** Even fruits may not be available when one wants them. The forest tracts are almost invisible. They are full of stones and thorns. **68.** The forest of Dandaka is characterised by many forbidding features like caves and caverns and the humming of stinging insects. **69.** There one has to walk on bare feet. There will be shivering cold and heat alternating, besides terrible winds. Frightened by the sight of the Rakshasas in the forest, you may even die.

(70-74). "Therefore, O handsome one, you stay back at this palace until my return." Hearing these words of Rama, Sita, sorrow-stricken and red in her face with a tinge of indignation, replied: "I am a wedded wife, blemishless, vowed to faithfulness to you and solely dependent on you. How can I ever think of staying away from you? You know all Dharma and you are inherently kind. Who in the forest will dare to injure me while I am staying with you? The remnants of fruits and roots that you have

त्वया सह चरन्त्या मे कुशाः काशाश्च कण्टकाः । पुष्पास्तरणतुल्या मे भविष्यन्ति न संशयः ॥ 74
अहं त्वां क्लेशये नैव भवेयं कार्यसाधिनी । बाल्ये मां वीक्ष्य कश्चिद्वै ज्योतिःशास्त्रविशारदः 75
प्राह ते विपिने वासः पत्या सह भविष्यति । सत्यवादी द्विजो भूयाद्गमिष्यामि त्वया सह॥ 76
अन्यत्किञ्चित्प्रवक्ष्यामि श्रुत्वा मां नय काननम् । रामायणानि बहुशः श्रुतानि बहुभिर्द्विजैः ॥ 77
सीतां विना वनं रामो गतः किं कुत्रचिद्वद । अतस्त्वया गमिष्यामि सर्वथा त्वत्सहायिनी ॥ 78
यदि गच्छसि मां त्यक्त्वा प्राणांस्त्यक्ष्यामि तेऽग्रतः। इति तं निश्चयं ज्ञात्वा सीताया रघुनन्दनः ॥79
अब्रवीद्देवि गच्छ त्वं वनं शीघ्रं मया सह । अरुन्धत्यै प्रयच्छाशु हारानाभरणानि च ॥ 80
ब्राह्मणेभ्यो धनं सर्वं दत्त्वा गच्छामहे वनम् । इत्युक्त्वा लक्ष्मणेनाशु द्विजानाहूय भक्तितः ॥ 81

दत्तौ गवां वृन्दशतं धनानि वस्त्राणि दिव्यानि विभूषणानि ।
कुटुम्बवद्भ्यः श्रुतशीलवद्भ्यो मुदा द्विजेभ्यो रघुवंशकेतुः ॥ 82

अरुन्धत्यै ददौ सीता मुख्यान्याभरणानि च । रामो मातुः सेवकेभ्यो ददौ धनमनेकधा ॥ 83
स्वकान्तःपुरवासिभ्यः सेवकेभ्यस्तथैव च । पौरजानपदेभ्यश्च ब्राह्मणेभ्यः सहस्रशः ॥ 84
लक्ष्मणोऽपि सुमित्रां तु कौसल्यायै समर्पयत् । धनुष्पाणिः समागत्य रामस्याग्रे व्यवस्थितः ॥ 85

eaten will taste like nectar itself to me. I shall live highly satisfied with that food. For me following you, the forest lands, full of grass, thorny shrubs and stones, will be like a place spread with beds of flowers. I have no doubts about it. (75-76). I shall give you no trouble in any way. On the other hand, I shall always be helpful. In my girlhood, a great astrologer, on seeing me, had predicted that I would have to live with my husband in a forest. May that scholar's words come true! I shall certainly go with you. (77-78). I shall tell you one thing more, and hearing that, please decide to take me into the forest. I have heard the various versions of the Rama-saga (Ramayana), recited by many scholars. In which of these, do you find Rama going to the forest without Sita? In none, to be sure. Therefore, I have to go with you. In every way, I shall only be helpful to you. (79-82). If you decide to go without me, I shall abandon my life in your very presence."

Hearing these determined words of Sita, Rama said to her: "O Lady! Then be ready quickly to start with me to the forest. Your necklaces and other jewellery may be given over to our preceptor's wife, Arundhati. We shall go to the forest after giving all our wealth as gift to holy men." Saying so, he asked Lakshmana to gather together a large number of pious Brahmanas, and he gave them as gift several hundreds of cows and valuable pieces of cloth and ornaments. They were all adepts in Vedas, of noble conduct and householders with families. **83.** Sita gave away all her important ornaments to Arundhati, while Rama gave much wealth as present to the attendants of his mother. **84.** Thus Rama gave numerous gifts to the residents of the palace, to his servants, to the residents of the city and villages and to many holy men. **85.** And as for Laksh-

रामः सीता लक्ष्मणश्च जग्मुः सर्वे नृपालयम् ॥ 86

श्रीरामः सह सीतया नृपपथे गच्छन् शनैः सानुजः ।
पौरान् जानपदान्कुतूहलदृशः सानन्दमुद्वीक्षयन् ।
श्यामः कामसहस्रसुन्दरवपुः कान्त्या दिशो भासयन्
पादन्यासपवित्रिताखिलजगत् प्रापालयं तत्पितुः ॥ 87

इति श्रीमदध्यात्मरामायणे उमामहेश्वरसंवादे
अयोध्याकाण्डे चतुर्थः सर्गः ॥ ४ ॥

mana, he entrusted his mother Sumitra to Kausalya's care, and then equipped with bow in hand, he stood in front of Rama ready to depart. **86.** Then Rama, Sita and Lakshmana went to the king's palace. **87.** Rama of blue complexion, who was more handsome than a hundred cupids, whose radiance illumined all the quarters, and whose foot-steps sanctified the three worlds, now went with Sita and Lakshmana leisurely on foot to his father's mansion, looking joyfully at the large crowd of the inhabitants of the city and villages that had gathered on the highway for the installation ceremony.

पञ्चमः सर्गः

आयान्तं नागरा दृष्ट्वा मार्गे रामं सजानकीम्। लक्ष्मणेन समं वीक्ष्य ऊचुः सर्वे परस्परम् ॥ 1
कैकेय्या वरदानादि श्रुत्वा दुःखसमावृताः । बत राजा दशरथः सत्यसन्धं प्रियं सुतम् ॥ 2
स्त्रीहेतोरत्यजत्कामी तस्य सत्यवता कुतः । कैकेयी वा कथं दुष्टा रामं सत्यं प्रियङ्करम् ॥ 3
विवासयामास कथं क्रूरकर्मातिमूढधीः । हे जना नात्र वस्तव्यं गच्छामोऽद्यैव काननम् ॥ 4

Chapter 5

RAMA'S DEPARTURE TO THE FOREST

The Reaction of the Citizens (1-9)

1. Seeing Rama coming along the public road with Lakshmana and Sita, the daughter of Janaka, all the citizens in the neighbourhood began to look at each other and remark about it among themselves. (2-4). Steeped in sorrow on hearing about the boon given to Kaikeyi, these citizens said: "Alas! On account of a woman's instigation, King Dasaratha has sacrificed a son so virtuous and truthful. The King is highly uxorious. How can such a person be given credit for being truthful? How has this Kaikeyi become so cruel-hearted? How could she think of getting expelled from the country a prince like Rama so truthful and beneficent to all? She must indeed be an extremely stupid and heartless woman. O fellow citizens! A country like this, where such injustice and cruelty are perpetrated, is

यत्र रामः सभार्यश्च सानुजो गन्तुमिच्छति । पश्यन्तु जानकीं सर्वे पादचारेण गच्छतीम् ॥ 5
पुंभिः कदाचिद्दृष्ट्वा वा जानकी लोकसुन्दरी । सापि पादेन गच्छन्ती जनसङ्घेष्वनावृता ॥ 6
रामोऽपि पादचारेण गजाश्वादिविवर्जितः । गच्छति द्रक्ष्यथ विभुं सर्वलोकैकसुन्दरम् ॥ 7
राक्षसी कैकेयीनाम्नी जाता सर्वविनाशिनी । रामस्यापि भवेद्दुःखं सीतायाः पादयानतः ॥ 8
बलवान्विधिरेवात्र पुंप्रयत्नो हि दुर्बलः । इति दुःखाकुले वृन्दे साधूनां मुनिपुङ्गवः ॥ 9
अब्रवीद्वामदेवोऽथ साधूनां सङ्घमध्यगः । मानुशोचथ रामं वा सीतां वा वच्मि तत्त्वतः ॥ 10
एष रामः परो विष्णुरादिनारायणः स्मृतः । एषा सा जानकी लक्ष्मीर्योगमायेति विश्रुता ॥ 11
असौ शेषस्तमन्वेति लक्ष्मणाख्यश्च साम्प्रतम् । एष मायागुणैर्युक्तस्तत्तदाकारवानिव ॥ 12
एष एव रजोयुक्तो ब्रह्माभूद्विश्वभावनः । सत्त्वाविष्टस्तथा विष्णुस्त्रिजगत्प्रतिपालकः ॥ 13
एष रुद्रस्तामसोऽन्ते जगत्प्रलयकारणम् । एष मत्स्यः पुरा भूत्वा भक्तं वैवस्वतं मनुम् ॥ 14
नाव्यारोप्य लयस्यान्ते पालयामास राघवः । समुद्रमथने पूर्वं मन्दरे सुतलं गते ॥ 15
अधारयत्स्वपृष्ठेऽद्रिं कूर्मरूपी रघूत्तमः । मही रसातलं याता प्रलये सूकरोऽभवत् ॥ 16
तोलयामास दंष्ट्राग्रे तां क्षोणीं रघुनन्दनः । नारसिंहं वपुः कृत्वा प्रह्लादवरदः पुरा ॥ 17

unfit for us to stay in any longer. Let us also go to the forest even today. **5.** We shall go where Rama is going with his wife and brother. See how Sita the daughter of Janaka is walking bare-footed along the road! **6.** Sita, a beauty without a peer anywhere in the world, was hitherto living in seclusion without being seen by any man outside the circle of her kith and kin. But see how she is walking bare-footed along the crowded public road without even a veil covering her face! **7.** Rama too is going on foot without any horse or elephant as a mount. See, there goes our noble Lord, the most handsome person in the whole world! **8.** That Rakshasi of a Kaikeyi will cause total ruin. Rama's heart must surely be wrenched by grief to see Sita trudging along the road. **9.** This is indeed a stroke of destiny against which all human effort is of no avail."

Vamadeva on Rama's spiritual Identity (10-31)

10. When all good men were thus mourning, the great sage Vamadeva, who was amidst them, came forward to comfort them. He said to them: "Do not be downcast with sorrow, thinking either of Rama or Sita. Listen to what I say regarding the truth about them. **(11-12).** This Rama is none but the Supreme Being—Mahavishnu Adi-Narayana. This Sita, the daughter of Janaka, is Mahalakshmi, famous as the Yogamaya of Vishnu. The one whom you know as Lakshmana is Adisesha now following him. The Lord, uniting Himself with Maya, has taken these different forms. **(13-17).** It is He who, assuming the qualities of Rajas, has become Brahma, the creator. So also, assuming the quality of Sattva, He has become Mahavishnu, the protector

त्रैलोक्यकण्टकं रक्षः पाटयामास तन्नखैः । पुत्रराज्यं हृतं दृष्ट्वा ह्यदित्या याचितः पुरा ॥ 18
वामनत्वमुपागम्य याच्ञया चाहरत्पुनः । दुष्टक्षत्रियभूभारनिवृत्त्यै भार्गवोऽभवत् ॥ 19
स एव जगतां नाथ इदानीं रामतां गतः । रावणादीनि रक्षांसि कोटिशो निहनिष्यति ॥ 20
मानुषेणैव मरणं तस्य दृष्टं दुरात्मनः । राज्ञा दशरथेनापि तपसाराधितो हरिः ॥ 21
पुत्रत्वाकाङ्क्षया विष्णोस्तदा पुत्रोऽभवद्धरिः । स एव विष्णुः श्रीरामो रावणादिवधाय हि ॥ 22
गन्ताद्यैव वनं रामो लक्ष्मणेन सहायवान् । एषा सीता हरेर्माया सृष्टिस्थित्यन्तकारिणी ॥ 23
राजा वा कैकेयी वापि नात्र कारणमण्वपि । पूर्वेद्युर्नारदः प्राह भूभारहरणाय च ॥ 24
रामोऽप्याह स्वयं साक्षाच्छ्वो गमिष्याम्यहं वनम् । अतो रामं समुद्दिश्य चिन्तां त्यजत बालिशाः ॥ 25
रामरामेति ये नित्यं जपन्ति मनुजा भुवि । तेषां मृत्यु भयादीनि न भवन्ति कदाचन ॥ 26
का पुनस्तस्य रामस्य दुःखशङ्का महात्मनः । रामनाम्नैव मुक्तिः स्यात्कलौ नान्येन केनचित् ॥ 27

of the worlds. In the end, assuming the quality of Tamas, He will be Rudra the cause of dissolution. In days of old, taking the form of a Fish, He enabled the devotee Vaivasvata Manu to get into a boat and get protection till the end of the great deluge. Again, when the Milk Ocean was churned and the churning rod Mandara mountain sank into the ocean up to Sutala, He, this leader of the Raghu's clan, assuming the form of a Tortoise, supported the mountain on His back. When at the time of Pralaya, the earth sank to the level of Rasatala, this noble one of Raghu's line took the shape of a Boar and lifted it out on His tusk. (18-23). In days of yore assuming the form of a Man-lion, He gave protection to Prahlada and tore open with his nails the chest of the demon Hiranyakasipu, the oppressor of all the worlds. When Aditi, the motherof the Devas, approached him to help her sons, the Devas, who had been deprived of their heavenly realm by Bali, He manifested himself in the form of a Dwarf, and through the tactics of begging, recovered that realm of the celestials. In order to relieve the earth of the burden of evil Kshatriyas, He incarnated Himself as Rama of Bhrigu's line. That same Lord of the universe has now incarnated as Rama. He will destroy Ravana and other Rakshasas in thousands. He has taken a human form because that evil Rakshasa Ravana can be killed only by the hands of a man. In a previous birth, King Dasaratha had adored Hari through austerities, desiring that He Himself should be born as a son to him. Rama is that Mahavishnu, now incarnated as man. In order to destroy Ravana and others, He will go even today to the forest accompanied by Lakshmana. This Sita is Maya, the power of Vishnu, who is the cause of creation, sustentation and dissolution of the universe. (24-25). Neither Kaikeyi nor King Dasaratha is in the least responsible for all these developments. It was even yesterday that Narada prayed to Rama to be pleased to relieve the earth of its burdens, and Rama himself replied to him that he would go to the forest the very next day. Therefore, you ignorant people can abandon all grief on account of Rama. (26-27) In this world, who-

मायामानुषरूपेण विडम्बयति लोककृत् । भक्तानां भजनार्थाय रावणस्य वधाय च ॥ 28

राज्ञश्चाभीष्टसिद्ध्यर्थं मानुषं वपुराश्रितः । इत्युक्त्वा विररामाथ वामदेवो महामुनिः ॥ 29

श्रुत्वा तेऽपि द्विजाः सर्वे रामं ज्ञात्वा हरिं विभुम् । जहुर्हृत्संशयग्रन्थिं राममेवान्वचिन्तयन् ॥ 30

य इदं चिन्तयेन्नित्यं रहस्यं रामसीतयोः । तस्य रामे दृढा भक्तिर्भवेद्विज्ञानपूर्विका ॥ 31

रहस्यं गोपनीयं वो यूयं वै राघवप्रियाः । इत्युक्त्वा प्रययौ विप्रस्तेऽपि रामं परं विदुः ॥ 32

ततो रामः समाविश्य पितृगेहमवारितः । सानुजः सीतया गत्वा कैकेयीमिदमब्रवीत् ॥ 33

आगताः स्मो वयं मातस्त्रयस्ते सम्मतं वनम् । गन्तुं कृतधियः शीघ्रमाज्ञापयतु नः पिता ॥ 34

इत्युक्ता सहसोत्थाय चीराणि प्रददौ स्वयम् । रामाय लक्ष्मणायाथ सीतायै च पृथक् पृथक् ॥ 35

रामस्तु वस्त्राण्युत्सृज्य वन्यचीराणि पर्यधात् । लक्ष्मणोऽपि तथा चक्रे सीता तन्न विजानती ॥ 36

हस्ते गृहीत्वा रामस्य लज्जया मुखमैक्षत । रामो गृहीत्वा तच्चीरमंशुके पर्यवेष्टयत् ॥ 37

तद् दृष्ट्वा रुरुदुः सर्वे राजदाराः समन्ततः । वसिष्ठस्तु तदाकर्ण्य रुदितं भर्त्सयन् रुषा ॥ 38

कैकेयीं प्राह दुर्वृत्ते राम एव त्वया वृतः । वनवासाय दुष्टे त्वं सीतायै किं प्रयच्छसि ॥ 39

ever repeats the name of Rama constantly, is never overcome by fear of death and other calamities. That being the case, how can you ever suspect this Rama to be overcome by grief? **(28-29).** In order to bless the world, He is imitating the ways of man. For providing devotees with an object for centring their devotion and service, for bringing about the destruction of Ravana, and for fulfilling the prayer of King Dasaratha, He has assumed this human form." Saying so, the sage Vamadeva resumed silence.

30. Hearing these words of Vamadeva, all those pious men had the doubts of their heart dispelled and began to meditate on Rama as a Divine Being. **31.** Whoever constantly contemplates on this esoteric teaching on Rama and Sita, will attain to firm devotion to Rama, accompanied by illumination. **32.** "This secret doctrine is to be jealously guarded," said sage Vamadeva, "you are all very dear to Rama." Saying so, the sage departed, and the pious devotees recognised the identity of Rama with the Supreme Being.

Scenes at Rama's Departure (33-46)

33. Now Rama, along with Sita and Lakshmana went straight to the palace of his father, and said to Kaikeyi as follows: **34.** "O mother! We three have come ready to go to any forest that you want us to go to. Let our father order us without delay." **35.** Hearing these words of Rama, Kaikeyi got up at once and gave them three tree-bark garments that ascetics wear, one each for Rama, Lakshmana and Sita. **(36-37.)** Rama now abandoned his royal dress and put on the tree-bark. Lakshmaṇa also followed suit. But Sita, not knowing how to wear a garment of that kind, stood puzzled, holding it in hand and looking at the face of Rama. Rama, thereupon took that piece of tree-bark and tied it over her dress. **(38-39).** Seeing this piteous scene, all the women in

यदि रामं समन्वेति सीता भक्त्या पतिव्रता । दिव्याम्बरधरा नित्यं सर्वाभरणभूषिता ॥ 40
रमयत्वनिशं रामं वनदुःखनिवारिणी । राजा दशरथोऽप्याह सुमन्त्रं रथमानय ॥ 41
रथमारुह्य गच्छन्तु वनं वनचरप्रियाः । इत्युक्त्वा राममालोक्य सीतां चैव सलक्ष्मणम् ॥42
दुःखाभिपतितो भूमौ रुरोदाश्रु परिप्लुतः । आरुरोह रथं सीता शीघ्रं रामस्य पश्यतः ॥ 43
रामः प्रदक्षिणं कृत्वा पितरं रथमारुहत् । लक्ष्मणः खड्गयुगलं धनुस्तूणीयुगं तथा ॥ 44
गृहीत्वा रथमारुह्य नोदयामास सारथिम् । तिष्ठ तिष्ठ सुमन्त्रेति राजा दशरथोऽब्रवीत् ॥45
गच्छ गच्छेति रामेण नोदितोऽचोदयद्रथम् । रामे दूरं गते राजा मूर्च्छितः प्रापतद्भुवि ॥ 46
पौरास्तु बालवृद्धाश्च वृद्धा ब्राह्मणसत्तमाः । तिष्ठ तिष्ठेति रामेति क्रोशन्तो रथमन्वयुः ॥ 47
राजा रुदित्वा सुचिरं मां नयन्तु गृहं प्रति । कौसल्याया राममातुरित्याह परिचारकान् ॥ 48
किञ्चित्कालं भवेत्तत्र जीवनं दुःखितस्य मे । अत ऊर्ध्वं न जीवामि चिरं रामं विना कृतः ॥49
ततो गृहं प्रविश्यैव कौसल्यायाः पपात ह । मूर्च्छितश्च चिराद्बुद्ध्वा तूष्णीमेवावतस्थिवान् ॥ 50

the palace began to cry aloud. The Preceptor Vasishtha, on hearing their cry,came into the palace. He grasped the situation and addressed Kaikeyi in a very angry mood. He said, "O wicked woman! According to the boon given to you, Rama alone is to go to the forest. Why are you then giving this ascetic's tree-bark dress to Sita? (**40-43**). If Sita, the chaste wife of Rama, prefers to follow him to the forest as a matter of duty, let her do so, always dressed in excellent clothes and bedecked with all ornaments. By accompanying him, she will be able to relieve Rama of much of his sufferings incidental to life in the forest."

Now King Dasaratha said, addressing his minister Sumantra, "These three, who are dear to the ascetics of the forest, should go from here only in a chariot." Saying so, he looked at Rama, Sita and Lakshmana, and immediately fell down on the earth crying aloud, overwhelmed by sorrow, and was almost drowned in his own tears. Now first Sita got into the chariot in the presence of Rama. (**44-46**). Circumambulating his father, Rama also got into the chariot and Lakshmana followed him, taking with him a pair each of sword, bow and quiver. When they directed their charioteer to proceed, King Dasaratha cried out, "O Sumantra! Stop, Stop." But Rama once again gave order to proceed and the charioteer started off. When they had moved out some distance, King Dasaratha fell unconscious on the floor.

47. Many citizens, including children, old men, pious Brahmanas and others ran after the chariot crying out, "O Rama! Stop, Stop." **48.** After weeping for a long time, King Dasaratha asked his attendants to take him to the quarters of Kausalya, the mother of Rama. **49.** He said, "If I am there in Kausalya's palace, the life of my sorrow-stricken self may last for a short time more. Separated from Rama, I am not going to live any longer." **50.** Reaching Kausalya's palace, he again became unconscious and fell down. Recover-

रामस्तु तमसातीरं गत्वा तत्रावसत्सुखी । जलं प्राश्य निराहारो वृक्षमूलेऽस्वपद्विभुः ॥ 51
सीतया सह धर्मात्मा धनुष्पाणिस्तु लक्ष्मणः । पालयामास धर्मज्ञः सुमन्त्रेण समन्वितः ॥ 52
पौराः सर्वे समागत्य स्थितास्तस्याविदूरतः । शक्ता रामं पुरं नेतुं नोचेद्गच्छामहे वनम् ॥ 53
इति निश्चयमाज्ञाय तेषां रामोऽतिविस्मितः । नाहं गच्छामि नगरमेते वै क्लेशभागिनः ॥ 54
भविष्यन्तीति निश्चित्य सुमन्त्रमिदमब्रवीत् । इदानीमेव गच्छामः सुमन्त्र रथमानय ॥ 55
इत्याज्ञप्तः सुमन्त्रोऽपि रथं वाहैरयोजयत् । आरुह्य रामः सीता च लक्ष्मणोऽपि ययुर्द्रुतम् ॥ 56
अयोध्याभिमुखं गत्वा किञ्चिद् दूरं ततो ययुः । तेऽपि राममदृष्ट्वैव प्रातरुत्थाय दुःखिताः ॥ 57
रथनेमिगतं मार्गं पश्यन्तस्ते पुरं ययुः । हृदि रामं ससीतं ते ध्यायन्तस्तस्थुरन्वहम् ॥ 58
सुमन्त्रोऽपि रथं शीघ्रं नोदयामास सादरम् । स्फीतान् जनपदान्पश्यन् रामः सीतासमन्वितः 59
गङ्गातीरं समागच्छच्छृङ्गवेराविदूरतः । गङ्गां दृष्ट्वा नमस्कृत्य स्नात्वा सानन्दमानसः ॥ 60
शिंशपावृक्षमूले स निषसाद रघूत्तमः । ततो गुहो जनैः श्रुत्वा रामागममहोत्सवम् ॥ 61
सखायं स्वामिनं द्रष्टुं हर्षात्तूर्णं समापतत् । फलानि मधुपुष्पादि गृहीत्वा भक्तिसंयुतः ॥ 62

ing consciousness after a long time, he sat there dazed without uttering a word

Meeting with Guha (51-73)

(51-52) Reaching the banks of the river Tamasa, Rama stayed there happily for the night. Without taking any food excepting water from the river, he slept under a tree. Sita also did the same. And Lakshmana, who knew all Dharma, along with Sumantra kept guard with bow in hand. **53.** The sorrow-stricken citizens too had followed Rama. They halted somewhere in the neighbourhood for the night with the resolution that either they would get back Rama to the city, or failing that, go with him to the forest. **(54-56)**. Astonished at their determination, Rama said, "I cannot go back to the city and if these people come to the forest, they will be put to great difficulties." Accordingly he addressed Sumantra, "O Sumantra! Get the chariot ready. We shall get away from here even now, while these people are asleep." Sumantra, as ordered, yoked the horses to the chariot, and Rama, Sita and Lakshmana started in it in great haste. **(57-58)**. The chariot was taken in the direction of Ayodhya for some distance and from there turned back to the forest. The citizens, waking up in the morning, were terribly grief-stricken to notice the absence of Rama there. They, however, tried to trace him, following the mark made by the chariot wheels. But that took them only back to the city. And so resigning themselves to their fate, they continued to stay in the city, constantly thinking of Rama and Sita.

(59-62). Sumantra now drove the chariot very fast. Moving through prosperous villages, Rama reached the banks of the Ganga where the Ashrama known as Sringavera was situated. Seeing the holy river Ganga and bathing in it, Rama was highly delighted to stay underneath a Simsapa tree. Now Guha, a local chief-

रामस्याग्रे विनिक्षिप्य दण्डवत्प्रापतद्भुवि । गुहमुत्थाप्य तं तूर्णं राघवः परिषस्वजे ॥ 63
संपृष्टकुशलो रामं गुहं प्राञ्जलिरब्रवीत् । धन्योऽहमद्य मे जन्म नैषादं लोकपावन ॥ 64
बभूव परमानन्दः स्पृष्ट्वा तेऽङ्गं रघूत्तम । नैषादराज्यमेतत्ते किङ्करस्य रघूत्तम ॥ 65
त्वदधीनं वसन्नत्र पालयास्मान् रघूद्वह । आगच्छ यामो नगरं पावनं कुरु मे गृहम् ॥ 66
गृहाण फलमूलानि त्वदर्थं सञ्चितानि मे । अनुगृह्णीष्व भगवन् दासस्तेऽहं सुरोत्तम ॥ 67
रामस्तमाह सुप्रीतो वचनं शृणु मे सखे । न वेक्ष्यामि गृहं ग्रामं नव वर्षाणि पञ्च च ॥ 68
दत्तमन्येन नो भुञ्जे फलमूलादि किञ्चन । राज्यं ममैतत्त्तं सर्वं त्वं सखा मेऽतिवल्लभः ॥69
वटक्षीरं समानाय्य जटामुकुटमादरात् । बबन्ध लक्ष्मणेनाथ सहितो रघुनन्दनः ॥ 70
जलमात्रं तु सम्प्राश्य सीतया सह राघवः । आस्तृतं कुशपर्णाद्यैः शयनं लक्ष्मणेन हि ॥ 71
उवास तत्र नगरप्रासादाग्रे यथा पुरा । सुष्वाप तत्र वैदेह्या पर्यङ्क इव संस्कृते ॥ 72

tain, knowing about the advent of Rama from his people, proceeded to meet him, who was both his friend and master. Carrying fruits, honey, flowers and the like in hand, he went quickly in a mood of high elation. **63.** Offering all these things to Rama, he made a full prostration at his feet, stretching his whole body on the ground. Rama lifted him up immediately and embraced him. **64.** After Rama had made kind enquiries of his welfare, Guha said to him with his palms joined in salutation: "O Thou, who art the sanctifier of the worlds! Today I am really fortunate and my birth in the tribe of hunters has come to its fulfilment. **(65-67).** O the noblest among the Raghus! I have had the thrill of spiritual joy by contacting Thy body today. This country of the hunters belongs to me, Thy servant. Therefore these places are under Thy sovereignty. O noble scion of Raghu's line! Be pleased to stay on here and rule over us. Let us go to the town, and there be Thou pleased to sanctify my house by Thy presence after accepting this offering of all the fruits and roots that I collected for Thee—O venerable one! Be gracious and bless Thy servant."

(68-69). Rama, who was delighted with Guha, said to him, "O friend! Hear my words. For fourteen years, I shall not enter a village or a house, nor shall I eat fruits and roots offered by others. True it is that all this kingdom is mine. You are indeed dear to my heart." **70.** Rama next had some sap of banyan tree brought, and with it he and Lakshmana had their hair matted and tied on their head like crowns. **(71-72).** That prince of Raghu's line, taking only water as his food, spent the night along with Sita on a bed of grass made for them by Lakshmana. On such beds, he and Sita slept as comfortably as they used to do on luxurious cots in the upper floor of the palace.

ततोऽविदूरे परिगृह्य चापं सबाणतूणीरधनुः स लक्ष्मणः
ररक्ष रामं परितो विपश्यन् गुहेन सार्धं सशरासनेन ॥ 73

इति श्रीमदध्यात्मरामायणे उमामहेश्वरसंवादे
अयोध्याकाण्डे पञ्चमः सर्गः ॥ ५ ॥

73. And Lakshmana, equipped with bow, arrow and quiver, along with the fully armed Guha, stood guard over Rama in the premises.

षष्ठः सर्गः

सुप्तं रामं समालोक्य गुहः सोऽश्रुपरिप्लुतः । लक्ष्मणं प्राह विनयाद् भ्रातः पश्यसि राघवम् ॥ 1
शयानं कुशपत्रौघसंस्तरे सीतया सह । यः शेते स्वर्णपर्यङ्के स्वास्तीर्णे भवनोत्तमे ॥ 2
कैकेयी रामदुःखस्य कारणं विधिना कृता । मन्थराबुद्धिमास्थाय कैकेयी पापमाचरत् ॥ 3
तच्छ्रुत्वा लक्ष्मणः प्राह सखे शृणु वचो मम । कः कस्य हेतुर्दुःखस्य कश्च हेतुः सुखस्य वा ॥ 4
स्वपूर्वार्जितकर्मैव कारणं सुखदुःखयोः ॥ 5
सुखस्य दुःखस्य न कोऽपि दाता परो ददातीति कुबुद्धिरेषा
अहं करोमीति वृथाभिमानः स्वकर्मसूत्रग्रथितो हि लोकः ॥ 6
सुहृन्मित्रार्युदासीनद्वेष्यमध्यस्थबान्धवाः । स्वयमेवाचरन्कर्म तथा तत्र विभाव्यते ॥ 7

Chapter 6

RAMA ON HIS WAY TO CHITRAKUTA

Lakshmana's advice to Guha (1-15)

(1-2). After Rama had fallen asleep, Guha, looking at him with eyes brimming with tears, said to Lakshmana in all humility, "O brother! Don't you see this prince of Raghu's line, who has been accustomed to sleep only on golden cots with excellent mattresses, now lying on a bed of grass along with Sita! **3.** It was destiny that made Kaikeyi bring about this sad condition for Rama. But this was done indirectly through Manthara, whose evil advice Kaikeyi accepted and so committed this sinful act."

4. Hearing this, Lakshmana replied, "O friend! Listen to me. In this world who is the cause of whose sorrow, and who is the cause of whose happiness too? **5.** The cause of one's enjoyment and suffering is one's own actions (Karmas) of past lives. **6.** There is none external to oneself causing one happiness and misery. It is a perverted intelligence that attributes these experiences as caused by another. It is vain pride that makes one think that 'I am doing' such an act. The world is strung, as it were, on the thread of one's own action. **7.** In this world, men think of others as friends, relatives,

सुखं वा यदि वा दुःखं स्वकर्मवशगो नरः । यद्यद्यथागतं तत्तद् भुक्त्वा स्वस्थमना भवेत् ॥ 8
न मे भोगागमे वाञ्छा न मे भोगविवर्जने । आगच्छत्वथ मागच्छत्वभोगवशगो भवेत् ॥ 9
स्वस्मिन् देशे च काले च यस्माद्वा येन केन वा । कृतं शुभाशुभं कर्म भोज्यं तत्तत्र नान्यथा ॥ 10
अलं हर्षविषादाभ्यां शुभाशुभफलोदये । विधात्रा विहितं यद्यत्तदलङ्घ्यं सुरासुरैः ॥ 11
सर्वदा सुखदुःखाभ्यां नरः प्रत्यवरुध्यते । शरीरं पुण्यपापाभ्यामुत्पन्नं सुखदुःखवत् ॥ 12
सुखस्यानन्तरं दुःखं दुःखस्यानन्तरं सुखम् । द्वयमेतद्धि जन्तूनामलङ्घ्यं दिनरात्रिवत् ॥ 13
सुखमध्ये स्थितं दुःखं दुःखमध्ये स्थितं सुखम् । द्वयमन्योन्यसंयुक्तं प्रोच्यते जलपङ्कवत् ॥ 14
तस्माद्धैर्येण विद्वांस इष्टानिष्टोपपत्तिषु । न हृष्यन्ति न मुह्यन्ति समं मायेति भावनात् 15
गुहलक्ष्मणयोरेवं भाषतोर्विमलं नभः । बभूव रामः सलिलं स्पृष्ट्वा प्रातः समाहितः ॥16
उवाच शीघ्रं सुदृढां नावमानय मे सखे । श्रुत्वा रामस्य वचनं निषादाधिपतिर्गुहः ॥ 17

enemies, neutrals etc. But the responsibility, for one's actions is entirely on oneself. We wrongly attribute them to the others mentioned. **8.** Man, who is subject to his own Karma, should submit himself to the happiness and the misery that befall him as a result of his own Karma. He should remain unperturbed while experiencing these, the fruits of one's own actions. **9.** Let him think, 'I have neither desire for Bhoga (enjoyments), nor do I avoid them. Let them come or let them go.' Thinking in this way, one should liberate oneself from enslavement to enjoyments. **10.** The fruits of one's own good and evil actions, accruing from whomever or in whatever manner and in whatever place and time, have to be experienced then and there. There is no remedy against this. **11.** One should not feel elated when happiness is experienced, nor depressed when misery overcomes one. What Destiny has accorded to one according to one's Karma cannot be overcome by anyone, be he a Deva or an Asura. **12.** This body of ours, which is a product of our virtuous and sinful actions, is always subject to happiness and misery. The life of man is a bundle of such experiences. **13.** Just as day and night follow each other irreversibly, so do men experience happiness now and after that misery, and after misery, happiness once again. **14.** In the midst of happiness, misery can occur, and in the midst of misery, happiness too can occur. As water and mire are mixed together intimately, so are happiness and misery. **15.** So, enlightened men, considering these favourable, and unfavourable experiences as Maya or mere appearances, remain unperturbed without yielding to elation or depression."

Parting with Guha (16-27)

16. As Guha and Lakshmana conversed in this way, a glimmer of light began to spread in the sky. It was now dawn, when Rama, getting up from sleep, bathed in the water of the river and performed his morning rites. **(17-20).** Next Rama said to Guha, "Get me a good boat." And Guha, the king of the hunters, accordingly brought a well-constructed boat, himself rowing it. He now said to Rama, "O Lord! Please

स्वयमेव दृढां नावमानिनाय सुलक्षणाम् । स्वामिन्नारुह्यतां नौकां सीतया लक्ष्मणेन च ॥ 18
वाहये ज्ञातिभिः सार्धमहमेव समाहितः । तथेति राघवः सीतामारोप्य शुभलक्षणाम् ॥ 19
गुहस्य हस्तावालम्ब्य स्वयं चारोहदच्युतः । आयुधादीन् समारोप्य लक्ष्मणोऽप्यारुरोह च ॥ 20
गुहस्तान्वाहयामास ज्ञातिभिः सहितः स्वयम् । गङ्गामध्ये गतां गङ्गां प्रार्थयामास जानकी ॥ 21
देवि गङ्गे नमस्तुभ्यं निवृत्ता वनवासतः । रामेण सहिताहं त्वां लक्ष्मणेन च पूजये ॥ 22
सुरामांसोपहारैश्च नानाबलिभिरादृता । इत्युक्त्वा परकूलं तौ शनैरुत्तीर्य जग्मतुः ॥ 23
गुहोऽपि राघवं प्राह गमिष्यामि त्वया सह । अनुज्ञां देहि राजेन्द्र नोचेत्प्राणांस्त्यजाम्यहम् ॥ 24
श्रुत्वा नैषादिवचनं श्रीरामस्तमथाब्रवीत् । चतुर्दश समाः स्थित्वा दण्डके पुनरप्यहम् ॥ 25
आयास्याम्युदितं सत्यं नासत्यं रामभाषितम् । इत्युक्त्वालिङ्ग्य तं भक्तं समाश्वास्य पुनःपुनः ॥ 26
निवर्तयामास गुहं सोऽपि कृच्छ्राद्ययौ गृहम् ॥ 27
तत्र मेध्यं मृगं हत्वा पक्त्वा हुत्वा च ते त्रयः । भुक्त्वा वृक्षतले सुप्त्वा सुखमासत तां निशाम् 28
ततो रामस्तु वैदेह्या लक्ष्मणेन समन्वितः ।
भरद्वाजाश्रमपदं गत्वा बहिरुपस्थितः । तत्रैकं बटुकं दृष्ट्वा रामः प्राह च हे बटो ॥ 29
रामो दाशरथिः सीतालक्ष्मणाभ्यां समन्वितः । आस्ते बहिर्वनस्येति ह्युच्यतां मुनिसन्निधौ ॥ 30

get into the boat along with Sita and Lakshmana. I shall myself row it with perfect dexterity." Agreeing to the proposal, Rama helped Sita to embark and himself followed, holding the hands of Guha. Next Lakshmana put all the weapons in the boat and himself got into it. **21.** As Guha rowed the boat along with his companions and the boat reached the middle of the Ganga, Sita prayed as follows to the river-goddess: **22.** "O Goddess of Ganga! Salutations to Thee! After I return from forest life along with Rama and Lakshmana, I shall worship Thee. **23.** With great devotion I shall adore Thee with plentiful offerings, including liquor and meat." Shortly after, they all reached the other shore.

(24-27). Guha now said to Rama, "O great king, I too shall go with you. Be pleased to give me permission for that. If you do not do so, I shall give up my life." Hearing these words of the hunter-chief, Sri Rama said to him, "After staying in the Dandaka forest for fourteen years, I shall be returning. What I say is true, Rama's words never prove untrue." With these words, he embraced the devotee, consoled him again and again, and managed to send him back, and Guha returned sorrowfully.

Rama at Bharadwaja's Ashrama (28-41)

28. In the forest nearby, Rama and Lakshmana hunted a permitted wild animal, cooked it, offered it, and took the meat for the day as meal. During the night, they peacefully slept under a tree. **(29-30).** In the morning, along with Sita and Lakshmana, Rama proceeded to the hermitage of Bharadwaja. In the neighbourhood of the hermitage, he

तत्श्रुत्वा सहसा गत्वा पादयोः पतितो मुनेः । स्वामिन् रामः समागत्य वनाद् बहिरवस्थितः ॥ 31
सभार्यः सानुजः श्रीमानाह मां देवसन्निभः । भरद्वाजाय मुनये ज्ञापयस्व यथोचितम् ॥ 32
तत्श्रुत्वा सहसोत्थाय भरद्वाजो मुनीश्वरः । गृहीत्वार्घ्यं च पाद्यं च रामसामीप्यमाययौ ॥ 33
दृष्ट्वा रामं यथान्यायं पूजयित्वा सलक्ष्मणम् । आह मे पर्णशालां भो राम राजीवलोचन ॥ 34
आगच्छ पादरजसा पुनीहि रघुनन्दन । इत्युक्त्वोटजमानीय सीतया सह राघवौ ॥ 35
भक्त्या पुनः पूजयित्वा चकारातिथ्यमुत्तमम् । अद्याहं तपसः पारं गतोऽस्मि तव सङ्गमात् ॥ 36
ज्ञातं राम तवोदन्तं भूतं चागामिकं च यत् । जानामि त्वां परात्मानं मायया कार्यमानुषम् ॥ 37
यदर्थमवतीर्णोऽसि प्रार्थितो ब्रह्मणा पुरा । यदर्थं वनवासस्ते यत्करिष्यसि वै पुनः ॥ 38
जानामि ज्ञानदृष्ट्याहं जातया त्वदुपासनात् । इतः परं त्वां किं वक्ष्ये कृतार्थोऽहं रघूत्तम ॥ 39
यस्त्वां पश्यामि काकुत्स्थं पुरुषं प्रकृतेः परम् । रामस्तमभिवाद्याह सीतालक्ष्मणसंयुतः ॥ 40
अनुग्राह्यास्त्वया ब्रह्मन्वयं क्षत्रियबान्धवाः । इति सम्भाष्य तेऽन्योन्यमुषित्वा मुनिसन्निधौ ॥ 41

saw a Brahmacharin, and accosting him, said, "Please inform your teacher, the sage, that Rama, the son of Dasaratha, is waiting at the fringe of the forest surrounding the hermitage." (31-32). The Brahmacharin thereupon went quickly into the hermitage and saluting the sage Bharadwaja, said, "O Master! Rama has come into the forest and is waiting outside in the neighbourhood of the Ashrama. He is accompanied by his wife and brother. He is a personage looking like a divinity. He asked me to inform you in the proper way about his arrival." **33.** Hearing these words, the great sage Bharadwaja got up immediately from his seat and went towards Rama, carrying with him the ingredients for the offerings of Arghya and Padya. **(34-36).** After making salutation to Rama and Lakshmana, the sage said, "O Rama, lotus-eyed one! Please visit my hermitage and deign to consecrate it with the dust of Thy feet." With these words, he led him into the hermitage along with Sita and Lakshmana, again adored him and extended to him a reception according to the noblest traditions. **37.** He then said, "By Thy advent, the austerities I have been practising have come to their fulfilment. I am acquainted, O Rama, with everything about Thee—Thy past and what Thou art going to do hereafter. I know Thee as the veritable Paramatman who has assumed a human form by His Maya. **(38-39).** By virtue of the insight I have gained by Thy adoration, I have come to understand how Thou wert prayed to by Brahma, how Thou hast incarnated Thyself, what the purpose of Thy residence in the forest is, and what Thou hast done while living in Ayodhya. What more am I to say? O the noblest one of Raghu's line! **(40-41).** I have come to my life's fulfilment by my contact with Thee. I am blessed by meeting Thee, who art the Purusha that transcends Prakriti, now incarnated in Kakutstha's line." Thereupon Rama, along with Sita and Lakshmana, saluted the sage and said, "O

प्रातरुत्थाय यमुनामुत्तीर्य मुनिदारकैः । कृताप्लवेन मुनिना दृष्टमार्गेण राघवः ॥ 42
प्रययौ चित्रकूटाद्रिं वाल्मीकेर्यत्र चाश्रमः । गत्वा रामोऽथवाल्मीकेराश्रमं ऋषिसङ्कुलम् ॥ 43
नानामृगद्विजाकीर्णं नित्यपुष्पफलाकुलम् । तत्र दृष्ट्वा समासीनं वाल्मीकिं मुनिसत्तमम् ॥44
ननाम शिरसा रामो लक्ष्मणेन च सीतया । दृष्ट्वा रामं रमानाथं वाल्मीकिर्लोकसुन्दरम् ॥45
जानकीलक्ष्मणोपेतं जटामुकुटमण्डितम् । कन्दर्पसदृशाकारं कमनीयाम्बुजेक्षणम् ॥ 46
दृष्ट्वैव सहसोत्तस्थौ विस्मयानिमिषेक्षणः । आलिङ्ग्य परमानन्दं रामं हर्षाश्रुलोचनः ॥ 47
पूजयित्वा जगत्पूज्यं भक्त्याऽर्घ्यादिभिरादृतः । फलमूलैः स मधुरैर्भोजयित्वा च लालितः ॥ 48
राघवः प्राञ्जलिः प्राह वाल्मीकिं विनयान्वितः । पितुराज्ञां पुरस्कृत्य दण्डकानागता वयम् ॥ 49
भवन्तो यदि जानन्ति किं वक्ष्यामोऽत्र कारणम् । यत्र मे सुखवासाय भवेत्स्थानं वदस्व तत् ॥ 50
सीतया सहितः कालं किञ्चित्तत्र नयाम्यहम् । इत्युक्तो राघवेणासौ मुनिः सस्मितमब्रवीत् ॥ 51
त्वमेव सर्वलोकानां निवासस्थानमुत्तमम् । तवापि सर्वभूतानि निवाससदनानि हि ॥ 52
एवं साधारणं स्थानमुक्तं ते रघुनन्दन । सीतया सहितस्येति विशेषं पृच्छतस्तव ॥
तद्वक्ष्यामि रघुश्रेष्ठ यत्ते नियतमन्दिरम् ॥ 53

great sage! We, who are mere Kshatriyas, beseech your blessings." Conversing in this way, they spent some time with the sage.

Rama at Valmiki's Ashrama (42-64)

(42-43). Next morning, after his bath and morning rites, the sage directed Rama to the banks of the Yamuna. Accompanied by some of the pupils of the sage, Rama crossed the Yamuna on his way to mount Chitrakuta, where the hermitage of sage Valmiki was situated. Soon, he reached that hermitage which was inhabited by a large number of sages. **(44-45).** That hermitage was full of animals and birds, and the trees there were laden with flowers and fruits. Meeting the sage Valmiki there, Rama, Lakshmana and Sita saluted him. **(46-48).** At the sight of Rama, the consort of Lakshmi and the most handsome one—of Rama who had a cupid-like form and attractive eyes of the shape of lotus petals, and who appeared now with a crown of matted locks on his head—,the sage Valmiki got up from his seat in great haste. With eyes brimming with tears and unwinking due to amazement and with a heart overflowing with bliss, he embraced Rama and offered Arghya and Padya with great devotion to him who was the object of worship for the whole world. He then fed him with sweet fruits and roots.

(49-50). Saluting the sage Valmiki with humility, Rama said to him, "At the command of our father, we have come to this Dandakaranya. To you, who are capable of knowing everything, it is needless for me to give the reason for this. I request you to advise me as to where I can stay in peace in these regions. **51.** At that place, I shall spend some length of time along with Sita." When Rama said this much, that sage spoke to him with a smile on his face. **(52-53).** "Thou art indeed the best residence for the

शान्तानां समदृष्टीनामद्वेष्टणां च जन्तुषु । त्वामेव भजतां नित्यं हृदयं तेऽधिमन्दिरम् ॥ 54
धर्माधर्मान्परित्यज्य त्वामेव भजतोऽनिशम् । सीतया सह ते राम तस्य हृत्सुखमन्दिरम् ॥ 55
त्वन्मन्त्रजापको यस्तु त्वामेव शरणं गतः । निर्द्वन्द्वो निःस्पृहस्तस्य हृदयं ते सुमन्दिरम् ॥ 56
निरहङ्कारिणः शान्ता ये रागद्वेषवर्जिताः । समलोष्टाश्मकनकास्तेषां ते हृदयं गृहम् ॥ 57
त्वयि दत्तमनोबुद्धिर्यः सन्तुष्ट सदाः भवेत् । त्वयि सन्त्यक्तकर्मा यस्तन्मनस्ते शुभं गृहम् ॥58
यो न द्वेष्टयप्रियं प्राप्य प्रियं प्राप्य न हृष्यति । सर्वं मायेति निश्चित्य त्वां भजेत्तन्मनो गृहम् ॥59
षडभावादिविकारान्यो देहे पश्यति नात्मनि । क्षुत्तृट् सुखं भयं दुःखं प्राणबुद्ध्योर्निरीक्षते ॥ 60
संसारधर्मैर्निर्मुक्तस्तस्य ते मानसं गृहम् ॥ 61

पश्यन्ति ये सर्वगुहाशयस्थं त्वां चिद्घनं सत्यमनन्तमेकम् ।
अलेपकं सर्वगतं वरेण्यं तेषां हृदब्जे सह सीतया वस ॥ 62
निरन्तराभ्यासदृढीकृतात्मनां त्वत्पादसेवापरिनिष्ठितानाम् ।

whole world, while at the same time all beings in the universe form a fitting residence for Thee too. O Rama! Thou scion of Raghu's line! What I have pointed out is Thy common place of residence. Thou hast asked for a special residence where Thou couldst stay with Sita. O Thou, the noblest of Raghu's line! I shall now point it out. **54.** The best residence for Thee is the heart of those who are peaceful, even-minded, friendly to all creatures and who ever adore Thee with great devotion. **55.** Those who are ever dependent on Thee abandoning all Dharma and Adharma—their heart, O Rama, is the happiest residence for Thee along with Sita. **56.** Those who ever repeat Thy name, those who are ever resigned to Thee, those who are above the pairs of opposites, those who are devoid of all desires—their heart is the happy residence for Thee. **57.** Those who are without self-conceit, who are peaceful, who are devoid of attachment and anger, and who view a clod of earth and a piece of gold as equal—their heart is the fitting residence for Thee. **58.** Those who have resigned their mind and intellect to Thee, those who are ever established in perfect contentment, those who have dedicated all their works to Thee—their hearts form the auspicious residence for Thee. **59.** Those who do not show any revulsion to unpleasant experiences and do not get elated with pleasant ones, and those who look upon the whole universe as Maya, a mere appearance, and remain devoted to Thee alone—their heart forms a fitting residence for Thee. **(60-61).** Whosoever sees the six transformations of one's being beginning with birth as occurring to the body and not to the Self, whoever sees hunger, thirst and fear, as also happiness and misery as belonging to the Prana and not to the Atman, and whoever is by such knowledge free from involvement in the processes of Samsara—the heart of such a person forms a fitting residence for Thee. **62.** Mayest Thou reside along with Sita in the heart-lotus of those who see Thee

त्वन्नामकीर्त्या हतकल्मषाणां सीतासमेतस्य गृहं हृदब्जे ॥ 63

राम त्वन्नाममहिमा वर्ण्यते केन वा कथम् । यत्प्रभावादहं राम ब्रह्मर्षित्वमवाप्तवान् ॥ 64

अहं पुरा किरातेषु किरातैः सह वर्धितः । जन्ममात्रद्विजत्वं मे शूद्राचाररतः सदा ॥ 65

शूद्रायां बहवः पुत्रा उत्पन्ना मेऽजितात्मनः । ततश्चोरश्च सङ्गम्य चौरोऽहमभवं पुरा ॥ 66

धनुर्बाणधरो नित्यं जीवानामन्तकोपमः । एकदा मुनयः सप्त दृष्टा महति कानने ॥ 67

साक्षान्मया प्रकाशन्तो ज्वलनार्कसमप्रभाः । तानन्वधावं लोभेन तेषां सर्वपरिच्छदान् ॥ 68

ग्रहीतुकामस्तत्राहं तिष्ठ तिष्ठेति चाब्रवम् । दृष्ट्वा मां मुनयोऽपृच्छन्किमायासि द्विजाधम॥ 69

अहं तानब्रवं किञ्चिदादातुं मुनिसत्तमाः । पुत्रदारादयः सन्ति बहवो मे बुभुक्षिताः ॥ 70

तेषां संरक्षणार्थाय चरामि गिरिकानने । ततो मामूचुरव्यग्राः पृच्छ गत्वा कुटुम्बकम् ॥ 71

यो यो मया प्रतिदिनं क्रियते पापसञ्चयः । यूयं तद्भागिनः किं वा नेति वेति पृथक्पृथक् ॥ 72

वयं स्थास्यामहे तावदागमिष्यसि निश्चयः । तथेत्युक्त्वा गृहं गत्वा मुनिभिर्यदुदीरितम् ॥ 73

अपृच्छं पुत्रदारादींस्तैरुक्तोऽहं रघूत्तम । पापं तवैव तत्सर्वं वयं तु फलभागिनः ॥ 74

as the resident of the inner recess of all beings, who understand Thee as Pure Consciousness, as the Truth, as the Immeasurable, as the One without a second, as the One Unaffected, as the One all-pervading and as the One superior to everything else. **63.** Those who have succeeded in concentrating their mind by continuous practice, those who are ever devoted to the service of Thy feet, those whose sins have been effaced by taking Thy name and singing about Thy glories—the heart-lotus of such persons is the fitting home for Thee to dwell with Sita.

Valmiki's previous History (64-92)

64. O Rama! Who can describe adequately the greatness of Thy name—the name by the power of which I attained to the status of a Brahmarshi. **65.** Long ago, I was living in the land of the hunters among a tribe of that community. A Brahmana by mere birth, I was given to the ways of the most ignoble people. **66.** The sensual man that I was, I had a brood of children by a low-born woman, and for their support I associated myself with thieves and robbers and took to their profession as the means of livelihood. **67.** Every day, equipped with bow and arrow, I moved about in the forest as death embodied, for the destruction of all living creatures. While doing so, I once saw seven Munis in a thick forest. **(68-69)** I saw them luminous like fire and the sun. Moved by greed, I desired to rob them of all their possessions, and for that purpose, I followed them and ordered them to stop. Seeing me, they addressed me thus, 'O degenerate **fellow** of a Brahmana! Why are you following us?' **70.** I replied, 'There are many hungry mouths in my house to feed. I am coming to rob you of your possessions to fulfil my needs. **(71-74)**. For the support of my family I am moving about on mountains and in forests.' **But** in a very gentle tone, they told me, 'You go to your family members

तत्श्रुत्वा जातनिर्वेदो विचार्य पुनरागमम् । मुनयो यत्र तिष्ठन्ति करुणापूर्णमानसाः ॥ 75
मुनीनां दर्शनादेव शुद्धान्तःकरणोऽभवम् । धनुरादीन्परित्यज्य दण्डवत्पतितोऽस्म्यहम् ॥ 76
रक्षध्वं मां मुनिश्रेष्ठा गच्छन्तं निरयार्णवम् । इत्यग्रे पतितं दृष्ट्वा मामूचुर्मुनिसत्तमाः ॥ 77
उत्तिष्ठोत्तिष्ठ भद्रं ते सफलः सत्समागमः । उपदेक्ष्यामहे तुभ्यं किञ्चित्तेनैव मोक्ष्यसे ॥ 78
परस्परं समालोच्य दुर्वृत्तोऽयं द्विजाधमः ।
उपेक्ष्य एव सद्वृत्तस्तथापि शरणं गतः । रक्षणीयः प्रयत्नेन मोक्षमार्गोपदेशतः ॥ 79
इत्युक्त्वा राम ते नाम व्यत्यस्ताक्षरपूर्वकम् । एकाग्रमनसात्रैव मरेति जप सर्वदा ॥ 80
आगच्छामः पुनर्यावत्तावदुक्तं सदा जप । इत्युक्त्वा प्रययुः सर्वे मुनयो दिव्यदर्शनाः ॥ 81
अहं यथोपदिष्टं तैस्तथाकरवमञ्जसा । जपन्नेकाग्रमनसा बाह्यं विस्मृतवानहम् ॥ 82
एवं बहुतिथे काले गते निश्चलरूपिणः । सर्वसङ्गविहीनस्य वल्मीकोऽभून्ममोपरि ॥ 83

and ask every one of them individually, whether they are willing to share the sins that you are accumulating to your credit every day. Until you return after making this enquiry, we shall remain here itself.' I, therefore, went home and communicated to my wife and children what the sages had said. But their reply was that they were willing to share only my earnings and not my sins. **75.** Their words drove me to a mood of tremendous repentance. I now hurried to the place where the merciful sages were awaiting my return. **76.** My mind being purified by the sight of these holy men, I abandoned my weapons like bow and arrow, and fell flat before them in salutation. **77.** I prayed to them, 'O great sages! Save me from the terrible hells I am destined to.' To me who was thus lying flat before them in prostration, the sages said: **(78-79).** 'Arise! Arise! You will be saved. The contact with holy men will certainly be fruitful. We shall give you some advice. By that you will attain salvation.' Then they had some consultation among themselves as follows: "He is certainly a man of evil ways. A Brahmana, who has degenerated by evil ways, has to be shunned by all good men. This is the law. Yet, he has taken shelter under us and as such, even though it may be difficult, he has to be helped with proper advice for the attainment of spiritual salvation.' **80.** With these words, O Rama, they initiated me into Thy name in the reverse order as '*Mara*' and asked me to repeat it continuously there itself with concentration of mind. **81.** 'Until we return to this place again,' said they, 'you go on repeating the name with which we have initiated you.' With this instruction, those holy and divine-looking sages departed.

82. "I immediately started to put their advice into practice in all sincerity. I repeated the name with such concentration that I lost awareness of all external things. **83.** Devoid of all worldly attachments, I went on with this practice for a long time without moving the body in the least, and as a consequence an ant-hill (Valmika) gathered

ततो युगसहस्रान्ते ऋषयः पुनरागमन् । मामूचुर्निष्क्रमस्वेति तत्श्रुत्वा तूर्णमुत्थितः ॥ 84
वल्मीकान्निर्गतश्चाहं नीहारादिव भास्करः । मामप्याहुर्मुनिगणा वाल्मीकिस्त्वं मुनीश्वर ॥ 85
वल्मीकात्सम्भवो यस्माद् द्वितीयं जन्म तेऽभवत् । इत्युक्त्वा ते ययुर्दिव्यगतिं रघुकुलोत्तम ॥ 86
अहं ते राम नाम्नश्च प्रभावादीदृशोऽभवम् । अद्य साक्षात्प्रपश्यामि ससीतं लक्ष्मणेन च ॥ 87
रामं राजीवपत्राक्षं त्वां मुक्तो नात्र संशयः । आगच्छ राम भद्रं ते स्थलं वै दर्शयाम्यहम् ॥ 88
एवमुक्त्वा मुनिः श्रीमाँल्लक्ष्मणेन समन्वितः । शिष्यैः परिवृतो गत्वा मध्ये पर्वतगङ्गयोः ॥ 89
तत्र शालां सुविस्तीर्णां कारयामास वासभूः । प्राक्पश्चिमं दक्षिणोदक् शोभनं मन्दिरद्वयम् ॥ 90
जानक्या सहितो रामो लक्ष्मणेन समन्वितः । तत्र ते देवसदृशा ह्यवसन् भवनोत्तमे ॥ 91

वाल्मीकिना तत्र सुपूजितोऽयं रामः ससीतः सह लक्ष्मणेन ।
देवैर्मुनीन्द्रैः सहितो मुदास्ते स्वर्गे यथा देवपतिः सशच्या ॥ 92

इति श्रीमदध्यात्मरामायणे उमामहेश्वरसंवादे
अयोध्याकाण्डे षष्ठः सर्गः ॥ ६ ॥

about me and rose above my head. **84.** At the end of a thousand divine years, those holy sages who instructed me returned to me, who was sitting covered by that ant-hill. Seeing me in that condtion they called out to me to come out. I then arose from my seat at once. **(85-86)**. As the sun emerges from the clouds, I got out of the mould of earth. The sages thereupon said. 'This emergence from a mould of earth is a second birth for you. O sage! You will hereafter be known as Valmiki—one born out of *Valmika* or ant-hill. Saying so, they departed to the heavenly regions. **(87-88)**. O the noblest of Raghu's line! By the power of Thy name 'Rama', I have attained to this state of life. Now, I have the privilege of seeing Thee with Sita and Lakshmana with my mortal eyes. I have thereby certainly become liberated. Come, O Rama! May everything good befall Thee. I shall show a place suitable for Thee to stay."

(89-90). Saying so, the sage Valmiki, along with Rama, Lakshmana and some of his own disciples went to a region between the Ganga and the Chitrakuta mountain. There, an extensive plot was located, and Rama, whose real residence is the whole world, had two spacious thatched constructions made, one extending from east to west and the other south to north. **91.** Like divine beings, Rama, Sita and Lakshmana took their residence in those abodes. **92.** Adored by sage Valmiki, Rama along with Sita and Lakshmana, resided there in joy just as Indra resides in heaven in the company of Sachi and great sages.

सप्तमः सर्गः

सुमन्त्रोऽपि तदायोध्यां दिनान्ते प्रविवेश ह । वस्त्रेण मुखमाच्छाद्य बाष्पाकुलितलोचनः । 1
बहिरेव रथं स्थाप्य राजानं द्रष्टुमाययौ । जय शब्देन राजानं स्तुत्वा तं प्रणनाम ह ॥ 2
ततो राजा नमन्तं तं सुमन्त्रं विह्वलोऽब्रवीत् । सुमन्त्र रामः कुत्रास्ते सीतया लक्ष्मणेन च ॥ 3
कुत्र त्यक्तस्त्वया रामः किं मां पापिनमब्रवीत् । सीता वा लक्ष्मणो वापि निर्दयं मां किमब्रवीत् ॥ 4
हा राम हा गुणनिधे हा सीते प्रियवादिनि । दुःखार्णवे निमग्नं मां म्रियमाणं न पश्यसि ॥ 5
विलप्यैवं चिरं राजा निमग्नो दुःखसागरे । एवं मन्त्री रुदन्तं तं प्राञ्जलिर्वाक्यमब्रवीत् ॥ 6
रामः सीता च सौमित्रिर्मया नीता रथेन ते । शृङ्गवेरपुराभ्याशे गङ्गाकूले व्यवस्थिताः ॥ 7
गुहेन किञ्चिदानीतं फलमूलादिकं च यत् । स्पृष्ट्वा हस्तेन सम्प्रीत्या नाग्रहीद्विससर्ज तत् ॥ 8
वटक्षीरः समानाय्य गुहेन रघुनन्दनः । जटामुकुटमाबद्ध्य मामाह नृपते स्वयम् । 9
सुमन्त्र ब्रूहि राजानं शोकस्तेऽस्तु न मत्कृते । साकेतादधिकं सौख्यं विपिने नो भविष्यति ॥10
मातुर्मे वन्दनं ब्रूहि शोकं त्यजतु मत्कृते । आश्वासयतु राजानं वृद्धं शोकपरिप्लुतम् ॥ 11

Chapter 7

KING DASARATHA'S DEMISE

Sumantra's return and after (1-19)

(1-2). Now Sumantra had returned to Ayodhya by evening. He covered his face with a cloth to hide the tears flowing from his eyes. Stationing the chariot outside, he went to the palace to see King Dasaratha. He greeted the King respectfully and made prostrations to him. **(3-4).** To Sumantra, who was thus waiting before him, King Dasaratha, said, distracted with grief, "O Sumantra! Where is Rama staying along with Sita and Lakshmana? Where did you leave him? What did he, Sita and Lakshmana ask you to report to me, a hard-hearted sinner? **5.** O virtuous Rama! O dear Sita! Don't you see me almost dying, submerged in an ocean of sorrow!" **6.** He bemoaned like this for a long time, completely overpowered by sorrow. To him, piteously crying like this, the Minister said, **7.** "I took Rama, Sita and Lakshmana in your chariot up to the banks of the Ganges where the city of Sringivera stands. **8.** There, Guha presented him with fruits and roots. With great joy, Rama accepted them, touching them with his hands, but did not eat anything. **(9-10).** That great prince of Raghu's line asked Guha to fetch him some sap of the banyan tree. With that he matted his hair as a crown on his head. Then, he said to me of his own accord: 'O Sumantra! Tell the king as follows: Please do not feel sorry on my account. We shall stay in the forest more happily than in Ayodhya. **11.** Convey my greetings to my mother. Let her abandon all sorrow on my

सीता चाश्रुपरीताक्षी मामाह नृपसत्तम । दुःखगद्गदया वाचा रामं किञ्चिद्वेक्षती ॥ 12

साष्टाङ्ग प्रणिपातं मे ब्रूहि श्वश्रोः पदाम्बुजे । इति प्ररुदती सीता गता किञ्चिदवाङ्मुखी ॥ 13

ततस्तेऽश्रुपरीताक्षा नावमारुरुहुस्तदा । यावद्गङ्गां समुत्तीर्य गतास्तावदहं स्थितः ॥ 14

ततो दुःखेन महता पुनरेवाहमागतः । ततो रुदन्ती कौसल्या राजानमिदमब्रवीत् ॥ 15

कैकेय्यै प्रियभार्यायै प्रसन्नो दत्तवान्वरम् । त्वं राज्यं देहि तस्यैव मत्पुत्रः किं विवासितः ॥ 16

कृत्वा त्वमेव तत्सर्वमिदानीं किं नु रोदिषि । कौसल्यावचनं श्रुत्वा क्षते स्पृष्ट इवाग्निना ॥ 17

पुनः शोकाश्रुपूर्णाक्षः कौसल्यामिदमब्रवीत् । दुःखेन म्रियमाणं मां किं पुनर्दुःखयस्यलम् ॥ 18

इदानीमेव मे प्राणा उत्क्रमिष्यन्ति निश्चयः । शप्तोऽहं बाल्यभावेन केनचिन्मुनिना पुरा ॥ 19

पुराहं यौवने दृप्तचापबाणधरो निशि । अचरं मृगयासक्तो नद्यास्तीरे महावने ॥ 20

तत्रार्धरात्रसमये मुनिः कश्चित्तृषार्दितः ।

पिपासार्दितयोः पित्रोर्जलमानेतुमुद्यतः । अपूरयज्जले कुम्भं तदा शब्दोऽभवन्महान् ॥ 21

गजः पिबति पानीयमिति मत्वा महानिशि । बाणं धनुषि सन्धाय शब्दवेधिनमक्षिपम् ॥ 22

account, and comfort the sorrow-stricken old king. **(12-13).** Next, Sita with tears flowing from her eyes and speech choked by sorrow, said, casting a glance at Rama: 'Convey my full prostrations to my father-in-law and mother-in-law!' So said Sita weeping and with face inclined downward. **(14-15).** Next, shedding tears, they got into a boat, and I watched them until they crossed the Ganges. After that, with my heart heavy with sorrow, I came over to this place." Now, Kausalya with tears in her eyes said to the king as follows:

16. She said, "Out of fondness for your dear wife Kaikeyi, you gave her a boon. According to that, let the kingdom go to her son. But why should my son be exiled to the forest? **(17-19).** You have been yourself responsible for the present situation. Then why weep so much over it?" These words of Kausalya, had on the king, the effect of a flame touching a festering wound. Again, with tears flowing from his eyes, he said to Kausalya as follows: "Why are you inflicting more sorrow on me, who am now going to die out of sorrow. My Prana will surely depart even now. All this is the effect of the curse of a sage for a thoughtless action of mine.

Muni's curse on Dasaratha (20-46)

20. "In my youth, equipped with bow and arrows, I was once hunting at night near a deep forest on a river bank. **(21-22).** There at midnight, came a sage to fetch water from the river in order to quench the thirst of himself and of his thirsty parents. He immersed the jug in the water, giving rise to a great gurgling sound. In that dark night, when nothing could be seen, I could hear only the sound, and I thought that it was an elephant drinking water. So, I shot in that direction an arrow, which could track a sound and strike the target

हा हतोऽस्मीति तत्राभूच्छब्दो मानुषसूचकः । कस्यापि न कृतो दोषो मया केन हतो विधे ॥23

प्रतीक्षते मां माता च पिता च जलकाङ्क्षया । तत्श्रुत्वा भयसन्त्रस्तस्ततोऽहं पौरुषं वचः ॥ 24

शनैर्गत्वाथ तत्पार्श्वं स्वामिन् दशरथोऽस्म्यहम् । अजानता मया विद्धस्त्रातुमर्हसि मां मुने ॥ 25

इत्युक्त्वा पादयोस्तस्य पतितो गद्गदाक्षरः । तदा मामाह स मुनिर्मा भैषीर्नृपसत्तम ॥ 26

ब्रह्महत्या स्पृशेन्न त्वां वैश्योऽहं तपसि स्थितः । पितरौ मां प्रतीक्षेते क्षुत्तृड्भ्यां परिपीडितौ ॥ 27

तयोस्त्वमुदकं देहि शीघ्रमेवाविचारयन् । न चेत्त्वां भस्मसात्कुर्यात्पिता मे यदि कुप्यति ॥28

जलं दत्त्वा तु तौ नत्वा कृतं सर्वं निवेदय । शल्यमुद्धर मे देहात्प्राणांस्त्यक्ष्यामि पीडितः ॥29

इत्युक्तो मुनिना शीघ्रं बाणमुत्पाट्य देहतः । सजलं कलशं धृत्वा गतोऽहं यत्र दम्पती ॥ 30

अतिवृद्धावन्धदृशौ क्षुत्पिपासार्दितौ निशि । नायाति सलिलं गृह्य पुत्रः किं वात्र कारणम् ॥31

अनन्यगतिकौ वृद्धौ शोच्यौ तृट्परिपीडितौ । आवामुपेक्षते किं वा भक्तिमानावयोः सुतः ॥ 32

इति चिन्ताव्याकुलौ तौ मत्पादन्यासजं ध्वनिम् । श्रुत्वा प्राह पिता पुत्र किं विलम्बः कृतस्त्वया ॥33

देह्यावयोः सुपानीयं पिब त्वमपि पुत्रक । इत्येवं लपतोर्भीत्या सकाशमगमं शनैः ॥ 34

पादयोः प्रणिपत्याहमब्रवं विनयान्वितः । नाहं पुत्रस्त्वयोध्याया राजा दशरथोऽस्म्यहम् ॥35

even without visibility. **(23-26).** 'Alas! I am dead,' came a human cry from that direction. Further the voice said, 'I have done no harm to anyone. O God! Who is it that is killing me? My father and mother are awaiting my arrival in a very thirsty condition.' Hearing these words, uttered by a human voice, I trembled with fear. I went close to the person stricken by the arrow and said, 'O holy Sir! I am Dasaratha. I shot the arrow unaware of the nature of the target. O sage, I seek your pardon.' I said so in a choked voice and fell at his feet. The sage thereupon said, 'O king! Do not be afraid. **27.** You will not be affected by the sin of Brahmahatya. I am only a Vaisya engaged in austerities. My parents, stricken with hunger and thirst, are awaiting my arrival. **(28-30)** Take some water to them. Don't waste time in vain thought. It should be done quickly. Otherwise, my father might get angry and reduce you to ashes. Give them water to drink and prostrate before them and inform them of what has happened. Now remove the arrow from my body so that I, who am in great agony, may die immediately.' At these words of the sage, I pulled out the arrow quickly, and then with a pot of water in my hand, I went to the sage and his wife.

(31-35). I found them very aged, blind and suffering from extreme hunger and thirst. They were preoccupied with the thought, 'Our son is not bringing water. What is it due to? Is it possible that such a devoted son would abandon his parents like us, who are old, thirsty and pitiable, and with no other support than he?' While troubled by such sorrowful thoughts they heard the sound of my footsteps. And the father said, 'O my son! Why is it that you have delayed? Give us some sweet water to drink, and you,

पापोऽहं मृगयासक्तो रात्रौ मृगविहिंसकः । जलावतारादूदूरेऽहं स्थित्वा जलगतं ध्वनिम् । 36
श्रुत्वाहं शब्दवेधित्वादेकं बाणमथात्यजम् । हतोऽस्मीति ध्वनिं श्रुत्वा भयात्तत्राहमागतः ॥ 37
जटां विकीर्य पतितं दृष्ट्वाहं मुनिदारकम् । भीतो गृहीत्वा तत्पादौ रक्ष रक्षेति चाब्रवम् ॥ 38
मा भैषीरिति मां प्राह ब्रह्महत्याभयं न ते । मत्पित्रोः सलिलं दत्त्वा नत्वा प्रार्थय जीवितम् ॥39
इत्युक्तो मुनिना तेन ह्यागतो मुनिहिंसकः । रक्षेतां मां दयायुक्तौ युवां हि शरणागतम् ॥40
इति श्रुत्वा तु दुःखार्तौ विलप्य बहु शोच्य तम् । पतितौ नौ सुतो यत्र नय तत्राविलम्बयन् ॥ 41
ततो नीतौ सुतो यत्र मया तौ वृद्धदम्पती । स्पृष्ट्वा सुतं तौ हस्ताभ्यां बहुशोऽथ विलेपतुः 42
हाहेति क्रन्दमानौ तौ पुत्रपुत्रेत्यवोचताम् । जलं देहीति पुत्रेति किमर्थं न ददास्यलम् ॥ 43
ततो मामूचतुः शीघ्रं चितिं रचय भूपते ।
मया तदैव रचिता चितिस्तत्र निवेशिताः । त्रयस्तत्राग्निरुत्सृष्टो दग्धास्ते त्रिदिवं ययुः ॥44
तत्र वृद्धः पिता प्राह त्वमप्येवं भविष्यसि । पुत्रशोकेन मरणं प्राप्स्यसे वचनान्मम ॥ 45
स इदानीं मम प्राप्तः शापकालोऽनिवारितः । इत्युक्त्वा विललापाथ राजा शोकसमाकुलः ॥46

too, drink of it.' To them, who were speaking this way, I slowly went, and making prostrations, said in all humility, 'I am not your son. I am Dasaratha, the King of Ayodhya. **(36-37).** Mad after chase, this sinful fellow was engaged in hunting and killing animals at night. Stationed at some distance from a source of water, I heard the gurgling sound of water. Mistaking it to be an animal drinking water in darkness, I shot an arrow that could pierce a target indicated by a sound. Next I heard the cry, 'Alas! I am killed!' Frightened at this, I went to the spot. **38.** I saw there lying a young sage with his matted hair dishevelled. Terrified at the sight, I fell at his feet and prayed to be pardoned. **39.** The young sage said, 'Do not be afraid of the sin of Brahmahatya. Give water to my parents to drink. Pray to them to spare your life.'

40. Directed thus by the young sage, this slayer of a holy person has come over to you. Be merciful towards me, who am taking refuge at your feet.' **41.** On hearing this account, they were stricken with unbearable grief. They gave expression to their sorrow by wailing. They gave vent to sorrowful reactions in many ways and fell on the ground. Then they said to me, 'Lead us to where our son is lying.' **42.** Next, I took them to the place where their son was lying dead. Those two aged couple touched that lifeless body with their hands and lamented over their dead son in many ways. **43.** They said, 'Ah our son! our son! Give us water. Why are you delaying?' **44.** And then turning to me they said, 'O King! Make a funeral pyre soon.' I made it according to their order and laid the bodies of the three on it, and as desired by them, set fire to the pyre. Their bodies were burnt and they attained to heaven. **(45-46).** Before dying, the old sage had cursed me, 'The same fate as ours will befall you. Your death will be caused on

हा राम पुत्र हा सीते हा लक्ष्मण गुणाकर । त्वद्वियोगादहं प्राप्तो मृत्युं कैकेयिसम्भवम् ॥ 47
वदन्नेवं दशरथः प्राणांस्त्यक्त्वा दिवं गतः । कौसल्या च सुमित्रा च तथान्या राजयोषितः ॥ 48
चुक्रुशुश्च विलेपुश्च उरस्ताडनपूर्वकम् । वसिष्ठः प्रययौ तत्र प्रातर्मन्त्रिभिरावृतः ॥ 49
तैलद्रोण्यां दशरथं क्षिप्त्वा दूतानाथाब्रवीत् । गच्छत त्वरितं साश्वा युधाजिन्नगरं प्रति ॥ 50
तत्रास्ते भरतः श्रीमाञ्छत्रुघ्नसहितः प्रभुः । उच्यतां भरतः शीघ्रमागच्छेति ममाज्ञया ॥ 51
अयोध्यां प्रति राजानं कैकेयीं चापि पश्यतु । इत्युक्तास्त्वरितं दूता गत्वा भरतमातुलम् ॥ 52
युधाजितं प्रणम्योचुर्भरतं सानुजं प्रति । वसिष्ठस्त्वब्रवीद्राजन् भरतः सानुजः प्रभुः ॥ 53
शीघ्रमागच्छतु पुरीमयोध्यामविचारयन् । इत्याज्ञप्तोऽथ भरतस्त्वरितं भयविह्वलः ॥ 54
आययौ गुरुणादिष्टः सह दूतैस्तु सानुजः । राज्ञो वा राघवस्यापि दुःखं किञ्चिदुपस्थितम् ॥ 55
इति चिन्तापरो मार्गे चिन्तयन्नगरं ययौ । नगरं भ्रष्टलक्ष्मीकं जनसम्बाधवर्जितम् ॥ 56
उत्सवैश्च परित्यक्तं दृष्ट्वा चिन्तापरोऽभवत् । प्रविश्य राजभवनं राजलक्ष्मीविवर्जितम् ॥ 57

account of sorrow connected with your son.' That curse which cannot in any way be prevented from fructifying is now taking effect." With these words, the king indulged in lamentations in many ways.

Bharata's return and confrontation with Kaikeyi (47-82)

47. He said, "O Rama, my son! O Sita! O virtuous Lakshmana! I shall now be dying because of separation from you. I am now face to face with death on account of Kaikeyi, who has brought about your separation from me." **(48-49).** With these words, Dasaratha breathed his last and attained to heaven. Then Kausalya, Sumitra and other ladies of the palace began to beat their breasts and cry. Early in the morning, Vasishtha along with the other ministers came to the palace. **50.** They immersed the dead body of Dasaratha in a vessel of oil for its preservation. Then they called royal messengers and said to them, "Go quickly to the city of King Yudhajit on horse back. **51.** The noble prince Bharata along with Satrughna is now staying there. Tell him that I want him to return immediately. **(52-56).** Coming to Ayodhya, they have got to meet the King and Kaikeyi, urgently." Instructed in this way, the messengers quickly reached the place of Yudhajit, the uncle of Bharata. They then said to Bharata and his brother, "Let Bharata along with his brother come to the city of Ayodhya quickly without wasting any time in speculation—Sage Vasishtha ordered us to communicate this to you." Bharata was very much agitated to hear these instructions of the preceptor. However, in obedience to these instructions, he immediately started for Ayodhya along with his brother and the messengers, fearing all along the way that some danger must have happened to the King or to Rama. **(57-58).** Seeing the city of Ayodhya overcast with gloom, deserted bv people and devoid of decorations, Bharata was all the more filled with vague fears. Immediately he went to

अपश्यत्कैकेयीं तत्र एकामेवासने स्थिताम् । ननाम शिरसा पादौ मातुर्भक्तिसमन्वितः ॥ 58

आगतं भरतं दृष्ट्वा कैकेयी प्रेमसम्भ्रमात् । उत्थायालिङ्ग्य रभसा स्वाङ्कमारोप्य संस्थिता 59

मूर्ध्न्यवघ्राय पप्रच्छ कुशलं स्वकुलस्य सा । पिता मे कुशली भ्राता माता च शुभलक्षणा ॥60

दिष्ट्या त्वमद्य कुशली मया दृष्टोऽसि पुत्रक । इति पृष्टः स भरतो मात्रा चिन्ताकुलेन्द्रियः ॥ 61

दूयमानेन मनसा मातरं समपृच्छत । मातः पिता मे कुत्रास्ते एका त्वमिह संस्थिता ॥62

त्वया विना न मे तातः कदाचिद्रहसि स्थितः । इदानीं दृश्यते नैव कुत्र तिष्ठति मे वद ॥ 63

अदृष्ट्वा पितरं मेऽद्य भयं दुःखं च जायते । अथाह कैकेयी पुत्रं किं दुःखेन तवानघ ॥ 64

या गतिर्धर्मशीलानामश्वमेधादियाजिनाम् । तां गतिं गतवानद्य पिता ते पितृवत्सल ॥ 65

तच्छ्रुत्वा निपपातोर्व्यां भरतः शोकविह्वलः । हा तात क्व गतोऽसि त्वं त्यक्त्वा मां वृजिनार्णवे 66

असमर्प्यैव रामाय राज्ञे मां क्व गतोऽसि भोः । इति विलपितं पुत्रं पतितं मुक्तमूर्धजम् ॥ 67

उत्थाप्यामृज्य नयने कैकेयी पुत्रमब्रवीत् । समाश्वसिहि भद्रं ते सर्वं सम्पादितं मया ॥ 68

तामाह भरतस्तातो म्रियमाणः किमब्रवीत् । तमाह कैकेयी देवी भरतं भयवर्जिता ॥ 69

the palace, which was without any royal splendour. There he saw Kaikeyi, sitting alone. To her, his mother, he made devout prostrations. **59.** Bharata's arrival, filled Kaikeyi with mental excitement arising from her love of her son. She got up at once from her seat, embraced him, and seated him in her lap. **(60-63).** She smelt the crown of her son's head and made enquiries of him about the welfare of the people at home—about her father, brother and beloved mother. She then expresed to him her great delight in seeing him return. Depressed in mind by these words of his mother, Bharata, moved by great sorrow, asked Kaikeyi, his mother, "O mother! Where is my father? I see you here alone. It's never the habit of my father to sit alone without you. I do not see him here now. Where is he? Please tell me where he is. **(64-65).** I feel very much concerned at not seeing my father, and my mind is filled with sorrow and fear on account of it." Then Kaikeyi said to her son, "O virtuous and loving boy! What's the use of your sorrowing? Your father has gone the way of all those righteous men who have performed great sacrificial rites like Aswamedha."

(66-68). At these words, Bharata, overwhelmed with grief, fell down on the ground and wailed: "O my father! Where have you gone abandoning me in this ocean of sorrow? Where have you gone without entrusting me to Rama, the rightful king?" Kaikeyi now raised up her son, who was lying on the floor highly agitated and with his hair dishevelled. She wiped his eyes and said to him, "Be comforted. Everything will be well with you. I have acquired for you everything." **69.** Bharata thereupon asked her, "What did my dying father say?" Without in anyway being concerned, Kai-

हा राम राम सीतेति लक्ष्मणेति पुनः पुनः । विलपन्नेव सुचिरं देहं त्यक्त्वा दिवं ययौ ॥ 70
तामाह भरतो हेऽम्ब रामः सन्निहितो न किम् । तदानीं लक्ष्मणो वापि सीता वा कुत्र ते गताः॥ 71
रामस्य यौवराज्यार्थं पित्रा ते सम्भ्रमः कृतः । तव राज्यप्रदानाय तदाहं विघ्नमाचरम् ॥ 72
राज्ञा दत्तं हि मे पूर्वं वरदेन वरद्वयम् । याचितं तदिदानीं मे तयोरेकेन तेऽखिलम् ॥ 73
राज्यं रामस्य चैकेन वनवासो मुनिव्रतम् । ततः सत्यपरो राज्यं दत्त्वा तदैव हि ॥ 74
रामं सम्प्रेषयाभास वनमेव पिता तव । सीताप्यनुगता रामं पातिव्रत्यमुपाश्रिता ॥ 75
सौभ्रात्रं दर्शयन्राममनुयातोऽपि लक्ष्मणः । वनं गतेषु सर्वेषु राजा तानेव चिन्तयन् ॥ 76
प्रलपन् रामरामेति ममार नृपसत्तमः । इति मातुर्वचः श्रुत्वा वज्राहत इव द्रुमः ॥ 77
पपात भूमौ निःसंज्ञस्तं दृष्ट्वा दुःखिता तदा । कैकेयी पुनरप्याह वत्स शोकेन किं तव ॥78
राज्ये महति सम्प्राप्ते दुःखस्यावसरः कुतः । इति ब्रुवन्तीमालोक्य मातरं प्रदहन्निव ॥ 79
असम्भाष्यासि पापे मे घोरे त्वं भर्तृघातिनी ।
पापे त्वद्गर्भजातोऽहं पापवानस्मि साम्प्रतम् । अहमग्निं प्रवेक्ष्यामि विषं वा भक्षयाम्यहम् ॥ 80

keyi replied: **70.** "He lamented long saying, 'O Rama! O Sita! O Lakshmana!' Again and again lamenting long like this, he abandoned his body and attained to heaven." **71.** Bharata now said to her, "O mother! Where are Rama, Lakshmana and Sita then? Were they not by his side, or had they gone anywhere?"

72. Kaikeyi replied, "Your father made hurried arrangements for installing Rama as Yuvaraja. I obstructed this arrangement so that the kingdom may come to you. **(73-78).** The liberal-minded King had given me two boons in days of old. I wanted him to fulfil these now. By one of them I secured the whole kingdom for you, and by the other, I got Rama expelled to the forest to lead an ascetic life there. Accordingly, your father, the King, has assigned the kingdom to you and sent Rama to the forest. Sita, according to the duties of a chaste wife, has opted to follow him to the forest, and Lakshmana, too, has done so impelled by his love for his brother. After their departure, the King was lamenting continuously, calling the name of Rama, and in the end died." Hearing these words of his mother, Bharata fell unconscious on the floor as if struck with a sharp weapon. Kaikeyi, who was grief-stricken to see her son in that condition, again said, "O dear son! Why are you sorrow-stricken? **(79-80)** When this great kingdom has come to you, where is the occasion for grief?" At these words of his mother, Bharata addressed her with a flaming, fiery look in his eyes, as if he were going to burn her up. He said, "O hideous and sinful creature! You are a murderer of your own husband. It is improper for me to converse with you. By being born in the womb of a sinful person like you, I have also become a sinner.

खड्गेन वाथ चात्मानं हत्वा यामि यमक्षयम् । भर्तृघातिनि दुष्टे त्वं कुम्भीपाकं गमिष्यसि ॥ 81
इति निर्भर्त्स्य कैकेयीं कौसल्याभवनं ययौ । सापि तं भरतं दृष्ट्वा मुक्तकण्ठा रुरोद ह ॥ 82
पादयोः पतितस्तस्या भरतोऽपि तदारुदत् । आलिङ्ग्य भरतं साध्वी राममाता यशस्विनी ॥
कृशातिदीनवदना साश्रुनेत्रेदमब्रवीत् ॥ 83
पुत्र त्वयि गते दूरमेवं सर्वमभूदिदम् । उक्तं मात्रा श्रुतं सर्वं त्वया ते मातृचेष्टितम्॥ 84
पुत्रः सभार्यो वनमेव यातः सलक्ष्मणो मे रघुरामचन्द्रः ।
चीराम्बरो बद्धजटाकलापः सन्त्यज्य मां दुःखसमुद्रमग्नाम् ॥ 85
हा राम हा मे रघुवंशनाथ जातोऽसि मे त्वं परतः परात्मा ।
तथापि दुःखं न जहाति मां वै विधिर्बलीयानिति मे मनीषा ॥ 86
स एवं भरतो वीक्ष्य विलपन्तीं भृशं शुचा । पादौ गृहीत्वा प्राहेदं शृणु मातर्वचो मम ॥ 87
कैकेय्या यत्कृतं कर्म रामराज्याभिषेचने । अन्यद्वा यदि जानामि सा मया नोदिता यदि ॥88
पापं मेऽस्तु तदा मातर्ब्रह्महत्याशतोद्भवम् । हत्वा वसिष्ठं खड्गेन अरुन्धत्या समन्वितम् ॥89
भूयात्तत्पापमखिलं मम जानामि यद्यहम् । इत्येवं शपथं कृत्वा रुरोद भरतस्तदा ॥ 90

(81-82). Therefore I am going to enter into a fire or end my life by taking poison. Or I shall slay myself with the sword and go to the realm of Yama, the king of death. O evil one! You murderer of your own husband! You are bound to be confined to the hell of Kumbhipaka." Abusing Kaikeyi in this way, Bharata now went to the house of Kausalya. Alas! At the sight of Bharata, Kausalya wept aloud without restraint.

Bharata seeking Kausalya's Pardon (83-91)

(83-85). Bharata, while prostrating at her feet, also wept along with her. Rama's mother Kausalya, the virtuous and chaste wife, had become very lean and pitiable to look at. She now embraced Bharata, and with tears flowing from her eyes, said to him: "O son! When you were far away, all these unfortunate events have happened. You must have already heard from your mother a report about all these achievements of hers. My son Rama, the gladdener of the hearts of all of Raghu's line, has along with his wife and Lakshmana gone to the forest, donning the tree-bark and matted locks of ascetics. He has thus left me plunged in the ocean of grief. **86.** O Rama! Thou art the Supreme Lord, born in me as my son. Still I am not able to overcome grief. I deem destiny is too strong for anyone to overcome."

87. Seeing her thus wailing out of inexpressible sorrow, Bharata, held her feet and said as follows to her: "O mother! Hear my words. **(88-90).** If I have any part in what Kaikeyi has done to obstruct Rama's installation and in other allied matters, if I had been responsible for prompting her in these respects, let, O mother, the sin of a hundred Brahmahatyas befall me. If these

कौसल्या तमथालिङ्ग्य पुत्र जानामि मा शुचः । एतस्मिन्नन्तरे श्रुत्वा भरतस्य समागमम् ॥ 91
वसिष्ठो मन्त्रिभिः सार्धं प्रययौ राजमन्दिरम् । रुदन्तं भरतं दृष्ट्वा वसिष्ठः प्राह सादरम् ॥ 92
वृद्धो राजा दशरथो ज्ञानी सत्यपराक्रमः । भुक्त्वा मर्त्यसुखं सर्वमिष्ट्वा विपुलदक्षिणैः ॥ 93
अश्वमेधादिभिर्यज्ञैर्लब्ध्वा रामं सुतं हरिम् । अन्ते जगाम त्रिदिवं देवेन्द्रार्द्धासनं प्रभुः ॥ 94
तं शोचसि वृथैव त्वमशोच्यं मोक्षभाजनम् । आत्मा नित्योऽव्ययः शुद्धो जन्मनाशादिवर्जितः 95
शरीरं जडमत्यर्थमपवित्रं विनश्वरम् । विचार्यमाणे शोकस्य नावकाशः कथञ्चन ॥ 96
पिता वा तनयो वापि यदि मृत्युवशं गतः । मूढास्तमनुशोचन्ति स्वात्मताडनपूर्वकम् ॥ 97
निःसारे खलु संसारे वियोगो ज्ञानिनां यदा । भवेद्वैराग्यहेतुः स शान्तिसौख्यं तनोति च ॥98
जन्मवान्यदि लोकेऽस्मिंस्तर्हि तं मृत्युरन्वगात् । तस्मादपरिहार्योऽयं मृत्युर्जन्मवतां सदा ॥ 99
स्वकर्मवशतः सर्वजन्तूनां प्रभवाप्ययौ । विजानन्नप्यविद्वान्यः कथं शोचति बान्धवान्॥ 100

have been done even with my slightest knowledge, let me be overcome by the sin of murdering Vasishta and his consort Arundhati with the sword." Giving expression to his innocence in this way, Bharata began to wail.

Vasishta's Advice to Bharata (91-114)

(91-92). Then Kausalya embraced him and said, "O Son! I understand you. Don't grieve." Meantime, hearing about the arrival of Bharata, Vasishtha in the company of Ministers went to the palace. Seeing Bharata weeping, he said to him lovingly: **(93-94).** "King Dasaratha was advanced in years. He was a wise one and noted for his truthfulness. Having enjoyed all that human life can offer, having performed great sacrifices like Aswamedha involving magnificent gifts,and having obtained Sri Hari himself as his son in the shape of Rama, he has now in the end attained to the realm of Indra where he has a seat along with Indra himself. **95.** He is eligible to get Moksha, liberation, and therefore it is meaningless to feel sorry for his death. Your sorrow is all misplaced. The Atman is eternal and indestructible. He is pure and devoid of birth, death and other transformations. There is thus no ground for you to mourn over your father's spirit which has attained liberation. **96.** And as for the body, it is insentient, impure and subject to destruction. When you reflect like this, you will find no reason for sorrow. **97.** Thoughtless and ignorant people wail beating their breast when a father or a son dies. **98.** But as for the wise ones, who understand this transitory life to be trivial, the phenomenon of death becomes a means for strengthening their spirit of renunciation and obtaining the bliss of peace. **99.** If a man is born in this world, death follows him, to be sure. Therefore, for all creatures that have birth, death is unavoidable. **100.** Even an ignorant man, who understands the common principle that birth and death of an individual are regulated by his Karma, will find no cause of sorrow when death occurs. Then, what

ब्रह्माण्डकोटयो नष्टाः सृष्टयो बहुशो गताः । शुष्यन्ति सागराः सर्वे कैवास्था क्षणजीविते ॥ 101
चलपत्रान्तलग्नाम्बुबिन्दुवत्क्षणभङ्गुरम् । आयुस्त्यजत्यवेलायां कस्तत्र प्रत्ययस्तव ॥ 102
देही प्राक्तनदेहोत्थकर्मणा देहवान्पुनः । तद्देहोत्थेन च पुनरेवं देहः सदात्मनः ॥ 103
यथा त्यजति वै जीर्णं वासो गृह्णाति नूतनम् । तथा जीर्णं परित्यज्य देही देहं पुनर्नवम् । 104
भजत्येव सदा तत्र शोकस्यावसरः कुतः । आत्मा न म्रियते जातु जायते न च वर्धते ॥ 105
षड्भावरहितोऽनन्तः सत्यप्रज्ञानविग्रहः । आनन्दरूपो बुद्ध्यादिसाक्षी लयविवर्जितः ॥ 106
एक एव परो ह्यात्मा ह्यद्वितीयः समः स्थितः । इत्यात्मानं दृढं ज्ञात्वा त्यक्त्वा शोकं कुरु क्रियाम् ।
तैलद्रोण्याः पितुर्देहमुद्धृत्य सचिवैः सह । कृत्यं कुरु यथान्यायमस्माभिः कुलनन्दन ॥ 108
इति सम्बोधितः साक्षाद् गुरुणा भरतस्तदा । विसृज्याज्ञानजं शोकं चक्रे सविधिवत्क्रियाम् ॥ 109
गुरुणोक्तप्रकारेण आहिताग्नेर्यथाविधि । संस्कृत्य स पितुर्देहं विधिदृष्टेन कर्मणा ॥ 110

justification is there for an enlightened man like you to be sorrow-stricken in this situation? **101.** Thousands of world systems are getting destroyed in the course of creative cycles, and many such creative cycles have passed. So also many oceans have dried up. Before this vision of Infinity, how can there be attachment for this very short span of a human life? **102.** Man's life is as fickle as a drop of water on a leaf, it being subject to destruction at any moment. You find beings meeting with untimely death even in infancy. Why then do you attach so much reality value to life? **103.** The embodied being (Jiva) has got his present embodiment as a result of the Karmas he has performed in a previous embodiment. The Jiva, who is thus embodied at present, gets still another embodiment after the death of the present body as a result of the Karmas he has performed in this birth. In this way, the Jiva gets body after body. **104.** Just as a man puts aside worn out clothes and puts on new ones, just like that the spirit within discards a body that has become decrepit and assumes a new body. This is an eternal process. **105.** What reason is there to be sorrowful because of this phenomenon? The spirit (Atman) never dies, is never born and it never grows **(106-107).** The spirit (Atman) that is embodied in one is the Supreme non-dual Self itself. He is devoid of the six forms of transformations. He is of the nature of Truth, Consciousness and Bliss—the witness of Buddhi and other changeful layers of personality. Free from dissolution, he is ever the same. Knowing full well that the Atman is like this, abandon grief and proceed to do what is next required of you. **108.** O noble one! Take the body of your father from the vessel of oil in which it is preserved, and along with your ministers and myself, proceed to perform all the usual funeral obsequies."

109. Abandoning the grief born of ignorance as a result of the preceptor's above instructions, Bharata performed all the funeral obsequies of his father in the proper form. **110.** He cremated the body

एकादशेऽहनि प्राप्ते ब्राह्मणान्वेदपारगान् । भोजयामास विधिवच्छतशोऽथ सहस्रशः ॥ 111
उद्दिश्य पितरं तत्र ब्राह्मणेभ्यो धनं बहु । ददौ गवां सहस्राणि ग्रामान् रत्नाम्बराणि च॥112
अवसत्स्वगृहे यत्र राममेवानुचिन्तयन् । वसिष्ठेन सह भ्रात्रा मन्त्रिभिः परिवारितः ॥ 113

रामेऽरण्यं प्रयाते सह जनकसुता-लक्ष्मणाभ्यां सुघोरं
माता मे राक्षसीव प्रदहति हृदयं दर्शनादेव सद्यः ।
गच्छाम्यारण्यमद्य स्थिरमतिरखिलं दूरतोऽपास्य राज्यं
रामं सीतासमेतं स्मितरुचिरमुखं नित्यमेवानुसेवे ॥ 114

इति श्रीमदध्यात्मरामायणे उमामहेश्वरसंवादे
अयोध्याकाण्डे सप्तमः सर्गः ॥ ७ ॥

of his father, who had performed many fire sacrifices, according to the rules of the scriptures as expounded by the preceptor. **111.** On the eleventh day after cremation he duly fed hundreds and thousands of holy men, who were versed in all the Vedas. **112.** In the name of his father, he gave them also many gifts—money, herds of cattle, villages, and bejewelled clothes. **113.** Surrounded by his ministers, besides the preceptor Vasishtha, he lived with his brother Satrughna in the palace, constantly thinking of Rama. **114.** He thought: "My heart burns with unbearable feelings as with fire, when I think of the circumstances under which Rama along with Sita and Lakshmana had to go to the forest and when I see the face of that demoness of my mother who is the cause of all this tragedy. So with a firm resolution, I shall abandon this kingdom and everything connected with it, and go to the forest to be in constant attendance on Rama, whose face is attractive by the bewitching smile playing on it."

अटष्मः सर्गः

वसिष्ठो मुनिभिः सार्धं मन्त्रिभिः परिवारितः । राज्ञः सभां देवसभासन्निभामविशद्विभुः ॥ 1
तत्रासने समासीनश्चतुर्मुख इवापरः । आनीय भरतं तत्र उपवेश्य सहानुजम् ॥ 2
अब्रवीद्वचनं देशकालोचितमरिन्दमम् । वत्स राज्येऽभिषेक्ष्यामस्त्वामद्य पितृशासनात्॥ 3

Chapter 8

BHARATA ON THE TRAILS OF RAMA

Bharata on the way to the forest to fetch Rama (1-14)

1. The great Vasishta accompanied by the sages and surrounded by the ministers entered the royal assembly which resembled the celestial assembly itself. **(2-3).** The preceptor Vasishtha now seated himself in the assembly even like Brahmā himself and directed

कैकेय्या याचितं राज्यं त्वदर्थे पुरुषर्षभ । सत्यसन्धो दशरथः प्रतिज्ञाय ददौ किल ॥ 4
अभिषेको भवत्वद्य मुनिभिर्मन्त्रपूर्वकम् । तत्श्रुत्वा भरतोऽप्याह मम राज्येन किं मुने॥ 5
रामो राजाधिराजश्च वयं तस्यैव किङ्कराः । श्वः प्रभाते गमिष्यामो राममानेतुमञ्जसा ॥ 6
अहं यूयं मातरश्च कैकेयीं राक्षसीं विना । हनिष्याम्यधुनैवाहं कैकेयीं मातृगन्धिनीम् ॥ 7
किन्तु मां नो रघुश्रेष्ठः स्त्रीहन्तारं सहिष्यते । तच्छ्वो भूते गमिष्यामि पादचारेण दण्डकान् । 8
शत्रुघ्नसहितस्तूर्णं यूयमायात वा न वा । रामो यथा वने यातस्तथाहं वल्कलाम्बरः ॥ 9
फलमूलकृताहारः शत्रुघ्नसहितो मुने । भूमिशायी जटाधारी यावद्रामो निवर्तते ॥ 10
इति निश्चित्य भरतस्तूष्णीमेवावतस्थिवान् । साधुसाध्विति तं सर्वे प्रशशंसुर्मुदान्विताः ॥ 11
ततः प्रभाते भरतं गच्छन्तं सर्वसैनिकाः । अनुजग्मुः सुमन्त्रेण नोदिताः साश्वकुञ्जराः ॥12
कौसल्याद्या राजदारा वसिष्ठप्रमुखा द्विजाः । छादयन्तो भुवं सर्वे पृष्ठतः पार्श्वतोऽग्रतः ॥ 13
श्रृङ्गवेरपुरं गत्वा गङ्गाकूले समन्ततः । उवास महती सेना शत्रुघ्नपरिचोदिता ॥ 14

Bharata along with his brother to the other seats and said to that heroic prince the following words appropriate for the occasion. He said, l, "O dear one! I am going to install you on the throne, after anointing you, as ordered by your father. **4.** O noble one! The Queen Kaikeyi requested the King to give you this kingdom and the truthful Raja Dasaratha in fulfilment of his promise, informed us that he had granted the request. **5.** Therefore, let the installation ceremony now start in this assembly of sages to the accompaniment of the chanting of appropriate Mantras." Hearing these words, Bharata said, "O great sage! Of what use is this kingdom to me? **(6-11)** Rama, the king of kings, is the ruler of us all, and we are his servants. Immediately, tomorrow morning itself, I shall go to fetch Rama in the company of you all and my mothers except that demoness of a Kaikeyi. I would have killed that so-called mother of mine now itself, had it not been for the fact that Rama would not approve the slaughter of a woman. Tomorrow itself at sun rise, I shall start with Satrughna to the Dandaka forest on foot, whether you all are ready to accompany me or not. In the same manner in which Rama went to the forest, I shall proceed—wearing the tree-bark cloth, eating fruits and roots, sleeping on the ground and having matted locks. I shall observe this rule until Rama returns." Announcing his resolution to this effect, Bharata resumed silence. All the sages, thereupon acclaimed his resolution.

12. When Bharata started in the morning as announced, the minister Sumantra directed the army with its regiments of horses and elephants to follow him. **13.** The royal ladies like Kausalya, the sages like Vasishtha and all others moved behind and on the sides of Bharata, all together covering an extensive area of land. **14.** Bharata and his followers now reached the town of Sringavera. The men of the army and the others who were under the command of

आगतं भरतं श्रुत्वा गुहः शङ्कितमानसः । महत्या सेनया सार्धमागतो भरतः किल ॥ 15
पापं कर्तुं न वा याति रामस्याविदितात्मनः । गत्वा तद्धृदयं ज्ञेयं यदि शुद्धस्तरिष्यति ॥ 16
गङ्गां नोचेत्समाकृष्य नावस्तिष्ठन्तु सायुधाः । ज्ञातयो मे समायत्ताः पश्यन्तः सर्वतोदिशम् ॥17
इति सर्वान्समादिश्य गुहो भरतमागतः । उपायनानि संगृह्य विविधानि बहून्यपि ॥ 18
प्रययौ ज्ञातिभिः सार्धं बहुभिर्विविधायुधैः । निवेद्योपायनान्यग्रे भरतस्य समन्ततः ॥ 19
दृष्ट्वा भरतमासीनं सानुजं सह मन्त्रिभिः । चीराम्बरं घनश्यामं जटामुकुटधारिणम् ॥ 20
राममेवानुशोचन्तं रामरामेति वादिनम् । ननाम शिरसा भूमौ गुहोऽहमिति चाब्रवीत् 21
शीघ्रमुत्थाप्य भरतो गाढमालिङ्ग्य सादरम् । पृष्ट्वा नामयमव्यग्रः सखायमिदमब्रवीत् ॥ 22
भ्रातस्त्वं राघवेणात्र समेतः समवस्थितः । रामेणालिङ्गितः सार्द्रनयनेनामलात्मना ॥ 23
धन्योऽसि कृतकृत्योऽसि यत्त्वया परिभाषितः । रामो राजीवपत्राक्षो लक्ष्मणेन च सीतया ॥ 24
यत्र रामस्त्वया दृष्टस्तत्र मां नय सुव्रत । सीतया सहितो यत्र सुप्तस्तद्दर्शयस्व मे ॥ 25

Satrughna camped on the bank of the Ganga.

Meeting with Guha (15-41)

(15-16) Hearing the arrival of Bharata in his principality, Guha with a suspicious mind reflected: "Bharata has arrived with a big army. Has he come to do some mischief to Rama, who does not know anything about his movements? I must know what is in his mind. If his intentions are good, I shall help him to cross the Ganga. **17.** If his intentions are mischievous, myself and my relatives and dependants shall withdraw all boats from the river and with weapons in hand guard the approaches on all sides." **18.** Directing all his followers in this way, Guha now went to where Bharata was camping, carrying with him many objects of presentation in his hand. **19.** It was in the company of a large number of friends and dependants, all bearing arms, that he went to see Bharata with those objects of presentation, which he now placed in front of him. **(20-21).** Guha saw Bharata there in the company of his brother and ministers—Bharata blue in complexion like a cloud, wearing a crown of matted locks, donned in tree-bark garment and constantly uttering the name of Rama. Guha now prostrated before him and announced himself by name. **22.** Bharata at once lifted him up and embraced him with great affection and made enquiries about his welfare. Then he spoke in a very peaceful tone the following words to that friend. **(23-25).** He said, "O brother! Is it in this place that you met Rama, the scion of Raghu's line? Is it in this place that Rama of kindly look and pure heart embraced you? You are, indeed, blessed and you have achieved the purpose of your life in that you were spoken to by the lotus-eyed Rama. Show me the spot where you met Rama along with Lakshmana and Sita, and conversed

त्वं रामस्य प्रियतमो भक्तिमानसि भाग्यवान् । इति संस्मृत्य संस्मृत्य रामं साश्रुविलोचनः ॥ 26

गुहेन सहितस्तत्र यत्र रामः स्थितो निशि । ययौ ददर्श शयनस्थलं कुशसमास्तृतम् ॥ 27

सीताऽऽभरणसंलग्नस्वर्णबिन्दुभिरर्चितम् । दुःखसन्तप्तहृदयो भरतः पर्यदेवयत् ॥ 28

अहोऽतिसुकुमारी या सीता जनकनन्दिनी । प्रासादे रत्नपर्यङ्के कोमलास्तरणे शुभे ॥ 29

रामेण सहिता शेते सा कथं कुशविष्टरे । सीता रामेण सहिता दुःखेन मम दोषतः ॥ 30

धिङ्मां जातोऽस्मि कैकेय्यां पापराशिसमानतः । मन्निमित्तमिदं क्लेशं रामस्य परमात्मनः ॥ 31

अहोऽतिसफलं जन्म लक्ष्मणस्य महात्मनः । राममेव सदान्वेति वनस्थमपि हृष्टधीः ॥ 32

अहं रामस्य दासा ये तेषां दासस्य किङ्करः । यदि स्यां सफलं जन्म मम भूयान्न संशयः ॥ 33

भ्रातर्जानासि यदि तत्कथयस्व ममाखिलम् । यत्र तिष्ठति तत्राहं गच्छाम्यानेतुमञ्जसा ॥ 34

गुहस्तं शुद्धहृदयं ज्ञात्वा सस्नेहमब्रवीत् । देव त्वमेव धन्योऽसि यस्य ते भक्तिरीदृशी ॥ 35

रामे राजीवपत्राक्षे सीतायां लक्ष्मणे तथा । चित्रकूटाद्रिनिकटे मन्दाकिन्यविदूरतः ॥ 36

मुनीनामाश्रमपदे रामस्तिष्ठति सानुजः । जानक्या सहितो नन्दात्सुखमास्ते किल प्रभुः ॥ 37

तत्र गच्छामहे शीघ्रं गङ्गां तर्तुमिहार्हसि । इत्युक्त्वा त्वरितं गत्वा नावः पञ्चशतानि ह ॥ 38

समानयत्ससैन्यस्य तर्तुं गङ्गां महानदीम् । स्वयमेवानिनायैकां राजनावं गुहस्तदा ॥ 39

with them. Lead me to that place where Rama and Sita slept. **(26-28).** You are extremely dear to Rama, and you are devoted to him too." Remembering Rama again and again in this way, Bharata, with tears brimming over his eyes. went in the company of Guha to the spot where Rama spent the night. Seeing there the grass bed, gleaming here and there with the gold-dust from Sita's jewels, Bharata, with a heart smitten with sorrow, wept bitterly. **(29-30).** He began to bemoan: "Sita, the tender-bodied daughter of Janaka, was always accustomed to sleep on golden cots with soft mattresses on the upper floor of the palace. Alas! That Sita, because of my fault, has now to sleep along with Rama on a bed of grass. How could she stand this ordeal? **31.** It is because of my enormous sin that I have been born as the son of Kaikeyi. I have been the cause of all this woe to Rama who is the Supreme Being Himself. **32.** The birth of high-souled Lakshmana is indeed fruitful. Though he is staying in the forest, he is able to follow Rama always. **33.** My birth would have been fulfilled, if I could have served even the servants of Rama's servants. **34.** Dear brother! If you know anything about Rama, tell all that to me. I shall go to him wherever he is, and get him back at once."

(35-37). Finding Bharata's motives to be pure, Guha said to him lovingly, "Lord, you are indeed fortunate to have this kind of devotion to the lotus-eyed Rama, Sita and Lakshmana. He is now staying along with Sita and brother Lakshmana in a colony inhabited by ascetics near the Chitrakuta mountain and not far from the Ganga. **(38-39).** We shall cross the Ganga here and

आरोप्य भरतं तत्र शत्रुघ्नं राममातरम् । वसिष्ठं च तथान्यत्र कैकेयीं चान्ययोषितः ॥ 40
तीर्त्वा गङ्गां ययौ शीघ्रं भरद्वाजाश्रमं प्रति । दूरे स्थाप्य महासैन्यं भरतः सानुजो ययौ ॥ 41
आश्रमे मुनिमासीनं ज्वलन्तमिव पावकम् । दृष्ट्वा ननाम भरतः साष्टाङ्गमतिभक्तितः ॥ 42
ज्ञात्वा दाशरथिं प्रीत्या पूजयामास मौनिराट् । पप्रच्छ कुशलं दृष्ट्वा जटावल्कलधारिणम् ॥43
राज्यं प्रशासतस्तेऽद्य किमेतद्वल्कलादिकम् । आगतोऽसि किमर्थं त्वं विपिनं मुनिसेवितम् ॥ 44
भरद्वाजवचः श्रुत्वा भरतः साश्रुलोचनः । सर्वं जानासि भगवन् सर्वभूताशयस्थितः ॥ 45
तथापि पृच्छसे किञ्चित्तदनुग्रह एव मे । कैकेय्या मत्कृतं कर्म रामराज्यविघातनम् ॥ 46
वनवासादिकं वापि न हि जानामि किञ्चन । भवत्पादयुगं मेऽद्य प्रमाणं मुनिसत्तम ॥ 47
इत्युक्त्वा पादयुगलं मुनेः स्पृष्ट्वाऽऽर्तमानसः । ज्ञातुमर्हसि मां देव शुद्धो वाशुद्ध एव वा ॥ 48
मम राज्येन किं स्वामिन् रामे तिष्ठति राजनि । किङ्करोऽहं मुनिश्रेष्ठ रामचन्द्रस्य शाश्वतः ॥ 49
अतो गत्वा मुनिश्रेष्ठ रामस्य चरणान्तिके । पतित्वा राज्यसम्भारान् समर्प्यात्रैव राघवम् ॥50
अभिषेक्ष्ये वसिष्ठाद्यैः पौरजानपदैः सह । नेष्येऽयोध्यां रमानाथं दासः सेवेतिनीचवत् ॥ 51

reach that place soon." With these words, he quickly went and gathered together five hundred boats for Bharata to cross the river with his troops. Guha himself brought a royal boat for Bharata's use. **(40-41).** Seating Bharata, Satrughna, Rama's mother and Vasishtha in that, and Kaikeyi and the other women in another, he crossed the Ganga and went towards the Ashrama of Bharadwaja. Stationing the army at a distance, Bharata along with his brother went to that Ashrama.

Bharata at Bharadwaja's Ashrama
(47-63)

42. Seeing sage Bharadwaja sitting there, radiant like fire, Bharata prostrated himself before him with great reverence. **43.** Hearing that the visitor, though donning tree-bark and matted locks, was the son of King Dasaratha, the sage received him with great joy and made enquiries about his welfare. **44.** The sage asked him, "You are now ruling the kingdom. How is it that you have put on the tree-bark garment? What is it that brings you to this forest inhabited by ascetics?"

(45-48) Hearing the words of Bharadwaja, Bharata said with tears flowing from his eyes. "O holy one! You, who can read the minds of all beings, are already acquianted with everything. Yet you are making this enquiry of me, this is indeed my good fortune, I had not the least inkling of the evil designs of Kaikeyi, by which Rama was expelled to the forest. O great sage! Your holy self is today the witness of this fact." With these words, Bharata, in a mood of extreme sorrow, held the feet of the sage and said, "O Master! You are capable of understanding whether I am innocent or not. **49.** O holy one! When Rama, the rightful king, is alive, what have I got to do with the kingdom? I am only the eternal servant of Rama. **(50-51).** O great sage! Therefore, I shall go to the place where Rama is and

इत्युदीरितमाकर्ण्य भरतस्य वचो मुनिः । आलिङ्ग्य मूर्ध्न्यवघ्राय प्रशशंस सविस्मयः ॥ 52
वत्स ज्ञातं पुरैवैतद्भविष्यं ज्ञानचक्षुषा । मा शुचस्त्वं परो भक्तः श्रीरामे लक्ष्मणादपि ॥ 53
आतिथ्यं कर्तुमिच्छामि ससैन्यस्य तवानघ । अद्य भुक्त्वा ससैन्यस्त्वं श्वो गन्ता रामसन्निधिम् ॥
यथाऽऽज्ञापयति भवांस्तथेति भरतोऽब्रवीत् । भरद्वाजस्तवपः स्पृष्ट्वा मौनी होमगृहे स्थितः ॥55
दध्यौ कामदुघां कामवर्षिणीं कामदो मुनिः । असृजत्कामधुक् सर्वं यथाकाममलौकिकम् ॥ 56
भरतस्य ससैन्यस्य यथेष्टं च मनोरथम् । यथा ववर्ष सकलं तृप्तास्ते सर्वसैनिकाः ॥ 57
वसिष्ठं पूजयित्वाग्रे शास्त्रदृष्टेन कर्मणा । पश्चात्ससैन्यं भरतं तर्पयामास योगिराट् ॥ 58
उषित्वा दिनमेकं तु आश्रमे स्वर्गसन्निभे । अभिवाद्य पुनः प्रातर्भरद्वाजं सहानुजः ॥ 59
भरतस्तु कृतानुज्ञः प्रययौ रामसन्निधिम् ।
चित्रकूटमनुप्राप्य दूरे संस्थाप्य सैनिकान् । रामसंदर्शनाकाङ्क्षी प्रययौ भरतः स्वयम् ॥ 60
शत्रुघ्नेन सुमन्त्रेण गुहेन च परन्तपः । तपस्विमण्डलं सर्वं विचिन्वानो न्यवर्तत ॥ 61
अदृष्ट्वा रामभवनमपृच्छदृषिमण्डलम् । कुत्रास्ते सीतया सार्धं लक्ष्मणेन रघूत्तमः ॥ 62

fall at his feet. Along with Vasishtha and the leading citizens, I shall have the installation ceremony of Rama performed here itself with all the necessary materials I have brought with me, and lead him, the consort of Ramā, to Ayodhya as the king. I shall remain with him as the humblest of his servants."

52. Amazed at these words of Bharata, the sage embraced him and approved of his words. **53.** He said, "Dear one! With the eye of wisdom, I have already been able to know the events that were to happen. Be not sorry. Your devotion to Rama is indeed greater than that of Lakshmana even.

54. O sinless one! I wish to extend hospitality to you and your following. So you have your food and stay here tonight and go to see Rama tomorrow."

(55-56). Bharata agreed to this proposal. Thereupon, Bharadwaja went to his sacrificial chamber in silence, and desirous of meeting all the needs of his guests, meditated on Kamadhenu, the heavenly cow of plenty. And Kamadhenu created by her mysterious power all the requirements of the party without any physical aid. **57.** According to Bharata's requirements, all things appeared in abundance to the great satisfaction of the troops constituting Bharata's retinue. **58.** The great Yogi Bharadwaja first extended his hospitality to Vasishtha according to the Sastras, and then did the same to Bharata and to the other members of his party.

(59-62). Afer spending the night in that heavenly Ashrama, Bharata did obeisance to the sage in the morning and with his permission started along with his brother to the presence of Rama. Reaching Chitrakuta he stationed his army at a distance, and in great eagerness to meet Rama, went along with Satrughna, Sumantra and Guha to the colony of ascetics staying there. He searched for Rama's residence everywhere in that place, but failing to locate it, made enquiries

ऊचुरग्रे गिरेः पश्चाद्गङ्गाया उत्तरे तटे । विविक्तं रामसदनं रम्यं काननमण्डितम् ॥ 63
सफलैराम्रपनसैः कदलीखण्डसंवृतम् । चम्पकैः कोविदारैश्च पुन्नागैर्विपुलैस्तथा ॥ 64
एवं दर्शितमालोक्य मुनिभिर्भरतोऽग्रतः । हर्षाद् ययौ रघुश्रेष्ठभवनं मन्त्रिणा सह ॥ 65
ददर्श दूरादतिभासुरं शुभं रामस्य गेहं मुनिवृन्दसेवितम् ।
वृक्षाग्रसंलग्नसुवल्कलाजिनं रामाभिरामं भरतः सहानुजः ॥ 66

इति श्रीमदध्यात्मरामायणे उमामहेश्वरसंवादे
अयोध्याकाण्डे अष्टमः सर्गः ॥ ८ ॥

of the Rishis there as to where Rama with Sita and Lakshmana was staying. (63-65). They told him, "There on the northern side of the Ganga, behind the mountain, you will see a solitary place surrounded by a thick growth of several fruit-laden trees like Amra, Panasa, Punnaga, Kovidara, Champaka and plantain. There you will find before you, Rama's residence." Thereupon, Bharata proceeded in great joy to that place with his brother and ministers. **66.** Bharata and his brother Satrughna saw at a distance, the glorious residence of Rama frequented by ascetics, where the tops of trees were distinguished by the tree-bark clothes and deer-skin hung on them for sunning.

नवमः सर्गः

अथ गत्वाऽऽश्रमपदसमीपं भरतो मुदा । सीतारामपदैर्युक्तं पवित्रमतिशोभनम् ॥ 1
स तत्र वज्राङ्कुशवारिजाञ्चितध्वजादिचिह्नानि पदानि सर्वतः ।
ददर्श रामस्य भुवोऽतिमङ्गलान्यचेष्टयत्पादरजःसु सानुजः ॥ 2
अहो सुधन्योऽहममूनि रामपादारविन्दाङ्कितभूतलानि ।
पश्यामि यत्पादरजो विमृग्यं ब्रह्मादिदेवैः श्रुतिभिश्च नित्यम् ॥ 3

Chapter 9

BHARATA'S RETURN AND AFTER

Performance of Dasaratha's Funeral Rites (1-20)

1. Now Bharata in great joy reached the precincts of that holy Ashrama of Rama, the ground of which was marked by the foot-prints of Rama and Sita. **2.** Seeing those footprints, with marks of Vajra, Ankusa, lotus, flag etc.—the merit-generating marks of Rama's feet—Bharata and his brother Satrughna covered themselves with the dust carrying these impressions. **3.** Bharata said, "What a great good fortune! I am indeed blessed to see this ground rendered

इत्यद्भुतप्रेमरसाप्लुताशयो विगाढचेता रघुनाथभावने ।
आनन्दजाश्रुस्नपितस्तनान्तरः शनैरवापाश्रमसन्निधिं हरेः ॥ 4
स तत्र दृष्ट्वा रघुनाथमास्थितं दूर्वादलश्यामलमायतेक्षणम् ।
जटाकिरीटं नववल्कलाम्बरं प्रसन्नवक्त्रं तरुणारुणद्युतिम् ॥ 5
विलोकयन्तं जनकात्मजां शुभां सौमित्रिणा सेवितपादपङ्कजम् ।
तदाभिदुद्राव रघूत्तमं शुचा हर्षाच्च तत्पादयुगं त्वराग्रहीत् ॥ 6
रामस्तमाकृष्य सुदीर्घबाहुदोर्भ्यां परिष्वज्य सिषिञ्च नेत्रजैः ।
जलैरथाङ्कोपरि संन्यवेशयत् पुनः पुनः संपरिषस्वजे विभुः ॥ 7
अथ ता मातरः सर्वाः समाजग्मुस्त्वरान्विताः । राघवं द्रष्टुकामास्तास्तृषार्ता गौर्यथा जलम् ॥ 8
रामः स्वमातरं वीक्ष्य द्रुतमुत्थाय पादयोः । ववन्दे साश्रु सा पुत्रमालिङ्ग्यातीव दुःखिता ॥ 9
इतराश्च तथा नत्वा जननी रघुनन्दनः । ततः समागतं दृष्ट्वा वसिष्ठं मुनिपुङ्गवम् ॥ 10
साष्टाङ्गं प्रणिपत्याह धन्योऽस्मीति पुनः पुनः । यथार्हमुपवेश्याह सर्वानेव रघूद्वहः ॥ 11
पिता मे कुशली किं वा मां किमाहातिदुःखितः । वसिष्ठस्तमुवाचेदं पिता ते रघुनन्दन ॥ 12
त्वद्वियोगाभितप्तात्मा त्वामेव परिचिन्तयन् । रामरामेति सीतेति लक्ष्मणेति ममार ह ॥ 13

holy by the feet of Rama, the dust of which is the quest of Brahma and other Devas as also of the Vedas." **4.** With his mind overflowing by the out-burst of divine love, his chest wet with tears of joy and his attention concentrated on Rama, Bharata slowly approached the residence of Rama, who was none but Sri Hari Himself. **(5-6).** There he saw Rama sitting along with Sita and attended upon by Lakshmana—Rama who was of blue complexion like Durva grass, who had long eyes, who wore a crown of matted locks on his head, who had on him a tree-bark garment as dress, whose face was calm and placid, and who had the radiance of the mid-day sun. Overcome by both sorrow and joy at the same time, Bharata hurried towards him and prostrating himself before him, held his feet with both his hands. **7.** Rama, who was possessed of long arms, now lifted him up, embraced him, and wetted his body with tears. Seating him in his lap, Rama, that All-pervading Being, embraced him again and again. **8.** As a thirsty cow hurries towards a water receptacle, the mothers of Rama, who were anxious to meet him, also went towards him quickly. **9.** Seeing his mother, Rama got up in haste and with tears flowing from his eyes, prostrated himself at her feet, and she embraced her son, extremely grief-stricken. **(10-11).** Rama did obeisance to his other mothers also. Seeing Vasishtha in the party, he made a full prostration before him and said that he was indeed blessed to see the sage. Then he seated them all in proper seats and said as follows: **(12-13).** He said, "How is my father? Sorrow-stricken by my departure, what message

श्रुत्वा तत्कर्णशूलाभं गुरोर्वचनमञ्जसा । हा हतोऽस्मीति पतितो रुदन् रामः सलक्ष्मणः॥ 14
ततोऽनुरुरुदुः सर्वा मातरश्च तथापरे । हा तात मां परित्यज्य क्व गतोऽसि घृणाकर ॥
अनाथोऽस्मि महाबाहो मां को वा लालयेदितः । सीता च लक्ष्मणश्चैव विलेपतुरता भृशम् ॥
वसिष्ठः शान्तवचनैः शमयामास तां शुचम् । ततो मन्दाकिनीं गत्वा स्नात्वा ते वीतकल्मषाः॥ 17
राज्ञे ददुर्जलं तत्र सर्वे ते जलकाङ्क्षिणे । पिण्डान्निर्वापयामास रामो लक्ष्मणसंयुतः ॥ 18
इङ्गुदीफलपिण्याकरचितान्मधुसम्प्लुतान् । वयं यदन्नाः पितरस्तदन्नाः स्मृतिनोदिताः ॥ 19
इति दुःखाश्रुपूर्णाक्षः पुनः स्नात्वा गृहं ययौ । सर्वे रुदित्वा सुचिरं स्नात्वा जग्मुस्तदाश्रमम् ॥20
तस्मिंस्तु दिवसे सर्वे उपासं प्रचक्रिरे । ततः परेद्युर्विमले स्नात्वा मन्दाकिनीजले ॥ 21
उपविष्टं समागम्य भरतो राममब्रवीत् । राम राम महाभाग स्वात्मानमभिषेचय ॥ 22
राज्यं पालय पित्र्यं ते ज्येष्ठस्त्वं मे पिता तथा । क्षत्रियाणामयं धर्मो यत्प्रजापरिपालनम् ॥ 23

has he sent to me through you?" To him Vasishtha replied, "O leader of Raghu's line! Your father, burning as it were in the fire of sorrow, was thinking constantly of you and always calling out, 'O, Rama! O Sita! O Lakshmana!' Alas! he is now dead."

14. These words of the preceptor went into Rama's ears like the piercing pain of an ear-cancer. Calling out, "O father! O father! woe unto me," he fell on the ground, and along with Lakshmana, began to weep. **15.** He cried aloud, "O merciful father! Where have you gone abandoning me?" Following him, all his mothers and others began to cry. **16.** He bemoaned saying, "O noble one! I am now orphaned. Who will hereafter fondle me?" Following him, Sita and Lakshmana cried out even more loudly. **(17-18).** Vasishtha now assuaged their grief with his consoling words. Then, they all went to the river and purifying themselves by bathing made offerings of water to the king as desired by him at the time of death. Lakshmana and Rama also performed the rite of offering morsels of food to the departed. **19.** The balls of food that they offered were made of the flour of a certain forest plant mixed with honey and rolled into lumps—a food which all ascetics took. "The scriptures have declared that we should offer to our ancestors whatever type of food we are taking"—with this thought they consoled themselves. **20.** After making this offering to the departed, Rama again took his bath, and weeping, returned to his Ashrama. After weeping for a considerable time, all the others also took their bath again and went back to the Ashrama.

Bharata Persuaded to Return (21-53)

(21-23). That day after the performance of the funeral obsequies, they all observed fast. Next day, after a bath in the pure water of the river, Bharata said to Rama who was seated, "O noble one! Permit us to have you installed as King. Come and rule over the kingdom that has come to you from our father. You are elder to me and so equal to father. So, following the Dharma of Kshatriyas, perform the

इष्ट्वा यज्ञैर्बहुविधैः पुत्रानुत्पाद्य तन्तवे । राज्ये पुत्रं समारोप्य गमिष्यसि ततो वनम् ॥ 24
इदानीं वनवासस्य कालो नैव प्रसीद मे । मातुर्मे दुष्कृतं किञ्चित्स्मर्तुं नार्हसि पाहि नः ॥ 25
इत्युक्त्वा चरणौ भ्रातुः शिरस्याधाय भक्तितः । रामस्य पुरतः साक्षाद्दण्डवत्पतितो भुवि ॥ 26
उत्थाप्य राघवः शीघ्रमारोप्याङ्केऽतिभक्तितः । उवाच भरतं रामः स्नेहार्द्रनयनः शनैः ॥ 27
शृणु वत्स प्रवक्ष्यामि त्वयोक्तं यत्तथैव तत् । किन्तु मामब्रवीत्तातो नव वर्षाणि पञ्च च ॥ 28
उषित्वा दण्डकारण्ये पुरं पश्चात्समाविश । इदानीं भरतायेदं राज्यं दत्तं मयाखिलम् ॥ 29
ततः पित्रैव सुव्यक्तं राज्यं दत्तं तवैव हि । दण्डकारण्यराज्यं मे दत्तं पित्रा तथैव च ॥ 30
अतः पितुर्वचः कार्यमावाभ्यामतियत्नतः । पितुर्वचनमुल्लङ्घ्य स्वतन्त्रो यस्तु वर्तते ॥ 31
स जीवन्नेव मृतको देहान्ते निरयं व्रजेत् । तस्माद्राज्यं प्रशाधि त्वं वयं दण्डकपालकाः ॥ 32

भरतस्त्वब्रवीद्रामं कामुको मूढधीः पिता ।
स्त्रीजितो भ्रान्तहृदय उन्मत्तो यदि वक्ष्यति । तत्सत्यमिति न ग्राह्यं भ्रान्तवाक्यं यथा सुधीः ॥ 33

श्रीराम उवाच

न स्त्रीजितः पिता ब्रूयान्न कामी नैव मूढधीः । पूर्वं प्रतिश्रुतं तस्य सत्यवादी ददौ भयात् ॥ 34

duty of ruling over the subjects. **(24-26).** After performing many Yajnas and procreating sons to continue your line, the proper time for you to abandon everything would come, then entrusting the responsibility of the kingdom to your son and successor, you can go to the forest: not now. Be gracious towards me. Please forget the evil deeds of my mother. Deign to come and rule over us all." Saying so, he placed his brother's feet on his own head and lay prostrate like a stick before him.

27. Rama quickly raised him up and seating him in his lap said to him slowly with his heart melting in affection. **(28-32)** "Dear brother!" said he, "hear what I say. There is much truth in what you have represented. Yet it is a fact that our father ordered me to spend fourteen years in the Dandaka forest and then only return to the city; and for that period, he has assigned the kingdom to you, Bharata. So it is clear that the kingdom has been given to you by our father himself. And to me likewise has been assigned the kingdom of Dandaka forest by our father. It is therefore the duty of us both to obey strictly the command of our father. One who disobeys his father and goes about doing things according to his own sweet will, is as good as dead even while living. He is sure to be consigned to hell after death. Therefore, you rule over the kingdom, and we shall look after the forest.

33. To this Bharata replied: "Our father when he gave the order was under infatuation for a woman, a victim of passion, and therefore out of his senses. His words need not be taken seriously any more than of any demented person." **34.** Rama corrected him saying, "You cannot say that our father was infatuated by a woman, or was a victim of passion and out of his senses. Truthful by nature, he was afraid of being

असत्याद्भीतिरधिका महतां नरकादपि । करोमीत्यहमप्येतत्सत्यं तस्यै प्रतिश्रुतम् ॥ 35
कथं वाक्यमहं कुर्यामसत्यं राघवो हि सन् । इत्युदीरितमाकर्ण्य रामस्य भरतोऽब्रवीत् ॥ 36
श्रीभरत उवाच
तथैव चीरवसनो वने वत्स्यामि सुव्रत । चतुर्दश समास्त्वं तु राज्यं कुरु यथासुखम् ॥ 37
श्रीराम उवाच
पित्रा दत्तं तवैवैतद्राज्यं मह्यं वनं ददौ । व्यत्ययं यद्यहं कुर्यामसत्यं पूर्ववत् स्थितम् ॥ 38
अहमप्यागमिष्यामि सेवे त्वां लक्ष्मणो यथा । नोचेत्प्रायोपवेशेन त्यजाम्येतत्कलेवरम् ॥ 39
इत्येवं निश्चयं कृत्वा दर्भानास्तीर्य चातपे । मनसापि विनिश्चित्य प्राङ्मुखोपविवेश सः ॥ 40
भरतस्यापि निर्बन्धं दृष्ट्वा रामोऽतिविस्मितः । नेत्रान्तसंज्ञां गुरवे चकार रघुनन्दनः ॥ 41
एकान्ते भरतं प्राह वसिष्ठो ज्ञानिनां वरः । वत्स गुह्यं शृणुष्वेदं मम वाक्यात्सुनिश्चितम् ॥42
रामो नारायणः साक्षाद् ब्रह्मणा याचितः पुरा । रावणस्य वधार्थाय जातो दशरथात्मजः ॥ 43
योगमायापि सीतेति जाता जनकनन्दिनी । शेषोऽपि लक्ष्मणो जातो राममन्वेति सर्वदा ॥44
रावणं हन्तुकामास्ते गमिष्यन्ति न संशयः । कैकेय्या वरदानादि यद्यन्निष्ठुरभाषणम् ॥ 45
सर्वं देवकृतं नोचेदेवं सा भाषयेत्कथम् । तस्मात्त्यजाग्रहं तात रामस्य विनिवर्तने ॥ 46

false to his plighted word if he failed to give to Kaikeyi the boon he had promised her long ago. **(35-36).** Noble personages fear untruth more than hell. I too have undertaken before Kaikeyi that I shall do as ordered by our father. Being one born in Raghu's line, how can I break the tradition of my family and fail to fulfil a promise?" Hearing these words of Rama, Bharata replied: **37.** "O truthful one! On your behalf I shall then live in the forest for fourteen years, donning the ascetic's tree-bark cloth. You rule over the kingdom and live happily." **38.** "The kingdom has been assigned to you by our father," said Rama, rejecting this proposal, "and to me he has given the forest. An agreed mutual exchange of these gifts will not save the situation, as even this would involve a breach of promise." **(39-40).** Bharata now pleaded: "In that case I too shall stay in the forest with you like Lakshmana and serve you. If you decide otherwise, I shall end my life by fasting." Resolving like that, he had some Darbha grass spread in the sun and sat on it facing the east.

41. Seeing that Bharata was determined about this course of action, Rama, by a sign of his eyes, requested the preceptor Vasishtha to intervene and save the situation. **42.** Then Vasishtha took Bharata aside to a solitary place and said to him: "Dear boy! Hear from me a secret concerning certain unalterable matters. **43.** Rama is really Lord Narayana Himself. Requested by Brahma He has incarnated Himself as the son of Dasaratha for destroying Ravana. **44.** And Yogamaya, the Sakti of Vishnu, has embodied Herself as Sita, the daughter of Janaka. Adisesha, the mystic serpent serving as Vishnu's bed, is born as Lakshmana in order to follow and attend on Rama always **(45-46).** They are therefore bound to proceed onward for the destruction of

निवर्तस्व महासैन्यैर्भ्रातृभिः सहितः पुरम् । रावणं सकुलं हत्वा शीघ्रमेत्रागमिष्यति ॥ 47
इति श्रुत्वा गुरोर्वाक्यं भरतो विस्मयान्वितः । गत्वा समीपं रामस्य विस्मयोत्फुल्ललोचनः ॥ 48
पादुके देहि राजेन्द्र राज्याय तव पूजिते । तयोः सेवां करोम्येव यावदागमनं तव ॥ 49
इत्युक्त्वा पादुके दिव्ये योजयामास पादयोः । रामस्य ते ददौ रामो भरतायातिभक्तितः ॥ 50
गृहीत्वा पादुके दिव्ये भरतो रत्नभूषिते । रामं पुनः परिक्रम्य प्रणनाम पुनः पुनः ॥ 51
भरतः पुनराहेदं भक्त्या गद्गदया गिरा । नवपञ्चसमान्ते तु प्रथमे दिवसे यदि ॥ 52
नागमिष्यसि चेद्राम प्रविशामि महानलम् । बाढमित्येव तं रामो भरतं संन्यवर्तयत् ॥ 53
ससैन्यः सवसिष्ठश्च शत्रुघ्नसहितः सुधीः । मातृभिर्मन्त्रिभिः साधं गमनायोपचक्रमे ॥ 54
कैकेयी राममेकान्ते स्रवन्नेत्रजलाकुला । प्राञ्जलिः प्राह हे राम तव राज्यविघातनम् ॥55
कृतं मया दुष्टधिया मायामोहितचेतसा । क्षमस्व मम दौरात्म्यं क्षमासारा हि साधवः ॥56

Ravana. The gift of boon to Kaikeyi and her heartless words in this connection were all the result of the will of Providence. Had it not been for this, how could she have spoken what she did? Therefore, dear one, give up your idea of getting Rama back. **47.** Along with your army and your brother, you now go back to the city. After destroying Ravana along with all his tribe, Rama will return soon."

(48-49). Hearing these words of the teacher, Bharata was amazed, and with eyes widened by wonder, approached Rama and said: "O greatest of monarchs! Give me your worship-worthy footwear to serve as a symbol of your rulership over the kingdom. Until your return I shall rule as your servant through the service of your footwear representing you." **50.** With these words Bharata put on Rama's feet a magnificent pair of sandals and Rama taking them up returned them solemnly to Bharata. **51.** Now Bharata, receiving these sandals made of precious metals and studded with jewels, circumambulated Rama and made prostrations to him again and again. **(52-53).** Then Bharata said, with his voice choked with an outburst of devotion, "If you do not return to Ayodhya on the very first day after the period of fourteen years, I will enter into a well-lit fire." Rama accepted this prayer of Bharata and sent him back on that understanding.

Kaikeyi's conversion and hymn (54-65)

54. Bharata along with his army, preceptor Vasishtha, brother Satrughna, his mothers, and the ministers, was about to start on his return journey to Ayodhya. **(55-56).** Just then Kaikeyi in a highly distressed mood and with tears flowing from her eyes, called Rama aside and said to him in privacy: "O Rama! Under a spell of delusion my evil mind prompted me to obstruct Thy installation as the Yuvaraja. I beseech Thee to pardon me for the bad turn I did to Thee thereby. Forgiveness is the very nature of good

त्वं साक्षाद्विष्णुरव्यक्तः परमात्मा सनातनः ।
मायामानुषरूपेण मोहयस्यखिलं जगत् । त्वयैव प्रेरितो लोकः कुरुते साध्वसाधु वा ॥ 57
त्वदधीनमिदं विश्वमस्वतन्त्रं करोति किम् । यथा कृत्रिमनर्तक्यो नृत्यन्ति कुहकेच्छया ॥ 58
त्वदधीना तथा माया नर्तकी बहुरूपिणी । त्वयैव प्रेरिताहं च देवकार्यं करिष्यता ॥ 59
पापिष्ठं पापमनसा कर्माचरमरिन्दम । अद्य प्रतीतोऽसि मम देवानामप्यगोचरः ॥ 60
पाहि विश्वेश्वरानन्त जगन्नाथ नमोऽस्तु ते । छिन्धि स्नेहमयं पाशं पुत्रवित्तादिगोचरम् ॥ 61
त्वज्ज्ञानानलखड्गेन त्वामहं शरणं गता । कैकेय्या वचनं श्रुत्वा रामः सस्मितमब्रवीत् ॥ 62
यदाह मां महाभागे नानृतं सत्यमेव तत् । मयैव प्रेरिता वाणी तव वक्त्राद्विनिर्गता ॥ 63
देवकार्यार्थसिद्ध्यर्थमत्र दोषः कुतस्तव । गच्छ त्वं हृदि मां नित्यं भावयन्ती दिवानिशम् ॥
सर्वत्र विगतस्नेहा मद्भक्त्या मोक्ष्यसेऽचिरात् । अहं सर्वत्र समदृग् द्वेष्यो वा प्रिय एव वा ॥ 65
नास्ति मे कल्पकस्येव भजतोऽनुभजाम्यहम् । मन्मायामोहितधियो मामम्ब मनुजाकृतिम् ॥ 66
सुखदुःखाद्यनुगतं जानन्ति न तु तत्त्वतः । दिष्ट्या मद्गोचरं ज्ञानमुत्पन्नं ते भवापहम् ॥ 67
स्मरन्ती तिष्ठ भवने लिप्यसे न च कर्मभिः । इत्युक्ता सा परिक्रम्य रामं सानन्दविस्मया ॥ 68
प्रणम्य शतशो भूमौ ययौ गेहं मुदान्विता । भरतस्तु सहामात्यैर्मातृभिर्गुरुणा सह ॥ 69

mèn. **57.** You are verily Mahavishnu, the Supreme Spirit and Eternal Being, whose nature is not clear to any one. Assuming the form of a man Thou art hiding Thy identity. Man performs good and evil acts only under Thy prompting. **(58-59).** This whole world is subject to Thy will, and is without any freedom. Just as puppet dolls dance according to the will of their hidden director who pulls the strings unseen, so is this multiformed Maya a dancer manipulated by Thy will. I too was prompted by Thee as a part of Thy scheme for the fulfilment of the purpose of the Devas. **60.** Under the influence of my evil mind, I have done this sinful act. Now alone have I understood Thee to be the indwelling Spirit in all—Thee who art beyond the ken even of the celestials. **(61-62).** Save me, O Infinite Being, Thou the lord and protector of the worlds. Deign to cut asunder with the sword of knowledge of Thy exalted Self, my bondage of attachment to son, wealth and other worldly objects. I have taken refuge in Thee."

Hearing these words of Kaikeyi, Rama said to her smilingly: **63.** "O noble lady! What you have just now said is the exact truth. The words that came out of your mouth, took shape under My prompting. **(64-69).** Thus by your choice of boons etc., which were prompted by Me for the attainment of the purpose of the Devas, you incur no sin. So you return home in peace. Let your mind be constantly absorbed in My thought. Abandon your attachment for all worldly objects, and be whole-heartedly devoted to Me. Soon will you gain liberation by following this way of life. I

अयोध्यामगमच्छीघ्रं राममेवानुचिन्तयन् । पौरजानपदान् सर्वानयोध्यायामुदारधीः ।। 70
स्थापयित्वा यथान्यायं नन्दिग्रामं ययौ स्वयम् । तत्र सिंहासने नित्यं पादुके स्थाप्य भक्तितः ।।71
पूजयित्वा यथा रामं गन्धपुष्पाक्षतादिभिः । राजोपचारैरखिलैः प्रत्यहं नियतव्रतः ॥ 72
फलमूलाशनो दान्तो जटावल्कलधारकः । अधःशायी ब्रह्मचारी शत्रुघ्नसहितस्तदा ॥ 73
राजकार्याणि सर्वाणि यावन्ति पृथिवीतले । तानि पादुकयोः सम्यङ्निवेदयति राघवः ॥ 74
गणयन् दिवसानेव रामागमनकाङ्क्षया । स्थितो रामार्पितमनाःसाक्षाद्ब्रह्ममुनिर्यथा ॥ 75
रामस्तु चित्रकूटाद्रौ वसन्मुनिभिरावृतः । सीतया लक्ष्मणेनापि किञ्चित्कालमुपावसत् ॥ 76
नागराश्च सदा यान्ति रामदर्शनलालसाः । चित्रकूटस्थितं ज्ञात्वा सीतया लक्ष्मणेन च ॥ 77

view all beings alike. None is inimical or dear to Me. I am like the heavenly tree Kalpaka-Vriksha. Whoever go under it and pray, get what they want, and whoever exclude themselves from it keeping away, do not get those favours. To those who resign themselves to Me, I respond by revealing Myself. Those whose minds are clouded by My Maya, see Me as a human being, subject to the happiness and sufferings of worldly life. They do not know Me in truth and in reality. Fortunately that enlightenment which liberates one from this transmigratory life, has dawned on you. Stay at home attending to your duties, but remembering Me always. That will save you from the bondage of that hankering after the fruits that Karma brings." Hearing these words of Rama, Kaikeyi was filled with wonder and joy. She circumambulated Rama, and prostrated before him several times. She then returned to the palace pacified in mind.

Bharata After his Return (70-75)

(70-75). Soon Bharata the noble-minded arrived at Ayodhya along with his preceptor, mothers and the ministers, constantly remembering Rama. After making all the necessary arrangements for the residence and administration of the citizens of Ayodhya, he himself went to stay in a village called Nandigrama. There on a throne he reverently installed the sandals of Rama he had brought with him and daily worshipped them as representing Rama, with flowers, sandal paste etc., as also with all objects that are considered as royal insignia. In his daily life he observed strict ascetic discipline. His food consisted of roots and fruits, and his attire, of a tree-bark garments and matted locks. He slept on the bare floor, and strictly observed the rule of celibacy. Satrughna kept him company. He transacted all the affairs of state after first representing them before the sandals of Rama in token of his taking orders from Rama. Counting the days of Rama's return, he lived like a Brahmarshi, dedicating his whole mind to Rama.

Rama at Atri's Ashrama (76-91)

76. As for Rama, though he took his residence in Chitrakuta with Sita and Lakshmana amidst the settlement of the ascetics of that place, he did not, however, continue to stay there long. **(77-79).** For,

दृष्ट्वा तज्जनसम्बाधं रामस्तत्याज तं गिरिम् । दण्डकारण्यगमने कार्यमप्यनुचिन्तयन् ॥ 78

अन्वगात्सीतया भ्रात्रा ह्यत्रेराश्रममुत्तमम् । सर्वत्र सुखसंत्रासं जनसम्बाधवर्जितम् ॥ 79

गत्वा मुनिमुपासीनं भासयन्तं तपोवनम् । दण्डवत्प्रणिपत्याह रामोऽहमभिवादये ॥ 80

पितुराज्ञां पुरस्कृत्य दण्डकाननमागतः । वनवासमिषेणापि धन्योऽहं दर्शनात्तव ॥ 81

श्रुत्वा रामस्य वचनं रामं ज्ञात्वा हरिं परम् । पूजयामास विधिवद्भक्त्या परमया मुनिः ॥ 82

वन्यैः फलैः कृतातिथ्यमुपविष्टं रघूत्तमम् । सीतां च लक्ष्मणं चैव संतुष्टो वाक्यमब्रवीत् ॥ 83

भार्या मेऽतीव संवृद्धा ह्यनसूयेति विश्रुता । तपश्चरन्ती सुचिरं धर्मज्ञा धर्मवत्सला ॥ 84

अन्तस्तिष्ठति तां सीता पश्यत्वरिनिषूदन । तथेति जानकीं प्राह रामो राजीवलोचनः ॥ 85

गच्छ देवीं नमस्कृत्य शीघ्रमेहि पुनः शुभे । तथेति रामवचनं सीता चापि तथाकरोत् ॥ 86

दण्डवत्पतितामग्रे सीतां दृष्ट्वातिहृष्टधीः । अनसूया समालिङ्ग्य वत्से सीतेति सादरम् ॥ 87

दिव्ये ददौ कुण्डले द्वे निर्मिते विश्वकर्मणा । दुकूले द्वे ददौ तस्यै निर्मले भक्तिसंयुता ॥ 88

अङ्गरागं च सीतायै ददौ दिव्यं शुभानना । न त्यक्ष्यतेऽङ्गरागेण शोभा त्वां कमलानने ॥ 89

पातिव्रत्यं पुरस्कृत्य राममन्वेहि जानकि । कुशली राघवो यातु त्वया सह पुनर्गृहम् ॥ 90

knowing that Rama was staying at Mount Chitrakuta, large numbers of people from the countryside began to visit that place because of their eagerness to meet him. To avoid the disturbance from the crowds, as also for the fulfilment of the ultimate object of his exile to the forest, he abandoned his residence at Chitrakuta, and proceeded towards Dandakaranya. On the way he along with Sita and his brother, reached the Ashrama of the sage Atri, which was situated at a very solitary place, with the necessary facilities for one to stay all round the year. **80.** There in that Ashrama was seated the sage Atri, illumining the whole place with his lustre. Rama prostrated before him and announced himself to the sage saying, "I am Rama, offering my salutations to you. **81.** According to my father's order, I have come to the Dandaka forest. In the guise of forest life an occasion has arisen for me to meet your holy self." **82.** Hearing Rama's words and knowing him to be Hari Himself, the sage Atri extended to him a very warm reception with great devotion. **83.** He gave hospitality by presenting to him fruits of the forest. Seating Rama, Sita and Lakshmana, the sage said the following in great joy: **(84-85)** "Inside the Ashrama, there is my aged wife Anasuya who has been performing austerities for a very long time, and who has a deep knowledge of Dharma and has been observing the same. O destroyer of enemies! Let Sita go in and see her." The lotus-eyed Rama asked Sita to do as requested by the sage. **86.** He said: "O good lady! Go in and make salutations to holy Anasuya and come back soon." And Sita did accordingly.

(87-90). Holy Anasuya was very glad to see Sita, who made a full prostration

भोजयित्वा यथान्यायं रामं सीतासमन्वितम् । लक्ष्मणं च तदा रामं पुनः प्राह कृताञ्जलिः ॥ 91

राम त्वमेव भुवनानि विधाय तेषां संरक्षणाय सुरमानुषतिर्यगादीन् ।
देहान्बिभर्षि न च देहगुणैर्विलिप्तस्त्वत्तो बिभेत्यखिलमोहकरी च माया ॥ 92

इति श्रीमदध्यात्मरामायणे उमामहेश्वरसंवादे
अयोध्याकाण्डे नवमः सर्गः ॥ ९ ॥

before her. Addressing her as "Dear Sita", Anasuya with great devotion presented her two heavenly ear ornaments made by Viswakarma, as also two lovely pieces of silk. She also gave Sita a unique paste for bodily application with the words, "O lotus-faced one! By the application of this paste, the lustre of your body will remain undimmed. O daughter of Janaka! Following the duty of a pious wife, you now follow Rama. May that great personage soon return to his palace with you!"

(91-92). Afterwards the sage Atri fed Rama, Sita and Lakshmana sumptuously, and with palms joined in salutation said: "O Rama! Thou alone art the creator of all these worlds. After creating them, Thou manifestest for their protection and orderly growth, as incarnations in the species of Devas, humans and brute creations. Though embodied in this way, the bodily traits do not affect Thee. Maya which deludes all, remains aloof from Thee out of fear of Thee."

ॐ

अध्यात्मरामायणम्

आरण्यकाण्डः

प्रथमः सर्गः

विराध-वधः

श्रीमहादेव उवाच

अथ तत्र दिनं स्थित्वा प्रभाते रघुनन्दनः । स्नात्वा मुनिं समामंत्र्य प्रयाणायोपचक्रमे ॥ 1
मुने गच्छामहे सर्वे मुनिमण्डलमण्डितम् । विपिनं दण्डकं यत्र त्वमाज्ञातुमिहार्हसि ॥ 2
मार्गप्रदर्शनार्थाय शिष्यानाज्ञप्तुमर्हसि ।
श्रुत्वा रामस्य वचनं प्रहस्यात्रिर्महायशाः । प्राह तत्र रघुश्रेष्ठं राम राम सुराश्रय ॥ 3
सर्वस्य मार्गद्रष्टा त्वं तव को मार्गदर्शकः । तथापि दर्शयिष्यन्ति तव लोकानुसारिणः ॥ 4
इति शिष्यान्समादिश्य स्वयं किंचित्तमन्वगात् । रामेण वारितः प्रीत्या अत्रिः स्वभवनं ययौ ॥ 5
क्रोशमात्रं ततो गत्वा ददर्श महतीं नदीम् । अत्रेः शिष्यानुवाचेदं रामो राजीवलोचनः ॥ 6

ARANYA KANDAM

Chapter 1

TOWARDS DANDAKARANYA

Redemption of Viradha (1-35)

1. Rama spent the rest of the day at that Ashrama and in the morning took leave of the sage and was ready to start on his journey. **2.** He said to the sage: "O holy one! We are all going to the forest known as Dandaka, where many ascetics are staying. We seek your blessing. **(3-5).** Please direct some of your disciples to show us the path." Hearing Rama's words, the great sage Atri said, smiling: "O Rama! Thou the support of even the celestials! Thou art the Pathfinder for all beings. How can any one therefore show Thee the Path? Still following the way of the world, we shall show the path." With these words, he deputed some of his disciples for the purpose, and himself followed Rama for some distance. Persuaded by Rama to return, the sage did accordingly, and went back to his Ashrama. **(6-9)** When they had walked the distance of about a Krosa,

नद्याः सन्तरणे कश्चिदुपायो विद्यते न वा । ऊचुस्ते विद्यते नौका सुदृढा रघुनन्दन ॥ 7
तारयिष्यामहे युष्मान्वयमेव क्षणादिह । ततो नावि समारोप्य सीतां राघवलक्ष्मणौ ॥ 8
क्षणात्सन्तारयामासुर्नदीं मुनिकुमारकाः । रामाभिनन्दिताः सर्वे जग्मुरत्रे रथाश्रमम् ॥ 9
तावेत्य विपिनं घोरं झिल्लीझङ्कारनादितम् । नानामृगगणाकीर्णं सिंहव्याघ्रादिभीषणम् ॥ 10
राक्षसैर्घोररूपैश्च सेवितं रोमहर्षणम् । प्रविश्य विपिनं घोरं रामो लक्ष्मणमब्रवीत् ॥ 11
इतः परं प्रयत्नेन गन्तव्यं सहितेन मे । धनुर्गुणेन संयोज्य शरानपि करे दधत् ॥ 12
अग्रे यास्याम्यहं पश्चात्त्वमन्वेहि धनुर्धर । आवयोर्मध्यगा सीता मायेवात्मपरात्मनोः ॥ 13
चक्षुश्चारय सर्वत्र दृष्टं रक्षोभयं महत् । विद्यते दण्डकारण्ये श्रुतपूर्वमरिन्दम ॥ 14
इत्येवं भाषमाणौ तौ जग्मतुः सार्धयोजनम् । तत्रैका पुष्करिण्यास्ते कह्लारकुमुदोत्पलैः ॥ 15
अम्बुजैः शीतलोदेन शोभमाना व्यदृश्यत । तत्समीपमथो गत्वा पीत्वा तत्सलिलं शुभम् ॥ 16
ऊषुस्ते सलिलाभ्याशे क्षणं छायामुपाश्रिताः । ततो ददृशुरायान्तं महासत्त्वं भयानकम् ॥ 17

they came across a great river. "How can we cross this river?" asked Rama, and the disciples of Atri replied: "O noble descendant of Raghu's line! There is an excellent boat for the purpose. We ourselves shall take you across the river in a short time." Then they fetched the boat, seated Rama, Sita and Lakshmana in it, and the young ascetics themselves rowed the party across the river. Rama appreciated very much the skill they displayed. They later returned to Atri's Ashrama.

(10-11). Now Rama and party entered into the terrifying and thickly wooded forest of Dandaka. With the shrill chirping of insects, with animals of various species everywhere, with dangerous wild animals like lions and tigers prowling about, and with fierce-looking Rakshasas infesting its precincts, that awesome forest would create horripilation on the body of anyone. Entering into the forest Rama said to Lakshmana, Sumitra's son: **(12-13).** "From here onwards we should travel very carefully. Along with me you should have your bow strung and arrows ready at hand. I shall walk in front and you behind. Sita will walk between us, just as Maya, the illusory power, stands between the Paramatma (Supreme Spirit) and the Jiva (the embodied spirit). **14.** Look around carefully. O heroic one! Dandakaranya is notorious for the many Rakshasas infesting it. I have heard of this even before."

(15-17). Travelling and conversing thus between themselves, they covered about a Yojana and a half when they came across a lake of cool and crystal waters full of lotuses and water lilies of various kinds. Approaching that lake, they drank of its sweet waters, and sat under a shade on its

करालदंष्ट्रवदनं भीषयन्तं स्वगर्जितैः । वामांसे न्यस्तशूलाग्रग्रथितानेकमानुषम् ॥ 18

भक्षयन्तं गजव्याघ्रमहिषं वनगोचरम् । ज्यारोपितं धनुर्धृत्वा रामो लक्ष्मणमब्रवीत् ॥ 19

पश्य भ्रातर्महाकायो राक्षसोऽयमुपागतः । आयात्यभिमुखं नोऽग्रे भीरूणां भयमावहन् ॥ 20

सज्जीकृतधनुस्तिष्ठ मा भैर्जनकनन्दिनि । इत्युक्त्वा बाणमादाय स्थितो राम इवाचलः ॥ 21

स तु दृष्ट्वा रमानाथं लक्ष्मणं जानकीं तदा । अट्टहासं ततः कृत्वा भीषयन्निदमब्रवीत् ॥ 22

कौ युवां बाणतूणीरजटावल्कलधारिणौ । मुनिवेषधरौ बालौ स्त्रीसहायौ सुदुर्मदौ ॥ 23

सुन्दरौ बत मे वक्त्रप्रविष्टकवलोपमौ । किमर्थमागतौ घोरं वनं व्यालनिषेवितम् ॥ 24

श्रुत्वा रक्षोवचो रामः स्मयमान उवाच तम् । अहं रामस्त्वयं भ्राता लक्ष्मणो मम सम्मतः ॥ 25

एषा सीता मम प्राणवल्लभा वयमागताः । पितृवाक्यं पुरस्कृत्य शिक्षणार्थं भवादृशाम् ॥ 26

श्रुत्वा तद्रामवचनमट्टहासमथाकरोत् । व्यादाय वक्त्रं बाहुभ्यां शूलमादाय सत्वरः ॥ 27

मां न जानासि राम त्वं विराधं लोकविश्रुतम् । मद्भयान्मुनयः सर्वे त्यक्त्वा वनमितो गताः ॥ 28

यदि जीवितुमिच्छास्ति त्यक्त्वा सीतां निरायुधौ । पलायत न चेच्छीघ्रं भक्षयामि युवामहम् ॥ 29

bank for some time. A terrible-looking monster now appeared in their sight **(18-19).** The monster had fierce fangs and his howls spread terror all around. On his left shoulder rested a trident, at the sharp end of which were impaled several human bodies. He was moving about, eating whatever wild animal he saw—be it elephant, tiger, lion or bison. At the sight of that monster, Rama lifted his bow in readiness for use and said to Lakshmana: **(20-21).** "Look, brother, at what is before us. There comes a Rakshasa with a huge body towards us. His form is fear-inspiring in those who are timid. Stand with your bow in readiness. Do not be frightened, O daughter of Janaka." Saying so, Rama stood firm like a mountain, bow and arrow in hand.

22. Seeing Rama along with Sita and Lakshmana, that monster gave out fierce howls and said as follows in a threatening manner: **(23-24).** "Who are you in the assumed forms of ascetics donning tree-bark and matted hair, but with bows and arrows in hand and accompanied by a woman? You are handsome and extremely wanton. Alas! You are almost in my mouth as a morsel of food for me. Why have you dared to come into this terrible forest infested by all kinds of fierce creatures?" **(25-26).** To these words of the Rakshasa, Rama replied smiling, "I am Rama. This is my dear brother Lakshmana and this my wife Sita. At the command of my father we have come here to free this place from menacing fellows like you."

(27-29). Hearing these words of Rama, the demon gave out a terrific howl, and with mouth wide open and grasping the trident with both his hands, shouted in haste: "O Rama! Haven't you heard of me, the world renowned Viradha? All the ascetics have left this region of the forest out of fear of me. If you want to save your life, you abandon your weapons and leave Sita here, and run away in all haste. Other-

इत्युक्त्वा राक्षसः सीतामादातुमभिदुद्रुवे । रामश्चिच्छेद तद्बाहू शरेण प्रहसन्निव ॥ 30

ततः क्रोधपरीतात्मा व्यादाय विकटं मुखम् । राममभ्यद्रवद्रामश्चिच्छेद परिधावतः ॥ 31

पदद्वयं विराधस्य तदद्भुतमिवाभवत् ॥ 32

ततः सर्प इवास्येन ग्रसितुं राममापतन् । ततोऽर्धचन्द्राकारेण बाणेनास्य महच्छिरः ॥ 33

चिच्छेद रुधिरौघेण पपात धरणीतले । ततः सीता समालिङ्ग्य प्रशशंस रघूत्तमम् ॥ 34

ततो दुन्दुभयो नेदुर्दिवि देवगणेरिताः । ननृतुश्चाप्सरा हृष्टा जगुर्गन्धर्वकिन्नराः ॥ 35

विराधकायादतिसुन्दराकृति विभ्राजमानो विमलाम्बरावृतः ।
प्रतप्तचामीकरचारुभूषणो व्यदृश्यताग्रे गगने रविर्यथा ॥ 36

प्रणम्य रामं प्रणतार्तिहारिणं भवप्रवाहोपरमं घृणाकरम् ।
प्रणम्य भूयः प्रणनाम दण्डवत् प्रपन्नसर्वार्तिहरं प्रसन्नधीः ॥ 37

विराध उवाच

श्रीराम राजीवदलायताक्ष विद्याधरोऽहं विमलप्रकाशः ।
दुर्वाससाकारणकोपमूर्तिना शप्तः पुरा सोऽद्य विमोचितस्त्वया ॥ 38

wise I am going to eat up both of you." **30.** With these words the Rakshasa rushed forward to get hold of Sita. At this Rama severed both his arms with a single arrow with utmost ease.

(31-32). Then with his mouth wide open out of great anger, he came running towards Rama. Confronting Viradha who came charging, Rama cut his two legs with utmost ease to the astonishment of all. **(33-34).** Viradha now crawled towards Rama like a serpent with a view to devour him. Now with a semi-circular arrow Rama cut off his head, which fell in a river of blood on the ground. Sita thereupon congratulated Rama on his great feat. **35.** The kettle drums of the heavens now sounded. The celestials and the Apsaras, the heavenly artistes, danced while the Gandharvas and the Kinnaras sang.

Viradha's Hymn (36-46)

36. There came out of Viradha's body a very handsome form, bright, dressed in excellent robes, decorated with shining golden ornaments, and luminous like the sun in the sky. **37.** That being with a very placid appearance, now fell again and again in prostration before Rama, who destroys the sorrows of all who prostrate before him and take shelter under him, who is capable of terminating the term of Jivas in Samsara, and who is a veritable treasure of mercy. **38.** Viradha said, "O Rama of lotus eyes! I am a Vidyadhara of luminous form. In days of old, I was cursed for no special reason by sage Durvasas, who is an embodiment of anger. Today I am liberated from the effect of it

इतः परं त्वच्चरणारविन्दयोः स्मृतिः सदा मेऽस्तु भवोपशान्तये ।
त्वन्नामसङ्कीर्तनमेव वाणी करोतु मे कर्णपुटं त्वदीयम् ॥ 39
कथामृतं पातु करद्वयं ते पादारविन्दार्चनमेव कुर्यात् ।
शिरश्च ते पादयुगप्रणामं करोतु नित्यं भवदीयमेवम् ॥ 40
नमस्तुभ्यं भगवते विशुद्धज्ञानमूर्तये । आत्मारामाय रामाय सीतारामाय, वेधसे ॥ 41
प्रपन्नं पाहि मां राम यास्यामि त्वदनुज्ञया । देवलोकं रघुश्रेष्ठ माया मां मा वृणोतु ते ॥ 42
इति विज्ञापितस्तेन प्रसन्नो रघुनन्दनः । ददौ वरं तदा प्रीतो विराधाय महामतिः ॥ 43
गच्छ विद्याधराशेषमायादोषगुणा जिताः । त्वया मद्दर्शनात्सद्यो मुक्तो ज्ञानवतां वरः ॥ 44
मद्भक्तिर्दुर्लभा लोके जाता चेन्मुक्तिदा यतः । अतस्त्वं भक्तिसम्पन्नः परं याहि ममाज्ञया ॥ 45
रामेण रक्षोनिधनं सुघोरं शापाद्विमुक्तिर्वरदानमेवम् ।
विद्याधरत्वं पुनरेव लब्धं रामं गृणन्नेति नरोऽखिलार्थान् ॥ 46

इति श्रीमदध्यात्मरामायणे उमामहेश्वरसंवादे
आरण्यकाण्डे प्रथमः सर्गः ॥ १ ॥

by Thee. **(39-40).** Freed from Samsara, may my mind always keep remembrance of Thy lotus-feet. May my speech be ever engaged in uttering Thy exalted names. May my ears ever imbibe the nectar of Thy stories. May my hands be constantly engaged in making offerings to Thee. May my head be ever laid at Thy feet in prostration. May the whole of my being, body, mind and soul be thus absorbed in the service of Thee. **(41-42).** Salutation to Thee, Rama with Sita—Thou the Supreme Being and creator of the worlds. Devoid of all attributes, Thou art of the natue of Pure Consciousness, ever absorbed in Thy own Self. Protect me, who am a refugee at Thy feet. With Thy permission, O the noblest one in Raghu's line, I would like to go to my heavenly abode. May Thy Maya never cloud my vision." **43.** When Viradha prayed in this way, the noble Rama was much pleased, and in a mood of great joy bestowed boons on Viradha. **44.** He said, "O Vidyadhara! You may now go. By seeing Me, you have overcome all the limitations of Maya. You have become liberated this very moment and have been elevated to the rank of the great knowing ones. **45.** In this world of living beings, pure devotion to Me is very seldom found; for if one has that type of Bhakti, he attains Mukti immediately and is no longer in this world of beings in bondage. So endowed with Bhakti, you will now at my command attain Mukti." **46.** Rama accomplished the destruction of this fierce Rakshasa, but the Rakshasa thereby gained liberation. He received Rama's blessings and boons, and attained the status of a Vidyadhara again. So will every man attain to all blessings of life if he would but serve Rama and sing hymns in praise of him.

द्वितीयः सर्गः

श्रीमहादेव उवाच

विराधे स्वर्गते रामो लक्ष्मणेन च सीतया । जगाम शरभङ्गस्य वनं सर्वसुखावहम् ॥ 1

शरभङ्गस्ततो दृष्ट्वा रामं सौमित्रिणा सह । आयान्तं सीतया सार्धं सम्भ्रमादुत्थितः सुधीः ॥ 2

अभिगम्य सुसम्पूज्य विष्टरेषूपवेशयत् । आतिथ्यमकरोत्तेषां कन्दमूलफलादिभिः ॥ 3

प्रीत्याह शरभङ्गोऽपि रामं भक्तपरायणम् । बहुकालमिहैवासं तपसे कृतनिश्चयः ॥ 4

तव सन्दर्शनाकाङ्क्षी राम त्वं परमेश्वरः ।
अद्य मत्तपसा सिद्धं यत्पुण्यं बहु विद्यते । तत्सर्वं तव दास्यामि ततो मुक्तिं व्रजाम्यहम् ॥ 5

समर्प्य रामस्य महत्सुपुण्यफलं विरक्तः शरभङ्गयोगी ।
चितिं समारोहयदप्रमेयं रामं ससीतं सहसा प्रणम्य ॥ 6

ध्यायंश्चिरं राममशेषहृत्स्थं दूर्वादलश्याममलमम्बुजाक्षम् ।
चीराम्बरं स्निग्धजटाकलापं सीतासहायं सहलक्ष्मणं तम् ॥ 7

को वा दयालुः स्मृतकामधेनुरन्यो जगत्यां रघुनायकादहो ।
स्मृतो मया नित्यमनन्यभाजा ज्ञात्वा स्मृतिं मे स्वयमेव यातः ॥ 8

Chapter 2

VISIT TO THE ASHRAMAS OF SARABHANGA AND SUTIKSHNA

At Sarabhanga's Ashrama (1-12)

1. After Viradha attained salvation, Rama along with Sita and Lakshmana went to the peaceful forest hermitage of the sage Sarabhanga. **2.** At the sight of Rama arriving at his place in the company of Sita and Lakshmana, the high-minded sage Sarabhanga got up from his seat in hot haste out of respect for the visitors. **3.** He went towards them, received them cordially and offered them seats. He then did hospitality to them with roots, fruits, etc., available in the forest. **(4-5).** Rejoiced at the presence of Rama, the refuge of all devotees, at his hermitage, the sage Sarabhanga said, "O Rama! Thou art verily the Lord of all. With a view to meet Thee, I have been staying here long, resolved to be engaged in austerities. Whatever merits I have acquired, all that I offer unto Thee so that I may obtain Moksha or Mukti." **6.** After thus offering all his merits at the feet of Rama the holy sage Sarabhanga, who was full of renunciation, prostrated before that immeasurable being Rama in the company of Sita. Then, without any more delay, he got ready to consign his body to the flames, holding his mind absorbed in Rama. **7.** He held his mind for long in meditation on that form of Rama—blue like Durva grass, lotus-eyed, dressed in tree-bark cloth, wearing matted locks, accompanied by Sita and Lakshmana, and established in the hearts of all. **8.** He thought, "Lo! Who

पश्यत्विदानीं देवेशो रामो दाशरथिः प्रभुः । दग्ध्वा स्वदेहं गच्छामि ब्रह्मलोकमकल्मषः ॥ 9
अयोध्याधिपतिर्मेऽस्तु हृदये राघवः सदा । यद्वामाङ्के स्थिता सीता मेघस्येव तटिल्लता ॥ 10
इति रामं चिरं ध्यात्वा दृष्ट्वा च पुरतः स्थितम् । प्रज्वाल्य सहसा वह्निं दग्ध्वा पश्चात्मकं वपुः ॥11
दिव्यदेहधरः साक्षाद्ययौ लोकपतेः पदम् ।
ततो मुनिगणाः सर्वे दण्डकारण्यवासिनः । आजग्मू राघवं द्रष्टुं शरभङ्गनिवेशनम् ॥ 12
दृष्ट्वा मुनिसमूहं तं जानकीरामलक्ष्मणाः । प्रणेमुः सहसा भूमौ मायामानुषरूपिणः ॥ 13
आशीर्भिरभिनन्द्याथ रामं सर्वहृदि स्थितम् । ऊचुः प्राञ्जलयः सर्वे धनुर्बाणधरं हरिम् ॥ 14
भूमेर्भारावताराय जातोऽसि ब्रह्मणार्थितः । जानीमस्त्वां हरिं लक्ष्मीं जानकीं लक्ष्मणं तथा ॥ 15
शेषांशं शङ्खचक्रे द्वे भरतं सानुजं तथा । अतश्चादौ ऋषीणां त्वं दुःखं भोक्तुमिहार्हसि ॥ 16
आगच्छ यामो मुनिसेवितानि वनानि सर्वाणि रघूत्तम क्रमात् ।
द्रष्टुं सुमित्रासुतजानकीभ्यां तदा दयास्मासु दृढा भविष्यति ॥ 17

is there so merciful, so liberal to his devotees other than Rama? Wonder of wonders, he has, of his own accord, come here to bless me, intuiting how I have been constantly thinking about him. **9.** Purified in mind and burning this body in fire, I shall attain the realm of Brahma in the very presence of Rama, the Supreme Being born as son of Dasaratha. **10.** May Rama, the Lord of Ayodhya, ever dwell in my heart—Rama in whose lap is seated Sita like lightning in the clouds." **(11-12).** Thus for a long time did he look at Rama standing in front of him and meditate on him in mind. Then setting fire to the pyre, he reduced his physical body to ashes, gained a divine body, and attained the realm of Brahma. Subsequently, a large number of ascetics inhabiting the Dandaka forest came to meet Rama at the hermitage of Sarabhanga.

Rama vows to extirpate the Rakshasas (13-24)

13. Seeing all those holy men, Rama, Lakshmana and Sita, who had by the power of Maya assumed human forms and manners, saluted them all in haste by making full prostrations. **14.** Pronouncing their blessings on Rama, the resident of the hearts of all, they said the following with joined palms to him, who was none but Hari, equipped with bow and arrow: **(15-16).** "We know Thee to be Mahavishnu, Sita to be Thy consort Lakshmi, Lakshmana to be Sesha and Bharata and his brother Satrughna to be Thy Conch and Discus. Beseeched by Brahma, Thou art incarnated in this world to rid the earth of its burdens. Therefore, it is among the principal objects of Thy mission to relieve the Rishis of their sorrows and difficulties. **17.** O Rama! May Thou be pleased to come along with Sita and Lakshmana to see the forest inhabited by ascetics. We shall lead Thee to those places. When Thou seest the sights there and know our conditions of life, Thou wouldst be moved by a powerful impulse of mercy towards us."

इति विज्ञापितो रामः कृताञ्जलिपुटैर्विभुः । जगाम मुनिभिः सार्थं द्रष्टुं मुनिवनानि सः ॥ 18

ददर्श तत्र पतितान्यनेकानि शिरांसि सः । अस्थिभूतानि सर्वत्र रामो वचनमब्रवीत् ॥ 19

अस्थीनि केषामेतानि किमर्थं पतितानि वै । तमूचुर्मुनयो राम ऋषीणां मस्तकानि हि ॥ 20

राक्षसैर्भक्षितानीश प्रमत्तानां समाधितः । अन्तरायं मुनीनां ते पश्यन्तोऽनुचरन्ति हि ॥ 21

श्रुत्वा वाक्यं मुनीनां स भयदैन्यसमन्वितम् । प्रतिज्ञामकरोद्रामो वधायाशेषरक्षसाम् ॥ 22

पूज्यमानः सदा तत्र मुनिभिर्वनवासिभिः । जानक्या सहितो रामो लक्ष्मणेन समन्वितः ॥ 23

उवास कतिचित्तत्र वर्षाणि रघुनन्दनः । एवं क्रमेण संपश्यन्नृषीणामाश्रमान्विभुः ॥ 24

सुतीक्ष्णस्याश्रमं प्रागात्प्रख्यातमृषिसङ्कुलम् । सर्वर्तुगुणसम्पन्नं सर्वकालसुखावहम् ॥ 25

रामममागतमाकर्ण्य सुतीक्ष्णः स्वयमागतः ।
अगस्त्यशिष्यो रामस्य मन्त्रोपासनतत्परः । विधिवत्पूजयामास भक्त्युत्कण्ठितलोचनः ॥ 26

सुतीक्ष्ण उवाच

त्वन्मन्त्रजाप्यहमनन्तगुणाप्रमेय सीतापते शिवविरिञ्चिसमाश्रिताङ्घ्रे ।
संसारसिन्धुतरणामलपोतपाद रामाभिराम सततं तव दासदासः ॥ 27

18. Being thus implored prayerfully by them, the all-powerful Rama went along with those ascetics to see their abodes. **19.** In all those places Rama saw here and there many skeletons of human heads. At this sight, Rama asked: **20.** "Whose are these skeletons of heads? How have they fallen here?" The ascetics replied, "Indeed they are the heads of Rishis. **21.** When the ascetics are unconscious of the external world in the state of meditation, the Rakshasas eat their heads and throw the bones here and there. They do this carefully watching the time when the sages in meditation are unaware of the conditions outside." **22.** Hearing these piteous words of the frightened Rishis and Munis, Rama then and there took the vow that he would destroy the whole tribe of Rakshasas there. **(23-24).** In this way the noble Rama of Raghu's line along with Sita and Lakshmana spent some years, seeing the Ashramas of the Rishis of those regions, receiving everywhere the cordial reception of these ascetics.

At the Ashrama of Sutikshna (25-40)

25. In the course of those travels, one day he reached the Ashrama of the sage Sutikshna, which had a pleasant climate in all seasons, which yielded the benefits of every season always, and which was inhabited by a large number of Rishis. **26.** Sutikshna was a disciple of the sage Agastya, and used to utter the sacred name of Rama always. Hearing about the arrival of Rama, he came himself, and moved by a great spirit of devotion which was manifest in his eyes, received him with due worship. Sutikshna said: **27.** "O Rama, consort of Sita, and the delight of all! Thou art beyond the bounds of Knowledge and endowed with excellences that are limitless

मामद्य सर्वजगतामविगोचरस्त्वं त्वन्मायया सुतकलत्रगृहान्धकूपे ।
मग्नं निरीक्ष्य मलपुद्गलपिण्डमोहपाशानुबद्धहृदयं स्वयमागतोऽसि ॥ 28

त्वं सर्वभूतहृदयेषु कृतालयोऽपि त्वन्मन्त्रजाप्यविमुखेषु तनोषि मायाम् ।
त्वन्मन्त्रसाधनपरेष्वपयाति माया सेवानुरूपफलदोऽसि यथा महीपः ॥ 29

विश्वस्य सृष्टिलयसंस्थितिहेतुरेकस्त्वं मायया त्रिगुणया विधिरीशविष्णू ।
भासीश मोहितधियां विविधाकृतिस्त्वं यद्वद्रविः सलिलपात्रगतो ह्यनेकः ॥ 30

प्रत्यक्षतोऽद्य भवतश्चरणारविन्दं पश्यामि राम तमसः परतः स्थितस्य ।
दृग्रूपतस्त्वमसतामविगोचरोऽपि त्वन्मन्त्रपूतहृदयेषु सदा प्रसन्नः ॥ 31

पश्यामि राम तव रूपमरूपिणोऽपि मायाविडम्बनकृतं सुमनुष्यवेषम् ।
कन्दर्पकोटिसुभगं कमनीयचापबाणं दयार्द्रहृदयं स्मितचारुवक्त्रम् ॥ 32

Thy feet are sought after even by Parameswara and Brahma. Thou art the one faultless boat for all Jivas to cross the ocean of Samsara. I am one given to the repetition of Thy holy Mantra and the servant of even Thy servants. **28.** I am one bound by the cord of identification with the body, which is nothing but a mass of filthy stuff. I am consigned to the disused well of family life, centering on wife and children and other worldly relationships. Yet, Thou, who art beyond the knowledge of all beings in this universe, hast deigned to come here, seeking me of Thy own accord. **29.** Though Thou art residing in the hearts of all, Thou hidest with Thy delusive power, the vision of those who are not disposed to take Thy name. But Maya's delusion does not affect those who are devoted to the repetition of Thy holy name. Just as in the case of the heavenly tree, the Kalpaka Vriksha, the fruits of Thy grace come to those who seek Thee. **30.** Thou art the one cause for the creation, sustentation and dissolution of the universe. By assuming Maya with its three Gunas of Sattva, Rajas and Tamas, Thou manifestest in a threefold way as Brahma, Vishnu and Maheswara. O Supreme One! As the one sun is reflected as many in different pots of water, so dost Thou assume different forms with different adjuncts. **31.** O Rama! Thou, who transcendest the darkness of Tamas and who art the Ultimate Subject, has been pleased today to reveal Thyself before me as an object of perception. Though unseen by unholy ones, Thou dost indeed reveal Thyself to those whose hearts have been purified by Thy sacred name. **32.** O Rama! Though formless, Thou hast assumed a form in association with Maya. I see Thee before me in such an assumed human form more handsome than countless Cupids—a form charming with a sweet smile that reveals a

सीतासमेतमजिनाम्बरमप्रधृष्यं सौमित्रिणा नियतसेवितपादपद्मम् ।
नीलोत्पलद्युतिमनन्तगुणं प्रशान्तं मद्भागधेयमनिशं प्रणमामि रामम् ॥ 33

जानन्तु राम तव रूपमशेषदेशकालाद्युपाधिरहितं घनचित्प्रकाशम् ।
प्रत्यक्षतोऽद्य मम गोचरमेतदेव रूपं विभातु हृदये न परं विकाङ्क्षे ॥ 34

इत्येवं स्तुवतस्तस्य रामः सुस्मितमब्रवीत् । मुने जानामि ते चित्तं निर्मलं मदुपासनात् ॥ 35
अतोऽहमागतो द्रष्टुं मदृते नान्यसाधनम् । मन्मन्त्रोपासका लोके मामेव शरणं गताः ॥ 36
निरपेक्षानान्यगतास्तेषां दृश्योऽहमन्वहम् । स्तोत्रमेतत्पठेद्यस्तु त्वत्कृतं मत्प्रियं सदा ॥ 37
सद्भक्तिर्मे भवेत्तस्य ज्ञानं च विमलं भवेत् । त्वं ममोपासनादेव विमुक्तोऽसीह सर्वतः ॥ 38
देहान्ते मम सायुज्यं लप्स्यसे नात्र संशयः ।
गुरुं ते द्रष्टुमिच्छामि ह्यगस्त्यं मुनिनायकम् । किञ्चित्कालं तत्र वस्तुं मनो मे त्वरयत्यलम् ॥39
सुतीक्ष्णोऽपि तथेत्याह श्वो गमिष्यसि राघव । अहमप्यागमिष्यामि चिराद् दृष्टो महामुनिः ॥40

heart melting in mercy, and with attractive bow and arrows in hand. **33.** Salutations to Thee ever more, O Rama! My sole wealth and fortune, who art accompanied by Sita and served by Lakshmana the son of Sumitra, who art dressed in deer skin, who hast the brightness of a blue lotus who art very calm, who art the centre of countless excellences and who art the object of service and devotion to all disciplined persons. **34.** O Rama! Let philosophers know Thee as transcending every kind of adjuncts like space and time and the luminosity of pure consciousness. But I, a devotee, aspire for nothing other than this form of Thine concretely present before me. May it shine in my consciousness at all times!"

35. To the sage Sutikshna who offered this hymn of praise, Rama said, smiling: "I know that by the adoration of Me, your heart has become very pure. **(36-39).** It is therefore that I have come to see you. There is no means other than devotion for realising Me. I reveal Myself always to those who repeat My Mantra, who seek shelter under Me without depending on anything or anyone else. The hymn that you have addressed Me is dear to Me. Whoever studies this hymn always, in them will be generated pure devotion and spiritual illumination. You have become free even in this world by your devotion to Me. After the fall of your body, you will attain Sayujya—liberation of becoming My very Being. There is no doubt about it. Now I desire to meet your teacher, the great sage Agastya. I am extremely desirous of living for some time in those precincts where that sage dwells."

(40-41). Sutikshna agreed to this proposal and said, "O Rama! We shall go there

अथ प्रभाते मुनिना समेतो रामःससीतः सह लक्ष्मणेन ।
अगस्त्यसम्भाषणलोलमानसः शनैरगस्त्यानुजमन्दिरं ययौ ॥ 41

इति श्रीमदध्यात्मरामायणे उमामहेश्वरसंवादे
आरण्यकाण्डे द्वितीयः सर्गः ॥ २ ॥

tomorrow. I too shall accompany you. It is now long since I have seen that sage." In the morning, accompanied by the sage Sutikshna, Sita and Lakshmana, Rama started for the residence of Agastya's brother with a mind eagerly interested in communing with that sage.

तृतीयः सर्गः

श्रीमहादेव उवाच

अथ रामः सुतीक्ष्णेन जानक्या लक्ष्मणेन च । अगस्त्यस्यानुजस्थानं मध्याह्ने समपद्यत ॥ 1
तेन सम्पूजितः सम्यग्भुक्त्वा मूलफलादिकम् । परेद्युः प्रातरुत्थाय जग्मुस्तेऽगस्त्यमण्डलम् ॥ 2
सर्वर्तुफलपुष्पाढ्यं नानामृगगणैर्युतम् । पक्षिसङ्घैश्च विविधैर्नादितं नन्दनोपमम् ॥ 3
ब्रह्मर्षिभिर्देवर्षिभिः सेवितं मुनिमन्दिरैः । सर्वतोऽलंकृतं साक्षाद् ब्रह्मलोकमिवापरम् ॥ 4
बहिरेवाश्रमस्याथ स्थित्वा रामोऽब्रवीन्मुनिम् । सुतीक्ष्ण गच्छ त्वं शीघ्रमागतं मां निवेदय ॥ 5

Chapter 3

AT THE ASHRAMA OF THE SAGE AGASTYA

Meeting with sage Agastya (1-16)

1. Towards noon, Rama along with Sutikshna, Sita and Lakshmana, reached the hermitage of the brother of Agastya, by name Agnijihwa. **2.** That sage gave him a warm reception and fed him with roots and fruits. Rising up early next morning, they started for Agastya's Ashrama. (3-4). That hermitage was noted for the presence of fruits and flowers of all seasons. It was full of animals of various species and its atmosphere was filled with the sweet warblings of many kinds of birds. It resembled Nandana, the garden of Heaven. It was a resort of Brahma Rishis, Deva Rishis and resident ascetics. It filled one with a feeling that it was another Brahma-Loka. **5.** Stopping outside the precincts of that Ashrama, Rama said to Sutikshna, "You please

अगस्त्यमुनिवर्याय सीतया लक्ष्मणेन च । महाप्रसाद इत्युक्त्वा सुतीक्ष्णः प्रययौ गुरोः ॥ 6
आश्रमं त्वरया तत्र ऋषिसङ्घसमावृतम् । उपविष्टं रामभक्तैर्विशेषेण समायुतम् ॥ 7
व्याख्यातराममन्त्रार्थशिष्येभ्यश्चातिभक्तितः । दृष्ट्वागस्त्यं मुनिश्रेष्ठं सुतीक्ष्णः प्रययौ मुनेः ॥ 8
दण्डवत्प्रणिपत्याह विनयावनतः सुधीः ।
रामो दाशरथिर्ब्रह्मन् सीतया लक्ष्मणेन च । आगतो दर्शनार्थं ते बहिस्तिष्ठति साञ्जलिः ॥ 9

अगस्त्य उवाच

शीघ्रमानय भद्रं ते रामं मम हृदिस्थितम् । तमेव ध्यायमानोऽहं काङ्क्षमाणोऽत्र संस्थितः ॥ 10
इत्युक्त्वा स्वयमुत्थाय मुनिभिः सहितो द्रुतम् । अभ्यगात्परया भक्त्या गत्वा राममथाब्रवीत् ॥ 11
आगच्छ राम भद्रं ते दिष्टया तेऽद्य समागमः । प्रियातिथिर्मम प्राप्तोऽस्यद्य मे सफलं दिनम् ॥ 12
रामोऽपि मुनिमायान्तं दृष्ट्वा हर्षसमाकुलः । सीतया लक्ष्मणेनापि दण्डवत्पतितो भुवि ॥ 13
द्रुतमुत्थाप्य मुनिराडाममालिङ्ग्य भक्तितः । तद्गात्रस्पर्शजाह्लादस्रवन्नेत्रजलाकुलः ॥ 14
गृहीत्वा करमेकेन करेण रघुनन्दनम् । जगाम स्वाश्रमं हृष्टो मनसा मुनिपुङ्गवः ॥ 15
सुखोपविष्टं सम्पूज्य पूजया बहुविस्तरम् । भोजयित्वा यथान्यायं भोज्यैर्वन्यैरनेकधा ॥ 16

go in and announce that I have come. **(6-9)**. Tell the sage that along with Sita and Lakshmana, I have come to see him." Saying that he would do so with great pleasure, Sutikshna entered the Ashrama of his teacher. There Sutikshna saw the sage sitting, surrounded by ascetics, especially by devotees of Rama, and expounding to these disciples the meaning of the sacred name of Rama. Sutikshna made full salutation to the sage by stretching his whole body at the feet of his Guru and announced: "O great and illumined sage! Rama, the son of Dasaratha, accompanied by Sita and Lakshmana, has arrived to see you. He is standing there with his palms joined in salutation to you."

(10-11). Agastya said, "Quickly bring here Rama, who is ever seated in my heart. May you prosper! I am staying here, ever meditating on him in my heart and ever aspiring to meet him." With these words, he got up from his seat, and along with the other ascetics, went to meet Rama in a spirit of great devotion and said: **12.** "O Rama! Deign to come in. I am indeed fortunate to meet Thee now. Thou hast condescended to come here as my guest. This indeed is the day that marks the fulfilment of my life's objective." **13.** Seeing the sage approaching them, Rama along with Sita and Lakshmana saluted him with overflowing joy, stretching themselves in salutation on the ground like sticks. **14.** The great sage lifted Rama up and embraced him with great devotion. The bliss arising from contact with Rama's body expressed itself in a constant flow of tears from Agastya's eyes. **15.** Holding Rama's hand with his own, that great sage took him to the Ashrama in a mood of high exaltation. **16.** He gave him a comfortable seat and

सुखोपविष्टमेकान्ते रामं शशिनिभाननम् । कृताञ्जलिरुवाचेदमगस्त्यो भगवानृषिः ॥ 17
त्वदागमनमेवाहं प्रतीक्षन्समवस्थितः । यदा क्षीरसमुद्रान्ते ब्रह्मणा प्रार्थितः पुरा ॥ 18
भूमेर्भारापनुत्त्यर्थं रावणस्य वधाय च ।
तदादि दर्शनाकाङ्क्षी तव राम तपश्चरन् । वसामि मुनिभिः सार्धं त्वामेव परिचिन्तयन् ॥ 19
सृष्टेः प्रागेक एवासीर्निर्विकल्पोऽनुपाधिकः । त्वदाश्रया त्वद्विषया माया ते शक्तिरुच्यते ॥ 20
त्वामेव निर्गुणं शक्तिरावृणोति यदा तदा । अव्याकृतमिति प्राहुर्वेदान्तपरिनिष्ठिताः ॥ 21
मूलप्रकृतिरित्येके प्राहुर्मायेति केचन । अविद्या संसृतिर्बन्ध इत्यादि बहुधोच्यते ॥ 22
त्वया संक्षोभ्यमाणा सा महत्तत्त्वं प्रसूयते । महत्तत्त्वादहङ्कारस्त्वया सञ्चोदितादभूत् ॥ 23
अहङ्कारो महत्तत्त्वसंवृतस्त्रिविधोऽभवत् । सात्त्विको राजसश्चैव तामसश्चेति भण्यते ॥ 24
तामसात्सूक्ष्मतन्मात्राण्यासन् भूतान्यतः परम् । स्थूलानि क्रमशो राम क्रमोत्तरगुणानि ह ॥ 25
राजसानीन्द्रियाण्येव सात्त्विका देवता मनः । तेभ्योऽभवत्सूत्ररूपं लिङ्गं सर्वगतं महत् ॥ 26

worshipped him in a very elaborate manner and fed him with several kinds of fruits and roots available in that forest.

Agastya's hymn (17-50).

17. Rama of moonlike face being now seated alone, the holy sage Agastya said as follows with palms joined in salutation: **(18-19).** "The day on which Brahma prayed to Thee on the shore of the Milk Ocean to relieve the earth of its burdens and to destroy Ravana, from that day I have been waiting here in expectation of Thy arrival· I have been staying with the ascetics of this place, performing austerities and constantly thinking about Thee in my eagerness to meet Thee. **(20-22).** Before the cycle of creation started, Thou alone didst exist with none else besides, unmodified, without any adjunct. There is Thy potency spoken of as Maya, which has no existence apart from Thee,and which was latent in Thy self with all the manifoldness and adjunct-potential in it. When that Power, on being assumed by Thee, manifests itself, the savants of Vedanta call it Avyakrita, the Unmanifested Whole. Some call it Mulaprakriti (Root-Nature), others as Maya (Mysterious Power), still others as Avidya (ignorance), and *samsriti* (transmigratory cycle) and *bandha* (bondage). **23.** Under Thy prompting, She (Maya) manifests Mahattattva (Great Element). Out of Mahattatva, under Thy stimulation, Ahamkara (the cosmic I-sense) evolves. **24.** Ahamkara, which is an expression of Mahattatva, manifests itself in three aspects—the Sattvika aspect, the Rajasika aspect and the Tamasika aspect. **25.** Out of Ahamkara dominated by Tamas, evolved the subtle essence of things (Tanmatra), and out of them in due order evolved the gross elements—Akasa (ether), Vayu (air), Agni (fire), Jala (water) and Bhumi, (earth). **26.** Out of Rajasa-ahamkara was evolved the Indriyas (senses) and out of Sattvika-ahamkara, the Devatas (deities) and Manas (mind). By the combination of all these (evolutes) was formed

ततो विराट् समुत्पन्नः स्थूलाद् भूतकदम्बकात् । विराजः पुरुषात्सर्वं जगत्स्थावरजङ्गमम् ॥ 27

देवतिर्यङ्मनुष्याश्च कालकर्मक्रमेण तु । त्वं रजोगुणतो ब्रह्मा जगतः सर्वकारणम् ॥ 28

सत्त्वाद्विष्णुस्त्वमेवास्य पालकः सद्भिरुच्यते । लये रुद्रस्त्वमेवास्य त्वन्मायागुणभेदतः ॥ 29

जाग्रत्स्वप्नसुषुप्त्याख्या वृत्तयो बुद्धिजैर्गुणैः । तासां विलक्षणो राम त्वं साक्षी चिन्मयोऽव्ययः ।

सृष्टिलीलां यदा कर्तुमीहसे रघुनन्दन । अङ्गीकरोषि मायां त्वं तदा वै गुणवानिव ॥ 31

राम माया द्विधा भाति विद्याविद्येति ते सदा ।

प्रवृत्तिमार्गनिरता अविद्यावशवर्तिनः । निवृत्तिमार्गनिरता वेदान्तार्थविचारकाः ॥ 32

त्वद्भक्तिनिरता ये च ते वै विद्यामयाः स्मृताः॥ 33

अविद्यावशगा ये तु नित्यं संसारिणश्च ते । विद्याभ्यासरता ये तु नित्यमुक्तास्त एव हि ॥ 34

लोके त्वद्भक्तिनिरतास्त्वन्मन्त्रोपासकाश्च ये । विद्या प्रादुर्भवेत्तेषां नेतरेषां कदाचन ॥ 35

the universal causal body (Linga), holding within it the whole potentiality of the universe. It is also called the Sutratma (the Pervading Self) and the Hiranyagarbha (Luminous Potentiality). **27.** From the Hiranyagarbha manifested the Cosmic Whole (Virat), whose gross body consists of the whole universe, with all its moving and unmoving beings. **28.** In the course of time or according to the manifestation of Karma potentialities, the Devas, men and the brute creations came into existence. Assuming the constituent of Rajas, Thou didst become Brahma, the creator of the universe. **29.** Wise men say that assuming the constituent of Sattva, Thou art Vishnu, the Protector, and assuming Tamas Thou art also Rudra, the destroyer of the universe. Thus what are called the Trimurti, the Triune Being, is nothing but Thyself. **30.** The three states of waking, dream and sleep, which are the three modes of Buddhi born of its constituents of Sattva, Rajas and Tamas, are verily Thyself, O Rama. Thou art also the Pure Consciousness, changeless and transcendent, distinct from the Buddhi and its modes of three states, standing as their witness. **31.** O the noblest of Raghu's line! When Thou willest to enact the play of creation, Thou assumest Thy Power Maya, and appearest as one endowed with the Gunas of Sattva, Rajas and Tamas **(32-33).** O Rama! Thy Maya has two aspects—Vidya (spiritual illumination) and Avidya (ignorance). Those who are devoted to works, Vedic and secular, are under the dominance of Avidya, while the followers of the path of renunciation, given to reflection on the purport of the Vedanta and the practice of devotion to Thee, are filled by the power of Vidya. **34.** Those who are dominated by Avidya are ever consigned to the transmigratory cycle, while those devoted to Vidya become ever-free. **35.** In this world, Vidya shines in those who have constant devotion to Thee and ever repeat Thy sacred name and reflect on it, but never in others devoid of devotion.

अतस्त्वद्भक्तिसम्पन्ना मुक्ता एव न संशयः। त्वद्भक्त्यमृतहीनानां मोक्षः स्वप्नेऽपि नो भवेत् ॥
किं राम बहुनोक्तेन सारं किञ्चिद् ब्रवीमि ते। साधुसङ्गतिरेवात्र मोक्षहेतुरुदाहृता ॥ 37
साधवः समचित्ता ये निःस्पृहा विगतैषिणः। दान्ताः प्रशान्तास्त्वद्भक्ता निवृत्ताखिलकामनाः॥
इष्टप्राप्तिविपत्त्योश्च समाः सङ्गविवर्जिताः। संन्यस्ताखिलकर्माणः सर्वदा ब्रह्मतत्पराः ॥ 39
यमादिगुणसम्पन्नाः सन्तुष्टा येन केनचित्। सत्सङ्गमो भवेद्यर्हि त्वत्कथाश्रवणे रतिः ॥ 40
समुदेति ततो भक्तिस्त्वयि राम सनातने। त्वद्भक्तावुपपन्नायां विज्ञानं विपुलं स्फुटम् ॥ 41
उदेति मुक्तिमार्गोऽयमाद्यश्चतुरसेवितः। तस्माद्राघव सद्भक्तिस्त्वयि मे प्रेमलक्षणा ॥ 42
सदा भूयाद्धरे सङ्गस्त्वद्भक्तेषु विशेषतः। अद्य मे सफलं जन्म भवत्सन्दर्शनादभूत् ॥ 43
अद्य मे क्रतवः सर्वे बभूवुः सफलाः प्रभो।
दीर्घकालं मया तप्तमनन्यमतिना तपः। तस्येह तपसो राम फलं तव यदर्चनम् ॥ 44

36. Therefore those who have devotion (Bhakti) are verily blessed with Mukti (liberation), while those devoid of that immortal excellence of devotion can never hope to experience Moksha (freedom from Samsara) even in dream.

37. "What is the good of speaking too much, O Rama? I shall place before Thee the most essential requirement of devotional life. Contact with holy men (Sadhus) is the one essential means for the attainment of Moksha. **(38-40).** A Sadhu (a true holy man) is one in whom the following excellences are found: even-mindedness towards all including friend, enemy and neutral; desirelessness; control of the senses in respect of external objects; abandonment of the three *eshanas* (desire for children, for wealth, and for heavenly enjoyment); placidity of mind arising from complete self-mastery; supreme devotion to Thee; equanimity of mind in success and failure; absence of all attachments; abandonment of all evil and selfish actions; abiding interest in contemplating on Brahman; the practice of Yama and other disciplines of Yoga; and satisfaction with whatever means of livelihood that comes spontaneously without seeking. Such are the characteristics of holy men. Intimate contact with them gives rise to delight in matters dealing with the Divine excellences and accounts. **(41-43).** When such delight is established in the mind, loving devotion to God (Bhakti) is generated. Devotion gives rise to clear and comprehensive realisation of the Divine. This is the royal road to Mukti adopted by men of sound discernment. Therefore, O Rama, may I ever have Bhakti characterised by intense love of Thee! May I, O Hari, particularly have contact with holy men completely devoted to Thee. My life's purpose has been attained today by this meeting I am having with Thee. **44.** Today all the Vedic rituals I have practised have come to their fruition. Long have I been practising austerities without any other thought in my mind except Thee. O Rama! The blessing I have got today through this opportunity to offer adoration to Thee in this form as the Incarnate, is the result of all the disciplines

सदा मे सीतया सार्धं हृदये वस राघव । गच्छतस्तिष्ठतो वापि स्मृतिः स्यान्मे सदा त्वयि ॥
इति स्तुत्वा रमानाथमगस्त्यो मुनिसत्तमः । ददौ चापं महेन्द्रेण रामार्थे स्थापितं पुरा ॥ 46
अक्षय्यौ बाणतूणीरौ खड्गं रत्नविभूषितः ।
जहि राघव भूभारभूतं राक्षसमण्डलम् । यदर्थमवतीर्णोऽसि मायया मनुजाकृतिः ॥ 47
इतो योजनयुग्मे तु पुण्यकाननमण्डितः ।
अस्ति पञ्चवटीनाम्ना आश्रमो गौतमीतटे । नेतव्यस्तत्र ते कालः शेषो रघुकुलोद्वह ॥ 48
तत्रैव बहुकार्याणि देवानां कुरु सत्पते ॥ 49
श्रुत्वा तदागस्त्यसुभाषितं वचः स्तोत्रं च तत्त्वार्थसमन्वितं विभुः ।
मुनिं समाभाष्य मुदान्वितो ययौ प्रदर्शितं मार्गमशेषविद्धरिः ॥ 50

इति श्रीमदध्यात्मरामायणे उमामहेश्वरसंवादे
आरण्यकाण्डे तृतीयः सर्गः ॥ ३ ॥

and austerities I have practised. **45.** May Thou dwell in my heart with Sita for ever. And May the remembrance of Thee occur constantly in my mind in all conditions, whether I am engaged in some work or am resting!"

(46-47). Adoring Rama, the consort of Ramā in this way, the great Rishi Agastya presented to him a bow which Indra had entrusted him with for the purpose of being handed over to Rama. He also gave him a quiver that is never exhausted of arrows and a sword studded with gems and said, "O scion of Raghu's line! Destroy with these the tribe of Rakshasas who have become a burden to this earth. It is for this purpose that Thou hast incarnated in a human body. **48.** About two Yojanas from here, there is an Ashrama named Panchavati on the banks of the river Gautami, surrounded by a sacred forest. O noblest of the descendents of Raghu! You can spend the rest of your forest life in that place. **49.** O protector of holy men! There you can accomplish many objectives for the benefit of the Devas." **50.** Rama, who was none but the all-knowing and all-powerful Hari, having heard the very meaningful hymn of Agastya and the guidance given by him, went away highly satisfied in the direction shown by the sage.

चतुर्थः सर्गः

श्रीमहादेव उवाच

मार्गे व्रजन्ददर्शाथ शैलशृङ्गमिव स्थितम्। वृद्धं जटायुषं रामः किमेतदिति विस्मितः ॥ 1

धनुरानय सौमित्रे राक्षसोऽयं पुरः स्थितः। इत्याह लक्ष्मणं रामो हनिष्याम्यृषिभक्षकम् ॥ 2

तच्छ्रुत्वा रामवचनं गृध्रराड् भयपीडितः। वधार्होऽहं न ते राम पितुस्तेऽहं प्रियः सखा ॥ 3

जटायुर्नाम भद्रं ते गृध्रोऽहं प्रियकृत्तव ॥ 4

पञ्चवटयामहं वत्स्ये तवैव प्रियकाम्यया। मृगयायां कदाचित्तु प्रयाते लक्ष्मणेऽपि च ॥ 5

सीता जनककन्या मे रक्षितव्या प्रयत्नतः। श्रुत्वा तद्गृध्रवचनं रामः सस्नेहमब्रवीत् ॥ 6

साधु गृध्र महाराज तथैव कुरु मे प्रियम्। अत्रैव मे समीपस्थो नातिदूरे वने वसन् ॥ 7

इत्यामन्त्रितमालिङ्ग्य ययौ पञ्चवटीं प्रभुः। लक्ष्मणेन सह भ्रात्रा सीतया रघुनन्दनः ॥ 8

गत्वा ते गौतमीतीरं पञ्चवटयां सुविस्तरम्। मन्दिरं कारयामास लक्ष्मणेन सुबुद्धिना ॥ 9

तत्र ते न्यवसन्सर्वे गङ्गाया उत्तरे तटे। कदम्बपनसाम्रादिफलवृक्षसमाकुले ॥ 10

विविक्ते जनसम्बाधवर्जिते नीरुजस्थले। विनोदयन् जनकजां लक्ष्मणेन विपश्चिता ॥ 11

अध्युवास सुखं रामो देवलोक इवापरः। कन्दमूलफलादीनि लक्ष्मणोऽनुदिनं तयोः ॥ 12

आनीय प्रददौ रामसेवातत्परमानसः। धनुर्बाणधरो नित्यं रात्रौ जागर्ति सर्वतः ॥ 13

Chapter 4

TOWARDS PANCHAVATI

Meeting with Jatayu (1-15)

1. While travelling along the path shown by the sage Agastya, Rama and party came across the aged eagle Jatayu, mountain-like in size and wondrous in appearance. **2.** Thereupon Rama said: "O Lakshmana, get my bow. What is standing before us must be one of those Rakshasas eating up the Rishis. He deserves to be killed." **3.** Frightened to hear those words of Rama, that king of the eagles said, "I do not deserve to be killed by you, O Rama! I am a close friend of your father. **(4-7)** I am the eagle named Jatayu. Desirous of serving you, I shall stay in Panchavati itself. If ever you and Lakshmana both happen to go into the forest to hunt, I shall guard and protect Sita, the daughter of Janaka." Hearing these words of the eagle, Rama said with great affection, "O King of eagles! Your words are praiseworthy. Please stay in this forest itself not very far off from my residence, and help me whenever I want." **8.** Addressing these words to the eagle and embracing him, the great Lord Rama, the delight of the Raghus, moved on with Lakshmana and Sita.

9. Reaching the bank of the river Gautami (Godavari), there in the region called Panchavati, Lakshmana built a roomy cottage for the party to stay. **(10-13).** That

स्नानं कुर्वन्त्यनुदिनं त्रयस्ते गौतमीजले । उभयोर्मध्यगा सीता कुरुते च गमागमौ ॥ 14
आनीय सलिलं नित्यं लक्ष्मणः प्रीतमानसः । सेवतेऽहरहः प्रीत्या एवमासन् सुखं त्रयः ॥ 15
एकदा लक्ष्मणो राममेकान्ते समुपस्थितम् । विनयावनतो भूत्वा पप्रच्छ परमेश्वरम् ॥ 16
भगवन् श्रोतुमिच्छामि मोक्षस्यैकान्तिकीं गतिम् । त्वत्तः कमलपत्राक्ष संक्षेपाद्वक्तुमर्हसि ॥ 17
ज्ञानं विज्ञानसहितं भक्तिवैराग्यबृंहितम् । आचक्ष्व मे रघुश्रेष्ठ वक्ता नान्योऽस्ति भूतले ॥

श्रीराम उवाच

शृणु वक्ष्यामि ते वत्स गुह्याद्गुह्यतरं परम् । यद्विज्ञाय नरो जह्यात्सद्यो वैकल्पिकं भ्रमम् ॥ 19
आदौ मायास्वरूपं ते वक्ष्यामि तदनन्तरम् । ज्ञानस्य साधनं पश्चाज्ज्ञानं विज्ञानसंयुतम् ॥ 20
ज्ञेयं च परमात्मानं यज्ज्ञात्वा मुच्यते भयात् । अनात्मनि शरीरादावात्मबुद्धिस्तु या भवेत् ॥21
सैव माया तयैवासौ संसारः परिकल्प्यते । रूपे द्वे निश्चिते पूर्वं मायायाः कुलनन्दन ॥22
विक्षेपावरणे तत्र प्रथमं कल्पयेज्जगत् । लिङ्गाद्यब्रह्मपर्यन्तं स्थूलसूक्ष्मविभेदतः ॥ 23
अपरं त्वखिलं ज्ञानरूपमावृत्य तिष्ठति । मायया कल्पितं विश्वं परमात्मनि केवले ॥ 24

place was situated on the northern bank of the Godavari, away from the madding crowds and surrounded by a thick growth of fruit-bearing trees like Kadamba, Panasa and Amra. Delighting Sita, Rama stayed there as immortals in heaven along with Lakshmana of deep insight. Lakshmana devoted himself to the service of Rama in every way. Every day he went out and collected the roots and fruits of the forest and fed Rama with them. At night he kept vigil with bow and arrow in hand, protecting the residence of Rama. **14.** All the three of them went every day for their ablutions to the Godavari. While going for, and returning from, bath, Rama and Lakshmana walked in front and behind with Sita in the middle. **15.** With great joy Lakshmana brought the water required for their use. Thus the three lived in great happiness.

Rama's sermon to Lakshmana (16-55)

16. During one of those days, while Rama was sitting in solitude, Lakshmana approached him in due form and humility and questioned him. **17.** He said "O Lotus-eyed One, all-knowing and all-powerful! I wish to know from Thee the sure means for the attainment of Moksha. Deign to expound it to me in brief. **18.** O the leader of Raghu's line! Deign to impart to me Jnana (knowledge) together with Vijnana (realisation of spiritual truth) augmented by devotion and renunciation of worldly values. In the world there is none other than Thee to expound this recondite theme."

19. Rama replied: "O dear brother! Listen. I shall speak to you on the most profound of all doctrines which frees one immediately from delusions of the figments of imagination. **(20-24).** First I shall expound to you the nature of Maya. Next I shall describe the steps that lead to knowledge (Jnana), and after that to Vijnana or knowledge accompanied with realisation, and to the Supreme Self (the Paramatman). The Paramatman is the object of the spiritual

रज्जौ भुजङ्गवद्भ्रान्त्या विचारे नास्ति किञ्चन । श्रूयते दृश्यते यद्यत्स्मर्यते वा नरैः सदा ॥ 25
असदेव हि तत्सर्वं यथा स्वप्नमनोरथौ । देह एव हि संसारवृक्षमूलं दृढं स्मृतम् ॥ 26
तन्मूलःपुत्र दारादिबन्धः किं तेऽन्यथात्मनः ॥ 27
देहस्तु स्थूलभूतानां पञ्च तन्मात्रपञ्चकम् । अहंकारश्च बुद्धिश्च इन्द्रियाणि तथा दश ॥ 28
चिदाभासो मनश्चैव मूलप्रकृतिरेव च । एतत्क्षेत्रमिति ज्ञेयं देह इत्यभिधीयते ॥ 29
एतैर्विलक्षणो जीवः परमात्मा निरामयः । तस्य जीवस्य विज्ञाने साधनान्यपि मे शृणु ॥ 30
जीवश्च परमात्मा च पर्यायो नात्र भेदधीः । मानाभावस्तथा दम्भहिंसादिपरिवर्जनम् ॥ 31
पराक्षेपादिसहनं सर्वत्रावक्रता तथा । मनोवाक्कायसद्भक्त्या सद्गुरोः परिसेवनम् ॥ 32
बाह्याभ्यन्तरसंशुद्धिः स्थिरता सत्क्रियादिषु । मनोवाक्कायदण्डश्च विषयेषु निरीहता ॥ 33

aspirant's quest. By knowing him one is released from Bhaya—fear consisting in the repeated experience of death and birth in Samsara. That by the power of which one falsely feels the sense of selfhood with regard to the body-mind, which in reality is not the Self at all—that is Maya. This Samsara, based on the false identification, is entirely a creation of Maya. O noble one! Maya is traditionally accepted as having two aspects—Vikshepa (projection) and Avarana (covering up). The whole of the objective universe in its gross and subtle form, embracing everything from the Mahattatva (all-comprehending category) to the Cosmic Being (Brahmā) is super-imposed by the power (Sakti) known as Vikshepa. The other aspect of Avidya known as Avarana (covering power) completely covers up the real nature of Pure Consciousness and thus paves the way for the super-imposition of this multifarious universe on Pure Consciousness by Maya (or the Vikshepa aspect of it). **(25-26).** On discriminating, the world of multiplicity is found only to be a product of delusion and not really existent, just like the rope experienced as snake. All that men constantly hear, see and remember—it is all unreal, just like the contents of a dream or imagination. The body is the firm root of the tree of Śamsara.

27. "It is because of the body that connection with wife and children and other members of the family is established. No other form of connection with these can be traced between them and oneself. The Atman does not in any way need them. **(28-29).** The body-mind is a combination of several factors. The five gross elements, the five subtle elements, the 'I' sense (Ahamkara), intellect (Buddhi), the ten senses, mind (Manas) which is a reflection of Pure Consciousness, Root-Nature (Mula-Prakriti)—the combination of all these is what is called Kshetra, also known as the body. **30.** The Jiva is distinct from this complex described above. He is the Spirit (Paramatman), free from happiness and sorrow. I shall now tell you the means by which the truth about the Jiva could be ascertained.

(31-37). "The terms Jiva (Individual spirit) and Paramatman (Supreme Spirit) are synon-

निरहङ्कारता जन्मजराद्यालोचनं तथा । असक्तिः स्नेहशून्यत्वं पुत्रदारधनादिषु ॥ 34
इष्टानिष्टागमे नित्यं चित्तस्य समता तथा । मयि सर्वात्मके रामे ह्यनन्यविषया मतिः ॥ 35
जनसम्बाधरहितशुद्धदेशनिषेवणम् । प्राकृतैर्जनसङ्घैश्च ह्यरतिः सर्वदा भवेत् ॥ 36
आत्मज्ञाने सदोद्योगो वेदान्तार्थावलोकनम् । उक्तैरेतैर्भवेज्ज्ञानं विपरीतैर्विपर्ययः ॥ 37
बुद्धिप्राणमनोदेहाहंकृतिभ्यो विलक्षणः । चिदात्माहं नित्यशुद्धो बुद्ध एवेति निश्चयम् ॥ 38
येन ज्ञानेन संवित्ते तज्ज्ञानं निश्चितं च मे । विज्ञानं च तदैवैतत्साक्षादनुभवेद्यदा ॥ 39
आत्मा सर्वत्र पूर्णः स्याच्चिदानन्दात्मकोऽव्ययः । बुद्ध्याद्युपाधिरहितः परिणामादिवर्जितः ॥ 40
स्वप्रकाशेन देहादीन् भासयन्ननपावृतः । एक एवाद्वितीयश्च सत्यज्ञानादिलक्षणः ॥ 41

ymous. There is no difference between these. Therefore, do not entertain identification with the body as oneself. Avoid fraud, oppression and infliction of pain on other beings. Bear with fortitude the criticisms and persecutions of others. Be without crookedness. Be devoted to a true teacher and serve him with mind, speech and body. Observe purity, mental and physical. Be steady in the performance of virtuous acts. Control your mind, speech and body. Have no longing for sense objects. Be free from egotism. Be always aware of the evils of birth, old age etc. Be non-attached to sons, wife etc.; avoid cherishing towards them affection that partakes of partiality. Be equanimous when desirable and undesirable experiences come. Have constant devotion to Me, Rama, who is the soul of all beings. Do not concern your mind with matters that are not spiritual; resort to holy places that are free from crowds of men. Never feel attraction for the company of worldly-minded people. Let the search for the Atman be your sole quest. Always be reflecting in your mind about the truth of scriptural dicta. The practice of these disciplines will lead to Jnana, the knowledge of the Spirit. In their absence, the result will be the contrary.

38. "Jnana (knowledge of the Spirit) is that knowledge by which one gets certitude that the real 'I' is distinct from Buddhi, Prana, Ahamkara (I-sense), Manas (Mind) and body, but is, on the other hand, one with Pure Consciousness, eternal, pure and wakeful. **39.** When this conviction becomes a constant realisation or actuality, that is called Vijnana (Enlightenment). **40.** The Atman infills everything. He is of the nature of Pure Consciousness and Bliss. He has no destruction. He is free from attachment, aversion etc., which are the characteristics of His adjuncts like Buddhi. He is free from all transformations(which are characteristics of the products of Prakriti and its evolutes). **41.** It is He who endows the body-mind with consciousness and Himself stands self-revealed. He is the One with out a second whose existence can never be-covered up or sublated. Truth, conscious-

असङ्गः स्वप्रभो द्रष्टा विज्ञानेनावगम्यते । आचार्यशास्त्रोपदेशाद्यैक्यज्ञानं यदा भवेत् ॥ 42
आत्मनोर्जीवपरयोर्मूलाविद्या तदैव हि । लीयते कार्यकरणैः सहैव परमात्मनि ॥ 43
सावस्था मुक्तिरित्युक्ता ह्युपचारोऽयमात्मनि । इदं मोक्षस्वरूपं ते कथितं रघुनन्दन ॥ 44
ज्ञानविज्ञानवैराग्यसहितं मे परात्मनः । किन्त्वेतद्दुर्लभं मन्ये मद्भक्तिविमुखात्मनाम् ॥ 45
चक्षुष्मतामपि तथा रात्रौ सम्यङ् न दृश्यते । पदं दीपसमेतानां दृश्यते सम्यगेव हि ॥ 46
एवं मद्भक्तियुक्तानामात्मा सम्यक् प्रकाशते । मद्भक्तेः कारणं किञ्चिद्वक्ष्यामि शृणु तत्त्वतः ॥47
मद्भक्तसङ्गो मत्सेवा मद्भक्तानां निरन्तरम् । एकादश्युवासादि मम पर्वानुमोदनम् ॥ 48
मत्कथाश्रवणे पाठे व्याख्याने सर्वदा रतिः । मत्पूजापरिनिष्ठा च मम नामानुकीर्तनम् ॥ 49
एवं सततयुक्तानां भक्तिरव्यभिचारिणी । मयि सञ्जायते नित्यं ततः किमवशिष्यते ॥ 50
अतो मद्भक्तियुक्तस्य ज्ञानं विज्ञानमेव च । वैराग्यं च भवेच्छीघ्रं ततो मुक्तिमवाप्नुयात् ॥51
कथितं सर्वमेतत्ते तव प्रश्नानुसारतः । अस्मिन्मनः समाधाय यस्तिष्ठेत्स तु मुक्तिभाक् ॥52

ness etc., are his characteristics. **(42-47)**. This Eternal Witness, unrelated to anything and self-revealing, comes to be understood through realisation. When, through the instruction of the scripture and the teacher, the understanding of unity of the individual Self with the Supreme Self dawns on the mind of an aspirant, then the root-ignorance (Mula-avidya) along with its cause and its effects dissolve into the Supreme Self. That state is called Mukti (Liberation). O scion of Raghu's line! I have expounded to you My true nature along with the teachings regarding its knowledge and its realisation. All this doctrine about bondage and liberation is secondary. (They are not actual; for the Atman is ever-free). But this Supreme Truth about the Atman never dawns in the minds of people who are without devotion to Me. At night, in darkness, even men with eyes cannot see their foot-steps. When they are provided with light they can see it. Even like that, to those who have devotion to Me, the Atman shines. I shall, therefore, tell you now some of those factors that generate devotion to Me.

(48-50). "Association with My devotees, adoring service of Me, constant service of My devotees, observance of the vow of Ekadasi and the like, keen interest in listening to, reading and exposition of accounts of, My excellences, adherence to My ceremonial worship, repetition of My name and hymning about my attributes-those whoare constantly devoted to these disciplines gain unshakable devotion to Me. What else is there to gain than this? **51.** Therefore, one who is endowed with devotion to me attains knowledge, non-attachment and enlightenment quickly. Thereby he attains Mukti (liberation). **52.** In accordance with your questions I have expounded to you all these Truths. One who remembers and follows

न वक्तव्यमिदं यत्नान्मद्भक्तिविमुखाय हि। मद्भक्ताय प्रदातव्यमाहूयापि प्रयत्नतः ॥ 53
य इदं तु पठेन्नित्यं श्रद्धाभक्तिसमन्वितः। अज्ञानपटलध्वान्तं विधूय परिमुच्यते ॥ 54
भक्तानां मम योगिनां सुविमलस्वान्तातिशान्तात्मनाँ
मत्सेवाभिरतात्मनां च विमलज्ञानात्मनाँ सर्वदा।
सङ्गं यः कुरुते सदोद्यतमतिस्तत्सेवनानन्यधी-
र्मोक्षस्तस्य करे स्थितोऽहमनिशं दृश्यो भवे नान्यथा ॥ 55

इति श्रीमदध्यात्मरामायणे उमामहेश्वरसंवादे
आरण्यकाण्डे चतुर्थः सर्गः ॥ ४ ॥

these teachings becomes fit to attain Mukti. **53.** You should never impart these teachings even under compulsion to those who have no trace of devotion to Me, but you must impart them to My devotees, even calling them to your side. **54.** Whoever studies this daily with faith and devotion succeeds in shattering the thick darkness of Ignorance and attaining liberation. **55.** Whoever is devoted to Me, practises communion with Me, is pure in heart and calm in mind, delights in the service of Me, understands the nature of the Self to be purity, is devoid of attachments and is ever striving in the spiritual path—to such a person whose mind never goes to anything other than the service of holy men and holy causes, Moksha is an achievement already in hand. They become fit to see My presence always and everywhere. There is no other way for this attainment.

पञ्चमः सर्गः

श्रीमहादेव उवाच

तस्मिन् काले महारण्ये राक्षसी कामरूपिणी। विचचार महासत्त्वा जनस्थाननिवासिनी ॥ 1
एकदा गौतमीतीरे पञ्चवट्याः समीपतः। पद्मवज्राङ्कुशाङ्कानि पदानि जगतीपतेः ॥ 2
दृष्ट्वा कामपरीतात्मा पादसौन्दर्यमोहिता। पश्यन्ती सा शनैरायाद्राघवस्य निवेशनम् ॥ 3

Chapter 5

SURPANAKHA'S MUTILATION

Surpanakha's arrival (1-17)

1. In those days, in the thick forest that surrounded Janasthana, there moved about a Rakshasa woman of enormous strength who had the capacity to assume any form she liked. **(2-3).** On a certain day this Rakshasa woman noticed on the banks of the Godavari the foot-prints of Rama, the Lord of the

तत्र सा तं रमानाथं सीतया सह संस्थितम् । कन्दर्पसदृशं रामं दृष्ट्वा कामविमोहिता ॥ 4
राक्षसी राघवं प्राह कस्य त्वं कः किमाश्रमे । युक्तो जटावल्कलाद्यैः साध्यं किं तेऽत्र मेवद ॥5
अहं शूर्पणखा नाम राक्षसी कामरूपिणी । भगिनी राक्षसेन्द्रस्य रावणस्य महात्मनः ॥ 6
खरेण सहिता भ्रात्रा वसाम्यत्रैव कानने । राज्ञा दत्तं च मे सर्वं मुनिभक्षा वसाम्यहम् ॥ 7
त्वां तु वेदितुमिच्छामि वद मे वदतां वर । तामाह रामनामाहमयोध्याधिपतेः सुतः ॥ 8
एषा मे सुन्दरी भार्या सीता जनकनन्दिनी । स तु भ्राता कनीयान्मे लक्ष्मणोऽतीवसुन्दरः ॥ 9
किं कृत्यं ते मया ब्रूहि कार्यं भुवनसुन्दरि । इति रामवचः श्रुत्वा कामार्ता साब्रवीदिदम् ॥ 10
एहि राम मया सार्धं रमस्व गिरिकानने । कामार्ताहं न शक्नोमि त्यक्तुं त्वां कमलेक्षणम् ॥
रामः सीतां कटाक्षेण पश्यन् सस्मितमब्रवीत् । भार्या ममैषा कल्याणी विद्यते ह्यनपायिनी ॥ 12
त्वं तु सापत्न्यदुःखेन कथं स्थास्यसि सुन्दरि । बहिरास्ते मम भ्राता लक्ष्मणोऽतीव सुन्दरः ॥13
तवानुरूपो भविता पतिस्तेनैव सञ्चर । इत्युक्ता लक्ष्मणं प्राह पतिर्मे भव सुन्दर ॥ 14

universe, with marks of Lotus, Vajra (diamond weapon) and Ankusa (hook). Seeing the extremely handsome nature of these foot-prints, she was struck with passionate love for the one to whom they belonged. So following the track of these foot-prints she arrived at the abode of Rama. **4-5.** Seeing there, in the company of Sita, the Cupid-like Rama, the consort of Lakshmi, this Rakshasa woman with intensified passion for him, asked him, "Whose son are you? What's your name? Why do you stay in the Ashrama donning tree-bark clothes and matted locks? What are you going to attain by staying here? **6.** I am a Rakshasa woman named Surpanakha, who can assume any form I like. I am a sister of the great Ravana, the lord of the Rakshasas. **7.** I am staying in this forest along with Khara, my brother. Our king Ravana has assigned this whole forest to me. I stay here eating up all the ascetics I come across. **(8-10).** I desire to be acquainted with you. O eloquent one! Tell me everything about yourself." To her Rama replied, "I am known as Rama, the son of the King of Ayodhya. This beautiful woman is my wife Sita, the daughter of Janaka. The other person with me is my handsome younger brother Lakshmana. Now, O beauty-queen of the whole universe! What do you want of me? Speak out." Hearing these words of Rama, that love-lorn Rakshasa woman said in reply: **11.** "O Rama! Come along with me. We shall have a very enjoyable time, moving about in this forest. I, who am in the grip of passion, cannot remain separated from you, O lotus-eyed one!"

(12-14). Casting a meaningful sidelong glance at Sita, Rama replied to that woman with a smile, "Here is this handsome woman, my wife who never remains separated from me. So you will have to be only a co-wife which will be intolerable to you. Here outside is my brother Lakshmana, who is very handsome in appearance. He will be a fitting husband for you. You enjoy life with him moving about in this forest." At

भ्रातुराज्ञां पुरस्कृत्य सङ्गच्छावोऽद्य मा चिरम् । इत्याह राक्षसी घोरा लक्ष्मणं काममोहिता ॥ 15
तामाह लक्ष्मणः साध्वि दासोऽहं तस्य धीमतः । दासी भविष्यसि त्वं तु ततो दुःखतरं नु किम् ॥ 16
तमेव गच्छ भद्रं ते स तु राजाखिलेश्वरः । ततश्च त्वा पुनरप्यागाद्राघवं दुष्टमानसा ॥ 17
क्रोधाद्राम किमर्थं मां भ्रामयस्यनवस्थितः । इदानीमेव तां सीतां भक्षयामि तवाग्रतः ॥ 18
इत्युक्त्वा विकटाकरा जानकीमनुधावति । ततो रामाज्ञया खड्गमादाय परिगृह्य ताम् ॥ 19
चिच्छेद नासां कर्णौ च लक्ष्मणोऽलघुविक्रमः । ततो घोरध्वनिं कृत्वा रुधिराक्तवपुर्द्रुतम् ॥ 20
क्रन्दमाना पपाताग्रे खरस्य परुषाक्षरा । किमेतदिति तामाह खरः खरतराक्षरः ॥ 21
केनैवं कारितासि त्वं मृत्योर्वक्त्रानुवर्तिना । वद मे तं वधिष्यामि कालकल्पमपि क्षणात् ॥ 22
तमाह राक्षसी रामः सीतालक्ष्मणसंयुतः । दण्डकं निर्भयं कुर्वन्नास्ते गोदावरीतटे ॥ 23
मामेवं कृतवांस्तस्य भ्राता तेनैव चोदितः । यदि त्वं कुलजातोऽसि वीरोऽसि जहि तौ रिपू ॥24
तयोस्तु रुधिरं पास्ये भक्षयेतौ सुदुर्मदौ । नो चेत्प्राणान्परित्यज्य यास्यामि यमसादनम् ॥25

these words of Rama, Surpanakha turned towards Lakshmana and said, "O handsome one! Be pleased to be my husband. **15.** According to the command of your brother, we both shall be united. Let there be no delay." Moved by intense sexual passion, that fierce Rakshasi said thus to Lakshmana.

(16-17). Lakshmana now said to her, "O good woman! I am only a servant of that highly intelligent person, Rama. Do you want to become a servant woman? What is more pitiable than that? So, you go to Rama again for your own good. He is the king and the lord of all." Hearing this, that evil-minded woman approached Rama again.

Surpanakha's mutilation and destruction of Khara (18-37)

(18-22). In great anger she said, "O Rama, fickle-minded as you are, why are you teasing me like this? Now itself, in your very presence, I shall devour this Sita, who is at the bottom of all this mischief." With these words, she rushed towards Sita, assuming a fierce form. Thereupon, on the orders of Rama, the powerful Lakshmana cut off her ears and nose with a sword. As blood flowed all over her body, that Rakshasa woman gave out a fierce howl. Shrieking and uttering abusive words, she went and fell before the Rakshasa Khara of fierce speech. He thereupon asked her, "How has this happened? This atrocity must have been done on you by one who is almost in the mouth of death. I am going to kill him, even if he be as powerful as Kala." **(23-25).** That Rakshasi, thereupon replied, "Rama, along with Sita and Lakshmana, is staying on the banks of the Godavari with the idea of making this forest of Dandaka free of fear for men. His brother Lakshmana, directed by him, has done this to me. If you are a man of a great family and a hero, you go and kill those two enemies. I shall drink their blood and you eat the bodies of those audacious men. If you do not do this, I shall give up my body and go to the abode of Yama."

ततश्श्रुत्वा त्वरितं प्रागात्खरः क्रोधेन मूर्च्छितः । चतुर्दश सहस्राणि रक्षसां भीमकर्मणाम् ॥ 26
चोदयामास रामस्य समीपं वधकाङ्क्षया । खरश्च त्रिशिराश्चैव दूषणश्चैव राक्षसः ॥ 27
सर्वे रामं ययुः शीघ्रं नानाप्रहरणोद्यताः । श्रुत्वा कोलाहलं तेषां रामः सौमित्रिमब्रवीत् ॥28
श्रूयते विपुलः शब्दो नूनमायान्ति राक्षसाः । भविष्यति महद्युद्धं नूनमद्य मया सह ॥ 29
सीतां नीत्वा गुहां गत्वा तत्र तिष्ठ महाबल । हन्तुमिच्छाम्यहं सर्वान् राक्षसान् घोररूपिणः॥ 30
अत्र किञ्चिन्न वक्तव्यं शापितोऽसि ममोपरि । तथेति सीतामादाय लक्ष्मणो गह्वरं ययौ ॥ 31
रामः परिकरं बद्ध्वा धनुरादाय निष्ठुरम् । तूणीरावक्षयशरौ बद्ध्वायत्तोऽभवत्प्रभुः ॥ 32
तत आगत्य रक्षांसि रामस्योपरि चिक्षिपुः । आयुधानि विचित्राणि पाषाणान्पादपानपि ॥ 33
तानि चिच्छेद रामोऽपि लीलया तिलशः क्षणात् । ततो बाणसहस्रेण हत्वा तान् सर्वराक्षसान् ॥ 34
खरं त्रिशिरसं चैव दूषणं चैव राक्षसम् । जघान प्रहरार्धेन सर्वानेव रघूत्तमः ॥ 35
लक्ष्मणोऽपि गुहामध्यात्सीतामादाय राघवे । समर्प्य राक्षसान्दृष्ट्वा हतान्विस्मयमाययौ ॥ 36
सीता रामं समालिङ्ग्य प्रसन्नमुखपङ्कजा । शस्त्रव्रणानि चाङ्गेषु ममार्ज जनकात्मजा ॥ 37

(26-28). The words of Surpranakha drove Khara into a fit of anger. He quickly started on an expedition. With an army of ferocious Rakshasas, fourteen thousand strong, he started for the destruction of Rama, accompanied by the Rakshasa leaders Trisiras and Dushana, all holding various kinds of weapons ready to strike. Hearing the tumultuous uproar produced by this army, Rama said to Lakshmana: **(29-31).** "A terrific sound is audible. It is certain that the Rakshasas are on the move. There is going to be a fierce fight between them and me. O powerful Lakshmana! Taking Sita, you go to the neighbouring cave for shelter. You remain there and I shall destroy all these Rakshasas of terror-inspiring forms. Don't say anything against this directive of mine. You are vowed to obey my words." Agreeing to this proposal, Lakshmana, leading Sita, went to the cave. **32.** And lordly Rama tying up his cloth and hair, stood there ready with his terrible bow in hand and his inexhaustible quiver tied to his back. **33.** The Rakshasas reached the spot quickly and they began to shower on Rama various kinds of weapons, rocks and trees. **(34-35).** Rama in reply cut all those missiles into shreds. With a thousand arrows, he killed all those Rakshasas, including the three leaders, Khara, Trisiras and Dushana within a short period of half a Yama. **36.** Lakshmana, now led Sita back from the cave to Rama's presence. Seeing the number of Rakshasas killed, all were astonished. **37.** Sita embraced Rama, with a face shinning like a full-blown lotus. She rubbed and healed the wounds on Rama's body with her hands.

सापि दुद्राव दृष्ट्वा तान्हतान् राक्षसपुङ्गवान् । लङ्कां गत्वा सभामध्ये क्रोशन्ती पादसन्निधौ ॥38

रावणस्य पपातोर्व्यां भगिनी तस्य रक्षसः । दृष्ट्वा तां रावणः प्राह भगिनीं भयविह्वलाम् ॥39

उत्तिष्ठोत्तिष्ठ वत्से त्वं विरूपकरणं तव । कृतं शक्रेण वा भद्रे यमेन वरुणेन वा ॥ 40

कुबेरेणाथवा ब्रूहि भस्मीकुर्यां क्षणेन तम् । राक्षसी तमुवाचेदं त्वं प्रमत्तो विमूढधीः ॥ 41

पानासक्तः स्त्रीविजितः षण्ढः सर्वत्र लक्ष्यसे । चारचक्षुर्विहीनस्त्वं कथं राजा भविष्यसि ॥ 42

खरश्च निहतः सङ्ख्ये दूषणस्त्रिशिरास्तथा । चतुर्दश सहस्राणि राक्षसानां महात्मनाम् ॥ 43

निहतानि क्षणेनैव रामेणासुरशत्रुणा ।

जनस्थानमशेषेण मुनीनां निर्भयं कृतम् । न जानासि विमूढस्त्वमत एव मयोच्यते ॥ 44

रावण उवाच

को वा रामः किमर्थं वा कथं तेनासुरा हताः । सम्यक्कथय मे तेषां मूलघातं करोम्यहम् ॥ 45

शूर्पणखोवाच

जनस्थानादहं याता कदाचित् गौतमीतटे । तत्र पञ्चवटी नाम पुरा मुनिजनाश्रया ॥ 46

तत्राश्रमे मया दृष्टो रामो राजीवलोचनः । धनुर्बाणधरः श्रीमान् जटावल्कलमण्डितः ॥ 47

कनीयाननुजस्तस्य लक्ष्मणोऽपि तथाविधः । तस्य भार्या विशालाक्षी रूपिणी श्रीरिवापरा ॥ 48

देवगन्धर्वनागानां मनुष्याणां तथाविधा । न दृष्टा न श्रुता राजन्द्योतयन्ती वनं शुभा ॥ 49

Surpanakha's Representation to Ravana (38-61)

(38-42). Seeing all those leading Rakshasas dead, Surpanakha, the sister of Ravana, rushed to Lanka. Crying aloud, she went into the royal assembly of Ravana and fell flat on the floor. Seeing his sister in such a frightened and distressed condition, Ravana said, "Dear sister, get up, get up. Who is it that mutilated you in this way? Be it Indra, Yama, Varuna or Kubera—tell me their name, and within a moment I shall reduce them to ashes." The Rakshasa woman, Surpanakha now replied to him, "You are a heedless fool given to drinking and the company of women. You are as good as a eunuch. That is what your conduct reveals. How can you call yourself a king, when you do not have an efficient system for gathering information? **(43-44)** Khara, Dushana and Trisiras have all been killed in battle and an army of fourteen thousand Rakshasas destroyed by Rama, the sworn enemy of Rakshasas. The whole of Janasthana has now been made a safe abode for ascetics. You have not known any of these events. It is therefore that I stigmatise you as a fool."

Hearing this, Ravana enquired: **45.** "Who is this Rama? Why has he killed all these Rakshasas? Tell me everything about it. I shall cause the total destruction of these enemies." Surpanakha then said: **(46-47).** "Recently I happened to go to Janasthana on the banks of the Godavari. In that region is located Panchavati, a place formerly inhabited by ascetics. At that place, I happened to meet Rama, handsome and lotus-eyed, equipped with bow and arrows, and donning tree-bark

आनेतुमहमुद्युक्ता तां भार्यार्थं तवानघ । लक्ष्मणो नाम तद्भ्राता चिच्छेद मम नासिकाम् 50
कर्णौ च नोदितस्तेन रामेण स महाबलः । ततोऽहमतिदुःखेन रुदती खरमन्वगाम् ॥ 51
सोऽपि रामं समासाद्य युद्धं राक्षसयूथपैः । अतः क्षणेन रामेण तेनैव बलशालिना ॥ 52
सर्वे तेन विनष्टा वै राक्षसा भीमविक्रमाः । यदि रामो मनः कुर्यात्त्रैलोक्यं निमिषार्धतः ॥ 53
भस्मीकुर्यान्न सन्देह इति भाति मम प्रभो । यदि सा तव भार्या स्यात्सफलं तव जीवितम् ॥ 54
अतो यतस्व राजेन्द्र यथा ते वल्लभा भवेत् । सीता राजीवपत्राक्षी सर्वलोकैकसुन्दरी ॥ 55
साक्षाद्रामस्य पुरतः स्थातुं त्वं न क्षमः प्रभो । मायया मोहयित्वा तु प्राप्स्यसे तां रघूत्तमम् ॥ 56
श्रुत्वा तत्सूक्तवाक्यैश्च दानमानादिभिस्तथा ।
आश्वास्य भगिनीं राजा प्रविवेश स्वकं गृहम् । तत्र चिन्तापरो भूत्वा निद्रां रात्रौ न लब्धवान् ॥ 57

एकेन रामेण कथं मनुष्य-मात्रेण नष्टः सबलः खरो मे ।
भ्राता कथं मे बलवीर्यदर्प-युतो विनष्टो बत राघवेण ॥ 58
यद्वा न रामो मनुजः परेशो मां हन्तुकामः सबलं बलौघैः ।
सम्प्रार्थितोऽयं द्रुहिणेन पूर्वं मनुष्यरूपोऽद्य रघोः कुलेऽभूत् ॥ 59

clothes and matted locks. **(48-49).** Equipped just like himself, there was by his side, his younger brother Lakshmana. With Rama,there was also his wife,an unparalleled beauty, the like of whom you will not find among the Devas, Gandharvas or men. O King! She looks veritably like another Sri and her presence illumines the forest. **(50-54).** O sinless one! I tried to get that women over here to be your wife, but Lakshmana, at the order of his brother cut off my nose and ears. Crying in great pain and distress, I approached Khara. He came with his army of Rakshasas to punish Rama, but the whole of that fierce and courageous army of Rakshasas was destroyed by that powerful man Rama. It seems to me that if he makes up his mind, Rama can reduce the whole world to ashes in half a moment. Now if that woman could be got as your wife, your life will really become fruitful. **(55-56).** O great King! You have now got to take steps to somehow secure the lotus-eyed Sita, the most noted among the world beauties, as your wife. But, O my Lord and King! You won't be able to do it directly by facing Rama. You will have to hoodwink him by some magical strategem and then approach her."

57. Hearing this representation of his sister, Ravana consoled her with good words and presents. He then went to his residential quarters. Immersed in thought, he could not get sleep that night. He thought: **58.** "How is it that Khara, with his army, was destroyed by Rama, a mere man? Proud of his own strength and courage as he was, it is a wonder to me that my brother Khara could thus be destroyed by Rama. **59.** In all probability, Rama may not be a mere man. He may be that Supreme Being, who has now

वध्यो यदि स्यां परमात्मनाहं वैकुण्ठराज्यं परिपालयेऽहम् ।
नो चेदिदं राक्षसराज्यमेव भोक्ष्ये चिरं राममतो व्रजामि ॥ 60

इत्थं विचिन्त्याखिलराक्षसेन्द्रो रामं विदित्वा परमेश्वरं हरिम् ।
विरोधबुद्ध्यैव हरिं प्रयामि द्रुतं न भक्त्या भगवान् प्रसीदेत् ॥ 61

इति श्रीमदध्यात्मरामायणे उमामहेश्वरसंवादे
आरण्यकाण्डे पञ्चमः सर्गः ॥ ५ ॥

assumed a human form in the line of the Raghus, and come with his forces to destroy me with my army, as implored by Brahma in days of old. **60.** If I am killed by the Supreme Self, I shall reign in the Supreme Realm of Vaikuntha. If I am not killed, I shall be enjoying this realm of the Rakshasas for a long time. So, I am going to oppose Rama." **61.** Reflecting in this way, that lord of the Rakshasas concluded that Rama must be Hari, the Supreme Lord, and resolved within himself, "I shall attain to Him through the attitude of confrontation; for, the Lord does not reveal himself quickly by ordinary forms of Bhakti (devotion)."

षष्ठः सर्गः

श्रीमहादेव उवाच

विचिन्त्यैवं निशायां स प्रभाते रथमास्थितः । रावणो मनसा कार्यमेकं निश्चित्य बुद्धिमान् ॥ 1

ययौ मारीचसदनं परं पारमुदन्वतः । मारीचस्तत्र मुनिवज्जटावल्कलधारकः ॥ 2

ध्यायन् हृदि परात्मानं निर्गुणं गुणभासकम् । समाधिविरमेऽपश्यद्रावणं गृहमागतम् ॥ 3

द्रुतमुत्थाय चालिङ्ग्य पूजयित्वा यथाविधि । कृतातिथ्यं सुखासीनं मारीचो वाक्यमब्रवीत् ॥ 4

Chapter 6

THE COMMISSIONING OF MAREECHA

Ravana at Mareecha's Abode (1-14).

(1-3). Reflecting thus at night, the intelligent Ravana made some resolutions in his mind. Ascending his chariot (the aerial vehicle Pushpaka), he went to the other side of the ocean, where the Rakshasa Mareecha was staying. There, Mareecha, donning tree-bark cloth and matted locks like an ascetic, was contemplating in his heart on that Supreme Being, who though transcending the Gunas of Prakriti, is yet reflected in the Gunas. After he obtained external consciousness from the depths of Samadhi, he saw Ravana who had arrived at his abode. **4.** He got up from his seat immediately, embraced Ravana, received him in the proper form, and did him hospitality. After giving him a comfortable

समागमनमेतत्ते रथेनैकेन रावण । चिन्तापर इवाभासि हृदि कार्यं विचिन्तयन् ॥ 5

ब्रूहि मे न हि गोप्यं चेत्करवाणि तव प्रियम् । न्याय्यं चेद् ब्रूहि राजेन्द्र वृजिनं मां स्पृशेन्नहि ॥ 6

रावण उवाच

अस्ति राजा दशरथः साकेताधिपतिः किल । रामनामा सुतस्तस्य ज्येष्ठः सत्यपराक्रमः ॥ 7

विवासयामास सुतं वनं वनजनप्रियम् । भार्यया सहितं भ्रात्रा लक्ष्मणेन समन्वितम् ॥ 8

स आस्ते विपिने घोरे पञ्चवटयाश्रमे शुभे । तस्य भार्या विशालाक्षी सीता लोकविमोहिनी 9

रामो निरपराधान्मे राक्षसान् भीमविक्रमान् । खरं च हत्वा विपिने सुखमास्तेऽतिनिर्भयः ॥ 10

भगिन्याः शूर्पणखाया निर्दोषायाश्च नासिकाम् । कर्णौ चिच्छेद दुष्टात्मा वने तिष्ठति निर्भयः ॥11

अतस्त्वया सहायेन गत्वा तत्प्राणवल्लभाम् । आनयिष्यामि विपिने रहिते राघवेण ताम् ॥ 12

त्वं तु मायामृगो भूत्वा ह्याश्रमादपनेष्यसि । रामं च लक्ष्मणं चैव तदा सीतां हराम्यहम् ॥13

त्वं तु तावत्सहायं मे कृत्वा स्थास्यसि पूर्ववत् । इत्येवं भाषमाणं तं रावणं वीक्ष्य विस्मितः ॥ 14

seat, Mareecha said to Ravana: **(5-6).** "O Ravana! How is it that you have come alone in a chariot? Your face reflects that you are caught up in some worrying train of thoughts. If it is not a secret, reveal to me what it is. O great King! If it is anything righteous and not attended by sinful consequences, I shall accomplish what is dear to you."

Now Ravana said: **7.** "You must know of a famous King of Ayodhya by name Dasaratha. His eldest son Rama is noted for his truthfulness and heroism. **8.** King Dasaratha has sent this son of his, along with his wife and his brother Lakshmana, to the forest, which is the abode of ascetics and forest-dwellers. **9.** He is now staying in an Ashrama at Panchavati amidst a dense fear-inspiring forest. He has a handsome wife Sita, who can be the beauty queen of the world. **10.** He is now staying fearlessly in the forest after killing my courageous army of Rakshasas including Khara, who were absolutely guiltless in this affair. **11.** This wicked fellow Rama has also cut off the nose and ears of my innocent sister Surpanakha, and yet is staying fearlessly in this forest. **12.** With your help, I shall manage to remove Rama from that region of the forest, and then, while he is away, abduct his wife. **13.** Assuming the form of an illusory deer, you should attract Rama and Lakshmana away from their Ashrama. Taking that opportunity, I shall carry away Sita. **14.** And after you have done me that much of service, you can come back and live as you are now doing." Mareecha was astounded to hear these words of Ravana and he gazed at him in wonder.

केनेदमुपदिष्टं ते मूलघातकरं वचः । स एव शत्रुर्वध्यश्च यस्त्वन्नाशं प्रतीक्षते ॥ 15
रामस्य पौरुषं स्मृत्वा चित्तमद्यापि रावण । बालोऽपि मां कौशिकस्य यज्ञसंरक्षणाय सः ॥ 16
आगतस्त्विषुणैकेन पातयामास सागरे । योजनानां शतं रामस्तदादि भयविह्वलः ॥ 17
स्मृत्वा स्मृत्वा तदेवाहं रामं पश्यामि सर्वतः ॥ 18
दण्डकेऽपि पुनरप्यहं वने पूर्ववैरमनुचिन्तयन् हृदि ।
तीक्ष्णशृङ्गमृगरूपमेकदा मादृशैर्बहुभिरावृतोऽभ्ययाम् ॥ 19
राघवं जनकजासमन्वितं लक्ष्मणेन सहितं त्वरान्वितः ।
आगतोऽहमथ हन्तुमुद्यतो मां विलोक्य शरमेकमक्षिपत् ॥ 20
तेन विद्धहृदयोऽहमुद्भ्रमन राक्षसेन्द्र पतितोऽस्मि सागरे ।
तत्प्रभृत्यहमिदं समाश्रितः स्थानमूर्जितमिदं भयार्दितः ॥ 21
राममेव सततं विभावये भीतभीत इव भोगराशितः ।
राजरत्नरमणीरथादिकं श्रोत्रयोर्यदि गतं भयं भवेत् ॥ 22
राम आगत इहेति शङ्कया बाह्यकार्यमपि सर्वमत्यजम् ।
निद्रया परिवृतो यदा स्वपे राममेव मनसानुचिन्तयन् ॥ 23

Conversation between Ravana and Mareecha (15-29)

Mareecha replied: **15.** Who is it that has given you this advice, which, if carried out, will bring about our total destruction? He must certainly be an enemy of ours, deserving slaughter. He must be devising a way for your destruction. **(16-18).** Even as a boy, when he came for giving protection to the sacrificial rites of Viswamitra, Rama, with a single arrow, hurled me into the ocean over a distance of a hundred Yojanas. O Ravana! Thinking of Rama's prowess, my mind gets overpowered by fear even now. Remembering those incidents, I am apprehending the presence of Rama everywhere out of fear. **19.** Even afterwards, retaining in mind my old enmity towards him, I went one day to the Dandaka forest in the form of a deer with sharp horns, surrounded by many other deer like myself. **20.** With a view to kill him, I rushed towards Rama, who was in the company of Sita and Lakshmana. Seeing me approaching, he sent one arrow at me. **21.** Struck by that arrow, O king of the Rakshasas, I was thrown into the ocean whirling. After that, I have in great fear taken shelter in this secluded place. **22.** Withdrawing myself from all objects of enjoyments, I am living here, constantly thinking of Rama out of fear. Not only that, I shake with fear even on hearing words indicating objects of enjoyments beginning with 'R'—words like Raja, Ratna, Ramani, Ratha, etc; for the very sound 'R', with which Rama's name begins, fills me with dread. **(23-24).** I have abandoned all external enterprises,

स्वप्नदृष्टिगतराघवं तदा बोधितो विगतनिद्र आस्थितः ।
तद्भवानपि विमुच्य चाग्रहं राघवं प्रति गृहं प्रयाहि भोः ॥ 24
रक्ष राक्षसकुलं चिरागतं तत्स्मृतौ सकलमेव नश्यति ।
तव हितं वदतो मम भाषितं परिगृहाण परात्मनि राघवे ।
त्यज विरोधमतिं भज भक्तितः परमकारुणिको रघुनन्दनः ॥ 25
अहमशेषमिदं मुनिवाक्यतोऽश्रृणवमादियुगे परमेश्वरः ।
ब्रह्मणार्थित उवाच तं हरिः किं तवेप्सितमहं करवाणि तत् ॥ 26
ब्रह्मणोक्तमरविन्दलोचन त्वं प्रयाहि भुवि मानुषं वपुः ।
दशरथात्मजभावमञ्जसा जहि रिपुं दशकन्धरं हरे ॥ 27
अतो न मानुषो रामः साक्षान्नारायणोऽव्ययः । मायामानुषवेषेण वनं यातोऽतिनिर्भयः ॥ 28
भूभारहरणार्थाय गच्छ तात गृहं सुखम् । श्रुत्वा मारीचवचनं रावणः प्रत्यभाषत ॥ 29
परमात्मा यदा रामः प्रार्थितो ब्रह्मणा किल । मां हन्तुं मानुषो भूत्वा यत्नादिह समागतः ॥ 30
करिष्यत्यचिरादेव सत्यसङ्कल्प ईश्वरः । अतोऽहं यत्नतः सीतामानेष्याम्येव राघवात् ॥ 31

fearing that Rama may come at me anywhere at any moment. Constantly thinking of Rama, when sleep overcomes me, I see Rama in dream, and getting awakened, I am spending sleepless nights sitting. Therefore, O great one! You abandon your designs against Rama and go home. **25.** Do not be the cause of the destruction of the tribe of Rakshasas, whom you have raised to a state of great prosperity for a very long period. Accept my advice which is given in good faith for your own welfare. Give up your enmity towards Rama, who is Paramatma Himself. Seek him with true devotion. He is supremely merciful. **26.** I have known everything about certain secret matters from the words of the sage Narada. In the Satya Yuga, the Supreme Being Hari had given word to Brahma that He would grant his prayers to him. **27.** Brahma had said to Hari, 'O Lotus-eyed one! Born in the world of men as the son of Dasaratha, deign to destroy the ten-headed Ravana, our enemy.' **28.** Therefore know that Rama is not a mere man. He is the Eternal Being Narayana who by His mysterious power Maya has assumed the form of a man and come to the forest. He is not afraid of any one. **29.** He has incarnated in order to relieve the earth of her burden. So, O dear one, return home, giving up your present enterprise." Hearing these words of Mareecha, Ravana replied:

Mareecha assumes the Form of a Golden Deer (30-41)

He said: **(30-31).** "If Rama is really the Supreme Being come on earth as man at Brahma's imploring in order to kill me, he will accomplish it easily, whatever you may do. For whatever God wills, comes to

वधे प्राप्ते रणे वीर प्राप्स्यामि परमं पदम् । यद्वा रामं रणे हत्वा सीतां प्राप्स्यामि निर्भयः ॥ 32
तदुत्तिष्ठ महाभाग विचित्रमृगरूपधृक् । रामं सलक्ष्मणं शीघ्रमाश्रमादतिदूरतः ॥ 33
आक्रम्य गच्छ त्वं शीघ्रं सुखं तिष्ठ यथा पुरा । अतः परं चेद्यत्किञ्चिद्भाषसे मद्विभीषणम् ॥ 34
हनिष्याम्यसिनानेन त्वामत्रैव न संशयः । मारीचस्तद्वचः श्रुत्वा स्वात्मन्येवान्वचिन्तयत् 35
यदि मां राघवो हन्यात्तदा मुक्तो भवार्णवात् । मां हन्याद्यदि चेद्दुष्टस्तदा मे निरयो ध्रुवम् 36
इति निश्चित्य मरणं रामादुत्थाय वेगतः । अब्रवीद्रावणं राजन्करोम्याज्ञां तव प्रभो ॥ 37
इत्युक्त्वा रथमास्थाय गतो रामाश्रमं प्रति । शुद्धजाम्बूनदप्रख्यो मृगोऽभूद्रौप्यबिन्दुकः ॥ 38
रत्नशृङ्गो मणिखुरो नीलरत्नविलोचनः । विद्युत्प्रभो विमुग्धास्यो विचचार वनान्तरे ॥ 39
रामाश्रमपदस्यान्ते सीतादृष्टिपथे चरन् ॥ 40
क्षणं च धावत्यवतिष्ठते क्षणं समीपमागत्य पुनर्भयावृतः
एवं स मायामृगवेषरूपधृक् चचार सीतां परिमोहयन्खलः ॥ 41

इति श्रीमदध्यात्मरामायणे उमामहेश्वरसंवादे
आरण्यकाण्डे षष्ठः सर्गः ॥ ६ ॥

pass. Therefore by hook or by crook I will take away Sita from Rama. **32.** O bold one! You know that if I die in battle, I shall attain the highest heaven. If I succeed in killing Rama in battle, I can enjoy Sita without the fear of a rival. **(33-35).** Therefore, O respected one, get ready. You are to attract Rama and Lakshmana to a far off distance from their Ashrama by assuming the form of an attractive magical deer. After that you can return and stay happily in retirement as now. If you speak a single word of intimidation to me, I shall cut off your head even now with my sword." Hearing these words of Ravana, Mareecha thought within himself: **(36-37).** "If Rama happens to kill me, I shall obtain freedom from this transmigratory cycle. But if I meet with death at the hands of this wicked fellow, I am sure to be consigned to hell." Thus preferring death at Rama's hands, Mareecha got up immediately and said to Ravana: "O great King! I shall do as you command."

(38-40). With these words he ascended a chariot and soon went to the place where Rama's Ashrama was situated. Then in the neighbouring forest he moved about as a silver-spotted deer of golden colour, having horns of gems, eyes of sapphire, hoofs of pearls, the brightness of lightning, and a face of great attractiveness. Moving about in that way, he reached the precincts of Rama's Ashrama and attracted the notice of Sita. **41.** While moving about, he would now run a little and then stop for a while; coming near, he would run away a little distance, as if out of fear. Thus captivating Sita's mind, that evil fellow of a Rakshasa moved about in the guise of a magical deer.

सप्तमः सर्गः

श्रीमहादेव उवाच

अथ रामोऽपि तत्सर्वं ज्ञात्वा रावणचेष्टितम् । उवाच सीतामेकान्ते श‍ृणु जानकि मे वचः ॥ 1
रावणो भिक्षुरूपेण आगमिष्यति तेऽन्तिकम् । त्वं तु छायां त्वदाकारां स्थापयित्वोटजे विश ॥ 2
अग्नावदृश्यरूपेण वर्षं तिष्ठ ममाज्ञया । रावणस्य वधान्ते मां पूर्ववत्प्राप्स्यसे शुभे ॥ 3
श्रुत्वा रामोदितं वाक्यं सापि तत्र तथाकरोत् । मायासीतां बहिः स्थाप्य स्वयमन्तर्दधेऽनले ॥ 4
मायासीता तदापश्यन्मृगं मायाविनिर्मितम् । हसन्ती राममभ्येत्य प्रोवाच विनयान्विता ॥ 5
पश्य राम मृगं चित्रं कानकं रत्नभूषितम् ।
विचित्रबिन्दुभिर्युक्तं चरन्तमकुतोभयम् । बद्ध्वा देहि मम क्रीडामृगो भवतु सुन्दरः ॥ 6
तथेति धनुरादाय गच्छन् लक्ष्मणमब्रवीत् । रक्ष त्वमतियत्नेन सीतां मत्प्राणवल्लभाम् ॥ 7
मायिनः सन्ति विपिने राक्षसा घोरदर्शनाः । अतोऽत्रावहितः साध्वीं रक्ष सीतामनिन्दिताम् ॥ 8
लक्ष्मणो राममाहेदं देवायं मृगरूपधृक् । मारीचोऽत्र न सन्देह एवंभूतो मृगः कुतः ॥ 9

Chapter 7

ABDUCTION OF SITA

The Destruction of Mareecha (1-25)

(1-3). Rama, divining beforehand the designs of Ravana, had called Sita alone one day and said to her: "O daughter of Janaka! Listen to my words. Ravana is going to approach you in the form of an ascetic for holy alms. Therefore you substitute in the Ashrama a magically created double of yours, and stationing her outside the Ashrama, you go in and hide yourself in fire in an invisible form. As desired by me you have to remain thus hidden for one year. When Ravana has been killed, you will join me again." **4.** Following this instruction of Rama, Sita projected outside a magical double of hers, and hid herself in fire.

5. Now the magical Sita saw the magical deer, and laughing in wonder at its sight, approached Rama and said to him in a humble tone: **6.** "See, see! Here is a wonderful wild deer, spotted, many-coloured and bejewelled. It is moving about everywhere fearlessly. Be pleased to capture it and give it to me to be taken care of as an attractive pet animal by me." **7.** Rama agreed to do so, and getting ready to start, took his bow in hand and said to Lakshmana: "Keep careful guard over my dear wife, Sita. **8.** In the forest there are many terrible Rakshasas who are adepts in deception by magic. You have therefore got to be very vigilant in this matter. In every way protect the virtuous and devoted Sita." **9.** But Lakshmana thereupon said to Rama, "O noble one, this is only Mareecha disguised as a deer. There is no doubt about it.

श्रीराम उवाच

यदि मारीच एवायं तदा हन्मि न संशयः । मृगश्चेदानयिष्यामि सीताविश्रमहेतवे ॥ 10

गमिष्यामि मृगं बद्ध्वा ह्यानयिष्यामि सत्वरः । त्वं प्रयत्नेन सन्तिष्ठ सीतासंरक्षणोद्यतः ॥ 11

इत्युक्त्वा प्रययौ रामो मायामृगमनुद्रुतः । माया यथाश्रया लोकमोहिनी जगदाकृतिः ॥ 12

निर्विकारश्चिदात्मापि पूर्णोऽपि मृगमन्वगात् । भक्तानुकम्पो भगवानिति सत्यं वचो हरिः ॥ 13

कर्तुं सीताप्रियार्थाय जानन्नपि मृगं ययौ । अन्यथा पूर्णकामस्य रामस्य विदितात्मनः । 14

मृगेण वा स्त्रिया वापि किं कार्यं परमात्मनः ॥ 15

कदाचिद् दृश्यतेऽभ्याशे क्षणं धावति लीयते ।

दृश्यते च ततो दूरादेवं राममपाहरत् । ततो रामोऽपि विज्ञाय राक्षसोऽयमिति स्फुटम् ॥ 16

विव्याध शरमादाय राक्षसं मृगरूपिणम् । पपात रुधिराक्तास्यो मारीचः पूर्वरूपधृक् ॥ 17

हा हतोऽस्मि महाबाहो त्राहि लक्ष्मण मां द्रुतम् । इत्युक्त्वा रामवद्वाचा पपात रुधिराशनः ॥ 18

यन्नामाज्ञोऽपि मरणे स्मृत्वा तत्साम्यमाप्नुयात् । किमुताग्रे हरिं पश्यंस्तेनैव निहतोऽसुरः ॥ 19

तद्देहादुत्थितं तेजः सर्वलोकस्य पश्यतः । राममेवाविशद्देवा विस्मयं परमं ययुः ॥ 20

For, a deer of this kind can occur nowhere." To this Rama said in reply: **10.** "If it is Mareecha, I shall certainly kill him. If it is really a deer, I shall capture it for the entertainment of Sita. **11.** I am anyway starting now, but shall return soon with the captured animal. You please guard Sita vigilantly."

(12-15). After instructing in this way Rama followed the magical deer (*Maya-mriga*)—Rama who is the support of the cosmic magic called Maya, which is world-bewitching and which manifests as the universe. In spite of being the Pure Spirit, self-fulfilled and changeless, he followed the deer for pleasing Sita, though knowing that the deer was really Mareecha. He did all this only to fulfil the dictum that the Supreme Lord is ever gracious to His devotees. (For Mareecha was a devotee who wanted death at his hand as a means of salvation, and Ravana too was one of those two devotees, Jaya and Vijaya, who were under a curse and were awaiting death at Rama's hands.) Otherwise, what significance has a deer or a woman got for that self-fulfilled and illumined being?

(16-17). Now appearing near, next running away and disappearing, now again emerging at a distance and next disappearing, the deer managed to draw Rama to a considerable distance. Rama now became convinced that that deer must really be an Asura and struck it with an arrow. Then the real Mareecha fell down in his natural form in a pool of blood. **18.** While falling, he cried out in a voice resembling that of Rama, "Alas! Alas! O powerful Lakshmana! I am dying. Come quickly and save me." **(19-20).** By merely uttering Rama's name at the time of death, Jivas attain to Him, Sri Hari. Then what glorious state must have been attained by that Asura who met with death at His hand and with His physical presence within his sight

किं कर्म कृत्वा किं प्राप्तः पातकी मुनिहिंसकः । अथवा राघवस्यायं महिमा नात्र संशयः ॥ 21
रामबाणेन संविद्धः पूर्वं राममनुस्मरन् । भयात्सर्वं परित्यज्य गृहवित्तादिकं च यत् ॥ 22
हृदि रामं सदा ध्यात्वा निर्धूताशेषकल्मषः । अन्ते रामेण निहतः पश्यन् राममवाप सः ॥ 23
द्विजो वा राक्षसो वापि पापी वा धार्मिकोऽपि वा । त्यजन्कलेवरं रामं स्मृत्वा याति परं पदम् ॥ 24
इति तेऽन्योन्यमाभाष्य ततो देवा दिवं ययुः ॥ 25
रामस्तच्चिन्तयामास म्रियमाणोऽसुराधमः ।
हा लक्ष्मणेति मद्वाक्यमनुकुर्वन्ममार किम् । श्रुत्वा मद्वाक्यसदृशं वाक्यं सीतापि किं भवेत् ॥26
इति चिन्तापरीतात्मा रामो दूरान्न्यवर्तत ॥ 27
सीता तद्भाषितं श्रुत्वा मारीचस्य दुरात्मनः ।
भीतातिदुःखसंविग्ना लक्ष्मणं त्विदमब्रवीत् । गच्छ लक्ष्मण वेगेन भ्राता तेऽसुरपीडितः ॥ 28
हा लक्ष्मणेति वचनं भ्रातुस्ते न शृणोषि किम् । तामाह लक्ष्मणो देवि रामवाक्यं न तद्भवेत् ॥ 29
यः कश्चिद्राक्षसो देवि म्रियमाणोऽब्रवीद्वचः । रामस्त्रैलोक्यमपि यः क्रुद्धो नाशयति क्षणात् ॥
स कथं दीनवचनं भाषतेऽमरपूजितः ॥ 31
क्रुद्धा लक्ष्मणमालोक्य सीता बाष्पविलोचना ।

To their utter astonishment, the Devas and all others who witnessed the scene saw a brilliance emerging from the body of the dead Rakshasa and entering into Rama.

(21-25). The Devas began talking among themselves, "By what meritorious work has this sinful Rakshasa, a killer of ascetics, attained to this highest spiritual state? Nothing but Rama's greatness can account for this. He has now been killed by Rama's arrows. Before this he has been thinking of Rama constantly.Out of fear of him, he had abandoned home, wealth etc. and was constantly engaged in the thought of Rama. Having thus burnt up all his sins, he has been fortunate to meet with death at the hands of Rama while seeing Him before, with his own eyes.

"Whether one is a Brahmana or a Rakshasa, whether one is a sinner or a righteous man—if one dies remembering Rama, one attains to the Supreme Status." Speaking to one another like this, the Devas went to their abode.

Sita's harsh Words to Lakshmana (26-37)

(26-27). Rama now began to think: "The dying Asura was heard to cry out 'Ah! Lakshmana!' imitating my voice. Why did he do so? What will Sita think on hearing that voice resembling mine?" With such worrying thoughts, Rama hastened to cover the distance and reach back his Ashrama. **(28-31).** Meantime in their Ashrama, the dying cry of Mareecha provoked great fear and sorrow in the mind of Sita. She said to Lakshmana: "O Lakshmana! go quickly. Your brother seems to be in danger from the Asura. Didn't you hear his distressed cry, 'Ah Lakshmana!' " Lakshmana tried

प्राह लक्ष्मण दुर्बुद्धे भ्रातुर्व्यसनमिच्छसि । प्रेषितो भरतेनैव रामनाशाभिकाङ्क्षिणा ॥ 32
मां नेतुमागतोऽसि त्वं रामनाश उपस्थिते । न प्राप्स्यसे त्वं मामद्य पश्य प्राणांस्त्यजाम्यहम् ॥
न जानातीदृशं रामस्त्वां भार्याहरणोद्यतम् । रामादन्यं न स्पृशामि त्वां वा भरतमेव वा ॥ 34
इत्युक्त्वा वध्यमाना सा स्वबाहुभ्यां रुरोद ह । तच्छ्रुत्वा लक्ष्मणः कर्णौ पिधायातीव दुःखितः॥ 35
मामेवं भाषसे चण्डि धिक् त्वां नाशमुपैष्यसि । इत्युक्त्वा वनदेवीभ्यः समर्प्य जनकात्मजाम् ॥ 36
ययौ दुःखातिसंविग्नो राममेव शनैः शनैः ॥ 37
ततोऽन्तरं समालोक्य रावणो भिक्षुवेषधृक् ।
सीतासमीपमगमत् स्फुरद्दण्डकमण्डलुः । सीता तमवलोक्याशु नत्वा सम्पूज्य भक्तितः ॥
कन्दमूलफलादीनि दत्त्वा स्वागतमब्रवीत् । मुने भुङ्क्ष्व फलादीनि विश्रमस्व यथासुखम् ॥ 39
इदानीमेव भर्ता मे ह्यागमिष्यति ते प्रियम् । करिष्यति विशेषेण तिष्ठ त्वं यदि रोचते ॥ 40

to console her: "O noble lady! That cry of distress cannot be that of Rama. It must be of some dying Rakshasa. For, if Rama is angry, he is capable of destroying the three worlds in no time. How can He who receives the adoration of even celestials utter a cry of distress?"

(32-34). At these words of Lakshmana, Sita, angry and weeping, looked at him and said, "O vicious fellow! I see, you want to see Rama killed. You have been prompted to come with us by that Bharata who wants to see Rama destroyed. You have come planning to possess me on Rama's death. But know for certain that you shall never get me. Look, I am going to end my life immediately. Rama is unaware that your intention is to steal his wife. I shall not touch any male other than Rama, whether it be you or Bharata." **(35-37).** Speaking in this vein, she beat her body with her own hands and wept. These harsh words cut Lakshmana to the quick, and closing his ears with his hand, he said with a heart full of sorrow: "Don't speak like that, O angry woman! Your vulgar speech will recoil on yourself. Your ruin is near at hand." With these words, entrusting Sita to the protection of the forest deities, Lakshmana went reluctantly in search of Rama in an extremely sorrow-stricken mood.

Ravana abducting Sita (38-66)

(38-40). Now taking advantage of this opportune moment, Ravana appeared before Sita, in the disguise of a mendicant with a fine Yogi's rod and water vessel in hand. Seeing him, Sita quickly made prostration before him. She adored him respectfully and offered him fruits and roots. Welcoming him she said, "O holy one! Please accept these fruits and roots and rest here for a while. In a short time my husband will be returning, and he will do you hospitality. So if you have time, please wait here for a

भिक्षुरुवाच

का त्वं कमलपत्राक्षि को वा भर्ता तवानघे।
किमर्थमत्र ते वासो वने राक्षससेविते। ब्रूहि भद्रे ततः सर्वं स्ववृत्तान्तं निवेदये॥ 41

सीतोवाच

अयोध्याधिपतिः श्रीमान् राजा दशरथो महान्। तस्य ज्येष्ठः सुतो रामः सर्वलक्षणलक्षितः॥ 42
तस्याहं धर्मतः पत्नी सीता जनकनन्दिनी। तस्य भ्राता कनीयांश्च लक्ष्मणो भ्रातृवत्सलः॥ 43
पितुराज्ञां पुरस्कृत्य दण्डके वस्तुमागतः। चतुर्दश समास्त्वं तु ज्ञातुमिच्छामि मे वद॥ 44

भिक्षुरुवाच

पौलस्त्यतनयोऽहं तु रावणो राक्षसाधिपः। त्वत्कामपरितप्तोऽहं त्वां नेतुं पुरमागतः॥ 45
मुनिवेषेण रामेण किं करिष्यसि मां भज। भुङ्क्ष्व भोगान्मया सार्धं त्यज दुःखं वनोद्भवम्
श्रुत्वा तद्वचनं सीता भीता किञ्चिदुवाच तम्। यद्येवं भाषसे मां त्वं नाशमेष्यसि राघवात्॥ 47
आगमिष्यति रामोऽपि क्षणं तिष्ठ सहानुजः। मां को धर्षयितुं शक्तो हरेर्भार्यां शशो यथा॥48
रामबाणैर्विभिन्नस्त्वं पतिष्यसि महीतले॥ 49
इति सीतावचः श्रुत्वा रावणः क्रोधमूर्च्छितः।
स्वरूपं दर्शयमास महापर्वतसन्निभम्। दशास्यं विंशतिभुजं कालमेघसमद्युतिम्॥ 50

while." **41.** At this the mendicant said: "O lotus-eyed one! Who are you? Who is your husband? Why are you staying in the forest resorted to by Rakshasas? O good lady! Please enlighten me on these matters, and then I shall tell you everything about myself."

Sita said in reply: **(42-44).** "There was a great and famous king named Dasaratha ruling over Ayodhya. His eldest son, possessed of all excellences, is Rama. I, the daughter of Janaka, am his wife. Lakshmana is his dear brother. As ordered by his father, Rama has come to the forest to stay here for fourteen years. Now I would like to know something about you."

The mendicant thereupon said: **(45-46).** "I am Ravana, a scion of Pulasthya's line and the king of all the Rakshasas. I am passionately infatuated with you, and I have come to take you away to my palace. Of what use to you is Rama who has taken to an ascetic's way of life? Come with me, and enjoy life with me. Don't remain any longer amidst this harsh forest life."

(47-49). Frightened by these words of Ravana, Sita spoke a few words in reply. She said: "Words of the kind you have spoken to me now, will attract the penalty of death at Rama's hands. He will soon arrive with his brother. You wait for a while. Your threat to carry me away—me who am the consort of Hari Himself—is as ridiculous as a hare seeking to carry away the wife of a Hari (lion). Soon will you fall down on the earth, pierced by the arrows of Rama."

50. At these words of Sita, Ravana, roused to a fit of violent wrath, now revealed his true form, resembling a mountain in stature, ten-headed and twenty-armed, and sombre

तद्दृष्ट्वा वनदेव्यश्च भूतानि च वितत्रसुः। ततो विदार्य धरणीं नखैरुद्धृत्य बाहुभिः ॥ 51
तोलयित्वा रथे क्षिप्त्वा ययौ क्षिप्रं विहायसा। हा राम हा लक्ष्मणेति रुदती जनकात्मजा ॥ 52
भयोद्विग्नमना दीना पश्यन्ती भुवमेव सा। श्रुत्वा तत्क्रन्दितं दीनं सीतायाः पक्षिसत्तमः ॥53
जटायुरुत्थितः शीघ्रं नगाग्रात्तीक्ष्णतुण्डकः। तिष्ठ तिष्ठेति तं प्राह को गच्छति ममाग्रतः ॥54
मुषित्वा लोकनाथस्य भार्यां शून्याद्वनालयात्। शुनको मन्त्रपूतं त्वं पुरोडाशमिवाध्वरे ॥ 55
इत्युक्त्वा तीक्ष्णतुण्डेन चूर्णयामास तद्रथम्। वाहान्विभेद पादाभ्यां चूर्णयामास तद्धनुः ॥56
ततः सीतां परित्यज्य रावणः खड्गमाददे। चिच्छेद पक्षौ सामर्षः पक्षिराजस्य धीमतः ॥ 57
पपात किञ्चिच्छेषेण प्राणेन भुवि पक्षिराट्। पुनरन्यरथेनाशु सीतामादाय रावणः ॥ 58
क्रोशन्ती रामरामेति त्रातारं नाधिगच्छति। हा राम हा जगन्नाथ मां न पश्यसि दुःखिताम् ॥
रक्षसा नीयमानां स्वां भार्यां मोचय राघव। हा लक्ष्मण महाभाग त्राहि मामपराधिनीम् ॥60
वाक्शरेण हतस्त्वं मे क्षन्तुमर्हसि देवर। इत्येवं क्रोशमानां तां रामागमनशङ्कया ॥ 61
जगाम वायुवेगेन सीतामादाय सत्वरः ॥ 62
विहायसा नीयमाना सीतापश्यदधोमुखी।
पर्वताग्रे स्थितान्पञ्च वानरान्वारिजानना। उत्तरीयार्धखण्डेन विमुच्याभरणादिकम् ॥ 63
बद्ध्वा चिक्षेप रामाय कथयन्त्विति पर्वते ॥ 64

like the dark blue cloud of the rainy season. **(51-56).** The forest-deities and other beings to whom Lakshmana had entrusted Sita, fled away at the very sight of that form. Ravana now scooped up the ground on which Sita was standing, and placing that block of earth along with Sita in his aerial car, hastened through the sky. Sita, shivering with terror and looking down towards the earth, kept on crying aloud, "Ah Rama! Ah Lakshmana!" Hearing the mournful cries of Sita, the eagle Jatayu, a leader of the tribe of birds, rose up from his arboreal home, and challenged Ravana with the words, "Stop, stop, you are stealing away the wife of the Lord of the worlds from their empty Ashrama, as a dog carries away the offerings prepared for a sacrifice. You cannot pass me unchallenged." With these words Jatayu with his sharp beak and claws attacked Ravana, killing the horses of the chariot and shattering his bow and vehicle. **57.** Thereupon Ravana gave up his hold of Sita, and taking a sword in great anger, severed the eagle's wings with it. **(58-62).** The king of the birds fell on the earth, with a little consciousness still left in him. Meanwhile, Sita kept on crying aloud, saying, "O Rama, lord of the earth! Don't you see me utterly distracted with sorrow? Save your wife, O scion of Raghu's line, from being abducted by this Rakshasa. O worshipful Lakshmana! Forgive me, forgetting my transgression. I railed at you with a volley of unspeakable words. Pardon me for the same." Afraid of Rama's arrival, Ravana put the weeping Sita in another vehicle, and moved on with the speed of wind. **(63-64).** While going through the sky the lotus-faced Sita kept on gazing

ततः समुद्रमुल्लङ्घ्य लङ्कां गत्वा स रावणः ।
स्वान्तःपुरे रहस्येतामशोकविपिनेऽक्षिपत् । राक्षसीभिः परिवृतां मातृबुद्ध्यान्वपालयत् ॥ 65
कृशातिदीना परिकर्मवर्जिता दुःखेन शुष्यद्वदनातिविह्वला ।
हा राम रामेति विलप्यमाना सीता स्थिता राक्षसवृन्दमध्ये ॥ 66
इति श्रीमदध्यात्मरामायणे उमामहेश्वरसंवादे
आरण्यकाण्डे सप्तमः सर्गः ॥ ७ ॥

below towards to the earth, and saw on the top of a mountain five monkeys assembled together. She tied up her jewels in a half of her upper cloth, and threw this bundle down to reach the monkeys, so that they might tell Rama about her, if they happened to meet him.

65. And as for Ravana, he crossed the sea and reached Lanka with Sita. He took her to his residential palace, and lodged her amidst a guard of Rakshasa women in an Ashoka grove, situated at a very sequestered region. He protected her, as one would do one's mother (*mātṛbudhyā*).

(It is pointed out that Ravana was at heart a devotee, and that the attitude of a lust-infatuated abductor adoptod by him was only a cloak he put on to hasten his death at the hands of Rama. It is parallel to Rama assuming the role of a man and undergoing all travails while in reality he was always the Supreme Being Himself).

66. Lean, miserable, untrimmed, and frightened to the core, Sita stayed amidst those Rakshasa women, with signs of complete dejection on her face and uttering piteous cries of "O Rama! O Rama!" frequently.

अष्टमः सर्गः

श्रीमहादेव उवाच

रामो मायाविनं हत्वा राक्षसं कामरूपिणम् । प्रतस्थे स्वाश्रमं गन्तुं ततो दूराद्ददर्श तम् ॥ 1
आयान्तं लक्ष्मणं दीनं मुखेन परिशुष्यता । राघवश्चिन्तयामास स्वात्मन्येव महामतिः ॥ 2
लक्ष्मणस्तन्न जानाति माया सीतां मया कृताम् । ज्ञात्वाप्येनं वञ्चयित्वा शोचामि प्राकृतो यथा॥ 3

Chapter 8

SALVATION OF JATAYU

Rama in Search of Sita (1-2)

(1-2). After destroying Mareecha capable of assuming any form by his mastery of deluding magic, Rama was on his way returning to the Ashrama when he saw at some distance Lakshmana coming towards him, with a face faded and miserable looking. At his sight, Rama, the great one, thought as follows: **3.** "Lakshmana does not know that I have created a magical Sita and replaced the real one with her. I know the truth, but still, I shall practise

यद्यहं विरतो भूत्वा तूष्णीं स्थास्यामि मन्दिरे । तदा राक्षसकोटीनां वधोपायः कथं भवेत् ॥ 4

यदि शोचामि तां दुःखसन्तप्तः कामुको यथा ।

तदा क्रमेणानुचिन्वन्सीतां यास्येऽसुरालयम् । रावणं सकुलं हत्वा सीतामग्नौ स्थितां पुनः ॥ 5

मयैव स्थापितां नीत्वा यातायोध्यामतन्द्रितः ॥ 6

अहं मनुष्यभावेन जातोऽस्मि ब्रह्मणार्थितः ।

मनुष्यभावमापन्नः किञ्चित्कालं वसामि कौ । ततो मायामनुष्यस्य चरितं मेऽनुशृण्वताम् ॥ 7

मुक्तिः स्यादप्रयासेन भक्तिमार्गानुवर्तिनाम् । निश्चित्यैवं तदा दृष्ट्वा लक्ष्मणं वाक्यमब्रवीत् ॥

किमर्थमागतोऽसि त्वं सीतां त्यक्त्वा मम प्रियाम् । नीता वा भक्षिता वापि राक्षसैर्जनकात्मजा ॥ 9

लक्ष्मणः प्राञ्जलिः प्राह सीताया दुर्वचो रुदन् । हा लक्ष्मणेति वचनं राक्षसोक्तं श्रुतं तया ॥ 10

त्वद्वाक्यसदृशं श्रुत्वा मां गच्छेति त्वराब्रवीत् ।

रुदन्ती सा मया प्रोक्ता देवि राक्षसभाषितम् । नेदं रामस्य वचनं स्वस्था भव शुचिस्मिते ॥ 11

इत्येवं सान्त्विता साध्वी मया प्रोवाच मां पुनः । यदुक्तं दुर्वचो राम न वाच्यं पुरतस्तव ॥ 12

कर्णौ पिधाय निर्गत्य यातोऽहं त्वां समीक्षितुम् ॥ 13

a deception on him by imitating the sorrow-stricken pose of an ignorant, worldly man. **4.** If I were to remain quiet in the Ashrama, there will be no occasion for the destruction of countless Rakshasas. **5.** So I shall behave like a grief-stricken lover on this occasion. This will lead us to institute a search for Sita and in the end take us to the habitat of the Rakshasas. **(6-8).** After destroying Ravana with all his tribe, I shall bring out the real Sita from the fire in which I have hidden her, and return to Ayodhya in great joy. At Brahma's request I have assumed the form and ways of a man, and shall continue to do so for some time more. These activities of mine in the disguise of a man shall become in future a subject of study for the followers of the path of devotion and provide an easy means for the attainment of Mukti." Resolving thus, Rama, on meeting Lakshmana, said to him, **9.** "Why have you come away, leaving my dear wife Sita alone? The Rakshasas might have taken her away or eaten her up." **(10-13).** Lakshmana, with tears in his eyes and hands joined in humble salutation reported to him about the very unseemly words spoken by Sita. He said: "When Sita heard the Rakshasa's cry 'Alas Lakshmana!' in a voice resembling yours, she asked me to come to your help without any delay. To her who was weeping, I said, comforting her, 'Good lady! These are not the words of Rama, but of a Rakshasa. Please remain at peace.' But at these words of mine, that chaste woman railed at me with unmentionable words of abuse. It is not befitting for me to utter those words before you. Closing my ears I have hastened to meet you."

रामस्तु लक्ष्मणं प्राह तथाप्यनुचितं कृतम् ।
त्वया स्त्रीभाषितं सत्यं कृत्वा त्यक्ता शुभानना । नीता वा भक्षिता वापि राक्षसैर्नात्र संशयः ॥ 14
इति चिन्तापरो रामः स्वाश्रमं त्वरितो ययौ । तत्रादृष्ट्वा जनकजां विललापातिदुःखितः ॥ 15
हा प्रिये क्व गतासि त्वं नासि पूर्ववदाश्रमे । अथवा मद्विमोहार्थं लीलया क्व विलीयसे ॥ 16
इत्याचिन्वन्वनं सर्वं नापश्यज्जानकीं तदा । वनदेव्यः कुतः सीतां ब्रुवन्तु मम वल्लभाम् ॥ 17
मृगाश्च पक्षिणो वृक्षा दर्शयन्तु मम प्रियाम् । इत्येवं विलपन्नेव रामः सीतां न कुत्रचित् ॥ 18
सर्वज्ञः सर्वथा क्वापि नापश्यद्रघुनन्दनः । आनन्दोऽप्यन्वशोचत्तामचलोऽप्यनुधावति ॥ 19
निर्ममो निरहङ्कारोऽप्यखण्डानन्दरूपवान् । मम जायेति सीतेति विललापातिदुःखितः ॥ 20
एवं मायामनुचरन्नसक्तोऽपि रघूत्तमः । आसक्त इव मूढानां भाति तत्त्वविदां न हि ॥ 21
एवं विचिन्वन्सकलं वनं रामः सलक्ष्मणः । भग्नं रथं छत्रचापं कूबरं पतितं भुवि ॥ 22
दृष्ट्वा लक्ष्मणमाहेदं पश्य लक्ष्मण केनचित् । नीयमानां जनकजां तं जित्वान्यो जहार ताम् ॥
ततः कश्चिद्द्रवो भागं गत्वा पर्वतसन्निभम् । रुधिरात्तवपुर्दृष्ट्वा रामो वाक्यमथाब्रवीत् ॥ 24

(14-15). Thereupon Rama said to Lakshmana: "Even if it be so, it was not right for you to have taken a woman's word so seriously and left my handsome wife alone. In our absence she must surely have been either abducted or eaten up by the Rakshasas." With great anxiety Rama spoke these words and hastened towards his Ashrama. Not finding Sita there, he was completely upset by sorrow and burst into the following mournful words: **(16-20).** "O dear one! Where have you gone? You are not to be seen in the Ashrama as before. Or are you hiding yourself somewhere to tease me by a false alarm?" Bemoaning in this way, he searched here and there all over that forest and enquired of the forest deities and birds and beasts, "Could you say where my Sita is? May the birds, beasts and the trees of the forest guide me to my wife." But Sita was nowhere to be seen, however much he moaned for her. Though Rama was all-knowing, he could find her nowhere. Though he was blissful by nature, he was subject to sorrow on her account. Though he was omnipresent and motionless, he ran about everywhere in search of her. Though he was egoless, devoid of the sense of 'I', and was of the nature of unbroken Bliss, he none the less experienced bitter sorrow and wept over Sita considering her as wife. **21.** Though devoid of all attachments, that great prince of Raghu's line appeared like one attached and a victim to the ways of Maya. But the truth-knowers know that the facts are otherwise.

Meeting Jatayu (22-43)

(22-23). Searching in this way all through the forest, Rama and Lakshmana came across a shattered chariot and a broken bow. Seeing these, Rama said to Lakshmana, "Look, look Lakshmana! Here the abductor of Sita must have been confronted by a rival who must have carried her away from him." **24.** A little away

एष वै भक्षयित्वा तां जानकीं शुभदर्शनाम् । शेते विविक्तेऽतितृप्तः पश्य हन्मि निशाचरम् ॥25
चापमानय शीघ्रं मे बाणं च रघुनन्दन । तत्श्रुत्वा रामवचनं जटायुः प्राह भीतवत् ॥ 26
मां न मारय भद्रं ते म्रियमाणं स्वकर्मणा । अहं जटायुस्ते भार्याहारिणं समनुद्रुतः ॥ 27
रावणं तत्र युद्धं मे बभूवारिविमर्दन । तस्य वाहान् रथं चापं छित्त्वाहं तेन घातितः ॥ 28
पतितोऽस्मि जगन्नाथ प्राणांस्त्यक्ष्यामि पश्य माम् । तत्श्रुत्वा राघवो दीनं कण्ठप्राणं ददर्श ह ॥ 29
हस्ताभ्यां संस्पृशन् रामो दुःखाश्रुवृतलोचनः ॥ 30
जटायो ब्रूहि मे भार्या केन नीता शुभानना । मत्कार्यार्थं हतोऽसि त्वमतो मे प्रियबान्धवः ॥31
जटायुः सन्नया वाचा वक्त्राद्रक्तं समुद्वमन् । उवाच रावणो राम राक्षसो भीमविक्रमः ॥ 32
आदाय मैथिलीं सीतां दक्षिणाभिमुखो ययौ । इतो वक्तुं न मे शक्तिः प्राणांस्त्यक्ष्यामि तेऽग्रतः ॥
दिष्ट्या दृष्टोऽसि राम त्वं म्रियमाणेन मेऽनघ । परमात्मासि विष्णुस्त्वं मायामनुजरूपधृक् ॥ 34
अन्तकालेऽपि दृष्ट्वा त्वां मुक्तोऽहं रघुसत्तम । हस्ताभ्यां स्पृश मां राम पुनर्यास्यामि ते पदम् 35
तथेति रामः पस्पर्श तदङ्गं पाणिना स्मयन् । ततः प्राणान्परित्यज्य जटायुः पतितो भुवि ॥ 36
रामस्तमनुशोचित्वा बन्धुवत्साश्रुलोचनः । लक्ष्मणेन समानाय्य काष्ठानि प्रददाह तम् ॥ 37

from there, seeing a huge blood-smeared body of the size of a hillock, Rama said to Lakshmana: **25.** "See here lies that fellow who, after deriving ample satisfaction by eating up Sita, is resting in a solitary place. **26.** Give my bow and arrows quickly." Hearing these words of Rama, Jatayu said like one frightened. **(27-30).** "I am at the end of my Karma and am about to die. There is no need of your killing me. Good wishes to you! I am Jatayu. I chased Ravana who was carrying away your wife. I fought with him and destroyed his vehicle and bow. Thereupon he severed my wings and threw me to the ground. Seeing you before me, I shall end my life." At the sight of him with his life ebbing away, Rama, grief-stricken and shedding tears, passed his hands over his body, and said: **31.** "Tell me, O Jatayu, who carried away my handsome wife. You have opted to meet with death for my sake. You are therefore my very dear friend." **(32-35).** In reply Jatayu who was vomitting blood, said as follows in a very low tone: "O Rama, Ravana, a very powerful Rakshasa, has carried away Sita in the southern direction. I am not able to speak more. I am dying in Thy presence. O holy one! It is my good fortune that I could die seeing Thee. Thou art Mahavishnu, the Supreme Being, who hast assumed a human form by Maya, Thy mysterious power. By seeing Thee even at the end of my life, I have become liberated. Deign to touch me again with Thy hands, so that I may attain Thy Status." **36.** Saying, "So be it," Rama stroked his body with his hands, and Jatayu breathed his last and fell down.

37. Rama shed tears at his death as of a close relative and bemoaned his loss in many ways. They took and cremated Jatayu's body in a pyre made by Lakshmana with firewood. **(38-40).** In deep sorrow

स्नात्वा दुःखेन रामोऽपि लक्ष्मणेन समन्वितः । हत्वा वने मृगं तत्र मांसखण्डान्समन्ततः ॥ 38

शाद्वले प्राक्षिपद्रामः पृथक् पृथगनेकधा । भक्षन्तु पक्षिणः सर्वे तृप्तो भवतु पक्षिराट् ॥ 39

इत्युक्त्वा राघवः प्राह जटायो गच्छ मत्पदम् । मत्सारूप्यं भजस्वाद्य सर्वलोकस्य पश्यतः ॥ 40

ततोऽनन्तरमेवासौ दिव्यरूपधरः शुभः । विमानवरमारुह्य भास्वरं भानुसन्निभम् ॥ 41

शङ्खचक्रगदापद्मकिरीटवरभूषणैः । द्योतयन्स्वप्रकाशेन पीताम्बरधरोऽमलः ॥ 42

चतुर्भिः पार्षदैर्विष्णोस्तादृशैरभिपूजितः ।

स्तूयमानो योगिगणै राममाभाष्य सत्वरः । कृताञ्जलिपुटो भूत्वा तुष्टाव रघुनन्दनम् ॥ 43

"जटायु उवाच" अगणितगुणमप्रमेयमाद्यं सकलजगत्स्थितिसंयमादिहेतुम् ।
उपरमपरमं परात्मभूतं सततमहं प्रणतोऽस्मि रामचन्द्रम् ॥ 44

निरवधिसुखमिन्दिराकटाक्षं क्षपितसुरेन्द्रचतुर्मुखादिदुःखम् ।
नरवरमनिशं नतोऽस्मि रामं वरदमहं वरचापबाणहस्तम् ॥ 45

त्रिभुवनकमनीयरूपमीड्यं रविशतभासुरमीहितप्रदानम् ।
शरणदमनिशं सुरागमूले कृतनिलयं रघुनन्दनं प्रपद्ये ॥ 46

Rama along with Lakshmana took his bath for performing obsequies. Rama scattered over the grassy ground round about, pieces of meat of a slaughtered wild animal with the words: "May all the birds of the forest eat this meat! May it fill the king of the birds with satisfaction!" Next in the presence of all onlookers, he addressed Jatayu, saying: "O Jatayu! You shall attain to My Status possessed of a form similar to Mine." **(41-43).** Immediately the spirit of Jatayu, embodied in a luminous divine form, ascended a heavenly vehicle resplendent like the sun. He got a form with four hands sporting the conch, discus, mace and lotus, and decorated with a diadem, attractive ornaments and robes of shining yellow cloth. Received lovingly by emissaries of Vishnu with similar forms, and praised by bands of Yogis, the transfigured Jatayu addressed Sri Rama as follows:

The Hymn of Jatayu (44-56)

Jatayu said: **44.** "Possessed of countless excellences; unlimited by time and space; the most ancient; the cause of the worlds, its sustentation and dissolution; endowed with the radiance of peace; the soul of all souls—such is Ramachandra whom I salute. **(45-46).** The seat of all bliss; the object of the Goddess Lakshmi's constant gaze; the redresser of the woes of all Devas including Brahma; the noblest among men; the bestower of all boons; sporting in hands an excellent bow and arrows; the acme of beauty of form in the whole universe; the most fitting object to be prayed to and hymned upon; possessing the brilliance of a hundred suns; the bestower of all desired

भवविपिनदवाग्निनामधेयं भवमुखदैवतदैवतं दयालुम् ।
दनुजपतिसहस्रकोटिनाशं रवितनयासदृशं हरिं प्रपद्ये ॥ 47

अविरतभवभावनातिदूरं भवविमुखैर्मुनिभिः सदैव दृश्यम् ।
भवजलधिसुतारणाङ्घ्रिपोतं शरणमहं रघुनन्दनं प्रपद्ये ॥ 48

गिरिशगिरिसुतामनोनिवासं गिरिवरधारिणमीहिताभिरामम् ।
सुरवरदनुजेन्द्रसेविताङ्घ्रिं सुरवरदं रघुनायकं प्रपद्ये ॥ 49

परधनपरदारवर्जितानां परगुणभूतिषु तुष्टमानसानाम् ।
परहितनिरतात्मनां सुसेव्यं रघुवरमम्बुजलोचनं प्रपद्ये ॥ 50

स्मितरुचिरविकासिताननाब्जमतिसुलभं सुरराजनीलनीलम् ।
सितजलरुहचारुनेत्रशोभं रघुपतिमीशगुरोर्गुरुं प्रपद्ये ॥ 51

हरिकमलजशम्भुरूपभेदात्त्वमिह विभासि गुणत्रयानुवृत्तः ।
रविरिव जलपूरितोदपात्रेष्वमरपतिस्तुतिपात्रमीशमीडे ॥ 52

objects; the grantor of refuge; the resident at the foot of the tree of Bhakti; the gladdener of all the members of Raghu's line—such is Rama, in whom I take refuge. **47.** Celebrated as the fire that destroys the forest of Samsara; the Supreme Being who is the Master of Siva and all the deities; the embodiment of grace; the destroyer of countless Rakshasa leaders; blue-complexioned like the waters of the Yamuna—such is Rama, verily Hari Himself, in whom I seek refuge. **48.** Far away from those whose minds are ever engrossed in worldly thoughts, but ever visible to sages who eschew worldly thoughts; a veritable boat for crossing the waters of Samsara—such is Rama of Raghu's line in whom I take refuge. **49.** The Resident of the hearts of 'the Lord of Mountains' (Siva) and his consort; the up-lifter of the mountain; the object of worship of the leaders of Devas and Asuras; the fulfiller of the prayers of Devas—such is Rama, the leader of Raghu's line, in whom I seek refuge. **50.** The one, who is fit to be worshipped by those who eschew others' possessions and women; who are ever particular about the welfare of others, and who delight in others' excellences and prosperity—such is the lotus-eyed Rama of Raghu's line in whom I take refuge. **51.** Possessed of a face like a fully blossomed lotus rendered charming by a smile; graciously revealing His presence in the consciousness of those who constantly keep up His remembrance; possessed of a blue complexion like the colour of Indraneela gem; endowed with eyes that are attractive like the petals of a white lotus; the preceptor of even Siva and Brahma— such is the lord of the Raghu's in whom I take shelter. **52.** Just as the one sun shines differently in different vessels filled with water, Thou appearest in different aspects as Hari, Brahma and Sambhu according to

रतिपतिशतकोटिसुन्दराङ्गं शतपथगोचरभावनाविदूरम् ।
यतिपतिहृदये सदा विभातं रघुपतिमार्तिहरं प्रभुं प्रपद्ये ॥ 53

इत्येवं स्तुवतस्तस्य प्रसन्नोऽभूद्रघूत्तमः । उवाच गच्छ भद्रं ते मम विष्णोः परं पदम् ॥ 54

शृणोति य इदं स्तोत्रं लिखेद्वा नियतः पठेत् । स याति मम सारूप्यं मरणे मत्स्मृतिं लभेत् ॥ 55

इति राघवभाषितं तदा श्रुतवान् हर्षसमाकुलो द्विजः ।
रघुनन्दनसाम्यमास्थितः प्रययौ ब्रह्मसुपूजितं पदम् ॥ 56

इति श्रीमदध्यात्मरामायणे उमामहेश्वरसंवादे
आरण्यकाण्डेऽष्टमः सर्गः ॥ ८ ॥

the three Gunas of Prakriti, that Thou assumest for cosmic purposes. I sing this hymn in praise of that Being who is the object of adoration of even Indra, the lord of the celestials. **53.** I take shelter in Him, Rama incarnated in Raghu's line, who is more handsome than a hundred Cupids, who is not far away for those who meditate on Him on the lines laid down in Satapatha Brahmana. who is ever shining in the heart of all-renouncing ascetics; and who is the remover of the miseries of all."

54. Immensely pleased with Jatayu, who was reciting this hymn of praise, Rama blessed him telling, "I, Mahavishnu, am granting you My Supreme Status. **55.** Besides, whoever studies this hymn everyday or hears it or writes it down, he will remember Me at his death and will attain to My form." **56.** Jatayu was filled with unspeakable joy on hearing the blessings of Rama. He got transformed into the form of Vishnu and attained to that Status which is the aspiration of even Brahma.

नवमः सर्गः

श्रीमहादेव उवाच

ततो रामो लक्ष्मणेन जगाम विपिनान्तरम् । पुनर्दुःखं समाश्रित्य सीतान्वेषणतत्परः ॥ 1

तत्राद्भुतसमाकारो राक्षसः प्रत्यदृश्यत । वक्षस्येव महावक्त्रश्चक्षुरादिविवर्जितः ॥ 2

Chapter 9

SALVATION OF KABANDHA

Rama's confrontation with Kabandha (1-14)

1. After these incidents, Rama, moved by intense sorrow, again started with Lakshmana on the search for Sita in another forest. **2.** As they proceeded, they came across a Rakshasa of wondrous form. He was a monster, whose huge face was in the chest and who was devoid of important

बाहू योजनमात्रेण व्याप्तौ तस्य रक्षसः । कबन्धो नाम दैत्येन्द्रः सर्वसत्त्वविहिंसकः ॥ 3
तद्बाह्वोर्मध्यदेशे तौ चरन्तौ रामलक्ष्मणौ । ददर्शतुर्महासत्त्वं तद्बाहुपरिवेष्टितौ ॥ 4
रामः प्रोवाच विहसन्पश्य लक्ष्मण राक्षसम् । शिरःपादविहीनोऽयं यस्य वक्षसि चाननम् ॥ 5
बाहुभ्यां लभ्यते यद्यत्तत्तद्भक्षन् स्थितो ध्रुवम् । आवामप्येतयोर्बाह्वोर्मध्ये सङ्कलितौ ध्रुवम् ॥ 6
गन्तुमन्यत्र मार्गो न दृश्यते रघुनन्दन । किं कर्तव्यमितोऽस्माभिरिदानीं भक्षयेत्स नौ ॥ 7
लक्ष्मणस्तमुवाचेदं किं विचारेण राघव । आवामेकैकमव्यग्रौ छिन्द्यावास्य भुजौ ध्रुवम् ॥ 8
तथेति रामः खड्गेन भुजं दक्षिणमच्छिनत् । तथैव लक्ष्मणो वामं चिच्छेद भुजमञ्जसा ॥ 9
ततोऽतिविस्मितो दैत्यः कौ युवां सुरपुङ्गवौ । मद्बाहुच्छेदकौ लोके दिवि देवेषु वा कुतः ॥ 10
ततोऽब्रवीद्धसन्नेव रामो राजीवलोचनः । अयोध्याधिपतिः श्रीमान् राजा दशरथो महान् 11
रामोऽहं तस्य पुत्रोऽसौ भ्राता मे लक्ष्मणः सुधीः । मम भार्या जनकजा सीता त्रैलोक्यसुन्दरी ॥ 12
आवां मृगयया यातौ तदा केनापि रक्षसा । नीतां सीतां विचिन्वन्तौ चागतौ घोरकानने । 13
बाहुभ्यां वेष्टितावत्र तव प्राणरिरक्षया । छिन्नौ तव भुजौ त्वं च को वा विकटरूपधृक् ॥ 14

organs like eyes. **3.** His two arms extended up to a Yojana. The destroyer of every kind of beings, he was known by the name Kabandha. **4.** When Rama and Lakshmana saw this creature of enormous size, they were already between his huge arms, which surrounded them on all sides. **5.** Laughing at the sight of him, Rama said to Lakshmana, "Look at this Rakshasa. He is without head or legs. His face is situated on his chest. **6.** It is sure that he subsists on whatever comes between the clutches of his huge arms. We are already between them. **7.** O Lakshmana! There is no way to get out elsewhere. What shall we do now? He will eat us up very soon." **8.** Lakshmana replied, "Why, O Lord, are you agitated over this? With an unperturbed mind, we shall cut off his two hands, each one cutting one arm." **9.** Agreeing to this proposal, Rama cut off the monster's left arm with a sword and Lakshmana did the same with the right. **10.** The Rakshasa, who was astonished at this, asked, "Are you two celestials? Tell me, who you are. For, neither in the world of men nor of celestials is there any one competent to cut off my arms." **(11-12).** Rama replied laughing: "There was a great king in Ayodhya called Dasaratha. I am his son Rama. This intelligent man accompanying me is my brother Lakshmana. My wife Sita is a world-renowned beauty. **13.** When we both had gone out of our residence hunting, some Rakshasa has abducted Sita. We have come to this awe-inspiring forest in search of her. **14.** We found ourselves within the clutches of your huge arms. For saving ourselves, we have cut off those arms of yours. Now tell us who you are with this monstrous form."

कबन्ध उवाच

धन्योऽहं यदि रामस्त्वमागतोऽसि ममान्तिकम् । पुरा गन्धर्वराजोऽहं रूपयौवनदर्पितः ॥ 15
विचरँल्लोकमखिलं वरनारीमनोहरः । तपसा ब्रह्मणो लब्धमवध्यत्वं रघूत्तम ॥ 16
अष्टावक्रं मुनिं दृष्ट्वा कदाचिदहसं पुरा । क्रुद्धोऽसावाह दुष्ट त्वं राक्षसो भव दुर्मते ॥ 17
अष्टावक्रः पुनः प्राह वन्दितो मे दयापरः । शापस्यान्तं च मे प्राह तपसा द्योतितप्रभः ॥ 18
त्रेतायुगे दाशरथिर्भूत्वा नारायणः स्वयम् । आगमिष्यति ते बाहू छिद्येते योजनायतौ ॥ 19
तेन शापाद्विनिर्मुक्तो भविष्यसि यथा पुरा । इति शप्तोऽहमद्राक्षं राक्षसीं तनुमात्मनः ॥ 20
कदाचिद्देवराजानमभ्याद्रवमहं रुषा । सोऽपि वज्रेण मां राम शिरोदेशेऽभ्यताडयत् ॥ 21
तदा शिरो गतं कुक्षिं पादौ च रघुनन्दन । ब्रह्मदत्तवरान्मृत्युर्नाभून्मे वज्रताडनात् ॥ 22
मुखाभावे कथं जीवेदयमित्यमराधिपम् । ऊचुः सर्वे दयाविष्टा मां विलोक्यास्यवर्जितम् ॥ 23
ततो मां प्राह मघवा जठरे ते मुखं भवेत् । बाहू ते योजनायामौ भविष्यत इतो व्रज ॥ 24
इत्युक्तोऽत्रवसन्नित्यं बाहुभ्यां वनगोचरान् । भक्षयाम्यधुना बाहू खण्डितौ मे त्वयानघा ॥ 25

Kabandha's Antecedents (15-28)

(15-16). Kabandha replied: "I am indeed fortunate if the one who has approached me is really Rama. In my previous embodiment, I was a leader of Gandharvas. Infatuated with the pride of youth and my handsome form, I went about the world in the company of the women dear to me, delighting them in every way. By austerities, O Rama, I had obtained the boon of indestructibility from Brahma. **17.** Once, meeting Ashtavakra, the sage with eight bends in his body, I laughed at him in ridicule. The sage, excited with anger, cursed me, telling, 'O evil fellow! You will become a Rakshasa.' **18.** When I beseeched him for pardon, the sage Ashtavakra, resplendent with the power of austerities, spoke to me about my release from the effect of the curse. **(19-20).** He said, 'In the Treta-yuga, Lord Narayana will be incarnated as the son of Dasaratha. He will come near you and cut off your arms of a Yojana's length. You will be free from the effect of the curse at that time and get your original form.' It is as a result of that sage's curse that I got this monstrous body of a Rakshasa. **21.** Once, excited with anger, I opposed Indra, the king of celestials. He, O Rama, struck me on my head with his thunderbolt weapon. **22.** As a result of this, my head entered into my trunk and my feet were also destroyed. But, O Rama, because of the boon given by Brahma, I did not die in spite of being struck with the thunderbolt weapon. **23.** All the Devas, who felt pity for me for not having a face, asked Indra, 'How will he live without a face?' **24.** Indra told me, 'Your face will hereafter be within your trunk. You will get arms, each a Yojana long. Now you go away from here.' **25.** Being so commanded, I have been staying here, catching and eating whoever travels through this forest. And now,

इतः परं मां श्वभ्रास्ये निक्षिपाग्नीन्धनावृते । अग्निना दह्यमानोऽहं त्वया रघुकुलोत्तम ॥ 26
पूर्वरूपमनुप्राप्य भार्यामार्गं वदामि ते ॥ 27
इत्युक्ते लक्ष्मणेनाशु श्वभ्रं निर्माय तत्र तम् ।
निक्षिप्य प्रादहत्काष्ठैस्ततो देहात्समुत्थितः । कन्दर्पसदृशाकारः सर्वाभरणभूषितः ॥ 28
रामं प्रदक्षिणं कृत्वा साष्टाङ्गं प्रणिपत्य च । कृताञ्जलिरुवाचेदं भक्तिगद्गदया गिरा ॥ 29

गन्धर्व उवाच

स्तोतुमुत्सहते मेऽद्य मनो रामातिसम्भ्रमात् । त्वामनन्तमनाद्यन्तं मनोवाचामगोचरम् ॥ 30
सूक्ष्मं ते रूपमव्यक्तं देहद्वयविलक्षणम् ।
दृग्रूपमितरत्सर्वं दृश्यं जडमनात्मकम् । तत्कथं त्वां विजानीयाद्व्यतिरिक्तं मनः प्रभो ॥31
बुद्ध्यात्माभासयोरैक्यं जीव इत्यभिधीयते । बुद्ध्यादि साक्षी ब्रह्मैव तस्मिन्निर्विषयेऽखिलम्॥32
आरोप्यतेऽज्ञानवशान्निर्विकारेऽखिलात्मनि । हिरण्यगर्भस्ते सूक्ष्मं देहं स्थूलं विराट् स्मृतम् ॥ 33
भावनाविषयो राम सूक्ष्मं ते ध्यातृमङ्गलम् । भूतं भव्यं भविष्यच्च यत्रेदं दृश्यते जगत् ॥34

O holy one, you have severed my arms.' **(26-27).** Next, O Rama, put me into a pit and fill it with fuel and make a blazing fire. Being thus burnt by you, I shall obtain my original form. After that, I shall tell you about the ways and means to get back your wife."

(28-29). Hearing these words, Rama had a pit made by Lakshmana in which the monster was put and burnt with firewood. Thereupon, there arose from the body, a form equal in beauty to Cupid, decorated with every kind of ornaments. He circumambulated Rama, made a full prostration before him, and with his palms joined in salutation and voice choked with devotional fervour, said as follows:

Kabandha's Hymn (30-56)

He said: **30.** "O Rama! I now feel desirous of praising Thee who art partless, limitless and beyond the scope of mind and words. **31.** Thou art beyond the two aspects of Thy cosmic embodiment—the subtle one known as Hiranyagarbha and the gross one as Virat, both of which together is Thy manifest form. Distinct from this is Thy unmanifest form as Pure Consciousness, the Subject. Everything other than this constitutes the Object, the unconscious non-self. Therefore, O Lord! How can one know Thee with the mind, which itself belongs to the sphere of the Object or the unconscious non-self? **(32-33).** What is called Jiva (embodied spirit) is a state of identity of the reflection of the Atman with the Buddhi in which the former is reflected. That which is the Witness (Pervader) of the Buddhi and other adjuncts, is Brahman Himself. He is not an object of perception to Buddhi, being the ultimate Subject. He is unmodified Consciousness and the Essence of everything. In Him, owing to ignorance, the universe is superimposed. What is called the Hiranyagarbha is the subtle aspect of this cosmic manifestation, and the Virat the gross aspect. **34.** Thy subtle body, O Rama, is fit to be meditated upon by spiritual aspirants. That sort of medi-

स्थूलेऽण्डकोशे देहे ते महदादिभिरावृते । सप्तभिरुत्तरगुणैर्वैराजो धारणाश्रयः ॥ 35
त्वमेव सर्वकैवल्यं लोकास्तेऽवयवाः स्मृताः । पातालं ते पादमूलं पार्ष्णिस्तव महातलम् ॥ 36
रसातलं ते गुल्फौ तु तलातलमितीर्यते । जानुनी सुतलं राम ऊरू ते वितलं तथा ॥ 37
अतलं च मही राम जघनं नाभिगं नभः । उरःस्थलं ते ज्योतींषि ग्रीवा ते मह उच्यते ॥ 38
वदनं जनलोकस्ते तपस्ते शङ्खदेशगम् । सत्यलोको रघुश्रेष्ठ शीर्षण्यास्ते सदा प्रभो ॥ 39
इन्द्रादयो लोकपाला बाहवस्ते दिशः श्रुती । अश्विनौ नासिके राम वक्त्रं तेऽग्निरुदाहृतः ॥ 40
चक्षुस्ते सविता राम मनश्चन्द्र उदाहृतः । भ्रूभङ्ग एव कालस्ते बुद्धिस्ते वाक्पतिर्भवेत् ॥ 41
रुद्रोऽहङ्काररूपस्ते वाचश्छन्दांसि तेऽव्यय । यमस्ते दंष्ट्रदेशस्थो नक्षत्राणि द्विजालयः ॥ 42
हासो मोहकरी माया सृष्टिस्तेऽपाङ्गमोक्षणम् । धर्मः पुरस्तेऽधर्मश्च पृष्ठभाग उदीरितः ॥ 43
निमिषोन्मेषणे रात्रिर्दिवा चैव रघूत्तम । समुद्राः सप्त ते कुक्षिर्नाड्यो नद्यस्तव प्रभो ॥ 44
रोमाणि वृक्षौषधयो रेतो वृष्टिस्तव प्रभो । महिमा ज्ञानशक्तिस्ते एवं स्थूलं वपुस्तव ॥ 45
यदस्मिन् स्थूलरूपे ते मनः सन्धार्यते नरैः । अनायासेन मुक्तिः स्यादतोऽन्यन्नहि किञ्चन॥ 46

tation will bring them the supreme good, and they will thereby perceive therein the past, present and future of the universe. **35.** Thy gross manifestation called the Virat is the Cosmic Whole, having seven coverings consisting of Mahat-tattva, Ahamkara, Akasa, Vayu, Tejas, Jala and Prithvi, each succeeding one being ten times more extensive than the preceding. This Virat-Purusha, Thy Cosmic manifestation, is a fit object for meditation, which is to be done as follows: **(36-39).** Thou, the Virat, art the unity of the whole manifested universe, and the various regions in the universe are Thy parts. The underpart of Thy feet forms Patala, and the upper part of it Mahatala; Thy ankles form Rasatala, and knees, Talatala; Thy two thighs constitute Sutala and Vitala, while their lower part forms Atala; Thy hips form Bhuloka, and Thy naval, Bhuvarloka; Thy chest forms the luminous regions (Jyotir-loka) and Thy neck the Maharloka; the lower part of Thy face forms the Janaloka, and the upper part of it the forehead, the Tapoloka. Thy head is Satyaloka, the most superior of all regions. **(40-41).** Indra and other Guardians of the Regions are Thy arms; the quarters, Thy ears; the Aswini Devas, Thy two nostrils; Agni, Thy face; Time, the movement of Thy brows; and the preceptor of the Devas, Thy intellect. **(42-43).** Thy 'I'sense is Rudra; Thy speech, Vedic Mantras; Thy fangs, Yama; Thy rows of teeth, the stars; Thy laughter, Maya that deludes the worlds; Thy side-long glance, creation; Thy front, Dharma, and Thy back, Adharma. **(44-45).** Thy winking constitutes night and day; Thy abdomen, the seven seas; Thy blood vessels, the rivers; Thy hair, the trees; Thy semen, rain; the power of Thy knowledge, the greatness manifested in the universe—such is Thy gross body. **46.** Concentration of mind on this gross form of Thine is the easy way for man to attain salvation.

अतोऽहं राम रूपं ते स्थूलमेवानुभावये । यस्मिन् ध्याते प्रेमरसः सरोमपुलको भवेत् ॥ 47
तदैव मुक्तिः स्याद्राम यदा ते स्थूलभावकः । तदप्यास्तां तवैवाहमेतद्रूपं विचिन्तये ॥ 48
धनुर्बाणधरं श्यामं जटावल्कलभूषितम् । अपीच्यवयसं सीतां विचिन्वन्तं सलक्ष्मणम् ॥ 49
इदमेव सदा मे स्यान्मानसे रघुनन्दन ॥ 50
सर्वज्ञः शङ्करः साक्षात्पार्वत्या सहितः सदा ।
त्वद्रूपमेवं सततं ध्यायन्नास्ते रघूत्तम । मुमूर्षूणां तदा काश्यां तारकं ब्रह्मवाचकम् ॥ 51
रामरामेत्युपदिशन्सदा सन्तुष्टमानसः । अतस्त्वं जानकीनाथ परमात्मा सुनिश्चितः ॥ 52
सर्वे ते मायया मूढास्त्वां न जानन्ति तत्त्वतः । नमस्ते रामभद्राय वेधसे परमात्मने ॥ 53
अयोध्याधिपते तुभ्यं नमः सौमित्रिसेवित । त्राहि त्राहि जगन्नाथ मां माया नावृणोतु ते ॥ 54

श्रीराम उवाच

तुष्टोऽहं देवगन्धर्व भक्त्या स्तुत्या च तेऽनघ । याहि मे परमं स्थानं योगिगम्यं सनातनम् ॥ 55
जपन्ति ये नित्यमनन्यबुद्ध्या भक्त्या त्वदुक्तं स्तवमागमोक्तम् ।
तेऽज्ञानसम्भूतभवं विहाय मां यान्ति नित्यानुभवानुमेयम् ॥ 56

इति श्रीमदध्यात्मरामायणे उमामहेश्वरसंवादे
आरण्यकाण्डे नवमः सर्गः ॥ ९ ॥

This form includes everything. **(47-50).** Therefore, O Rama, I am always meditating on this form of Thine, a practice by which intense devotion is generated in the mind with the hairs on the body standing on end. When one succeeds in meditating on this gross form of Thine, immediately one obtains liberation. Let that topic rest. I now think of Thy form present here before me—the form holding bow and arrows in hand, blue in complexion, donning tree-bark clothes and matted locks, endowed with the freshness of youth, engaged in the search for Sita, and accompanied by Lakshmana. Let this form of Thine, O Rama, be the object of my constant meditation. **(51-52).** The all-knowing Lord Siva, along with Parvati, is always meditating on this form of Thine. At Kasi, He imparts with joy to dying Jivas Thy Name, the *tarakabrahma* (the saving Mantra), for their spiritual redemption. Therefore, O Lord of Janaka's daughter! Thou art indeed the Supreme Spirit. There is no doubt about it. **(53-54).** Veiled by Thy power of Maya, the ignorant man does not understand Thee in Truth. Salutation to Thee, Rama, the creator of everything. Salutation to Thee, the Prince of Ayodhya, attended upon by Lakshmana. Save me! Save me! May not Thy Maya veil my insight!"

Now Rama said: **55.** "O Gandharva of celestial class! O sinless one! I am very much pleased with your devotion and your hymn. You shall attain to my eternal Status, the goal of all Yogis. **56.** Whoever recites every day with devotion and concentration this hymn sung by you, they shall overcome Samsara, the product of Ajnana, and attain to the state of perpetual intuition of Me."

दशमः सर्गः

श्रीमहादेव उवाच

लब्ध्वा वरं स गन्धर्वः प्रयास्यन् राममब्रवीत् । शबर्यास्ते पुरोभागे आश्रमे रघुनन्दन ॥ 1
भक्त्या त्वत्पादकमले भक्तिमार्गविशारदा । तां प्रयाहि महाभाग सर्वं ते कथयिष्यति ॥ 2
इत्युक्त्वा प्रययौ सोऽपि विमानेनार्कवर्चसा । विष्णोः पदं रामनामस्मरणे फलमीदृशम् ॥ 3
त्यक्त्वा तद्विपिनं घोरं सिंहव्याघ्रादिदूषितम् । शनैरथाश्रमपदं शबर्या रघुनन्दनः ॥ 4
शबरी राममालोक्य लक्ष्मणेन समन्वितम् । आयान्तमाराद्धर्षेण प्रत्युत्थायाचिरेण सा ॥ 5
पतित्वा पादयोरग्रे हर्षपूर्णाश्रुलोचना । स्वागतेनाभिनन्द्याथ स्वासने संन्यवेशयत् ॥ 6
रामलक्ष्मणयोः सम्यक्पादौ प्रक्षाल्य भक्तितः । तज्जलेनाभिषिच्याङ्गमथार्घ्यादिभिरादृता ॥ 7
सम्पूज्य विधिवद्रामं ससौमित्रिं सपर्यया । सङ्गृहीतानि दिव्यानि रामार्थं शबरी मुदा ॥ 8
फलान्यमृतकल्पानि ददौ रामाय भक्तितः । पादौ सम्पूज्य कुसुमैः सुगन्धैः सानुलेपनैः ॥ 9
कृतातिथ्यं रघुश्रेष्ठमुपविष्टं सहानुजम् । शबरी भक्तिसम्पन्ना प्राञ्जलिर्वाक्यमब्रवीत् 10

Chapter 10

THE MEETING WITH SABARI

Sabari and her Antecedents (1-19)

(1-2). The Gandharva, who was about to depart after getting the Lord's grace, now said to Rama, "O scion of Raghu's line! At a little distance on your way there is an Ashrama where an ascetic woman named Sabari, devoted to the practice of Bhakti, lives, constantly meditating on Thy feet. O worshipful one! Go to her and she will give you all information." **3.** With these words, he ascended a heavenly vehicle luminous like the sun and attained to the realm of Vishnu. Such is the fruit of taking the name of Rama. **4.** Now, moving away from that dense forest infested by fierce animals like lions and tigers, Rama went towards the Ashrama of Sabari. **(5-6).** Seeing Rama in the company of Lakshmana arriving at her Ashrama, Sabari immediately got up with great joy and made prostrations at his feet. With eyes filled with tears of joy, she welcomed Rama and offered him a suitable seat. **(7-10).** She washed the feet of Rama and Lakshmana with great devotion and sprinkled that water on herself. Offering Arghya and other ceremonial honours, she worshipped Rama according to the scriptural injunctions. Then she offered him the choicest nectar-like fruits that she had collected specially for him. She worshipped his feet with sweet-smelling flowers smeared with unguents. To Rama who was thus received with due hospitality and was seated along

अत्राश्रमे रघुश्रेष्ठ गुरवो मे महर्षयः । स्थिताः शुश्रूषणं तेषां कुर्वती समुपस्थिता ॥ 11
बहुवर्षसहस्राणि गतास्ते ब्रह्मणः पदम् । गमिष्यन्तोऽब्रुवन्मां त्वं वसात्रैव समाहिता ॥ 12
रामो दाशरथिर्जातः परमात्मा सनातनः । राक्षसानां वधार्थाय ऋषीणां रक्षणाय च ॥ 13
आगमिष्यति चैकाग्रध्याननिष्ठा स्थिरा भव । इदानीं चित्रकूटाद्रावाश्रमे वसति प्रभुः ॥ 14
यावदागमनं तस्य तावद्रक्ष कलेवरम् । दृष्ट्वैव राघवं दग्ध्वा देहं यास्यसि तत्पदम् ॥ 15
तथैवाकरवं राम त्वद्ध्यानैकपरायणा । प्रतीक्ष्यागमनं तेऽद्य सफलं गुरुभाषितम् ॥ 16
तव सन्दर्शनं राम गुरूणामपि मे न हि । योषिन्मूढाप्रमेयात्मन् हीनजातिसमुद्भवा ॥ 17
तव दासस्य दासानां शतशङ्ख्योत्तरस्य वा । दासीत्वे नाधिकारोऽस्ति कुतः साक्षात्तवैव हि ॥ 18
कथं रामाद्य मे दृष्टस्त्वं मनोवागगोचरः । स्तोतुं न जाने देवेश किं करोमि प्रसीद मे ॥ 19

श्रीराम उवाच

पुंस्त्वे स्त्रीत्वे विशेषो वा जातिनामाश्रमादयः । न कारणं मद्भजने भक्तिरेव हि कारणम् ॥ 20

with his brother, Sabari, moved by a great upsurge of devotion, spoke with palms joined in salutation.

She said: **(11-12).** "O the greatest among the Raghus! This Ashrama is the place where some great Rishis, who were my teachers, stayed. For several hundred years, I stayed here attending upon them. They have now abandoned their bodies and attained to the world of Brahman. At the time of departing from the body, they asked me to stay on here in peace. They said to me: **(13-15).** 'The Supreme Spirit, who exists eternally, has embodied Himself as Rama, the son of Dasaratha, in order to destroy the Rakshasas and protect the Rishis. He will be coming to this place. You remain here till then, concentrating your mind on the Supreme Being. Just now, that great one is staying at Chitrakuta. Retain your body till He comes here and after that you can burn it in the fire of Yoga and attain His Status.' **16.** O Rama! Engaged solely in meditation on Thee, I have been staying here awaiting Thy arrival. It has now happened exactly as my teachers said. **(17-18).** O Rama! Even the Rishis, my teachers, had not the good fortune of seeing Thee. O Thou immeasurable Being! I am an ignorant and low-born woman. I have not the qualification to be the servant of Thy servants at the hundredth remove. What then to speak of my qualification to serve Thee! **19.** How is it that I am able to see Thee with my eyes—Thee who art beyond the ken of mind and speech! O Rama! Thou the Lord of all gods! I am not capable of praising Thee with a hymn. What am I to do? Bestow Thy grace on me!"

Rama on the disciplines of Devotion (20-33)

Rama said to her in reply: **20.** "The state of being a man or a woman, or belonging to a particular class or Ashrama or a state of life, or bearing any special name is not the qualification for my adoration.

यज्ञदानतपोभिर्वा वेदाध्ययनकर्मभिः । नैव द्रष्टुमहं शक्यो मद्भक्तिविमुखैः सदा ॥ 21

तस्माद्भामिनि सङ्क्षेपाद्वक्ष्येऽहं भक्तिसाधनम् ॥ 22

सतां सङ्गतिरेवात्र साधनं प्रथमं स्मृतम् ।

द्वितीयं मत्कथालापस्तृतीयं मद्गुणेरणम् । व्याख्यातृत्वं मद्वचसां चतुर्थं साधनं भवेत् ॥ 23

आचार्योपासनं भद्रे मद्बुद्ध्यामायया सदा । पञ्चमं पुण्यशीलत्वं यमादि नियमादि च ॥ 24

निष्ठा मत्पूजने नित्यं षष्ठं साधनमीरितम् । मम मन्त्रोपासकत्वं साङ्गं सप्तममुच्यते ॥ 25

मद्भक्तेष्वधिका पूजा सर्वभूतेषु मन्मतिः । बाह्यार्थेषु विरागित्वं शमादिसहितं तथा ॥ 26

अष्टमं नवमं तत्त्वविचारो मम भामिनि । एवं नवविधा भक्तिः साधनं यस्य कस्य वा ॥ 27

स्त्रियो वा पुरुषस्यापि तिर्यग्योनिगतस्य वा । भक्तिः सञ्जायते प्रेमलक्षणा शुभलक्षणे ॥ 28

भक्तौ सञ्जातमात्रायां मत्तत्त्वानुभवस्तदा । ममानुभवसिद्धस्य मुक्तिस्तत्रैव जन्मनि ॥ 29

स्यात्तस्मात्कारणं भक्तिर्मोक्षस्येति सुनिश्चितम् । प्रथमं साधनं यस्य भवेत्तस्य क्रमेण तु ॥ 30

भवेत्सर्वं ततो भक्तिर्मुक्तिरेव सुनिश्चितम् । यस्मान्मद्भक्तियुक्ता त्वं ततोऽहं त्वामुपस्थितः ॥ 31

Devotion is the only qualification. **(21-22).** If a man has no devotion to me, neither sacrifice nor charities, neither Tapas nor the study of Vedas and performance of rituals can help one to see Me. By Bhakti alone am I attained. Therefore, O good lady! I shall now speak to you about the means for the attainment of Bhakti. **(23-27).** The first and foremost of these is association with holy men; the second is the recital of accounts about me; the third, the singing of My glories; the fourth, the hearing and exposition of My teachings; and the fifth, sincere and devoted service of the teacher, seeing Me in him; the practice of meritorious habits, the control of the inner senses, the observance of external rules of purity and devoted ceremonial worship of Me constitute the sixth discipline; the seventh is a devoted repetition and contemplation of My Mantra with all its parts. The worshipful service of My devotees, seeing My presence in all beings, and the cultivation of non-attachment for all external objects combined with practice of self-control and other inner virtues constitute the eight discipline. Investigation of My true nature is the ninth. Whoever has such devotion with these nine limbs, is eligible to worship Me. **28.** O noble lady! Whoever is endowed with these disciplines, whether it be woman, man or brute creation, that person will have Bhakti characterised by intense love. **29.** When such Bhakti is generated, the truth about My nature will dawn upon him. Realising Me in that way one will attain Mukti in this very birth. **(30-31).** Therefore, it is firmly established that Bhakti is the cause of Mukti. If a person has succeeded in the first of these disciplines, namely, the association with holy men, then the others will follow one by one gradually. Therefore, it has been declared that Bhakti is Mukti. You being thus

इतो मद्दर्शनान्मुक्तिस्तव नास्त्यत्र संशयः । यदि जानासि मे ब्रूहि सीता कमललोचना ॥32
कुत्रास्ते केन वा नीता प्रिया मे प्रियदर्शना ॥ 33

शबर्युवाच

देव जानासि सर्वज्ञ सर्वं त्वं विश्वभावन । तथापि पृच्छसे यन्मां लोकाननुसृतः प्रभो ॥ 34
ततोऽहमभिधास्यामि सीता यत्राधुना स्थिता । रावणेन हृता सीता लङ्कायां वर्ततेऽधुना ॥ 35
इतः समीपे रामास्ते पम्पानाम सरोवरम् । ऋष्यमूकगिरिर्नाम तत्समीपे महानगः ॥ 36
चतुर्भिर्मन्त्रिभिः सार्धं सुग्रीवो वानराधिपः । भीतभीतः सदा यत्र तिष्ठत्यतुलविक्रमः ॥ 37
वालिनश्च भयाद् भ्रातुस्तदगम्यमृषेर्भयात् । वालिनस्तत्र गच्छ त्वं तेन सख्यं कुरु प्रभो ॥38
सुग्रीवेण स सर्वं ते कार्यं सम्पादयिष्यति । अहमग्निं प्रवेक्ष्यामि तवाग्रे रघुनन्दन ॥ 39
मुहूर्तं तिष्ठ राजेन्द्र यावद्दग्ध्वा कलेवरम् । यास्यामि भगवन् राम तव विष्णोः परं पदम् ॥ 40
इति रामं समामन्त्र्य प्रविवेश हुताशनम् ।
क्षणान्निर्धूय सकलमविद्याकृतबन्धनम् । रामप्रसादाच्छबरी मोक्षं प्रापातिदुर्लभम् ॥41
किं दुर्लभं जगन्नाथे श्रीरामे भक्तवत्सले । प्रसन्नेऽधमजन्मापि शबरी मुक्तिमाप सा ॥ 42

endowed with Bhakti towards Me, I have come before you. **(32-33).** It is certain that you will attain Mukti, because you have Bhakti. I have Myself come before you. Now, have you any idea where my handsome wife Sita is? Who has taken her away? If you know anything about it, please tell me."

Sabari on Sita's Whereabouts (34-44)

Sabari said: **(34-35).** "O Omniscient one! Creator of all the worlds! Thou knowest everything. Yet, Thou, the master of all the worlds, only to follow the ways of the world, art putting me this question. Nevertheless, I shall now tell where Sita is. Sita has been abducted by Ravana and is now in Lanka. **(36-40).** Not far away from here is a vast lake called Pampa. Close to it is a great mountain called Rishyamooka. There, the monkey-leader Sugreeva is staying with his four ministers in terrible dread of his brother Vali. Vali cannot go to the top of that mountain, being afraid of a curse on him by a sage. Deign to go there, O Lord, and enter into an alliance with Sugreeva. He will be able to achieve everything for you. Now, in Thy presence, I wish to enter into the fire, burn my body in it, and attain Thy Status—the Status of Mahavishnu. So please, wait for a while here." **41.** Making this request to Rama, Sabari entered into a well-lit fire. With all shackles of ignorance burnt in a moment, she, by Rama's grace, attained to Moksha, which is very difficult of attainment. **42.** If Rama, the Lord of the universe is pleased, what is there difficult of achievement? Sabari, though low-born, attained Mukti by

किं पुनर्ब्राह्मणा मुख्याः पुण्याः श्रीरामचिन्तकाः । मुक्तिं यान्तीति तद्भक्तिर्मुक्तिरेव न संशयः ॥ 43

भक्तिर्मुक्तिविधायिनी भगवतः श्रीरामचन्द्रस्य हे
लोकाः कामदुघाङ्घ्रिपद्मयुगलं सेवध्वमत्युत्सुकाः ।
नानाज्ञानविशेषमन्त्रविततिं त्यक्त्वा सुदूरे भृशं
रामं श्यामतनुं स्मरारिहृदये भान्तं भजध्वं बुधाः ॥ 44

इति श्रीमदध्यात्मरामायणे उमामहेश्वरसंवादे
आरण्यकाण्डे दशमः सर्गः ॥ १० ॥

Rama's grace. **43.** It is then needless to say that a man of high birth, if he be devoted to Rama will certainly attain to Mukti. There is no doubt in the statement that devotion to Rama is Mukti itself. **44.** Devotion to Sri Rama gives rise to Mukti. O men all the world over! Abandon all the various types of Mantras which are only the product of Ajnana (ignorance), and with great devotion, adore and serve the feet of Rama, which can fulfil all your needs. O wise men! Worship Rama, the blue complexioned one, who ever shines in the heart of Siva.

ॐ

अध्यात्मरामायणम्

किष्किन्धाकाण्ड :

प्रथमः सर्गः

श्रीमहादेव उवाच

ततः सलक्ष्मणो रामः शनैः पम्पासरस्तटम् । आगत्य सरसां श्रेष्ठं दृष्ट्वा विस्मयमाययौ ॥ 1
क्रोशमात्रं सुविस्तीर्णमगाधामलशम्बरम् । उत्फुल्लाम्बुजकह्लारकुमुदोत्पलमण्डितम् ॥ 2
हंसकारण्डवाकीर्णं चक्रवाकादिशोभितम् । जलकुक्कुटकोयष्टिक्रौञ्चनादोपनादितम् ॥ 3
नानापुष्पलताकीर्णं नानाफलसमावृतम् । सतां मनःस्वच्छजलं पद्मकिञ्जल्कवासितम् ॥ 4
तत्रोपस्पृश्य सलिलं पीत्वा श्रमहरं विभुः । सानुजः सरसस्तीरे शीतलेन पथा ययौ ॥ 5
ऋष्यमूकगिरेः पार्श्वे गच्छन्तौ रामलक्ष्मणौ ।
धनुर्बाणकरौ दान्तौ जटावल्कलमण्डितौ । पश्यन्तौ विविधान्वृक्षान् गिरेः शोभां सुविक्रमौ 6

KISHKINDHA KANDAM

Chapter 1

ALLIANCE WITH SUGREEVA

Hanuman's meeting with Rama (1-26)

1. Next Rama and Lakshmana slowly proceeded to the banks of the great lake Pampa. They were amazed to see that extensive and impressive lake. **(2-4).** About a Krosa in extent, Pampa was a deep lake with water free from the pollution of mud and mire, and clear like the minds of holy men. On the surface of its waters were various kinds of water-born flowers in bloom like lotus, Kalhara, water-lily and blue lotus. Numerous types of birds like Hamsa, Karandava, Chakravaka, water-fowl, Koyeshti and Krauncha were swimming on, or hovering over, the waters of that lake, producing a symphony of humming sounds. Its banks were crowded with trees and creepers bearing flowers and fruits, the fragrance of which spread all around. **5.** Rama and Lakshmana now washed themselves and drank of the refreshing waters of the lake to assuage their exhaustion. They then walked along the cool shores of the lake. **6.** Donning matted locks and tree-bark cloth, and equipped

सुग्रीवस्तु गिरेर्मूर्ध्नि चतुर्भिः सह वानरैः । स्थित्वा ददर्श तौ यान्तावारुरोहगिरेः शिरः ॥ 7
भयादाह हनूमन्तं कौ तौ वीरवरौ सखे । गच्छ जानीहि भद्रं ते वटुर्भूत्वा द्विजाकृतिः ॥ 8
वालिना प्रेषितौ किं वा मां हन्तुं समुपागतौ । ताभ्यां सम्भाषणं कृत्वा जानीहि हृदयं तयोः ॥ 9
यदि तौ दुष्टहृदयौ संज्ञां कुरु कराग्रतः । विनयावनतो भूत्वा एवं जानीहि निश्चयम् ॥ 10
तथेति वटुरूपेण हनुमान् समुपागतः । विनयावनतो भूत्वा रामं नत्वेदमब्रवीत् ॥ 11
कौ युवां पुरुषव्याघ्रौ युवानौ वीरसम्मतौ । द्योतयन्तौ दिशः सर्वाः प्रभयाभास्कराविव ॥ 12
युवां त्रैलोक्यकर्तारविति भाति मनो मम । युवां प्रधानपुरुषौ जगद्धेतू जगन्मयौ ॥ 13
मायया मानुषाकारौ चरन्ताविव लीलया । भूभारहरणार्थाय भक्तानां पालनाय च ॥ 14
अवतीर्णाविह परौ चरन्तौ क्षत्रियाकृती । जगत्स्थितिलयौ सर्गं लीलया कर्तुमुद्यतौ ॥ 15
स्वतन्त्रौ प्रेरकौ सर्वहृदयस्थाविहेश्वरौ । नरनारायणौ लोके चरन्ताविति मे मतिः ॥ 16

with bow and arrow in hands, the two heroic brothers, Rama and Lakshmana, proceeded towards the Rishyamooka mountain, viewing the beauty of the mountain and the various types of trees that they saw round about.

7. From the top of that mountain, Sugreeva, the monkey chief, along with his four monkey companions saw from a distance Rama and Lakshmana approaching the mountain, whereupon he ran to the highest peak of the mountain. **8.** Full of fear he addressed Hanuman, "O Friend! who could those two persons probably be? Adopting the form of a Brahmacharin, you go and find out all the particulars about them. **9.** Are they here sent by Vali to kill me? You talk with them and try to find out what they have in mind. **10.** If they are coming with evil intentions, indicate the same by a sign of your hand. Putting on an attitude of humility and prostrating before them, try to find out their motive."

11. Hanuman agreed to do so, and approaching Rama in the form of a Brahmacharin, saluted him in all humility and said: **12.** "Who are you great men, young in age and impressive in every way, as heroic personages are. Your radiance is illumining all the surroundings like the sun and the moon. **13.** It dawns on my mind that you are the personages that create, sustain and dissolve the world systems, now manifest in human forms for the benefit of the world. **14.** It occurs to me that assuming the form of men you are here moving about, as in sport, to free the world of its burdens and to protect the devotees. **15.** Performing the protection, dissolution and creation of these worlds as a play, you, supreme personages, have now adopted the form of Kshatriyas and incarnated yourselves in this world. **16.** I believe that you two are Nara-Narayana, the ever-free Lord dwelling in the hearts of all as their impeller, now moving about in this world in human forms."

श्रीरामो लक्ष्मणं प्राह पश्यैनं वटुरूपिणम् । शब्दशास्त्रमशेषेण श्रुतं नूनमनेकधा ॥ 17
अनेन भाषितं कृत्स्नं न किञ्चिदपशब्दितम् । ततः प्राह हनूमन्तं राघवो ज्ञानविग्रहः ॥ 18
अहं दाशरथी रामस्त्वयं मे लक्ष्मणोऽनुजः । सीतया भार्यया सार्धं पितुर्वचनगौरवात् ॥ 19
आगतस्तत्र विपिने स्थितोऽहं दण्डके द्विज । तत्र भार्या हृता सीता रक्षसा केनचिन्मम ॥ 20
तामन्वेष्टुमिहायातौ त्वं को वा कस्य वा वद ।

वटुरुवाच

सुग्रीवो नाम राजा यो वानराणां महामतिः । चतुर्भिर्मन्त्रिभिः सार्धं गिरिमूर्धनि तिष्ठति ॥ 21
भ्राता कनीयान् सुग्रीवो वालिनः पापचेतसः । तेन निष्कासितो भार्या हृता तस्येह वालिना ॥ 22
तद्भयादृष्यमूकाख्यं गिरिमाश्रित्य संस्थितः । अहं सुग्रीवसचिवो वायुपुत्रो महामते ॥ 23
हनूमान्नाम विख्यातो ह्यञ्जनीगर्भसम्भवः । तेन सख्यं त्वया युक्तं सुग्रीवेण रघूत्तम ॥ 24
भार्यापहारिणं हन्तुं सहायस्ते भविष्यति । इदानीमेव गच्छाम आगच्छ यदि रोचते ॥ 25

श्रीराम उवाच

अहमप्यागतस्तेन सख्यं कर्तुं कपीश्वर । सख्युस्तस्यापि यत्कार्यं तत्करिष्याम्यसंशयम् ॥ 26
हनूमान् स्वस्वरूपेण स्थितो राममथाब्रवीत् । आरोहतां मम स्कन्धौ गच्छामः पर्वतोपरि ॥ 27
यत्र तिष्ठति सुग्रीवो मन्त्रिभिर्वालिनो भयात् । तथेति तस्यारुरोह स्कन्धं रामोऽथ लक्ष्मणः ॥28

(17-18). Rama now said to Lakshmana, "Look at this Brahmacharin! He seems to be a master of grammar. His entire speech is flawless." Speaking thus to Lakshmana, Rama, who was knowledge-embodied, now said to Hanuman: **(19-21).** "I am Rama, the son of Dasaratha, and this is my brother Lakshmana. Honouring the words of my father, I have come to stay in the Dandaka forest, accompanied by my wife Sita. While staying here, O Brahmacharin, my wife Sita has been carried away by some Rakshasa. I am here in search of her. Now tell me who you are and whose son?" The Brahmacharin replied, "Sugreeva, the highly intelligent king of the monkeys, along with his four ministers is staying at the top of this mountain. **22.** Sugreeva, is the younger brother of Vali. This evil-minded Vali has expelled him from the country and appropriated his wife for himself. **(23-24).** Afraid of this Vali, he has taken refuge on this mountain Rishyamooka. I am a minister of Sugreeva. I am born of the Wind-deity as my father, and my mother's name is Anjana. O great scion of Raghu's line! It is proper that you and Sugreeva become allies. **25.** He will be helpful to you in destroying him who has abducted your wife. If this arrangement will suit you, we shall go to Sugreeva immediately." **26.** Sri Rama said in reply, "O great monkey! I too have come here to enter into an alliance with Sugreeva. I shall also surely accomplish his purpose and become his ally."

Rama's Alliance with Sugreeva (27-59)

(27-28). Hanuman now stood before them in his real form and said to Rama, "Both

उत्पपात गिरेर्मूर्ध्नि क्षणादेव महाकपिः । वृक्षच्छायां समाश्रित्य स्थितौ तौ रामलक्ष्मणौ ॥29
हनूमानपि सुग्रीवमुपगम्य कृताञ्जलिः । व्येतु ते भयमायातौ राजन् श्रीरामलक्ष्मणौ ॥ 30
शीघ्रमुत्तिष्ठ रामेण सख्यं ते योजितं मया । अग्निं साक्षिणमारोप्य तेन सख्यं द्रुतं कुरु ॥ 31
ततोऽतिहर्षात्सुग्रीवः समागम्य रघूत्तमम् । वृक्षशाखां स्वयं छित्त्वा विष्टराय ददौ मुदा ॥32
हनूमान्लक्ष्मणायादात्सुग्रीवाय च लक्ष्मणः । हर्षेण महताविष्टाः सर्व एवावतस्थिरे ॥ 33
लक्ष्मणस्त्वब्रवीत्सर्वं रामवृत्तान्तमादितः । वनवासाभिगमनं सीताहरणमेव च ॥ 34
लक्ष्मणोक्तं वचः श्रुत्वा सुग्रीवो राममब्रवीत् । अहं करिष्ये राजेन्द्र सीतायाः परिमार्गणम् ॥ 35
साहाय्यमपि ते राम करिष्ये शत्रुघातिनः । शृणु राम मया दृष्टं किञ्चित्ते कथयाम्यहम् ॥36
एकदा मन्त्रिभिः सार्धं स्थितोऽहं गिरिमूर्धनि । विहायसा नीयमानां केनचित्प्रमदोत्तमाम् ॥ 37
क्रोशन्तीं राम रामेति दृष्ट्वास्मान्पर्वतोपरि । आमुच्याभरणान्याशु स्वोत्तरीयेण भामिनी ॥ 38
निरीक्ष्याधः परित्यज्य क्रोशन्ती तेन रक्षसा । नीताहं भूषणान्याशु गुहायामक्षिपं प्रभो ॥ 39
इदानीमपि पश्य त्वं जानीहि तव वा न वा । इत्युक्त्वानीय रामाय दर्शयामास वानरः ॥ 40

of you can get upon my shoulders and go to the top of the mountain where Sugreeva is staying with his ministers." Agreeing to do so, Rama and Lakshmana mounted the shoulders of Hanuman. **(29-31).** In a moment, Hanuman jumped to the top of the mountain and placed Rama and Lakshmana under the shadow of a tree to rest. He then went to Sugreeva and said to him making salutation in all humility, "O King! Cast away all fear. Rama and Lakshmana have come here. Get up soon to receive them. I have requested Rama to enter into an alliance with you. Immediately that alliance has to be solemnised before fire as witness."

32. Then Sugreeva came to the presence of Rama in great joy. Cutting the branch of a tree, he himself made a seat for Rama to sit upon. **33.** Hanuman made a seat for Lakshmana, and Lakshmana one for Sugreeva. All of them then sat in great joy. **34.** Lakshmana then narrated all matters connected with Rama from the time of his coming to the forest to the time of Sita's abduction. **(35-36).** Hearing the words of Lakshmana, Sugreeva said to Rama, "O noble Lord! I shall take up the responsibility of instituting a search for Sita. I shall render you all the help I can to destroy your enemy. Now, O Rama! Hear from me a report on certain matters that have come to my notice. **(37-40).** One day, I was sitting with my ministers at the top of this mountain. I saw from there a noble lady being carried away through the sky by someone. She was crying, 'O Rama, O Rama'. Seeing us on the top of the mountain, she bundled up her ornaments in her upper cloth and threw the bundle down to us. She was crying as she was being carried away by the Rakshasa. I picked up the bundle of ornaments and deposited them in a cave.

विमुच्य रामस्तद्दृष्ट्वा हा सीतेति मुहुर्मुहुः । हृदि निक्षिप्य तत्सर्वं रुरोद प्राकृतो यथा ॥ 41
आश्वास्य राघवं भ्राता लक्ष्मणो वाक्यमब्रवीत् ।
अचिरेणैव ते राम प्राप्यते जानकी शुभा । वानरेन्द्रसहायेन हत्वा रावणमाहवे ॥ 42
सुग्रीवोऽप्याह हे राम प्रतिज्ञां करवाणि ते । समरे रावणं हत्वा तव दास्यामि जानकीम् । 43
ततो हनूमान्प्रज्वाल्य तयोरग्निं समीपतः । तावुभौ रामसुग्रीवावग्नौ साक्षिणि तिष्ठति ॥ 44
बाहू प्रसार्य चालिङ्ग्य परस्परमकल्मषौ । समीपे रघुनाथस्य सुग्रीवः समुपाविशत् ॥ 45
स्वोदन्तं कथयामास प्रणयाद्रघुनायके । सखे शृणु ममोदन्तं वालिना यत्कृतं पुरा ॥ 46
मयपुत्रोऽथ मायावी नाम्ना परमदुर्मदः । किष्किन्धां समुपागत्य वालिनं समुपाह्वयत् ॥47
सिंहनादेन महता वाली तु तदमर्षणः । निर्ययौ क्रोधताम्राक्षो जघान दृढमुष्टिना ॥ 48
दुद्राव तेन संविग्नो जगाम स्वगुहां प्रति ।
अनुदुद्राव तं वाली मायाविनमहं तथा । ततः प्रविष्टमालोक्य गुहां मायाविनं रुषा ॥ 49
वाली मामाह तिष्ठ त्वं बहिर्गच्छाम्यहं गुहाम् । इत्युक्त्वाविश्य स गुहां मासमेकं न निर्ययौ ॥50
मासादूर्ध्वं गुहाद्वारान्निर्गतं रुधिरं बहु । तद्दृष्ट्वा परितप्ताङ्गो मृतो वालीति दुःखितः॥51
गुहाद्वारि शिलामेकां निधाय गृहमागतः । ततोऽब्रवं मृतो वाली गुहायां रक्षसा हतः ॥ 52

You can see them even now and ascertain whether they are yours or not." With these words he brought and placed the bundle of ornaments before Rama. **41.** Rama untied the bundle, and on seeing its contents burst out again and again, 'Alas Sita! Alas Sita!' Then placing those ornaments on his chest, he began to cry like an ignorant person. **42.** Lakshmana now comforted Rama saying, "With the help of this great monkey-leader, we shall kill Ravana in battle and recover Sita without much delay." **43.** Sugreeva now said, "O Rama! I shall kill Ravana in battle and present Sita to you. I make this solemn promise to you." **(44-45).** Then Hanuman lit a fire, and the sinless pair, Rama and Sugreeva, with the fire as the witness, embraced each other with their extended arms in token of their alliance. Next Sugreeva sat by the side of Rama.

46. In a mood of great confidence, Sugreeva now narrated his story to Rama. He said, "O friend! Hear from me, what Vali has done to me sometime back. **(47-48).** The city of Kishkindha was once attacked by an Asura named Mayavi, the son of Maya. Making great lion-roars, he challenged Vali. Provoked terribly by it, Vali came out and with eyes reddened with anger, hit the Asura with his fist. **(49-50).** Terribly bruised by the blow, that Asura ran away and took shelter in a cave. Vali and myself went after him. Seeing that he had entered the cave, Vali said to me in great anger, 'You stand outside. I shall enter into the cave.' With these words, he went in, and for a whole month he did not come out. **(51-53).** At the end of a month, I found much blood flowing out of the cave. I broke down in sorrow on

तत्श्रुत्वा दुःखिताः सर्वे मामनिच्छन्तमप्युत । राज्येऽभिषेचनं चक्रुः सर्वे वानरमन्त्रिणः ॥ 53
शिष्टं तदा मया राज्यं किञ्चित्कालमरिन्दम । ततः समागतो वाली मामाह परुषं रुषा ॥ 54
बहुधा भर्त्सयित्वा मां निजघान च मुष्टिभिः । ततो निर्गत्य नगरादधावं परया भिया ॥ 55
लोकान् सर्वान्परिक्रम्य ऋष्यमूकं समाश्रितः । ऋषेः शापभयात्सोऽपि नायातीमं गिरिं प्रभो॥56
तदादि मम भार्यां स स्वयं भुङ्क्ते विमूढधीः । अतो दुःखेन सन्तप्तो हृतदारो हृताश्रयः ॥ 57
वसाम्यद्य भवत्पादसंस्पर्शात्सुखितोऽस्म्यहम् । मित्रदुःखेन सन्तप्तो रामो राजीवलोचनः ॥ 58
हनिष्यामि तव द्वेष्यं शीघ्रं भार्यापहारिणम् । इति प्रतिज्ञामकरोत्सुग्रीवस्य पुरस्तदा ॥ 59
सुग्रीवोऽप्याह राजेन्द्र वाली बलवतां बली । कथं हनिष्यति भवान्देवैरपि दुरासदम् ॥ 60
शृणु ते कथयिष्यामि तद्बलं बलिनां वर । कदाचिद्दुन्दुभिर्नाम महाकायो महाबलः ॥ 61
किष्किन्धामगमद्राम महामहिषरूपधृक् । युद्धाय वालिनं रात्रौ समाह्वयत भीषणः ॥ 62
तत्श्रुत्वासहमानोऽसो वाली परमकोपनः । महिषं शृङ्गयोर्धृत्वा पातयामास भूतले ॥ 63
पादेनैकेन तत्कायमाक्रम्यास्य शिरो महत् । हस्ताभ्यां भ्रामयंश्छित्वातोलयित्वाक्षिपद्भुवि 64
पपात तच्छिरो राम मातङ्गाश्रमसन्निधौ । योजनात्परितं तस्मान्मुनेरांश्रममण्डले ॥ 65

seeing it, thinking that Vali was dead. I closed the mouth of the cave with a stone and returned home and announced that Vali had ben killed by the Rakshasa. Our ministers were all very much distressed to hear this, and much against my will, they installed me as king. **(54-56).** O destroyer of enemies! For some days I ruled the kingdom. And then, Vali came back to the city. In great anger, he abused me in harsh words and delivered punches on me with his fist. In great fear, I fled away from the city, and going about many places, at last took shelter in this mountain Rishyamooka. Due to the curse of a Rishi, Vali cannot come to this mountain. **(57-59).** That vulgar fellow appropriated my wife. I am very much aggrieved by that. With my wife taken away from me, I am staying here in great sorrow. Today, I have got great relief by touching your feet." And now Rama, much moved by the distressed condition of his friend, said to him, "I shall soon put an end to the life of your enemy who has taken away your wife." Rama took this vow before Sugreeva and others.

Sugreeva calls for tests of Rama's strength (60-75)

60. Thereupon Sugreeva said to him, "O great king! Vali is the strongest among the strong. He cannot be confronted even by the Devas. How are you going to destroy him? **(61-62).** I shall tell you about his strength, please listen. Once a very powerful Asura named Dundubhi in the form of a huge buffalo attacked Kishkindha and challenged Vali for a duel at night. **(63-65).** Provoked and overwhelmed with anger, Vali caught hold of the buffalo by its horns, and whirling it round and round threw him on the ground. Then placing one foot on the Asura's body,

रक्तवृष्टिः पपातोच्चैर्दृष्ट्वा तां क्रोधमूर्च्छितः । मातङ्गो वालिनं प्राह यद्यागन्तासि मे गिरिम् ॥66
इतः परं भग्नशिरा मरिष्यसि न संशयः । एवं शप्तस्तदारभ्य ऋष्यमूकं न यात्यसौ ॥ 67
एतज्ज्ञात्वाहमप्यत्र वसामि भयवर्जितः । राम पश्य शिरस्तस्य दुन्दुभेः पर्वतोपमम् ॥ 68
तत्क्षेपणे यदा शक्तः शक्तस्त्वं वालिनो वधे । इत्युक्त्वा दर्शयामास शिरस्तद्गिरिसन्निभम् ॥ 69
दृष्ट्वा रामः स्मितं कृत्वा पादाङ्गुष्ठेन चाक्षिपत् । दशयोजनपर्यन्तं तदद्भुतमिवाभवत् ॥ 70
साधु साध्विति सम्प्राह सुग्रीवो मन्त्रिभिः सह । पुनरप्याह सुग्रीवो रामं भक्तपरायणम् ॥ 71
एते ताला महासाराः सप्त पश्य रघूत्तम । एकैकं चालयित्वासौ निष्पत्रान्कुरुतेऽञ्जसा ॥ 72
यदि त्वमेकबाणेन विद्ध्वा छिद्रं करोषि चेत् । हतस्त्वया तदा वाली विश्वासो मे प्रजायते ॥ 73
तथेति धनुरादाय सायकं तत्र सन्दधे । बिभेद च तदा रामः सप्त तालान्महाबलः ॥ 74
तालान्सप्त विनिर्भिद्य गिरिं भूमिं च सायकः ।
पुनरागत्य रामस्य तूणीरे पूर्ववत् स्थितः । ततोऽतिहर्षात्सुग्रीवो राममाहातिविस्मितः ॥ 75

Vali twisted its head with his hands and severed it from the body. In order to test the weight of that head, he threw it to a distance, and it fell on the ground about a Yojana away near the Ashrama of the sage Matanga. **(66-68).** From that severed head, a rain of blood poured near that sage's Ashrama. Being enraged at this, the sage Matanga cursed Vali, declaring that if he ever approached the mountain Rishyamuka where the sage's Ashrama was situated, his (Vali's) head would be shattered to pieces. From that time Vali never goes to that mountain. Knowing this secret, I have taken refuge in this mountain Rishyamuka and am staying here without fear of Vali. Please see there, O Rama, the head of Dundubhi lying like a mountain. **69.** If you can hurl it, it would be proof that you are strong enough to kill Vali. With these words Sugreeva showed that head, hill-like in size. **70.** Rama looked at it with a smile, and lo! he kicked it to a distance of ten Yojanas with his toe.

71. "Well done! Well done!" declared Sugreeva and his ministers. Then Sugreeva further said to Rama, the lover of all devotees: **72** "Here are seven huge palmyra trees. See them, O lord of the Raghus! Vali used to shake each of them at a time, until all its leaves fell down. **73.** If you can pass an arrow through all these trees, then I can believe that Vali's death at your hand is like an accomplished fact." **(74-75).** Rama agreed to stand this test also. Possessed of unlimited power, he strung his bow, and shot an arrow which not only passed through all the seven trees, but penetrated even through the mountain and the earth, and returned to Rama's quiver. Overjoyed and amazed at this feat, Sugreeva said as follows to Rama.

देव त्वं जगतां नाथः परमात्मा न संशयः । मत्पूर्वकृतपुण्यौघैः सङ्गतोऽद्य मया सह ॥ 76
त्वां भजन्ति महात्मानः संसारविनिवृत्तये । त्वां प्राप्य मोक्षसचिवं प्रार्थयेऽहं कथं भवम् ॥77
दाराः पुत्रा धनं राज्यं सर्वं त्वन्मायया कृतम् । अतोऽहं देवदेवेश नाकाङ्क्षेऽन्यत्प्रसीद मे ॥ 78
आनन्दानुभवं त्वाद्य प्राप्तोऽहं भाग्यगौरवात् । मृदर्थं यतमानेन निधानमिव सत्पते ॥ 79
अनाद्यबिद्यासंसिद्धं बन्धनं छिन्नमद्य नः । यज्ञदानतपःकर्मपूर्तेष्टादिभिरप्यसौ ॥ 80
न जीर्यते पुनर्दार्ढ्यं भजते संसृतिः प्रभो । त्वत्पाददर्शनात्सद्यो नाशमेति न संशयः ॥ 81
क्षणार्धमपि यच्चित्तं त्वयि तिष्ठत्यचञ्चलम् । तस्याज्ञानमनर्थानां मूलं नश्यति तत्क्षणात् ॥ 82
तत्तिष्ठतु मनो राम त्वयि नान्यत्र मे सदा । रामरामेति यद्वाणी मधुरं गायति क्षणम् ॥ 83
स ब्रह्महा सुरापो वा मुच्यते सर्वपातकैः ॥ 48
न काङ्क्षे विजयं राम न च दारसुखादिकम् । भक्तिमेव सदा काङ्क्षे त्वयि बन्धविमोचनीम् ॥85
त्वन्मायाकृतसंसारस्त्वदंशोऽहं रघूत्तम । स्वपादभक्तिमादिश्य त्राहि मां भवसङ्कटात् ॥86

Sugreeva's praise of Rama (76-93)

76. Sugreeva said: "O great Lord! Thou art the Paramatman, the protector of all the worlds. Some meritorious actions of mine in the past, have drawn Thee to me and given me Thy association. **77.** Holy men adore Thee for the cessation of their entanglement in Samsara. So having gained association with Thee, the bestower of Moksha, how can I pray to Thee for worldly goods, which means a further lease of entanglement in Samsara. **78.** Children, wealth, wife, kingdom etc., are infatuations caused by Maya, Thy mysterious power. I do not therefore seek them. Except Thy grace I do not seek anything. So, O Lord of all lords, bestow Thy grace on me. **79.** By a rare piece of good fortune I, who have been seeking my worldly welfare, have come to Thee, the bestower of supreme spiritual bliss, just like a man who digging the earth comes across a treasure trove. **(80-81).** My bondage resulting from primeval ignorance has been cut asunder today. This Samsara is not exhausted through sacrifice, charity, austerity, welfare work and the like; on the contrary, it only gets strengthened. But on seeing Thy lotus-feet it undoubtedly gets effaced. **82.** He whose mind remains in Thee unwavering even for a moment—his ignorance, the cause of all entanglement in Samsara, gets destroyed immediately. **(83-84).** Therefore, O Rama, may my mind remain on Thee at all times. May it not stray into anything else. Whoever takes even for a short time, Thy sweet name, chanting, 'Rama, Rama', such a person is freed from the effects of serious sins like murder and drunkenness. **85.** I seek, O Rama, neither victory over the enemy nor the happiness of the company of my wife. I desire only for devotion to Thee, which frees one from all bondages. **86.** O leader of Raghu's clan! I am a particle of Thy own Self subjected to the bondage created by Thy Maya. Bestowing on me devotion to Thy feet, save me from this

पूर्वं मित्रार्युदासीनास्त्वन्मायाऽऽवृतचेतसः । आसन्मेऽद्य भवत्पाददर्शनादेव राघव ॥ 87
सर्वं ब्रह्मैव मे भाति क्व मित्रं क्व च मे रिपुः । यावत्त्वन्मायया बद्धस्तावद्गुणविशेषता ॥ 88
सा यावदस्ति नानात्वं तावद्भवति नान्यथा । यावन्नानात्वमज्ञानात्तावत्कालकृतं भयम् ॥ 89
अतोऽविद्यामुपास्ते यः सोऽन्धे तमसि मज्जति ।
मायामूलमिदं सर्वं पुत्रदारादिबन्धनम् । तदुत्सारय मायां त्वं दासीं तव रघूत्तम ॥ 90
त्वत्पादपद्मार्पितचित्तवृत्तिस्त्वन्नामसङ्गीतकथासु वाणी ।
त्वद्भक्तसेवानिरतौ करौ मे त्वदङ्गसङ्गं लभतां मदङ्गम् ॥ 91
त्वन्मूर्तिभक्तान् स्वगुरुं च चक्षुः पश्यत्वजस्रं स शृणोतु कर्णः ।
त्वज्जन्मकर्माणि च पादयुग्मं व्रजत्वजस्रं तव मन्दिराणि ॥ 92
अङ्गानि ते पादरजोविमिश्रतीर्थानि बिभ्रत्वहिशत्रुकेतो ।
शिरस्त्वदीयं भवपद्मजाद्यैर्जुष्टं पदं राम नमत्वजस्रम् ॥ 93
इति श्रीमदध्यात्मरामायणे उमामहेश्वरसंवादे
किष्किन्धाकाण्डे प्रथमः सर्गः ॥ १ ॥

anguish of Samsara. **(87-88).** Formerly when my mind was clouded by Thy Maya, I entertained the distinctions between enemy, friend and neutral in my attitude towards others. But now on account of my having Thy holy communion, all these differences are gone, sublated by the perception of everything as Brahman. Where is friend, and where enemy to one having this experience? The differentiations made by the Gunas of Prakriti are experienced only when the bondage of Thy Maya operates. **89.** So long as ignorance facilitates the operation of the Gunas, this multiplicity is experienced as a hard reality, and so long as multiplicity is experienced due to ignorance, Time generates the fear of death. **90.** Therefore he who is satisfied with the life of ignorance, is submerged in the darkness of Tamas consisting in attachment for wife, children, wealth etc., which are all rooted in Maya. Therefore, O the noblest of Raghus, destroy this Maya, which is Thy bond slave. **91.** Let all the movements of my mind be offerings at Thy feet. Let my speech be devoted to the recital of Thy name and Thy excellences. Let my hands be engaged in Thy service and let my body have opportunities of contact with Thine. **92.** May my eyes ever see Thy images, Thy devotees and my spiritual teacher (Guru). May these ears of mine always hear accounts of Thy doings in Thy incarnation. And may my feet be constantly engaged in making pilgrimages to Thy shrines. **93.** O Vishnu, the eagle-vehicled one! May my limbs bear the dust of the holy spots sanctified by Thy feet. And may my head, O Rama, be ever prostrating at Thy feet, which are adored even by Siva and Brahma."

द्वितीयः सर्गः

श्रीमहादेव उवाच

इत्थं स्वात्मपरिष्वङ्गनिर्धूताशेषकल्मषम् । रामः सुग्रीवमालोक्य सस्मितं वाक्यमब्रवीत् ॥ 1
मायां मोहकरीं तस्मिन्वितन्वन् कार्यसिद्धये । सखे त्वदुक्तं यत्तन्मां सत्यमेव न संशय ॥ 2
किन्तु लोका वदिष्यन्ति मामेव रघुनन्दनः । कृतवान् किं कपीन्द्राय सख्यं कृत्वाग्निसाक्षिकम् ॥
इति लोकापवादो मे भविष्यति न संशयः । तस्मादाह्वय भद्रं ते गत्वा युद्धाय वालिनम् ॥ 4
बाणेनैकेन तं हत्वा राज्ये त्वामभिषेचये । तथेति गत्वा सुग्रीवः किष्किन्धोपवनं द्रुतम् ॥ 5
कृत्वा शब्दं महानादं तमाह्वयत वालिनम् । तच्छ्रुत्वा भ्रातृनिनदं रोषताम्रविलोचनः ॥ 6
निर्जगाम गृहाच्छीघ्रं सुग्रीवो यत्र वानरः । तमापतन्तं सुग्रीवः शीघ्रं वक्षस्यताडयत् ॥ 7
सुग्रीवमपि मुष्टिभ्यां जघान क्रोधमूर्च्छितः । वाली तमपि सुग्रीव एवं क्रुद्धौ परस्परम् ॥ 8
अयुद्ध्येतामेकरूपौ दृष्ट्वा रामोऽतिविस्मितः । न मुमोच तदा बाणं सुग्रीववधशङ्कया ॥ 9
ततो दुद्राव सुग्रीवो वमन् रक्तं भयाकुलः । वाली स्वभवनं यातः सुग्रीवो राममब्रवीत् ॥ 10

Chapter 2

THE DESTRUCTION OF VALI

Fight between Vali and Sugreeva (1-18)

1. To Sugreeva, whose sins were all eradicated by being embraced by him, Rama said smiling. **2.** Applying his delusion-generating power of Maya on Sugreeva in the interest of the success of his mission, Rama said, "O friend! Whatever you have said is true **3.** But the world will say, 'With the fire as witness, Rama took the vow of helping Sugreeva. What has he done to fulfil his obligations to Sugreeva?' People will bring such criticism against me. **4.** To prevent the circulation of such aspersions against me, you challenge Vali for a fight. It will end in good for you. **(5-7).** With a single arrow, I will kill Vali and install you as king." Agreeing to this proposal, Sugreeva went to the grove adjacent to Kishkindha and with a terrific roar, challenged Vali for a fight. Hearing that sound produced by his brother, Vali, his eyes red with anger, emerged soon from his abode, and went to the place where Sugreeva had stationed himself. He rushed at Sugreeva, who thereupon hit him on his chest. **(8-9).** Vali too, provoked to extreme wrath, delivered punch after punch on Sugreeva with his fist, and Sugreeva did the same to him in return. Thus, these two, resembling each other very much, fought between themselves. Rama was watching them in great astonishment, but did not release the arrow for fear of striking Sugreeva, for Vali and Sugreeva resembled each other so much. **10.** Shaken with fear, Sugreeva ran away

किं मां घातयसे राम शत्रुणा भ्रातृरूपिणा । यदि मद्धनने वाञ्छा त्वमेव जहि मां विभो ॥11
एवं मे प्रत्ययं कृत्वा सत्यवादिन् रघूत्तम । उपेक्षसे किमर्थं मां शरणागतवत्सल ॥ 12
श्रुत्वा सुग्रीववचनं रामः साश्रुविलोचनः । आलिङ्ग्य मास्म भैषीस्त्वं दृष्ट्वावामेकरूपिणौ ॥13
मित्रघातित्वमाशङ्क्य मुक्तवान्सायकं न हि । इदानीमेव ते चिह्नं करिष्ये भ्रमशान्तये ॥ 14
गत्वाह्वय पुनः शत्रुं हतं द्रक्ष्यसि वालिनम् । रामोऽहं त्वां शपे भ्रातर्हनिष्यामि रिपुं क्षणात् ॥15
इत्याश्वास्य स सुग्रीवं रामो लक्ष्मणमब्रवीत् । सुग्रीवस्य गले पुष्पमालामामुच्य पुष्पिताम् ॥ 16
प्रेषयस्व महाभाग सुग्रीवं वालिनं प्रति । लक्ष्मणस्तु तदा बद्ध्वा गच्छगच्छेति सादरम् ॥
प्रेषयामास सुग्रीवं सोऽपि गत्वा तथाकरोत् । पुनरप्यद्भुतं शब्दं कृत्वा वालिनमाह्वयत् । 18
तच्छ्रुत्वा विस्मितो वाली क्रोधेन महतावृतः । बद्ध्वा परिकरं सम्यग्गमनायोपचक्रमे ॥ 19
गच्छन्तं वालिनं तारा गृहीत्वा निषिषेध तम् । न गन्तव्यं त्वयेदानीं शङ्का मेऽतीव जायते ॥20
इदानीमेव ते भग्नः पुनरायाति सत्वरः । सहायो बलवांस्तस्य कश्चिन्नूनं समागतः ॥ 21

defeated, vomitting blood; and victorious Vali returned to his abode. Now Sugreeva said to Rama. **11.** "O Rama! Do you want me to be killed by the enemy, my brother? If your object is to kill me, you can yourself do it directly, O Lord! **(12-14).** O adherent of Truth and lover of those who seek refuge in you! Why have you abandoned me after generating confidence in you in my mind?" Hearing Sugreeva's words, Rama with tears in his eyes embraced him and said, "Be not afraid, O friend! Both of you being alike, I could not release my arrow fearing that it might strike you, my friend. Therefore, to avoid this mistake by confusion, I am giving you a distinguishing mark. **15.** Now go again and challenge Vali, and you will see him dead. I, Rama, am swearing this to you. O brother! In a moment, I will destroy your enemy."

(16-18). Consoling Sugreeva in this manner, Rama said to Lakshmana, "O high-souled one! Make a garland of fully blossomed flowers and put it on the neck of Sugreeva. Send him against Vali, thus marked with a garland." Lakshmana did accordingly, and prompted Sugreeva to set forth again for battle. Sugreeva went out once more and with a terrific sound challenged Vali.

Tara's plea to Vali (19-41)

19. Surprised at this new challenge, Vali in great wrath, girded up his loins and got ready to take up the challenge. **20.** While thus getting ready to start, he was obstructed by Tara, who said, "I do not think it is correct for you to go now. I have got great apprehensions in my mind. **21.** It is only just now that Sugreeva ran away defeated by you. He is again returning for combat in great haste. He must have some very powerful ally behind him for support." **22.** To her Vali said, "O handsome lady! You give up these apprehensions regarding him. Release your hold on my hand. Let me

वाली तामाह हे सुभ्रु शङ्का ते व्येतु तद्गता ।	प्रिये करं परित्यत्य गच्छ गच्छामि तं रिपुम् ॥	22
हत्वा शीघ्रं समायास्ये सहायस्तस्य को भवेत् ।	सहायो यदि सुग्रीवस्ततो हत्वोभयं क्षणात् ॥	23
आयास्ये मा शुचः शूरः कथं तिष्ठेद् गृहे रिपुम् ।	ज्ञात्वाप्याह्वयमान हि हत्वा यास्यामि सुन्दरि ॥	24

तारोवाच

मत्तोऽन्यच्छृणु राजेन्द्र श्रुत्वा कुरु यथोचितम् ।	आह मामङ्गदः पुत्रो मृगयायां श्रुतं वचः ॥	25
अयोध्याधिपतिः श्रीमान् रामो दाशरथिः किल ।	लक्ष्मणेन सह भ्रात्रा सीतया भार्यया सह ॥	26
आगतो दण्डकारण्यं तत्र सीता हृता किल ।	रावणेन सह भ्रात्रा मार्गमाणोऽथ जानकीम् ॥	27
आगतो ऋष्यमूकाद्रिं सुग्रीवेण समागतः ।	चकार तेन सुग्रीवः सख्यं चानलसाक्षिकम् ॥	28
प्रतिज्ञां कृतवान् रामः सुग्रीवाय सलक्ष्मणः ।	वालिनं समरे हत्वा राजानं त्वां करोम्यहम् ॥	29
इति निश्चित्य तौ यातौ निश्चितं शृणु मद्वचः ।	इदानीमेव ते भग्नः कथं पुनरुपागतः ॥	30
अतस्त्वं सर्वथा वैरं त्यक्त्वा सुग्रीवमानय ।	यौवराज्येऽभिषिञ्चाशु रामं त्वं शरणं व्रज ॥	31
पाहि मामङ्गदं राज्यं कुलं च हरिपुङ्गव ।	इत्युक्त्वाश्रुमुखी तारा पादयोः प्रणिपत्य तम् ॥	32
हस्ताभ्यां चरणौ धृत्वा रुरोद भयविह्वला ।	तामालिङ्ग्य तदा वाली सस्नेहमिदमब्रवीत् ॥	33

go to meet the enemy. **(23-24).** I shall be returning very soon after killing him. Who can be his ally? If there is any such ally for Sugreeva, I shall kill him too in an instant and return. Grieve not. When challenged by an enemy, which courageous person can stand without responding? So, O handsome lady! I shall return soon after destroying him."

25. Tara said in reply. "O great ruler! Hear from me some news that I have learnt. After that you can do as you think fit. When son Angada had gone on a hunt, he heard some news which he reported to me. **(26-33).** It is as follows: They say there is a great personage by name Rama, the son of King Dasaratha of Ayodhya. Along with his brother Lakshmana and wife Sita, he has come to stay in the Dandaka forest. It appears that Rama's wife Sita has been abducted by Ravana. Searching for her everywhere, he along with Lakshmana arrived at Rishyamuka and entered into an alliance with Sugreeva, taking an oath of rendering mutual help, with fire as witness. The agreement between them, it seems, is that killing you in battle, he will install Sugreeva in your place. With this resolve, they are staying in their abodes nearby. Now hear my advice. It's only just now that Sugreeva ran away defeated. Then, how can he come for battle so soon? (This gives credence to my fear that he has a powerful ally behind.) Therefore, it is better that you abandon your enmity with Sugreeva and bring him to your city and install him as the heir apparent. You, therefore, seek shelter in Rama. O great monkey leader! Thus be pleased to save your country, community, Angada and myself from destruction." With these words, Tara, shedding tears, prostrated

स्रीस्वभावाद्बिभेषि त्वं प्रिये नास्ति भयं मम । रामो यदि समायातो लक्ष्मणेन समं प्रभुः ॥ 34
तदा रामेण मे स्नेहो भविष्यति न संशयः । रामो नारायणः साक्षादवतीर्णोऽखिलप्रभुः ॥ 35
भूभारहरणार्थाय श्रुतं पूर्वं मयानघे । स्वपक्षः परपक्षो वा नास्ति तस्य परात्मनः ॥ 36
आनेष्यामि गृहं साध्वि नत्वा तच्चरणाम्बुजम् । भजतोऽनुभजत्येष भक्तिगम्यः सुरेश्वरः ॥ 37
यदि स्वयं समायाति सुग्रीवो हन्मि तं क्षणात् । यदुक्तं यौवराज्याय सुग्रीवस्याभिषेचनम् ॥ 38
कथमाहूयमानोऽहं युद्धाय रिपुणा प्रिये । शूरोऽहं सर्वलोकानां सम्मतः शुभलक्षणे ॥ 39
भीतभीतमिदं वाक्यं कथं वाली वदेत्प्रिये । तस्माच्छोकं परित्यज्य तिष्ठ सुन्दरि वेश्मनि ॥40
एवमाश्वास्य तारां तां शोचन्तीमश्रुलोचनाम् । गतो वाली समुद्युक्तः सुग्रीवस्य वधाय सः ॥ 41
दृष्ट्वा वालिनमायान्तं सुग्रीवो भीमविक्रमः । उत्पपात गले बद्धपुष्पमालः मतङ्गवत् ॥ 42
मुष्टिभ्यां ताडयामास वालिनं सोऽपि तं तथा । अहन्वाली च सुग्रीवं सुग्रीवो वालिनं तथा ॥ 43
रामं विलोकयन्नेव सुग्रीवो युयुधे युधि । इत्येवं युद्ध्यमानौ तौ दृष्ट्वा रामः प्रतापवान् ॥ 44
बाणमादाय तूणीरादैन्द्रे धनुषि सन्दधे । आकृष्य कर्णपर्यन्तमदृश्यो वृक्षखण्डगः ॥ 45
निरीक्ष्य वालिनं सम्यग्लक्ष्यं तद्धृदयं हरिः । उत्ससर्जाशनिसमं महावेगं महाबलः ॥ 46
बिभेद स शरो वक्षो वालिनः कम्पयन्महीम् । उत्पपात महाशब्दं मुञ्चन्स निपपात ह ॥ 47

before Vali and caught hold of his feet with her hands and wept bitterly out of fear. Then Vali, embracing her, said to her with great affection. **(34-36).** He said, "Dear wife! Your words are the mere promptings of your womanly timidity. I have no such fear. If Lord Rama along with Lakshmana has come here, I shall certainly get into friendship with him. I have heard formerly that the Supreme Lord Narayana has incarnated Himself as Rama for relieving the earth of her burdens. He is the Supreme Self and He is not likely to have any distinction between friend and foe. **37.** O virtuous woman! Saluting His feet, I shall fetch Him home. He, the God of gods, seeks those who seek Him. He is approachable through devotion. **(38-41).** If Sugreeva comes alone to fight, I shall kill him in no time. You spoke to me about cultivating friendship with Sugreeva and making him the heir-apparent. How can I, O dear lady—I, the celebrated Vali whose heroism is recognised by the whole world—follow the suggestions prompted by fear, when challenged by the enemy to fight? How can I think or speak like that? Therefore, O handsome lady! abandon your sorrow and remain at home." Consoling the grief-stricken and weeping Tara in this way, Vali went out determined to kill Sugreeva.

Death of Vali (42-71)

(42-43). Powerful Sugreeva, now with a garland of flowers around his neck, seeing Vali advancing, rushed at him with great speed like an elephant in rut, and delivered punches on him with his fist. Vali did the same to Sugreeva. Thus their fight went on. **(44-47).** Sugreeva fought all along, casting

तदा मुहूर्तं निःसंज्ञो भूत्वा चेतनमाप सः । ततो वाली ददर्शाग्रे रामं राजीवलोचनम् ॥ 48
धनुरालम्ब्य वामेन हस्तेनान्येन सायकम् । बिभ्राणं चीरवसनं जटामुकुटधारिणम् ॥ 49
विशालवक्षसं भ्राजद्वनमालाविभूषितम् ।
पीनचार्वायतभुजं नवदूर्वादलच्छविम् । सुग्रीवलक्ष्मणाभ्यां च पार्श्वयोः परिसेवितम् 50
विलोक्य शनकैः प्राह वाली रामं विगर्हयन् । किं मयापकृतं राम तव येन हतोऽस्म्यहम् ॥ 51
राजधर्ममविज्ञाय गर्हितं कर्म ते कृतम् । वृक्षखण्डे तिरोभूत्वा त्यजता मयि सायकम् ॥52
यशः किं लप्स्यसे राम चोरवत्कृतसङ्गरः । यदि क्षत्रियदायादो मनोर्वंशसमुद्भवः ॥ 53
युद्धं कृत्वा समक्षं मे प्राप्स्यसे तत्फलं तदा । सुग्रीवेण कृतं किं ते मया वा न कृतं किमु ॥ 54
रावणेन हृता भार्या तव राम महावने । सुग्रीवं शरणं यातस्तदर्थमिति शुश्रुम ॥ 55
पत राम न जानीषे मद्बलं लोकविश्रुतम् । रावणं सकुलं बद्ध्वा ससीतं लङ्कया सह ॥ 56
आनयामि मुहूर्त्तार्द्धाद्यदि चेच्छामि राघव । धर्मिष्ठ इति लोकेऽस्मिन् कथ्यसे रघुनन्दन ॥57

glances at Rama. Looking at these two, engaged in mortal combat, Rama took up an arrow from his quiver and attached it to his divine bow. Hiding himself behind the stump of a tree and pulling the bow string up to his ear, Rama of great prowess released at the chest of Vali that arrow, which was powerful like the thunderbolt weapon. The missile smashed the chest of Vali, who jumped up causing earth-tremors and then with a terrific howl fell to the ground.

(48-50). Vali lay unconscious for a time. Then regaining consciousness, he saw before him, the lotus-eyed Rama, holding bow in his left hand and an arrow in the other, donning tree-bark cloth and a crown of matted hair, broad-chested, resplendent with a wreath of wild flowers, and stout, long arms, shining with the lustre of new Durva grass, and accompanied by Sugreeva and Lakshmana on either side. **51.** Seeing Rama before him, Vali spoke to him the following words of insult. He said: "O Rama! What harm have I done to you to justify your slaughtering me? **52.** In shooting an arrow at me hiding behind the stump of a tree, you have violated the code of conduct of royal personages. You have committed an extremely heinous crime. **(53-54).** O Rama! What gain are you going to reap by fighting with me adopting the conduct of a thief? If you are a Kshatriya born in the line of Manu, fight with me facing me and reap its consequences. What favour has Sugreeva done to you and what is it that I have left undone? **55.** I have heard, O Rama, that while staying in the forest, your wife has been abducted by Ravana and that you have taken refuge with Sugreeva in order to recover her. **(56-57).** O Rama! Have you not heard of my strength, which is so well-known all over the world? I am capable of capturing Ravana along with all his tribe and bringing the whole of Lanka along with Sita in no time, if I wish to do so. I have heard people saying that you are a strict adherent

वानरं व्याधवद्धत्वा धर्मं कं लप्स्यसे वद । अभक्ष्यं वानरं मांसं हत्वा मां किं करिष्यसि ॥58
इत्येवं बहु भाषन्तं वालिनं राघवोऽब्रवीत् । धर्मस्य गोप्ता लोकेऽस्मिंश्चरामि सशरासनः ॥ 59
अधर्मकारिणं हत्वा सद्धर्मं पालयाम्यहम् । दुहिता भगिनी भ्रातुर्भार्या चैव तथा स्नुषा ॥60
समा यो रमते तासामेकामपि विमूढधीः । पातकी स तु विज्ञेयः स वध्यो राजभिः सदा ॥61
त्वं तु भ्रातुः कनिष्ठस्य भार्यायां रमसे बलात् । अतो मया धर्मविदा हतोऽसि वनगोचर ॥ 62
त्वं कपित्वान्न जानीषे महान्तो विचरन्ति यत् । लोकं पुनानाः सञ्चारैरतस्तान्नातिभाषयेत् ॥ 63
तत् श्रुत्वा भयसन्त्रस्तो ज्ञात्वा रामं रमापतिम् । वाली प्रणम्य रभसाद्रामं वचनमब्रवीत् ॥ 64
राम राम महाभाग जाने त्वां परमेश्वरम् । अजानता मया किञ्चिदुक्तं तत्क्षन्तुमर्हसि ॥ 65
साक्षात्त्वच्छरघातेन विशेषेण तवाग्रतः । त्यजाम्यसून्महायोगिदुर्लभं तव दर्शनम् ॥ 66
यन्नाम विवशो गृह्णन् म्रियमाणः परं पदम् । याति साक्षात्स एवाद्य मुमूर्षोर्मे पुरः स्थितः ॥ 67
देव जानामि पुरुषं त्वां श्रियं जानकीं शुभाम् । रावणस्य वधार्थाय जातं त्वां ब्रह्मणार्थितम् ॥ 68

of righteousness. **58.** Tell me what rules of righteousness you have observed in killing a monkey, hiding like a hunter. The flesh of monkeys is not fit for consumption. What have you gained by killing me?"

(59-61). To Vali, who was thus speaking at length such insulting words, Rama, born in Raghu's line, replied: "I am moving on this earth, with bow in hand in order to enforce the rules of Dharma in this world. Destroying the perpetrators of Adharma, I am here to establish Dharma. A daughter, a sister, a sister-in-law, the daughter-in-law—all these are alike. If a foolish man takes a woman of any of these relations as a wife or mistress, he is to be considered a sinner, and he deserves to be executed by the king. **62.** You have forcibly appropriated for yourself the wife of your younger brother. So, O monkey leader, I, who know Dharma, have killed you. **63.** Great men move about in this world to sanctify it. Because of your monkey nature, you are not able to understand it. So do not indulge in insulting criticism."

64. Hearing these words, the terror-stricken Vali, recognised Rama as Mahavishnu Himself. So making prostrations to him with an agitated mind, he said to Rama: **65.** "O high-souled Rama! Thou art verily the Supreme Being. The ignorant monkey that I am, I have made these irreverent remarks. Be gracious to pardon me for the same. **66.** I am going to die, struck with Thy arrow and particularly in Thy very presence. It is not given even to great Yogis to see Thee in this way. **67.** He, by repeating whose name in a mood of helplessness at the time of one's death, a Jiva attains to the Supreme Status—even He is now standing before me. **68.** O Divine Being! I recognise Thee as the Supreme Purusha, Maha-Vishnu, and Sita as Thy consort Sri.

अनुजानीहि मां राम यान्तं तत्पदमुत्तमम् । मम तुल्यबले बाले अङ्गदे त्वं दयां कुरु ॥ 69
विशल्यं कुरु मे राम हृदयं पाणिना स्पृशन् ।
तथेति बाणमुद्धृत्य रामः पस्पर्श पाणिना । त्यक्त्वा तद्वानरं देहममरेन्द्रोऽभवत्क्षणात् ॥ 70
वाली रघूत्तमशराभिहतो विमृष्टो रामेण शीतलकरेण सुखाकरेण ।
सद्यो विमुच्य कपिदेहमनन्यलभ्यं प्राप्तं परं परमहंसगणैर्दुरापम् ॥ 71

इति श्रीमदध्यात्मरामायणे उमामहेश्वरसंवादे
किष्किन्धाकाण्डे द्वितीयः सर्गः ॥ २ ॥

Prayed to by Brahma, Thou art born in this world for the destruction of Ravana. **69.** Give me Thy permission, O Rama, to attain to Thy Supreme Status. And may Thou be gracious to my son Angada, who is equal in strength to me. **70.** O Rama! Stroking my chest, be Thou gracious enough to pull out the arrow." Rama, thereupon removed the arrow, holding him by the hand. That monkey-chief now left his physical body and his spirit became identified with Indra. **71.** Struck by the arrow of Rama, and stroked by his cooling and comforting hands, Vali immediately left his monkey body and attained to a Status, which is difficult even for Paramahamsas to gain.

तृतीयः सर्गः

श्रीमहादेव उवाच

निहते वालिनि रणे रामेण परमात्मना । दुद्रुवुर्वानराः सर्वे किष्किन्धां भयविह्वलाः ॥ 1
तारामूचुर्महाभागे हतो वाली रणाजिरे । अङ्गदं परिरक्षाद्य मन्त्रिणः परिनोदय ॥ 2
चतुर्द्वारकपाटादीन् बद्ध्वा रक्षामहे पुरीम् । वानराणां तु राजानमङ्गदं कुरु भामिनि ॥ 3
निहतं वालिनं श्रुत्वा तारा शोकविमूर्च्छिता । अताडयत्स्वपाणिभ्यां शिरो वक्षश्च भूरिशः ॥ 4

Chapter 3

AFTERMATH OF VALI'S DEATH

Tara distracted at Vali's death (1-11)

1. When Rama, the Supreme Self, killed Vali in battle, all the monkeys, terrified beyond measure, rushed to Kishkindha. **2.** The monkeys went and reported to Tara, "O Noble lady! Vali has been killed in battle. Take measures to protect Prince Angada. Instruct the ministers in this respect. **3.** Closing all the gates of the city, we shall guard it. Proclaim Angada as the king of the monkeys." **4.** Hearing that Vali

किमङ्गदेन राज्येन नगरेण धनेन वा । इदानीमेव निधनं यास्यामि पतिना सह ॥ 5
इत्युक्त्वा त्वरिता तत्र रुदती मुक्तमूर्धजा । ययौ तारातिशोकार्ता यत्र भर्तृकलेवरम् ॥ 6
पतितं वालिनं दृष्ट्वा रक्तैः पांसुभिरावृतम् । रुदती नाथनाथेति पतिता तस्य पादयोः ॥ 7
करुणं विलपन्ती सा ददर्श रघुनन्दनम् । राम मां जहि बाणेन येन वाली हतस्त्वया ॥ 8
गच्छामि पतिसालोक्यं पतिर्मामभिकाङ्क्षते । स्वर्गेऽपि न सुखं तस्य मां विना रघुनन्दन ॥ 9
पत्नीवियोगजं दुःखमनुभूतं त्वयानघ । वालिने मां प्रयच्छाशु पत्नीदानफलं भवेत् ॥ 10
सुग्रीव त्वं सुखं राज्यं दापितं वालिघातिना । रामेण रुमया सार्धं भुङ्क्ष्व सापत्नवर्जितम् ॥ 11
इत्येवं विलपन्तीं तां तारां रामो महामनाः । सान्त्वयामास दयया तत्त्वज्ञानोपदेशतः ॥ 12
किं भीरु शोचसि व्यर्थं शोकस्याविषयं पतिम् । पतिस्तवायं देहो वा जीवो वा वद तत्त्वतः ॥ 13
पञ्चात्मको जडो देहस्त्वङ्मांसरुधिरास्थिमान् । कालकर्मगुणोत्पन्नः सोऽप्यास्तेऽद्यापि ते पुरः ॥14
मन्यसे जीवमात्मानं जीवस्तर्हि निरामयः । न जायते न म्रियते न तिष्ठति न गच्छति ॥15

was dead, Tara was overcome by sorrow and she beat her chest with her hands several times. **5.** She cried, "What am I to achieve by Angada, by the kingdom, by the city, by wealth? I shall die together with my husband even now." **6.** Speaking in this way and weeping in bitter sorrow, she walked quicklywith her locks dishevelled to the place where her husband's dead body was lying. **7.** On seeing Vali's body lying on the ground, covered with blood and dust, she cried aloud, "O my husband! O my husband!" and fell at his feet. **8.** With tears flowing from her eyes, she looked at Rama and said to him, "O Rama! Kill me also with the same arrow with which you killed Vali. **9.** I want to attain to the same realm as my husband and be with him. O scion of Raghu's line! Without me, he will not be happy even in heaven. **10.** O holy one! You have experienced the sorrow arising from separation from one's wife. So, send me soon to Vali. You will thereby gain the merit equal to arranging for a person's marriage. **11.** And, O Sugreeva, the kingdom being assigned to you by Vali's killer, you have easily gained kingship over it. You now enjoy it in the company of your wife Ruma without fear of any enemy."

Rama's sermon to Tara (12-39)

12. Tara, who was bemoaning her fate in this way, was graciously comforted by the high-souled Rama by imparting to her the knowledge of Truth. **13.** Rama said to her, "O timid lady! It befits you not to mourn over your husband's death. Who is your husband—is it this body or the Jiva? Think of the true state of affairs. **14.** The body is a combination of the five elements and inert. It consists of skin, flesh, blood, bones etc., and is born of the functioning of Time, Karma and Gunas. It is lying here now before you. **15.** If you consider that your husband is the Atman, then as the Spirit, he is deathless. He, as the Spirit, is neither born nor dead, nor

न स्त्री पुमान्वा षण्ढो वा जीवः सर्वगतोऽव्ययः ।
एक एवाद्वितीयोऽयमाकाशवदलेपकः । नित्यो ज्ञानमयः शुद्धः स कथं शोकमर्हति ॥ 16

तारोवाच

देहोऽचित्काष्ठवद्राम जीवो नित्यश्चिदात्मकः । सुखदुःखादिसम्बन्धः कस्य स्याद्राम मे वद ॥ 17

श्रीराम उवाच

अहङ्कारादिसम्बन्धो यावद्देहेन्द्रियैः सह । संसारस्तावदेव स्यादात्मनस्त्वविवेकिनः ॥ 18
मिथ्यारोपितसंसारो न स्वयं विनिवर्तते । विषयाध्यायमानस्य स्वप्ने मिथ्यागमो यथा ॥ 19
अनाद्यविद्यासम्बन्धात्तत्कार्याहङ्कृतेस्तथा । संसारोऽपार्थकोऽपि स्याद्रागद्वेषादिसङ्कुलः ॥ 20
मन एव हि संसारो बन्धश्चैव मनः शुभे । आत्मा मनः समानत्वमेत्य तद्गतबन्धभाक् ॥ 21
यदा विशुद्धः स्फटिकोऽलक्तकादिसमीपगः । तत्तद्वर्णयुगाभाति वस्तुतो नास्ति रञ्जनम् ॥ 22
बुद्धीन्द्रियादिसामीप्यादात्मनः संसृतिर्बलात् । आत्मा स्वलिङ्गं तु मनः परिगृह्य तदुद्भवान् ॥ 23
कामान् जुषन् गुणैर्बद्धः संसारे वर्ततेऽवशः । आदौ मनोगुणान् सृष्ट्वा ततः कर्माण्यनेकधा ॥ 24
शुक्ललोहितकृष्णानि गतयस्तत्समानतः । एवं कर्मवशाज्जीवो भ्रमत्याभूतसम्प्लवम् ॥ 25

sitting anywhere. **16.** The Jiva is all-pervading and endless. He is neither a man, nor a woman, nor a neuter. He is one without a second, unaffected by anything, just like the sky. He is eternal, pure, and of the nature of Consciousness. What reason is there for you to mourn for him?"

17. Tara now questioned Rama, "O Rama! The body is an insentient thing like a piece of wood. The Jiva is deathless and of the nature of Pure Consciousness. If it be so, whose is this bondage? Who is it that experiences pleasure and pain and is affected by them?"

18. Sri Rama replied, "So long as one feels the 'I-sense' with regard to the body, subtle or gross, and the Indriyas, so long that ignorant person (Atma) is subject to Samsara, birth and death. **19.** The false and superimposed bondage of Samsara, of one contemplating on the objects of the senses, does not pass off by itself, just as the false experience of a dream does not. It is eradicated only when the sleep ends. **20.** By its connection with the beginningless Avidya, the I-sense, which is itself a product of Avidya, experiences Samsara, characterised by attraction, aversion etc., though it is entirely meaningless. **21.** O Noble lady! Samsara and the bondage experienced in that state belong to the Manas. The Spirit getting identified with the Manas becomes a participant of the bondage accruing to the latter. **22.** This phenomenon can be understood from the analogy of how a clear piece of crystal placed near a red paint appears as stained by that colour. Though the crystal looks red in appearance, it is not really stained. **(23-25).** Similarly owing

सर्वोपसंहृतौ जीवो वासनाभिः स्वकर्मभिः । अनाद्यविद्यावशगस्तिष्ठत्यभिनिवेशतः ॥ 26
सृष्टिकाले पुनः पूर्ववासनामानसैः सह । जायते पुनरप्येवं घटीयन्त्रमिवावशः ॥ 27
यदा पुण्यविशेषेण लभते सङ्गतिं सताम् । मद्भक्तानां सुशान्तानां तदा मद्विषया मतिः ॥28
मत्कथाश्रवणे श्रद्धा दुर्लभा जायते ततः । ततः स्वरूपविज्ञानमनायासेन जायते ॥ 29
तदाचार्यप्रसादेन वाक्यार्थज्ञानतः क्षणात् । देहेन्द्रियमनःप्राणाहङ्कृतिभ्यः पृथक्स्थितम् ॥ 30
स्वात्मानुभवतः सत्यमानन्दात्मानमद्वयम् । ज्ञात्वा सद्यो भवेन्मुक्तः सत्यमेव मयोदितम् ॥ 31
एवं मयोदितं सम्यगालोचयति योऽनिशम् । तस्य संसारदुःखानि न स्पृशन्ति कदाचन ॥ 32
त्वमप्येतन्मया प्रोक्तमालोचय विशुद्धधीः । नस्पृश्यसे दुःखजालैः कर्मबन्धाद्विमोक्ष्यसे ॥ 33

to the proximity of Buddhi, Indriyas and the like, the experience of Samsara is forced upon the Atman. The Atman identifying itself with the Manas—whose reflected sentiency helps one infer its matrix, the Atman, as Pure Sentiency—,enjoys the sense objects which are born of Manas itself in association with the Atman. Thus the Atman comes to be involved in Samsara, helplessly bound by the Gunas or the objects of the senses. First, the mind in association with Atman, generates the sense objects and superimposes on them their painful and pleasurable nature. From this arise their repulsiveness and attractiveness, which make the Jiva perform works, some pure (*Sukla*), some impure (*Krishna*), and some others a mixture of these two (*Lohita*). Subject to these various types of Karmas, the Jiva is involved in Samsara for the whole cosmic cycle. **26.** When everything is dissolved into the primitive condition at the end of the cosmic cycle, the Jiva along with all its acquired tendencies and its Karma potential gets dissolved in beginningless Avidya, owing to its identification with mind, senses etc., and remains in that condition. **27.** When the time of creation comes at the end of the cosmic cycle, the Jiva gains manifestation once again, wrapped in mind and tendencies acquired in the past. Helplessly, he is thus submerged and projected into Samsara, just like a water-lifting machine. **(28-29).** When, as a result of some meritorious deeds, the embodied Jiva gets association with My devotees or holy men, established in peace, then he gradually turns his attention towards Me. He then gains that rare good fortune of hearing recitals of My actions and excellences. When he seriously takes to these devotional disciplines, he will without much difficulty gradually gain an understanding of the real nature of the Self. **(30-31).** Instructed by a competent spiritual teacher, the sense of the Vedic dictums dawns on him. He comes to have the intuitive experience that his Self is identical with the supreme and blissful Self, non-dual, eternal and distinct from body, senses, mind, Prana and the I-sense (*Ahamkara*). Gaining this knowledge, he becomes liberated immediately. Know that what I have said is the Truth. **32.** Whoever always contemplates seriously on these teachings that I have given out, him the travails of Samsara will never affect. **33.** You

पूर्वजन्मनि ते सुभ्रु कृता मद्भक्तिरुत्तमा । अतस्तव विमोक्षाय रूपं मे दर्शितं शुभे ॥ 34

ध्यात्वा मद्रूपमनिशमालोचय मयोदितम् । प्रवाहपतितं कार्यं कुर्वन्त्यपि न लिप्यसे ॥ 35

श्रीरामेणोदितं सर्वं श्रुत्वा तारातिविस्मिता । देहाभिमानजं शोकं त्यक्त्वा नत्वा रघूत्तमम् ॥ 36

आत्मानुभवसन्तुष्टा जीवन्मुक्ता बभूव ह । क्षणसङ्गममात्रेण रामेण परमात्मना ॥ 37

अनादिबन्धं निर्धूय मुक्ता सापि विकल्मषा ॥ 38

सुग्रीवोऽपि च तत्श्रुत्वा रामवक्त्रात्समीरितम् । जहावज्ञानामखिलं स्वस्थचित्तोऽभवत्तदा ।

ततः सुग्रीवमाहेदं रामो वानरपुङ्गवम् । 39

भ्रातुर्ज्येष्ठस्य पुत्रेण यद्युक्तं साम्परायिकम् । कुरु सर्वं यथान्यायं संस्कारादि ममाज्ञया ॥ 40

तथेति बलिभिर्मुख्यैर्वानरैः परिणीय तम् । वालिनं पुष्पके क्षिप्त्वा सर्वराजोपचारकैः ॥ 41

भेरीदुन्दुभिनिर्घोषैर्ब्राह्मणैर्मन्त्रिभिः सह । यूथपैर्वानरैः पौरैस्तारया चाङ्गदेन च ॥ 42

गत्वा चकार तत्सर्वं यथाशास्त्रं प्रयत्नतः । स्नात्वा जगाम रामस्य समीपं मन्त्रिभिः सह ॥ 43

too, think over these teachings of Mine with a pure and concentrated mind. Then you will not be afflicted by miseries. You will be free from the bondage of Karma. **34.** O handsome lady! In your previous birth, you had practised devotional discipline. Therefore, for your liberation from Samsara, this form of Mine has been revealed to you. **35.** If you constantly contemplate on this form of Mine and think over these teachings, then Karmas will not bind you, even if you be engaged in activities brought about by life in Samsara."

(36-38). Tara heard all these instructions of Rama with great interest and attention. She overcame her grief born of identification with the body, and made prostrations before Rama. Rejoicing in being established in the Self, she became a Jivanmukta—one liberated in this very life. By her contact with Rama, the Supreme Self, for a short time, Tara became freed from all stains and from the beginningless bondage of Avidya. **39.** Hearing all these instructions of Rama, Sugreeva also overcame the influence of ignorance totally and became established in peace.

Coronation of Sugreeva (40-54).

40. Rama now said to Sugreeva, the great monkey, "You make arrangements now for the cremation and obsequies of your elder brother at my command. Make his son perform all the rites of funeral obsequies as laid down in the Sastra." **(41-43).** Agreeing to do so, Sugreeva had the body of Vali lifted by many powerful monkeys and kept on a specially decorated vehicle. To the accompaniment of the sound of kettle-drums and big drums and of all other forms of royal insignia, and followed by Brahmanas, ministers, monkey governors, citizens. Tara and Angada, the body of Vali was taken to the place of cremation and all rites were performed according to scriptural injunctions. Then Sugreeva took his bath and along with the ministers went to Rama's presence.

नत्वा रामस्य चरणौ सुग्रीवः प्राह हृष्टधीः । राज्यं प्रशाधि राजेन्द्र वानराणां समृद्धिमत् ॥44
दासोऽहं ते पादपद्मं सेवे लक्ष्मणवच्चिरम् । इत्युक्तो राघवः प्राह सुग्रीवं सस्मितं वचः ॥ 45
त्वमेवाहं न सन्देहः शीघ्रं गच्छ ममाज्ञया । पुरराज्याधिपत्ये त्वं स्वात्मानमभिषेचय ॥ 46
नगरं न प्रवेक्ष्यामि चतुर्दश समाः सखे । आगमिष्यति मे भ्राता लक्ष्मणः पत्तनं तव ॥ 47
अङ्गदं यौवराज्ये त्वमभिषेचय सादरम् । अहं समीपे शिखरे पर्वतस्य सहानुजः ॥ 48
वत्स्यामि वर्षदिवसांस्ततस्त्वं यत्नवान् भव । किञ्चित्कालं पुरे स्थित्वा सीतायाः परिमार्गणे ॥ 49
साष्टाङ्गं प्रणिपत्याह सुग्रीवो रामपादयोः । यदाज्ञापयसे देव तत्तथैव करोम्यहम् ॥ 50
अनुज्ञातश्च रामेण सुग्रीवस्तु सलक्ष्मणः । गत्वा पुरं तथा चक्रे यथा रामेण चोदितः ॥ 51
सुग्रीवेण यथान्यायं पूजितो लक्ष्मणस्तदा । आगत्य राघवं शीघ्रं प्रणिपत्योपतस्थिवान् ॥ 52
ततो रामो जगामाशु लक्ष्मणेन समन्वितः । प्रवर्षणगिरेरूर्ध्वं शिखरं भूरिविस्तरम् ॥ 53
तत्रैकं गह्वरं दृष्ट्वा स्फाटिकं दीप्तिमच्छुभम् ।
वर्षवातातपसहं फलमूलसमीपगम् । वासाय रोचयामास तत्र रामः सलक्ष्मणः ॥ 54

(44-45). Prostrating at Rama's feet, Sugreeva said with a sense of deep statisfaction: "O great royal personage! Rule over this prosperous realms of the monkeys. I shall be your attendant just like Lakshmana and serve you for a long time." To Sugreeva who spoke these words, Rama said with a smile: **46.** "You are verily myself. There is no doubt about this. At my order, you install yourself as the ruler of the city and the kingdom. **47.** O dear friend! For fourteen years, I will not enter into any city. So my brother Lakshmana will go with you to the city. **(48-49).** Install Angada as the heir-apparent. I along with brother Lakshmana, shall spend the rainy season on the peak of this neighbouring mountain. You go and live in your city for some time. After that, you can begin the search for Sita." **50.** Sugreeva prostrated before Rama and said, "O great one! Whatever you order me, I shall do accordingly." **51.** Permitted by Rama, Sugreeva went to the city in the company of Lakshmana and did everything as instructed by Rama. **52.** Received and honoured properly by Sugreeva, Lakshmana soon finished his work and reported himself to Rama by prostrating at his feet.

53. Next Rama and Lakshmana proceeded to a high peak of the mountain called Pravarshana. **54.** There Rama came across a cave which had the brilliance of crystal, which gave shelter from sun, rain and wind and where fruits and roots were in easy reach. He resolved to stay

दिव्यमूलफलपुष्पसंयुते मौक्तिकोपमजलौघपल्वले ।
चित्रवर्णमृगपक्षिशोभिते पर्वते रघुकुलोत्तमोऽवसत् ॥ 55

इति श्रीमदध्यात्मरामायणे उमामहेश्वरसंवादे
किष्किन्धाकाण्डे तृतीयः सर्गः ॥ ३ ॥

within that cave. **55.** He took his residence in that mountain which had an abundance of delicious fruits and roots and fragrant flowers, and of lakes with waters sparkling like pearls and which was filled with many-coloured birds and animals.

चतुर्थः सर्गः

श्रीमहादेव उवाच

तत्र वार्षिकदिनानि राघवो लीलया मणिगुहासु सञ्चरन् ।
पक्वमूलफलभोगतोषितो लक्ष्मणेन सहितोऽवसत्सुखम् ॥ 1

वातनुन्नजलपूरितमेघानन्तरस्तनितवैद्युतगर्भान् ।
वीक्ष्य विस्मयमगाद् गजयूथान्यद्वदाहितसुकाञ्चनकक्षान् ॥ 2

नवघासं समास्वाद्य हृष्टपुष्टमृगद्विजाः । धावन्तः परितो रामं वीक्ष्य विस्फारितेक्षणाः ॥ 3

न चलन्ति सदाध्याननिष्ठा इव मुनीश्वराः । रामं मानुषरूपेण गिरिकाननभूमिषु ॥ 4

चरन्तं परमात्मानं ज्ञात्वा सिद्धगणा भुवि । मृगपक्षिगणा भूत्वा राममेवानुसेविरे ॥ 5

Chapter 4

RAMA IN RETREAT AT PRAVARSHANA

Rama instructing Lakshmana on his ritualistic worship (1-42).

1. Rama and Lakshmana spent happily the rainy season, moving about for recreation among the caves made of precious stones on the mountain side and subsisting with great satisfaction on the fruits and roots available there in abundance. **2.** There Rama saw with wonder masses of rain-clouds in the sky moving before the wind with peals of thunder and flashes of lightning coming from within their watery mass. They resembled a herd of elephants in rut with golden seats spread on their top. **3.** On the grassy mountain surface could be seen moving about birds and beasts, happy and plumpy by consuming an abundance of fresh green grass. Seeing Rama's presence there, they stood looking at him with wide-open eyes. **(4-5).** Like ascetics ever immersed in meditation, there stood those birds and beasts gazing at Rama—birds and beasts who were verily Siddhas come to serve the Supreme Being, as he moved

सौमित्रिरेकदा राममेकान्ते ध्यानतत्परम् । समाधिविरमे भक्त्या प्रणयाद्विनान्वितः ॥ 6

अब्रवीद् देव ते वाक्यात्पूर्वोक्ताद्विगतो मम । अनाद्यविद्यासम्भूतः संशयो हृदि संस्थितः ॥ 7

इदानीं श्रोतुमिच्छामि क्रियामार्गेण राघव । भवदाराधनं लोके यथा कुर्वन्ति योगिनः ॥ 8

इदमेव सदा प्राहुर्योगिनो मुक्तिसाधनम् । नारदोऽपि तथा व्यासो ब्रह्मा कमलसम्भवः ॥ 9

ब्रह्मक्षत्रादिवर्णानामाश्रमाणां च मोक्षदम् ।

स्त्रीशूद्राणां च राजेन्द्र सुलभं मुक्तिसाधनम् । तव भक्ताय मे भ्रात्रे ब्रूहि लोकोपकारकम् ॥10

श्रीराम उवाच

मम पूजाविधानस्य नान्तोऽस्ति रघुनन्दन । तथापि वक्ष्ये सङ्क्षेपाद्यथावदनुपूर्वशः ॥ 11

स्वगृह्योक्तप्रकारेण द्विजत्वं प्राप्य मानवः । सकाशात्सद्गुरोर्मन्त्रं लब्ध्वा मद्भक्तिसंयुतः ॥12

तेन सन्दर्शितविधिर्मामेवाराधयेत्सुधीः । हृदये वानले वार्चेत्प्रतिमादौ विभावसौ ॥ 13

शालग्रामशिलायां वा पूजयेन्मामतन्द्रितः । प्रातःस्नानं प्रकुर्वीत प्रथमं देहशुद्धये ॥ 14

वेदतन्त्रोदितैर्मन्त्रैर्मृल्लेपनविधानतः । सन्ध्यादि कर्मयन्नित्यं तत्कुर्याद्विधिना बुधः ॥15

about in the form of a man amidst those forests and mountains.

(6-7). On one of those days, when Rama after his meditation was sitting in solitude in a contemplative mood, Lakshmana approached him in all affection and humility, and said: "O Lord! By the instructions Thou gave me on past occasions, the doubts of my mind born of beginningless Avidya, have been cleared. **(8-10).** I now wish to hear from Thee how Karma Yogis offer Thee their ritualistic worship. This path is always claimed by the Yogins as a way for the attainment of Mukti. Besides, Narada, Vyasa and the lotus-born Brahma speak of it as a way that confers Mukti alike to Brahmanas, Kshatriyas and Vaisyas as also to women and Sudras. O great one! Please speak to me, Thy brother and devotee, about this way of quick and universal access to Mukti, so that the whole world besides myself may be benefited thereby."

Sri Rama said in reply: **11.** "The ways of My ritualistic worship are endless. I shall therefore give you a brief exposition of it in its essential parts according to their importance. **(12-14).** After being invested with the sacred thread according to the traditions of the family, a person must get initiated into My Mantra and worship from a proper Guru. He should then proceed to perform My worship as shown by the teacher, with deep devotion and attention. Worship can be offered to Me as residing in the heart, or fire, or an image, or the sun, or the Salagrama. First an aspirant should cleanse his body by taking a morning bath **15.** He should utter appropriate Mantras, Vedic and Tantric, while bathing, and apply mud or other ingredients allowed by the scriptures for purifying his

सङ्कल्पमादौ कुर्वीत सिद्ध्यर्थं कर्मणां सुधीः । स्वगुरुं पूजयेद्भक्त्या मद्बुद्ध्या पूजको मम ॥16

शिलायां स्नपनं कुर्यात्प्रतिमासु प्रमार्जनम् । प्रसिद्धैर्गन्धपुष्पाद्यैर्मत्पूजा सिद्धिदायिका ॥ 17

अमायिकोऽनुवृत्त्या मां पूजयेन्नियतव्रतः । प्रतिमादिष्वलङ्कारः प्रियो मे कुलनन्दन ॥ 18

अग्नौ यजेत हविषा भास्करे स्थण्डिले यजेत् । भक्तेनोपहृतं प्रीत्यै श्रद्धया मम वार्यपि ॥ 19

किं पुनर्भक्ष्यभोज्यादि गन्धपुष्पाक्षतादिकम् । पूजाद्रव्याणि सर्वाणि सम्पाद्यैवं समारभेत् ॥ 20

चैलाजिनकुशैः सम्यगासनं परिकल्पयेत् । तत्रोपविश्य देवस्य सम्मुखे शुद्धमानसः ॥ 21

ततो न्यासं प्रकुर्वीत मातृकाबहिरान्तरम् । केशवादि ततः कुर्यात्तत्त्वन्यासं ततः परम् ॥ 22

मन्मूर्तिपञ्जरन्यासं मन्त्रन्यासं ततो न्यसेत् । प्रतिमादावपि तथा कुर्यान्नित्यमतन्द्रितः ॥ 23

body. Then he should perform Sandhya and other daily rites. **16.** With a pure mind he should at the beginning of worship utter the Sankalpa (the right resolution) for the successful performance of the rite. The worshipper should then adore the Guru in mind with the conviction that the Guru is Myself. **(17-18).** If the worship is done on a stone medium, ceremonial bath of the Deity with water should be performed. If the object of worship is an image, rubbing is necessary. Then offerings should be made with well-known ingredients like flower, sandal paste etc. If the worship is to bear fruit, it should be done with purity and sincerity of mind, and with observance of austere disciplines, and adherence to the procedure of worship according to the tradition as imparted by the Guru. Decoration of the image with flower garlands etc., is highly pleasing to Me. **(19-20).** If the worship is done through the medium of fire, then oblations with ghee accompanied with other ingredients should be made. If the sun is the medium of worship, then a ritualistic design to represent the sun must be made on the floor and worship should be offered on it. As for ingredients, offering of even mere water with firm faith by a devotee, is pleasing to Me. Not to speak then of how pleased I am when worshipped with flowers, sandal paste, incense, and offerings of fruits, sweets, Payasa and other delicious preparations. **21.** The worshipper should sit on a seat made with Kusa grass at the bottom and deer skin and cloth over it. He should sit facing the Deity, with his mind pure and filled with holy thoughts. **22.** Then one should do Nyasa or placement of fingers with Mantras. The first Nyasa to be performed is Matrika-Nyasa, which consists in placing the fifty one alphabets on the body and on the worshipping image. Then should be done *Kesavadi Nyasa* by placement of twentyfour divine names, and this is to be followed by the *Tattva-Nyasa*. (The details about thee Nyasas are given in the *Narada Pancharatra*). **23.** Next should be done *Murtipangara-Nyasa* (which consists in the placement of the divine names given in *Vishnu-Panjara-stotra* from the head to the feet). After that *Mantra-Nyāsa* should be done. All these have to

कलशं स्वपुरो वामे क्षिपेत्पुष्पादि दक्षिणे। अर्घ्यपाद्यप्रदानार्थं मधुपर्कार्थमेव च ॥ 24
तथैवाचमनार्थं तु न्यसेत्पात्रचतुष्टयम्। हृत्पद्मे भानुविमले मत्कलां जीवसंज्ञिताम् ॥ 25
ध्यायेत्स्वदेहमखिलं तया व्याप्तमरिन्दम। तामेवावाहयेन्नित्यं प्रतिमादिषु मत्कलाम् ॥ 26
पाद्यार्घ्याचमनीयाद्यैः स्नानवस्त्रविभूषणैः। यावच्छक्योपचारैर्वा त्वर्चयेन्मामममायया ॥ 27
विभवे सति कर्पूरकुङ्कुमागरुचन्दनैः। अर्चयेन्मन्त्रवन्नित्यं सुगन्धकुसुमैः शुभैः ॥ 28
दशावरणपूजां वै ह्यागमोक्तां प्रकारयेत्। नीराजनैर्धूपदीपैर्नैवेद्यैर्बहुविस्तरैः ॥ 29
श्रद्धयोपहरेन्नित्यं श्रद्धाभुगहमीश्वरः। होमं कुर्यात्प्रयत्नेन विधिना मन्त्रकोविदः ॥ 30
अगस्त्येनोक्तमार्गेण कुण्डेनागमवित्तमः। जुहुयान्मूलमन्त्रेण पुंसूक्तेनाथवा बुधः ॥ 31
अथवौपासनाग्नौ वा चरुणा हविषा तथा। तप्तजाम्बूनदप्रख्यं दिव्याभरणभूषितम् ॥ 32
ध्यायेदनलमध्यस्थं होमकाले सदा बुधः। पार्षदेभ्यो बलिं दत्त्वा होमशेषं समापयेत् ॥ 33
ततो जपं प्रकुर्वीत ध्यायेन्मां यतवाक् स्मरन्। मुखवासं च ताम्बूलं दत्त्वा प्रीतिसमन्वितः ॥ 34
मदर्थे नृत्यगीतादि स्तुतिपाठादि कारयेत्। प्रणमेद्दण्डवद्भूमौ हृदये मां निधाय च ॥ 35

be done also to the image scrupulously. **(24-25).** Then a little to the left in front of oneself, the water pot must be kept and on the right side the flowers to be offered. In the same way, four vessels must be arranged for Arghya, Padya, Achamana and Madhuparka. One should then meditate on the Jiva (embodied spirit), who is a particle of Myself, in the heart-lotus luminous like the sun. **26.** Then one should think that He is permeating the whole of the body from head to foot. Next one should transfer every day that Divine-Consciousness within oneself into the image to be worshipped and feel it as a living presence. **27.** Then one should adore Me with great sincerity, according to one's means, with Padya, Arghya, Achamaniya, water for bath, cloth and decorations. **28.** Those who have plenty of means should everyday make offerings of Karpura, Kumkuma, Akil, sandal paste and fragrant flowers. **(29-30).** An aspirant can do with the help of experts the Dasavarana Puja as given in Agastya Samhita. Everyday worship should be done with incense, light, various kinds of food offerings, bath etc. with great faith (Sraddha). I, the Lord of all, is a consumer of whatever is offered with great faith and sincerity. Those who are experts in Mantras, should every day make offerings in fire (Homa) also according to scriptural dictates. **31.** In a sacrificial pit designed according to the rules laid down in Agastya-Samhita, one versed in Agamas should make oblations of ghee and other ingredients with the chanting of Mula-Mantra or the Purusha-Sukta. **(32-33).** Or without making any special sacrificial pit, one can make oblations with Charu in the sacred fire kept by oneself. During the time of offering, one should contemplate on Me, golden in colour and decorated with divine ornaments, and as dwelling in the middle of the flame. In conclusion, offerings should be made to My attendants. **(34-35).** Next, one should make

शिरस्याधाय मद्दत्तं प्रसादं भावनामयम् । पाणिभ्यां मत्पदे मूर्ध्नि गृहीत्वा भक्ति संयुतः 36

रक्ष मां घोरसंसारादित्युक्त्वा प्रणमेत्सुधीः । उद्वासयेद्यथापूर्वं प्रत्यग्ज्योतिषि संस्मरन् ॥ 37

एवमुक्तप्रकारेण पूजयेद्विधिवद्यदि । इहामुत्र च संसिद्धिं प्राप्नोति मदनुग्रहात् ॥ 38

मद्भक्तो यदि मामेवं पूजां चैव दिने दिने । करोति मम सारूप्यं प्राप्नोत्येव न संशयः ॥ 39

इदं रहस्यं परमं च पावनं मयैव साक्षात्कथितं सनातनम् ।
पठत्यजस्रं यदि वा शृणोति यः स सर्वपूजाफलभाङ् न संशयः ॥ 40

एवं परात्मा श्रीरामः क्रियायोगमनुत्तमम् । पृष्टः प्राह स्वभक्ताय शेषांशाय महात्मने ॥ 41

पुनः प्राकृतवद्रामो मायामालंब्य दुःखितः । हा सीतेति वदन्नैव निद्रां लेभे कथञ्चन ॥ 42

एतस्मिन्नन्तरे तत्र किष्किन्धायां सुबुद्धिमान् । हनूमान्प्राह सुग्रीवमेकान्ते कपिनायकम् ॥ 43

शृणु राजन् प्रवक्ष्यामि तवैव हितमुत्तमम् । रामेण ते कृतः पूर्वमुपकारो ह्यनुत्तमः ॥ 44

silent repetition of My Mantra with the mind dwelling on Me. After that, he should offer Me betel leaves with a joyful mind, and next engage himself in dance, song, praise, chanting and reading of the scriptures. Next, he should make a full prostration contemplating on Me in his mind. **(36-37).** He should next imagine in his mind, the Deity as giving the offered flowers etc., to him as Prasada as a mark of His grace, and he should place them on his head. Then he should mentally grasp the feet of the Deity and touch his head on them and pray, "O Lord! Lift me from this terrible life in Samsara of repeated births and deaths." With this prayer one should make prostration. Then, just as he brought out the Deity from his consciousness, for the purpose of worship, he should also take Him back into himself, according to the rite called Udvāsa. **38.** If a man worships Me, in the way I have expounded, he will attain to spiritual well-being by My grace in this world and the next. **39.** If a devotee worships Me everyday in this way, he attains Sarupya or salvation by getting My own form. There is no doubt about it. **40.** Whoever either reads or hears this supremely holy and esoteric exposition of My worship as given by Myself, will attain to the fruits of doing all forms of daily worship." **41.** Thus, the Supreme Being incarnated as Sri Rama, on being questioned, expounded this doctrine of ritualistic worship to His brother Lakshmana, who was himself an incarnation of Adisesha. **42.** But afterwards assuming the attitude of an ordinary man, through the power of his own Maya, Rama, stricken with sorrow, spent sleepless nights calling aloud, 'O Sita'.

Hanuman's advice to Sugreeva (43-54)

43. In the meantime, in Kishkindha, intelligent Hanuman had a private conversation with Sugreeva, the king of the monkeys. **44.** Hanuman said, "O King! I shall speak to you of certain matters in your real interest. Rama has already done for you a favour

कृतघ्नवत्त्वया नूनं विस्मृतः प्रतिभाति मे । त्वत्कृते निहतो वाली वीरस्त्रैलोक्यसम्मतः ॥45
राज्ये प्रतिष्ठितोऽसि त्वं तारां प्राप्तोऽसि दुर्लभाम् । स रामः पर्वतस्याग्रे भ्रात्रा सह वसन्सुधीः ॥ 46
त्वदागमनमेकाग्रमीक्षते कार्यगौरवात् । त्वं तु वानरभावेन स्त्रीसक्तो नावबुद्ध्यसे ॥ 47
करोमीति प्रतिज्ञाय सीतायाः परिमार्गणम् । न करोषि कृतघ्नस्त्वं हन्यसे वालिवद्द्रुतम् ॥ 48
हनूमद्वचनं श्रुत्वा सुग्रीवो भयविह्वलः । प्रत्युवाच हनूमन्तं सत्यमेव त्वयोदितम् ॥ 49
शीघ्रं कुरु ममाज्ञां त्वं वानराणां तरस्विनाम् । सहस्राणि दशेदानीं प्रेषयाशु दिशो दश ॥ 50
सप्तद्वीपगतान्सर्वान्वानरानानयन्तु ते । पक्षमध्ये समायान्तु सर्वे वानरपुङ्गवाः ॥ 51
ये पक्षमतिवर्तन्ते ते वध्या मे न संशयः । इत्याज्ञाप्य हनूमन्तं सुग्रीवो गृहमाविशत् ॥ 52
सुग्रीवाज्ञां पुरस्कृत्य हनूमान्मन्त्रिसत्तमः । तत्क्षणे प्रेषयामास हरीन्दश दिशः सुधीः ॥ 53
अगणितगुणसत्त्वान्वायुवेगप्रचारान्वनचरणमुख्यान् पर्वताकाररूपान् ।
पवनहितकुमारः प्रेषयामास दूतानतिरभसतरात्मा दानमानादितृप्तान् ॥ 54

इति श्रीमदध्यात्मरामायणे उमामहेश्वरसंवादे
किष्किन्धाकाण्डे चतुर्थः सर्गः ॥ ४ ॥

of a very valuable type. **45.** But I find that like an ungrateful person, you seem to have forgotten all that. For your sake, he has destroyed Vali, celebrated for his strength and heroism in all the three worlds.

(46-47). You have been installed as king. You have also got back your very handsome wife Tara. The high-souled Rama, however, is living on the top of the mountain with his brother, and perhaps he may be eagerly awaiting your arrival before him with the news about Sita. But you are not aware of these facts, being absorbed in women's company, following the ways of monkeys. **48.** After promising to find out the whereabouts of Sita, if you fail to do so,you will, like an ungrateful person, meet with the same fate as Vali."

(49-50). Hearing Hanuman's words, Sugreeva was filled with fear and he said to Hanuman, "What you have said is correct. Now in all haste, please send ten thousand powerful monkeys in all the ten directions for the search for Sita. Please enforce this order of mine quickly. **(51-52).** Let all the monkeys dwelling in the seven continents be called. All of them should come within a fortnight. Those who fail to do so will be condemned to death." Giving these orders to Hanuman, Sugreeva went to his abode. **53.** The intelligent and competent minister that he was, Hanuman immediately put Sugreeva's order into practice and sent monkey messengers in all the directions **54.** With great care and attention, Hanuman deputed, after honouring them with good words and presents, a number of monkey messengers who were possessed of great excellences like courage and quickness of movement like the wind, and who were huge in size like mountains.

पञ्चमः सर्गः

श्रीमहादेव उवाच

रामस्तु पर्वतस्याग्रे मणिसानौ निशामुखे। सीताविरहजं शोकमसहन्निदमब्रवीत्। 1
पश्य लक्ष्मण मे सीता राक्षसेन हृता बलात्। मृतामृता वा निश्चेतुं न जानेऽद्यापि भामिनीम्॥
जीवतीति मम ब्रूयात्कश्चिद्वा प्रियकृत्स मे। यदि जानामि तां साध्वीं जीवन्तीं यत्र कुत्र वा॥
हठादेवाहरिष्यामि सुधामिव पयोनिधेः। प्रतिज्ञां शृणु मे भ्रातर्येन मे जनकात्मजा॥ 4
नीता तं भस्मसात्कुर्यां सपुत्रबलवाहनम्। हे सीते चन्द्रवदने वसन्ती राक्षसालये॥ 5
दुःखार्त्ता मामपश्यन्ती कथं प्राणान् धरिष्यसि। चन्द्रोऽपि भानुवद्भाति मम चन्द्राननां विना॥ 6
चन्द्र त्वं जानकीं स्पृष्ट्वा करैर्मां स्पृश शीतलैः। सुग्रीवोऽपि दयाहीनो दुःखितं मां न पश्यति॥ 7
राज्यं निष्कण्टकं प्राप्य स्त्रीभिः परिवृतो रहः। कृतघ्नो दृश्यते व्यक्तं पानासक्तोऽतिकामुकः॥ 8
नायाति शरदं पश्यन्नपि मार्गयितुं प्रियाम्। पूर्वोपकारिणं दुष्टः कृतघ्नो विस्मृतो हि माम्॥ 9
हन्मि सुग्रीवमप्येव सपुरं सहबान्धवम्। वाली यथा हतो मेऽद्य सुग्रीवोऽपि तथा भवेत्॥10

Chapter 5

LAKSHMANA'S ULTIMATUM TO SUGREEVA

Rama's grief, thinking of Sita (1-25)

1. Meantime, dwelling on that resplendent mountain, Rama, distressed extremely by separation from Sita, said as follows: **2.** He said, "O Lakshmana! See, my Sita has been forcibly abducted by the Rakshasa. I have not yet been able to determine whether she is dead or alive. **(3-6).** If anybody gives news about her survival, he will be doing me a service, which I shall appreciate very much. If I come to know about the whereabouts of that chaste wife of mine, I shall by force get her back, as Amrita was got from the ocean. Now, this, O my brother, is my vow. Whoever has taken Sita, I shall burn him with all his sons and his armies into ashes. Alas! O Sita of moon-like face, I can imagine how miserable you must be to sustain life without seeing me, in that Rakshasa's abode. Separated from that moon-faced wife of mine, even this moonlight appears to me to be as hot as the rays of the sun. **7.** O moon! Touch my body after you have cooled your rays by contacting Sita, the daughter of Janaka. It looks that this Sugreeva is heartless. He does not understand how distressed I am. **8.** Having obtained a kingdom free of all enemies, he is now living in privacy with ladies, giving himself to drink and over-indulgences. He has proved himself to be absolutely ungrateful. **9.** Even after the spring season has come, there is no sign of his starting in search of my wife. Wicked and thankless as he is, he has forgotten me, his great benefactor. **10.** I shall destroy

इति रुष्टं समालोक्य राघवं लक्ष्मणोऽब्रवीत् । इदानीमेव गत्वाहं सुग्रीवं दुष्टमानसम् ॥ 11
मामाज्ञापय हत्वा तमायास्ये राम तेऽन्तिकम् । इत्युक्त्वा धनुरादाय स्वयं तूणीरमेव च ॥ 12
गन्तुमभ्युद्यतं वीक्ष्य रामो लक्ष्मणमब्रवीत् । न हन्तव्यस्त्वया वत्स सुग्रीवो मे प्रियः सखा ॥13
किन्तु भीषय सुग्रीवं वालिवत्त्वं हनिष्यसे । इत्युक्त्वा शीघ्रमादाय सुग्रीवप्रतिभाषितम् ॥ 14
आगत्य पश्चाद्यत्कार्यं तत्करिष्याम्यसंशयम् । तथेति लक्ष्मणोऽगच्छत्त्वरितो भीमविक्रमः ॥15
किष्किन्धां प्रति कोपेन निर्दहन्निव वानरान् । सर्वज्ञो नित्यलक्ष्मीको विज्ञानात्मापि राघवः ॥16
सीतामनुशुशोचार्त्तः प्राकृतः प्राकृतामिव । बुद्ध्यादिसाक्षिणस्तस्य मायाकार्यातिवर्तिनः ॥ 17
रागादिरहितस्यास्य तत्कार्यं कथमुद्भवेत् । ब्राह्मणोक्तमृतं कर्तुं राज्ञो दशरथस्य हि ॥ 18
तपसः फलदानाय जातो मानुषवेषधृक् । मायया मोहितः सर्वे जना अज्ञानसंयुताः ॥ 19
कथमेषां भवेन्मोक्ष इति विष्णुर्विचिन्तयन् । कथां प्रथयितुं लोके सर्वलोकमलापहाम् ॥ 20
रामायणाभिधां रामो भूत्वा मानुषचेष्टकः । क्रोधं मोहं च कामं च व्यवहारार्थसिद्धये ॥ 21
तत्तत्कालोचितं गृह्णन् मोहयत्यवशाः प्रजाः । अनुरक्त इवाशेषगुणेषु गुणवर्जितः ॥ 22

Sugreeva along with his city and all his tribe. I shall send him the same way as I have sent Vali."

(11-13). Seeing Rama in this angry mood, Lakshmana now said, "Command me whatever you want to be done. Even now I shall go and kill that Sugreeva and come back." Saying so, Lakshmana, equipped with bow, quiver and sword, was ready to start. Rama thereupon said to him: "Dear brother! Sugreeva is my close friend and it is not proper for you to kill him.

(14-15). Only frighten him that he too will be killed like Vali. Communicating this, return soon with his reply. I shall decide what should be done after that." Agreeing to do so, Lakshmana of great prowess went without delay, towards Kishkindha determined, as it were, to burn the whole tribe of monkeys with the fire of his anger.

(16-22). But, how is it that Rama, who is all-knowing, who has Lakshmi ever abiding with Him, who is of the nature of Pure Consciousness, is seen as distracted like an ordinary worldly man because of separation from Sita? How can He, who is the witness of Buddhi, who transcends Maya and its effects, who is in truth without attachment and aversion, be afflicted by the effect of Maya, namely, the sorrows of the world? The answer to this mystery is this. In order to fulfil the request made to Him by Brahma, and also to give the proper reward to King Dasaratha for his austerities, He incarnated assuming the form of a man. Besides, He, who is Mahavishnu Himself, wanted to provide men engrossed in Samsara with the story of Ramayana as a means for the eradication of all their sins. So He assumed this form of a man as Rama, in order to teach man how to behave in worldly life and how to attain the highest

विज्ञानमूर्तिर्विज्ञानशक्तिः साक्ष्यगुणान्वितः । अतः कामादिभिर्नित्यमविलिप्तो यथा नभः ॥23
विन्दन्ति मुनयः केचिज्जानन्ति सनकादयः । तद्भक्ता निर्मलात्मानः सम्यग् जानन्ति नित्यदा ॥
भक्तचित्तानुसारेण जायते भगवानजः । 25
लक्ष्मणोऽपि तदा गत्वा किष्किन्धानगरान्तिकम् । ज्याघोषमकरोत्तीव्रं भीषयन् सर्ववानरान्॥
तं दृष्ट्वा प्राकृतास्तत्र वानरा वप्रमूर्धनि । चक्रुः किलकिलाशब्दं धृतपाषाणपादपाः ॥27
तान्दृष्ट्वा क्रोधताम्राक्षो वानरान् लक्ष्मणस्तदा । निर्मूलान्कर्तुमुद्युक्तो धनुरानम्य वीर्यवान् ॥
ततः शीघ्रं समाप्लुत्य ज्ञात्वा लक्ष्मणमागतम् ।
निवार्य वानरान् सर्वानङ्गदो मन्त्रिसत्तमः । गत्वा लक्ष्मणसामीप्यं प्रणनाम स दण्डवत् ॥ 29
ततोऽङ्गदं परिष्वज्य लक्ष्मणः प्रियवर्धनः । उवाच वत्स गच्छ त्वं पितृव्याय निवेदय ॥ 30
मामागतं राघवेण चोदितं रौद्रमूर्तिना । तथेति त्वरितं गत्वा सुग्रीवाय न्यवेदयत् ॥ 31

spiritual destiny; and for this, He, the One transcending all the Gunas of Prakriti, behaved according to time and circumstance like one infatuated by anger, delusion, lust etc.—in fact, as a helpless man subject to the love of a woman. **23.** He is, in truth, of the form of Pure Consciousness and is endowed with the power of Pure Consciousness. He is the pure witness transcending the Gunas of Prakriti. Therefore, as the sky is unaffected by anything, He is not affected by lust, anger and other passions. **24.** The ordinary people in ignorance may credit Rama with attachment, aversion and weaknesses, but Sanaka and other great Rishis know the truth about Him and attained to Him through that. So too, is this truth known to others, who are pure at heart and are endowed with devotion to the Lord. **25.** The Lord, who is unborn and ever existent, presents Himself to devotees, according to the degree of their mental purity and spiritual capacity.

Lakshmana in a threatening mood (26-63)

(26-28). Now Lakshmana approached the city of Kishkindha and twanged his bowstring, spreading terror into the minds of all monkeys. Thereupon, several of the ordinary monkeys, in order to put up a defence got upon the rampart, with rocks and trees in hand, producing a tumultuous sound. Seeing the monkeys in such a menacing mood Lakshmana bent his bow in order to bring about their total destruction. **29.** Hearing about Lakshmana's arrival, Angada, the chief of the ministers, came quickly to meet him. He dispersed all the monkeys, and going near Lakshmana, made prostrations to him. **(30-31).** Lakshmana, possessed of winning manners, then embraced Angada and said to him, "Dear one! Rama is in an extremely angry mood. I have come here at his command. Convey this news to your uncle." Agreeing to do so, Angada went back quickly and informed Sugreeva of

लक्ष्मणः क्रोधताम्राक्षः पुरद्वारि बहिःस्थितः । तत् श्रुत्वातीव सन्त्रस्तः सुग्रीवो वानरेश्वरः॥ 32
आहूय मन्त्रिणां श्रेष्ठं हनूमन्तमथाब्रवीत् । गच्छ त्वमङ्गदेनाशु लक्ष्मणं विनयान्वितः ॥ 33
सान्त्वयन्कोपितं वीरं शनैरानय सादरम् । प्रेषयित्वा हनूमन्तं तारामाह कपीश्वरः ॥ 34
त्वं गच्छ सान्त्वयन्ती तं लक्ष्मणं मृदुभाषितैः । शान्तमन्तःपुरं नीत्वा पश्चाद्दर्शय मेऽनघे ॥ 35
भवत्विति ततस्तारा मध्यकक्षं समाविशत् । हनूमानङ्गदेनैव सहितो लक्ष्मणान्तिकम् ॥ 36
गत्वा ननाम शिरसा भक्त्या स्वागतमब्रवीत् । एहि वीर महाभाग भवद्गृहमशङ्कितम् ॥ 37
प्रविश्य राजदारादीन् दृष्ट्वा सुग्रीवमेव च । यदाज्ञापयसे पश्चात्तत्सर्वं करवाणि भोः ॥ 38
इत्युक्त्वा लक्ष्मणं भक्त्या करे गृह्य स मारुतिः । आनयामास नगरमध्याद्राजगृहं प्रति ॥ 39
पश्यंस्तत्र महासौधान् यूथपानां समन्ततः । जगाम भवनं राज्ञः सुरेन्द्रभवनोपमम् ॥ 40
मध्यकक्षे गता तारा ताराधिपानना । सर्वाभरणसंम्पन्ना मदरक्तान्तलोचना ॥ 41
उवाच लक्ष्मणं नत्वा स्मितपूर्वाभिभाषिणी । याहि देवर भद्रं ते साधुस्त्वं भक्तवत्सलः ॥ 42
किमर्थं कोपमाकार्षीर्भक्ते भृत्ये कपीश्वरे । बहुकालमनाश्वासं दुःखमेवानुभूतवान् ॥ 43
इदानीं बहुदुःखौघाद्भवद्भिरभिरक्षितः । भवत्प्रसादात्सुग्रीवः प्राप्तसौख्यो महामतिः ॥ 44
कामासक्तो रघुपतेः सेवार्थं नागतो हरिः । आगमिष्यन्ति हरयो नानादेशगताः प्रभो ॥ 45
प्रेषिता दशसाहस्रा हरयो रघुसत्तम । आनेतुं वानरान् दिग्भ्यो महापर्वतसन्निभान् ॥ 46

Lakshmana's arrival. **(32-34).** Hearing that Lakshmana had arrived at the gate of the city in a very angry mood, Sugreeva was terribly frightened and called his trusted minister, Hanuman. He said to Hanuman, "Go quickly with Angada and try to pacify the angry Lakshmana, and persuade him to come into the palace." Commissioning Hanuman in this way, the king of the monkeys said to Tara: **35.** "You please go, and with sweet words try to pacify Lakshmana and bring him to the inner apartments. After he is thus pacified, I shall meet him."

(36-38). Agreeing to do so, Tara went towards the middle region of the palace. Angada with Hanuman now went and saluted Lakshmana at the gate. They said to him, "O great one! O worshipful one! O hero! Considering this as your own home, please come in and after meeting Sugreeva and his consort, order us what we have to do. We shall do accordingly." **39.** Saying so with great devotion, Hanuman, the son of the wind-god, held Lakshmana by hand and led him from the middle of the street into the palace. **40.** On all sides, Lakshmana saw the huge mansions of the chiefs of the community and reached the palace of the king, which was comparable to the abode of Indra. **(41-46).** When he reached the middle region of the palace, he was greeted by Tara, the moon-faced beauty, bedecked with jewellery and with eyes crimson-tinged through intoxication. After saluting Lakshmana

सुग्रीवः स्वयमागत्य सर्ववानरयूथपैः । वधयिष्यति दैत्यौघान् रावणं च हनिष्यति ॥ 47
त्वयैव सहितोऽद्यैव गन्ता वानरपुङ्गवः । पश्यान्तर्भवनं तत्र पुत्रदारसुहृद्वृतम् ॥ 48
दृष्ट्वा सुग्रीवमभयं दत्त्वा नय सहैव ते । ताराया वचनं श्रुत्वा कृशक्रोधोऽथ लक्ष्मणः ॥49
जगामान्तःपुरं यत्र सुग्रीवो वानरेश्वरः । रुमामालिङ्ग्य सुग्रीवः पर्यङ्के पर्यवस्थितः ॥ 50
दृष्ट्वा लक्ष्मणमत्यर्थमुत्पपतातिभीतवत् । तं दृष्ट्वा लक्ष्मणः क्रुद्धो मदविह्वलितेक्षणम् ॥51
सुग्रीवं प्राह दुर्वृत्त विस्मृतोऽसि रघूत्तमम् । वाली येन हतो वीरः स बाणोऽद्य प्रतीक्षते ॥ 52
त्वमेव वालिनो मार्गं गमिष्यसि मया हतः । एवमत्यन्तपरुषं वदन्तं लक्ष्मणं तदा ॥ 53
उवाच हनुमान् वीरः कथमेवं प्रभाषते । त्वत्तोऽधिकतरो रामे भक्तोऽयं वानराधिपः ॥ 54
रामकार्यार्थमनिशं जागर्ति न तु विस्मृतः । आगताः परितः पश्य वानराः कोटिशः प्रभो॥ 55
गमिष्यन्त्यचिरेणैव सीतायाः परिमार्गणम् । साधयिष्यति सुग्रीवो रामकार्यमशेषतः ॥ 56

she said to him smiling, "O Kinsman! I pray for your welfare. You are one of noble conduct and extremely loving towards your devotees. Why are you angry at the king of the monkeys, who is a devoted servant? He has for a long time been suffering from sorrows and hardships continuously. Now he has been rescued from that difficult situation by you. By your grace, he has been restored to prosperity. But do not think that the noble-minded Sugreeva, being addicted to sexual enjoyments, has failed to come and meet Rama. O Lord! Monkeys will come from all directions. O scion of Raghu's line! Ten thousand monkeys have already gone to different places to mobilise a big army of mountain-sized monkeys. **47.** Sugreeva himself will go with the army of monkeys and destroy all the Rakshasas including Ravana. **(48-50).** The monkey chief Sugreeva will go with you immediately to Rama. Now please come into the palace and see Sugreeva in the midst of his family. After he is relieved of his fear, you can take him with you." Lakshmana, with his anger assuaged a little by Tara's words, now went into the inner apartment of the palace where Sugreeva was seated on a cot with his wife Ruma. **(51-52).** Seeing Lakshmana, Sugreeva got up like one extremely frightened, with his eyes rolling in intoxication. Angry Lakshmana now said to him, "O you wretch! You seem to have forgotten Rama, the greatest of Raghu's line. Remember, that the arrow which killed the heroic Vali is still with him. **(53-56).** Killed by me, you too will go the way of Vali." To Lakshmana who was speaking in this very harsh tone, the heroic Hanuman said, "Why do you speak in this vein? This monkey-chief is more devoted to Rama than even yourself. He is ever awake to Rama's interests. He has not forgotten anything. Crores of monkeys have already arrived. Look all around. Soon they will start in search of Sita, and Sugreeva will fully achieve the purposes of Rama."

श्रुत्वा हनुमतो वाक्यं सौमित्रिर्लज्जितोऽभवत् । सुग्रीवोऽप्यर्घ्यपाद्याद्यैर्लक्ष्मणं समपूजयत् ॥ 57
आलिङ्ग्य प्राह रामस्य दासोऽहं तेन रक्षितः । रामः स्वतेजसा लोकान् क्षणार्द्धेनैव जेष्यति ॥ 58
सहायमात्रमेवाहं वानरैः सहितः प्रभो । सौमित्रिरपि सुग्रीवं प्राह किञ्चिन्मयोदितम् ॥ 59
तत्क्षमस्व महाभाग प्रणयाद्भाषितं मया । गच्छामोऽद्यैव सुग्रीव रामस्तिष्ठति कानने ॥ 60
एक एवातिदुःखार्तो जानकीविरहात्प्रभुः । तथेति रथमारुह्य लक्ष्मणेन समन्वितः ॥ 61
वानरैः सहितो राजा राममेवान्वपद्यत ॥ 62
भेरीमृदङ्गैर्बहुऋक्षवानरैः श्वेतातपत्रैर्व्यजनैश्च शोभितः ।
नीलाङ्गदाद्यैर्हनुमत्प्रधानैः समावृतो राघवमभ्यगाद्धरिः ॥ 63

इति श्रीमदध्यात्मरामायणे उमामहेश्वरसंवादे
किष्किन्धाकाण्डे पञ्चमः सर्गः ॥ ५ ॥

57. Lakshmana felt ashamed of his conduct on hearing the words of Hanuman. And just then Sugreeva also came forward and received Lakshmana in the proper way with Arghya and Padya. **(58-62).** Embracing Lakshmana, Sugreeva said, "I am the servant of Rama. I have been saved by him. Rama can conquer the whole world in a trice by his own power. My monkey armies are only a small help in this enterprise." Lakshmana then said to Sugreeva, "I have perhaps talked too much. O worshipful one! I said all that out of love only. Please pardon me for the same, O Sugreeva! We shall even now go to see Rama. He is staying alone on the mountain, steeped in sorrow on account of separation from Sita, the daughter of Janaka." Agreeing to do so, Sugreeva got into a chariot along with Lakshmana. Accompanied by monkeys he proceeded to the place where Rama was staying. **63.** To the accompaniment of drums, Mridanga and other musical instruments, and provided with royal insignias like white ceremonial umbrella and peacock-feather fans, and accompanied by a band of ministers headed by Hanuman, Neela, Angada, and a big following of bears and monkeys—Sugreeva now went to Rama's presence.

षष्ठः सर्गः

श्रीमहादेव उवाच

दृष्ट्वा रामं समासीनं गुहाद्वारि शिलातले । चैलाजिनधरं श्यामं जटामौलिविराजितम् ॥ 1
विशालनयनं शान्तं स्मितचारुमुखाम्बुजम् । सीताविरहसन्तप्तं पश्यन्तं मृगपक्षिणः ॥ 2
रथाद्दूरात्समुत्पत्य वेगात्सुग्रीवलक्ष्मणौ । रामस्य पादयोरग्रे पेततुर्भक्तिसंयुतौ ॥ 3
रामः सुग्रीवमालिङ्ग्य पृष्ट्वानामयमन्तिके । स्थापयित्वा यथान्यायं पूजयामास धर्मवित् ॥ 4
ततोऽब्रवीद्रघुश्रेष्ठं सुग्रीवो भक्तिनम्रधीः । देव पश्य समायान्तीं वानराणां महाचमूम् ॥ 5
कुलाचलाद्रिसम्भूता मेरुमन्दरसन्निभाः । नानाद्वीपसरिच्छैलवासिनः पर्वतोपमाः ॥ 6
असंख्याताः समायान्ति हरयः कामरूपिणः । सर्वे देवांशसम्भूताः सर्वे युद्धविशारदाः ॥ 7
अत्र केचिद्गजबलाः केचिद्दशगजोपमाः । गजायुतबलाः केचिदन्येऽमितबलाः प्रभो ॥ 8
केचिदञ्जनकूटाभाः केचित्कनकसन्निभाः । केचिद्रक्तान्तवदनाः दीर्घवालास्तथापरे ॥ 9
शुद्धस्फटिकसङ्काशाः केचिद्राक्षससन्निभाः । गर्जन्तः परितो यान्ति वानरा युद्धकाङ्क्षिणः ॥10

Chapter 6

SEARCH OF THE MONKEYS

Monkeys Commissioned on the search (1-29)

(1-3). Sugreeva and Lakshmana saw Rama at a distance sitting at the mouth of a cave—Rama, who was dressed in a deer skin and torn clothes, who had matted locks adorning his crown, who was broad-eyed and smiling, who was distracted by separation from Sita, and who was there peacefully sitting and watching the birds and animals nearby. Seeing Rama of blue complexion, they both got down from the chariot, and approaching him, fell down at his feet in prostration. **4.** Rama, a master of all codes of right conduct, embraced Sugreeva, made enquiries about his welfare, and seating him by his side, extended to him a reception according to tradition. **5.** Now Sugreeva, in an attitude expressive of his deep devotion, said as follows: "O Lord! See the great army of monkeys that is gathering. **(6-7).** Here is assembled an army of countless numbers of monkeys come from their abodes in various continents, lakes and mountains. Born in principal mountain ranges, they have all originated from parts of the Devas. In size they are like the Meru and Mandara mountains, and they can take any form they like. They are also well-versed in all forms of warfare. **8.** Besides, they are all incredibly strong—some equal in strength to one elephant and others equal to ten or even ten thousand elephants. There are still others whose strength cannot be estimated. **(9-10).** These monkey heroes are of varied complexions—some shining like anitmony,

त्वदाज्ञाकारिणः सर्वे फलमूलाशनाः प्रभो । ऋक्षाणामधिपो वीरो जाम्बवान्नाम बुद्धिमान् ॥ 11
एष मे मन्त्रिणां श्रेष्ठः कोटिभल्लूकवृन्दपः । हनूमानेष विख्यातो महासत्त्वपराक्रमः ॥ 12
वायुपुत्रोऽतितेजस्वी मन्त्री बुद्धिमतां वरः । नलो नीलश्च गवयो गवाक्षो गन्धमादनः ॥ 13
शरभो मैन्दवश्चैव गजः पनस एव च । बलीमुखो दधिमुखः सुषेणस्तार एव च ॥ 14
केसरी च महासत्त्वः पिता हनुमतो बली । एते ते यूथपा राम प्राधान्येन मयोदिताः ॥ 15
महात्मानो महावीर्याः शक्रतुल्यपराक्रमाः । एते प्रत्येकतः कोटिकोटिवानरयूथपाः ॥ 16
तवाज्ञाकारिणः सर्वे सर्वे देवांशसम्भवाः । एष वालिसुतः श्रीमानङ्गदो नाम विश्रुतः ॥ 17
वालितुल्यबलो वीरो राक्षसानां बलान्तकः । एते चान्ये च बहवस्त्वदर्थे त्यक्तजीविताः ॥ 18
योद्धारः पर्वताग्रैश्च निपुणाः शत्रुघातने । आज्ञापय रघुश्रेष्ठ सर्वे ते वशवर्तिनः ॥ 19
रामः सुग्रीवमालिङ्ग्य हर्षपूर्णाश्रुलोचनः । प्राह सुग्रीव जानासि सर्वं त्वं कार्यगौरवम् ॥ 20
मार्गणार्थं हि जानक्या नियुङ्क्ष्व यदि रोचते । श्रुत्वा रामस्य वचनं सुग्रीवः प्रीतमानसः ॥ 21
प्रेषयामास बलिनो वानरान् वानरर्षभः । दिक्षु सर्वासु विविधान्वानरान् प्रेष्य सत्वरम् ॥ 22

some golden-coloured, some with red faces, some long-tailed, some crystal-clear, and some demon-like. All these monkeys of various sizes and appearance are roaming about roaring, thus expressing their war-lust. **11.** O Lord! All these monkey-heroes, subsisting on roots and fruits, are now assembled here to carry out your orders. Besides them, there is the army of bears, whose leader is the wise and heroic Jambavan. **(12-19).** Here is another, my famous chief minister Hanuman, who is the leader of a crore of bears and noted for his great strength and courage. He is the off-spring of the Wind-deity, possessed of unlimited prowess, the best among intellectuals and an adept in diplomacy. Next, O Rama, hear the names of my other generals in the order of their importance. They are: Nala, Neela, Gavaya, Gavaksha, Gandhamadana, Sarabha, Maindava, Gaja, Panasa, Balimukha, Dadhimukha, Sushena, Tara and Kesari, the highsouled and mighty father of Hanuman. All of them are endowed with great character and in their warlike quality equal to Indra himself. Everyone of them is a leader of a crore of monkeys. All of them, born of Devas, are assembled here to carry out your orders. Here is Vali's son Angada equal to Vali himself in strength, and capable of destroying armies of Rakshasas. All these and several others, capable of catapulting pieces of mountain and adepts in destroying enemy forces, are assembled here ready to give up their lives for your sake. O the noblest of Raghu's line! All these are at your disposal, ready to carry out your orders."

(20-24). Thereupon Rama, embracing Sugreeva with tears of joy in his eyes, said, "O Sugreeva, you know the serious nature of the mission we are to undertake. If it pleases you, you have to institute a

दक्षिणां दिशमत्यर्थं प्रयत्नेन महाबलान् । युवराजं जाम्बवन्तं हनूमन्तं महाबलम् ॥ 23
नलं सुषेणं शरभं मैन्दं द्विविदमेव च । प्रेषयामास सुग्रीवो वचनं चेदमब्रवीत् ॥ 24
विचिन्वन्तु प्रयत्नेन भवन्तो जानकीं शुभाम् । मासादर्वाङ्निवर्तध्वं मच्छासनपुरःसराः ॥ 25
सीतामदृष्ट्वा यदि वो मासादूर्ध्वं दिनं भवेत् । तदा प्राणान्तिकं दण्डं मत्तः प्राप्स्यथ वानराः ॥26
इति प्रस्थाप्य सुग्रीवो वानरान् भीमविक्रमान् । रामस्य पार्श्वे श्रीरामं नत्वा चोपविवेश सः ॥ 27
गच्छन्तं मारुतिं दृष्ट्वा रामो वचनमब्रवीत् । अभिज्ञानार्थमेतन्मे ह्यङ्गुलीयकमुत्तमम् ॥ 28
मन्नामाक्षरसंयुक्तं सीतायै दीयतां रहः ।
अस्मिन् कार्ये प्रमाणं हि त्वमेव कपिसत्तम । जानामि सत्त्वं ते सर्वं गच्छ पन्थाः शुभस्तव॥ 29
एवं कपीनां राज्ञा ते विसृष्टाः परिमार्गणे । सीताया अङ्गदमुखा बभ्रमुस्तत्र तत्र ह ॥ 30
भ्रमन्तो विन्ध्यगहने ददृशुः पर्वतोपमम् । राक्षसं भीषणाकारं भक्षयन्तं मृगान् गजान् ॥ 31
रावणोऽयमिति ज्ञात्वा केचिद्वानरपुङ्गवाः । जघ्नुः किलकिलाशब्दं मुञ्चतो मुष्टिभिः क्षणात् ॥

search for the whereabouts of Sita, the daughter of Janaka." With great pleasure Sugreeva thereupon directed all his powerful monkey followers to take up this search for Sita While sending various types of monkeys in different directions, he selected after much deliberation, a special band of his followers to go in the southern direction. In this group he specially included his heir-apparent Angada, Jambavan, Hanuman of mighty prowess, Nala, Sushena, Sarabha, Mainda and Dvivida. He gave the following order to the search party. **(25-27).** "You have to spare no effort in searching for the virtuous and handsome Sita. You have to finish your search within the period of a month. Any one returning even a day after the lapse of that period without finding out Sita, will have to face severe punishment at my hand, including execution." After giving these directions and sending off those powerful monkeys, Sugreeva prostrated before Rama, and sat by his side.

(28-29). Seeing Hanuman about to start, Rama called him aside and said to him: "As a token for recognition, you privately give to Sita this signet ring of mine, having my name inscribed on it. I deem you, O monkey leader, as the principal agent in this enterprise. I have understood the full extent of your prowess. Now go ahead. May success attend your effort!"

Meeting with Svayamprabha (30-58)

30. Angada and other monkeys who were thus commissioned by their king to search for Sita, wandered here and there for long on their quest. **31.** In the forest of the name Vindhya they came across a fierce and gigantic Rakshasa subsisting on the deer and elephants he came across. **32.** Some of these great monkeys took this monster to be Ravana, and with enthusiastic

नायं रावण इत्युक्त्वा ययुरन्यन्महद्वनम् । तृषार्ताः सलिलं तत्र नाविन्दन् हरिपुङ्गवाः ॥33
विभ्रमन्तो महारण्ये शुष्ककण्ठोष्ठतालुकाः । ददृशुर्गह्वरं तत्र तृणगुल्मावृतं महत् ॥ 34
आर्द्रपक्षान् क्रौञ्चहंसान्निःसृतान्ददृशुस्ततः । अत्रास्ते सलिलं नूनं प्रविशामो महागुहाम् ॥ 35
इत्युक्त्वा हनुमानग्रे प्रविवेश तमन्वयुः । सर्वे परस्परं धृत्वा बाहून्बाहुभिरुत्सुकाः ॥ 36
अन्धकारे महद्दूरं गत्वापश्यन् कपीश्वराः । जलाशयान्मणिनिभतोयान् कल्पद्रुमोपमान् ॥ 37
वृक्षान् पक्वफलैर्नम्रान्मधुद्रोणसमन्वितान् । गृहान् सर्वगुणोपेतान् मणिवस्त्रादिपूरितान् ॥ 38
दिव्यभक्ष्यान्नसहितान्मानुषैः परिवर्जितान् । विस्मितास्तत्र भवने दिव्ये कनकविष्टरे ॥ 39
प्रभया दीप्यमानां तु ददृशुः स्त्रियमेककाम् । ध्यायन्तीं चीरवसनां योगिनीं योगमास्थिताम् 40
प्रणेमुस्तां महाभागां भक्त्या भीत्या च वानराः । दृष्ट्वा तान् वानरान्देवी प्राह यूयं किमागताः॥ 41
कुतो वा कस्य दूता वा मत्स्थानं किं प्रधर्षथ । तत् श्रुत्वा हनुमानाह शृणु वक्ष्यामि देवि ते ॥42
अयोध्याधिपतिः श्रीमान् राजा दशरथः प्रभुः । तस्य पुत्रो महाभागो ज्येष्ठो राम इति श्रुतः ॥ 43
पितुराज्ञां पुरस्कृत्य सभार्यः सानुजो वनम् । गतस्तत्र हृता भार्या तस्य साध्वी दुरात्मना ॥ 44

cries hit him with their fists. **33.** On realising that he was not Ravana, they proceeded to another forest where they were faced with the problem of drinking water. **34.** Wandering through the dense forests with their throat and tongue parched, they came across a big cave hidden by the growth of grass and creepers. **(35-36).** They found coming out of it, birds like Crouncha and Hamsa with water dripping from their wings. Concluding therefore that there must be water within, they decided to go into it. Hanuman entered the cave first, and led by him, several of them, who were greatly excited by the prospect of finding water, followed him linking hands. **(37-40).** After they had penetrated a long distance through darkness, those monkeys came across a very strange place. They found there water reservoirs with crystal-clear water. There were trees resembling Kalpaka-Vriksha, the heavenly wish-yielding tree, bending with fruits having about sixteen measures of juice in each. They saw there well-designed houses, full of precious gems, wearing-clothes and excellent food materials. But the place was without any living inhabitants. When they surveyed the place in extreme wonder, they saw in one of the houses, the luminous form of a lady dressed in tree-bark clothes and sitting alone completely absorbed in meditation. **(41-42).** The monkeys, full of fear and devotion in their mind, made prostrations to that ascetic woman. She, on her part, asked the monkeys, "Whence and for what purpose have you come here? Whose messengers are you? Why have you invaded my residence?" To these queries, Hanuman replied, "O venerable lady! I shall tell you everything about ourselves. **(43-47).** There was a great king, prosperous and powerful, named Dasaratha ruling over Ayodhya. His eldest son of great nobility and fame is named

रावणेन ततो रामः सुग्रीवं सानुजो ययौ । सुग्रीवो मित्रभावेन रामस्य प्रियवल्लभाम् ॥ 45
मृगयध्वमिति प्राह ततो वयमुपागताः । ततो वनं विचिन्वन्तो जानकीं जलकाङ्क्षिणः॥ 46
प्रविष्टा गह्वरं घोरं दैवादत्र समागताः । त्वं वा किमर्थमत्रासि का वा त्वं वद नः शुभे ॥47
योगिनी च तथा दृष्ट्वा वानरान् प्राह हृष्टधीः । यथेष्टं फलमूलानि जग्ध्वा पीत्वामृतं पयः ॥ 48
आगच्छत ततो वक्ष्ये मम वृत्तान्तमादितः । तथेति भुक्त्वा पीत्वा च हृष्टास्ते सर्ववानराः ॥49
देव्याः समीपं गत्वा ते बद्धाञ्जलिपुटाः स्थिताः । ततः प्राह हनूमन्तं योगिनी दिव्यदर्शना ॥ 50
हेमा नाम पुरा दिव्यरूपिणी विश्वकर्मणः । पुत्री महेशं नृत्येन तोषयामास भामिनी ॥ 51
तुष्टो महेशः प्रददाविदं दिव्यपुरं महत् । अत्र स्थिता सा सुदती वर्षाणामयुतायुतम् ॥ 52
तस्या अहं सखी विष्णुतत्परा मोक्षकाङ्क्षिणी । नाम्ना स्वयम्प्रभा दिव्यगन्धर्वतनया पुरा ॥ 53
गच्छन्ती ब्रह्मलोकं सा मामाहेदं तपश्चर । अत्रैव निवसन्ती त्वं सर्वप्राणिविवर्जिते ॥ 54
त्रेतायुगे दाशरथिर्भूत्वा नारायणोऽव्ययः । भूभारहरणार्थाय विचरिष्यति कानने ॥ 55

Rama. Obeying the command of his father, he along with his wife Sita and brother Lakshmana, came to stay in the forest. There, his devoted wife was abducted by evil-minded Ravana. Subsequently, Rama along with his brother happened to meet Sugreeva and entered into an alliance with him. As an ally, Sugreeva instituted a search for Rama's wife and has sent us all on the task of searching for Sita. Searching for Sita all through this forest, we found ourselves very thirsty and entered into a terribly dark cave, driven by thirst. Fortunately, we have now come across you. We would like to know who you are and why you are staying here. Please tell us about this, O noble lady!"

(48-50). The ascetic woman, who was highly pleased to see the monkeys, asked them to come and hear about her story after they had partaken of the delicious fruits there and drunk of the nectar-like water to their fill. The monkeys did so accordingly, and with their hunger and thirst appeased, gathered round her and stood with palms joined in salutation. That divine-looking ascetic woman then said, addressing Hanuman: **51.** "Once upon a time, there was a daughter of Viswakarma named Hema who looked like a divinity in appearance. Through the art of dance, she propitiated Parameswara. **52.** Pleased with her, Lord Parameswara gave her this wonderful place as her abode. She lived in this place for a long number of years. **53.** I am her friend. I am devoted to Mahavishnu and am an aspirant for Moksha. My name is Svayamprabha and I am the daughter of a Gandharva named Divya. **54.** Before my friend Hema attained to Brahmaloka, she said to me, 'You stay in this solitary place devoid of other living beings and perform austerity. **55.** In the Treta Yuga, the eternal and undecaying being Narayana will be born as the son of Dasaratha, and for lightening the burdens

मार्गन्तो वानरास्तस्य भार्यामायान्ति ते गुहाम् । पूजयित्वाथ तान् नत्वा रामं स्तुत्वा प्रयत्नतः ॥56
यातासि भवनं विष्णोर्योगिगम्यं सनातनम् । इतोऽहं गन्तुमिच्छामि रामं द्रष्टुं त्वरान्विता ॥57
यूयं पिदध्वमक्षीणि गमिष्यथ बहिर्गुहाम् । तथैव चक्रुस्ते वेगाद् गताः पूर्वस्थितं वनम् ॥ 58
सापि त्यक्त्वा गुहां शीघ्रं ययौ राघवसन्निधिम् । तत्र रामं ससुग्रीवं लक्ष्मणं च ददर्श ह ॥ 59
कृत्वा प्रदक्षिणं रामं प्रणम्य बहुशः सुधीः । आह गद्गदया वाचा रोमाञ्चिततनूरुहा ॥ 60
दासी तवाहं राजेन्द्र दर्शनार्थमिहागता । बहुवर्षसहस्राणि तप्तं मे दुश्चरं तपः ॥ 61
गुहायां दर्शनार्थं ते फलितं मेऽद्य तत्तपः । अद्य हि त्वां नमस्यामि मायायाः परतः स्थितम् 62
सर्वभूतेषु चालक्ष्यं बहिरन्तरवस्थितम् । योगमायाजवनिकाच्छन्नो मानुषविग्रहः ॥ 63
न लक्ष्यसेऽज्ञानदृशां शैलूष इव रूपधृक् । महाभागवतानां त्वं भक्तियोगविधित्सया ॥ 64
अवतीर्णोऽसि भगवन् कथं जानामि तामसी । लोके जानातु यः कश्चित्तत्र तत्त्वं रघूत्तम ॥ 65
ममैतदेव रूपं ते सदा भातु हृदालये । राम ते पादयुगलं दर्शितं मोक्षदर्शनम् ॥ 66

of the earth, he will move about in this forest. **(56-57).** In search of his wife Sita, a troop of monkeys will come to the cave where you are residing. Extend a proper reception to them and then do heartfelt salutation to Rama. After that, you will attain to the Status of Vishnu, which is the goal of Yogis alone.' So now, I am in a hurry to meet Rama. **58.** All of you close your eyes. You will then be out of this cave in a trice.'' The monkeys did accordingly and they found themselves in the forest where they were before.

Swayamprabha's Hymn (59-84)

(59-60). Next that ascetic woman Swayamprabha immediately left her cave and went to the place where Rama was. Seeing Rama in the company of Lakshmana and Sugreeva, that high-minded lady made repeated circumambulations round him, and after prostrating herself before him with horripilations all over her body, she said with a voice choked with emotion: **(61-66).** "O great Lord! I am Thy servant come here to see Thee. For getting a sight of Thee, I have been staying in a cave for countless years, performing great austerities. Those austerities of mine have come to fruition today. Though Thou art residing within the hearts of all as well as without, Thou art invisible, being beyond the bounds of Maya. That Supreme Being, I am now fortunate to salute. Like an actor, Thou art hidden behind a curtain of Maya. Embodied as a human being, Thou art unrecognisable to those whose insight is vitiated by ignorance. Thou hast incarnated Thyself in order to provide a means of communion through devotion for great aspirants after Bhakti. O Supreme Lord! Immersed as I am in Tamas, how can I recognise Thee? O Lord of Raghu's line! Let philosophers seek to know Thy true nature, but as for me, I am satisfied with this form of Thine. May this form shine ever in my

अदर्शनं भवार्णानां सन्मार्गपरिदर्शनम् । धनपुत्रकलत्रादिविभूतिपरिदर्पितः ॥ 67
अकिञ्चनधनं त्वाद्य नाभिधातुं जनोऽर्हति ॥ 68
निवृत्तगुणमार्गाय निष्किञ्चनधनाय ते ।
नमः स्वात्माभिरामाय निर्गुणाय गुणात्मने । कालरूपिणमीशानमादिमध्यान्तवर्जितम् ॥ 69
समं चरन्तं सर्वत्र मन्ये त्वां पुरुषं परम् । देव ते चेष्टितं कश्चिन्न वेद नृविडम्बनम् ॥ 70
न तेऽस्ति कश्चिद्दयितो द्वेष्यो वापर एव च । त्वन्मायापिहितात्मानस्त्वां पश्यन्ति तथाविधम् ।
अजस्याकर्तुरीशस्य देवतिर्यङ्नरादिषु । जन्मकर्मादिकं यद्यत्तदत्यन्तविडम्बनम् ॥ 72
त्वामाहुरक्षरं जातं कथाश्रवणसिद्धये । केचित्कोसलराजस्य तपसः फलसिद्धये ॥ 73
कौसल्यया प्रार्थ्यमानं जातमाहुः परे जनाः । दुष्टराक्षसभूभारहरणायार्थितो विभुः ॥ 74
ब्रह्मणा नररूपेण जातोऽयमिति केचन । शृण्वन्ति गायन्ति च ये कथास्ते रघुनन्दन ॥ 75
पश्यन्ति तव पादाब्जं भवार्णवसुतारणम् । त्वन्मायागुणबद्धाहं व्यतिरिक्तं गुणाश्रयम् ॥ 76
कथं त्वां देव जानीयां स्तोतुं वाविषयं विभुम् ।
नमस्यामि रघुश्रेष्ठं बाणासनशरान्वितम् । लक्ष्मणेन सह भ्रात्रा सुग्रीवादिभिरन्वितम् ॥ 77
एवं स्तुतो रघुश्रेष्टः प्रसन्नः प्रणताघहृत् । उवाच योगिनीं भक्तां किं ते मनसि काङ्क्षितम् ॥

heart. I have now seen Thy feet which show the path of Moksha. **(67-68).** Beyond the vision of those who are immersed in Samsara, Thou, the revealer of the Truth to all seekers after Moksha and the wealth of those who have no possessions, canst never be even an object of speech for those who are established in the pride of wealth, relatives and power. **(69-70).** Salutation to Thee, who art beyond the Gunas of Prakriti. Salutation to Thee, who art the wealth of those who have no other wealth than Thee. Salutation to Thee, who art ever immersed in the Bliss of Thyself. Salutation to Thee, who transcendest the Gunas but yet manifestest as Gunas. I look upon Thee as Time, as the lord of all, as the one without beginning and end, as the one abiding unmodified in everything, and as the one Supreme Being that transcends everything. None, O Lord, can understand the mystery of Thy human advent. **71.** None is dear to Thee, none inimical, none indifferent. These differences are only attributed to Thee by those whose vision is clouded by Thy Maya. **72.** Birthless, actionless and endowed with supremacy over all, the talk of birth and actions by Thee in Thy incarnations among Devas, men and sub-human beings relate merely to appearances assumed by Thyself. **(73-78).** Though Thou art really birthless and deathless, some say that Thou art born, so that devotees may hear accounts about Thee and Thy deeds as a means for salvation. Some say that Thy birth is in fulfilment of the austerities of King Dasaratha of Kosala, and some that it is the result of the prayers of Kausalya. Still others say that in answer to the prayer of Brahma, Thou art born as man in order to relieve the earth of the

सा प्राह राघवं भक्त्या भक्तिं ते भक्तवत्सल । यत्र कुत्रापि जाताया निश्चलां देहि मे प्रभो ॥79
त्वद्भक्तेषु सदा सङ्गो भूयान्मे प्राकृतेषु न । जिह्वा मे राम रामेति भक्त्या वदतु सर्वदा ॥80
मानसं श्यामलं रूपं सीतालक्ष्मणसंयुतम् । धनुर्बाणधरं पीतवाससं मुकुटोज्ज्वलम् ॥ 81
अङ्गदैर्नूपुरैर्मुक्ताहारैः कौस्तुभकुण्डलैः । भान्तं स्मरतु मे राम वरं नान्यं वृणे प्रभो ॥ 82

श्रीराम उवाच

भवत्वेवं महाभागे गच्छ त्वं बदरीवनम् ।
तत्रैव मां स्मरन्ती त्वं त्यक्त्वेदं भूतपञ्चकम् । मामेव परमात्मानमचिरात्प्रतिपद्यसे ॥ 83
श्रुत्वा रघूत्तमवचोऽमृतसारकल्पं गत्वा तदैव बदरीतरुखण्डजुष्टम् ।
तीर्थं तदा रघुपतिं मनसा स्मरन्ती त्यक्त्वा कलेवरमवाप परं पदं सा ॥ 84

इति श्रीमदध्यात्मरामायणे उमामहेश्वरसंवादे
किष्किन्धाकाण्डे षष्ठः सर्गः ॥ ६ ॥

burden of evil Rakshasas. O Lord of the Raghus! Whoever hears or sings about Thy actions and excellences, attain Thy feet, which help them cross the ocean of Samsara. How can I know or praise Thee, who art distinct from the I-sense resulting from the limitation of the Gunas of Thy Maya—Thee who art not an Object perceivable, but yet art existent everywhere. I salute the Lord of the Raghus, equipped with bow and arrow and accompanied by brother Lakshmana and Sugreeva." To that devoted ascetic woman who sang his praise in this way, Rama, the eradicator of the sins of those who prostrate to Him, said, "Ask what you want of me."

79. She replied with great devotion, "In whatever womb I may be born, O Lord of devotees, grant me unswerving devotion to Thee. **80.** May I ever have association with Thy devotees and never with worldly-minded people! May my tongue ever utter with devotion, 'Rama, Rama', Thy sacred name. **(81-82).** May my mind ever contemplate on Thy form of blue complexion —bedecked with armlets, anklets, pearl necklaces, ear pendants and Kaustubha gem, donning a brilliant crown and yellow wearing cloth, equipped with a bow and arrows, and accompanied by Sita and Lakshmana."

83. Rama said, "O high-souled lady! I grant you your prayer. You resort to the Badari forest and there, contemplating on Me, you will abandon this physical body made of five elements and attain to Me, the Supreme Being, without much delay." **84.** Hearing these nectarine words of Rama, the ascetic woman Swayamprabha went to the Badari forest, and there meditating on Rama, abandoned her physical body and attained to the supreme State.

सप्तमः सर्गः

श्रीमहादेव उवाच

अथ तत्र समासीना वृक्षखण्डेषु वानराः । चिन्तयन्तो विमुह्यन्तः सीतामार्गणकर्षिताः ॥ 1
तत्रोवाचाङ्गदः कांश्चिद्वानरान् वानरर्षभः । भ्रमतां गह्वरेऽस्माकं मासो नूनं गतोऽभवत् ॥ 2
सीता नाधिगतास्माभिर्न कृतं राजशासनम् । यदि गच्छामः किष्किन्धां सुग्रीवोऽस्मान् हनिष्यति ।
विशेषतः शत्रुसुतं मां मिषान्निहनिष्यति । मयि तस्य कुतः प्रीतिरहं रामेण रक्षितः ॥ 4
इदानीं रामकार्यं मे न कृतं तन्मिषं भवेत् । तस्य मद्धनने नूनं सुग्रीवस्य दुरात्मनः ॥ 5
मातृकल्पां भ्रातृभार्यां पापात्मानुभवत्यसौ । न गच्छेयमतः पार्श्वं तस्य वानरपुङ्गवाः ॥ 6
त्यक्ष्यामि जीवितं चात्र येन केनापि मृत्युना । इत्यश्रुनयनं केचिद् दृष्ट्वा वानरपुङ्गवाः ॥ 7
व्यथिताः साश्रुनयना युवराजमथाब्रुवन् ॥ 8
किमर्थं तव शोकोऽत्र वयं ते प्राणरक्षकाः । भवामो निवसामोऽत्र गुहायां भयवर्जिताः ॥ 9
सर्वसौभाग्यसहितं पुरं देवपुरोपमम् । शनैः परस्परं वाक्यं वदतां मारुतात्मजः ॥ 10
श्रुत्वाङ्गदं समालिङ्ग्य प्रोवाच नयकोविदः ॥ 11

Chapter 7

MEETING WITH SAMPATI

Anxiety of the Monkeys (1-11)

1. Now the monkeys, resting on the trees of the forest for a while on account of weakness arising from the search for Sita, immersed themselves in very anxious thoughts. **2.** Angada said to a group of monkeys: "Wandering in the cave, we have already exhausted the period of one month given to us for the search. **3.** We have not been able to find out Sita yet and accomplish the king's order. If we now return to Kishkindha, Sugreeva will execute us. **4.** Particularly he will kill me, I being the son of his enemy. He has no affection for me. I have been saved only by Rama. **5.** Now that I have not been able to fulfil Rama's purpose, the evil-minded Sugreeva will surely kill me, making my failure a pretext. **6.** That evil-minded Sugreeva is now consorting with his elder brother's wife, whom he should look upon as his mother. Therefore, O great monkeys., I shall never go to him. **(7-8).** I shall therefore give up my life here in some way or other." Some of the monkey chiefs who saw him sitting with tears in his eyes, now spoke to him, shedding tears in sympathy with him. **9.** They said, "Why are you sorry like this? We shall protect you and save your life. We shall stay on with you in this cave free from all fear. **(10-11).** This cave has an abundance of all desirable things and is verily like the city of the Devas." Hearing such private conversations going on among the

विचार्यते किमर्थं ते दुर्विचारो न युज्यते ।
राज्ञोऽत्यन्तप्रियस्त्वं हि तारापुत्रोऽतिवल्लभः । रामस्य लक्ष्मणात्प्रीतस्त्वयि नित्यं प्रवर्धते ॥ 12
अतो न राघवाद्भीतिस्तव राज्ञो विशेषतः । अहं तव हिते सक्तो वत्स नान्यं विचारय ॥ 13
गुहावासश्च निर्भेद्य इत्युक्तं वानरैस्तु यत् । तदेतद्रामबाणानामभेद्यं किं जगत्त्रये ॥ 14
ये त्वां दुर्बोधयन्त्येते वानरा वानरर्षभ । पुत्रदारादिकं त्यक्त्वा कथं स्थास्यन्ति ते त्वया ॥ 15
अन्यद्गुह्यतमं वक्ष्ये रहस्यं श्रृणु मे सुत । रामो न मानुषो देवः साक्षान्नारायणोऽव्ययः ॥ 16
सीता भगवती माया जनसम्मोहकारिणी । लक्ष्मणो भुवनाधारः साक्षाच्छेषः फणीश्वरः ॥ 17
ब्रह्मणा प्रार्थिताः सर्वे रक्षोगणविनाशने । मायामानुषभावेन जाता लोकैकरक्षकाः ॥ 18
वयं च पार्षदाः सर्वे विष्णोर्वैकुण्ठवासिनः । मनुष्यभावमापन्ने स्वेच्छया परमात्मनि ॥ 19
वयं वानररूपेण जातास्तस्यैव मायया । वयं तु तपसा पूर्वमाराध्य जगतां पतिम् ॥ 20
तेनैवानुगृहीताः स्मः पार्षदत्वमुपागताः । इदानीमपि तस्यैव सेवां कृत्वैव मायया ॥ 21
पुनर्वैकुण्ठमासाद्य सुखं स्थास्यामहे वयम् । इत्यङ्गदमथाश्वास्य गता विन्ध्यं महाचलम् ॥ 22

monkeys, Hanuman, the son of the Wind-god, who was versed in the art of administering consolation to people, embraced Angada and spoke to him.

Hanumam assuages their fears (12-22)

He said: **(12-15).** "Why are you thinking like this? This kind of pessimistic thought does not befit you. You are very dear to our king, being the son of Tara. You are also a person of great capacity. Rama loves you even more than Lakshmana. Therefore you have nothing to fear from Rama and especially from our king also. I am your well-wisher. Do not be under any misapprehension. What the other monkeys have advised you about absolute safety of life within this cave, is not to be believed in; for, there is nothing in the three worlds into which Rama's arrows cannot penetrate. Those monkeys who are giving you this wrong advice will not stay with you. For they have their wives and children. Abandoning them, how will they stay with you? **(16-22).** I shall reveal to you a highly esoteric truth. O child! Rama is not a mere man. He is the Divinity, the eternal Being Narayana Himself. Sita is His Maya Sakti, who infatuates the whole world. Lakshmana is Adisesha, who supports the whole universe. In response to the prayer of Brahma all these protectors of the world are born assuming human forms in order to destroy the tribe of Rakshasas. All of us monkeys too are denizens of Vaikuntha, the Lord's Abode. When that Supreme Being assumed a human form, we too, by the power of His Maya, have been born in the form of monkeys. In our previous births, we had propitiated the Lord by our austerities and received His blessing. As a consequence, we have attained the status of his attendants. Now also, we shall, as occasioned by the power of Maya, be doing His service, and after that attain to Vaikuntha and abide there happily."

विचिन्वन्तोऽथ शनकैर्जानकीं दक्षिणाम्बुधेः । तीरे महेन्द्राख्यगिरेः पवित्रं पादमाययुः ॥ 23
दृष्ट्वा समुद्रं दुष्पारमगाधं भयवर्धनम् । वानरा भयसन्त्रस्ताः किं कुर्म इति वादिनः ॥ 24
निषेदुरुदधेस्तीरे सर्वे चिंतासमन्विताः । मन्त्रयामासुरन्योन्यमङ्गदाद्या महाबलाः ॥ 25
भ्रमतो मे वने मासो गतोऽत्रैव गुहान्तरे । न दृष्टो रावणो वाद्य सीता वा जनकात्मजा ॥ 26
सुग्रीवस्तीक्ष्णदण्डोऽस्मान्निहन्त्येव न संशयः । सुग्रीववधतोऽस्माकं श्रेयः प्रायोपवेशनम् ॥ 27
इति निश्चित्य तत्रैव दर्भानास्तीर्य सर्वतः । उपाविविशुस्ते सर्वे मरणे कृतनिश्चयाः ॥ 28
एतस्मिन्नन्तरे तत्र महेन्द्राद्रिगुहान्तरात् । निर्गत्य शनकैरागाद्गृध्रः पर्वतसन्निभः ॥ 29
दृष्ट्वा प्रायोपवेशेन स्थितान्वानरपुङ्गवान् । उवाच शनकैर्गृध्रः प्राप्तो भक्ष्योऽद्य मे बहुः ॥ 30
एकैकशः क्रमात्सर्वान् भक्षयामि दिने दिने । श्रुत्वा तद्गृध्रवचनं वानरा भीतमानसाः ॥ 31
भक्षयिष्यति नः सर्वानसौ गृध्रो न संशयः । रामकार्यं च नास्माभिःकृतं किञ्चिद्धरीश्वराः ॥ 32
सुग्रीवस्यापि च हितं न कृतं स्वात्मनामपि । वृथानेन वधं प्राप्ता गच्छामो यमसादनम् ॥ 33
अहो जटायुर्धर्मात्मा रामस्यार्थे मृतः सुधीः । मोक्षं प्राप दुरावापं योगिनामप्यरिन्दमः ॥ 34

Comforting Angada in this way, Hanuman with all the monkeys went to the great Vindhya mountains.

Meeting with Sampati (23-56).

23. Afterwards, moving forward little by little in search of Sita, the monkeys reached the valley of the great mountain Mahendra, near the shore of the southern sea. **(24-25).** Seeing that ocean, extending with no shore in sight and deep and awe-inspiring, they were all frightened. They stopped near the sea shore thinking over what they should do thereafter. Angada and other powerful monkeys all jointly conferred on their next move. **26.** They thought, "Wandering in that cave, we spent a month without locating either Ravana or Sita **(27-28).** Sugreeva is in the habit of giving very severe punishments. He will certainly kill us all. Fasting unto death is better than death by Sugreeva's hands." Deciding this way, they spread beds of Darbha grass and laid themselves on it, determined to die by fasting.

29. Just then, there emerged from a cave of the Mahendra mountain, an eagle mountain-like in size, who went slowly to the place where the monkeys were lying. **(30-31).** Seeing the monkeys preparing to die of fasting, the eagle said, "I have now got plenty to eat. I shall eat these one after another every day." The monkeys were frightened to hear these words of the eagle. **32.** They now began to speak among themselves, "This vulture will eat up all of us. There is no doubt about it. O great monkeys! We have not done even a little service to Rama. **33.** Nor have we done any service to Sugreeva, or to ourselves. So by dying at the hands of this vulture without any merit to our credit, we shall be consigned to the realm of Yama. **34.** Look at Jatayu —how he sacrificed himself for a righteous

सम्पातिस्तु तदा वाक्यं श्रुत्वा वानरभाषितम् । के वा यूयं मम भ्रातुः कर्णपीयूषसन्निभम् ॥ 35
जटायुरिति नामाद्य व्याहरन्तः परस्परम् । उच्यतां वो भयं मा भून्मत्तः प्लवगसत्तमाः ॥36
तमुवाचाङ्गदः श्रीमानुत्थितो गृध्रसन्निधौ । रामो दाशरथिः श्रीमान् लक्ष्मणेन समन्वितः ॥37
सीतया भार्यया सार्धं विचचार महावने । तस्य सीता हृता साध्वी रावणेन दुरात्मना ॥ 38
मृगयां निर्गते रामे लक्ष्मणे च हृता बलात् । रामरामेति क्रोशन्ती श्रुत्वा गृध्रः प्रतापवान् ॥ 39
जटायुर्नाम पक्षीन्द्रो युद्धं कृत्वा सुदारुणम् । रावणेन हतो वीरो राघवार्थं महाबलः ॥ 40
रामेण दग्धो रामस्य सायुज्यमगमत्क्षणात् । रामः सुग्रीवमासाद्य सख्यं कृत्वाग्निसाक्षिकम् ॥41
सुग्रीवचोदितो हत्वा वालिनं सुदुरासदम् । राज्यं ददौ वानराणां सुग्रीवाय महाबलः ॥ 42
सुग्रीवः प्रेषयामास सीतायाः परिमार्गणे । अस्मान्वानरवृन्दान्वै महासत्त्वान्महाबलः ॥ 43
मासादर्वाङ् निवर्तध्वं नोचेत्प्राणान्हरामि वः । इत्याज्ञया भ्रमन्तोऽस्मिन्वने गह्वरमध्यगाः ॥ 44
गतो मासो न जानीमः सीतां वा रावणं च वा । मर्तुं प्रायोपविष्टाः स्मस्तीरे लवणवारिधेः ॥ 45
यदि जानासि हे पक्षिन्सीतां कथय नः शुभाम् । अङ्गदस्य वचः श्रुत्वा सम्पातिर्हृष्टमानसः ॥ 46
उवाच मत्प्रियो भ्राता जटायुः प्लवगेश्वराः । बहुवर्षसहस्रान्ते भ्रातृवार्ता श्रुता मया ॥ 47

cause. Opposing the enemies of Rama he laid down his life for the cause of Rama. Thereby he attained Moksha, which even Rishis cannot have."

(35-36). That vulture Sampati, hearing these words of the monkeys, said, "You are speaking among yourselves about my brother Jatayu, a name very dear to me. You please tell me who you are. O monkey-heroes! You shall have nothing to fear from me." **(37-40).** Thereupon, the noble Angada got up and went to the vulture and said to him as follows: "Rama, the son of Dasaratha, along with his brother Lakshmana and wife Sita was staying in this dense forest. The wicked Ravana abducted Sita when Rama and Lakshmana had gone out for hunting. As Sita was crying aloud, 'Rama, Rama' while being carried away, the powerful eagle named Jatayu heard these cries and joined battle with Ravana. Thus fighting for the cause of Rama, he met with a hero's death. **41.** Rama cremated him. For these reasons, he has attained unity with Rama. Next Rama happened to meet Sugreeva and enter into an alliance with him before fire as witness. **42.** At the request of Sugreeva, Rama killed Vali whom none can ordinarily overcome. Thus the mighty Rama wrested the kingdom from Vali and awarded it to Sugreeva. **43.** After that, powerful Sugreeva deputed us, monkeys of great strength, to find out the whereabouts of Sita. **(44-45).** 'You must return within a month; failing that I shall execute you'—such was the order of Sugreeva. Now wandering in a cave in these mountains, we spent more than a month. We have not been able to locate Ravana or Sita. We have reached the shore of this salty ocean and are lying here resolved to die by fasting. **(46-48).** O great bird!

वाक्साहाय्यं करिष्येऽहं भवतां प्लवगेश्वराः । भ्रातुः सलिलदानाय नयध्वं मां जलान्तिकम् 48
पश्चात्सर्वं शुभं वक्ष्ये भवतां कार्यसिद्धये । तथेति निन्युस्ते तीरं समुद्रस्य विहङ्गमम् ॥ 49
सोऽपि तत्सलिले स्नात्वा भ्रातुर्दत्त्वा जलाञ्जलिम् ।
पुनः स्वस्थानमासाद्य स्थितो नीतो हरीश्वरैः । सम्पातिः कथयामास वानरान्परिहर्षयन् ॥ 50
लङ्का नाम नगर्यास्ते त्रिकूटगिरिमूर्धनि । तत्राशोकवने सीता राक्षसीभिः सुरक्षिता ॥ 51
समुद्रमध्ये सा लङ्का शतयोजनदूरतः । दृश्यते मे न सन्देहः सीता च परिदृश्यते ॥ 52
गृध्रत्वाद् दूरदृष्टिर्मे नात्र संशयितुं क्षमम् । शतयोजनविस्तीर्णं समुद्रं यस्तु लङ्घयेत् ॥ 53
स एव जानकीं दृष्ट्वा पुनरायास्यति ध्रुवम् ।
अहमेव दुरात्मानं रावणं हन्तुमुत्सहे । भ्रातुर्हन्तारमेकाकी किन्तु पक्षविवर्जितः ॥ 54
यतध्वमतियत्नेन लङ्घितुं सरितां पतिम् । ततो हन्ता रघुश्रेष्ठो रावणं राक्षसाधिपम् ॥ 55
उल्लङ्घ्य सिन्धुं शतयोजनायतं लङ्कां प्रविश्याथ विदेहकन्यकाम् ।
दृष्ट्वा समाभाष्य च वारिधिं पुनस्तर्तुं समर्थः कतमो विचार्यताम् ॥ 56
इति श्रीमदध्यात्मरामायणे उमामहेश्वरसंवादे
किष्किन्धाकाण्डे सप्तमः सर्गः ॥ ७ ॥

If you know anything about that glorious lady Sita, please tell us." Hearing the words of Angada, Sampati said with great joy, "O great monkeys! Jatayu is my dear brother. Now after the passing of many years, I am getting some news about him from you. I shall be able to give you some helpful suggestions in regard to your quest. But before that, please lead me to the shore of the ocean, so that I may do the obsequies of my brother. **(49-50).** After that I shall speak to you on matters that will be helpful to you in your mission." Agreeing to this proposal, the monkeys led him to the shore of the ocean. He took his bath in the ocean and made libations of water to his dead brother. After that the monkey leaders led him back to his seat. Sampati now spoke to them words that brought cheer to the heart of the monkeys.

(51-55). He said, "On a peak of the Trikuta mountain, is situated the city of Lanka. There guarded by a body of Rakshasa women, Sita is confined in an Ashoka grove. This city of Lanka is situated a hundred Yojanas across the sea. Being endowed with distant vision natural to vultures, I can see from here the city of Lanka and Sita confined there. Whoever can cross this span of a hundred Yojanas of ocean and find Sita there, can also return with the news of her discovery. I myself would have striven to destroy that Ravana, the murderer of my brother. But now I am wingless. So you now try your best to cross the ocean. After that Rama, the leader of Raghu's clan, can destroy Ravana. **56.** Now you confer and decide who among you can reach Lanka, crossing this hundred Yojanas of distance across the ocean, meet and talk with Sita, and recross the ocean with the news of her discovery."

अष्टमः सर्गः

श्रीमहादेव उवाच

अथ ते कौतुकाविष्टाः सम्पातिं सर्ववानराः । पप्रच्छुर्भगवन् ब्रूहि स्वमुदन्तं त्वमादितः ॥ 1
सम्पातिः कथयामास स्ववृत्तान्तं पुरा कृतम् । अहं पुरा जटायुश्च भ्रातरौ रूढयौवनौ ॥ 2
बलेन दर्पितावावां बलजिज्ञासया खगौ । सूर्यमण्डलपर्यन्तं गन्तुमुत्पतितौ मदात् ॥ 3
बहुयोजनसाहस्रं गतौ तत्र प्रतापितः । जटायुस्तं परित्रातुं पक्षैराच्छाद्य मोहतः ॥ 4
स्थितोऽहं रश्मिभिर्दग्धपक्षोऽस्मिन्विन्ध्यमूर्धनि । पतितो दूरपतनान्मूर्च्छितोऽहं कपीश्वराः ॥ 5
दिनत्रयात्पुनः प्राणसहितो दग्धपक्षकः । देशं वा गिरिकूटान्वा न जाने भ्रान्तमानसः ॥ 6
शनैरुन्मील्य नयने दृष्ट्वा तत्राश्रमं शुभम् । शनैः शनैराश्रमस्य समीपं गतवानहम् ॥ 7
चन्द्रमा नाम मुनिराड् दृष्ट्वा मां विस्मितोऽब्रवीत् । सम्पाते किमिदं तेऽद्य विरूपं केन वा कृतम् ॥ 8
जानामि त्वामहं पूर्वमत्यन्तं बलवानसि । दग्धौ किमर्थं ते पक्षौ कथ्यतां यदि मन्यसे ॥ 9

Chapter 8

SERMON OF CHANDRAMAS TO SAMPATI

Sampati's previous history (1-12)

1. All the monkeys, being very much intrigued to see Sampati and hear his words, wanted to know more about him. So they said to him, "O great one! Tell us all about your story from the beginning." **(2-3).** Sampati thereupon narrated the past incidents of his life. He said, "Myself and my brother Jatayu, being very proud of our strength in our youth, wanted to test it once by flying up to the region of the sun. **(4-5).** We flew several thousand Yojanas up, when Jatayu felt unable to bear the heat of the sun. In order to protect him, I sheltered him under my wings on account of my love for him. When I was thus protecting him, my wings were burnt by the heat of the sun, and from that great height, I fell on the top of the Vindhya mountain, losing consciousness. **6.** Three days after, I recovered consciousness, but wingless and confused in mind. I could not recognise the countryside or the mountain peaks. **7.** When I slowly opened my eyes, I saw there a very attractive Ashrama. I slowly moved up to that Ashrama. **(8-9).** The sage Chandramas, who was living in that Ashrama, saw me with great astonishment and said, 'O Sampati! How do you happen to be like this, deformed? Who did this? I knew you before as one endowed with very great strength. How is it that both your wings have been burnt? Please tell me all about it, if you have no objection.'

ततः स्वचेष्टितं सर्वं कथयित्वातिदुःखितः । अब्रवं मुनिशार्दूलं दह्येऽहं दाववह्निना ॥ 10
कथं धारयितुं शक्तो विपक्षो जीवितं प्रभो । इत्युक्तोऽथमुनिर्वीक्ष्य मां दयार्द्रत्रिलोचनः ॥ 11
शृणु वत्स वचो मेऽद्य श्रुत्वा कुरु यथेप्सितम् । देहमूलमिदं दुःखं देहः कर्मसमुद्भवः ॥ 12
कर्म प्रवर्तते देहेऽहंबुद्ध्या पुरुषस्य हि । अहङ्कारस्त्वनादिः स्यादविद्यासम्भवो जडः ॥ 13
चिच्छायया सदा युक्तस्तप्तायःपिण्डवत्सदा । तेन देहस्य तादात्म्याद्देहश्चेतनवान्भवेत् ॥ 14
देहोऽहमिति बुद्धिः स्यादात्मनोऽहङ्कृतेर्बलात् । तन्मूल एष संसारः सुखदुःखादिसाधकः ॥ 15
आत्मनो निर्विकारस्य मिथ्या तादात्म्यतः सदा । देहोऽहं कर्मकर्ताहमिति सङ्कल्प्य सर्वदा ॥ 16
जीवः करोति कर्माणि तत्फलैर्बद्ध्यतेऽवशः । ऊर्ध्वाधो भ्रमते नित्यं पापपुण्यात्मकः स्वयम् ॥17
कृतं मयाधिकं पुण्यं यज्ञदानादि निश्चितम् । स्वर्गं गत्वा सुखं भोक्ष्य इति सङ्कल्पवान्भवेत् ॥18
तथैवाध्यासतस्तत्र चिरं भुक्त्वा सुखं महत् । क्षीणपुण्यः पतत्यर्वागनिच्छन्कर्मचोदितः ॥ 19

(10-12). I thereupon narrated to him the whole of my story, and with great sorrow in my heart, asked that great sage: 'O holy one! All my body is burning as if I have fallen into a forest fire. Without my wings, how am I to sustain my life?' That sage thereupon addressed me, casting a kindly look. He said, 'Dear one! Listen to my words, and after that do as you please. All this sorrow of yours springs from the body, and the body is born of one's own past Karmas.

Chandramas Expounds the Philosophy of the Atman (13-19)

(13-14). 'Because man thinks of his body as himself, Karma becomes operative. This I-sense, which binds one to the body, is beginningless and is a result of ignorance. In itself it is inert without consciousness, but being in association with the reflection of pure consciousness, it appears conscious, just as a red hot piece of iron appears hot and shining in association with fire. Because the body is in identification with this I-sense, the body too appears to be endowed with consciousness. **15.** Dominated by the I-sense, the Atman thinks of himself as the body and becomes subject to the cycle of births and deaths, and to the consequent experience of happiness and misery. **(16-17).** The Atman in itself is changeless but because of this false identification, he thinks: I am the body and I am the doer of various actions. Thus, the embodied being becomes the performer of many actions and is helplesslybound by their consequences. He finds himself fettered and wanders hither and thither in this transmigratory cycle as a victim of sinful and meritorious actions. **18.** He makes a resolution: 'I have done many meritorious actions like sacrifices and charities. I shall therefore attain to heaven and enjoy heavenly felicities.' **19.** By the same sense of identification, he enjoys these heavenly pleasures for a long period, and then when the effect of these meritorious deeds has dwindled, the same power of Karma sends him down, however much he may dislike it.

पतित्वा मण्डले चेन्दोस्ततो नीहारसंयुतः । भूमौ पतित्वा व्रीह्यादौ तत्र स्थित्वा चिरं पुनः ॥20
भूत्वा चतुर्विधं भोज्यं पुरुषैर्भुज्यते ततः । रेतो भूत्वा पुनस्तेन ऋतौ स्त्रीयोनिसिञ्चितः ॥21
योनिरक्तेन संयुक्तं जरायुपरिवेष्टितम् । दिनेनैकेन कललं भूत्वा रूढत्वमाप्नुयात् ॥ 22
तत्पुनः पञ्चरात्रेण बुद्बुदाकारतामियात् । सप्तरात्रेण तदपि मांसपेशित्वमाप्नुयात् ॥ 23
पक्षमात्रेण सा पेशी रुधिरेण परिप्लुता । तस्या एवाङ्कुरोत्पत्तिः पञ्चविंशतिरात्रिषु ॥ 24
ग्रीवा शिरश्च स्कन्धश्च पृष्ठवंशस्तथोदरम् । पञ्चधाङ्गानि चैकैकं जायन्ते मासतः क्रमात् ॥25
पाणिपादौ तथा पार्श्वः कटिर्जानु तथैव च । मासद्वयात्प्रजायन्ते क्रमेणैव न चान्यथा ॥ 26
त्रिभिर्मासैः प्रजायन्ते अङ्गानां सन्धयः क्रमात् । सर्वाङ्गुल्यः प्रजायन्ते क्रमान्मासचतुष्टये ॥ 27
नासा कर्णौ च नेत्रे च जायन्ते पञ्चमासतः । दन्तपङ्क्तिर्नखा गुह्यं पञ्चमे जायते तथा ॥ 28
अर्वाक्षण्मासतश्छिद्रं कर्णयोर्भवति स्फुटम् । पायुर्मेढ्रमुपस्थं च नाभिश्चापि भवेन्नृणाम् ॥ 29
सप्तमे मासि रोमाणि शिरः केशास्तथैव च । विभक्तावयवत्वं च सर्वं सम्पद्यतेऽष्टमे ॥ 30
जठरे वर्धते गर्भः स्त्रिया एवं विहङ्गम । पञ्चमे मासि चैतन्यं जीवः प्राप्नोति सर्वशः ॥31
नाभिसूत्राल्परन्ध्रेण मातृभुक्तान्नसारतः । वर्धते गर्भगः पिण्डो न म्रियेत स्वकर्मतः ॥ 32

Travails of the Jiva (20-41)

(20-22). 'The descending Jiva, reaches the sphere of the moon, and from there, united with a drop of water, comes down to earth, and falling on cereals, gets identified with them. After remaining in that condition for long, he becomes any of the four types of food and in that condition is eaten by man. In the human body he is reduced to the seed, which being deposited in the womb of a woman and becoming united with the blood therein, becomes solidified within a day into the state called Kalala ensheathed by the placenta. **23.** Within five nights the foetus develops into a foam-like substance, and within seven nights into a muscular tissue. **24.** Within fifteen days blood will appear in it, and within twenty five nights a small shoot develops from it. **25.** In one month the neck, head, shoulder, backbone and abdomen will be formed one after another. **26.** Then in the second month, the arms, legs, hips and knee-caps develop one after another. **27.** In the third month, all the joints of organs are formed, and the fingers, in the fourth. **28.** In the fifth month the nose, ears, eyes, teeth, nails and the genitals develop. **29.** In the sixth month, the orifice of the ears, anus, the sex organ and navel are formed. **30.** In the seventh month, hair on the body, and the skull and the distinctiveness of all organs are formed. By the eighth month, the full human form comes into shape. **31.** In this way, the foetus gradually develops in the womb. By the fifth month, signs of life are seen throughout the foetus. **32.** Through the small orifice in the umbilical cord the foetus draws a little of the essence of the food consumed by the mother. It is by the power of its own Karma that it develops without perishing.

स्मृत्वा सर्वाणि जन्मानि पूर्वकर्माणि सर्वशः । जठरानलतप्तोऽयमिदं वचनमब्रवीत् ॥ 33

नानायोनिसहस्रेषु जायमानोऽनुभूतवान् । पुत्रदारादि सम्बन्धं कोटिशः पशुबान्धवान् ॥ 34

कुटुम्बभरणासक्त्या न्यायान्यायैर्धनार्जनम् । कृतं नाकरवं विष्णुचिन्तां स्वप्नेऽपि दुर्भगः ॥ 35

इदानीं तत्फलं भुञ्जे गर्भदुःखं महत्तरम् । अशाश्वते शाश्वतवद्देहे तृष्णासमन्वितः ॥ 36

अकार्याण्येव कृतवान्न कृतं हितमात्मनः । इत्येवं बहुधा दुःखमनुभूय स्वकर्मतः ॥ 37

कदा निष्क्रमणं मे स्याद् गर्भान्निरयसन्निभात् । इत ऊर्ध्वं नित्यमहं विष्णुमेवानुपूजये ॥ 38

इत्यादि चिन्तयञ्जीवो योनियन्त्रप्रपीडितः । जायमानोऽतिदुःखेन नरकात्पातकी यथा ॥ 39

पूतिव्रणान्निपतितः कृमिरेष इवापरः । ततो बाल्यादिदुःखानि सर्व एवं विभुञ्जते ॥ 40

त्वया चैवानुभूतानि सर्वत्र विदितानि च । न वर्णितानि मे गृध्र यौवनादिषु सर्वतः ॥ 41

एवं देहोऽहमित्यस्मादभ्यासान्निरयादिकम् । गर्भवासादिदुःखानि भवन्त्यभिनिवेशतः ॥ 42

तस्माद्देहद्वयादन्यमात्मानं प्रकृतेः परम् । ज्ञात्वा देहादिममतां त्यक्त्वात्मज्ञानवान् भवेत् 43

जाग्रदादिविनिर्मुक्तं सत्यज्ञानादिलक्षणम् । शुद्धं बुद्धं सदा शान्तमात्मानमवधारयेत् ॥ 44

33. 'The foetus now gets the memory of its previous lives and actions. With that memory, and suffering from the heat of the abdomen, the foetus thinks as follows: **34.** Born in innumerable wombs, I had associations with many wives and children, relatives and possessions. **35.** Preoccupied with the maintenance of the family, I managed to earn money in righteous and unrighteous ways. But unfortunate that I am, I never thought of the Lord even in dream. **(36-38).** As a consequence of it, I am now undergoing tortures in the womb, considering the impermanent body as permanent. I have done things which I should not do. I never did things beneficial for the Atman. After undergoing the sufferings due to all such actions, when I get out of this hell-like womb, I shall hereafter engage myself always in adoration of Mahavishnu.

(39-40). While thinking like this, he is ejected by the powerful forces of parturition, subjecting him to very great sufferings. Just as a sinner emerges from hell, he comes out of the foul smelling bodily orifice, resembling a worm in appearance. Thereafter, he undergoes all the sufferings of infancy. **41.** O vulture! I am not going to describe them or the sufferings of youth and other periods of life, as they are well-known to you and all other creatures. **42.** Thus as a result of identifying oneself with the body, the Jiva undergoes the sufferings of hell and the life in the womb.

43. 'Therefore, abandoning this sense of identification with the subtle and gross bodies, one should recognise oneself as the Self transcending Prakriti. Abandoning the feeling that 'I am the body', he should know himself as Atman. **44.** He should know himself as the Self, who is not involved in the states of waking, dream, and sleep, who is distinguished as Truth and Con-

चिदात्मनि परिज्ञाते नष्टे मोहेऽज्ञसम्भवे । देहः पततु प्रारब्धकर्मवेगेन तिष्ठतु ॥ 45
योगिनो न हि दुःखं वा सुखं वाज्ञानसम्भवम् । तस्माद्देहेन सहितो यावत्प्रारब्धसङ्क्षयः ॥ 46
तावत्तिष्ठ सुखेन त्वं धृतकञ्चुकमर्पवत् । अन्यद्वक्ष्यामि ते पक्षिन् शृणु मे परमं हितम् ॥ 47
त्रेतायुगे दाशरथिर्भूत्वा नारायणोऽव्ययः । रावणस्य वधार्थाय दण्डकानागमिष्यति ॥ 48
सीतया भार्यया सार्धं लक्ष्मणेन समन्वितः । तत्राश्रमे जनकजां भ्रातृभ्यां रहिते वने ॥ 49
रावणश्चौरवन्नीत्वा लङ्कायां स्थापयिष्यति । तस्याः सुग्रीवनिर्देशाद्वानराः परिमार्गणे ॥ 50
आगमिष्यन्ति जलधेस्तीरं तत्र समागमः । त्वया तैः कारणवशाद्भविष्यति न संशयः ॥ 51
तदा सीतास्थितिं तेभ्यः कथयस्व यथार्थतः । तदैव तव पक्षौ द्वावुत्पत्स्येते पुनर्नवौ ॥ 52

सम्पातिरुवाच

बोधयामास मां चन्द्रनामा मुनिकुलेश्वरः । पश्यन्तु पक्षौ मे जातौ नूतनावतिकोमलौ ॥ 53
स्वस्ति वोऽस्तु गमिष्यामि सीतां द्रक्ष्यथ निश्चयम् यत्नं कुरुध्वं दुर्लङ्घ्यसमुद्रस्य विलङ्घने ॥ 54

sciousness, who is pure, wakeful and peaceful. **(45-47).** When the Atman, who is of the nature of Truth and Consciousness, is realised and the infatuation caused by ignorance erased, it is immaterial whether the body dies or continues to live as a consequence of the operative Karma (Prarabdha Karma). A man of realisation will not identify himself with the body, and he has as a consequence neither enjoyments nor sufferings afterwards. Therefore until your operative Karma is exhausted and the body perishes, you live in the body without identification with it, just as a snake carries on its external sheath of skin, until the time for it to separate comes. O Vulture! I shall tell you another thing also which will contribute to your supreme good.

Conclusion of the Sampati Episode (48-55)

48. 'The Eternal Being Narayana will incarnate Himself in the Treta Yuga as a son of Dasaratha. He will come to the forest of Dandaka for the destruction of Ravana. **(49-51).** While he will be staying in a forest Ashrama along with his wife Sita and brother Lakshmana, Ravana will steal away Sita like a thief and take her to Lanka when the two brothers would have gone out into the forest. Directed by Sugreeva a host of monkeys will come up to the seashore in search of Sita. You will have occasion to meet them for your own good. **52.** You inform them about the true location of Sita. When you do that, your two wings will again sprout.' "

53. Sampati continued, "The sage Chandramas communicated all this to me. Now you see how extremely handsome wings are sprouting on my body. **54.** May you succeed and prosper. You will certainly be able to find out Sita. Now

यन्नामस्मृतिमात्रतोऽपरिमितं संसारवारांनिधिं
तीर्त्वा गच्छति दुर्जनोऽपि परमं विष्णोः पदं शाश्वतम् ।
तस्यैव स्थितिकारिणस्त्रिजगतां रामस्य भक्ताः प्रिया
यूयं किं न समुद्रमात्रतरणे शक्ताः कथं वानराः ॥ 55

इति श्रीमदध्यात्मरामायणे उमामहेश्वरसंवादे
किष्किन्धाकाण्डेऽष्टमः सर्गः ॥ ८ ॥

take steps to go across the ocean, which is very difficult to accomplish. **55.** He, by the remembrance of whose name even evil men are able to cross the ocean of Samsara and attain to the eternal status of Mahavishnu, He who is the protector of all the three worlds—of that Being you, O monkeys, are the dear devotees. What difficulty can this terrestrial ocean pose to you?"

नवमः सर्गः

श्रीमहादेव उवाच

गते विहायसा गृध्रराजे वानरपुङ्गवाः । हर्षेण महताविष्टाः सीतादर्शनलालसाः ॥ 1
ऊचुः समुद्रं पश्यन्तो नक्रचक्रभयङ्करम् । तरङ्गादिभिरुन्नद्धमाकाशमिव दुर्ग्रहम् ॥ 2
परस्परमवोचन्वै कथमेनं तरामहे । उवाच चाङ्गदस्तत्र श्रृणुध्वं वानरोत्तमाः ॥ 3
भवन्तोऽत्यन्तबलिनः शूराश्च कृतविक्रमाः । को वात्र वारिधिं तीर्त्वा राज्यकार्यं करिष्यति ॥ 4
एतेषां वानराणां स प्राणदाता न संशयः । तदुत्तिष्ठतु मे शीघ्रं पुरतो यो महाबलः ॥ 5

Chapter 9

EMERGENCE OF HANUMAN THE HERO

The Monkeys Confer Again (1-14)

1. Great was the joy of the monkeys intent on finding out Sita when they saw that lordly vulture flying high up into the sky. **2.** Looking at the sea expansive and unapproachable like the sky and augmented by its mighty waves and filled with whales and other dangerous aquatic creatures, the monkeys began to speak among themselves as follows: **3.** "How shall we cross this ocean?" Then Angada said, "O noble monkeys! Hear what I say. **4.** You are all endowed with very great strength, courage and adventurous spirit. Who among you will be able to cross this ocean and accomplish the king's directive? **5.** That one will be really the protector of the lives of all of us. Therefore, I request

वानराणां च सर्वेषां रामसुग्रीवयोरपि । स एव पालको भूयान्नात्र कार्या विचारणा ॥ 6
इत्युक्ते युवराजेन तूष्णीं वानरसैनिकाः । आसन्नोचुः किञ्चिदपि परस्परविलोकिनः ॥ 7

अङ्गद उवाच

उच्यतां वै बलं सर्वैः प्रत्येकं कार्यसिद्धये । केन वा साध्यते कार्यं जानीमस्तदनन्तरम् ॥ 8
अङ्गदस्य वचः श्रुत्वा प्रोचुर्वीरा बलं पृथक् । योजनानां दशारभ्य दशोत्तरगुणं जगुः ॥ 9
शतादर्वाग्जाम्बवांस्तु प्राह मध्ये वनौकसाम् । पुरा त्रिविक्रमे देवे पादं भूमानलक्षणम् ॥ 10
त्रिःसप्तकृत्वोऽहमगां प्रदक्षिणविधानतः । इदानीं वार्धकग्रस्तो न शक्नोमि विलङ्घितुम् ॥ 11
अङ्गदोऽप्याह मे गन्तुं शक्यं पारं महोदधेः । पुनर्लङ्घनसामर्थ्यं न जानाम्यस्ति वा न वा ॥ 12
तमाह जाम्बवान्वीरस्त्वं राजा नो नियामकः । न युक्तं त्वां नियोक्तुं मे त्वं समर्थोऽसि यद्यपि ॥ 13

अङ्गद उवाच

एवं चेत्पूर्ववत्सर्वे स्वप्स्यामो दर्भविष्टरे । केनापि न कृतं कार्यं जीवितुं च न शक्यते ॥ 14
तमाह जाम्बवान्वीरो दर्शयिष्यामि ते सुत । येनास्माकं कार्यसिद्धिर्भविष्यत्यचिरेण च ॥ 15

him who is powerful enough to do this, to come forward before me. **6.** That person will undoubtedly be the saviour of the lives of all the monkeys as also of Rama and Sugreeva. There is no doubt about it." **7.** When Angada, the heir-apparent, said like this, all the monkey heroes remained silent, looking at one another.

8. Angada again said, "For the accomplishment of this task, let each one declare out the strength he possesses. After that we shall determine who will be able to accomplish this task." **9.** Hearing Angada's speech, those monkey heroes one after another began to specify the extent they could leap. From ten Yojanas onwards, each succeeding monkey leader offered to leap ten Yojanas more than the previous speaker. **(10-11).** From among the monkeys Jambavan now said, "I can leap upto ninety Yojanas. In a previous age, when Mahavishnu incarnated Himself as Vamana and measured the whole world by one step, I circumambulated His foot twenty one times. But now I am old and my capacity to leap is very limited." **12.** Now Angada said, "I shall be able to leap across the ocean to the other shore, but I do not know whether I am capable of leaping back." **13.** The heroic Jambavan said, "But you are our leader and king. Even if you are powerful enough, I do not think it is proper to give this task to you." **14.** To this Angada said, "If matters stand like that, let all of us once again stretch ourselves on Darbha beds to die of starvation. Without accomplishing this task none can hope to live."

Jambavan's Prompting of Hanuman (15-29)

(15-17). Now the heroic Jambavan intervened again and said, "O child! I shall now show you him who can accomplish this task very easily and expeditiously."

इत्युक्त्वा जाम्बवान्प्राह हनूमन्तमवस्थितम् । हनुमन्किं रहस्तूष्णीं स्थीयते कार्यगौरवे ॥ 16
प्राप्तेऽङ्गेनेव सामर्थ्यं दर्शयाद्य महाबल । त्वं साक्षाद्वायुतनयो वायुतुल्यपराक्रमः ॥ 17
रामकार्यार्थमेव त्वं जनितोऽसि महात्मना । जातमात्रेण ते पूर्वं दृष्ट्वोद्यन्तं विभावसुम् ॥ 18
पक्वं फलं जिघृक्षामीत्युत्प्लुतं बालचेष्टया । योजनानां पञ्चशतं पतितोऽसि ततो भुवि ॥ 19
अतस्त्वद्बलमाहात्म्यं को वा शक्नोति वर्णितुम् । उत्तिष्ठ कुरु रामस्य कार्यं नः पाहि सुव्रत ॥ 20
श्रुत्वा जाम्बवतो वाक्यं हनुमानतिहर्षितः । चकार नादं सिंहस्य ब्रह्माण्डं स्फोटयन्निव ॥ 21
बभूव पर्वताकारस्त्रिविक्रम इवापरः । लङ्घयित्वा जलनिधिं कृत्वा लङ्कां च भस्मसात् ।22
रावणं सकुलं हत्वा नेष्ये जनकनन्दिनीम् । 23
यद्वा बद्ध्वा गले रज्ज्वा रावणं वामपाणिना । लङ्कां सपर्वतां धृत्वा रामस्याग्रे क्षिपाम्यहम् ॥24
यद्वादृष्ट्वैव यास्यामि जानकीं शुभलक्षणाम् । श्रुत्वा हनुमतो वाक्यं जाम्बवानिदमब्रवीत् ॥ 25
दृष्ट्वैवागच्छ भद्रं ते जीवन्तीं जानकीं शुभाम् । पश्चाद्रामेण सहितो दर्शयिष्यसि पौरुषम् ॥ 26
कल्याणं भवताद्भद्र गच्छतस्ते विहायसा । गच्छन्तं रामकार्यार्थं वायुस्त्वामनुगच्छतु ॥ 27

After saying so, he addressed Hanuman who was standing aloof. He said, "O Hanuman! In this grave situation, why are you standing aloof and silent? This, O powerful one, is the occasion for you to demonstrate your strength. You are the offspring of the Wind-god and are as powerful as he. **(18-20).** You are begotten by that deity in order to accomplish Rama's purpose. Long before, at your very birth, seeing the rising sun, you jumped towards him mistaking the disc of the sun for a ripe fruit. After going up about five hundred Yojanas you fell down on the earth. When you could accomplish such a feat, who can really estimate the extent of your strength? Wake up, accomplish the purpose of Rama and save us all."

21. Highly elated at these words of Jambavan, Hanuman gave out a lion-roar loud enough to split the cosmos. **(22-23).** He then grew into a huge mountain-like dimension like another Vamana and declared, "Crossing the ocean, I shall reduce Lanka to ashes. Destroying Ravana with all his tribe, I shall bring Sita, the daughter of Janaka. **24.** Dragging Ravana, by my left hand, with a halter round his neck and with my right lifting up the whole of Lanka along with the mountain on which it is situated, I shall go to Rama and **deposit** them before him. **25.** Or, after discovering the location of noble Sita, I shall return." Hearing these words of Hanuman, Jambavan said: **26.** "Now, finding out the whereabouts of Sita, whether she is alive or not, you should return. Afterwards, accompanied by Rama, you can go to Lanka and demonstrate your strength. **27.** O dear one! May good fortune befall you who have decided to go by the sky across the ocean. May the winds blow favouring you!"

इत्याशीर्भिः समामन्त्र्य विसृष्टः प्लवगाधिपैः । महेन्द्राद्रिशिरो गत्वा बभूवाद्भुतदर्शनः ॥ 28

महानगेन्द्रप्रतिमो महात्मा सुवर्णवर्णोऽरुणचारुवक्त्रः ।
महाफणीन्द्राभसुदीर्घबाहुर्वातात्मजोऽदृश्यत सर्वभूतैः ॥ 29

इति श्रीमदध्यात्मरामायणे उमामहेश्वरसंवादे
किष्किन्धाकाण्डे नवमः सर्गः ॥ ९ ॥

28. Backed by the blessings of the great monkey leaders, Hanuman went up to the top of Mahendra mountain, assuming a form that created wonder in the minds of all onlookers. **29.** All the onlookers saw that great personage Hanuman, the son of the Wind-god, there, mountain-like in size, golden in colour, pink and handsome in face and possessed of arms long and powerful like the king of the serpents.

———

ॐ

अध्यात्मरामायणम्

सुन्दरकाण्डः

प्रथमः सर्गः

श्रीमहादेव उवाच

शतयोजनविस्तीर्णं समुद्रं मकरालयम् । लिलङ्घयिषुरानन्दसन्दोहो मारुतात्मजः ॥ 1
ध्यात्वा रामं परात्मानमिदं वचनमब्रवीत् । पश्यन्तु वानराः सर्वे गच्छन्तं मां विहायसा ॥ 2
अमोघं रामनिर्मुक्तं महाबाणमिवाखिलाः । पश्याम्यद्यैव रामस्य पत्नीं जनकनन्दिनीम् ॥ 3
कृतार्थोऽहं कृतार्थोऽहं पुनः पश्यामि राघवम् । प्राणप्रयाणसमये यस्य नाम सकृत्स्मरन् ॥ 4
नरस्तीर्त्वा भवाम्भोधिमपारं याति तत्पदम् ॥ 5
किं पुनस्तस्य दूतोऽहं तदङ्गाङ्गुलिमुद्रिकः ।
तमेव हृदये ध्यात्वा लङ्घयाम्यल्पवारिधिम् । इत्युक्त्वा हनुमान्बाहू प्रसार्यायतवालधिः ॥ 6
ऋजुग्रीवोर्ध्वदृष्टिः सन्नाकुञ्चितपदद्वयः । दक्षिणाभिमुखस्तूर्णं पुप्लुवेऽनिलविक्रमः ॥ 7

SUNDARA KANDAM

Chapter 1

HANUMAN'S CROSSING OF THE SEA

Hanuman Takes the Leap
(1-7)

(1-4). Desirous of leaping across the hundred Yojanas of ocean infested by aquatic creatures, Hanuman, the son of the Wind-god, meditated in mind on Rama the Supreme Self, and said as follows in a mood of high elation: "O ye comrade monkeys! Be ye the witness of how I go through the sky like an unfailing arrow shot by Rama. I shall now itself find the whereabouts of Sita and return to Rama after accomplishing my task. **(5-7).** He by uttering whose name even once at the time of death a Jiva is able to cross the otherwise unspanable ocean of Samsara and attain to His divine Status—that Rama's signet ring with His name engraved, I carry with me. How insignificant then is this small ocean for me? Meditating on Him in my mind, I shall cross it with utmost ease." With these words Hanuman took a leap through the sky in the southern direction with the speed of wind—his arms spread, tail erect, neck straightened, legs contracted and eyes looking up.

आकाशात्त्वरितं देवैर्वीक्ष्यमाणो जगाम सः । दृष्ट्वानिलसुतं देवा गच्छन्तं वायुवेगतः ॥ 8
परीक्षणार्थं तत्त्वस्य वानरस्येदमब्रुवन् । गच्छत्येष महासत्त्वो वानरो वायुविक्रमः ॥ 9
लङ्कां प्रवेष्टुं शक्तो वा न वा जानीमहे बलम् । एवं विचार्य नागानां मातरं सुरसाभिधाम् ॥ 10
अब्रवीद् देवतावृन्दः कौतूहलसमन्वितः । गच्छ त्वं वानरेन्द्रस्य किंचिद्विघ्नं समाचर ॥ 11
ज्ञात्वा तस्य बलं बुद्धिं पुनरेहि त्वरान्विता । इत्युक्ता सा ययौ शीघ्रं हनुमद्विघ्नकारणात् ॥ 12
आवृत्य मार्गं पुरतः स्थित्वा वानरमब्रवीत् । एहि मे वदनं शीघ्रं प्रविशस्व महामते ॥ 13
देवैस्त्वं कल्पितो भक्ष्यः क्षुधासम्पीडितात्मनः । तामाह हनुमान्मातरहं रामस्य शासनात् ॥ 14
गच्छामि जानकीं द्रष्टुं पुनरागम्य सत्वरः । रामाय कुशलं तस्याः कथयित्वा त्वदाननम् ॥ 15
निवेक्ष्ये देहि मे मार्गं सुरसायै नमोऽस्तु ते ॥ 16
इत्युक्त्वा पुनरेवाह सुरसा क्षुधितास्म्यहम् ।
प्रविश्य गच्छ मे वक्त्रं नो चेत्त्वां भक्षयाम्यहम् । इत्युक्तो हनुमानाह मुखं शीघ्रं विदारय ॥ 17
प्रविश्य वदनं तेऽद्य गच्छामि त्वरयान्वितः । इत्युक्त्वा योजनायामदेहो भूत्वा पुरः स्थितः ॥ 18
दृष्ट्वा हनुमतो रूपं सुरसा पञ्चयोजनम् । मुखं चकार हनुमान् द्विगुणं रूपमादधत् ॥ 19

Surasa Episode (8-25)

(8-12). As Hanuman was leaping through the sky the Devas, who were observing with keen interest from the sky, felt that they should test the power of the monkey and said among themselves: "This powerful monkey equal to the wind in prowess is speeding towards Lanka. But we do not know whether he is powerful enough to reach Lanka or not." Thinking on these lines, that host of interested Devas said to Surasa, the mother of serpents, as follows: "You go and create some obstruction to the great monkey. Testing thus his intelligence and power, you can come back soon." Being thus instructed, she proceeded soon on the mission of obstructing Hanuman's passage. **(13-16).** She went and blocked the passage of Hanuman and said to him, "O wise one! Enter into my mouth quickly. Verily the Devas have offered you to me as food to appease my hungry stomach." Thereupon Hanuman said to her: "O mother! I am going at Rama's command to find out the whereabouts of Sita. Finding her out, I shall return quickly and, after conveying to Rama the news about her welfare, I shall enter into your mouth. Now please give me passage. Salutation to you Surasa."

(17-18) To this Surasa replied: "I am very hungry. You may go after entering into my mouth. Otherwise I shall eat you up." On being thus addressed by her, Hanuman asked her: "Then open your mouth quickly. I shall enter into it and proceed without delay." With these words Hanuman stood before her expanding his size to the extent of a Yojana. **19.** Seeing Hanuman's form, Surasa made her mouth five Yojanas in extent, whereupon Hanuman

ततश्चकार सुरसा योजनानां च विंशतिम् । वक्त्रं चकार हनुमांस्त्रिंशद्योजनसम्मितम् ॥ 20

ततश्चकार सुरसा पञ्चाशद्योजनायतम् । वक्त्रं तदा हनूमांस्तु बभूवाङ्गुष्ठसन्निभः ॥ 21

प्रविश्य वदनं तस्याः पुनरेत्य पुरः स्थितः । प्रविष्टो निर्गतोऽहं ते वदनं देवि ते नमः ॥ 22

एवं वदन्तं दृष्ट्वा सा हनूमन्तमथाब्रवीत् । गच्छ साधय रामस्य कार्यं बुद्धिमतां वर ॥ 23

देवैः सम्प्रेषिताहं ते बलं जिज्ञासुभिः कपे । दृष्टवा सीतां पुनर्गत्वा रामं द्रक्ष्यसि गच्छ भोः 24

इत्युक्त्वा सा ययौ देवलोकं वायुसुतः पुनः । जगाम वायुमार्गेण गरुत्मानिव पक्षिराट् ॥ 25

समुद्रोऽप्याह मैनाकं मणिकाञ्चनपर्वतम् । गच्छत्येष महासत्त्वो हनुमान्मारुतात्मजः ॥ 26

रामस्य कार्यसिद्ध्यर्थं तस्य त्वं सचिवो भव । सगरैर्वर्द्धितो यस्मात्पुराहं सागरोऽभवम् ॥ 27

तस्यान्वये बभूवासौ रामो दाशरथिः प्रभुः । तस्य कार्यार्थसिद्ध्यर्थं गच्छत्येष महाकपिः ॥ 28

त्वमुत्तिष्ठ जलात्तूर्णं त्वयि विश्रम्य गच्छतु । स तथेति प्रादुरभूज्जलमध्यान्महोन्नतः ॥ 29

नानामणिमयैः शृङ्गैस्तस्योपरि नराकृतिः । प्राह यान्तं हनूमन्तं मैनाकोऽहं महाकपे ॥ 30

made his form double that size. **20.** Surasa now stood with a mouth twenty Yojanas wide, whereupon Hanuman assumed a size of thirty Yojanas. **(21-22).** Surasa, now increased the extent of her open mouth to fifty Yojanas. Hanuman immediately reduced himself to the size of a thumb, entered her mouth, came out and addressed her, saying, "I have now entered into your mouth and come out of it, as wanted by you. Salutation to you, O Mother!"

(23-25). Seeing Hanuman before her and hearing these words of his, Surasa said to him: "O thou the wisest among intelligent personages! Now proceed and accomplish the mission on which Rama has sent you. I have been sent here by the Devas to test your strength. You will be able to see Sita and report to Rama about it." With these words, she went away to her heavenly abode. Next Hanuman, the son of the Wind-god, traversed through the atmosphere like Garuda.

Mainaka Episode (26-33)

(26-28). Now the Sea-god said to Mount Mainaka which had huge deposits of gold and precious gems: "Powerful Hanuman, the son of the Wind-god, is going for fulfilling the objectives of Rama. You must go and do some service to him. I have got the name of Sagara, because the sons of King Sagara augmented my extent. The noble Lord Rama, the son of Dasaratha, is one born in the line of that King Sagara. Now this great monkey is on an errand for the achievement of some purpose of Rama. **29.** You raise yourself to the water surface soon. Let Hanuman rest on you for a while and then proceed." That mountain of enormous size agreed to this proposal and rose above the water surface.

समुद्रेण समादिष्टस्त्वद्विश्रामाय मारुते । आगच्छामृतकल्पानि जग्ध्वा पक्वफलानि मे ॥
विश्रम्यात्र क्षणं पश्चाद्गमिष्यसि यथासुखम् । एवमुक्तोऽथ तं प्राह हनूमान्मारुतात्मजः ॥ 32
गच्छतो रामकार्यार्थं भक्षणं मे कथं भवेत् । विश्रामो वा कथं मे स्याद् गन्तव्यं त्वरितं मया ॥33
इत्युक्त्वा स्पृष्टशिखरः कराग्रेण ययौ कपिः ॥ 34
किञ्चिद्दूरं गतस्यास्य छायां छायाग्रहोऽग्रहीत् ।
सिंहिका नाम सा घोरा जलमध्ये स्थिता सदा । आकाशगामिनां छायामाक्रम्याकृष्य भक्षयेत् ॥35
तथा गृहीतो हनुमांश्चिन्तयामास वीर्यवान् । केनेदं मे कृतं वेगरोधनं विघ्नकारिणा ॥ 36
दृश्यते नैव कोऽप्यत्र विस्मयो मे प्रजायते । एवं विचिन्त्य हनुमानधो दृष्टिं प्रसारयत् ॥ 37
तत्र दृष्ट्वा महाकायां सिंहिकां घोररूपिणीम् । पपात सलिले तूर्णं पद्भ्यामेवाहनद्रुषा ॥ 38
पुनरुत्प्लुत्य हनुमान्दक्षिणाभिमुखो ययौ । ततो दक्षिणमासाद्य कूलं नानाफलद्रुमम् ॥ 39
नानापक्षिमृगाकीर्णं नानापुष्पलतावृतम् । ततो ददर्श नगरं त्रिकूटाचलमूर्धनि ॥ 40

(30-32). Towering over its many peaks with quarries of precious stones, the mountain appeared in a human form and said to Hanuman who was on his onward journey: "O noble monkey! I am Mount Mainaka. I have been sent here by the ocean for affording you some rest on your way. Descend on me and after assuaging your hunger with the nectarine fruits growing on me and taking rest for a while on my surface, you can proceed further at your ease." To him who spoke thiswise, Hanuman replied as follows: **33.** "For me who am going on Rama's errand, where is the need for food, where is the need for rest? My foremost duty is to proceed as quickly as possible without any delay. With these words he just touched the peak of the mountain with his hands, and proceeded towards Lanka.

Simhika Episode (34-42)

(34-35). When he had covered a little distance after this incident, he was held up by a fierce demoness called Simhika, who, stationing herself amidst the waters, had the power to grip anything by catching its shadow. **(36-37).** Being caught by her, Hanuman of great prowess thought: "Who or what is this obstructing cause, curbing my speed? I do not see any one before me. It is very puzzling indeed!" Revolving in this way in his mind, Hanuman looked down. **38.** Thereupon he saw the mighty and terrific form of Simihika. Immediately he swooped down to the surface of the sea in great anger, and killed that demoness with a kick of his feet.

(39-40). After that Hanuman rose up into the sky again and directed his course to the south. Soon he sighted the southern shore of the ocean full of many fruit-bearing trees, covered everywhere with creepers with luxuriant growth of flowers, and populated by various kinds of birds and beasts. He also saw the Trikuta mountain

प्रकारैर्बहुभिर्युक्तं परिखाभिश्च सर्वतः । प्रवेक्ष्यामि कथं लङ्कामिति चिन्तापरोऽभवत् ॥ 41
रात्रौ वेक्ष्यामि सूक्ष्मोऽहं लंकां रावणपालिताम् । एवं विचिन्त्य तत्रैव स्थित्वा लंकां जगाम सः ॥42
धृत्वा सूक्ष्मं वपुर्द्वारं प्रविवेश प्रतापवान् । तत्र लङ्कापुरी साक्षाद्राक्षसीवेषधारिणी ॥ 43
प्रविशन्तं हनूमन्तं दृष्ट्वा लंङ्का व्यतर्जयत् । कस्त्वं वानररूपेण मामनादृत्य लङ्किनीम् ॥ 44
प्रविश्य चोरवद्रात्रौ किं भवान्कर्तुमिच्छति । इत्युक्त्वा रोषताम्राक्षी पादेनाभिजघान तम् ॥ 45
हनुमानपि तां वाममुष्टिनावज्ञयाहनत् । तदैव पतिता भूमौ रक्तमुद्वमती भृशम् ॥ 46
उत्थाय प्राह सा लङ्का हनुमन्तं महाबलम् । हनूमन् गच्छ भद्रं ते जिता लङ्का त्वयानघ ॥47
पुराहं ब्रह्मणा प्रोक्ता ह्यष्टाविंशतिपर्यये । त्रेतायुगे दाशरथी रामो नारायणोऽव्ययः ॥ 48
जनिष्यते योगमाया सीता जनकवेश्मनि । भूभारहरणार्थाय प्रार्थितोऽयं मया क्वचित् ॥ 49
सभार्यो राघवो भ्रात्रा गमिष्यति महावनम् । तत्र सीतां महामायां रावणोऽपहरिष्यति ॥ 50
पश्चाद्रामेण साचिव्यं सुग्रीवस्य भविष्यति । सुग्रीवो जानकीं द्रष्टुं वानरान्प्रेषयिष्यति ॥ 51

on the top of which was situated the city of Lanka. **41.** He found that Lanka was surrounded by several high walls, one behind another and separated by extensive moats. He now began to think how he would enter such a well-protected city. He thought: **42.** "At night, assuming a very small body, I shall enter Lanka protected by Ravana." Deciding so, he remained there till nightfall and then entered Lanka.

Confrontation with Lanka-Sri (43-58)

(43-45). Making his body very small, Hanuman now entered the city through its gate, where stood Lanka-Lakshmi, the spirit of Lanka, guarding the city in the form of a fierce Rakshasa woman. Seeing Hanuman entering the city, she challenged him, saying: "Who are you entering Lanka at night like a thief in the form of a monkey, without caring for me. Pray, what is your business here?" Saying so, with eyes reddened by anger, she gave a kick to Hanuman. **46.** Hanuman, treating her as an insignificant opponent, delivered a punch on her with his left fist. Immediately she fell on the ground vomiting a large quantity of blood. **47.** Lanka-Lakshmi soon stood up and said to that powerful Hanuman: "O Hanuman! Go in. Good fortune will attend you. O faultless one! Lanka has already been conquered by you. **(48-49).** In times gone by, Brahma told me the following: 'In the twentyeighth Tretāyuga of this cycle of time, Narayana, the Eternal Being, will incarnate Himself as Rama, the son of King Dasaratha, and His Yoga-maya will embody Herself as Sita in the house of Janaka. This is in consequence of my prayer to the Lord for relieving the earth of her burdens. **50.** Rama with his wife and his brother will go to reside in the great forest of Dandaka. Then Ravana will abduct Sita, who is none but Mahamaya. **51.** Subsequently, Rama will enter into an alliance with the monkey king Sugreeva, who will depute his monkey followers

तत्रैको वानरो रात्रावागमिष्यति तेऽन्तिकम् । त्वया च भर्त्सितः सोऽपि त्वां हनिष्यति मुष्टिना ॥
तेनाहता त्वं व्यथिता भविष्यसि यदानघे । तदैव रावणस्यान्तो भविष्यति न संशयः ॥ 53
तस्मात्त्वया जिता लङ्का जितं सर्वं त्वयानघ । रावणान्तःपुरवरे क्रीडाकाननमुत्तमम् ॥ 54
तन्मध्येऽशोकवनिक दिव्यपादपसङ्कुला । अस्ति तस्यां महावृक्षः शिंशपानाम मध्यगः ॥ 55
तत्रास्ते जानकी घोरराक्षसीभिः सुरक्षिता । दृष्ट्वा गच्छ त्वरितं राघवाय निवेदय ॥ 56

धन्याहमप्यद्य चिराय राघवस्मृतिर्ममासीद्भवपाशमोचिनी ।
तद्भक्तसङ्गोऽप्यतिदुर्लभो मम प्रसीदतां दाशरथिः सदा हृदि ॥ 57
उल्लङ्घितेऽब्धौ पवनात्मजेन धरासुतायाश्च दशाननस्य ।
पुस्फोर वामाक्षि भुजश्च तीव्रं रामस्यदक्षाङ्गमतीन्द्रियस्य ॥ 58

इति श्रीमदध्यात्मरामायणे उमामहेश्वरसंवादे
सुन्दरकाण्डे प्रथमः सर्गः ॥ १ ॥

to find out the whereabouts of Sita. **52.** From among them one monkey will come near you at night. Being challenged by you, he will strike you with his fist. **53.** When you suffer injury from his blow, know for certain that the end of Ravana would be near at hand.' **(54-56).** Therefore I deem that you have already conquered Lanka, O noble one! You have subdued every one and everything here. In the women's quarters of Ravana, there is a fine woody grove for sport and relaxation. In the middle of it there is a grove full of a very rare type of trees called Ashoka. In the centre of it stands a huge Simsapa tree. Sita, the daughter of Janaka, is confined there, securely protected by a guard of fearsome Rakshasa women. Meeting her, you return soon and convey the news to Rama. **57.** For long have I been entertaining in my mind the thought of Rama which liberates one from the bondage of Samsara. Today I am indeed fortunate to have association with a devotee of his, which is ordinarily very difficult to get. May the Lord Rama ever dwell in my heart." **58.** When Hanuman, the son of the Wind-god, crossed the ocean, both Sita and Ravana got pronounced quivering of the left eye and arm, while for Rama, who transcends the senses, this happened on his right side.

द्वितीयः सर्गः

श्रीमहादेव उवाच

ततो जगाम हनुमान् लङ्कां परमशोभनाम्। रात्रौ सूक्ष्मतनुर्भूत्वा बभ्राम परितः पुरीम् ॥ 1
सीतान्वेषणकार्यार्थी प्रविवेश नृपालयम्। तत्र सर्वप्रदेशेषु विविच्य हनुमान्कपिः ॥ 2
नापश्यज्जानकीं स्मृत्वा ततो लङ्काभिभाषितम्। जगाम हनुमान् शीघ्रमशोकवनिकां शुभाम् ॥ 3
सुरपादपसम्बाधां रत्नसोपानवापिकाम्। नानापक्षिमृगाकीर्णां स्वर्णप्रासादशोभिताम्॥ 4
फलैरानम्रशाखाग्रपादपैः परिवारिताम्। विचिन्वन् जानकीं तत्र प्रतिवृक्षं मरुत्सुतः ॥ 5
ददर्शाभ्रंलिहं तत्र चैत्यप्रासादमुत्तमम्। दृष्ट्वा विस्मयमापन्नो मणिस्तम्भशतान्वितम् ॥ 6
समतीत्य पुनर्गत्वा किञ्चिद्दूरं स मारुतिः। ददर्श शिंशपावृक्षमत्यन्तनिबिडच्छदम् ॥ 7
अदृष्टातपमाकीर्णं स्वर्णवर्णविहङ्गमम्। तन्मूले राक्षसीमध्ये स्थितां जनकनन्दिनीम् ॥ 8
ददर्श हनुमान् वीरो देवतामिव भूतले। एकवेणीं कृशां दीनां मलिनाम्बरधारिणीम् ॥ 9
भूमौ शयानां शोचन्तीं रामरामेतिभाषिणीम्। त्रातारंनाधिगच्छन्तीमुपवासकृशां शुभाम् ॥ 10

Chapter 2

HANUMAN'S SEARCH

Hanuman sees Sita (1-12)

1. Assuming a form of small size, Hanuman entered resplendent Lanka and walked through all parts of the city. **(2-3).** Engaged in the search for Sita, he entered the residential quarters of Ravana and searched everywhere there, but could not discover Sita in any place. Now remembering the words of Lanka-Sri, he directed his search towards the Ashoka grove. **(4-6).** That Ashoka grove into which Hanuman entered had in it a dense growth of heavenly trees, with tanks here and there having steps studded with precious gems. There many types of birds and animals were moving about amidst trees whose branches were touching the earth with the weight of fruits on them. Here and there, were terraced buildings shining like gold. The son of the Wind-god searched for Sita under every tree there but could not find her. Then he came to a towering building on a mount so high, that it looked as if it touched the sky. He was astonished to see the numerous pillars of precious stones in that edifice. **(7-10).** As he proceeded some distance further from it, he came across a Simsapa tree having so dense a foliage that it gave complete shelter from the sun. Its branches spread extensively, and there were many birds of golden colour perching on them. Underneath that tree, amidst a guard of Rakshasa women, he found Sita, the daughter of Janaka, who looked like a goddess on earth. Her locks were unbraided and her body had become extremely lean and weak. Dressed with a much

शाखान्तच्छदमध्यस्थो ददर्श कपिकुञ्जरः । कृतार्थोऽहं कृतार्थोऽहं दृष्ट्वा जनकनन्दिनीम् ॥11
मयैव साधितं कार्यं रामस्य परमात्मनः ॥ 12
ततः किलकिलाशब्दो बभूवान्तःपुराद्बहिः ।
किमेतदिति सँल्लीनो वृक्षपत्रेषु मारुतिः । आयान्तं रावणं तत्र स्त्रीजनैः परिवारितम् ॥ 13
दशास्यं विंशतिभुजं नीलाञ्जनचयोपमम् । दृष्ट्वा विस्मयमापन्नः पत्रखण्डेष्वलीयत ॥ 14
रावणो राघवेणाशु मरणं मे कथं भवेत् । सीतार्थमपि नायाति रामः किं कारणं भवेत् ॥15
इत्येवं चिन्तयन्नित्यं राममेव सदा हृदि । तस्मिन्दिनेऽपररात्रौ रावणो राक्षसाधिपः ॥ 16
स्वप्ने रामेण सन्दिष्टः कश्चिदागत्य वानरः । कामरूपधरः सूक्ष्मो वृक्षाग्रस्थोऽनुपश्यति ॥ 17
इति दृष्ट्वाद्भुतं स्वप्नं स्वात्मन्येवानुचिन्त्य सः । स्वप्नः कदाचित्सत्यः स्यादेवं तत्र करोम्यहम् ॥ 18
जानकीं वाक्शरैर्विद्ध्वा दुःखितां नितरामहम् । करोमि दृष्ट्वा रामाय निवेदयतु वानरः ॥ 19
इत्येवं चिन्तयन्सीतासमीपमगमद्द्रुतम् ॥ 20
नूपुराणां किङ्किणीनां श्रुत्वा शिञ्जितमङ्गना ।
सीता भीता लीयमाना स्वात्मन्येव सुमध्यमा । अधोमुख्यश्रुनयना स्थिता रामार्पितान्तरा ॥ 21

soiled cloth, she was lying on the bare ground, extremely sorrow-stricken and crying, 'Rama, Rama' from time to time. Though she had every auspicious physical feature, she had become very lean by fasting and by the failure to find any way of being rescued from her plight. **(11-12)** Seated behind the shelter of the leaves of the Simsapa tree, that great monkey saw Sita and said within himself, "O I have achieved my purpose! I have achieved my purpose! I have accomplished the errand on which the Supreme Being, Rama, has sent me."

Ravana courting Sita (13-43)

(13-14). Now from outside the women's quarters of Ravana, Hanuman heard some jingling sounds, and wondering what it might be, he looked in that direction from his sheltered position amidst the leaves of the tree. To his great astonishment, he saw Ravana coming, surrounded by a bevy of women. Possessed of ten heads and twenty arms, he looked like a mountain of antimony.

(15-20). Meantime, Ravana had all along been thinking, "What could hasten my death at the hands of Rama? I do not find Rama as yet coming in quest of Sita. Why is it so?" Thinking thus always about Rama, Ravana had a dream the previous night. He saw in the dream that a monkey deputed by Rama, and capable of taking any form, had come assuming a very small form, and was watching from the top of the trees. Experiencing this wonderful dream, Ravana thought within himself: "Dreams sometime come true. So let me decide to do like this: I shall wound the feelings of Sita by harsh words and make her extremely sorrow-stricken. Let the monkey see it and report it to Rama." It was while thinking this way after he had this dream experience that he started to the place where Sita was confined.

21. Hearing the tinkling sound of anklets

रावणोऽपि तदा सीतामालोक्याह सुमध्यमे । मां दृष्ट्वा किं वृथा सुभ्रु स्वात्मन्येव विलीयसे ॥
रामो वनचराणां हि मध्ये तिष्ठति सानुजः । कदाचिद्दृश्यते कैश्चित्कदाचिन्नैव दृश्यते ॥ 23
मया तु बहुधा लोकाः प्रेषितास्तस्य दर्शने । न पश्यन्ति प्रयत्नेन वीक्षमाणाः समन्ततः ॥ 24
किं करिष्यसि रामेण निःस्पृहेण सदा त्वयि । त्वया सदालिङ्गितोऽपि समीपस्थोऽपि सर्वदा ॥ 25
हृदयेऽस्य न च स्नेहस्त्वयि रामस्य जायते । त्वत्कृतान्सर्वभोगांश्च त्वद्गुणानपि राघव ॥ 26
भुञ्जानोऽपि न जानाति कृतघ्नो निर्गुणोऽधमः । त्वमानीता मया साध्वी दुःखशोकसमाकुला ॥ 27
इदानीमपि नायाति भक्तिहीनः कथं व्रजेत् । निःसत्त्वो निर्ममो मानी मूढः पण्डितमानवान् ॥ 28
नराधमं त्वद्विमुखं किं करिष्यसि भामिनि । त्वय्यतीव समासक्तं मां भजस्वासुरोत्तमम् ॥ 29
देवगन्धर्वनागानां यक्षकिन्नरयोषिताम् । भविष्यसि नियोक्त्री त्वं यदि मां प्रतिपद्यसे ॥30
रावणस्य वचः श्रुत्वा सीतामर्षसमन्विता । उवाचाधोमुखी भूत्वा निधाय तृणमन्तरे ॥ 31
राघवाद्बिभ्यता नूनं भिक्षुरूपं त्वया धृतम् । रहिते राघवाभ्यां त्वं शुनीव हविरध्वरे ॥ 32

and **tiny** bells, Sita knew that Ravana was approaching, and she shrank into herself out of fear. That handsome lady now shed tears and kept gazing downwards, with her mind fully concentrated on Rama. **(22-29).** Now, seeing Sita in this condition, Ravana said to her, "O handsome lady! Why are you shrinking into yourself out of fear on seeing me? Rama, along with his brother Lakshmana, is living amidst forest tribes. He may be seen sometimes and sometimes not. I sent many spies to spot him. In spite of vigorous search everywhere they could not find him. What will you do with this Rama who does not seem to have any desire for you? You may always sit by his side embracing him; this Rama will never have any longing for you even then. All the delights that you can give him and all your excellences are known to him by experience, but still he has no feeling for you. He is a fool without any excellence. He is also thankless, O virtuous woman. I have carried you away into my abode and you are stricken with extreme grief because of it. Still he has not come to rescue you. Why do you then think of a man who has no love for you? He is without strength, self-respect and a sense of duty to his own people. Though an ignorant fool, he thinks of himself as a great scholar. O great beauty! What are you going to achieve by thinking of this low type of a man who has no inclination towards you? And in contrast, here am I, the greatest among Rakshasas, extremely infatuated with you. Why should you not then accept my advances? **30.** If you accept me, you will become the mistress of the women of various species of beings like Devas, Gandharvas, Nagas, Yakshas and Kinnaras."

31. Angry at these words of Ravana, Sita put a blade of grass between him and herself, and began to speak with downcast eyes: **(32-36).** "Out of fear for Rama you

हृतवानसि मां नीच तत्फलं प्राप्स्यसेऽचिरात् । यदा रामशराघातविदारितवपुर्भवान् ॥ 33
ज्ञास्यसेऽमानुषं रामं गमिष्यसि यमान्तिकम् । समुद्रं शोषयित्वा वा शरैर्बद्ध्वाथ वारिधिम् ॥ 34
हन्तुं त्वां समरे रामो लक्ष्मणेन समन्वितः । आगमिष्यत्यसन्देहो द्रक्ष्यसे राक्षसाधम ॥ 35
त्वां सपुत्रं सहबलं हत्वा नेष्यति मां पुरम् । 36
श्रुत्वा रक्षःपतिः क्रुद्धो जानक्याः परुषाक्षरम् ।
वाक्यं क्रोधसमाविष्टः खड्गमुद्यम्य सत्वरः । हन्तुं जनकराजस्य तनयां ताम्रलोचनः ॥ 37
मन्दोदरी निवार्याह पतिं पतिहिते रता । त्यजैनां मानुषीं दीनां दुःखितां कृपणां कृशाम् ॥
देवगन्धर्वनागानां बह्व्यः सन्ति वराङ्गनाः । त्वामेव वरयन्त्युच्चैर्मदमत्तविलोचनाः ॥ 39
ततोऽब्रवीद्दशग्रीवो राक्षसीर्विकृताननाः ।
यथा मे वशगा सीता भविष्यति सकामना । तथा यतध्वं त्वरितं तर्जनादरणादिभिः ॥ 40
द्विमासाभ्यन्तरे सीता यदि मे वशगा भवेत् । तदा सर्वसुखोपेता राज्यं भोक्ष्यति सा मया ॥ 41
यदि मासद्वयादूर्ध्वं मच्छय्यां नाभिनन्दति । तदा मे प्रातराशाय हत्वा कुरुत मानुषीम् ॥ 42
इत्युक्त्वा प्रययौ स्त्रीभी रावणोऽन्तःपुरालयम् ॥ 43
राक्षस्यो जानकीमेत्य भीषयन्त्यः स्वतर्जनैः ।

put on the disguise of an ascetic, and when Rama and Lakshmana were out, you carried me away, O low born one! as a bitch knocks away some sacrificial offering. Soon, you shall reap the consequences of it, when your body will be rent asunder by Rama's arrows. You think of Rama as a mere man. You will understand the folly of it when you are soon despatched to the realm of Yama. Either by drying up the ocean or by bridging it by his arrows, Rama will come here with Lakshmana to destroy you. There is no doubt about it. O despicable Rakshasa! You will soon see how Rama destroys you along with all your sons and army, and takes me back to his city."

37. The stinging words of Sita roused the wrath of that King of the Rakshasas, and moved by extreme anger indicated by his reddened eyes he lifted his sword and approached to strike at Sita. **38.** But Mandodari, Ravana's wife, came between them and restrained him from his rash act, saying, "Leave off this human female who is griefstricken and famished. **39.** You have got innumerable handsome women of Devas, Gandharvas and Nagas. They are always looking at you with love-lorn eyes." **40.** Ravana then turned towards the Rakshasi guards of distorted faces and said to them: "Deal with this woman sternly by threats or kind persuasion in such a way that she is attracted to me and comes under my control. **41.** If she comes under my control within two months, she will, along with me, have every kind of enjoyment available in this country. **(42-43).** If within two months, she does not agree to be my wife, you kill this human female and give her

तत्रैका जानकीमाह यौवनं ते वृथा गतम् । रावणेन समासाद्य सफलं तु भविष्यति ॥ 44

अपरा चाह कोपेन किं विलम्बेन जानकि । इदानीं छेद्यतामङ्गं विभज्य च पृथक्पृथक् ॥ 45

अन्या तु खड्गमुद्यम्य जानकीं हन्तुमुद्यता । अन्या करालवदना विदार्यास्यमभीषयत् ॥ 46

एवं तां भीषयन्तीस्ता राक्षसीर्विकृताननाः । निवार्य त्रिजटा वृद्धा राक्षसी वाक्यमब्रवीत् ॥ 47

शृणुध्वं दुष्टराक्षस्यो मद्वाक्यं वो हितं भवेत् ॥ 48

न भीषयध्वं रुदतीं नमस्कुरुत जानकीम् । इदानीमेव मे स्वप्ने रामः कमललोचनः ॥ 49

आरुह्यैरावतं शुभ्रं लक्ष्मणेन समागतः । दग्ध्वा लङ्कापुरीं सर्वां हत्वा रावणमाहवे ॥ 50

आरोप्य जानकीं स्वाङ्के स्थितो दृष्टोऽगमूर्धनि । रावणो गोमयह्रदे तैलाभ्यक्तो दिगम्बरः ॥ 51

अगाहत्पुत्रपौत्रैश्च कृत्वा वदनमालिकाम् । विभीषणस्तु रामस्य सन्निधौ हृष्टमानसः ॥ 52

सेवां करोति रामस्य पादयोर्भक्तिसंयुतः । सर्वथा रावणं रामो हत्वा सकुलमञ्जसा ॥ 53

विभीषणायाधिपत्यं दत्त्वा सीतां शुभाननाम् । अङ्के निधाय स्वपुरीं गमिष्यति न संशयः ॥ 54

त्रिजटाया वचः श्रुत्वा भीतास्ता राक्षसस्त्रियः । तूष्णीमासंस्तत्र तत्र निद्रावशमुपागताः ॥ 55

flesh for my breakfast." Ordering in this way, Ravana went back to his inner apartments along with all his female retinue.

Rakshasis' Threats and Trijata's Dream (44-55)

44. Immediately, the Rakshasa women began to terrify Sita with harsh words. One of them said to her, "Your youth is ebbing away without serving any purpose. If you live with Ravana, it will become fruitful." **45.** Another said in an angry mood, "O Janaki why do you delay? Let us even now sever her limbs and cut them to pieces." **46.** Another Rakshasa woman now raised her sword as if to kill Sita. Still another, having a terrific face, tried to frighten Sita by opening her formidable mouth. **47.** But an elderly Rakshasa woman named Trijata restrained the others from frightening Sita and said, **48.** "O cruel women! Hear my words for your own good. **(49-54).** Do not frighten the weeping Sita. On the other hand, you prostrate before her. I have just now had a dream, which is as follows: The lotus-eyed Rama along with Lakshmana had burnt the whole of Lanka and killed Ravana in battle. Then he was seated at the top of the mountain with Sita on his lap. On the other hand, I saw Ravana naked and smeared all over with oil. Holding in his hand a garland made of his own heads, he was entering into a deep pit of dung along with all his sons and grandsons. Vibhishana, I saw on the contrary prostrating at Rama's feet with great devotion and doing service to Rama. Soon Rama will destroy Ravana with all his tribe and install Vibhishana as a ruler and will go back to his city carrying Sita with him. This is certainly going to happen." **55.** Hearing these words of Trijata, the frightened Rakshasa women became silent and began to sleep lying here and there.

तर्जिता राक्षसीभिः सा सीता भीतातिविह्वला । त्रातारं नाधिगच्छन्ती दुःखेन परिमूर्च्छिता ॥ 56
अश्रुभिः पूर्णनयना चिन्तयन्तीदमब्रवीत् ।
प्रभाते भक्षयिष्यन्ति राक्षस्यो मां न संशयः । इदानीमेव मरणं केनोपायेन मे भवेत् ॥ 57
एवं सुदुःखेन परिप्लुता सा विमुक्तकण्ठं रुदती चिराय ।
आलम्ब्य शाखां कृतनिश्चया मृतौ न जानती कञ्चिदुपायमङ्गना ॥ 58

इति श्रीमदध्यात्मरामायणे उमामहेश्वरसंवादे
सुन्दरकाण्डे द्वितीयः सर्गः ॥ २ ॥

Sita in a desperate mood (56-58)

t56-57). Thus addressed by the Rakshasis, Sita broke down with fear, as she found none to protect her. Reduced to a mood of extreme grief, she began to reflect with tears flowing down from her eyes, and said, "These Rakshasis will eat me up in the morning. There is no doubt about it. So is there any way by which I can die even now?" **58.** Thus steeped in grief and weeping aloud, Sita, failing to see any way out, decided to kill herself and remained there for some time, holding a branch of the tree.

तृतीयः सर्गः

श्रीमहादेव उवाच

उद्बन्धनेन वा मोक्ष्ये शरीरं राघवं विना । जीवितेन फलं किं स्यान्मम रक्षोऽधिमध्यतः ॥ 1
दीर्घा वेणी ममात्यर्थमुद्बन्धाय भविष्यति । एवं निश्चितबुद्धिं तां मरणायाथ जानकीम् ॥ 2
विलोक्य हनुमान्किञ्चिद्विचार्यैतदभाषत । शनैः शनैः सूक्ष्मरूपो जानक्याः श्रोत्रगं वचः ॥ 3

Chapter 3

HANUMAN DELIVERING RAMA'S MESSAGE TO SITA

Hanuman's stratagem to draw Sita's attention (1-19)

1. Sita thought within herself: "I shall free myself from this body that is separated from Rama, by hanging myself. What is the good of living in the midst of these Rakshasa women? My locks are pretty long and are enough to put a knot on my neck." **(2-3).** Hanuman saw Sita, the daughter of Janaka, in this condition, determined to kill herself. He thought for a while and then adopting a small form spoke

इक्ष्वाकुवंशसम्भूतो राजा दशरथो महान् । अयोध्याधिपतिस्तस्य चत्वारो लोकविश्रुताः ॥ 4
पुत्रा देवसमाः सर्वे लक्षणैरुपलक्षिताः । रामश्च लक्ष्मणश्चैव भरतश्चैव शत्रुहा ॥ 5
ज्येष्ठो रामः पितुर्वाक्याद्दण्डकारण्यमागतः । लक्ष्मणेन सह भ्रात्रा सीतया भार्यया सह ॥ 6
उवास गौतमीतीरे पञ्चवट्यां महामनाः । तत्र नीता महाभागा सीता जनकनन्दिनी ॥ 7
रहिते रामचन्द्रेण रावणेन दुरात्मना । ततो रामोऽतिदुःखार्तो मार्गमाणोऽथ जानकीम् ॥ 8
जटायुषं पक्षिराजमपश्यत्पतितं भुवि । तस्मै दत्त्वा दिवं शीघ्रमृष्यमूकमुपागमत ॥ 9
सुग्रीवेण कृता मैत्री रामस्य विदितात्मनः । तद्भार्याहारिणं हत्वा वालिनं रघुनन्दनः ॥ 10
राज्येऽभिषिच्य सुग्रीवं मित्रकार्यं चकार सः । सुग्रीवस्तु समानाय्य वानरान्वानरप्रभुः ॥ 11
प्रेषयामास परितो वानरान्परिमार्गणे । सीतायास्तत्र चैकोऽहं सुग्रीवसचिवो हरिः ॥ 12
सम्पातिवचनाच्छीघ्रमुल्लङ्घ्य शतयोजनम् । समुद्रं नगरीं लङ्कां विचिन्वञ्जानकीं शुभाम् ॥ 13
शनैरशोकवनिकां विचिन्वन् शिंशपातरुम् । अद्राक्षं जानकीमत्र शोचन्तीं दुःखसम्प्लुताम् ॥ 14
रामस्य महिषीं देवीं कृतकृत्योऽहमागतः । इत्युक्त्वोपररामाथ मारुतिर्बुद्धिमत्तरः । 15
सीता क्रमेण तत्सर्वं श्रुत्वा विस्मयमाययौ । किमिदं मे श्रुतं व्योम्नि वायुना समुदीरितम् ॥ 16

the following words just loud enough to reach the ears of Sita. **(4-15).** He said, "In the line of Ikshvakus, there was a great king called Dasaratha ruling over Ayodhya. He has four famous sons equal to divinities, possessed of all auspicious signs and qualities. Their names are Rama, Lakshmana, Bharata and Satrughna. Of them the eldest brother, in compliance with his father's order, had come to reside in the forest of Dandaka accompanied by his brother Lakshmana and wife Sita. They were staying at Panchavati on the banks of the Godavari. When Rama was away from his abode, the wicked Ravana abducted his wife, the worshipful Sita. Extremely sorrow-stricken by this, Rama instituted a search for Sita and in the course of it came across the kingly vulture Jatayu lying fallen on the ground. Sending him to the heavenly realm, Rama soon reached the Rishyamuka mountain. There Sugreeva entered into an alliance with the high-souled Rama. Rama helped his ally Sugreeva by destroying Vali who had deprived Sugreeva of his wife, and afterwards installing Sugreeva as the king. Now King Sugreeva gathered together his monkey followers and sent them to search for Sita. Myself, one of them, who is a minister of Sugreeva, has, as directed by the vulture named Sampati, managed to cross over the ocean a hundred Yojanas wide and reach the city of Lanka. Searching here slowly every where, I have come to the Asoka grove and therein the Simsapa tree. Here I see Rama's consort Sita sitting immersed in sorrow. Having come here I have accomplished my mission." Saying this much, the intelligent Hanuman resumed silence.

(16-19). Sita listened to the whole narrative step by step with great astonish-

स्वप्नो वा मे मनोभ्रान्तिर्यदि वा सत्यमेव तत् । निद्रा मे नास्ति दुःखेन जानाम्येतत्कुतो भ्रमः ॥ 17
येन मे कर्णपीयूषं वचनं समुदीरितम् । स दृश्यतां महाभागः प्रियवादी ममाग्रतः ॥ 18
श्रुत्वा तज्जानकीवाक्यं हनुमान्पत्रखण्डतः । अवतीर्य शनैः सीतापुरतः समवस्थितः ॥ 19
कलविङ्कप्रमाणाङ्गो रक्तास्यः पीतवानरः । ननाम शनकैः सीतां प्राञ्जलिः पुरतः स्थितः ॥ 20
दृष्ट्वा तं जानकी भीता रावणोऽयमुपागतः । मां मोहयितुमायातो मायया वानराकृतिः ॥ 21
इत्येवं चिन्तयित्वा सा तूष्णीमासीदधोमुखी ॥ 22
पुनरप्याह तां सीतां देवि यत्त्वं विशङ्कसे ।
नाहं तथाविधो मातस्त्यज शङ्कां मयि स्थिताम् । दासोऽहं कोसलेन्द्रस्य रामस्य परमात्मनः ॥ 23
सचिवोऽहं हरीन्द्रस्य सुग्रीवस्य शुभप्रदे । वायोः पुत्रोऽहमखिलप्राणभूतस्य शोभने ॥ 24
तच्छ्रुत्वा जानकी प्राह हनूमन्तं कृताञ्जलिम् । वानराणां मनुष्याणां सङ्गतिर्घटते कथम् ॥ 25
यथा त्वं रामचन्द्रस्य दासोऽहमिति भाषसे । तामाह मारुतिः प्रीतो जानकीं पुरतः स्थितः ॥ 26
ऋष्यमूकमगाद्रामः शबर्या नोदितः सुधीः । सुग्रीवो ऋष्यमूकस्थो दृष्टवान् रामलक्ष्मणौ ॥ 27
भीतो मां प्रेषयामास ज्ञातुं रामस्य हृद्गतम् । ब्रह्मचारिवपुर्धृत्वा गतोऽहं रामसन्निधिम् ॥ 28
ज्ञात्वा रामस्य सद्भावं स्कन्धोपरि निधाय तौ । नीत्वा सुग्रीवसामीप्यं सख्यं चाकरवं तयोः ॥ 29

ment and entered into the following soliloquy: "What is it that I just now heard from the sky above! Is it the speech of the Wind-deity? Or is it a dream or a delusion of mine? Or is it a true experience? Grief has deprived me of sleep and therefore it cannot be a dream. And how can it be a delusion too? Let that great personage, who spoke these welcome words, which are like nectar to my ears, appear before me, if the words are factual." Hearing these words of Sita, Hanuman slowly emerged from the thick foliage of the trees and stood before her.

Hanuman's Conversation with Sita (20-36)

20. A monkey of the size of the bird called Kalavinga, yellow in colour but red in face, now came forward slowly, made prostration to Sita and stood before her. **(21-22).** On seeing him, Sita was at first frightened, thinking that Ravana, who was a master of the magical art, had again come disguised as a monkey to deceive her. So she sat there silently with downcast eyes. **(23-24).** Divining Sita's fear, Hanuman said again to Sita: "O divine lady! I am not at all what you suspect me to be. So please cast away all your suspicions about me. I am the servant of the Supreme Being incarnated as Rama, the King of Kosala. I am also the minister of Sugreeva the king of the monkeys. I am the offspring of Vayu, the Wind-deity, who is the Cosmic Prana of the universe."

(25-29). Hearing these words, Sita, the daughter of Janaka, asked Hanuman, who was standing before her with palms joined in salutation: "You say you are a servant of Sri Ramachandra. How has this kind of an alliance between men and monkeys

सुग्रीवस्य हृता भार्या वालिना तं रघूत्तमः । जघानैकेन बाणेन ततो राज्येऽभ्यषेचयत् ॥ 30
सुग्रीवं वानराणां स प्रेषयामास वानरान् । दिग्भ्यो महाबलान्वीरान् भवत्याः परिमार्गणे ॥ 31
गच्छन्तं राघवो दृष्ट्वा मामभाषत सादरम् । 32
त्वयि कार्यमशेषं मे स्थितं मारुतनन्दन । ब्रूहि मे कुशलं सर्वं सीतायै लक्ष्मणस्य च ॥ 33
अङ्गुलीयकमेतन्मे परिज्ञानार्थमुत्तमम् । सीतायै दीयतां साधु मन्नामाक्षरमुद्रितम् ॥ 34
इत्युक्त्वा प्रददौ मह्यं कराग्रादङ्गुलीयकम् । प्रयत्नेन मयानीतं देवि पश्याङ्गुलीयकम् ॥ 35
इत्युक्त्वा प्रददौ देव्यै मुद्रिकां मारुतात्मजः । नमस्कृत्य स्थितो दूराद्बद्धाञ्जलिपुटो हरिः ॥ 36
दृष्ट्वा सीता प्रमुदिता रामनामाङ्कितां तदा । मुद्रिकां शिरसा धृत्वा स्रवदानन्दनेत्रजा ॥ 37
कपे मे प्राणदाता त्वं बुद्धिमानसि राघवे । भक्तोऽसि प्रियकारी त्वं विश्वासोऽस्ति तवैव हि 38
नो चेन्मत्सन्निधिं चान्यं पुरुषं प्रेषयेत्कथम् । हनूमन्दृष्टमखिलं मम दुःखादिकं त्वया ॥ 39

come into existence? How is it believable?" Thereupon, Hanuman, the son of the Wind-deity, said to Sita, facing her: "The high-souled Rama, as directed by the ascetic woman Sabari, went to Mount Rishyamooka. Sugreeva, who had taken shelter on Rishyamooka, was frightened to see Rama and Lakshmana approaching and sent me to them to know their real intention. In the form of a Brahmacharin I approachedRama, and on becoming sure that his intentions were good, I took both the brothers on my shoulders to the presence of Sugreeva and arranged for an alliance between Rama and Sugreeva. **(30-32).** Sugreeva's wife had been forcibly taken away by Vali. That Vali, Sri Rama killed with a single arrow, and installed Sugreeva as the king of the monkeys. Sugreeva deputed very powerful monkeys to institute a search for your venerable self. When Rama saw me among the search party getting ready to start, he called me aside and spoke to me lovingly. **(33-34).** He said: 'O Hanuman, the son of the Wind-god! The success of this enterprise of mine depends entirely on you. Convey to Sita all news about the welfare of Lakshmana and myself. Here is my signet ring with my name engraved on it. Present it to Sita as a token for recognising you as a genuine messenger.' **(35-36).** With these words Rama took off the ring from his finger and handed it over to me. I have taken every care to preserve it and bring it with me. O high-souled lady! 'Here it is.' With these words Hanuman presented the ring to Sita, and then prostrating before her, withdrew a little and stood holding his joined palms on his head in salutation.

After the Presentation of the Signet Ring (37-51).

(37-44). Seeing the signet ring of Rama with his name engraved on it, Sita was overwhelmed with joy. With tears streaming down her face, she took the ring and placed it on her head in adoration.

सर्वं कथय रामाय यथा मे जायते दया । मासद्वयावधि प्राणाः स्थास्यन्ति मम सत्तम ॥40
नागमिष्यति चेद्रामो भक्षयिष्यति मां खलः । अतः शीघ्रं कपीन्द्रेण सुग्रीवेण समन्वितः ॥ 41
वानरानीकपैः सार्धं हत्वा रावणमाहवे । सपुत्रं सबलं रामो यदि मां मोचयेत्प्रभुः ॥ 42
तत्तस्य सदृशं वीर्यं वीर वर्णय वर्णितम् । यथा मां तारयेद्रामो हत्वा शीघ्रं दशाननम् ॥ 43
तथा यतस्व हनुमन्वाचा धर्ममवाप्नुहि । 44
हनूमानपि तामाह देवि दृष्टो यथा मया । रामः सलक्ष्मणः शीघ्रमागमिष्यति सायुधः ॥ 45
सुग्रीवेण ससैन्येन हत्वा दशमुखं बलात् । समानेष्यति देवि त्वामयोध्यां नात्र संशयः ॥46
तमाहजानकी रामः कथं वारिधिमाततम् । तीर्त्वा यास्यत्यमेयात्मा वानरानीकपैःसह ॥ 47
हनूमानाह मे स्कन्धवारुह्य पुरुषर्षभौ ।
आयास्यतः ससैन्यश्च सुग्रीवो वानरेश्वरः । विहायसा क्षणेनैव तीर्त्वा वारिधिमाततम् ॥ 48
निर्दहिष्यति रक्षौघांस्त्वत्कृते नात्र संशयः । अनुज्ञां देहि मे देवि गच्छामि त्वरयान्वितः ॥49
द्रष्टुं रामं सह भ्रात्रा त्वरयामि तवान्तिकम् । देवि किञ्चिदभिज्ञानं देहि मे येन राघवः ॥ 50
विश्वसेन्मां प्रयत्नेन ततो गन्ता समुत्सुकः ॥ 51

She then said, "O monkey! You are verily the saviour of my life. You are highly intelligent, whole-heartedly devoted to Rama and bent on doing what is pleasing to him. Rama must have reposed absolute confidence in you, for he would not have selected an unknown stranger as a messenger to me. O Hanuman! You have seen in what a miserable state I am. You report about all this to Rama in a way that will produce intense compassion in his mind. O noble one! I have now only two more months of life. If Rama does not come and rescue me within that time, this wicked fellow will eat me up. If within that time the lordly Rama comes over here with the monkey king Sugreeva and his monkey forces, and destroys Ravana with his whole family and army and releases me—then his heroic achievement will be a topic of naration and praise for generations to come. O hero! Report in such a way that he feels forced to kill Ravana at the earliest and rescue me. O Hanuman! Do your best to achieve this. Through your words you will then be achieving a great and righteous purpose."

(45-46). To this appeal of Sita, Hanuman replied: "O divine lady! Immediately I return and meet Rama and Lakshmana, they will come along with Sugreeva and his army, all fully equipped with weapons, and destroy Ravana and take you back to Ayodhya. There is no doubt about this."

47. On hearing this, Sita put him a question: "How will Rama the great cross the wide ocean with the generals of the monkey army and come to this place?"

(48-51). For clearing her doubt Hanuman replied: "Those two great men will arrive riding on my shoulders. Sugreeva with his monkey army will leap across the

ततः किञ्चिद्विचार्याथ सीता कमललोचना ।
विमुच्य केशपाशान्ते स्थितं चूडामणिं ददौ । अनेन विश्वसेद्रामस्त्वां कपीन्द्र सलक्ष्मणः ॥ 52
अभिज्ञानार्थमन्यच्च वदामि तव सुव्रत । चित्रकूटगिरौ पूर्वमेकदा रहसि स्थितः ॥ 53
मदङ्के शिर आधाय निद्राति रघुनन्दनः । ऐन्द्रः काकस्तदागत्य नखैस्तुण्डेन चासकृत् ॥ 54
मत्पादाङ्गुष्ठमारक्तं विददारामिषाशया । ततो रामः प्रबुद्ध्याथ दृष्ट्वा पादं कृतव्रणम् ॥
केन भद्रे कृतं चैतद्विप्रियं मे दुरात्मना । इत्युक्त्वा पुरतोऽपश्यद्वायसं मां पुनः पुनः ॥ 56
अभिद्रवन्तं रक्ताक्तनखतुण्डं चुकोप ह । तृणमेकमुपादाय दिव्यास्त्रेणाभियोज्य तत् ॥ 57
चिक्षेप लीलया रामो वायसोपरि तज्ज्वलत् । अभ्यद्रवद्वायसश्च भीतो लोकान् भ्रमन्पुनः ॥58
इन्द्रब्रह्मादिभिश्चापि न शक्यो रक्षितुं तदा । रामस्य पादयोरग्रेऽपतद्भीत्या दयानिधेः ॥ 59
शरणागतमालोक्य रामस्तमिदमब्रवीत् । अमोघमेतदस्त्रं मे दत्त्वैकाक्षमितो व्रज ॥ 60
सव्यं दत्त्वा गतः काक एवं पौरुषवानपि । उपेक्षते किमर्थं मामिदानीं सोऽपि राघवः ॥ 61

ocean through the sky. Crossing the ocean in this way, they will, for your sake, reduce the whole of this tribe of Rakshasas to ashes. Please have no doubt about this. Now, O great lady, give me permission to return. It is necessary that I return very soon, so that I may meet the two brothers, come back here fetching them, and meet you again at the earliest opportunity. Now give me some thing as a token that will be recognised by Rama and will make him convinced that I have actually seen you. Rama will then come here soon in high spirits fully prepared."

Sita Gives the Crest-jewel and Narrates the Crow Incident (52-88)

52. Sita, the lotus-eyed, then thought for a while, and taking from within her locks a crest-jewel handed it over to Hanuman saying, "O noble monkey! This will enable Rama along with Lakshmana to accept the veracity of your report. **(53-61).** Further as a token for recognition, I shall tell you something more, O pure-souled one! Sometime back when we were staying in Chitrakuta, Rama was one day sleeping in privacy with his head resting on my lap. Now there came a son of Indra in the form of a crow, and with a view to get some flesh to eat, began to tear my crimson-tinged toes with his beak and claws. Meanwhile, Rama woke up, and seeing my wounded feet, exclaimed, 'Who is it that has done this offence against me?' . Seeing the crow with bloodstained face and claws attacking me repeatedly, he got angry at it, and invoking a divine missile. in a blade of grass, threw it at the crow. The divine missile went flaming towards the crow, which thereupon flew away to save itself. It flew to all the realms in the universe followed by the missile. Finding that even celestials like Brahma could not give it shelter from the missile, it at last came to Rama and fell at his feet in great fright seeking refuge. Rama then told the crow: 'This missile of mine

हनूमानपपि तामाह श्रुत्वा सीतानुभाषितम् । देवि त्वां यदि जानाति स्थितामत्र रघूत्तमः ॥ 62

करिष्यति क्षणाद्भस्म लङ्कां राक्षसमण्डिताम् । जानकी प्राह तं वत्स कथं त्वं योत्स्यसेऽसुरैः ॥ 63

अतिसूक्ष्मवपुः सर्वे वानराश्च भवादृशाः । श्रुत्वा तद्वचनं देव्यै पूर्वरूपमदर्शयत् ॥ 64

मेरुमन्दरसङ्काशं रक्षोगणविभीषणम् । दृष्ट्वा सीता हनूमन्तं महापर्वतसन्निभम् ॥ 65

हर्षेण महताविष्टा प्राह तं कपिकुञ्जरम् ।

समर्थोऽसि महासत्त्व द्रक्ष्यन्ति त्वां महाबलम् । राक्षस्यस्ते शुभः पन्था गच्छ रामान्तिकं द्रुतम् 66

बुभुक्षितः कपिः प्राह दर्शनात्पारणं मम । भविष्यति फलैः सर्वैस्तव दृष्टौ स्थितैर्हि मे ॥ 67

तथेत्युक्तः स जानक्या भक्षयित्वा फलं कपिः ।

ततः प्रस्थापितोऽगच्छज्जानकीं प्रणिपत्य सः । किञ्चिद्दूरमथो गत्वा स्वात्मन्येवानुचिन्तयत् ॥

कार्यार्थमागतो दूतः स्वामिकार्याविरोधतः । अन्यत्किञ्चिदसम्पाद्य गच्छत्यधम एव सः ॥ 69

अतोऽहं किञ्चिदन्यच्च कृत्वा दृष्ट्वाथ रावणम् । सम्भाष्य च ततो रामदर्शनार्थं व्रजाम्यहम् ॥ 70

इति निश्चित्य मनसा वृक्षखण्डान्महाबलः । उत्पाट्याशोकवनिकां निर्वृक्षामकरोत्क्षणात् ॥ 71

cannot go in vain. Give one of your eyes as a target for it, and go away from here.' Its left eye was destroyed by the missile and the crow then went away. How is it that Rama of such invincible puissance has chosen to neglect me unvindicated?"

(62-64). Hearing the words of Sita, Hanuman said to her, "O respected lady! If Rama, the greatest of Raghu's line, comes to know that you are here, he would reduce this glorious city of the Rakshasas into ashes in no time." Thereupon Sita asked him, "Dear one! You are of a small size and so must be the other monkeys too. How will you fight the Rakshasas?" At these words of Sita, Hanuman revealed his real form to her. **(65-66).** It was of the size of the mountain Meru and capable of terrifying the Rakshasas. She was glad to see that mountain-like form of Hanuman and said to that great monkey hero, "O paragon of strength! You will indeed be capable of accomplishing what you say. Now these Rakshasa women will notice you of tremendous size and strength. So leave this place immediately and hurry on to Rama. I wish you a happy return journey." **67.** Hanuman who was by now very hungry asked, "After having met you, may I not satisfy my hunger a little? You need not in any way be concerned thinking what you could give me to eat. I shall be able to satisfy my hunger with all the fruits in these trees before you." **68.** Being permitted to do so by Sita, Hanuman ate all those fruits. Sita then gave him permission once again to go. He started after prostrating before her. But having gone some distance, he began to think within himself.

(69-71). He thought: "A messenger who has been sent for one purpose, if he returns merely after accomplishing his mission but

सीताश्रयनगं त्यक्त्वा वनं शून्यं चकार सः । उत्पाटयन्तं विपिनं दृष्ट्वा राक्षसयोषितः ॥ 72
अपृच्छञ् जानकीं कोऽसौ वानराकृतिरुद्भटः ॥ 73

सीता उवाच

भवत्य एव जानन्ति मायां राक्षसनिर्मिताम् । नाहमेनं विजानामि दुःखशोकसमाकुला ॥ 74
इत्युक्तास्त्वरितं गत्वा राक्षस्यो भयपीडिताः । हनूमता कृतं सर्वं रावणाय न्यवेदयन् ॥ 75
देव कश्चिन्महासत्त्वो वानराकृतिदेहभृत् ।
सीतया सह सम्भाष्य ह्यशोकवनिकां क्षणात् । उत्पाट्य चैत्यप्रासादं बभञ्जामितविक्रमः ॥ 76
प्रासादरक्षिणः सर्वान्हत्वा तत्रैव तस्थिवान् । तच्छ्रुत्वा तूर्णमुत्थाय वनभङ्गं महाप्रियम् ॥ 77
किङ्करान्प्रेषयामास नियुतं राक्षसाधिपः ॥ 78
निभग्नचैत्यप्रासादप्रथमान्तरसंस्थितः ।
हनुमान्पर्वताकारो लोहस्तम्भकृतायुधः । किञ्चिल्लाङ्गूलचलनो रक्तास्यो भीषणाकृतिः ॥ 79
आपतन्तं महासङ्घं राक्षसानां ददर्श सः । चकार सिंहनादं च श्रुत्वा ते मुमुहुर्भृशम् ॥ 80

without doing something more in extension of it, is the most inferior type of a messenger. Therefore, I will accomplish something more here and try to meet Ravana and talk with him. After that I shall proceed to meet Rama." Resolving like this in his mind, the mighty Hanuman began to pull out the trees of that Ashoka grove and soon made that place devoid of all trees. **(72-73).** With the exception of the tree under which Sita was sitting, what was previously a grove became almost a bare ground. By that time the Rakshasa women, getting sight of Hanuman uprooting the trees, asked Sita, "Who is that fellow who has the form of a monkey but seems to be a great fighter too?" **(74-75).** Sita replied, "The secret of these magical feats of Rakshasas is known to you only and not to me, distressed as I am by intense sorrow. I know nothing about this monkey." The Rakshasis were now filled with fear and reported to Ravana about all that Hanuman did in the Ashoka grove. **76.** They said, "O great king! A gigantic figure in the form of a monkey and possessed of great strength, after having conversed with Sita, has uprooted the trees of the Ashoka grove in no time and has also levelled the mansion on the mound. **(77-78).** After killing all the guards of the mansion, he is now standing there." On hearing about the destruction of the Ashoka grove, which was very dear to him, Ravana got up immediately in great anger and despatched a large body of his troops called Kinkaras.

(79-80). Where the mansion once stood the Kinkaras now saw Hanuman, mountain-like in size, terrific in form, red in face, equipped with an iron pillar as weapon and slowly moving his tail. At the sight of the advancing Rakshasa army, Hanuman gave out a lion-roar, at which many of his opponents fell

हनूमन्तमथो दृष्ट्वा राक्षसा भीषणाकृतिम् । निर्जघ्नुर्विविधास्त्रौघैः सर्वराक्षसघातिनम् ॥ 81
तत उत्थाय हनुमान्मुद्गरेण समन्ततः । निष्पिपेष क्षणादेव मशकानिव यूथपः ॥ 82
निहतान्किङ्कराञ्श्रुत्वा रावणः क्रोधमूर्च्छितः । पञ्च सेनापतींस्तत्र प्रेषयामास दुर्मदान् ॥ 83
हनूमानपि तान्सर्वाल्लोहस्तम्भेन चाहनत् । ततः क्रुद्धो मन्त्रिसुतान्प्रेषयामास सप्त सः ॥ 84
आगतानपि तान्सर्वान्पूर्ववद्वानरेश्वरः । क्षणान्निःशेषतो हत्वा लोहस्तम्भेन मारुतिः ॥ 85
पूर्वस्थानमुपाश्रित्य प्रतीक्षन् राक्षसान् स्थितः । ततो जगाम बलवान्कुमारोऽक्षः प्रतापवान् ॥ 86
तमुत्पपात हनुमान् दृष्ट्वाकाशे समुद्गरः । गगनात्त्वरितो मूर्ध्नि मुद्गरेण व्यताडयत् ॥ 87
हत्वा तमक्षं निःशेषं बलं सर्वं चकार सः ॥ 88
ततः श्रुत्वा कुमारस्य वधं राक्षसपुङ्गवः । क्रोधेन महताविष्ट इन्द्रजेतारमब्रवीत् ॥ 89
पुत्र गच्छाम्यहं तत्र यत्रास्ते पुत्रहा रिपुः । हत्वा तमथवा बद्ध्वा आनयिष्यामि तेऽन्तिकम् ॥
इन्द्रजित्पितरं प्राह त्यज शोकं महामते । मयि स्थिते किमर्थं त्वं भाषसे दुःखितं वचः ॥ 91
बद्ध्वानेष्ये द्रुतं तात वानरं ब्रह्मपाशतः । इत्युक्त्वा रथमारुह्य राक्षसैर्बहुभिर्वृतः ॥ 92
जगाम वायुपुत्रस्य समीपं वीरविक्रमः ॥ 93

unconscious. **81.** On seeing Hanuman of frightening form, who had killed all the Rakshasa guards of the mansion earlier, the newly arrived Rakshasa troups attacked him with all kinds of weapons. **82.** Hanuman now rushed at the Rakshasa troops, and striking at them on all sides with an iron mace, made a paste of them like a lordly elephant crushing mosquitoes.

83. The news of the destruction of the Kinkaras raised the wrath of Ravana to its summit, and he sent against Hanuman his five generals who were possessed of great war-lust. **84.** Hanuman killed all of them with iron mace-pestle, and angry Ravana thereupon sent the seven sons of his ministers next. **(85-86).** That monkey lord, the son of the Wind-god, quickly despatched all of them too with his iron mace in no time and stationed himself in the same old place awaiting more Rakshasas to come for attack. Now came for battle, the powerful Akshakumara, the youngest son of Ravana. **87.** As Akshakumara advanced, Hanuman leaped at him through the skies and delivered a fatal blow on his head with his iron mace. **88.** After thus killing Akshakumara, Hanuman did the same with the troops whom he was leading.

Indrajit binds Hanuman (89-100)

89. The news of the death of his son Aksha incensed Ravana in the extreme and he now summoned his eldest son Indrajit, the victor over Indra. **90.** Ravana said, "O my son! I am now going to attack that fellow who killed my boy Aksha. I shall now bring him to you, either killed or bound." **(91-93).** Thereupon Indrajit said to his father, "O high souled one! Abandon grief. When I am there, why are

ततोऽतिगर्जितं श्रुत्वा स्तम्भमुद्यम्य वीर्यवान् ।
उत्पपात नभोदेशं गरुत्मानिव मारुतिः । ततो भ्रमन्तं नभसि हनूमन्तं शिलीमुखैः ॥ 94
विद्‌ध्वा तस्य शिरोभागमिषुभिश्चाष्टभिः पुनः । हृदयं पादयुगलं षड्भिरेकेन वालधिम् ॥ 95
भेदयित्वा ततो घोरं सिंहनादमथाकरोत् ॥ 96
ततोऽतिहर्षाद्धनुमान् स्तम्भमुद्यम्य वीर्यवान् । जघान सारथिं साश्वं रथं चाचूर्णयत्क्षणात् ॥ 97
ततोऽन्यं रथमादाय मेघनादो महाबलः ।
शीघ्रं ब्रह्मास्त्रमादाय बद्‌ध्वा वानरपुङ्गवम् । निनाय निकटं राज्ञो रावणस्य महाबलः ॥ 98
यस्य नाम सततं जपन्ति येऽज्ञानकर्मकृतबन्धनं क्षणात् ।
सद्य एव परिमुच्य तत्पदं यान्ति कोटिरविभासुरं शिवम् ॥ 99
तस्यैव रामस्य पदाम्बुजं सदा हृत्पद्ममध्ये सुनिधाय मारुतिः ।
सदैव निर्मुक्तसमस्तबन्धनः किं तस्य पाशैरितरैश्च बन्धनैः ॥ 100
इति श्रीमदध्यात्मरामायणे उमामहेश्वरसंवादे
सुन्दरकाण्डे तृतीयः सर्गः ॥ ३ ॥

you giving yourself up to grief so much? O father! Binding the monkey with the Brahma missile, I shall bring him to you very soon." With these words, heroic Indrajit sallied forth against the Wind-god's son, surrounded by a large body of Rakshasa troops. **(94-96).** Hearing the loud and tumultuous sound of the Rakshasa forces, Hanuman rose into the sky with the iron mace raised in his hand. As he hovered over the army like an eagle, Indrajit wounded him with arrows. He shot eight arrows on his head, six at his chest and legs, and one at his tail. Thus wounding him all over, Indrajit gave out a terrific lion-roar. **97.** Hanuman of great prowess, delighted at this opportunity for battle, raised his iron mace, and delivering blows with it, killed Indrajit's charioteer and reduced his chariot along with its horses to powder. **98.** Powerful Indrajit now ascended another chariot and releasing his Brahma-missile, bound up the mighty Hanuman and took him to Ravana.

(99-100). He, by uttering whose name constantly Jivas get release from the bondage of Karma born of ignorance, and attain the status Divine which is of the nature of Supreme Bliss more luminous than countless suns—that Rama's feet were ever established in the heart of Hanuman, and all his bondage of Samsara had thereby been removed. For such a person, what harm can the bondage of cords or missiles do?

चतुर्थः सर्गः

श्रीमहादेव उवाच

यान्तं कपीन्द्रं धृतपाशबन्धनं विलोकयन्तं नगरं विभीतवत् ।
अताडयन्मुष्टितलैः सुकोपनाः पौराः समन्तादनुयन्त ईक्षितुम् ॥ 1
ब्रह्मास्त्रमेनं क्षणमात्रसङ्गमं कृत्वा गतं ब्रह्मवरेण सत्वरम् ।
ज्ञात्वा हनूमानपि फल्गुरज्जुभिर्धृतो ययौ कार्यविशेषगौरवात् ॥ 2
सभान्तरस्थस्य च रावणस्य तं पुरो निधायाह बलारिजित्तदा ।
बद्धो मया ब्रह्मवरेण वानरः समागतोऽनेन हता महासुराः ॥ 3
यद्युक्तमत्रार्य विचार्य मन्त्रिभिर्विधीयतामेष न लौकिको हरिः ।
ततो विलोक्याह स राक्षसेश्वरः प्रहस्तमग्रे स्थितमञ्जनाद्रिभम् ॥ 4
प्रहस्त पृच्छैनमसौ किमागतः किमत्र कार्यं कुत एव वानरः ।
वनं किमर्थं सकलं विनाशितं हताः किमर्थं मम राक्षसा बलात् ॥ 5

Chapter 4

THE BURNING OF LANKA

Hanuman As Captive (1-14).

1. Holding with his hands the binding cords as if in pain, and looking at the city here and there as if in fright, Hanuman allowed himself to be led by the Rakshasas through the streets of Lanka. To see him, the angry Rakshasa citizens followed the party, raining blows on him with their fists. **2.** On account of the boon given by Brahma, Hanuman was released from the bondage of that Brahma missile within a short time. He knew it, but yet he allowed himself to be subjected to bondage by inconsequential cords and went with his captors in order that he may fulfil an important purpose. **3.** Hanuman was now brought before Ravana who was seated in the assembly of his ministers and courtiers. Presenting him, Indrajit said, "With the help of the boon given to me by Brahma, I have been able to bind and bring before you this monkey who was responsible for the slaughter of so many Asuras. **4.** O father! Order whatever you decide about him in consultation with your ministers. He is not an ordinary monkey." Thereupon, that lord of the Rakshasas looked at his minister Prahasta who was of the complexion of an antimony mountain, and was then standing before him. **5.** He said: "O Prahasta! Question him on these lines: 'Why has this monkey come over here?

ततः प्रहस्तो हनुमन्तमादरात्पप्रच्छ केन प्रहितोऽसि वानर ।
भयं च ते मास्तु विमोक्ष्यसे मया सत्यं वदस्वाखिलराजसन्निधौ॥ 6
ततोऽतिहर्षात्पवनात्मजो रिपुं निरीक्ष्य लोकत्रयकण्टकासुरम् ।
वक्तुं प्रचक्रे रघुनाथसत्कथां क्रमेण रामं मनसा स्मरन्मुहुः ॥ 7
शृणु स्फुटं देवगणाद्यमित्र हे रामस्य दूतोऽहमशेषहृत्स्थितेः ।
यस्याखिलेशस्य हृताधुना त्वया भार्या स्वनाशाय शुनेव सद्धविः ॥ 8
स राघवोऽभ्येत्य मतङ्गपर्वतं सुग्रीवमैत्रीमनलस्य सन्निधौ ।
कृत्वैकबाणेन निहत्य वालिनं सुग्रीवमेवाधिपतिं चकार तम् ॥ 9
स वानराणामधिपो महाबली महाबलैर्वानरयूथकोटिभिः ।
रामेण सार्धं सह लक्ष्मणेन भोः प्रवर्षणेऽमर्षयुतोऽवतिष्ठते ॥ 10
सञ्चोदितास्तेन महाहरीश्वरा धरासुतां मार्गयितुं दिशो दश ।
तत्राहमेकः पवनात्मजः कपिः सीतां विचिन्वञ्छनकैः समागतः ॥ 11
दृष्ट्वा मया पद्मपलाशलोचना सीता कपित्वाद्विपिनं विनाशितम् ।
दृष्ट्वा ततोऽहं रभसा समागतान्मां हन्तुकामान् धृतचापसायकान् ॥ 12

What is his business here? Where does he come from? Why did he destroy my Ashoka grove? Why has he killed my Rakshasa troops by force?' " **6.** Thereupon Prahasta in obedience to his master's order, questioned Hanuman politely: "O monkey! Who has sent you over here? Do not entertain any fear. I shall get you released, if you tell the truth about yourself before His majesty, the king of all kings."

7. Thereupon Hanuman, delighted to see face to face the enemy Ravana, the oppressor of the three worlds, and remembering Rama again and again within himself, started narrating the sanctifying story of Rama from the very beginning. **8.** He said: "O Ravana, the enemy of the Devas! Listen to me carefully.I am the messenger of Rama, who resides in the hearts of all beings.You have recently, stolen away his wife, like a dog stealthily taking away sacrificial offerings. You have thereby paved the way for your own destruction. **9.** Know that coming to the Rishyamuka mountain, Rama has entered into an alliance with Sugreeva before the sacred fire as witness, and subsequently killed Vali with a single arrow and installed Sugreeva as the king of the kingdom of the monkeys. **10.** That powerful king of the monkeys is now staying in great anger on Mount Praharshana along with Rama and Lakshmana and a huge army of powerful monkeys. **11.** That monkey king has deputed powerful monkey leaders to search and find out the whereabouts of Sita. I, the off-spring of the Wind-god, am one such monkey come here after much search. **(12-13).** I have been able to find out the lotus-eyed Sita. Being a monkey, my nature prompted

मया हतास्ते परिरक्षितं वपुः प्रियो हि देहोऽखिलदेहिनां प्रभो ।
ब्रह्मास्त्रपाशेन निबध्य मां ततः समागमन्मेघनिनादनामकः ॥ 13

स्पृष्ट्वैव मां ब्रह्मवरप्रभावतस्त्यक्त्वा गतं सर्वमवैमि रावण ।
तथाप्यहं बद्ध इवागतो हितं प्रवक्तुकामः करुणारसार्द्रधीः ॥ 14

विचार्य लोकस्य विवेकतो गतिं न राक्षसीं बुद्धिमुपैहि रावण ।
दैवीं गतिं संसृतिमोक्षहैतुकीं समाश्रयात्यन्तहिताय देहिनः ॥ 15

त्वं ब्रह्मणो ह्युत्तमवंशसम्भवः पौलस्त्यपुत्रोऽसि कुबेरबान्धवः ।
देहात्मबुद्ध्यापि च पश्य राक्षसो नास्यात्मबुद्ध्या किमु राक्षसो न हि ॥ 16

शरीरबुद्धीन्द्रियदुःखसन्ततिर्न ते न च त्वं तव निर्विकारतः ।
अज्ञानहेतोश्च तथैव सन्ततेरसत्त्वमस्याः स्वपतो हि दृश्यवत् ॥ 17

me to destroy the trees of the Ashoka grove. Thereafter I found many of your emissaries equipped with bows and arrows coming in great anger to attack and kill me. So I had to kill them in defence of myself. O great king! You know very well how dear one's body is to all creatures. Finally Meghanada (Indrajit) came to put me in bondage with the Brahma missile. **14.** Because of a boon given to me by Brahma, the effect of that missile lasted only for a moment; and I was released after that. O Ravana! I know this fact, but yet out of pity for you, I wanted to give you some good advice, and so allowed myself to be brought here, as if I were still in bondage.

Hanuman's sermon to Ravana (15-26)

15. "By the practice of discrimination, understand the extremely trivial and temporary nature of this world, O Ravana, and with the help of that understanding, abandon your evil nature of a Rakshasa. For the ultimate good of your soul, practice virtuous conduct that will lead to liberation from the travails of Samsara. **16.** You are born in the great lineage of Brahma, being the son of Rishi Pulastya and the brother of Kubera. So, even granting the wrong view that the self of one is the body, you are not a Rakshasa in a physical sense even. And from the point of view of the spirit, it is needless to say that there is no Rakshasahood in you.

17. "The real 'You' or the Self has none of the series of miseries arising from body, intellect and the senses, because the real 'you' is only the unperturbed and unaffected witness of all these changes. The actual involvement in these changes belongs to the body-mind complex. It is just like the experience of one sleeping. The series of dream experiences which sleep brings about, end with the dream; they are the effects of the delusive ignorance characteristic of sleep. As far as the real Self is concerned, the bodily experiences are unreal in the same

इदं तु सत्यं तव नास्ति विक्रिया विकारहेतुर्न च तेऽद्वयत्वतः ।
यथा नभः सर्वगतं न लिप्यते तथा भवान्देहगतोऽपि सूक्ष्मकः ॥ 18

देहेन्द्रियप्राणशरीरसङ्गतस्त्वात्मेति बुद्ध्वाखिलबन्धभाग्भवेत् ।
चिन्मात्रमेवाहमजोऽहमक्षरो ह्यानन्दभावोऽहमिति प्रमुच्यते ॥ 19

देहोऽप्यनात्मा पृथिवीविकारजो न प्राण आत्मानिल एष एव सः ।
मनोऽप्यहङ्कारविकार एव नो न चापि बुद्धिः प्रकृतेर्विकारजा ॥ 20

आत्मा चिदानन्दमयोऽविकारवान्देहादि सङ्घाद्व्यतिरिक्त ईश्वरः ।
निरञ्जनो मुक्त उपाधितः सदा ज्ञात्वैवमात्मानमितो विमुच्यते ॥ 21

अतोऽहमात्यन्तिकमोक्षसाधनं वक्ष्ये शृणुष्वावहितो महामते ।
विष्णोर्हि भक्तिः सुविशोधनं धियस्ततो भवेज्ज्ञानमतीव निर्मलम् । 22

विशुद्धतत्त्वानुभवो भवेत्ततः सम्यग्विदित्वा परमं पदं व्रजेत् ।
अतो भजस्वाद्य हरिं रमापतिं रामं पुराणं प्रकृतेः परं विभुम् ॥ 23

way. **18.** This unperturbedness and unaffectedness is the truth in regard to the nature of your real Self . You are by nature changeless; for the Self being non-dual, there can be no cause to effect change in it. Like the all-pervading Akasa which pervades objects but is not affected by it, your real Self, though pervading the body, is not affected by the bodily experiences because of its subtlety. **19.** All bondage arises from the sense of identification of the complex—body-mind-Prana—with the real Self. And liberation consists in experiencing: 'I am Pure Consciousness, I am the Unbound I am the Deathless, I am pure Bliss.' **20.** The body which is born of the element earth is not the Self. Nor is Prana the Atman, because it is a modification of the element air. Mind too is not the Self, because it is an effect of Ahamkara, the I-sense. As for Buddhi, intellect, it is a modification of Prakriti and is not the Self. **21.** The Atman is Pure Consciousness and Bliss, He is devoid of changes like birth and death, and He, being separate from the body-mind combination, is only their witness and director. He is separate from all adjuncts through which He manifests. By himself He is ever pure. Knowing the Atman as such, one attains liberation from the bondage of Samsara.

22. "Therefore, I shall now tell you the means for attaining ultimate liberation. Hear it attentively. O intelligent one! Listen to it carefully. First of all cultivate devotion to Maha-Vishnu. That will purify your intellect and you will thereby gain pure knowledge too. **23.** You will then have the knowledge of the ever-pure and unaffected Truth. This knowledge being fully established, you will attain to the Supreme Status of Brahman. There-

विसृज्य मौर्ख्यं हृदि शत्रुभावनां भजस्व रामं शरणागतप्रियम् ।
सीतां पुरस्कृत्य सपुत्रबान्धवो रामं नमस्कृत्य विमुच्यसे भयात् ॥ 24

रामं परात्मानमभावयञ्जनो भक्त्या हृदिस्थं सुखरूपमद्वयम् ।
कथं परं तीरमवाप्नुयाज्जनो भवाम्बुधेर्दुःखतरङ्गमालिनः ॥ 25

नो चेत्त्वमज्ञानमयेन वह्निना ज्वलन्तमात्मानमरक्षितारिवत् ।
नयस्यधोऽधः स्वकृतैश्च पातकैर्विमोक्षशङ्का न च ते भविष्यति ॥ 26

श्रुत्वामृतास्वादसमानभाषितं तद्वायुसूनोर्दशकन्धरोऽसुरः ।
अमृष्यमाणोऽतिरुषा कपीश्वरं जगाद रक्तान्तविलोचनो ज्वलन् ॥ 27

कथं ममाग्रे विलपस्यभीतवत् प्लवङ्गमानामधमोऽसि दुष्टधीः ।
क एष रामः कतमो वनेचरो निहन्मि सुग्रीवयुतं नराधमम् ॥ 28

त्वां चाद्य हत्वा जनकात्मजां ततो निहन्मि रामं सहलक्ष्मणं ततः ।
सुग्रीवमग्रे बलिनं कपीश्वरं सवानरं हन्म्यचिरेण वानर ।
श्रुत्वा दशग्रीववचः स मारुतिर्विवृद्धकोपेन दहन्निवासुरम् ॥ 29

fore, worship with all devotion Rama who is none but Hari, the consort of Lakshmi, who transcends Prakriti and is all-pervading. **24.** Abandoning your stupidity and your mood of antagonism, take shelter at the feet of Rama, to whom all who surrender are very dear. Along with your sons and relatives, take Sita to Rama and restore her to him, making a full prostration as the sign of your submission. Then you will be free from fear. **25.** How can thoughtless persons cross over the ocean of Samsara with waves of misery raging in it, without taking shelter in Rama, with perfect devotion —Rama who is the essence of Bliss, Non-dual Being and Supreme Self residing in the hearts of all? **26.** If you do not do this, you will sink into the depths of spiritual degradation without anyone to protect you from the burning fire of ignorance. You will never have an opportunity of being lifted from the travails of Samsara."

Sentence of torture by fire on Hanuman (27-36)

27. Hearing these nectar-like words of Hanuman, the son of the Wind-god, the ten-headed Rakshasa,Ravana,felt unbearable anger, and in high excitement and with eyes reddened, said to that lordly monkey: **28.** "Who are you to talk this kind of nonsense before me without any fear? You must be the most degenerate and evil-minded among the monkeys. Who is this Rama? Who is this forest dweller Sugreeva? Look, you fool of a monkey! I am going to kill that evil man who has sought alliance with Sugreeva. **29.** But you are going to be killed immediately, and then Sita, the daughter of Janaka. After that, before long,

न मे समा रावणकोटयोऽधम रामस्य दासोऽहमपारविक्रमः ।
श्रुत्वातिकोपेन हनूमतो वचो दशाननो राक्षसमेवमब्रवीत् ॥ 30
पार्श्वे स्थितं मारय खण्डशः कपिं पश्यन्तु सर्वेऽसुरमित्रबान्धवाः । 31
निवारयामास ततो विभीषणो महासुरं सायुधमुद्यतं वधे ।
राजन्वधार्हो न भवेत्कथञ्चन प्रतापयुक्तैः परराजवानरः ॥ 32
हतेऽस्मिन्वानरे दूते वार्तां को वा निवेदयेत् । रामाय त्वं यमुद्दिश्य वधाय समुपस्थितः ॥ 33
अतो वधसमं किञ्चिदन्यच्चिन्तय वानरे । सचिह्नो गच्छतु हरिर्यं दृष्ट्वा यास्यति द्रुतम् ॥ 34
रामः सुग्रीवसहितस्ततो युद्धं भवेत्तव । विभीषणवचः श्रुत्वा रावणोऽप्येतदब्रवीत् ॥ 35
वानराणां हि लाङ्गूले महामानो भवेत्किल । अतो वस्त्रादिभिः पुच्छं वेष्टयित्वा प्रयत्नतः ॥36
वह्निना योजयित्वैनं भ्रामयित्वा पुरेऽभितः । विसर्जयत पश्यन्तु सर्वे वानरयूथपाः ॥ 37
तथेति शणपट्टैश्च वस्त्रैरन्यैरनेकशः । तैलाक्तैर्वेष्टयामासुर्लाङ्गूलं मारुतेर्दृढम् ॥ 38

I am going to destroy Rama and Lakshmana and the powerful monkey Sugreeva along with all his followers." Hearing these words of the ten-headed Ravana, Hanuman, the son of Wind-god, was inflamed with anger and said as follows in a threatening mood, as if he were going to burn him up.

30. He said: "O most degenerate fellow! Even a crore of Ravanas will not be equal to me; for I, the messenger of Rama, have inexhaustible puissance." These words of Hanuman drove Ravana to a mad fury, and he said, addressing a Rakshasa standing nearby: **31.** "Kill this monkey, cutting him into pieces. Let all other Asuras and friends and relatives witness this execution." Thereupon, Vibhishana intervened and warded off the Asura who was advancing with his weapon for the execution. **32.** Vibhishana said, "O great king! He is a monkey sent as a messenger by another king. How can a monarch noted for his courage and nobility order him to be killed? That is highly improper. **33.** If you kill this messenger monkey now, how can Rama, whose destruction is your ultimate purpose, come to know that Sita is here, and go over to Lanka for battle? **(34-35).** Therefore, think of some other kind of punishment that is equal to execution. Let the monkey go with the marks of punishment inflicted on his body. Seeing him, Rama will soon come here with Sugreeva and engage himself in battle with you." On hearing these words of Vibhishana, Ravana said as follows: **(36-37).** "Monkeys are very proud of their tail. Therefore, let his tail be wrapped with cloth and set fire to. Let him then be dragged through the whole city and then allowed to go away, so that all the leaders of the monkey army may see him in that deformed condition."

(38-40). Afterwards, the Rakshasas wrapped round Hanuman's tail pieces of sack and various kinds of cloth soaked in oil and set fire to the tip of the tail. They then bound him up with cords and a group of powerful Rakshasas carried him round

पुच्छाग्रे किञ्चिदनलं दीपयित्वाथ राक्षसाः । रज्जुभिः सुदृढं बद्ध्वा धृत्वा तं बलिनोऽसुराः ॥39
समन्ताद् भ्रामयामासुश्चोरोऽयमिति वादिनः । तूर्यघोषैर्घोषयन्तस्ताडयन्तो मुहुर्मुहुः ॥ 40
हनूमतापि तत्सर्वं सोढं किञ्चिच्चिकीर्षणा । गत्वा तु पश्चिमद्वारसमीपं तत्र मारुतिः ॥ 41
सूक्ष्मो बभूव बन्धेभ्यो निःसृतः पुनरप्यसौ । बभूव पर्वताकारस्तत उत्प्लुत्य गोपुरम् ॥ 42
तत्रैकं स्तम्भमादाय हत्वा तान् रक्षिणः क्षणात् । विचार्य कार्यशेषं स प्रासादाग्राद्गृहाद्गृहम् ॥ 43
उत्प्लुत्योत्प्लुत्य सन्दीप्तपुच्छेन महता कपिः । ददाह लङ्कामखिलां साट्टप्रासादतोरणाम् ॥ 44
हा तात पुत्र नाथेति क्रन्दमानाः समन्ततः । व्याप्ताः प्रासादशिखरेऽप्यारूढा दैत्ययोषितः ॥ 45
देवता इव दृश्यन्ते पतन्त्यः पावकेऽखिलाः । विभीषणगृहं त्यक्त्वा सर्वं भस्मीकृतं पुरम् ॥ 46
तत उत्प्लुत्य जलधौ हनूमान्मारुतात्मजः । लाङ्गूलं मज्जयित्वान्तः स्वस्थचित्तो बभूव सः ॥
वायोः प्रियसखित्वाच्च सीतया प्रार्थितोऽनिलः । न ददाह हरेः पुच्छं बभूवात्यन्तशीतलः ॥ 48

यन्नामसंस्मरणधूतसमस्तपापास्तापत्रयानलमपीह तरन्ति सद्यः ।
तस्यैव किं रघुवरस्य विशिष्टदूतः सन्तप्यते कथमसौ प्रकृतानलेन ॥ 49

इति श्रीमदध्यात्मरामायणे उमामहेश्वरसंवादे
सुन्दरकाण्डे चतुर्थः सर्गः ॥ ४ ॥

the city to the beating of drums and declaring again and again, "Come and see! Here is the thief—" all the while people raining blows on him. **(41-44).** With a strategem in his mind, Hanuman bore all that persecution patiently. On reaching the western gate, he shrunk his body into a small size and thus released himself from the bondage of all the cords. Then he again assumed his gigantic size and leaped on to the top of the gate-tower, and pulling out one of the pillars of that edifice, smashed all the Rakshasa emissaries. In order to complete his work in Lanka, he hopped from one building to another in the city with his burning tail and set fire to all the mansions and other edifices there. **45.** Now was heard everywhere in Lanka, the cries of women, 'O father', 'O son', 'O husband'! Many a Rakshasa women got on to the top of buildings in order to escape from fire, only to find that the fire had spread all around. **46.** As beings drop from the skies, these Rakshasa women fell into the fire from above. With the exception of Vibhishana's house, all Lanka was thus reduced to ashes. **47.** Having done all these, Hanuman jumped into the sea and extinguished the fire on his tail by dipping it into water. He now felt satisfied that he had accomplished his task. **48.** Thanks to the friendship of the Fire-deity with the Wind-deity, the father of Hanuman, and thanks to Sita's prayers, the fire did not burn his tail in the least. On the other hand, he felt it as very cool. **49.** He, by uttering whose name men are rid of the effects of all the sins, by which men in this world overcome the three fires of life (*Tāpatraya*)—to the special messenger of that Rama, how can this ordinary fire of this world inflict injury?

पञ्चमः सर्गः

श्रीमहादेव उवाच

ततः सीतां नमस्कृत्य हनुमानब्रवीद्वचः । आज्ञापयतु मां देवि भवती रामसन्निधिम् ॥ 1
गच्छामि रामस्त्वां द्रष्टुमागमिष्यति सानुजः । इत्युक्त्वा त्रिः परिक्रम्य जानकीं मारुतात्मजः ॥ 2
प्रणम्य प्रस्थितो गन्तुमिदं वचनमब्रवीत् । देवि गच्छामि भद्रं ते तूर्णं द्रक्ष्यसि राघवम् ॥ 3
लक्ष्मणं च ससुग्रीवं वानरायुतकोटिभिः । ततः प्राह हनूमन्तं जानकी दुःखकर्शिता ॥ 4
त्वां दृष्ट्वा विस्मृतं दुःखमिदानीं त्वं गमिष्यसि । इतः परं कथं वर्ते रामवार्ताश्रुतिं विना ॥ 5

मारुतिरुवाच

यद्येवं देवि मे स्कन्धमारोह क्षणमात्रतः । रामेण योजयिष्यामि मन्यसे यदि जानकि ॥ 6

सीतोवाच

रामः सागरमाशोष्य बद्ध्वा वा शरपञ्जरैः । आगत्य वानरैः सार्धं हत्वा रावणमाहवे ॥ 7
मां नयेद्यदि रामस्य कीर्तिर्भवति शाश्वती । अतो गच्छ कथं चापि प्राणान्सन्धारयाम्यहम् ॥
इति प्रस्थापितो वीर सीतया प्रणिपत्य ताम् । जगाम पर्वतस्याग्रे गन्तुं पारं महोदधेः ॥ 9

Chapter 5

HANUMAN'S TRIUMPHANT RETURN

Hanuman bids farewell to Sita and returns (1-17).

(1-4). Afterwards Hanuman went to see Sita, made prostrations to her and said, "O great lady! Now give me permission to return to Rama. Rama, along with his brother, will come soon to see you." With these words, he circumambulated Sita thrice, made prostrations to her again and made ready to go. He now addressed the following words to Sita, "O noble lady! I am now starting. Good fotune will soon dawn on you. Accompanied by a huge army, Sugreeva, Rama and Lakshmana will be seen here in this city very soon." To Hanuman, Sita said sorrow-stricken: **5.** "Seeing you, I have forgotten all my sorrows. Alas, now you are going. How can I now sustain my life without hearing about Rama?" **6.** Hanuman replied to Sita saying, "If that be the case, O noble lady, you get on my shoulders. If you want, I shall then take you in no time to Rama's presence." **(7-9).** Now Sita said, "Let Rama come along with the monkey army, drying the sea or bridging it with arrows, kill Ravana in battle and rescue me. Then Rama will gain everlasting fame. Therefore, you go now. I shall somehow sustain my life." Being thus permitted to go once again, Hanuman made prostrations to her and then went to the top of the

तत्र गत्वा महासत्त्वः पादाभ्यां पीडयन् गिरिम् । जगाम वायुवेगेन पर्वतश्च महीतलम् ॥ 10

गतो महीसमानत्वं त्रिंशद्योजनमुच्छ्रितः । मारुतिर्गगनान्तःस्थो महाशब्दं चकार सः ॥ 11

तं श्रुत्वा वानराः सर्वे ज्ञात्वा मारुतिमागतम् । हर्षेण महताविष्टाः शब्दं चक्रुर्महास्वनम् ॥ 12

शब्देनैव विजानीमः कृतकार्यः समागतः । हनूमानेव पश्यध्वं वानरा वानरर्षभम् ॥ 13

एवं ब्रुवत्सु वीरेषु वानरेषु स मारुतिः । अवतीर्य गिरेर्मूर्ध्नि वानरानिदमब्रवीत् ॥ 14

दृष्टा सीता मया लङ्का धर्षिता च सकानना । सम्भाषितो दशग्रीवस्ततोऽहं पुनरागतः ॥ 15

इदानीमेव गच्छामो रामसुग्रीवसन्निधिम् । इत्युक्ता वानराः सर्वे हर्षेणालिङ्ग्य मारुतिम् ॥ 16

केचिच्चुचुम्बुर्लाङ्गूलं ननृतुः केचिदुत्सुकाः । हनूमता समेतास्ते जग्मुः प्रस्रवणं गिरिम् ॥ 17

गच्छन्तो ददृशुर्वीरा वनं सुग्रीवरक्षितम् । मधुसंज्ञं तदा प्राहुरङ्गदं वानरर्षभाः ॥ 18

क्षुधिताः स्मो वयं वीर देह्यनुज्ञां महामते । भक्षयामः फलान्यद्य पिबामोऽमृतवन्मधु ॥ 19

सन्तुष्टा राघवं द्रष्टुं गच्छामोऽद्यैव सानुजम् ॥ 20

mountain Trikuta in order to prepare for crossing the sea.

10. In his effort to leap, Hanuman of tremendous size pressed his legs with such force on the mountain that the latter went deep into the bowels of the earth. With the speed of wind, he lifted himself up in the sky. **11.** Due to the force generated, that mountain, which was thirty Yojanas in height, became levelled to the ground. Ascending to the sky, Hanuman gave out a terrific roar. **12.** That sound reached the ears of the monkey hosts on the other shore of the ocean, and in great glee, they all together shouted in return like an echo. **(13-14).** "After achieving his object, Hanuman is returning. From the sound he has produced we can know it. O monkeys! Wait and see the arrival of that leader of ours." As the monkey chiefs were speaking thus amongst themselves, the son of the Wind-god descended on the top of a mountain and said to the monkeys thus: **(15-17).** "I have discovered Sita and I have destroyed Lanka along with its woody groves. I spoke with Ravana. I am now returning after achieving all these. Now we shall go to the presence of Rama and Sugreeva." When Hanuman spoke these words, all the monkeys were delighted. Some embraced Hanuman. Some kissed their tails, and some others danced enthusiastically. They all started along with Hanuman to mount Prasravana where Rama was staying.

Destruction of Madhuvana (18-15)

18. As the monkeys were travelling, they reached the forest named Madhu, which was under Sugreeva's special protection. Then all those monkey leaders said to Angada as follows: **19.** "O hero! We are all extremely hungry. If you, our noble-minded leader, give us permission, we would like to eat the fruits and drink the sweet honey abounding in this forest. **20.** Satisfied with eating and drinking, we shall

अङ्गद उवाच

हनूमान्कृतकार्योऽयं पिबतैतत्प्रसादतः । जक्षध्वं फलमूलानि त्वरितं हरिसत्तमाः ॥ 21
ततः प्रविश्य हरयः पातुमारेभिरे मधु । रक्षिणस्ताननादृत्य दधिवक्त्रेण नोदितान् ॥ 22
पिबतस्ताडयामासुर्वानरान्वानरर्षभाः । ततस्तान्मुष्टिभिः पादैश्चूर्णयित्वा पपुर्मधु ॥ 23
ततो दधिमुखः क्रुद्धः सुग्रीवस्य स मातुलः । जगाम रक्षिभिः सार्धं यत्र राजा कपीश्वरः ॥ 24
गत्वा तमब्रवीदेव चिरकालाभिरक्षितम् । नष्टं मधुवनं तेऽद्य कुमारेण हनूमता ॥ 25
श्रुत्वा दधिमुखेनोक्तं सुग्रीवो हृष्टमानसः । दृष्ट्वागतो न सन्देहः सीतां पवननन्दनः ॥ 26
नो चेन्मधुवनं द्रष्टुं समर्थः को भवेन्मम । तत्रापि वायुपुत्रेण कृतं कार्यं न संशयः ॥ 27
श्रुत्वा सुग्रीववचनं हृष्टो रामस्तमब्रवीत् । किमुच्यते त्वया राजन्वचः सीताकथान्वितम् ॥ 28
सुग्रीवस्त्वब्रवीद्वाक्यं देव दृष्टावनीसुता । हनूमत्प्रमुखाः सर्वे प्रविष्टा मधुकाननम् ॥ 29
भक्षयन्ति स्म सकलं ताडयन्ति स्म रक्षिणः । अकृत्वा देवकार्यं ते द्रष्टुं मधुवनं मम ॥ 30
न समर्थास्ततो देवी दृष्टा सीतेति निश्चितम् । रक्षिणो वो भयं मास्तु गत्वा ब्रूत ममाज्ञया ॥ 31
वानरानङ्गदमुखानानयध्वं ममान्तिकम् । श्रुत्वा सुग्रीववचनं गत्वा ते वायुवेगतः ॥ 32

go immediately to the presence of Rama and Lakshmana." **21.** Angada thereupon said, "Here is Hanuman, who has fulfilled the mission on which we are sent. In honour of him, O monkey-chiefs, consume the fruits and roots quickly and be on the move." **(22-23).** The monkeys now began to consume the honey. Noticing it, Dadhimukha, the keeper of the forest, sent a body of his guards to ward them off. But without minding them, the monkeys continued to consume the honey. When the forest guards attempted to beat the monkeys, they gave them kicks and blows, and continued to eat and drink.

24. Now Dadhimukha was an uncle of Sugreeva. Extremely angry at the conduct of the monkeys, he along with his forest guards went to the place where Sugreeva was staying. **25.** And he said to the king "O master! The Madhuvana that you have been maintaining for such a long time has been destroyed today by prince Angada and Hanuman." **(26-27).** On hearing Dadhimuka's representation, Sugreeva said in a joyous mood: "The son of the Wind-god must have certainly discovered Sita. There is no doubt about it. Otherwise, who would have dared even to look at my Madhuvana? Therefore their action only indicates that Hanuman has succeeded in his mission. There is no doubt about this."

28. Delighted at these words of Sugreeva, Rama asked him, "O royal friend! What is it that you are speaking about Sita?" **(29-34).** Hearing these words, Sugreeva said, "O noble one! Sita has been discovered. Hanuman and other monkeys are reported to have entered Madhuvana and eaten

हनूमत्प्रमुखान् चुर्गच्छतेश्वरशासनात् । द्रष्टुमिच्छति सुग्रीवः सरामो लक्ष्मणान्वितः ॥ 33
युष्मानतीव हृष्टास्ते त्वरयन्ति महाबलाः । तथेत्यम्बरमासाद्य ययुस्ते वानरोत्तमाः ॥ 34
हनूमन्तं पुरस्कृत्य युवराजं तथाङ्गदम् । रामसुग्रीवयोरग्रे निपेतुर्भुवि सत्वरम् ॥ 35
हनूमान्राघवं प्राह दृष्टा सीता निरामया । साष्टाङ्गं प्रणिपत्याग्रे रामं पश्चाद्धरीश्वरम् ॥ 36
कुशलं प्राह राजेन्द्र जानकी त्वां शुचान्विता । अशोकवनिकामध्ये शिंशपामूलमाश्रिता ॥ 37
राक्षसीभिः परिवृता निराहारा कृशा प्रभो । हा राम राम रामेति शोचन्ती मलिनाम्बरा ॥38
एकवेणी मया दृष्टा शनैराश्वासिता शुभा । वृक्ष शाखान्तरे स्थित्वा सूक्ष्मरूपेण ते कथाम् ॥ 39
जन्मारभ्य तवात्यर्थं दण्डकागमनं तथा । दशाननेन हरणं जानक्या रहिते त्वयि ॥ 40
सुग्रीवेण यथा मैत्री कृत्वा वालिनिबर्हणम् । मार्गणार्थं च वैदेह्याः सुग्रीवेण विसर्जिताः ॥ 41
महाबला महासत्त्वा हरयो जितकाशिनः । गताः सर्वत्र सर्वे वै तत्रैकोऽहमिहागतः ॥ 42
अहं सुग्रीवसचिवो दासोऽहं राघवस्य हि । दृष्टा यज्जानकी भाग्यात्प्रयासः फलितोऽद्यमे ॥

everything there and attacked the guards. Unless they have achieved the purpose of your divine Self, they would not have dared even to look at my Madhuvana. So from their action you can infer that they have certainly discovered Sita." And turning to his guards he said, "O guards! Entertain no fear. Returning to your place, communicate to Angada and others that it is my order that they return soon." The forest guards on hearing Sugreeva's words returned very soon and said to Hanuman and others, "It is the order of the King that you return soon. Sugreeva, along with Rama and Lakshmana, is anxious to meet you. Those powerful personages are immensely delighted with your conduct. They want to see you immediately." Hearing these words of Dadhimukha and his guards, the monkey leaders proceeded quickly through the sky. **35.** With Hanuman and the heir apparent Angada leading them, they descended at the place where Rama and Sugreeva were.

Hanuman's report to Rama (36-64)

(36-42). Hanuman now reported to Rama, "I have seen Sita in a healthy condition." Then he first prostrated before Rama and next before Sugreeva, and continued: "O great King! Sita, the daughter of Janaka, has in a very joyous mood asked me about your welfare. Surrounded by a guard of Rakshasa women, she is kept in the Ashoka grove underneath a Simsapa tree. O great one! Lean because of abstinence from food, she is always bemoaning, calling out 'O Rama, O Rama'. I saw her dressed in soiled clothes, with locks unbraided. I was able to comfort her a little. Hiding myself in a dimunitive form amidst the branches, I began to narrate your story from birth onwards. Your departure to the formidable forest of Dandaka, Ravana's abduction of Sita

इत्युदीरितमाकर्ण्य सीता विस्फारितेक्षणा । केन वा कर्णपीयूषं श्रावितं मे शुभाक्षरम् ॥ 44
यदि सत्यं तदायातु मद्दर्शनपथं तु सः । ततोऽहं वानराकारः सूक्ष्मरूपेण जानकीम् ॥ 45
प्रणम्य प्राञ्जलिर्भूत्वा दूरादेव स्थितः प्रभो । पृष्टोऽहं सीतया 'कस्त्वमित्यादि बहुविस्तरम् ॥46
मया सर्वक्रमेणैव विज्ञापितमरिन्दम । पश्चान्मयार्पितं देव्यै भवद्दत्ताङ्गुलीयकम् ॥ 47
तेन मामतिविश्वस्ता वचनं चेदमब्रवीत् । यथा दृष्टासि हनुमन्पीडयमाना दिवानिशम् ॥48
राक्षसीनां तर्जनैस्तत्सर्वं कथय राघवे । मयोक्तं देवि रामोऽपि त्वच्चिन्तापरिनिष्ठितः ॥49
परिशोचत्यहोरात्रं त्वद्वार्तां नाधिगम्य सः । इदानीमेव गत्वाहं स्थितिं रामाय ते ब्रुवे ॥ 50
रामः श्रवणमात्रेण सुग्रीवेण सलक्ष्मणः । वानरानीकपैः सार्धमागमिष्यति तेऽन्तिकम् ॥ 51
रावणं सकुलं हत्वा नेष्यति त्वां स्वकं पुरम् । अभिज्ञां देहि मे देवि यथा मां विश्वसेद्विभुः॥ 52
इत्युक्ता सा शिरोरत्नं चूडापाशे स्थितं प्रियम् । दत्त्वा काकेन यद्वृत्तं चित्रकूटगिरौ पुरा ॥ 53
तदप्याहाश्रुपूर्णाक्षी कुशलं ब्रूहि राघवम् । लक्ष्मणं ब्रूहि मे किञ्चिद्दुरुक्तं भाषितं पुरा ॥ 54

in your absence, your entering into alliance with Sugreeva, the destruction of Vali, Sugreeva's deputation of powerful and quick-moving monkey teams in search of Sita in all directions, and the arrival of one of them, myself, in Lanka—all these I narrated. **43.** I further said in conclusion: 'I am the minister of Sugreeva and the servant of Rama. Overcoming very great difficulties, I have now been able to discover the daughter of Janaka.' **(44-46)** Hearing these words of mine, Sita said with wide-open eyes: 'Who is speaking all these words that are like nectar to my ears? If what you say is all genuine you must appear before my eyes.' Then I appeared and prostrated myself before Sita in the form of a small monkey, and with my palms joined in salutation, stood at a little distance from her. I gave replies to the detailed questions she put to me about myself and all other matters. **47.** O valiant hero! I told her everything in proper order. Afterwards I presented to her the signet ring that you had sent with me. **(48-52).** Convinced now of my bona fides she said to me, 'O Hanuman! Tell Rama what you have seen—how I am living day and night under the oppression of these Rakshasa women.' To her I replied, 'Rama, who is constantly thinking of you, is sorrowing day and night that there is no news about you. Returning to him immediately, I shall report everything. Be sure that immediately after knowing the facts, Rama and Lakshmana, accompanied by Sugreeva and his army of monkeys will come to you. Destroying Ravana along with his whole tribe, he will take you back to your place. Now please give me some token of recognition which will make Rama convinced that I really met you.' **(53-56).** On my requesting her in this way, she gave me a crest-jewel from inside her locks. She also told me the story of the crow, which took place formerly at the Chitrakuta mountain. Then with tears flowing down her eyes, she added, 'Convey my enquiries about his welfare to Rama. Ask Lakshmana to excuse me for

तत्क्षमस्वाज्ञभावेन भाषितं कुलनन्दन । तारयेन्मां यथा रामस्तथा कुरु कृपान्वितः ॥ 55
इत्युक्त्वा रुदती सीता दुःखेन महतावृता । मयाप्याश्वासिता राम वदता सर्वमेव ते ॥ 56
ततः प्रस्थापितो राम त्वत्समीपमिहागतः । तदागमनवेलायामशोकवनिकां प्रियाम् ॥ 57
उत्पाट्य राक्षसांस्तत्र बहून्हत्वा क्षणादहम् । रावणस्यसुतं हत्वा रावणेनाभिभाष्य च ॥ 58
लङ्कामशेषतो दग्ध्वा पुनरप्यागमं क्षणात् । श्रुत्वा हनूमतो वाक्यं रामोऽत्यन्तप्रहृष्टधीः ॥ 59
हनूमंस्ते कृतं कार्यं देवैरपि सुदुष्करम् । उपकारं न पश्यामि तव प्रत्युपकारिणः ॥ 60
इदानीं ते प्रयच्छामि सर्वस्वं मम मारुते । इत्यालिङ्ग्य समाकृष्य गाढं वानरपुङ्गवम् ॥ 61
सार्द्रनेत्रो रघुश्रेष्ठः परां प्रीतिमवाप सः । हनूमन्तमुवाचेदं राघवो भक्तवत्सलः ॥ 62
परिरम्भो हि मे लोके दुर्लभः परमात्मनः । अतस्त्वं मम भक्तोऽसि प्रियोऽसि हरिपुङ्गव ॥ 63

यत्पादपद्मयुगलं तुलसीदलाद्यैः सम्पूज्य विष्णुपदवीमतुलां प्रयान्ति ।
तेनैव किं पुनरसौ परिरब्धमूर्ती रामेण वायुतनयः कृतपुण्यपुञ्जः ॥ 64

इति श्रीमदध्यात्मरामायणे उमामहेश्वरसंवादे
सुन्दरकाण्डे पञ्चमः सर्गः ॥ ५ ॥
समाप्तमिदं सुन्दरकाण्डम् ।

my thoughtless and unseemly speech to him. Then kindly do everything that may help Rama to rescue me at the earliest.' Speaking in this way, Sita began to weep, steeped in deep sorrow. I tried my best to comfort her with words concerning you.

(57-62). "Afterwards, O Rama, I made preparations to come back with the permission of the Devi. But before starting I did something more. I destroyed the Ashoka grove that is very dear to Ravana. Then I killed many Rakshasas including a son of Ravana. I got an a opportunity to speak face to face with Ravana. Then after setting fire to the whole of Lanka, I have come back immediately to you." Hearing these words of Hanuman, Rama was extremely delighted and said to him, "You have done something that is very difficult even for Devas to achieve. I find no way of making adequate returns to the service you have done me. O son of the Wind-god! I now offer to you all that I have." Speaking in this way, with tears flowing from his eyes, Rama held Hanuman in his tight embrace and felt great delight. Rama, the lover of devotees, next said to Hanuman as follows:

63. He said, "In this world it is very difficult for any one to be embraced in this manner by Me, the Supreme Spirit. Therefore, O the noblest of monkeys! You are My devotee and one dear to Me." **64.** He by worshipping whose lotus-feet with Tulasi and other ingredients one attains to the unparalleled Status of Vishnu—when one is embraced by that Being manifest as Rama, what doubt is there that such a person will attain to the summit of spiritual excellence?

ॐ

अध्यात्मरामायणम्

युद्धकाण्डः

प्रथमः सर्गः

श्रीमहादेव उवाच

यथावद्भाषितं वाक्यं श्रुत्वा रामो हनूमतः। उवाचानन्तरं वाक्यं हर्षेण महतावृतः। 1
कार्यं कृतं हनुमता देवैरपि सुदुष्करम्। मनसापि यदन्येन स्मर्तुं शक्यं न भूतले ॥ 2
शतयोजनविस्तीर्णं लङ्घयेत्कः पयोनिधिम्। लङ्कां च राक्षसैर्गुप्तां को वा धर्षयितुं क्षमः ॥ 3
भृत्यकार्यं हनुमता कृतं सर्वमशेषतः। सुग्रीवस्येदृशो लोके न भूतो न भविष्यति ॥ 4
अहं च रघुवंशश्च लक्ष्मणश्च कपीश्वरः। जानक्या दर्शनेनाद्य रक्षिताः स्मो हनूमता ॥ 5
सर्वथा सुकृतं कार्यं जानक्याः परिमार्गणम्। समुद्रं मनसा स्मृत्वा सीदतीव मनो मम ॥ 6
कथं नक्रझषाकीर्णं समुद्रं शतयोजनम्। लङ्घयित्वा रिपुं हन्यां कथं द्रक्ष्यामि जानकीम् ॥ 7

YUDDHA KANDAM

Chapter 1

THE MONKEY ARMY ON THE MARCH TO LANKA

Deliberations of Rama with Sugreeva and Hanuman (1-26)

1. Delighted at what Hanuman spoke, Rama said: **2.** 'Hanuman has performed a task which is impossible of achievement with great effort even by Devas. None in this world can do even in imagination what he has done. **3.** Who can leap over the sea a hundred Yojanas wide?' Who can destroy Lanka which is defended on all sides by Rakshasas? **4.** As a servant of Sugreeva, he has fully and perfectly achieved the task that was set for him. Such a servant has never existed before in this world and will never exist in future. **5.** By Hanuman's discovery of Sita, he has saved the honour of myself, of the royal line of Raghu, of Lakshmana and of Sugreeva, the king of monkeys. **6.** The search and the discovery of Sita has been fully accomplished. Now what is to be done hereafter? My mind reels when I think of crossing that ocean which Hanuman has achieved so easily. **7.** How shall I be able to rescue Sita, killing the enemy after crossing this ocean of a hundred Yojanas extent, full of dangerous aquatic creatures like sharks and crocodiles?"

श्रुत्वा तु रामवचनं सुग्रीवः प्राह राघवम् । समुद्रं लङ्घयिष्यामो महानक्रझषाकुलम् ॥ 8
लङ्कां च विधमिष्यामो हनिष्यामोऽद्य रावणम् । चिन्तां त्यज रघुश्रेष्ठ चिन्ता कार्यविनाशिनी ॥
एतान्पश्य महासत्त्वान् शूरान्वानरपुङ्गवान् । त्वत्प्रियार्थं समुद्युक्तान्प्रवेष्टुमपि पावकम् ॥ 10
समुद्रतरणे बुद्धिं कुरुष्व प्रथमं ततः । दृष्ट्वा लङ्कां दशग्रीवो हत इत्येव मन्महे ॥ 11
नहि पश्याम्यहं कश्चित्त्रिषु लोकेषु राघव । गृहीतधनुषो यस्ते तिष्ठेदभिमुखो रणे ॥ 12
सर्वथा नो जयो राम भविष्यति न संशयः । निमित्तानि च पश्यामि तथाभूतानि सर्वशः ॥ 13
सुग्रीववचनं श्रुत्वा भक्तिवीर्यसमन्वितम् । अङ्गीकृत्याब्रवीद्रामो हनूमन्तं पुरः स्थितम् ॥ 14
येन केन प्रकारेण लङ्घयामो महार्णवम् । लङ्कास्वरूपं मे ब्रूहि दुःसाध्यं देवदानवैः ॥ 15
ज्ञात्वा तस्य प्रतीकारं करिष्यामि कपीश्वर ।
श्रुत्वा रामस्य वचनं हनूमान्विनयान्वितः । उवाच प्राञ्जलिर्देव यथा दृष्टं ब्रवीमि ते ॥ 16
लङ्का दिव्यपुरी देव त्रिकूटशिखरे स्थिता ॥ 17
स्वर्णप्राकारसहिता स्वर्णाट्टालकसंयुता । परिखाभिः परिवृता पूर्णाभिर्निर्मलोदकैः ॥ 18

8. Hearing these words of Rama, Sugreeva said to him, "We shall be able to cross this ocean abounding in dangerous creatures like crocodiles and sharks **9.** We shall sack Lanka and kill Ravana. O Lord of Raghu's line! Abandon all worrying thoughts. Such worrying thoughts stand in the way of one's achieving one's objective. **10.** Here are these huge monkeys ready to please you by doing anything, if necesssary even by passing through fire. **11.** First let us think of the ways and means of crossing the ocean. Once we gain access to Lanka, then believe me, it is as good as our having killed Ravana. **12.** O Lord of the Raghus! I do not find anyone in the three worlds who can stand in the battlefield against you equipped with your bow. **13.** O Rama! Everywhere I see omens indicating that victory will surely be ours."

14. Accepting these words of Sugreeva couched in a language that was both devotional and heroic, Rama now said to Hanuman standing before him: **15.** "We might somehow manage to cross the great ocean. After that how shall we proceed? You therefore describe to me the features of this Lanka which is said to be difficult for even Devas and Asuras to penetrate. **16.** O great monkey! After knowing from you the difficulties of entering Lanka, we shall think of the strategy for overcoming them." At these words of Rama, Hanuman, joining his palms in salutation, said to Rama with great humility: "O great one! I shall describe the features of Lanka as I saw. **(17-18).** The city of Lanka is situated on the heights of the Trikuta mountain in a heavenly set-up. Filled with buildings and walls golden in appearance, it is surrounded by moats that are full of pure water.

नानोपवनशोभाढ्या दिव्यवापीभिरावृता । गृहैर्विचित्रशोभाढ्यमणिस्तम्भमयैः शुभैः ॥ 19
पश्चिमद्वारमासाद्य गजवाहाः सहस्रशः ॥ 20
तिष्ठन्त्यर्बुदसङ्ख्याकाः प्राच्यामपि तथैव च । रक्षिणो राक्षसा वीरा द्वारं दक्षिणमाश्रिताः ॥ 21
मध्यकक्षेऽप्यसङ्ख्याता गजाश्वरथपत्तयः । रक्षयन्ति सदा लङ्कां नानास्त्रकुशलाः प्रभो ॥ 22
सङ्क्रमैर्विविधैर्लङ्का शतघ्नीभिश्च संयुता । एवं स्थितेऽपि देवेश शृणु मे तत्र चेष्टितम् ॥ 23
दशाननबलौघस्य चतुर्थांशो मया हतः । दग्ध्वा लङ्का पुरीं स्वर्णप्रासादो धर्षितो मया ॥24
शतघ्न्यः सङ्क्रमाश्चैव नाशिता मे रघूत्तम । देव त्वद्दर्शनादेव लङ्का भस्मीकृता भवेत् ॥ 25
प्रस्थानं कुरु देवेश गच्छामो लवणाम्बुधेः । तीरं सह महावीरैर्वानरौघैः समन्ततः ॥ 26
श्रुत्वा हनूमतो वाक्यमुवाच रघुनन्दनः । सुग्रीव सैनिकान्सर्वान्प्रस्थानायाभिनोदय ॥ 27
इदानीमेव विजयो मुहूर्तः परिवर्तते । अस्मिन्मुहूर्ते गत्वाहं लङ्कां राक्षससङ्कुलाम् ॥ 28
सप्राकारां सुदुर्धर्षां नाशयामि सरावणाम् । आनेष्यामि च सीतां मे दक्षिणाक्षि स्फुरत्यधः 29
प्रयातु वाहिनी सर्वा वानराणां तरस्विनाम् । रक्षन्तु यूथपाः सेनामग्रे पृष्ठे च पार्श्वयोः ॥ 30

19. It is full of beautiful flower gardens, extensive tanks, pillars of precious stones, and mansions of great splendour. **20.** At its western gate, regiments of elephants are stationed and in the northern, regiments of cavalry and infantry. **21.** In the same way numerous troops of heroic Rakshasas are stationed at the eastern and southern gates of Lanka too. **22.** O Lord! In the middle of the city also are stationed innumerable elephants, horses, chariots and foot soldiers with leaders well versed in the use of all missiles. **23.** Lanka is defended with all these troops, besides with rockets (*Sataghni*) that can kill a hundred people at a time. Though defended so strongly in this way, hear, O Lord, what I was able to do there. **24.** A fourth of Ravana's forces was destroyed. The city was set fire to and its golden gate towers were shattered to pieces. **25.** I could destroy its batteries and secret places of defence. I see that by your very look, you will be able to reduce Lanka to ashes. **26.** O Supreme Lord! We can start immediately, with the army of heroic monkeys on all sides, and proceed to the shore of the ocean."

The army on the march (27-48)

27. Hearing Hanuman's speech Rama said, "O Sugreeva! Order your armies to march. **(28-29).** The auspicious time indicating victory has already begun. I shall start at this time with a view to destroy that well-defended Lanka along with Rávana and the whole tribe of Rakshasas inhabiting it. I shall succeed in rescuing Sita also. My right eye is throbbing, indicating that good fortune awaits us. **30.** Let the armies of powerful monkeys march forward. Let the leaders take positions behind, in front

हनूमन्तमथारुह्य गच्छाम्यग्रेऽङ्गदं ततः । आरुह्य लक्ष्मणो यातु सुग्रीव त्वं मया सह ॥ 31

गयो गवाक्षो गवयो मैन्दो द्विविद एव च । नलो नीलः सुषेणश्च जाम्बवांश्च तथापरे ॥ 32

सर्वे गच्छन्तु सर्वत्र सेनायाः शत्रुघातिनः ।

इत्याज्ञाप्य हरीन् रामः प्रतस्थे सहलक्ष्मणः । सुग्रीवसहितो हर्षात्सेनामध्यगतो विभुः ॥ 33

वारणेन्द्रनिभाः सर्वे वानराः कामरूपिणः । क्ष्वेलन्तः परिगर्जन्तो जग्मुस्ते दक्षिणां दिशम् ॥34

भक्षयन्तो ययुः सर्वे फलानि च मधूनि च । ब्रुवन्तो राघवस्याग्रे हनिष्यामोऽद्य रावणम् ॥ 35

एवं ते वानरश्रेष्ठा गच्छन्त्यतुलविक्रमाः । 36

हरिभ्यामुह्यमानौ तौ शुशुभाते रघूत्तमौ । नक्षत्रैः सेवितौ यद्वच्चन्द्रसूर्याविवाम्बरे ॥ 37

आवृत्य पृथिवीं कृत्स्नां जगाम महती चमूः । प्रस्फोटयन्तः पुच्छाग्रानुद्वहन्तश्च पादपान् ॥ 38

शैलानारोहयन्तश्च जग्मुर्मारुतवेगतः । असङ्ख्याताश्च सर्वत्र वानराः परिपूरिताः ॥ 39

हृष्टास्ते जग्मुरत्यर्थं रामेण परिपालिताः । गता चमू दिवारात्रं क्वचिन्नासज्जत क्षणम् ॥ 40

काननानि विचित्राणि पश्यन्मलयसह्ययोः । ते सह्यं समतिक्रम्य मलयं च तथा गिरीन् ॥41

आययुश्चानुपूर्व्येण समुद्रं भीमनिःस्वनम् । अवतीर्य हनूमन्तं रामः सुग्रीवसंयुतः ॥ 42

and on the sides to guard the forces. **31.** I shall travel in front mounting the shoulders of Hanuman, and Lakshmana behind me on Angada, and you, O Sugreeva, should march with me. **(32-33).** On all the sides of the forces, let all the army leaders march—the leaders of great destructive capacity like Gaya, Gavaya, Gavaksha, Mainda, Dwivida, Nala, Neela, Sushena and Jambavan." Giving these orders to the monkey forces, the all powerful Rama along with Sugreeva and Lakshmana started with the army. **34.** All the monkey troops, capable of assuming any form and equal to the heavenly elephant Airavata in power, marched towards the southern sea, demonstrating war-like movements and giving out terrific war cries. **(35-36).** Consuming all the fruits and honey on the way and declaring their resolve to destroy Ravana, all these monkey leaders of unparalleled power moved on. **37.** The two leaders of Raghu s clan, riding on the shoulders of the monkey leaders amidst these monkey forces, looked like the sun and the moon accompanied by luminous stars. **(38-40).** The countless monkey heroes of the army filling all space struck the ground with their tails, pulled out trees as their weapons, and climbed over mountains as they moved on with the speed of wind. That army of tremendous size, led and protected by Rama, marched with great enthusiasm by day and by night without rest.

(41-44). Seeing the grand forests of mounts Malaya and Sahya they joyously passed through those mountain ranges and duly

सलिलाभ्याशमासाद्य रामो वचनमब्रवीत् । आगताः स्मो वयं सर्वे समुद्रं मकरालयम् ॥ 43

इतो गन्तुमशक्यं नो निरुपायेन वानराः । तत्र सेनानिवेशोऽस्तु मन्त्रयामोऽस्य तारणे ॥ 44

श्रुत्वा रामस्य वचनं सुग्रीवः सागरान्तिके । सेनां न्यवेशयत्क्षिप्रं रक्षितां कपिकुञ्जरैः ॥ 45

ते पश्यन्तो विषेदुस्तं सागरं भीमदर्शनम् । महोन्नततरङ्गाढ्यं भीमनक्रभयङ्करम् ॥ 46

अगाधं गगनाकारं सागरं वीक्ष्य दुःखिताः । तरिष्यामः कथं घोरं सागरं वरुणालयम् ॥ 47

हन्तव्योऽस्माभिरद्यैव रावणो राक्षसाधमः । इति चिन्ताकुलाः सर्वे रामपार्श्वे व्यवस्थिताः ॥ 48

रामः सीतामनुस्मृत्य दुःखेन महतावृतः । विलप्य जानकीं सीतां बहुधा कार्यमानुषः ॥ 49

अद्वितीयश्चिदात्मैकः परमात्मा सनातनः । यस्तु जानाति रामस्य स्वरूपं तत्त्वतो जनः ॥ 50

तं न स्पृशति दुःखादि किमुतानन्दमव्ययम् । दुःखहर्षभयक्रोधलोभमोहमदादयः ॥ 51

अज्ञानलिङ्गान्येतानि कुतः सन्ति चिदात्मनि । देहाभिमानिनो दुःखं न देहस्य चिदात्मनः ॥ 52

सम्प्रसादे द्वयाभावात्सुखमात्रं हि दृश्यते ।

बुद्ध्याद्यभावात्संशुद्धे दुखं तत्र न दृश्यते । अतो दुःखादिकं सर्वं बुद्धेरेव न संशयः ॥ 53

reached the sea-shore, where the roaring sound of the ocean could be heard. Descending from the shoulder of Hanuman, Rama along with Sugreeva went to the sea-shore. He said, "We have all now reached the shore of the mighty ocean, the home of all aquatic creatures. We cannot proceed further from here without devising some way of crossing the ocean. Let us think about it, and meanwhile let the army rest."

45. Hearing these words of Rama, Sugreeva arranged for the orderly stay of that army on that sea shore under the protection of their leaders. **(46-48).** They all felt depressed to see before them the formidable ocean full of waves of enormous size, dangerous on account of its huge aquatic creatures, fathomless in depth, and extensive like the sky. Filled with sorrow at the sight of this awe-inspring abode of Varuna, they spoke among themselves, "How shall we cross this ocean and kill that evil fellow of a Ravana?" Distressed with such thought they all gathered round Rama.

The philosophy behind Rama's sorrow (49-54)

(49-53). Remembering Sita, Rama who had assumed a human form for a certain purpose, wailed piteously, thinking about Sita's condition. But it is the ignorant people, who do not understand the real nature of Rama, that attribute sorrow to him. In His true nature, Rama is the One without a second, Pure Consciousness, Eternal Being, and the Supreme Self. Not knowing this—that sorrow and such weaknesses like joy, fear, anger, greed, delusion, pride etc., which are the signs of ignorance, never affect Him who is Pure Consciousness —men attribute all these signs of ignorance

रामः परात्मा पुरुषः पुराणो नित्योदितो नित्यसुखो निरीहः ।
तथापि मायागुणसङ्गतोऽसौ सुखीव दुखीव विभाव्यतेऽबुधैः ॥ 54

इति श्रीमदध्यात्मरामायणे उमामहेश्वरसंवादे
युद्धकाण्डे प्रथमः सर्गः ॥ १ ॥

to Him. Sorrow is a characteristic of one who thinks, 'I am the body'. How can it be present in one who has no identification with the body and is established in the experience that he is Pure Consciousness? Even in deep sleep, there is no sorrow or joy. In the absence of relative joy and sorrow, sleep is declared to be one of Pure Bliss (which is however covered by ignorance). Owing to the absence of Buddhi there is no sorrow in one who is established in Pure Consciousness. So sorrow and all these relative experiences are only affectations of the Buddhi and never of the true Self. **54.** Rama is the Supreme Self, the all-inclusive and ever-shining Being, who existed even before creation. He is eternal and unbroken Bliss, unaffected by any change. People who are ignorant of this real nature of His, think of Him as possessed of the attributes of Maya and speak of Him as happy or afflicted.

द्वितीयः सर्गः

श्रीमहादेव उवाच

लङ्कायां रावणो दृष्ट्वा कृतं कर्म हनूमता । दुष्करं दैवतैर्वापि ह्रिया किञ्चिदवाङ्मुखः ॥ 1
आहूय मन्त्रिणः सर्वानिदं वचनमब्रवीत् । हनूमता कृतं कर्म भवद्भिर्दृष्टमेव तत् ॥ 2
प्रविश्य लङ्कां दुर्धर्षां दृष्ट्वा सीतां दुरासदाम् । हत्वा च राक्षसान्वीरानक्षं मन्दोदरीसुतम् ॥ 3
दग्ध्वा लङ्कामशेषेण लङ्घयित्वा च सागरम् । युष्मान्सर्वानतिक्रम्य स्वस्थोऽगात्पुनरेव सः ॥ 4
किं कर्तव्यमितोऽस्माभिर्यूयं मन्त्रविशारदाः । मन्त्रयध्वं प्रयत्नेन यत्कृतं मे हितं भवेत् ॥ 5

Chapter 2

EXPULSION OF VIBHEESHANA

Ravana deliberating with his ministers (1-19)

(1-4). In Lanka, Ravana, who felt humiliated by all that Hanuman did there—what is incapable of performance even by Devas—now said with a touch of shame, in the assembly of all his ministers: "You have all seen what Hanuman has done. He entered into this impregnable city of Lanka. He met Sita who is unapproachable to anyone. He destroyed many heroic Rakshasas including my son Aksha. Crossing the ocean, he set fire to the whole of Lanka and then overcoming you all, he has returned unhurt. **5.** What are we to do hereafter? What is it by doing which things

रावणस्य वचः श्रुत्वा राक्षसास्तमथाब्रुवन् । देव शङ्का कुतो रामात्तव लोकजितो रणे ॥ 6
इन्द्रस्तु बद्ध्वा निक्षिप्तः पुत्रेण तव पत्तने । जित्वा कुबेरमानीय पुष्पकं भुज्यते त्वया ॥ 7
यमो जितः कालदण्डाद्भयं नाभूत्तव प्रभो । वरुणो हुङ्कृतेनैव जितः सर्वेऽपि राक्षसाः ॥ 8
मयो महासुरो भीत्या कन्यां दत्त्वा स्वयं तव । त्वद्वशे वर्ततेऽद्यापि किमुतान्ये महासुराः ॥ 9
हनूमद्धर्षणं यत्तु तदवज्ञाकृतं च नः । वानरोऽयं किमस्माकमस्मिन्पौरुषदर्शने ॥ 10
इत्युपेक्षितमस्माभिर्धर्षणं तेन किं भवेत् । वयं प्रमत्ताः किं तेन वञ्चिताः स्मो हनूमता ॥ 11
जानीमो यदि तं सर्वे कथं जीवन् गमिष्यति । आज्ञापय जगत्कृत्स्नमवानरममानुषम् ॥ 12
कृत्वायास्यामहे सर्वे प्रत्येकं वा नियोजय ॥ 13
कुम्भकर्णस्तदा प्राह रावणं राक्षसेश्वरम् ।
आरब्धं यत्त्वया कर्म स्वात्मनाशाय केवलम् । न दृष्टोऽसि तदा भाग्यात्त्वं रामेण महात्मना ॥14
यदि पश्यति रामस्त्वां जीवन्नायासि रावण । रामो न मानुषो देवः साक्षान्नारायणोऽव्ययः ॥ 15
सीता भगवती लक्ष्मी रामपत्नी यशस्विनी । राक्षसानां विनाशाय त्वयानीता सुमध्यमा ॥ 16
विषपिण्डमिवागीर्य महामीनो यथा तथा । आनीता जानकी पश्चात्त्वया किं वा भविष्यति ॥17

will turn in my favour? You, who are experts in diplomacy, are required to think about this."

6. Hearing Ravana's words, those Rakshasa ministers said to him, "O our lord and master! How is it that you entertain any fear about this Rama—you who are the conqueror of all the worlds! **7.** Your son Indrajit bound up Indra himself and brought him before you. You have conquered Kubera and have taken away from him the aerial mansion Pushpaka, which now you are enjoying. **8.** You have conquered Yama, and therefore, O Lord, there is no reason for you to fear the rod, the weapon of that Lord of death even. You have subdued Varuna by a mere Humkara. You have subdued also Rakshasas of every kind. **9.** The great Asura Maya, out of fear, has given his own daughter to you, and he is even today your subordinate. Not to speak then of other Asuras. **(10-11).** Hanuman was able to behave so impudently here only because we did not take him seriously. We thought this insignificant fellow of a monkey could do nothing here and it was vain to show our heroism against him. Because of this way of thinking, we became a bit careless. What that Hanuman did was only deception. **(12-13).** If we had taken him seriously, do you imagine that he would ever have gone back alive? You order us, and we shall make this whole world devoid of the tribe of monkeys and of men. We shall all go together or go one by one according to your order."

14. Hearing these words of the time-serving ministers, Kumbhakarna said to Ravana, the lord of the Rakshasas, "What you have done at the start would itself have been the cause of your destruction. Fortunately for you, the great Rama did not see you when you went to abduct Sita. **(15-18).**

यद्यप्यनुचितं कर्म त्वया कृतमजानता । सर्वं समं करिष्यामि स्वस्थचित्तो भव प्रभो ॥ 18

कुम्भकर्णवचः श्रुत्वा वाक्यमिन्द्रजिदब्रवीत् ।
देहि देव ममानुज्ञां हत्वा रामं सलक्ष्मणम् । सुग्रीवं वानरांश्चैव पुनर्यास्यामि तेऽन्तिकम् ॥ 19

तत्रागतो भागवतप्रधानो विभीषणो बुद्धिमतां वरिष्ठः ।
श्रीरामपादद्वय एकतानः प्रणम्य देवारिमुपोपविष्टः ॥ 20

विलोक्य कुम्भश्रवणादिदैत्यान्मत्तप्रमत्तानतिविस्मयेन ।
विलोक्य कामातुरमप्रमत्तो दशाननं प्राह विशुद्धबुद्धिः ॥ 21

न कुम्भकर्णेन्द्रजितौ च राजंस्तथा महापार्श्वमहोदरौ तौ ।
निकुम्भकुम्भौ च तथातिकायः स्थातुं न शक्ता युधि राघवस्य ॥ 22

सीताभिधानेन महाग्रहेण ग्रस्तोऽसि राजन् न च ते विमोक्षः ।
तामेव सत्कृत्य महाधनेन दत्त्वाभिरामाय सुखी भव त्वम् ॥ 23

यावन्न रामस्य शिताः शिलीमुखा लङ्कामभिव्याप्य शिरांसि रक्षसाम् ।
छिन्दन्ति तावद्रघुनायकस्य भो तां जानकीं त्वं प्रतिदातुमर्हसि ॥ 24

O Ravana! If Rama had seen you, you would not have come back alive. Rama is not a mere man. He is divine—Narayana, the Supreme Being. His famous consort Sita is the divine Lakshmi. Just as fish swallows a poisoned bait inviting its own destruction, so have you brought Sita here for the destruction of the whole tribe of Rakshasas. Now you are worrying, thinking of the consequences of your own action. But, O lord, even though what you have done is improper, I shall set things right. Do not worry."

19. On hearing Kumbhakarna's words Indrajit rose up and said, "O my Lord! Command me. I shall destroy this Rama and Lakshmana along with Sugreeva and all his monkeys, and come back to you."

Vibheeshana's Expulsion (20-33)

(20-21). Now came forward Vibheeshana, who was highly devotional, intelligent, pure-minded and entirely devoted to Rama. After saluting Ravana, he sat by his side and spoke words that astounded the arrogant Rakshasas from Kumbhakarna downwards and the love-lorn Ravana as well. He spoke deliberately as follows: **22.** "O King! None of these Rakshasas—Kumbhakarna, Indrajit, Mahaparsva, Mahodara, Nikumbha, Kumbha, Adikaya etc.—can be a match to Rama in battle. **23.** O King! You have been possessed, as it were, of a spirit which is Sita. You have to be exorcised of that spirit if you want to survive. The way for that is to take her, along with rich presents, to Rama and hand her over to him. You can then be a happy man. **24.** If you do not want to see Rama's sharp arrows flying everywhere in Lanka and severing the heads of Rakshasas, then return Sita to him immediately.

यावन्नगाभा कपयो महाबला हरीन्द्रतुल्या नखदंष्ट्रयोधिनः ।
लङ्कां समाक्रम्य विनाशयन्ति ते तावद्द्रुतं देहि रघूत्तमाय ताम् ॥ 25
जीवन्न रामेण विमोक्ष्यसे त्वं गुप्तः सुरेन्द्रैरपि शङ्करेण ।
न देवराजाङ्कगतो न मृत्योः पातालत्लोकानपि सम्प्रविष्टः ॥ 26
शुभं हितं पवित्रं च विभीषणवचः खलः । प्रतिजग्राह नैवासौ म्रियमाण इवौषधम् ॥ 27
कालेन नोदितो दैत्यो विभीषणमथाब्रवीत् । मद्दत्तभोगैः पुष्टाङ्गो मत्समीपे वसन्नपि ॥ 28
प्रतीपमाचरत्येष ममैव हितकारिणः । मित्रभावेन शत्रुर्मे जातो नास्त्यत्र संशयः ॥ 29
अनार्येण कृतघ्नेन सङ्गतिर्मे न युज्यते । विनाशमभिकाङ्क्षन्ति ज्ञातीनां ज्ञातयः सदा ॥30
योऽन्यस्त्वेवंविधं ब्रूयाद्वाक्यमेकं निशाचरः । हन्मि तस्मिन् क्षणे एव धिक् त्वां रक्षःकुलाधमम् 31
रावणेनैवमुक्तः सन्परुषं स विभीषणः । उत्पपात सभामध्याद्गदापाणिर्महाबलः ॥ 32
चतुर्भिर्मन्त्रिभिः सार्धं गगनस्थोऽब्रवीद्वचः । क्रोधेन महताविष्टो रावणं दशकन्धरम् ॥ 33
मा विनाशमुपैहि त्वं प्रियवादिनमेव माम् । धिक्करोषि तथापि त्वं ज्येष्ठो भ्राता पितुः समः 34

25. If you do not want to see the mountain-like monkeys, strong as lions and capable of fighting with teeth and claws, attacking and sacking the whole of Lanka, then return Sita to Rama immediately. **26.** Even if you are protected by Indra or Sankara, even if you get a place of refuge in the lap of the lord of the celestials or the god of. death, or even if you take refuge in Patala, you will not be able to save your life from Rama."

27. These well-meant, noble and beneficial words were unacceptable to that evil-minded Ravana just as a medicine is to a man doomed to die. **(28-29).** Ravana, who was under the influence of destructive Time, now said to Vibheeshana, "You have been fattened by the food and the comforts of life bestowed by me. Though you are staying with me, you are inimical to me who have done only good to you. You are doing what is contrary to my interest. Though appearing to be a friend, you are a born enemy of mine. There is no doubt about it. **30.** It does not befit me to associate with such an ungrateful and impudent person like you. It is well known that one's close relatives often look forward to one's destruction. **31.** If any other Rakshasa had spoken such words as you have done, I would have executed him immediately. I do not, however, want to kill you. But begone, you scum of the Rakshasa tribe! Never again appear before me."

(32-33). On hearing these harsh words of Ravana, powerful Vibheeshana, with his mace in hand and accompanied by four ministers, leapt up into the sky from the assembly hall and in a mood of great anger, said to the ten-headed Ravana, stationing himself in the sky:

कालो राघवरूपेण जातो दशरथालये । काली सीताभिधानेन जाता जनकनन्दिनी ॥ 35
तावुभावागतावत्र भूमेर्भारापनुत्तये । तेनैव प्रेरितस्त्वं तु न शृणोषि हितं मम ॥ 36
श्रीरामः प्रकृतेः साक्षात्परस्तात्सर्वदा स्थितः । बहिरन्तश्च भूतानां समः सर्वत्र संस्थितः ॥ 37
नामरूपादिभेदेन तत्तन्मय इवामलः । यथा नानाप्रकारेषु वृक्षेष्वेको महानलः ॥ 38
तत्तदाकृतिभेदेन भिद्यतेऽज्ञानचक्षुषाम् ॥ 39
पञ्चकोशादिभेदेन तत्तन्मय इवाबभौ ।
नीलपीतादियोगेन निर्मलः स्फटिको यथा । स एव नित्यमुक्तोऽपि स्वमायागुणबिम्बितः ॥ 40
कालः प्रधानं पुरुषोऽव्यक्तं चेति चतुर्विधः । प्रधानपुरुषाभ्यां स जगत्कृत्स्नं सृजत्यजः ॥ 41
कालरूपेण कलनां जगतः कुरुतेऽव्ययः । कालरूपी स भगवान् रामरूपेण मायया ॥ 42
ब्रह्मणा प्रार्थितो देवस्त्वद्वधार्थमिहागतः । तदन्यथा कथं कुर्यात्सत्यसंकल्प ईश्वरः ॥ 43
हनिष्यति त्वां रामस्तु सपुत्रबलवाहनम् । हन्यमानं न शक्नोमि द्रष्टुं रामेण रावण ॥ 44

Vibheeshana's Sermon (34-46)

34. He said "May you not meet with destruction! You are my elder brother and therefore equal to my father himself. I have spoken only what is for your good and yet you are expelling me. **(35-36).** Kāla (Destructive Time) has been born in Dasaratha's house in the form of Rama and Kālī (feminine of Kāla) in the house of Janaka under the name of Sita. In order to relieve the earth of its burdens, they two have come here for your destruction. It is under their inducement that you refuse to hear my beneficial words of advice **(37-39).** Though Rama appears to be a man, he is really the Supreme Spirit who transcends Prakriti. He is Omnipresent, being within and without all beings. He is devoid of all impurity and ever the same. Under different names and forms, He appears as if divided, just as the one universal fire appears in different forms and sizes through different wooden pieces according to their shape and size. It is only the people who look at this phenomenon through the eye of ignorance that would consider the fire as different. **(40-41).** Just as a clear crystal appears as blue, yellow etc., in the proximity of those colours, so in the presence of the five sheaths (Kosas), He who is Pure Spirit appears like them. He is ever unbound and unlimited. But reflecting Himself in the Gunas of His own Maya, He appears in the four forms as Kala, Pradhana, Purusha and Avyakta. With Pradhana and Purusha as the cause, He, the unborn One manifests this whole universe. **(42-43).** The changeless Being that He is, He as Time effects the dissolution of the universe. Being prayed to by Brahma, He, the embodiment of Time, has assumed the form of Rama by His own mysterious power (Maya) and has come here for your destruction. How can you alter this? The will of the Lord comes always true. **(44-45).** Rama

त्वां राक्षसकुलं कृत्स्नं ततो गच्छामि राघवम् । मयि याते सुखी भूत्वा रमस्व भवने चिरम् ॥45

विभीषणो रावणवाक्यतः क्षणाद्विसृज्य सर्वं सपरिच्छदं गृहम् ।
जगाम रामस्य पदारविन्दयोः सेवाभिकाङ्क्षी परिपूर्णमानसः ॥ 46

इति श्रीमदध्यात्मरामायणे उमामहेश्वरसंवादे
युद्धकाण्डे द्वितीयः सर्गः ॥ २ ॥

is going to destroy you along with your sons, army and all equipments. I cannot bear to see you and the whole tribe of Rakshasas being destroyed. Therefore, O Ravana, I am going to seek shelter under Rama. When I am gone, you will certainly feel very happy and enjoy life in your palace." **46.** So goaded by Ravana's words, Vibheeshana in a moment abandoned everything, his home and his possessions, and went to Rama fully satisfied to spend his time in his service.

तृतीयः सर्गः

श्रीमहादेव उवाच

विभीषणो महाभागश्चतुर्भिर्मन्त्रिभिः सह । आगत्य गगने रामसम्मुखे समवस्थितः ॥ 1

उच्चैरुवाच भोः स्वामिन् राम राजीवलोचन । रावणस्यानुजोऽहं ते दारहर्तुर्विभीषणः ॥ 2

नाम्ना भ्रात्रा निरस्तोऽहं त्वामेव शरणं गतः । हितमुक्तं मया देव तस्य चाविदितात्मनः ॥ 3

सीतां रामाय वैदेहीं प्रेषयेति पुनः पुनः । उक्तोऽपि न शृणोत्येव कालपाशवशं गतः ॥ 4

हन्तुं मां खड्गमादाय प्राद्रवद्राक्षसाधमः । ततोऽचिरेण सचिवैश्चतुर्भिः सहितो भयात् ॥ 5

Chapter 3

SELF-SURRENDER OF VIBHEESHANA

Vibheeshana seeking shelter at Rama's feet (1-14)

1. The high-souled Vibheeshana with his four ministers went to the place where Rama was, and stationed himself in the sky facing Rama. **(2-4).** He then said aloud, "O Lord! Lotus-eyed Rama! I am Vibheeshana, the brother of Ravana who has abducted your wife. Being expelled by my brother, I am seeking shelter under you. O noble one! I spoke words that are beneficial to him, Ravana, who is bent on improper conduct. I advised him again and again to return Sita to you. Still, subject to the influence of Time, he would not listen to me. **(5-6).** On the other hand, the heinous Rakshasa approached, sword in hand, to kill me. So with my four ministers, I have left the place and, seeking liberation from Samsara, I take

त्वामेव भवमोक्षाय मुमुक्षुः शरणं गतः । विभीषणवचः श्रुत्वा सुग्रीवो वाक्यमब्रवीत् ॥ 6
विश्वासार्हो न ते राम मायावी राक्षसाधमः । सीताहर्तुर्विशेषेण रावणस्यानुजो बली ॥ 7
मन्त्रिभिः सायुधैरस्मान् विवरे निहनिष्यति । तदाज्ञापय मे देव वानरैर्हन्यतामयम् ॥ 8
ममैवं भाति ते राम बुद्ध्या किं निश्चितं वद । श्रुत्वा सुग्रीववचनं रामः सस्मितमब्रवीत् ॥ 9
यदीच्छामि कपिश्रेष्ठ लोकान्सर्वान्सहेश्वरान् । निमिषार्धेन संहन्यां सृजामि निमिषार्धतः ॥ 10
अतो मयाभयं दत्तं शीघ्रमानय राक्षसम् ।
सकृदेव प्रपन्नाय तवास्मीति च याचते ।
अभयं सर्वभूतेभ्यो ददाम्येतद्व्रतं मम ॥ 11
रामस्य वचनं श्रुत्वा सुग्रीवो हृष्टमानसः । विभीषणमथानाय्य दर्शयामास राघवम् ॥ 12
विभीषणस्तु साष्टाङ्गं प्रणिपत्य रघूत्तमम् । हर्षगद्गदया वाचा भक्त्या च परयान्वितः ॥ 13
रामं श्यामं विशालाक्षं प्रसन्नमुखपङ्कजम् ।
धनुर्बाणधरं शान्तं लक्ष्मणेन समन्वितम् । कृताञ्जलिपुटो भूत्वा स्तोतुं समुपचक्रमे ॥ 14

shelter under you without any loss of time." Hearing these words of Vibheeshana, Sugreeva said: **(7-9).** "O Rama! He must be a notorious Rakshasa, an expert in magical tricks. Besides he is the brother of Ravana, strong in body and accompanied by ministers bearing arms. When he gets an opportunity, he will kill us. Therefore, O Lord, order me to have him executed by monkey guards. This is the course that suggests itself to my mind. Now you order what you think is right." On hearing Sugreeva's words, Rama smiled and said: **10.** "O monkey leader! At my will, I create the whole universe along with Indra and other Devas in half a moment and destroy them also in a trice. **11.** Thus, being the Lord of all, I am giving him shelter from all fear. Bring that Rakshasa soon before Me. It is My vow to give shelter to whomsoever among the creatures that come to Me saying even once, 'I am thine' " **12.** Thereupon Sugreeva, who was delighted to hear Rama's words, brought Vibheeshana and presented him to Rama. **(13-14).** Vibheeshana now made a full prostration to Rama. In a voice choked with intense devotion and with palms joined in salutation, he began to chant a hymn in praise of Rama who was peaceful and joyous in facial expression, who was large-eyed and blue in complexion, who was equipped with bow and arrow, and who was accompained by Lakshmana.

Vibheeshana's Hymn (15-30)

Vibheeshana now said: **(15-20).** "Salutation to Thee great leader—to Thee the gladdener of Sita's heart, to Thee equipped with the terrible bow, to Thee lover of devotees, to Thee Infinite Being, to Thee of unlimited brilliance, to Thee the friend of Sugreeva, to Thee the Lord of Raghu's clan, to Thee the cause of the creation,

विभीषण उवाच

नमस्ते राम राजेन्द्र नमःसीतामनोरम । नमस्ते चण्डकोदण्ड नमस्ते भक्तवत्सल ॥ 15
नमोऽनन्ताय शान्ताय रामायामिततेजसे । सुग्रीवमित्राय च ते रघूणां पतये नमः ॥ 16
जगदुत्पत्तिनाशानां कारणाय महात्मने । त्रैलोक्यगुरवेऽनादिगृहस्थाय नमो नमः ॥ 17
त्वमादिर्जगतां राम त्वमेव स्थितिकारणम् । त्वमन्ते निधनस्थानं स्वेच्छाचारस्त्वमेव हि ॥ 18
चराचराणां भूतानां बहिरन्तश्च राघव । व्याप्यव्यापकरूपेण भवान् भाति जगन्मयः ॥ 19
त्वन्मायया हृतज्ञाना नष्टात्मानो विचेतसः । गतागतं प्रपद्यन्ते पापपुण्यवशात्सदा ॥ 20
तावत्सत्यं जगद्भाति शुक्तिकारजतं यथा । यावन्न ज्ञायते ज्ञानं चेतसानन्यगामिना ॥ 21
त्वदज्ञानात्सदा युक्ताः पुत्रदारगृहादिषु । रमन्ते विषयान्सर्वानन्ते दुःखप्रदान्विभो ॥ 22
त्वमिन्द्रोऽग्निर्यमो रक्षो वरुणश्च तथानिलः । कुबेरश्च तथा रुद्रस्त्वमेव पुरुषोत्तम ॥ 23
त्वमणोरप्यणीयांश्च स्थूलात् स्थूलतरः प्रभो । त्वं पिता सर्वलोकानां माता धाता त्वमेव हि ॥24
आदिमध्यान्तरहितः परिपूर्णोऽच्युतोऽव्ययः । त्वं पाणिपादरहितश्चक्षुःश्रोत्रविवर्जितः ॥ 25

sustentation and dissolution of the universe, to Thee the great Being who is the teacher of all the worlds, to Thee the primeval householder (being the Lord of Prakriti from the beginning of time),to Thee who preceded all the worlds! Thou art the cause of the worlds, Thou sustainest it and into Thee it dissolves. Thy will is unobstructed by anything. Thou alone existest within and without all beings as the Pervader and the Pervaded. Thou manifestest in the form of the universe. Carried away by the power of Thy Maya, Jivas steeped in ignorance, devoid of discriminative power and subject to merits and demerits, revolve in the Samsara consisting of births and deaths. **21.** Until one knows Thee with a purified mind which does not go after anything else other than Thee, the Jiva perceives this universe as real, just as silver is seen in the mother of pearl by one under illusory perception. **22.** Not knowing Thee, man, O Lord, remains ever attached to son, wife and relatives, and takes delight in all these objects of the senses, which will ultimately bring him sorrow. **(23-30).** Thou art verily Indra, Agni, Yama, Niruti,Varuna, Vayu,Kubera, Rudra and the Supreme Purusha. Thou art subtler than the subtlest atom, and bigger than the grossest of objects. The creator and Protector of the worlds, Thou art without beginning, middle or end, Thou art ever full. Thou art devoid of loss and destruction, devoid of hands and feet, devoid of eyes and ears. Thou movest fast without legs, Thou graspest everything without hands, Thou seest everything without eyes, and Thou hearest everything without ears. Thou art beyond the limitation of the five Kosas (sheaths of the Jiva), Thou art without the limitation of the Gunas, requiring no support other than Thyself.

निजघ्नुस्तानि रक्षांसि नखैर्दन्तैश्च वेगिताः । राक्षसाश्च तदा भीमा द्वारेभ्यः सर्वतो रुषा ॥ 57
निर्गत्य भिन्दिपालैश्च खड्गैः शूलैः परश्वधैः । निजघ्नुर्वानरानीकं महाकाया महाबलाः ॥ 58
राक्षसांश्च तथा जघ्नुर्वानरा जितकाशिनः । तदा बभूव समरो मांसशोणितकर्दमः ॥ 59
रक्षसां वानराणां च सम्बभूवाद्भुतोपमः । 60
ते हयैश्च गजैश्चैव रथैः काञ्चनसन्निभैः ।
रक्षोव्याघ्रा युयुधिरे नादयन्तो दिशो दश । राक्षसाश्च कपीन्द्राश्च परस्परजयैषिणः ॥ 61
राक्षसान्वानरा जघ्नुर्वानरांश्चैव राक्षसाः । रामेण विष्णुना दृष्टा हरयो दिविजांशजाः ॥ 62
बभूवुर्बलिनो हृष्टास्तदा पीतामृता इव । सीताभिमर्शपापेन रावणेनाभिपालितान् ॥ 63
हतश्रीकान्हतबलान् राक्षसान् जघ्नुरोजसा । चतुर्थांशावशेषेण निहतं राक्षसं बलम् ॥ 64
स्वसैन्यं निहतं दृष्ट्वा मेघनादोऽथ दुष्टधीः । ब्रह्मदत्तवरः श्रीमानन्तर्धानं गतोऽसुरः ॥ 65
सर्वास्त्रकुशलो व्योम्नि ब्रह्मास्त्रेण समन्ततः । नानाविधानि शस्त्राणि वानरानीकमर्दयन् ॥ 66
ववर्ष शरजालानि तदद्भुतमिवाभवत् । रामोऽपि मानयन्ब्राह्ममस्त्रमस्त्रविदां वरः ॥ 67

Dvivida, Jambavan, Dadhivaktra, Kesari, Tara etc., leapt over the gate towers of Lanka and obstructed the exit passages with trees and rocks. **(57-58).** The monkeys with very speedy movements killed with their nails and teeth many Rakshasas of huge size. Roused to great anger the Rakshasas came out of the portals of the fortress and killed many monkeys also with catapults, swords, spears, and hatchets. **(59-60).** The victorious monkeys killed many Rakshasas and the battlefield was made miry with the blood and flesh of the forces destroyed, thus presenting a sight of awe-inspiring bloodshed. **(61-64).** Reverberating the quarters with their battle cries, the Rakshasas fought, mounted on horses, elephants and chariots of golden hue. Fighting with an eye on victory, the Rakshasas and the monkeys clashed with great violence, causing mutual destruction. But blessed by the glance of Rama, the monkeys who were the off-spring of Devas, fought with great enthusiasm and joy like those who had drunk nectar. But the Rakshasas had their prowess and good fortune eclipsed by the fact of their being under the protection of Ravana accursed by the monstrous sin of having touched the holy body of Sita. They therefore suffered terrible destruction, a fourth of their forces being annihilated.

Meghanada's devastating attack (65-70)

(65-67). Seeing the Rakshasa army being thus destroyed, the evil-minded Asura named Meghanada came for its protection. He was once blessed with boons by Brahma and was a master in the use of all missiles. He was also noted for the various victories he had won. Now remaining unseen in the sky, he attacked the monkey forces with Brahma missile and various other kinds of weapons. Everyone was astonished at

क्षणं तूष्णीमुवासाथ ददर्श पतितं बलम् । वानराणां रघुश्रेष्ठश्चुकोपानलसन्निभः ॥ 68
चापमानय सौमित्रे ब्रह्मास्त्रेणासुरं क्षणात् । भस्मीकरोमि मे पश्य बलमद्य रघूत्तम ॥ 69
मेघनादोऽपि तच्छ्रुत्वा रामवाक्यमतन्द्रितः । तूर्णं जगाम नगरं मायया मायिकोऽसुरः ॥ 70
पतितं वानरानीकं दृष्ट्वा रामोऽतिदुःखितः । उवाच मारुतिं शीघ्रं गत्वा क्षीरमहोदधिम् ॥ 71
तत्र द्रोणगिरिर्नाम दिव्यौषधिसमुद्भवः । तमानय द्रुतं गत्वा सञ्जीवय महामते ॥ 72
वानरौघान्महासत्त्वान्कीर्तिस्ते सुस्थिरा भवेत् । आज्ञाप्रमाणमित्युक्त्वा जगामानिलनन्दनः ॥ 73
आनीय च गिरिं सर्वान्वानरान्वानरर्षभः । जीवयित्वा पुनस्तत्र स्थापयित्वा ययौ द्रुतम् ॥ 74
पूर्ववद्भैरवं नादं वानराणां बलौघतः । श्रुत्वा विस्मयमापन्नो रावणो वाक्यमब्रवीत् ॥ 75
राघवो मे महान् शत्रुः प्राप्तो देवविनिर्मितः । हन्तुं तं समरे शीघ्रं गच्छन्तु मम यूथपाः ॥ 76
मन्त्रिणो बान्धवाः शूरा ये च मत्प्रियकाङ्क्षिणः । सर्वे गच्छन्तु युद्धाय त्वरितं मम शासनात् ॥ 77
ये न गच्छन्ति युद्धाय भीरवः प्राणविप्लवात् । तान्हनिष्याम्यहं सर्वान्मच्छासनपराङ्मुखान् । 78
तच्छ्रुत्वा भयसन्त्रस्ता निर्जग्मू रणकोविदाः । अतिकायः प्रहस्तश्च महानादमहोदरौ ॥ 79
देवशत्रुर्निकुम्भश्च देवान्तकनरान्तकौ । अपरे बलिनः सर्वे ययुर्युद्धाय वानरैः ॥ 80

this feat of his. **(68-69).** Rama, who was a master of archery, for a time remained silent and passive in order to show respect to the Brahma missile. Then seeing the troops of the monkey army falling down, he flew into a fiery rage and said to Lakshmana, "O Lakshmana! Bring my bow. I shall reduce this Asura to ashes with Brahma missile. You witness my prowess." **70.** But over-hearing Rama's words, Meghanada, who was an adept in magic, took care to go back invisible to the city immediately.

Hanuman revives the monkeys (71-74)

(71-73). Rama was very much afflicted to see a very large number of monkey troops fallen down by Meghanada's attack. So he said to Hanuman, "Go quickly to the Milk Ocean where there is a mountain called Drona, on which many medicinal herbs grow. Go and bring it quickly in order to rejuvenate these monkeys. This will bring you eternal fame." Hanuman accepted the order implicity and went away immediately on that mission **74.** The mountain was brought and all the monkeys were revived with its help. Hanuman took back the mountain to replace it and came back quickly.

The Rout of the Rakshasas (75-86)

75. Now terrific sounds again arose from the ranks of the monkeys as before to the great astonishment of Ravana. Wondering at it, Ravana said: **(76-78).** "Rama, my great enemy deputed by the Devas, is standing there knocking at our gates. In order to kill him in battle soon, let all my army commanders, ministers, relatives and other brave persons who want to serve my interests go forward for battle at my order. Whoever out of fear shall not thus go in violation of my order, will be executed. **(79-80).** Trem-

एते चान्ये च बहवः शूराः शतसहस्रशः । प्रविश्य वानरं सैन्यं ममन्थुर्बलदर्पिताः ॥ 81

भुशुण्डीभिन्दिपालैश्च बाणैः खड्गैः परश्वधैः । अन्यैश्च विविधैरस्त्रैर्निजघ्नुर्हरियूथपान् ॥ 82

ते पादपैः पर्वताग्रैर्नखदंष्ट्रैश्च मुष्टिभिः । प्राणैर्विमोचयामासुः सर्वराक्षसयूथपान् ॥ 83

रामेण निहताः केचित्सुग्रीवेण तथापरे ।
हनूमता चाङ्गदेन लक्ष्मणेन महात्मना । यूथपैर्वानराणां ते निहताः सर्वराक्षसाः ॥ 84

रामतेजः समाविश्य वानरा बलिनोऽभवन् । रामशक्तिविहीनानामेवं शक्तिः कुतो भवेत् ॥ 85

सर्वेश्वरः सर्वमयो विधाता मायामनुष्यत्वविडम्बनेन ।
सदा चिदानन्दमयोऽपि रामो युद्धादिलीलां वितनोति मायाम् ॥ 86

इति श्रीमदध्यात्मरामायणे उमामहेश्वरसंवादे
युद्धकाण्डे पञ्चमः सर्गः ॥ ५ ॥

bling with fear at this order of Ravana, all the highly skilled Rakshasa warriors like Atikaya, Prahasta, Mahanada, Mohodara Devasatru, Nikumbha, Devantaka, Narantaka etc., went out for battle with the monkeys. **(81-82).** These and other numerous courageous warriors who were proud of their strength attacked the vast monkey forces with various kinds of weapons like Bhusundi, Bhindipala, arrows, swords, battleaxes and a variety of missiles. **83.** And the monkeys in their turn counter-attacked and killed the Rakshasas with trees, mountain-cliffs and with their teeth and claws. **84.** Consequently that Rakshasa army was largely destroyed, some by Rama and others by Sugreeva, Hanuman, Angada, the high-souled Lakshmana and various monkey leaders. **85.** By the infusion of Rama's prowess, the strength of the monkeys was augmented. How can others not blessed in this way by Rama's power gain strength? **86.** Rama is God of all and the creator who has become this All. He is ever established in His inherent Bliss-Consciousness. Still assuming the form of a man by His own Maya and consequently following human ways, he engages Himself in war and other activities as a sport.

षष्ठः सर्गः

श्रीमहादेव उवाच

श्रुत्वा युद्धे बलं नष्टमतिकायमुखं महत् । रावणो दुःखसन्तप्तः क्रोधेन महताऽऽवृतः ॥ 1

निधायेन्द्रजितं लङ्कारक्षणार्थं महाद्युतिः । स्वयं जगाम युद्धाय रामेण सह राक्षसः ॥ 2

दिव्यं स्यन्दनमारुह्य सर्वशस्त्रास्त्रसंयुतम् । राममेवाभिदुद्राव राक्षसेन्द्रो महाबलः ॥ 3

वानरान्बहुशो हत्वा बाणैराशीविषोपमैः । पातयामास सुग्रीवप्रमुखान्यूथनायकान् ॥ 4

गदापाणिं महासत्त्वं तत्र दृष्ट्वा विभीषणम् । उत्ससर्ज महाशक्तिं मयदत्तां विभीषणे ॥ 5

तामापतन्तीमालोक्य विभीषणविघातिनीम् । दत्ताभयोऽयं रामेण वधार्हो नायमासुरः ॥ 6

इत्युक्त्वा लक्ष्मणो भीमं चापमादाय वीर्यवान् । विभीषणस्य पुरतः स्थितोऽकम्प इवाचलः ॥ 7

सा शक्तिर्लक्ष्मणतनुं विवेशामोघशक्तितः । यावन्त्यः शक्तयो लोके मायायाः सम्भवन्ति हि ॥

तासामाधारभूतस्य लक्ष्मणस्य महात्मनः । मायाशक्त्या भवेत्किं वा शेषांशस्य हरेस्तनोः ॥ 9

Chapter 6

RAVANA SEEKS KALANEMI'S HELP

Ravana's attack and discomfiture (1-34)

(1-2). Ravana was overcome both by grief and anger to know of the destruction of that great army consisting of Atikaya and others. So stationing Indrajit for the protection of Lanka, Ravana himself sallied forth with a big army to give battle to Rama. **3.** Seating himself in a chariot equipped with all kinds of missiles and weapons, the mighty Ravana went forth to challenge Rama himself directly. **4.** While thus charging towards Rama, Ravana destroyed numerous monkeys with his arrows, sharp and penetrating like poison. Many a monkey leader including Sugreeva fell down on the battle field under this attack. **5.** When he saw there the powerful Vibheeshana equipped with a mace, Ravana threw at him a powerful weapon called Sakti (dart or javelin) given to him by Maya. **(6-7).** Noticing that the weapon was directed towards Vibheeshana for his destruction, mighty Lakshmana thought, "Rama has given shelter to this Asura. It is not befitting that he is killed." With this resolution, he took his mighty bow and stood in front of Vibheeshana like an immovable mountain for the latter's protection. **(8-9)** That weapon Sakti released by Ravana was irresistible and must necessarily strike its target. So it struck at Lakshmana, but what can the Sakti (Power) of a weapon do against him, Lakshmana, the incarnation

तथापि मानुषं भावमापन्नस्तदनुव्रतः । मूर्च्छितः पतितो भूमौ तमादातुं दशाननः ॥ 10
हस्तैस्तोलयितुं शक्तो न बभूवातिविस्मितः । सर्वस्य जगतः सारं विराजं परमेश्वरम् ॥ 11
कथं लोकाश्रयं विष्णुं तोलयेल्लघुराक्षसः ॥ 12
ग्रहीतुकामं सौमित्रिं रावणं वीक्ष्य मारुतिः ।
आजघानोरसि क्रुद्धो वज्रकल्पेन मुष्टिना । तेन मुष्टिप्रहारेण जानुभ्यामपतद्भुवि ॥ 13
आस्यैश्च नेत्रश्रवणैरुद्वमन् रुधिरं बहु । विघूर्णमाननयनो रथोपस्थ उपाविशत् ॥ 14
अथ लक्ष्मणमादाय हनूमान् रावणार्दितम् । आनयद्रामसामीप्यं बाहुभ्यां परिगृह्य तम् ॥ 15
हनूमतः सुहृत्त्वेन भक्त्या च परमेश्वरः । लघुत्वमगमद्देवो गुरूणां गुरुरप्यजः ॥ 16
सा शक्तिरपि तं त्यक्त्वा ज्ञात्वा नारायणांशजम् । रावणस्य रथं प्रागाद्रावणोऽपि शनैस्ततः ॥ 17
संज्ञामवाप्य जग्राह बाणासनमथो रुषा । राममेवाभिदुद्राव दृष्ट्वा रामोऽपि तं क्रुधा ॥ 18
आरुह्य जगतां नाथो हनूमन्तं महाबलम् । रथस्थं रावणं दृष्ट्वा अभिदुद्राव राघवः ॥ 19
ज्याशब्दमकरोत्तीव्रं वज्रनिष्पेषनिष्ठुरम् । रामो गम्भीरया वाचा राक्षसेन्द्रमुवाच ह ॥ 20
राक्षसाधम तिष्ठाद्य क्व गमिष्यसि मे पुरः । कृत्वापराधमेवं मे सर्वत्र समदर्शिनः ॥ 21

of Adisesha who is the support of all the Saktis (the powers) of Maya? **(10-12).** Still in compliance with his present human status, he fell unconscious on the ground. Ravana now approached the fallen Lakshmana and tried to lift him up with his hands, but to his great astonishment he could not do so. For how can this little fellow of a Rakshasa lift up him who was none but the All-formed Cosmic Being (the Virat Purusha) who supports the worlds—an aspect of Mahavishnu the Supreme Lord?

(13-14). On seeing Ravana attempting to lift up Lakshmana, Hanuman in great anger hit the former on his chest with his powerful fist. Being thus hit, Ravana fell down on his knees with blood profusely flowing through his mouth, nose and ears. He became dizzy and sat in his chariot. **15.** Next Hanuman lifted up the unconscious Lakshmana who had fallen down by the impact of Ravana's Sakti, and took him to the presence of Rama. **16.** Though himself the supreme Master of all masters, Rama felt obliged and grateful to Hanuman on seeing his devotion and faithfulness. **(17-19).** That weapon Sakti, finding Lakshmana to be a part of Narayana Himself and impossible therefore to be killed, went back to Ravana's chariot. Ravana too was little by little restored to consciousness. Then, bow in hand, he rushed towards Rama. Moved by great anger at the sight of Ravana coming for attack seated in his chariot, Rama the Lord of the worlds, faced him, ascending on the shoulders of the powerful Hanuman.

20. Twanging his bow strings and producing terrific sounds like that of an explosive, Rama said to the Rakshasa king in a deep and grave voice: **21.** "O despicable fellow of a Rakshasa! Remain before me for a while. Having done such a serious offence

येन बाणेन निहता राक्षसास्ते जनालये । तेनैव त्वां हनिष्यामि तिष्ठाद्य मम गोचरे ॥ 22
श्रीरामस्य वचः श्रुत्वा रावणो मारुतात्मजम् । वहन्तं राघवं सङ्ख्ये शरैस्तीक्ष्णैरताडयत् ॥ 23
हतस्यापि शरैस्तीक्ष्णैर्वायुसूनोः स्वतेजसा । व्यवर्धत पुनस्तेजो ननर्द च महाकपिः ॥ 24
ततो दृष्ट्वा हनूमन्तं सव्रणं रघुसत्तमः । क्रोधमाहारयामास कालरुद्र इवापरः ॥ 25
साश्वं रथं ध्वजं सूतं शस्त्रौघं धनुरञ्जसा । छत्रं पताकां तरसा चिच्छेद शितसायकैः ॥ 26
ततो महाशरेणाशु रावणं रघुसत्तमः । विव्याध वज्रकल्पेन पाकारिरिव पर्वतम् ॥ 27
रामबाणहतो वीरश्चचाल च मुमोह च । हस्तान्निपतितश्चापस्तं समीक्ष्य रघूत्तमः ॥ 28
अर्धचन्द्रेण चिच्छेद तत्किरीटं रविप्रभम् । अनुजानामि गच्छ त्वमिदानीं बाणपीडितः ॥ 29
प्रविश्य लङ्कामाश्वास्य श्वः पश्यसि बलं मम ॥ 30
रामबाणेन संविद्धो हतदर्पोऽथ रावणः । महत्या लज्जया युक्तो लङ्कां प्राविशदातुरः ॥ 31
रामोऽपि लक्ष्मणं दृष्ट्वा मूर्च्छितं पतितं भुवि । मानुषत्वमुपाश्रित्य लीलयानुशुशोच ह ॥ 32
ततः प्राह हनूमन्तं वत्स जीवय लक्ष्मणम् ।

against one who looks upon all beings with an equal eye, how can you now escape? **22.** That arrow by which your Rakshasa followers at Janasthana were destroyed, with that very arrow you are now going to be killed. Stand in my presence for a while."

23. On hearing these words of Rama, Ravana sent sharp arrows at Hanuman, on whom Rama was mounted. **24.** Though thus struck with those sharp arrows, Hanuman's strength only increased on account of the infusion of Rama's prowess into him. So, that great monkey leader now gave out terrific lion-roars. **25.** Now Rama seeing Hanuman thus wounded, assumed a mood of anger like Rudra, the destroyer Himself. **26.** In an instant he destroyed with powerful arrows, Ravana's chariot with its horses, standard, the charioteer, umbrella and his assemblage of weapons. **27.** Next Rama, the noblest of Raghu's line, wounded Ravana with his arrows, sharp like the thunderbolt weapon even as Indra smashes mountains. **(28-30).** Wounded in this way by Rama's arrows, the powerful Ravana trembled and swooned and his bow fell down from his hand. When he saw Ravana in this plight, Rama cut off the crowns on his heads with his semi-circular arrow and said to him, "As you are terribly distressed by the wounds caused by my arrows, I let you go now. Go to Lanka and take rest. Tomorrow you shall have more experience of my prowess." **31.** With his body torn by Rama's arrows, Ravana felt humbled very much and he entered Lanka in great grief and shame.

32. Now Rama again looked at Lakshmana, who was still lying unconscious, and in keeping with his human appearance, he indulged in mourning.

महौषधीः समानीय पूर्ववद्वानरानपि । तथेति राघवेणोक्तो जगामाशु महाकपिः ॥ 33
हनूमान्वायुवेगेन क्षणात्तीर्त्वा महोदधिम् ॥ 34
एतस्मिन्नन्तरे चारा रावणाय न्यवेदयन् ।
रामेण प्रेषितो देव हनूमान् क्षीरसागरम् । गतो नेतुं लक्ष्मणस्य जीवनार्थं महौषधीः ॥ 35
श्रुत्वा तच्चारवचनं राजा चिन्तापरोऽभवत् । जगाम रात्रावेकाकी कालनेमिगृहं क्षणात् ॥ 36
गृहागतं समालोक्य रावणं विस्मयान्वितः ।
कालनेमिरुवाचेदं प्राञ्जलिर्भयविह्वलः । अर्घ्यादिकं ततः कृत्वा रावणस्याग्रतः स्थितः ॥ 37
किं ते करोमि राजेन्द्र किमागमनकारणम् । कालनेमिमुवाचेदं रावणो दुःखपीडितः ॥ 38
ममापि कालवशतः कष्टमेतदुपस्थितम् । मया शक्त्या हतो वीरो लक्ष्मणः पतितो भुवि ॥39
तं जीवयितुमानेतुमोषधीर्हनुमान् गतः । यथा तस्य भवेद्विघ्नं तथा कुरु महामते ॥ 40
मायया मुनिवेषेण मोहयस्व महाकपिम् । कालात्ययो यथा भूयात्तथा कृत्वैहि मन्दिरे ॥ 41
रावणस्य वचः श्रुत्वा कालनेमिरुवाच तम् । रावणेश वचो मेऽद्य श‍ृणु धारय तत्त्वतः ॥ 42
प्रियं ते करवाण्येव न प्राणान् धारयाम्यहम् । मारीचस्य यथारण्ये पुराभून्मृगरूपिणः ॥ 43
तथैव मे न सन्देहो भविष्यति दशानन । हताः पुत्राश्च पौत्राश्च बान्धवा राक्षसाश्च ते ॥

(33-34). Then he said to Hanuman, "Dear one! As before, go and get those great herbal remedies once more in order to revive Lakshmana and the monkeys." Ordered in this way by Rama, Hanuman proceeded with the speed of wind, crossing the ocean.

Kalanemi Episode (35-46)

35. Meanwhile, Ravana's spies went and reported to him, "O Lord! For the revival of Lakshmana, Hanuman has been sent by Rama to get herbal remedies from the shores of the milk ocean." **36.** These words of the spy set Ravana thinking. At night, he went alone to the house of Kalanemi. **37.** Kalanemi was taken aback with fear and wonder to see Ravana at his house. After receiving him with Arghya and Padya, he stood before Ravana in all humility. **(38-40).** Kalanemi said, "O Lord! What shall I do for you? What is it that has brought you to me?" Ravana, who was distressed with great sorrow, said as follows to Kalanemi: "Bad times have overtaken me too, and misfortunes are befalling me one after another. Now in order to revive the powerful Lakshmana who has been hit by my weapon Sakti, Hanuman has gone to fetch herbal remedies. You do what you can to obstruct him in his course.

41. "Adopting the form of an ascetic, you deceive that great monkey and delay him in his mission. Doing this much, you return home." **42.** Hearing Ravana's words, Kalanemi said to him, "O my master Ravana! Hear my words and take them in their true spirit. **(43-46).** I shall certainly do what

घातयित्वासुरकुलं जीवितेनापि किं तव । राज्येन वा सीतया वा किं देहेन जडात्मना ॥45
सीतां प्रयच्छ रामाय राज्यं देहि विभीषणे । वनं याहि महाबाहो रम्यं मुनिगणाश्रयम् ॥ 46
स्नात्वा प्रातः शुभजले कृत्वा सन्ध्यादिकाः क्रियाः तत एकान्तमाश्रित्य सुखासनपरिग्रहः ॥ 47
विसृज्य सर्वतः सङ्गमितरान्विषयान्बहिः । बहिःप्रवृत्ताक्षगणं शनैः प्रत्यक् प्रवाहय ॥ 48
प्रकृतेर्भिन्नमात्मानं विचारय सदानघ । चराचरं जगत्कृत्स्नं देहबुद्धीन्द्रियादिकम् ॥ 49
आब्रह्मस्तम्बपर्यन्तं दृश्यते श्रूयते च यत् । सैषा प्रकृतिरित्युक्ता सैव मायेति कीर्तिता ॥ 50
सर्गस्थितिविनाशानां जगद्वृक्षस्य कारणम् । लोहितश्वेतकृष्णादिप्रजाः सृजति सर्वदा ॥ 51
कामक्रोधादिपुत्राद्यान्हिंसातृष्णादिकन्यकाः । मोहयन्त्यनिशं देवमात्मानं स्वैर्गुणैर्विभुम् ॥ 52
कर्तृत्वभोक्तृत्वमुखान् स्वगुणानात्मनीश्वरे । आरोप्य स्ववशं कृत्वा तेन क्रीडति सर्वदा ॥ 53
शुद्धोऽप्यात्मा यया युक्तः पश्यतीव सदा बहिः । विस्मृत्य च स्वमात्मानं मायागुणविमोहितः ॥ 54

is pleasing to you but know for certain that I shall not be able to return alive from this mission. What happened in the forest earlier to Mareecha who went in the guise of a deer, the same is going to happen to me also. O ten-headed one! After all your relatives are dead, after seeing the whole of the Rakshasa tribe destroyed, of what use is life for you, of what use is kingdom, of what use is even Sita? What will you achieve even with your body which will be as good as a corpse? Therefore give away Sita to Rama and the kingdom to Vibheeshana, and you, O powerful one, take to the life of an ascetic in the forest.

Kalanemi's Sermon (47-63)

(47-51). "Taking your bath early in the morning in clean water, perform the rites like Sandhya and others, resort to solitude, and sitting in a convenient posture and abandoning all attachment to all persons and external objects, slowly but steadily withdraw your mind away from them towards the inner Self, and think constantly of the Atman who is distinct from Prakriti (the objective universe). O great one! All this universe of moving and unmoving beings, objects like body, intellect and the senses, the whole universe from Brahma down to a blade of grass—in fact all that can be seen and heard—are manifestations of Prakriti, also known as Maya. It is the cause of this tree of the Universe—of its creation, preservation and dissolution. Its three aspects of Sattva, Rajas and Tamas constantly generate beings akin to them. **52.** Desire, anger and other passions are its sons, and cruelty, avarice and other tendencies, its daughters. It continuously deludes the Atman, who is luminous and all-pervading. **53.** It continues to sport for ever by superimposing on the Atman, who is really the Lord, the experiences that are born of its own Gunas (constituents), namely, the sense of agency and enjoyership. **54.** Though by nature ever pure, the Atman, by association with Prakriti, is deluded by

यदा सद्गुरुणा युक्तो बोध्यते बोधरूपिणा । निवृत्तदृष्टिरात्मानं पश्यत्येव सदा स्फुटम् ॥ 55
जीवन्मुक्तः सदा देही मुच्यते प्राकृतैर्गुणैः । त्वमप्येवं सदात्मानं विचार्य नियतेन्द्रियः ॥ 56
प्रकृतेरन्यमात्मानं ज्ञात्वा मुक्तो भविष्यसि । ध्यातुं यद्यसमर्थोऽसि सगुणं देवमाश्रय ॥ 57
हृत्पद्मकर्णिके स्वर्णपीठे मणिगणान्विते । मृदुश्लक्ष्णतरे तत्र जानक्या सह संस्थितम् ॥ 58
वीरासनं विशालाक्षं विद्युत्पुञ्जनिभाम्बरम् । किरीटहारकेयूरकौस्तुभादिभिरन्वितम् ॥ 59
नूपुरैः कटकैर्भान्तं तथैव वनमालया । लक्ष्मणेन धनुर्द्वन्द्वकरेण परिसेवितम् ॥ 60
एवं ध्यात्वा सदात्मानं रामं सर्वहृदि स्थितम् । भक्त्या परमया युक्तो मुच्यते नात्र संशयः ॥ 61
शृणु वै चरितं तस्य भक्तैर्नित्यमनन्यधीः ।
एवं चेत्कृतपूर्वाणि पापानि च महान्त्यपि । क्षणादेव विनश्यन्ति यथाग्नेस्तूलराशयः ॥ 62
भजस्व रामं परिपूर्णमेकं विहाय वैरं निजभक्तियुक्तः ।
हृदा सदा भावितभावरूपमनामरूपं पुरुषं पुराणम् ॥ 63

इति श्रीमदध्यात्मरामायणे उमामहेश्वरसंवादे
युद्धकाण्डे षष्ठः सर्गः ॥ ६ ॥

its Guna (constituents), and forgetting His own real nature, becomes outward-going. **55.** Instructed by a teacher who has realised himself as Pure Consciousness and thereby knowing that the Atman is different from Prakriti, the Jiva turns his outlook from the external to the internal and realises his own ever pure spiritual nature. **(56-57).** Then the Jiva, who is really free even in the embodied state, recognises his freedom from the clutches of the Gunas. You, too, by controlling your senses and ever reflecting on the Atman as distinct from Prakriti. can become liberated. If you cannot reflect in this way, you practise devotion for the Supreme Being as endowed with attributes.

(58-61). "Meditate on the shining form of Rama, the resident of the hearts of all, as served by Lakshmana holding the couple of bows. Meditate on Him as seated in the lotus of your heart in the heroic pose on a seat made of pure gold, studded with costly gems and covered with a soft-cushion. Meditate on Him seated beside Sita, as endowed with large eyes, as dressed with clothes shining like lightning, as adorned with a crown, necklaces, armlets, Kaustubha gem, anklets, wristlets and floral wreath. Meditating thus with supreme devotion, you can undoubtedly gain liberation. **62.** Hear always accounts about Him in the company of other devotees with a concentrated mind. By doing so, all your sins, however heinous, will in no time get burnt like a heap of cotton by fire. **63.** Abandoning enmity, cultivate devotion to Rama. He is that Pure Existence to be ever meditated upon with a concentrated mind, the one without a name and form, the unitary Eternal Being infilling everything."

सप्तमः सर्गः

श्रीमहादेव उवाच

कालनेमिवचः श्रुत्वा रावणोऽमृतसन्निभम् । जज्वाल क्रोधताम्राक्षः सर्पिरद्भिरिवाग्निमत् ॥ 1

निहन्मि त्वां दुरात्मानं मच्छासनपराङ्मुखम् । परैः किञ्चिद्गृहीत्वा त्वं भाषसे रामकिंकरः ॥ 2

कालनेमिरुवाचेदं रावणं देव किं क्रुधा । न रोचते मे वचनं यदि गत्वा करोमि तत् ॥ 3

इत्युक्त्वा प्रययौ शीघ्रं कालनेमिर्महासुरः । नोदितो रावणेनैव हनूमद्विघ्नकारणात् ॥ 4

स गत्वा हिमवत्पार्श्वं तपोवनमकल्पयत् । तत्र शिष्यैः परिवृतो मुनिवेषधरः खलः ॥ 5

गच्छतो मार्गमासाद्य वायुसूनोर्महात्मनः । ततो गत्वा ददर्शाथ हनूमानाश्रमं शुभम् ॥ 6

चिन्तयामास मनसा श्रीमान्पवननन्दनः । पुरा न दृष्टमेतन्मे मुनिमण्डलमुत्तमम् ॥ 7

मार्गो विभ्रंशितो वा मे भ्रमो वा चित्तसम्भवः । यद्वाविश्याश्रमपदं दृष्ट्वा मुनिमशेषतः ॥ 8

पीत्वा जलं ततो यामि द्रोणाचलमनुत्तमम् । इत्युक्त्वा प्रविवेशाथ सर्वतो योजनायतम् ॥ 9

आश्रमं कदलीशालखर्जूरपनसादिभिः । समावृतं पक्वफलैर्नम्रशाखैश्च पादपैः ॥ 10

Chapter 7

HANUMAN IN QUEST OF THE DIVINE MEDICINAL HERB

Kalanemi in the guise of an ascetic (1-33)

1. These nectarine words of Kalanemi went only to inflame the anger of Ravana and turn his eyes red as copper, just as boiling ghee emits fire when cool water is poured on it. **2.** Ravana said, "I am going to kill you, evil minded fellow, who behaves contrary to my orders. Bribed by the enemy, you are speaking to me like a servant of Rama." **3.** Kalanemi replied, "O Lord! What is the use of being angry with me! If my words are not to your liking, I shall go and do as commanded by you."

4. The great Asura Kalanemi, being thus directed by Ravana to cause obstruction to Hanuman, started quickly. **(5-7).** He went to the valley of the mount Himalayas. Assuming the form of an ascetic, he created there a hermitage with his magical powers and sat within it surrounded by many disciples. Being situated on the way, the Ashrama with its inhabitants came to the notice of Hanuman, who thought for a while on seeing it and felt that he had not seen such an Ashrama when he came here earlier. **(8-9).** Hanuman thought within himself, "Have I lost my way? Or is what I see before me a mere delusion of my mind? Anyway I shall enter into the Ashrama, see all these ascetics, drink water, and then proceed to Mount Drona."

Reflecting in this way, he went into the Ashrama campus, which was about one Yojana in length **(10-12).** That Ashrama was full of varieties of fruit-bearing trees like

वैरभावविनिर्मुक्तं शुद्धं निर्मललक्षणम् । तस्मिन्महाश्रमे रम्ये कालनेमिः स राक्षसः ॥ 11
इन्द्रयोगं समास्थाय चकार शिवपूजनम् । हनूमानभिवाद्याह गौरवेण महासुरम् ॥ 12
भगवन् रामदूतोऽहं हनूमन्नाम नामंतः । रामकार्येण महता क्षीराब्धिं गन्तुमुद्यतः ॥ 13
तृषा मां बाधते ब्रह्मन्नुदकं कुत्र विद्यते । यथेच्छं पातुमिच्छामि कथ्यतां मे मुनीश्वर ॥ 14
तच्छ्रुत्वा मारुतेर्वाक्यं कालनेमिस्तमब्रवीत् । कमण्डलुगतं तोयं मम त्वं पातुमर्हसि ॥ 15
भुङ्क्ष्व चेमानि पक्वानि फलानि तदनन्तरम् । निवसस्व सुखेनात्र निद्रामेहि त्वरास्तु मा ॥ 16
भूतं भव्यं भविष्यं च जानामि तपसा स्वयम् । उत्थिता लक्ष्मणः सर्वे वानरा रामवीक्षिताः ॥ 17
तच्छ्रुत्वा हनुमानाह कमण्डलुजलेन मे । न शाम्यत्यधिका तृष्णा ततो दर्शय मे जलम् ॥
तथेत्याज्ञापयामास वटुं मायाविकल्पितम् । वटो दर्शय विस्तीर्णं वायुसूनोर्जलाशयम् ॥ 19
निमील्य चाक्षिणी तोयं पीत्वागच्छ ममान्तिकम् । उपदेक्ष्यामि ते मन्त्रं येन द्रक्ष्यसि चौषधीः ॥ 20
तथेति दर्शितं शीघ्रं वटुना सलिलाशयम् । प्रविश्य हनूमांस्तोयमपिबन्मीलितेक्षणः ॥ 21
ततश्चागत्य मकरी महामाया महाकपिम् । अग्रसत्तं महावेगान्मारुतिं घोररूपिणी ॥ 22

plantain, Sal, plam and jack. Their branches were bending under the load of the fruits. Even animals that were naturally antagonistic to one another, lived there in peace. Seated in the pure and enchanting surroundings of that illusory Ashrama, the great Rakshasa Kalanemi was performing the worship of Siva. Respectfully saluting that Asura in the form of an ascetic, Hanuman said: **(13-14).**"O holy one! I am the messenger of Rama. My name is Hanuman. For the achievement of an important purpose of Rama, I am going to the milk ocean. I am now extremely thirsty. Where can I get water to drink my fill? O holy one! Please direct me." **(15-17).** At these words of Hanuman, Kalanemi said, "Drink all the water in my water pot and eat all these ripe fruits you see here. After that you can stay here peacefully for a time and have a nap. You need not in anyway be in a hurry. By the power of my psychic insight, I know all the past, present and future. I see that by Rama's look, Lakshmana and all the monkeys have revived." **18.** Hanuman thereupon replied, "My intense thirst cannot be quenched by that much of water as is contained in a Kamandalu (water pot). Show me, therefore, a bigger reservoir of water, a river or a lake." **19.** Agreeing to do so, Kalanemi called one of his magically created disciples and said to him, "Go and show an extensive water resevoir to Hanuman." **20.** And turning to Hanuman he said, "With your eyes closed, drink as much water as you like and return. I shall impart to you a Mantra which will enable you to recognise the medicinal herb you want to get."

(21-22). Accordingly, Hanuman quickly went to the lake shown by the ascetic disciple and entering into it began to drink the water with closed eyes. Immediately, a fierce crocodile quickly came and grasped

ततो ददर्श हनुमान् ग्रसन्तीं मकरीं रुषा । दारयामास हस्ताभ्यां वदनं सा ममार ह ॥ 23
ततोऽन्तरिक्षे ददृशे दिव्यरूपधराङ्गना । धान्यमालीति विख्याता हनूमन्तमथाब्रवीत् ॥ 24
त्वत्प्रसादादहं शापाद्विमुक्तास्मि कपीश्वर । शप्ताहं मुनिना पूर्वमप्सरा कारणान्तरे ॥ 25
आश्रमे यस्तु ते दृष्टः कालनेमिर्महासुरः । रावणप्रहितो मार्गे विघ्नं कर्तुं तवानघ ॥ 26
मुनिवेषधरो नासौ मुनिर्विप्रविहिंसकः । जहि दुष्टं गच्छ शीघ्रं द्रोणाचलमनुत्तमम् ॥ 27
गच्छाम्यहं ब्रह्मलोकं त्वत्स्पर्शाद्धुतकल्मषा । इत्युक्त्वा सा ययौ स्वर्गं हनूमानप्ययथाश्रमम् ॥ 28
आगतं तं समालोक्य कालनेमिरभाषत । किं विलम्बेन महता तव वानरसत्तम ॥ 29
गृहाण मत्तो मन्त्रांस्त्वं देहि मे गुरुदक्षिणाम् । इत्युक्तो हनुमान्मुष्टिं दृढं बद्ध्वाह राक्षसम् ॥ 30
गृहाण दक्षिणामेतामित्युक्त्वा निजघान तम् ॥ 31
विसृज्य मुनिवेषं स कालनेमिर्महासुरः ।
युयुधे वायुपुत्रेण नानामायाविधानतः । महामायिकदूतोऽसौ हनूमान्मायिनां रिपुः ॥ 32
जघान मुष्टिना शीर्ष्णि भग्नमूर्धा ममार सः ॥ 33
ततः क्षीरनिधिं गत्वा दृष्ट्वा द्रोणं महागिरिम् ।
अदृष्ट्वा चौषधीस्तत्र गिरिमुत्पाट्य सत्वरः । गृहीत्वा वायुवेगेन गत्वा रामस्य सन्निधिम् ॥ 34

Hanuman in its poweful jaws. **23.** Hanuman now caught hold of the jaws of the crocodile that was trying to devour him and split the creature into two. **24.** Thereupon he saw in the sky the form of a heavenly woman known as Dhanyamali. **25.** She said to Hanuman, "O great monkey! I am an Apsara woman who was formerly cursed by an ascetic for certain reasons. By your grace I have now been liberated from the effect of that curse. **(26-28).** The one you saw in the hermitage is not an ascetic but the great Asura Kalanemi who was despatched here by Ravana to cause obstruction to your passage. He has only put on the false garb of an ascetic. In truth he is a persecutor of ascetics. O noble one! Kill that evil fellow and hurry on to the Mount Drona. I have been purified of my sins by your touch. I am now going to the realm of Brahma, all my taints removed by your touch." With these words, she departed to her heavenly abode. Hanuman now returned to the Ashrama.

(29-31). Seeing Hanuman returning, Kalanemi said, "O great monkey! Why delay any more? Receive from me the Mantra and give me the Dakshina (the holy offering given to a Guru)." Being thus accosted, Hanuman, displaying his clenched fist, said to him. "This is the Dakshina for you!" and gave him a punch. **(32-33).** Now Kalanemi gave up his disguise of an ascetic and fought with Hanuman adopting various magical stratagems. But Hanuman, who was the messenger of the master magician, Rama, killed that delusion-creating enemy by delivering a blow on his head with his fist. With his head thus split, the Rakshasa died.

Lakshmana's revival (34-35).

Hanuman now hurried to the milk ocean

उवाच हनुमान् राममानीतोऽयं महागिरिः । यद्युक्तं कुरु देवेश विलम्बो नात्र युज्यते ॥ 35
श्रुत्वा हनूमतो वाक्यं रामः सन्तुष्टमानसः । गृहीत्वा चौषधीः शीघ्रं सुषेणेन महामतिः ॥ 36
चिकित्सां कारयामास लक्ष्मणाय महात्मने । ततः सुप्तोत्थित इव बुद्ध्वा प्रोवाच लक्ष्मणः ॥ 37
तिष्ठ तिष्ठ क्व गन्तासि हन्मीदानीं दशानन । इति ब्रुवन्तमालोक्य मूर्ध्न्यवघ्राय राघवः ॥ 38
मारुतिं प्राह वत्साद्य त्वत्प्रसादान्महाकपे । निरामयं प्रपश्यामि लक्ष्मणं भ्रातरं मम ॥ 39
इत्युक्त्वा वानरैः सार्धं सुग्रीवेण समन्वितः । विभीषणमतेनैव युद्धाय समवस्थितः ॥ 40
पाषाणैः पादपैश्चैव पर्वताग्रैश्च वानराः । युद्धायाभिमुखा भूत्वा ययुः सर्वे युयुत्सवः ॥ 41
रावणो विव्यथे रामबाणैर्विद्धो महासुरः । मातङ्ग इव सिंहेन गरुडेनेव पन्नगः ॥ 42
अभिभूतोऽगमद्राजा राघवेण महात्मना । सिंहासने समाविश्य राक्षसानिदमब्रवीत् ॥ 43
मानुषेणैव मे मृत्युमाह पूर्वं पितामहः । मानुषो हि न मां हन्तुं शक्तोऽसि भुवि कश्चन ॥ 44
ततो नारायणः साक्षान्मानुषोऽभून्न संशयः । रामो दाशरथिर्भूत्वा मां हन्तुं समुपस्थितः ॥ 45

where he saw Mount Drona. He could not, however, find out the particular medicinal herb that he wanted. So lifting up the mountain itself, he went to the presence of Rama with the speed of wind and said to him, "O great one! Here I have brought the mountain Drona. You do with it what you like. There need not be any more delay." **(36-37).** The high-souled Rama, on hearing Hanuman's words, was very much pleased. He called Sushena and asked him to treat Lakshmana with the specific medicinal herb that was available on that, mountain. Thereupon Lakshmana came to consciousness like one awakened from sleep and said, **(38-39)**: "O Ravana! Stop stop. Where are you going? I shall kill you even now." Seeing him speaking in this way, Rama smelt the crown of his head out of affection, and then looking at Hanuman, said: "O great monkey hero! O dear one! By your good offices my brother. Lakshmana has been relieved of his ailment."

Awakening of Kumbhakarna

(40-41). With these words Rama, along with monkeys and Sugreeva, following the advise of Vibheeshana, started for battle. All the war-like monkeys, equipped with stones, trees and tops of mountains, started for the battlefield. **(42-43).** The great Rakshasa Ravana, wounded by Rama's arrows like an elephant by a lion or a serpent by a Garuda, had been defeated and forced to withdraw to his palace. Sitting on his throne, he addressed the Rakshasas thus: **(44-45).** "In times of yore Brahma had said that my death will take place at the hands of a human being only, but there is no man living, powerful enough to kill me. Therefore Narayana himself must have undoubtedly come as a man in the shape of Rama, son of Dasaratha, in order to

अनरण्येन यत्पूर्वं शप्तोऽहं राक्षसेश्वर। उत्पत्स्यते च मद्वंशे परमात्मा सनातनः॥ 46
तेन त्वं पुत्रपौत्रैश्च बान्धवैश्च समन्वितः। हनिष्यसे न सन्देह इत्युक्त्वा मां दिवं गतः॥ 47
स एव रामः संजातो मदर्थे मां हनिष्यति।
कुम्भकर्णस्तु मूढात्मा सदा निद्रावशं गतः। तं विबोध्य महासत्त्वमानयन्तु ममान्तिकम्॥ 48
इत्युक्तास्ते महाकायास्तूर्णं गत्वा तु यत्नतः। विबोध्य कुम्भश्रवणं निन्यू रावणसन्निधिम्॥ 49
नमस्कृत्य स राजानमासनोपरि संस्थितः। तमाह रावणो राजा भ्रातरं दीनया गिरा॥ 50
कुम्भकर्ण निबोध त्वं महत्कष्टमुपस्थितम्। रामेण निहताः शूराः पुत्राः पौत्राश्च बान्धवाः॥ 51
किं कर्तव्यमिदानीं मे मृत्युकाल उपस्थिते। एष दाशरथी रामः सुग्रीवसहितो बली॥ 52
समुद्रं सबलस्तीर्त्वा मूलं नः परिकृन्तति। ये राक्षसा मुख्यतमास्ते हता वानरैर्युधि॥ 53
वानराणां क्षयं युद्धे न पश्यामि कदाचन। नाशयस्व महाबाहो यदर्थं परिबोधितः॥ 54
भ्रातुरर्थे महासत्त्व कुरु कर्म सुदुष्करम्॥ 55
श्रुत्वा तद्रावणेन्द्रस्य वचनं परिदेवितम्। कुम्भकर्णो जहासोच्चैर्वचनं चेदमब्रवीत्॥ 56
पुरा मन्त्रविचारे ते गदितं मन्मया नृप। तदद्य त्वामुपगतं फलं पापस्य कर्मणः॥ 57

kill me. **(46-48).** O Rakshasas! In times of old a Rajarshi of the solar dynasty named Anaranya, when killed by me, pronounced a curse on me, saying, 'The Supreme Being will one day incarnate in my line. You along with your sons and relatives will be destroyed by him. Have no doubt about this.' So saying, he left for heaven. Therefore that Supreme Being alone must have been born as Rama to kill me." The dull-witted Kumbhakarna is always asleep. Wake up that Leviathan and bring him to me."

49. Hearing these words of Ravana, those gigantic Rakshasas went immediately to awaken Kumbhakarna. With great effort they woke him up and brought him to the presence of Ravana. **50.** He saluted the King and took his seat. King Ravana now addressed his brother in plaintive tone: **(51-55).** "O Kumbhakarna! Hear what I have got to say. I am in a very difficult situation. My heroic sons and grandsons have all been destroyed by Rama, and the time of my death also seems to be near at hand. What shall I do now? Rama, the powerful son of Dasaratha, in combination with Sugreeva has crossed the ocean with an army, and is about to cause the total destruction of our tribe. All the leading Rakshasas have already been killed in battle by the monkeys. But on the other hand I do not find the monkeys on their side being destroyed in any way. It is for you to effect their destruction. I awakened you for this purpose. Accomplish this difficult task for the sake of your brother."

Kumbhakarna's Sermon
(56-70)

56. On hearing these words of the King

पूर्वमेव मया प्रोक्तो रामो नारायणः परः । सीता च योगमायेति बोधितोऽपि न बुध्यसे ॥ 58
एकदाहं वने सानौ विशालायां स्थितो निशि । दृष्टो मया मुनिः साक्षान्नारदो दिव्यदर्शनः ॥ 59
तमब्रवं महाभाग कुतो गन्तासि मे वद । इत्युक्तो नारदः प्राह देवानां मन्त्रणे स्थितः ॥ 60
तत्रोत्पन्नमुदन्तं ते वक्ष्यामि शृणु तत्त्वतः । युवाभ्यां पीडिता देवाः सर्वे विष्णुमुपागताः ॥ 61
ऊचुस्ते देवदेवेशं स्तुत्वा भक्त्या समाहिताः । जहि रावणमक्षोभ्यं देव त्रैलोक्यकण्टकम् ॥ 62
मानुषेण मृतिस्तस्य कल्पिता ब्रह्मणा पुरा । अतस्त्वं मानुषो भूत्वा जहि रावणकण्टकम् ॥ 63
तथेत्याह महाविष्णुः सत्यसङ्कल्प ईश्वरः । जातो रघुकुले देवो राम इत्यभिविश्रुतः ॥ 64
स हनिष्यति वः सर्वानित्युक्त्वा प्रययौ मुनिः । अतो जानीहि रामं त्वं परं ब्रह्म सनातनम् ॥ 65
त्यज वैरं भजस्वाद्य मायामानुषविग्रहम् । भजतां भक्तिभावेन प्रसीदति रघूत्तमः ॥ 66
भक्तिर्जनित्री ज्ञानस्य भक्तिर्मोक्षप्रदायिनी । भक्तिहीनेन यत्किञ्चित्कृतं सर्वमसत्समम् ॥ 67
अवताराः सुबहवो विष्णोर्लीलानुकारिणः । तेषां सहस्रसदृशो रामो ज्ञानमयः शिवः ॥ 68

of the Rakshasas, Kumbhakarna laughed loudly and said: **57.** "O King, at the time of our deliberations I told you that the effects of your evil deeds were soon going to befall you. Now those sins of yours are coming to fruition. **58.** I told you even before that Rama is Supreme Narayana, and Sita, his Yogamaya. But you did not heed my words. **59.** Once when I was sitting at night on a mountain top on an expansive slab of stone, I saw the sage Narada who is usually seen by the Devas only. **(60-61).** I asked him, 'O worshipful one! Where are you coming from?' Addressed by me in this way Narada replied, 'I am coming from the assembly of the Devas. I shall speak to you about certain matters that were discussed there. **62.** The Devas who had been suffering oppression from the Rakshasas approached Mahavishnu with a mind concentrated on Him and full of devotion, and said to that Supreme Being: 'O Lord! Destroy this Ravana who is an oppresser of the three worlds and who cannot be overcome by any other being. **63.** Brahma had long ago given him the boon that his death can occur only at the hands of a human being. Therefore deign to be incarnated as a man and destroy the monster Ravana.' **64.** Mahavishnu accepted their prayer. That Supreme Being, whose will ever becomes true, is now born in the line of Raghu under the famous name of Rama. **65.** He will wipe you all out completely." 'Saying so, the sage departed. So please understand that Rama is the eternal Para-Brahman. **66.** Therefore abandon your enmity to him and resign to him who has assumed the form of a man by his Maya. Rama, the leader of the Raghus, is always gracious to those who are devoted to him. **67.** Devotion generates knowledge. Devotion bestows Moksha. Whatever is done by one without devotion is as good as non-existent. **68.** The sportive incarnations of Mahavishnu are many. Among them that as Rama, who is the pure embodiment of

रामं भजन्ति निपुणा मनसा वचसानिशम् । अनायासेन संसारं तीर्त्वा यान्ति हरेः पदम् ॥ 69

ये राममेव सततं भुवि शुद्धसत्त्वा ध्यायन्ति तस्य चरितानि पठन्ति सन्तः ।
मुक्तास्त एव भवभोगमहाहिपाशैः सीतापतेः पदमनन्तसुखं प्रयान्ति ॥ 70

इति श्रीमदध्यात्मरामायणे उमामहेश्वरसंवादे
युद्धकाण्डे सप्तमः सर्गः ॥ ७ ॥

knowledge and purity, is equal to thousand such incarnations. **69.** Intelligent people worship Rama always, and without difficulty they attain the Status of Hari. **70.** Whoever with purity of mind meditates on Rama and studies accounts of his doings, becomes liberated from the coils of the terrible python of Samsara and attains to the extremely blissful Status of Vishnu."

अष्टमः सर्गः

श्रीमहादेव उवाच

कुम्भकर्णवचः श्रुत्वा भ्रुकुटीविकटाननः । दशग्रीवो जगादेदमासनादुत्पतन्निव ॥ 1

त्वमानीतो न मे ज्ञानबोधनाय सुबुद्धिमान् ।
मया कृतं समीकृत्य युध्यस्व यदि रोचते । नोचेद्गच्छ सुषुप्त्यर्थं निद्रा त्वां बाधतेऽधुना ॥ 2

रावणस्य वचः श्रुत्वा कुम्भकर्णो महाबलः । रुष्टोऽयमिति विज्ञाय तूर्णं युद्धाय निर्ययौ ॥ 3

स लङ्घयित्वा प्राकारं महापर्वतसन्निभः । निर्ययौ नगरात्तूर्णं भीषयन्हरिसैनिकान् ॥ 4

स ननाद महानादं समुद्रमभिनादयन् । वानरान्कालयामास बाहुभ्यां भक्षयन् रुषा ॥ 5

Chapter 8

DESTRUCTION OF KUMBHAKARNA

Kumbhakarna's Meeting with Vibheeshana (1-16).

1. Hearing these words of Kumbhakarna, Ravana with his eyesbrows arched in anger, sprang up from his seat as it were and said: **2.** "You are indeed a wise man! I did not call you here to advise me on spiritual matters. If it is acceptable to you, look upon my actions as yours, and go for battle. If not, you can relapse into your sleep. Probably sleep has already overtaken you." **3.** Inferring from Ravana's words that he was in a wrathful mood, the powerful Kumbhakarna started quickly for battle. **4.** Mountain-like in size, he passed the ramparts and emerged out of the city, causing terror among the monkeys. **5.** He raised terrific war cries louder than

कुम्भकर्णं तदा दृष्ट्वा सपक्षमिव पर्वतम् । दुद्रुवुर्वानराः सर्वे कालान्तकमिवाखिलाः ॥ 6
भ्रमन्तं हरिवाहिन्यां मुद्गरेण महाबलम् । कालयन्तं हरीन्वेगाद्भक्षयन्तं समन्ततः ॥ 7
चूर्णयन्तं मुद्गरेण पाणिपादैरनेकधा । कुम्भकर्णं तदा दृष्ट्वा गदापाणिर्विभीषणः ॥ 8
ननाम चरणं तस्य भ्रातुर्ज्येष्ठस्य बुद्धिमान् । विभीषणोऽहं भ्रातुर्मे दयां कुरु महामते ॥ 9
रावणस्तु मया भ्रातर्बहुधा परिबोधितः । सीतां देहीति रामाय रामः साक्षाज्जनार्दनः ॥ 10
न शृणोति च मां हन्तुं खड्गमुद्यम्य चोक्तवान् । धिक् त्वां गच्छेति मां हत्वा पदा पापिभिरावृतः ॥
चतुर्भिर्मन्त्रिभिः सार्धं रामं शरणमागतः ॥ 12
तच्छ्रुत्वा कुम्भकर्णोऽपि ज्ञात्वा भ्रातरमागतम् ।
समालिङ्ग्य च वत्स त्वं जीव रामपदाश्रयात् । कुलसंरक्षणार्थाय राक्षसानां हिताय च ॥ 13
महाभागवतोऽसि त्वं पुरा मे नारदाच्छ्रुतम् । गच्छ तात ममेदानीं दृश्यते न च किञ्चन ॥ 14
मदीयो वा परो वापि मदमत्तविलोचनः । इत्युक्तोऽश्रुमुखो भ्रातुश्चरणावभिवन्द्य सः ॥ 15
रामपार्श्वमुपागत्य चिन्तापर उपस्थितः ॥ 16
कुम्भकर्णोऽपि हस्ताभ्यां पदाभ्यां पेषयन्हरीन् । चचार वानरीं सेनां कालयन् गन्धहस्तिवत् ॥ 17

the waves of the ocean, and gathering the monkeys in his hand, began to eat them up. **6.** Seeing this Yama-like Kumbhakarna equal to a mountain with wings, all the monkeys began to run away in fright. **(7-9).** Kumbhakarna moved amidst the monkey forces destroying them on all sides partly by his Mudgara, partly by eating them up, and partly by crushing them by his hands and feet.

The wise Vibheeshana who had a mace in his hand now saw his elder brother in the battlefield. Approaching him he prostrated at his feet and said, "O High souled one! I am Vibheeshana, your brother. Have mercy on me. **(10-12).** O brother! I rendered advice to Ravana respectfully in many ways. I advised him to restore Sita to Rama who is Mahavishnu Himself. But he refused to take my advice. Lifting his sword, he ordered me to go out. Surrounded by a band of evil-minded courtiers, he kicked me out of his presence. I came away with four ministers and took shelter under Rama." **(13-16).** Hearing these words of Vibheeshana, Kumbhakarna embraced his brother and said, "O my dear boy! Seeking shelter under Rama, you will be the saviour and protector of the tribe of Rakshasas. I have heard from Narada that you are a great devotee of the Lord. Dear one! You now go away from my presence. Under the influence of liquor my eyes now make no difference between friend and foe." Hearing these words of Kumbhakarna, Vibheeshana prostrated at the feet of his brother and went to the presence of Rama in a very pensive mood.

17. Kumbhakarna now continued to move about like an elephant in rut amidst the

दृष्ट्वा तं राघवः क्रुद्धो वायव्यं शस्त्रमादरात् ।

चिक्षेप कुम्भकर्णाय तेन चिच्छेद रक्षसः । समुद्गरं दक्षहस्तं तेन घोरं ननाद सः ॥ 18

स हस्तः पतितो भूमावनेकानर्दयन्कपीन् । पर्यन्तमाश्रिताः सर्वे वानरा भयवेपिताः ॥ 19

रामराक्षसयोर्युद्धं पश्यन्तः पर्यवस्थिताः । कुम्भकर्णश्छिन्नहस्तः शालमुद्यम्य वेगतः ॥ 20

समरे राघवं हन्तुं दुद्राव तमथोऽच्छिनत् । शालेन सहितं वामहस्तमैन्द्रेण राघवः ॥ 21

छिन्नबाहुमथायान्तं नर्दन्तं वीक्ष्य राघवः । द्वावर्धचन्द्रौ निशितावादायास्य पदद्वयम् ॥ 22

चिच्छेद पतितौ पादौ लङ्काद्वारि महास्वनौ । निकृत्तपाणिपादोऽपि कुम्भकर्णोऽतिभीषणः ॥ 23

बडवामुखवद्वक्त्रं व्यादाय रघुनन्दनम् । अभिदुद्राव निनदन्राहुश्चन्द्रमसं यथा ॥ 24

अपूरयच्छिताग्रैश्च सायकैस्तद्रघूत्तमः । शरपूरितवक्त्रोऽसौ चुक्रोशातिभयङ्करः ॥ 25

अथ सूर्यप्रतीकाशमैन्द्रं शरमनुत्तमम् । वज्राशनिसमं रामश्चिक्षेपासुरमृत्यवे ॥ 26

स तत्पर्वतसङ्काशं स्फुरत्कुण्डलदंष्ट्रकम् । चकर्त रक्षोऽधिपतेः शिरो वृत्रमिवाशनिः ॥ 27

तच्छिरः पतितं लङ्काद्वारि कायो महोदधौ । शिरोऽस्य रोधयद्द्वारं कायो नक्राद्यचूर्णयत् ॥ 28

ततो देवाः सऋषयो गन्धर्वाः पन्नगाः खगाः । सिद्धा यक्षा गुह्यकाश्च अप्सरोभिश्च राघवम् ॥ 29

monkey army destroying them with his hands and feet. **18.** Angry at the sight of this, Rama directed the missile of the wind-god against Kumbhakarna and cut off his right hand that held the mace. At this Kumbhakarna raised a terrific yell. **(19-21).** That severed arm of his crashed to the ground causing injury to many monkeys. The frightened monkeys withdrew to some distance from the battle-field and watched the battle between Rama and Kumbhakarna. Though his right arm was severed, Kumbhakarna now came forward to attack Rama with a palmyra tree held in his left hand. But Rama cut off that hand also with Indra-missile. **(22-24).** With both his hands cut off, Kumbhakarna continued to rush at Rama howling. Rama thereupon severed both his legs with two semi-circular-headed arrows, which threw those .limbs upto the gates of Lanka with a big bang. Though bereft of hands and feet, the terrible Kumbhakarna with his mouth wide open like the concavity of a submarine fire, rushed howling towards Rama to swallow him as Rahu does towards the moon. **25.** Rama thereupon filled his wide open mouth with sharp and powerful arrows, at which the Rakshasa raised terrific howls. **26.** Then with the idea of killing the Rakshasa, Rama released at him a powerful arrow imparted to him by Indra which shone like the sun and was sharp like the thunderbolt weapon. **27.** Just as Indra's thunderbolt severed the head of Vritra, Rama's arrow cut off the Rakshasa prince's head which was massive like a mountain and glitterd because of his ear-pendents and fangs. **28.** Hit by that missile, Kumbhakarna's head fell at the gate of Lanka obstructing its passage, while his body fell in the mighty ocean crushing many aquatic creatures. **29.** Thereupon Rishis

ईडिरे कुसुमासारैर्वषन्तश्चाभिनन्दिताः ॥
आजगाम तदा रामं द्रष्टुं देवमुनीश्वरः ॥ 30
नारदो गगनात्तूर्णं स्वभासा भासयन्दिशः । राममिन्दीवरश्याममुदाराङ्गं धनुर्धरम् ॥ 31
ईषत्ताम्रविशालाक्षमैन्द्रास्त्राश्चितबाहुकम् । दयार्द्रदृष्टया पश्यन्तं वानराञ्छरपीडितान् ॥ 32
दृष्ट्वा गद्गदया वाचा भक्त्या स्तोतुं प्रचक्रमे ॥ 33

नारद उवाच

देवदेव जगन्नाथ परमात्मन् सनातन । नारायणाखिलाधार विश्वसाक्षिन्नमोऽस्तुते ॥ 34
विशुद्धज्ञानरूपोऽपि त्वं लोकानतिवञ्चयन् । मायया मनुजाकारः सुखदुःखादिमानिव ॥ 35
त्वं मायया गुह्यमानः सर्वेषां हृदि संस्थितः । स्वयंज्योतिः स्वभावस्त्वं व्यक्त एवामलात्मनाम् ॥
उन्मीलयन् सृजस्येतन्नेत्रे राम जगत्त्रयम् । उपसंह्रियते सर्वं त्वया चक्षुर्निमीलनात् ॥ 37
यस्मिन्सर्वमिदं भाति यतश्चैतच्चराचरम् । यस्मान्न किञ्चिल्लोकेऽस्मिंस्तस्मै ते ब्रह्मणे नमः 38
प्रकृतिं पुरुषं कालं व्यक्ताव्यक्तस्वरूपिणम् ।
यं जानन्ति मुनिश्रेष्ठास्तस्मै रामाय ते नमः ॥ 39

Devas, Gandharvas, Pannagas, Pakshis, Siddhas, Yakshas, Guhyakas and Apsaras showered a rain of flowers in their joy and sang Rama's praise.

Narada's Hymn (30-52)

(30-33). To see Rama whose body was beautiful and blue-complexioned, who held a bow in his hand, whose broad eyes had turned a little crimson, whose arms were resplendent with the arrow of Indra held in it, who was casting merciful glances at the monkeys suffering from the wounds caused by arrows,—to see Rama of such description, the great sage Narada came down from the sky, illumining all the quarters by his radiance, and began to sing a hymn of praise with great devotion in a choked voice.

34. Narada said, "Salutation to Thee, O Lord of Lords! O Master of the worlds! O Supreme Spirit! O Eternal Being! O Lord Narayana! O Support of all! O Witness of the universe! **35.** Though Thou art of the nature of Pure Consciousness, out of Thy Maya Thou hast assumed a human form and deludest the world by behaving like one subject to happiness and sorrow. **36.** Though residing in the hearts of all and partaking of the nature of self-resplendent Self-consciousness, Thou coverest Thyself with Thy Maya. Only men of pure minds are able to recognise Thee through that veil of Maya. **37.** O Rama! With the opening of Thy eyelids, Thou createst this universe and with their closing Thou withdrawest it into Thyself. **38.** He in whom all this universe is seen, He out of whom all that is moving and unmoving originated, He outside of whom nothing else exists—to Thee Brahman, my salutations! **39.** He whom the sages know as the one that has taken the forms of Prakriti, Purusha, Time, the manifested state and the

विकाररहितं शुद्धं ज्ञानरूपं श्रुतिर्जगौ । त्वां सर्वजगदाकारमूर्तिं चाप्याह सा श्रुतिः ॥ 40
विरोधो दृश्यते देव वैदिको वेदवादिनाम् । निश्चयं नाधिगच्छन्ति त्वत्प्रसादं विना बुधाः 41
मायया क्रीडतो देव न विरोधो मनागपि । रश्मिजालं रवेर्यद्वद्दृश्यते जलवद् भ्रमात् ॥ 42
भ्रान्तिज्ञानात्तथा राम त्वयि सर्वं प्रकल्प्यते । मनसोऽविषयो देव रूपं ते निर्गुणं परम् ॥ 43
कथं दृश्यं भवेद्देव दृश्याभावे भजेत्कथम् । अतस्त्वद्वतारेषु रूपाणि निपुणा भुवि ॥ 44
भजन्ति बुद्धिसम्पन्नास्तरन्त्येव भवार्णवम् । कामक्रोधादयस्तत्र बहवः परिपन्थिनः ॥ 45
भीषयन्ति सदा चेतो मार्जारा मूषकं यथा । त्वन्नाम स्मरतां नित्यं त्वद्रूपमपि मानसे ॥ 46
त्वत्पूजानिरतानां ते कथामृतपरात्मनाम् । त्वद्भक्तसङ्गिनां राम संसारो गोष्पदायते ॥ 47
अतस्ते सगुणं रूपं ध्यात्वाहं सर्वदा हृदि । मुक्तश्चरामि लोकेषु पूज्योऽहं सर्वदैवतैः ॥ 48
राम त्वया महत्कार्यं कृतं देवहितेच्छया । कुम्भकर्णवधेनाद्य भूभारोऽयं गतः प्रभो ॥ 49
श्वो हनिष्यति सौमित्रिरिन्द्रजेतारमाहवे । हनिष्यसेऽथ राम त्वं परश्वो दशकन्धरम् ॥ 50
पश्यामि सर्वं देवेश सिद्धैः सह नभोगतः । अनुगृह्णीष्व मां देव गमिष्यामि सुरालयम् ॥ 51
इत्युक्त्वा राममामन्त्र्य नारदो भगवानृषिः । ययौ देवैः पूज्यमानो ब्रह्मलोकमकल्मषम् ॥ 52

unmanifested condition—to Thee Rama, my salutations! **40.** The Veda which has described Thee as changeless, as unconnected with Maya, as Pure Consciousness—that very Veda describes Thee also as having the whole universe for Thy body. **41.** This view of the Vedic teaching appears contradictory to some, but the truth about this contradiction will not be clear even to wise men without Thy grace. **42.** In this play of Thine with Thy Maya, there is really not the slightest contradiction. It is like mirage in which sun's light appears as water in our visual illusion (wherein light and illusory water coexist). **43.** O Rama! It is due to illusory perception that all this universe is attributed to Thee. When the mind is properly instructed, one is able to understand Thy real nature that transcends the Gunas. **(44-47).** How can limited beings understand Thy formless aspect—the aspect without any attributes and transcending the Gunas? How is worship and devotion possible without an object to be loved and worshipped? Therefore, in this world the really intelligent people adore Thee through Thy incarnations and cross this ocean of Samsara. Various inimical forces like desire, anger etc., oppose and terrify those who address themselves to this task, as cats do with mice. But Thy form shines in the minds of those who ever think of Thee. This ocean of Samsara is indeed like a puddle made by a calf's hoof-mark to those who are devoted to Thy worship, who ever imbibe the nectar of the accounts of Thy glories, and who associate themselves with Thy devotees. **48.** Therefore I always meditate in my heart about your form with attributes and wander over all the worlds freely, adored by all the gods. **(49-52).** For the benefit of the Devas, Thou didst achieve many great things. By the destruc-

भ्रातरं निहतं श्रुत्वा कुम्भकर्णं महाबलम् । रावणः शोकसन्तप्तो रामेणाक्लिष्टकर्मणा ॥ 53
मूर्च्छितः पतितो भूमावुत्थाय विललाप ह । पितृव्यं निहतं श्रुत्वा पितरं चातिविह्वलम् ॥ 54
इन्द्रजित्प्राह शोकार्तं त्यज शोकं महामते । मयि जीवति राजेन्द्र मेघनादे महाबले ॥ 55
दुःखस्यावसरः कुत्र देवान्तक महामते । व्येतु ते दुःखमखिलं स्वस्थो भव महीपते ॥ 56
सर्वं समीकरिष्यामि हनिष्यामि च वै रिपून् । गत्वा निकुम्भिलां सद्यस्तर्पयित्वा हुताशनम् ॥57
लब्ध्वा रथादिकं तस्मादजेयोऽहं भवाम्यरेः । इत्युक्त्वा त्वरितं गत्वा निर्दिष्टं हवनस्थलम् ॥58
रक्तमाल्याम्बरधरो रक्तगन्धानुलेपनः । निकुम्भिलास्थले मौनी हवनायोपचक्रमे ॥ 59
विभीषणोऽथ तच्छ्रुत्वा मेघनादस्य चेष्टितम् । प्राह रामाय सकलं होमारम्भं दुरात्मनः ॥ 60
समाप्यते चेद्धोमोऽयं मेघनादस्य दुर्मतेः । तदाजेयो भवेद्राम मेघनादः सुरासुरैः ॥ 61
अतः शीघ्रं लक्ष्मणेन घातयिष्यामि रावणिम् ।
आज्ञापय मया सार्धं लक्ष्मणं बलिनां वरम् । हनिष्यति न संदेहो मेघनादं तवानुजः ॥ 62

tion of Kumbhakarna, much of the burden of the world has been removed. Tomorrow, Lakshmana the son of Sumitra is going to destroy Indrajit in battle, and the day after Thou art Thyself going to kill the ten-headed Ravana. I shall be watching all these from the sky along with the Siddhas. Be gracious now to bless me and permit me to go to the abode of the celestials." Having thus hymned and taken leave of Rama, and having received the adoration of the celestials, the holy sage Narada departed to the sinless abode of Brahma.

Indrajit's resolve (53-59)

(53-56). Hearing of the destruction of his powerful brother Kumbhakarna at the hands of Rama of matchless prowess, Ravana was stricken with deep sorrow and fell on the floor in a swoon. Recovering consciousness, he sat up and began to bemoan the loss of his brother. Now Indrajit, hearing of his uncle's death and witnessing his father's sorrow, came forward and said to the afflicted Ravana, "O great one! Abandon your grief. Where is the cause of grief so long as I, Meghanada, am alive? There is absolutely no reason for you to be downcast. Abandoning all your grief, be at peace. **(57-59).** I shall set everything right. I shall destroy all your enemies. I have no doubt about it. I shall immediately go to the Nikumbhila (the place for the fire-sacrifices for black magic), propitiate the fire-deity, and obtain the chariot and equipments necessary to become invincible by the enemy." Saying so, he went to the Nikumbhila, put on robes and garlands of red colour, applied red sandal paste to his body, and observing silence, began the fire sacrifice.

Vibheeshana's advice (60-68)

(60-62). Coming to know about this

श्रीरामचन्द्र उवाच

अहमेवागमिष्यामि हन्तुमिन्द्रजितं रिपुम् । आग्नेयेन महास्त्रेण मर्वराक्षसघातिना ॥ 63

विभीषणोऽपि तं प्राह नासावन्यैर्निहन्यते । यस्तु द्वादश वर्षाणि निद्राहारविवर्जितः ॥ 64

तेनैव मृत्युर्निर्दिष्टो ब्रह्मणास्य दुरात्मनः । लक्ष्मणस्तु अयोध्याया निर्गम्यायात्त्वया सह ॥65

तदादि निद्राहारादीन्न जानाति रघूत्तम । सेवार्थं तव राजेन्द्र ज्ञातं सर्वमिदं मया ॥ 66

तदाज्ञापय देवेश लक्ष्मणं त्वरया मया । हनिष्यति न सन्देहः शेषः साक्षाद्धराधरः ॥ 67

त्वमेव साक्षाज्जगतामधीशो नारायणो लक्ष्मण एव शेषः ।
युवां धराभारनिवारणार्थं जातौ जगन्नाटकसूत्रधारौ ॥ 68

इति श्रीमदध्यात्मरामायणे उमामहेश्वरसंवादे
युद्धकाण्डे अष्टमः सर्गः ॥ ८ ॥

enterprise of Meghanada, Vibheeshana informed Rama of it and said, "If the evil-minded Meghanada is allowed to complete the sacrifice, he will become invincible by Devas and Asuras. There fore, I would like to have him killed immediately by Lakshmana. So deign to send mighty Lakshmana with me on this mission. Your brother will surely be able to destroy Meghanada." **63.** Thereupon Rama said, "I shall myself go to destroy the whole tribe of Rakshasas with the missile of Agni," **(64-68).** To this Vibheeshana replied, "The death of this evil-minded Asura can be effected only by one who has been without food or sleep for twelve years. None else can kill him. This is a boon given to him by Brahma. Now Lakshmana ever since he left Ayodhya with you, from that day onwards has never cared to eat or sleep on account of his engrossment in your service. I have come to know all about this. Therefore, O great Lord, please ask Lakshmana to come with me quickly. He is none but that Adisesha who bears the weight of the world. He is sure to kill Indrajit. Thou art the supreme Narayana, the master of the whole universe and Lakshmana is Adisesha. You two, who are the directors of the play of this universe, are now born on this earth in order to free it of its burdens."

नवमः सर्गः

श्रीमहादेव उवाच

विभीषणवचः श्रुत्वा रामो वाक्यमथाब्रवीत् । जानामि तस्य रौद्रस्य मायां कृत्स्नां विभीषण ॥ 1

स हि ब्रह्मास्त्रविच्छूरो मायावी च महाबलः । जानामि लक्ष्मणस्यापि स्वरूपं मम सेवनम् ॥ 2

ज्ञात्वैवासमहं तूष्णीं भविष्यत्कार्यगौरवात् । इत्युक्त्वा लक्ष्मणं प्राह रामो ज्ञानवतां वरः ॥ 3

गच्छ लक्ष्मण सैन्येन महता जहि रावणिम् । हनूमत्प्रमुखैः सर्वैर्यूथपैः सह लक्ष्मण ॥ 4

जाम्बवानृक्षराजोऽयं सह सैन्येन संवृतः । विभीषणश्च सचिवैः सह त्वामभियास्यति ॥ 5

अभिज्ञस्तस्य देशस्य जानाति विवराणि सः । रामस्य वचनं श्रुत्वा लक्ष्मणः सविभीषणः ॥ 6

जग्राह कार्मुकं श्रेष्ठमन्यद्भीमपराक्रमः । रामपादाम्बुजं स्पृष्ट्वा हृष्टः सौमित्रिरब्रवीत् ॥ 7

अद्य मत्कार्मुकान्मुक्ताः शरा निर्भिद्य रावणिम् । गमिष्यन्ति हि पातालं स्नातुं भोगवतीजले ॥ 8

एवमुक्त्वा स सौमित्रिः परिक्रम्य प्रणम्य तम् । इन्द्रजिन्निधनाकाङ्क्षी ययौ त्वरितविक्रमः ॥ 9

वानरैर्बहुसाहस्रैर्हनूमान्पृष्ठतोऽन्वगात् । विभीषणश्च सहितो मन्त्रिभिस्त्वरितं ययौ ॥ 10

Chapter 9

FALL OF INDRAJIT

Interception of the Homa (1-24)

(1-3). Hearing these words of Vibheeshana, Rama said as follows: "O Vibheeshana! I know everything about that terrible Asura—that he is a master of all magic, that he is very brave, that he knows the use of the Brahma missile, and that he is an adept in magical warfare. I know also about the vow observed by Lakshmana during my service. I kept silent over his abandonment of food etc., only with the fore-knowledge of the great things he would have to accomplish." He then called Lakshmana and said, **(4-7).** "O Lakshmana! Go for battle accompanied by the great army and its leaders like Hanuman, and destroy Indrajit, the son of Ravana. Also Jambavan with his army and Vibheeshana with his ministers will accompany you. The wise Vibheeshana is well-acquainted with those places where the battle is to take place." At these words of Rama, Lakshmana, the mighty, selected a new bow, and getting ready to start with Vibheeshana, touched the feet of Rama and said: **8.** "Now the arrows shot from my bow after piercing the son of Ravana, will go down to the Patala to take a dip in the river Bhogavati."

9. Having said so and having circumambulated Rama, Lakshmana started for the destruction of Indrajit, impatient to demonstrate his prowess. **10.** Accomp-

जाम्बवत्प्रमुखा ऋक्षाः सौमित्रिं त्वरयान्वयुः । गत्वा निकुम्भिलादेशं लक्ष्मणो वानरैः सह ॥ 11
अपश्यद्बलसङ्घातं दूराद्राक्षससङ्कुलम् । धनुरायम्य सौमित्रिर्यत्तोऽभूद् भूरिविक्रमः ॥ 12
अङ्गदेन च वीरेण जाम्बवान् राक्षसाधिपः । तदा विभीषणः प्राह सौमित्रिं पश्य राक्षसान् ॥13
यदेतद्राक्षसानीकं मेघश्यामं विलोक्यते । अस्यानीकस्य महतो भेदने यत्नवान् भव ॥ 14
राक्षसेन्द्रसुतोऽप्यस्मिन् भिन्ने दृश्यो भविष्यति । अभिद्रवाशु यावद्वै नैतत्कर्म समाप्यते ॥ 15
जहि वीर दुरात्मानं हिंसापरमधार्मिकम् ॥ 16
विभीषणवचः श्रुत्वा लक्ष्मणः शुभलक्षणः ।
ववर्ष शरवर्षाणि राक्षसेन्द्रसुतं प्रति । पाषाणैः पर्वताग्रैश्च वृक्षैश्च हरियूथपाः ॥ 17
निर्जघ्नुः सर्वतो दैत्यांस्तेऽपि वानरयूतपान् । परश्वधैः शितैर्बाणैरसिभिर्यष्टितोमरैः ॥ 18
निर्जघ्नुर्वानरानीकं तदा शब्दो महानभूत् । स सम्प्रहारस्तुमुलः संजज्ञे हरिरक्षसाम् ॥ 19
इन्द्रजित्स्वबलं सर्वमद्यमानं विलोक्य सः । निकुम्भिलां च होमं च त्यक्त्वा शीघ्रं विनिर्गतः॥20
रथमारुह्य सधनुः क्रोधेन महतागमत् । समाह्वयन् स सौमित्रिं युद्धाय रणमूर्धनि ॥ 21
सौमित्रे मेघनादोऽहं मया जीवन्न मोक्ष्यसे । तत्र दृष्ट्वा पितृव्यं स प्राह निष्ठुरभाषणम् ॥ 22

anied by a big army of monkeys, Hanuman followed him. So did Vibheeshana hurry with his ministers. **(11-12).** Jambavan and his force of bears hurried behind Lakshmana. Reaching the premises of the sacrificial hall, Lakshmana saw there a huge army of Rakshasas. The highly skilled archer that he was, he strung his bow and got ready for battle. **(13-14).** Now Jambavan along with Angada, as also Vibheeshana the Rakshasa leader, said to Lakshmana, "See that huge army of Rakshasas spread like a mass of blue clouds. We have now to take steps to pierce the ranks of that Rakshasa army arrayed for battle. **(15-16).** When the army of Rakshasas is pierced, Indrajit the son of Ravana, will be visible. Before he completes his fire sacrifice, you have to face him in battle. Annihilate that evil-minded fellow, who is a destructive genius and a violator of Dharma.

(17-19). Hearing these words of Vibheeshana, Lakshmana of auspicious form, released a volley of arrows against the army of Indrajit, and the monkey leaders attacked them with boulders, hillocks and trees. The Rakshasas too fought back with battle-axes, sharp arrows, swords, pestles and Tomoras. Great was the tumult when the two armies thus clashed in fierce battle. **20'** On seeing his army thus attacked, Indrajit stopped the sacrifice and left the sacrificial hall and came out immediately.**(21-22).** Taking a bow, he ascended his chariot and in great anger addressed Lakshmana, "Know that I am Meghanada. You shall not go away alive from my presence." With this

इहैव जातः संवृद्धः साक्षाद् भ्राता पितुर्मम। यस्त्वं स्वजनमुत्सृज्य परभृत्यत्वमागतः॥ 23
कथं द्रुह्यसि पुत्राय पापीयानसि दुर्मतिः॥ 24
इत्युक्त्वा लक्ष्मणं दृष्ट्वा हनूमत्पृष्ठतः स्थितम्। उद्यदायुधनिस्त्रिंशे रथे महति संस्थितः॥ 25
महाप्रमाणमुद्यम्य घोरं विस्फारयन्धनुः। अद्य वो मामका बाणाः प्राणान्पास्यन्ति वानराः॥ 26
ततः शरं दाशरथिः सन्धायामित्रकर्षणः।
ससर्ज राक्षसेन्द्राय क्रुद्धः सर्प इव श्वसन्। इन्द्रजिद्रक्तनयनो लक्ष्मणं समुदैक्षत॥ 27
शक्राशनिसमस्पर्शैर्लक्ष्मणेनाहतः शरैः। मुहूर्तमभवन्मूढः पुनः प्रत्याहृतेन्द्रियः॥ 28
ददर्शावस्थितं वीरं वीरो दशरथात्मजम्। सोऽभिचक्राम सौमित्रिं क्रोधसंरक्तलोचनः॥ 29
शरान्धनुषि सन्धाय लक्ष्मणं चेदमब्रवीत्। यदि ते प्रथमे युद्धे न दृष्टो मे पराक्रमः॥ 30
अद्य त्वां दर्शयिष्यामि तिष्ठेदानीं व्यवस्थितः। इत्युक्त्वा सप्तभिर्बाणैरभिविव्याध लक्ष्मणम्॥ 31
दशभिश्च हनूमन्तं तीक्ष्णधारैः शरोत्तमैः। ततः शरशतेनैव सम्प्रयुक्तेन वीर्यवान्॥ 32
क्रोधद्विगुणसंरब्धो निर्बिभेद विभीषणम्। लक्ष्मणोऽपि तथा शत्रुं शरवर्षैरवाकिरत्॥ 33

challenge, he came to the midst of battle. **(23-24).** He saw before him his uncle Vibheeshana and addressed these harsh words to him, "You were born and brought up among us. You are a direct brother of my father. Still abandoning your own people, you have become a servant of our enemy.. You are demonstrating your treachery against me, who am like a son to you. You are the most sinful among the sinners."

Fight with Indrajit and his death (25-68)

(25-26). Having said so, he looked at Lakshmana sitting on the shoulders of Hanuman. Seated in his magnificent chariot, which was equipped with all kinds of missiles and other weapons,he lifted his great bow and twanging it, declared, "O monkey! My arrows are now going to consume your Prana." **27.** Thereupon Lakshmana, the destroyer of all foes, began to shower arrows, hissing like an angry serpent. Now Indrajit, roused to great anger, looked at Lakshmana with his reddened eyes. **(28-31).** Struck by Lakshmana's arrows sharp as the thunderbolt weapon of Indra, Indrajit lost his consciousness for a moment. Recovering from it presently he said to Lakshmana in great anger, with arrows attached to his bow: "In my first battle with you, you do not seem to have had sufficient experience of my prowess. I shall now demonstrate it to you. Stand here for a while." With these words, he struck Lakshmana with seven arrows. **(32-33).** With ten sharp and powerful arrows, he wounded Hanuman. Then highly excited with anger, he sent a hundred arrows at Vibheeshana. In return,

तस्य बाणैः सुसंविद्धं कवचं काञ्चनप्रभम् । व्यशीर्यत रथोपस्थे तिलशः पतितं भुवि ॥ 34
ततः शरसहस्रेण सङ्क्रुद्धो रावणात्मजः । बिभेद समरे वीरं लक्ष्मणं भीमविक्रमम् ॥ 35
व्यशीर्यतापतद्दिव्यं कवचं लक्ष्मणस्य च । कृतप्रतिकृतान्योन्यं बभूवतुरभिद्रुतौ ॥ 36
अभीक्ष्णं निःश्वसन्तौ तौ युध्येतां तुमुलं पुनः । शरसंवृतसर्वाङ्गौ सर्वतो रुधिरोक्षितौ ॥ 37
सुदीर्घकालं तौ वीरावन्योन्यं निशितैः शरैः । अयुध्येतां महासत्त्वौ जयाजयविवर्जितौ ॥ 38
एतस्मिन्नन्तरे वीरो लक्ष्मणः पञ्चभिः शरैः । रावणेः सारथिं साश्वं रथं च समचूर्णयत् ॥ 39
चिच्छेद कार्मुकं तस्य दर्शयन्हस्तलाघवम् । सोऽन्यत्तु कार्मुकं भद्रं सज्यं चक्रे त्वरान्वितः ॥ 40
तच्चापमपि चिच्छेद लक्ष्मणस्त्रिभिराशुगैः । तमेव छिन्नधन्वानं विव्याधानेकसायकैः ॥ 41
पुनरन्यत्समादाय कार्मुकं भीमविक्रमः । इन्द्रजिल्लक्ष्मणं बाणैः शितैरादित्यसन्निभैः ॥ 42
बिभेद वानरान्सर्वान्बाणैरापूरयन्दिशः । तत ऐन्द्रं समादाय लक्ष्मणो रावणिं प्रति ॥ 43
सन्धायाकृष्य कर्णान्तं कार्मुकं दृढनिष्ठुरम् । उवाच लक्ष्मणो वीरः स्मरन् रामपदाम्बुजम् ॥ 44
धर्मात्मा सत्यसन्धश्च रामो दाशरथिर्यदि । त्रिलोक्यामप्रतिद्वन्द्वस्तदैनं जहि रावणिम् ॥ 45
इत्युक्त्वा बाणमाकर्णाद्विकृष्य तमजिह्मगम् । लक्ष्मणः समरे वीरः ससर्जेन्द्रजितं प्रति ॥ 46
स शरः सशिरस्त्राणं श्रीमज्ज्वलितकुण्डलम् । प्रमथ्येन्द्रजितः कायात्पातयामास भूतले ॥ 47

Lakshmana also covered him with arrows. **34.** Struck by Lakshmana's arrows, the shining armour of Indrajit was shattered into bits and fell into the back of the chariot and on the ground. **(35-37).** Ravana's son, now full of wrath, sent numerous arrows at Lakshmana and shattered his armour also. Thus returning blow for blow, they traversed the battlefield up and down, locked in fierce combat. **38.** With their limbs covered with arrows and bleeding wounds, those two heroes fought for long a drawn battle. **(39-41).** In the meantime, heroic Lakshmana destroyed with five arrows the chariot of Indrajit along with its horses and charioteer. He showed his expertise by cutting off the enemy's bow also. In great haste, Indrajit took up another bow and strung it, but Lakshmana cut off that also with three arrows and wounded him with many shafts. **(42-44).** Heroic Indrajit now took up a third bow and with arrows shining like the sun's beams wounded Lakshmana and filled all the quarters with volleys of arrows. Lakshmana next took up the Indra missile. Drawing the string of his strong bow upto the ear and attaching to it that missile and aiming it at Indrajit as the target, he said with remembrance of Rama's feet in his mind: **(45-46).** "If Rama, the unrivalled hero is devoted to Dharma and truth, may this arrow destroy the son of Ravana." With these words, he drew the bow-string to his ear and let the unswerving missile speed towards Indrajit. **47.** That

ततः प्रमुदिता देवाः कीर्तयन्तो रघूत्तमम् । ववर्षुः पुष्पवर्षाणि स्तुवन्तश्च मुहुर्मुहुः ॥ 48
जहर्ष शक्रो भगवान्सह देवैर्महर्षिभिः । आकाशेऽपि च देवानां शुश्रुवे दुन्दुभिस्वनः ॥ 49
विमलं गगनं चासीत्स्थिराभूद्विश्वधारिणी । निहतं रावणिं दृष्ट्वा जयजल्पसमन्वितः ॥ 50
गतश्रमः स सौमित्रिः शङ्खमापूरयद्रणे । सिंहनादं ततः कृत्वा ज्याशब्दमकरोद्विभुः ॥ 51
तेन नादेन संहृष्टा वानराश्च गतश्रमाः । वानरेन्द्रैश्च सहितः स्तुवद्भिर्हृष्टमानसैः ॥ 52
लक्ष्मणः परितुष्टात्मा ददर्शाभ्येत्य राघवम् । हनूमद्राक्षसाभ्यां च सहितो विनयान्वितः ॥ 53
ववन्दे भ्रातरं रामं ज्येष्ठं नारायणं विभुम् । त्वत्प्रसादाद्रघुश्रेष्ठ हतो रावणिराहवे ॥ 54
श्रुत्वा तल्लक्ष्मणाद्भक्त्या तमालिङ्ग्य रघूत्तमः । मूर्ध्न्यवघ्राय मुदितः सस्नेहमिदमब्रवीत् ॥ 55
साधु लक्ष्मण तुष्टोऽस्मि कर्म ते दुष्करं कृतम् । मेघनादस्य निधने जितं सर्वमरिन्दम ॥ 56
अहोरात्रैस्त्रिभिर्वीरः कथञ्चिद्विनिपातितः । निःसपत्नः कृतोऽस्म्यद्य निर्यास्यति हि रावणः ॥
पुत्रशोकान्मया योद्धुं तं हनिष्यामि रावणम् ॥ 57
मेघनादं हतं श्रुत्वा लक्ष्मणेन महाबलम् । 58
रावणः पतितो भूमौ मूर्च्छितः पुनरुत्थितः । विललापातिदीनात्मा पुत्रशोकेन रावणः ॥ 59

arrow cut off the head of Indrajit, shining with ear-pendents and crowned by a diadem, and threw it on the ground.

(48-51). Delighted at the destruction of Indrajit, the Devas sang the praise of Rama again and again, and addressed hymns to him. They showered a rain of flowers. Indra, the celestials and the Maharshis joyously gathered in the sky. The kettle drums of the Devas sounded on high. The sky became clear and the earth became firm. Now with everyone there raising cries of hail to him, Lakshmana who had got over his exhaustion, sounded his conch, and with a lion-roar twanged his bow-string again and again. **(52-54).** That sound of victory refreshed and gladdened the monkeys, and they became free from exhaustion. Lakshmana, with all the joyous monkey leaders glorifying his deeds, now went along with Hanuman and Vibheeshana to Rama in great humility. He saluted his brother who was none but Narayana and said, "O noblest of Raghu's line! By your blessing Indrajit has been killed." **55.** Hearing these devoted words of Lakshmana, Rama embraced him and with great affection, smelt the crown of his head and said: **56.** "O Lakshmana! You have done well. I am much pleased with you. You have accomplished a very difficult task. With the death of Indrajit, victory over the Rakshasas is an accomplished task. **(57-58).** In three days, you have managed to destroy him. Now, really speaking, I am without an antagonist. Spurred by his sorrow at the death of his son, Ravana is sure to come for a fight with me. I shall then kill him."

पुत्रस्य गुणकर्माणि संस्मरन्पर्यदेवयन् । अद्य देवगणाः सर्वे लोकपाला महर्षयः ॥ 60
हतमिन्द्रजितं ज्ञात्वा सुखं स्वप्स्यन्ति निर्भयाः । इत्यादि बहुशः पुत्रलालसो विललाप ह ॥ 61
ततः परमसंक्रुद्धो रावणो राक्षसाधिपः । उवाच राक्षसान्सर्वान्विनाशयिषुराहवे ॥ 62
स पुत्रवधसन्तप्तः शूरः क्रोधवशं गतः । संवीक्ष्य रावणो बुद्ध्या हन्तुं सीतां प्रदुद्रुवे ॥ 63
खड्गपाणिमथायान्तं क्रुद्धं दृष्ट्वा दशाननम् । राक्षसीमध्यगा सीता भयशोकाकुलाभवत् ॥ 64
एतस्मिन्नन्तरे तस्य सचिवो बुद्धिमान् शुचिः । सुपार्श्वो नाम मेधावी रावणं वाक्यमब्रवीत् ॥ 65
ननु नाम दशग्रीव साक्षाद्वैश्रवणानुजः । वेदविद्याव्रतस्नातः स्वकर्मपरिनिष्ठितः ॥ 96
अनेकगुणसम्पन्नः कथं स्त्रीवधमिच्छसि ।
अस्माभिः सहितो युद्धे हत्वा रामं च लक्ष्मणम् । प्राप्स्यसे जानकीं शीघ्रमित्युक्तः स न्यवर्तत ॥ 67
ततो दुरात्मा सुहृदा निवेदितं वचः सुधर्म्यं प्रतिगृह्य रावणः ।
गृहं जगामाशु शुचा विमूढधीः पुनः सभां च प्रययौ सुहृद्वृतः ॥ 68

इति श्रीमदध्यात्मरामायणे उमामहेश्वरसंवादे
युद्धकाण्डे नवमः सर्गः ॥ ९ ॥

(59-61). Hearing about the death of the mighty Meghanada, Ravana swooned and fell on the floor. He bemoaned the loss of his son very bitterly. Afflicted by sorrow, he recalled the actions and qualities of his dead son and said, "Henceforward, with the death of Indrajit, the Devas, the Maharshis and the protectors of the quarters will sleep in peace." Ravana bemoaned his son's death in many ways like this. **(62-63).** Then seized by great wrath, he ordered all the Asuras to go for battle, even knowing that total destruction was before them. That heroic Ravana, stricken by the sorrow of his son's death, now gave himself up to thoughtless anger and resolved to kill Sita. **64.** Seeing Ravana approaching her in a wrathful mood, sword in hand, Sita, who was surrounded by Rakshasis, was stricken with great fear and sorrow. **65.** Fortunately, Suparsva, an intelligent and pure-minded minister of Ravana, intervened and said to him: **(66-67).** "You are the brother of Vaisravana and an adept in the rituals and practices of the Veda. You are noted for your devotion to duty and for your many virtues. How then can you even think of killing a woman? All of us together shall go to war and kill Rama and Lakshmana. After that you can make Sita your own." With such advice he turned back Ravana from his resolve to kill Sita. **68.** Now the evil-minded Ravana, accepting the righteous words of his adviser, came back to his palace with his mind stupefied by sorrow. Then he entered the assembly along with all his friends and advisers.

दशमः सर्गः

श्रीमहादेव उवाच

स विचार्य सभामध्ये राक्षसैः सह मन्त्रिभिः । निर्ययौ येऽवशिष्टास्तै राक्षसैः सह राघवम् ॥ 1
शलभः शलभैर्युक्तः प्रज्वलन्तमिवानलम् । ततो रामेण निहता सर्वे ते राक्षसा युधि ॥ 2
स्वयं रामेण निहतस्तीक्ष्णबाणेन वक्षसि । व्यथितस्त्वरितं लङ्कां प्रविवेश दशाननः ॥ 3
दृष्ट्वा रामस्य बहुशः पौरुषं चाप्यमानुषम् । रावणो मारुतेश्चैव शीघ्रं शुक्रान्तिकं ययौ ॥ 4
नमस्कृत्य दशग्रीवः शुक्रं प्राञ्जलिरब्रवीत् । भगवन् राघवेणैवं लङ्का राक्षसयूथपैः ॥ 5
विनाशिता महादैत्या निहताः पुत्रबान्धवाः । कथं मे दुःखसन्दोहस्त्वयि तिष्ठति सद्गुरौ ॥ 6
इति विज्ञापितो दैत्यगुरुः प्राह दशाननम् । होमं कुरु प्रयत्नेन रहसि त्वं दशानन ॥ 7
यदि विघ्नो न चेद्धोमे तर्हि होमानलोत्थितः । महान् रथश्च वाहाश्च चापतूणीरसायकाः ॥ 8
सम्भविष्यन्ति तैर्युक्तस्त्वमजेयो भविष्यसि ॥ 9
गृहाण मन्त्रान्मद्दत्तान् गच्छ होमं कुरु द्रुतम् ।
इत्युक्तस्त्वरितं गत्वा रावणो राक्षसाधिपः । गुहां पातालसदृशीं मन्दिरे स्वे चकार ह ॥ 10

Chapter 10

OBSTRUCTING RAVANA'S HOMA

Ravana's Fire-Sacrifice (1-10)

(1-3). Taking counsel in that assembly of Rakshasas and ministers, Ravana, with whatever forces were left, now resolved to go to attack Rama, just like a moth in the company of many other moths rushing towards fire. All those Rakshasas were killed in battle by Rama. The ten-headed Ravana was also wounded in his chest by Rama's arrows. He therefore turned back and entered Lanka quickly.

4. Having experienced the prowess of Rama and Hanuman several times, Ravana now went to his teacher Sukra immediately. **(5-6).** The ten-headed Ravana, after prostrating before Sukra said, "O holy one! Rama has destroyed Lanka along with the Rakshasa overlords and all our sons and relatives. All the powerful Asuras are already dead. How is it that such a vast calamity has befallen me when you my teacher are there?" **(7-9).** Hearing this representation of Ravana, Sukra, the teacher of Asuras, said to him, "Even exerting yourself to the utmost, do in secrecy a fire-sacrifice. If you are able to do it without obstruction, you will get out of that sacrificial fire a mighty chariot along with horses, bow and quiver. Equipped with all these, you will be invincible. **10.** Learn the necessary Mantras from me and go home and do the fire-sacrifice quickly." Following this instruction, Ravana returned

लङ्काद्वारकपाटादि बद्ध्वा सर्वत्र यत्नतः । होमद्रव्याणि सम्पाद्य यान्युक्तान्याभिचारिके ॥ 11
गुहां प्रविश्य चैकान्ते मौनी होमं प्रचक्रमे ॥ 12
उत्थितं धूममालोक्य महान्तं रावणानुजः ।
रामाय दर्शयामास होमधूमं भयाकुलः । पश्य राम दशग्रीवो होमं कर्तुं समारभत् ॥ 13
यदि होमः समाप्तः स्यात्तदाजेयो भविष्यति । अतो विघ्नाय होमस्य प्रेषयाशु हरीश्वरान् ॥ 14
तथेति रामः सुग्रीवसम्मतेनाङ्गदं कपिम् । हनूमत्प्रमुखान्वीरानादिदेश महाबलान् ॥ 15
प्राकारं लङ्घयित्वा ते गत्वा रावणमन्दिरम् । दशकोटयः प्लवङ्गानां गत्वा मन्दिररक्षकान् ॥ 16
चूर्णयामासुरश्वांश्च गजाश्च न्यहनन् क्षणात् । ततश्च सरमा नाम प्रभाते हस्तसंज्ञया ॥ 17
विभीषणस्य भार्या सा होमस्थानमसूचयत् ॥ 18
गुहापिधानपाषाणमङ्गदः पादघट्टनैः ।
चूर्णयित्वा महासत्त्वः प्रविवेशः महागुहाम् । दृष्ट्वा दशाननं तत्र मीलिताक्षं दृढासनम् ॥ 19
ततोऽङ्गदाज्ञया सर्वे वानरा विविशुर्द्रुतम् । तत्र कोलाहलं चक्रुस्ताडयन्तश्च सेवकान् ॥ 20
सम्भारांश्चिक्षिपुस्तस्य होमकुण्डे समन्ततः । स्त्रुवमाच्छिद्य हस्ताच्च रावणस्य बलाद्रुषा ॥ 21
तेनैव सञ्जघानाशु हनूमान् प्लवगाग्रणीः । घ्नन्ति दन्तैश्च काष्ठैश्च वानरास्तमितस्ततः ॥22

to his palace and made there a cave as deep as Patala.

Monkeys Obstructing the Fire-Sacrifice (11-34)

(11-12). Bolting all the gates of Lanka and collecting with great effort all the requisites for black magic, Ravana entered into the cave observing silence, and began the fire-sacrifice. **(13-14).** When the columns of smoke issuing from the sacrificial fire became visible, Vibheeshana, the brother of Ravana, was stricken with fear. Showing these columns of smoke to Rama, he said, "The ten-headed Ravana has started a fire-sacrifice. If he is able to complete it, he will become invincible. Therefore it is necessary to direct the monkey forces to obstruct the Homa." **15.** Rama agreed to do so and with the concurrence of Sugreeva, directed the great monkeys like Angada, Hanuman and other powerful heroes to accomplish this task. **(16-18).** They crossed the walls and entered the residence of Ravana. About ten crores of monkey forces went and plastered the Asura guard of the palace and all the horses and the elephants they found there. In the morning, Vibheeshana's wife, Sarama, showed by signs where the underground sacrificial chamber was located. **(19-20).** Angada the powerful, by a kick of his foot, broke open the stone door of the cave and entered into it. He saw there the ten-headed Ravana sitting in a steady posture with his eyes closed. Angada ordered all the monkeys to enter into the cave. They created an uproar, beating all the attendants there. **(21-22.)** All the materials for the Homa were scattered by them pell-mell. Hanuman forcibly

न जहौ रावणो ध्यानं हतोऽपि विजिगीषया ॥ 23

प्रविश्यान्तःपुरे वेश्मन्यङ्गदो वेगवत्तरः ।
समानयत्केशबन्धे धृत्वा मन्दोदरीं शुभाम् । रावणस्यैव पुरतो विलपन्तीमनाथवत् ॥ 24
विददाराङ्गदस्तस्याः कञ्चुकं रत्नभूषितम् । मुक्ता विमुक्ताः पतिताः समन्ताद्रत्नसञ्चयैः ॥ 25
श्रोणिसूत्रं निपतितं त्रुटितं रत्नचित्रितम् । कटिप्रदेशाद्विस्रंस्ता नीवी तस्यैव पश्यतः ॥ 26
भूषणानि च सर्वाणि पतितानि समन्ततः । देवगन्धर्वकन्याश्च नीता हृष्टैः प्लवङ्गमैः ॥ 27
मन्दोदरी रुरोदाथ रावणस्याग्रतो भृशम् । क्रोशन्ती करुणं दीना जगाद दशकन्धरम् ॥ 28
निर्लज्जोऽसि परैरेवं केशपाशे विकृष्यते ॥ 29
भार्या तवैवं पुरतः किं जुहोषि न लज्जसे । हन्यते पश्यते यस्य भार्या पापैश्च शत्रुभिः ॥ 30
मर्तव्यं तेन तत्रैव जीवितान्मरणं वरम् । हा मेघनाद ते माता क्लिश्यते बत वानरैः ॥ 31
त्वयि जीवति मे दुःखमीदृशं च कथं भवेत् । भार्या लज्जा च सन्त्यक्ता भर्त्रा मे जीविताशया ॥
श्रुत्वा तद्देवितं राजा मन्दोदर्या दशाननः । उत्तस्थौ खड्गमादाय त्यज देवीमिति ब्रुवन् ॥ 33
जघानाङ्गदमव्यग्रः कटिदेशे दशाननः । तदोत्सृज्य ययुः सर्वे विध्वंस्य हवनं महत् ॥ 34

took away from Ravana's hand the sacrificial ladle and delivered blows on him with it. The monkeys bit him with their teeth and thrashed him with sticks. **23.** But in spite of all this, Ravana did not give up his meditation because of his desire for victory. **24.** The fast-moving Angada now went into the inner apartment of Ravana's residence, and catching hold of Ravana's wife Mandodari by her locks, dragged her to the presence of Ravana, whereupon she began to weep like a masterless woman. Angada now tore away her gem-embedded overcoat. **25.** Many a precious gem and necklace was scattered all round her person. **26.** Her gem-bedecked waist-belt also fell down causing her lower garment to drop. **27.** All the ornaments she was wearing dropped down. The jubilant monkeys now brought in all the daughters of the Devas and the Gandharvas also from Ravana's inner apartments. **28.** Mandodari, weeping bitterly before Ravana, began to say to him: **29.** "In your very presence, your wife is being dragged by her locks by your enemies. You are a shameless man to tolerate it. **(30-34).** What is the good of your Homa? Have you no sense of shame? A man whose wife is molested by his enemies must court death then and there in an effort to save her. Death is better than life in such a situation. Alas! O Meghanada! Your mother is being molested by the monkeys. Alas! If you were alive, I would not have had to stand such sufferings. My husband has renounced both shame and wife in his anxiety to live". Ravana, on hearing these laments of Mandodari, got up from his seat, and taking hold of a sword, struck Angada on his waist, saying, "Hands off her." Thereupon the monkeys freed Mandodari and left the place, after having thus obstructed

रामपार्श्वमुपागम्य तस्थुः सर्वे प्रहर्षिताः । रावणस्तु ततो भार्यामुवाच परिसान्त्वयन् ॥ 35
दैवाधीनमिदं भद्रे जीवता किं न दृश्यते । त्यज शोकं विशालाक्षि ज्ञानमालम्ब्य निश्चितम् ॥
अज्ञानप्रभवः शोकः शोको ज्ञानविनाशकृत् । अज्ञानप्रभवाहन्धीः शरीरादिष्वनात्मसु ॥ 37
तन्मूलः पुत्रदारादि सम्बन्धः संसृतिस्ततः । हर्षशोकभयक्रोधलोभमोहस्पृहादयः । 38
अज्ञानप्रभवा ह्येते जन्ममृत्युजरादयः । आत्मा तु केवलं शुद्धो व्यतिरिक्तो ह्यलेपकः॥ 39
आनन्दरूपो ज्ञानात्मा सर्वभावविवर्जितः । न संयोगो वियोगो वा विद्यते केनचित्सतः॥ 40
एवं ज्ञात्वा स्वमात्मानं त्यज शोकमनिन्दिते । इदानीमेव गच्छामि हत्वा रामं सलक्ष्मणम् ॥ 41
आगमिष्यामि नोचेन्मां दारयिष्यति सायकैः । श्रीरामो वज्रकल्पैश्च ततो गच्छामि तत्पदम् ॥ 42
तदा त्वया मे कर्तव्या क्रिया मच्छासनात्प्रिये । सीतां हत्वा मया सार्धं त्वं प्रवेक्ष्यसि पावकम् ॥43
एवं श्रुत्वा वचस्तस्य रावणस्यातिदुःखिता । उवाच नाथ मे वाक्यं शृणु सत्यं तथा कुरु ॥44
शक्यो न राघवो जेतुं त्वया चान्यैः कदाचन । रामो देववरः साक्षात्प्रधानपुरुषेश्वरः ॥ 45

Ravana's great fire-sacrifice.

Ravana's Advice to Mandodari (35-43).

35. All of them now went to Rama in great joy. Ravana, for consoling his wife, now began to say as follows: **(36-43).** "O glorious lady! This world is under the decree of Providence. A man born here has to undergo all kinds of experiences. O handsome lady! Resorting to knowledge, you abandon your sorrow. Sorrow is the result of ignorance. Sorrow destroys knowledge. We associate 'I-sense' with the non-spirit i.e. the body, out of ignorance only. Attachment to sons, wives etc., arises from the above misunderstanding, out of which comes this cycle of births and deaths. Joy, sorrow, fear, anger, greed, delusion and desire, as also birth death, old age etc., are all born of ignorance. The real Self is alone, unaffected, pure, distinct from all objects and untainted. He is of the nature of bliss and consciousness, and free from every kind of change. For that pure existence, there is no coming together with, or separation from, anything. Knowing this, be free from fear, O perfect one! I shall now go immediately and return after killing Rama and Lakshmana. If it happens otherwise, I shall be killed by Rama's arrows, powerful like the thunderbolt weapon. If that happens, I shall be attaining to His Status. In that case, O my dear wife, according to my instructions, you perform my funeral rites. Kill Sita and you immolate yourself in the flames in which my body is burnt.

Conversation between Mandodari & Ravana (44-61)

44. On hearing these words of Ravana, the sorrow-stricken Mandodari said, "Hear my words which are nothing but the truth, and act accordingly. **45.** Rama cannot be

मत्स्यो भूत्वा पुरा कल्पे मनुं वैवस्वतं प्रभुः। ररक्ष सकलापद्भ्यो राघवो भक्तवत्सलः ॥ 46
रामः कूर्मोऽभवत्पूर्वं लक्षयोजनविस्तृतः। समुद्रमथने पृष्ठे दधार कनकाचलम् ॥ 47
हिरण्याक्षोऽतिदुर्वृत्तो हतोऽनेन महात्मना। क्रोडरूपेण वपुषा क्षोणीमुद्धरता क्वचित् ॥ 48
त्रिलोककण्टकं दैत्यं हिरण्यकशिपुं पुरा। हतवान्नारसिंहेन वपुषा रघुनन्दनः ॥ 49
विक्रमैस्त्रिभिरेवासौ बलिं बद्ध्वा जगत्त्रयम्। आक्रम्यादात्सुरेन्द्राय भृत्याय रघुसत्तमः ॥ 50
राक्षसाः क्षत्रियाकारा जाता भूमेर्भरावहाः। तान्हत्वा बहुशो रामो भुवं जित्वा ह्यदान्मुनेः ॥ 51
स एव साम्प्रतं जातो रघुवंशे परात्परः। भवदर्थे रघुश्रेष्ठो मानुषत्वमुपागतः ॥ 52
तस्य भार्या किमर्थं वा हृता सीता वनाद्बलात्। मम पुत्रविनाशार्थं स्वस्यापि निधनाय च ॥ 53
इतः परं वा वैदेहीं प्रेषयस्व रघूत्तमे। विभीषणाय राज्यं तु दत्त्वा गच्छामहे वनम् ॥ 54

मन्दोदरीवचः श्रुत्वा रावणो वाक्यमब्रवीत्।
कथं भद्रे रणे पुत्रान् भ्रातॄन् राक्षसमण्डलम्। घातयित्वा राघवेण जीवामि वनगोचरः ॥ 55
रामेण सह योत्स्यामि रामबाणैः सुशीघ्रगैः। विदार्यमाणो यास्यामि तद्विष्णोः परमं पदम् ॥ 56

conquered by you or by anybody else. He is none but the Supreme Lord of all Nature and all living beings. **46.** In an earlier Kalpa, the Supreme Lord Rama, the lover of devotees, took the shape of a Fish and saved Vaivasvata Manu from all dangers. **47.** At the time of the churning of the milk ocean, he assumed the form of a Tortoise, about a lakh of Yojanas in dimension and held up the golden mountain on His back. **48.** Taking the form of a Boar, He lifted the earth from the ocean after destroying Hiranyaksha noted for his evil deeds. **49.** Rama, assuming the form of a Man-lion, killed Hiranyakasipu, the son of Diti and the enemy of all the worlds. **50.** As Vamana, Rama the lord of Raghus, measured the whole universe by three strides, bound up Bali and gave the three worlds to His devotee Indra. **51.** Born as Rama with the battle axe, He destroyed numerous Rakshasas born as Kshatriyas on earth and made a gift of the earth to the sage Kasyapa. **52.** That same Supreme Being, in order to effect your destruction, is now born as man in the line of the Raghus. **53.** For the destruction of my children and for your own destruction, you have forcibly abducted his wife Sita from the forest. Why have you done this? **54.** At least now, you send away Sita to Rama's presence and bestow the kingdom to Vibheeshana. Let us afterwards take to the life of forest-dwelling asectics."

55. On hearing these words of Mandodari, Ravana replied, "O good lady! After having caused the destruction of my sons, of my brother and of the community of the Rakshasas through Rama, how can I now even think of saving my life by departing to the forest? **56.** I shall fight with Rama. Pierced by the speedy arrows of his, I

जानामि राघवं विष्णुं लक्ष्मीं जानामि जानकीम् । ज्ञात्वैव जानकी सीता मयानीता वनाद्बलात् ॥57

रामेण निधनं प्राप्य यास्यामीति परं पदम् । विमुच्य त्वां तु संसाराद्गमिष्यामि सह प्रिये ॥ 58

परानन्दमयी शुद्धा सेव्यते या मुमुक्षुभिः । तां गतिं तु गमिष्यामि हतो रामेण संयुगे ॥ 59

प्रक्षाल्य कल्मषाणीह मुक्तिं यास्यामि दुर्लभाम् ॥ 60

क्लेशादिपञ्चकतरङ्गयुतं भ्रमाढ्यं दारात्मजाप्तधनबन्धुझषाभियुक्तम् ।
और्वानलाभनिजरोषमनङ्गजालं संसारसागरमतीत्य हरिं व्रजामि ॥ 61

इति श्रीमदध्यात्मरामायणे उमामहेश्वरसंवादे
युद्धकाण्डे दशमः सर्गः ॥ १० ॥

shall attain to the Status of Vishnu. **57.** I know that Rama is Vishnu and that Sita, the daughter of Janaka, is Lakshmi. It is with the full knowlege of this that I forcibly abducted Sita from the forest. **58.** By courting death at the hands of Rama, I shall leave you in this world of Samsara and myself attain to the Supreme Status of Vishnu. O dear one! For this purpose, I brought Sita and now I am going to die with my relatives. **59.** That State, pure and blissful, which liberation-seekers attain—that very goal, I shall gain by being killed by Rama in battle. **60.** All my sins done in this world shall be washed off by death at Rama's hand and I shall gain liberation, which is a rare attainment for a Jiva. **61.** I shall cross this ocean of Samsara having for its waves the five Klesas (ignorance, I-sense with regard to the body, attachment, anger and fear); and filled with aquatic creatures constituted of wife, children, friends, wealth, relatives and the like; terrific by the submarine fire of one's own anger; and dangerous with the net of sexuality."

एकादशः सर्गः

श्रीमहादेव उवाच

इत्युक्त्वा वचनं प्रेम्णा राज्ञीं मन्दोदरीं तदा । रावणः प्रययौ योद्धुं रामेण सह संयुगे ॥ 1

दृढं स्यन्दनमास्थाय वृतो घोरैर्निशाचरैः । चक्रैः षोडशभिर्युक्तं सवरूथं सकूबरम् ॥ 2

पिशाचवदनैर्घोरैः खरैर्युक्तं भयावहम् । सर्वास्त्रशस्त्रसहितं सर्वोपस्करसंयुतम् ॥

निश्चक्रामाथ सहसा रावणो भीषणाकृतिः ॥ 3

आयान्तं रावणं दृष्ट्वा भीषणं रणकर्कशम् । सन्त्रस्ताभूत्तदा सेना वानरी रामपालिता ॥ 4

हनूमानथ चोत्प्लुत्य रावणं योद्धुमाययौ । आगत्य हनुमान् रक्षोवक्षस्यतुलविक्रमः ॥ 5

मुष्टिबन्धं दृढं बद्ध्वा ताडयामास वेगतः । तेन मुष्टिप्रहारेण जानुभ्यामपतद्रथे ॥ 6

मूर्च्छितोऽथ मुहूर्तेन रावणः पुनरुत्थितः । उवाच च हनूमन्तं शूरोऽसि मम सम्मतः ॥ 7

हनूमानाह तं धिङ्मां यस्त्वं जीवसि रावण । त्वं तावन्मुष्टिना वक्षो मम ताडय रावण ॥ 8

पश्चान्मया हतः प्राणान्मोक्ष्यसे नात्र संशयः ॥ 9

तथेति मुष्टिना वक्षो रावणेनापि ताडितः । विघूर्णमाननयनः किञ्चित्कश्मलमाययौ ॥ 10

Chapter 11

DESTRUCTION OF RAVANA

Ravana in the Battlefield (1-11)

1. After speaking lovingly as above to his queen Mandodari, Ravana hurried to join battle with Rama. **(2-3).** Surrounded by fierce Rakshasas, Ravana of terrific appearance quickly started, seated in his massive chariot. The chariot with sixteen wheels was drawn by donkeys with their faces resembling devils. It was heavily armour-plated and had a strong central pole for yoking the horses. It was equipped with all kinds of weapons and missiles and every kind of equipment needed for battle. **4.** Seeing the fierce and relentless warrior Ravana approaching, the monkey forces under Rama were stricken with fear. **(5-6).** Hanuman of matchless prowess now sprang up to give battle to Ravana. He clenched his fist firmly and delivered a punch on Ravana's chest. Stricken that way, Ravana fell down on his knees in a swoon. **7.** Within a few minutes he recovered and said to Hanuman that he was a hero deserving recognition. **(8-9).** Hanuman replied, "O Ravana! It is a matter of shame for me that you are still alive after receiving my blow. Now you strike me and after that I shall give you a blow which will deprive you of your life." **(10-11).** Agreeing to this, Ravana struck Hanuman on his chest with his fist. Hanuman became dizzy, and

संज्ञामवाप्य कपिराड् रावणं हन्तुमुद्यतः । ततोऽन्यत्र गतो भीत्या रावणो राक्षसाधिपः ॥ 11

हनूमानङ्गदश्चैव नलो नीलस्तथैव च । चत्वारः समवेत्याग्रे दृष्ट्वा राक्षसपुङ्गवान् ॥ 12

अग्निवर्णं तथा सर्परोमाणं खड्गरोमकम् । तथा वृश्चिकरोमाणं निर्जघ्नुः क्रमशोऽसुरान् ॥ 13

चत्वारश्चतुरो हत्वा राक्षसान् भीमविक्रमान् ।

सिंहनादं पृथक् कृत्वा रामपार्श्वमुपागताः । ततः क्रुद्धो दशग्रीवः सन्दश्य दशनच्छदम् ॥14

विवृत्य नयने क्रूरो राममेवान्वधावत । दशग्रीवो रथस्थस्तु राम वज्रोपमैः शरैः ॥ 15

आजघान महाघोरैर्धाराभिरिव तोयदः । रामस्य पुरतः सर्वान्वानरानपि विव्यथे ॥ 16

ततः पावकसङ्काशैः शरैः काञ्चनभूषणैः । अभ्यवर्षद्रणे रामो दशग्रीवं समाहितः ॥ 17

रथस्थं रावणं दृष्ट्वा भूमिष्ठं रघुनन्दनम् । आहूय मातलिं शक्रो वचनं चेदमब्रवीत् ॥ 18

रथेन मम भूमिष्ठं शीघ्रं याहि रघूत्तमम् । त्वरितं भूतलं गत्वा कुरु कार्यं ममानघ ॥ 19

एवमुक्तोऽथ तं नत्वा मातलिर्देवसारथिः । ततो हयैश्च संयोज्य हरितैः स्यन्दनोत्तमम् ॥ 20

स्वर्गाज्जयार्थं रामस्य ह्युपचक्राम मातलिः । प्राञ्जलिर्देवराजेन प्रेषितोऽस्मि रघूत्तम ॥ 21

was for a short while unconscious. After recovery, he was about to kill Ravana with his fist, but frightened by the prospect of Hanuman's blow, Ravana escaped to another part of the battlefield.

Attack on Rama (12-25)

(12-16). In battle, Hanuman, Angada, Nala and Neela destroyed the Rakshasas named Agnivarna the fire-coloured one, Sarparoma the serpent-haired one, Khadgaroma the sword-haired one, and Vrischikaroma the scorpion haired one. The four on destroying these four Asuras in battle, individually raised lion-roars as a sign of victory and went to meet Rama. Terribly incensed by the death of his followers, the cruel-hearted Ravana, biting his lips and rolling his eye balls, rushed at Rama himself to join battle with him. Seated in his chariot, the ten-headed Ravana showered very sharp arrows on Rama as a cloud showers rain. He wounded also all the monkeys standing in front of Rama. **17.** Rama with his mind concentrated, now sent volleys of fiery and gold-embellished arrows at Ravana.

18. Seeing that Ravana was seated in his chariot and Rama standing on the ground, Indra the king of the Devas called his charioteer Matali and said: **19.** "O virtuous one! Take my chariot to Rama, the chief of the Raghus, who is fighting, standing on the ground; go quickly to the earth and accomplish this task." **20.** On being so instructed, Matali the charioteer of Indra, saluted him and harnessed the green-coloured horses to the chariot. **21.** To bring about the victory of Rama, Matali arrived on the earth with incredible speed.

रथोऽयं देवराजस्य विजयाय तव प्रभो। प्रेषितश्च महाराज धनुरैन्द्रं च भूषितम् ॥ 22
अभेद्यं कवचं खड्गं दिव्यतूणीयुगं तथा। आरुह्य च रथं राम रावणं जहि राक्षसम् ॥ 23
मया सारथिना देव वृत्रं देवपतिर्यथा। इत्युक्तस्तं परिक्रम्य नमस्कृत्य रथोत्तमम् ॥ 24
आरुरोह रथं रामो लोकाँल्लक्ष्म्या नियोजयन् ॥ 25
ततोऽभवन्महायुद्धं भैरवं रोमहर्षणम्।
महात्मनो राघवस्य रावणस्य च धीमतः। आग्नेयेन च आग्नेयं दैवं दैवेन राघवः ॥ 26
अस्त्रं राक्षसराजस्य जघान परमास्त्रवित्। ततस्तु ससृजे घोरं राक्षसं चास्त्रमस्त्रवित् ॥ 27
क्रोधेन महताविष्टो रामस्योपरि रावणः ॥ 28
रावणस्य धनुर्मुक्ताः सर्पा भूत्वा महाविषाः। शराः काञ्चनपुङ्खाभा राघवं परितोऽपतन् ॥ 29
तैः शरैः सर्पवदनैर्वमद्भिरनलं मुखैः। दिशश्च विदिशश्चैव व्याप्तास्तत्र तदाभवन् ॥30
रामः सर्पांस्ततो दृष्ट्वा समन्तात्परिपूरितान्। सौपर्णमस्त्रं तद् घोरं पुरः प्रावर्तयद्रणे ॥ 31
रामेण मुक्तास्ते बाणा भूत्वा गरुडरूपिणः। चिच्छिदुः सर्पबाणांस्तान्समन्तात्सर्पशत्रवः ॥ 32
अस्त्रे प्रतिहते युद्धे रामेण दशकन्धरः। अभ्यवर्षत्ततो रामं घोराभिः शरवृष्टिभिः ॥ 33
ततः पुनः शरानीकै राममक्लिष्टकारिणम्। अर्दयित्वा तु घोरेण मातलिं प्रत्यविध्यत ॥ 34

With palms folded in salutation, he said to Rama, "O chief of the Raghus! I have been sent here by Indra the king of the gods. **(22-25).** The chariot belongs to Lord Indra, the king of the gods. It has been sent to help you to gain victory. It is equipped with the well-decorated bow of Indra, unbreakable armours, swords and a pair of celestial quivers. O Rama! Ascend this chariot, and accompanied by me, destroy Ravana as Indra did Vritra." On being so requested, Rama, after circumambulating that divine chariot, ascended it in order to bring about welfare and prosperity in the world.

Fight Between Rama & Ravana (26-50)

(26-28). Afterwards there took place a hair-raising and terrible battle between Rama and the powerful Ravana. The great archer that he was, Rama neutralised the fire-missile of Ravana with fire-missile, and celestial missile with celestial missile. Terribly excited, Ravana now directed the fierce Rakshasa-missile against Rama. **29.** The shining missiles released from Ravana's bow took the form of numerous poisonous serpents which surrounded Rama. **30.** All the quarters were filled with arrows having the face of serpents and vomiting fire. **31.** Seeing serpents everywhere, Rama now released the terrible Sauparna missile. **32.** The missiles released by Rama took the shape of Garuda and destroyed the serpents on all sides. **33.** When Rama thus counteracted his missiles, the ten-headed Ravana once more began to shower arrows on Rama. **(34-35).** Wounding Rama with numerous arrows, Ravana now wounded

पातयित्वा रथोपस्थे रथकेतुं च काञ्चनम् । ऐन्द्रानश्वानभ्यहनद्रावणः क्रोधमूर्च्छितः ॥ 35

विषेदुर्देवगन्धर्वांश्चारणाः पितरस्तथा । आर्त्ताकारं हरिं दृष्ट्वा व्यथिताश्च महर्षयः ।
व्यथिता वानरेन्द्राश्च बभूवुः सविभीषणाः ॥ 36

दशास्यो विंशतिभुजः प्रगृहीतशरासनः । ददृशे रावणस्तत्र मैनाक इव पर्वतः ॥ 37

रामस्तु भ्रुकुटिं बद्ध्वा क्रोधसंरक्तलोचनः । कोपं चकार सदृशं निदहन्निव राक्षसम् ॥ 38

धनुरादाय देवेन्द्रधनुराकारमद्भुतम् । गृहीत्वा पाणिना बाणं कालानलसमप्रभम् ॥ 39
निर्दहन्निव चक्षुर्भ्यां ददृशे रिपुमन्तिके । 40

पराक्रमं दर्शयितुं तेजसा प्रज्वलन्निव । प्रचक्रमे कालरूपी सर्वलोकस्य पश्यतः ॥ 41

विकृष्य चापं रामस्तु रावणं प्रतिविध्य च । हर्षयन्वानरानीकं कालान्तक इवाबभौ ॥ 42

क्रुद्धं रामस्य वदनं दृष्ट्वा शत्रुं प्रधावतः । तत्रसुः सर्वभूतानि चचाल च वसुन्धरा ॥ 43

रामं दृष्ट्वा महारौद्रमुत्पातांश्च सुदारुणान् । त्रस्तानि सर्वभूतानि रावणं चाविशद्भयम् ॥ 44

विमानस्थाः सुरगणाः सिद्धगन्धर्वकिन्नराः । ददृशुः सुमहायुद्धं लोकसंवर्तकोपमम् ॥ 45

ऐन्द्रमस्त्रं समादाय रावणस्य शिरोऽच्छिनत् । मूर्धानो रावणस्याथ बहवो रुधिरोक्षिताः ।
गगनात्प्रपतन्ति स्म तालादिव फलानि हि ॥ 46

Matali the charioteer, cut down the golden standard, and inflicted wounds on the horses drawing the chariot of Indra. **36.** Seeing Rama in a difficult situation, the Devas, Gandharvas, Charanas, manes and Maharshis grew anxious. So also did Vibheeshana and the monkey leaders.

37. The ten-headed Ravana holding bows and arrows in his twenty arms appeared like the mount Mainaka. **38.** Highly incensed Rama's eyes now became red and his eyebrows got knitted. He now looked at Ravana as if he were going to burn him up in a mood of anger that was appropriate for the occasion. **(39-40).** Holding the wonderful bow resembling the bow of Indra himself, he released fiery arrows at the enemy from close quarters and looked at him as if he were going to burn him by his looks. **41.** Rama, now realising that the time for the destruction of Ravana was approaching, revealed his prowess to all through his shining brilliance. **42.** Drawing his bow and aiming at Ravana, Rama appeared like death at the time of the world's dissolution—a sight which gave great joy to the monkey army. **43.** Seeing the angry face of Rama as he approached the enemy, all beings trembled in fear, and there were tremors on the earth. **44.** Rama's terrific form and the evil-foreboding omens filled all beings with fear. Even Ravana got frightened. **45.** In order to see the battle that resembled in its ferocity the world's dissolution, all the Devas, Siddhas and Gandharvas assembled in the sky in their aerial vehicles.

46. Now Rama took up the Indra-missile and cut off Ravana's heads one by one.

न दिनं न च वै रात्रिर्न सन्ध्या न दिशोऽपि वा ।
प्रकाशन्ते न तद्रूपं दृश्यते तत्र सङ्गरे । ततो रामो बभूवाथ विस्मयाविष्टमानसः ॥ 47
शतमेकोत्तरं छिन्नं शिरसां चैकवर्चसाम् । न चैव रावणः शान्तो दृश्यते जीवितक्षयात् ॥ 48
ततः सर्वास्त्रविद्वीरः कौशल्यानन्दवर्धनः । अस्त्रैश्च बहुभिर्युक्तश्चिन्तयामास राघवः ॥ 49
यैर्यैर्बाणैर्हता दैत्या महासत्त्वपराक्रमाः । त एते निष्फलं याता रावणस्य निपातने ॥ 50
इति चिन्ताकुले रामे समीपस्थो विभीषणः । उवाच राघवं वाक्यं ब्रह्मदत्तवरो ह्यसौ । 51
विच्छिन्ना बाहवोऽप्यस्य विच्छिन्नानि शिरांसि च । उत्पत्स्यन्ति पुनः शीघ्रमित्याह भगवानजः ॥ 52
नाभिदेशेऽमृतं तस्य कुण्डलाकारसंस्थितम् । तच्छोषयानलास्त्रेण तस्य मृत्युस्ततो भवेत् ॥ 53
विभीषणवचः श्रुत्वा रामः शीघ्रपराक्रमः । पावकास्त्रेण संयोज्य नाभिं विव्याध रक्षसः ॥54
अनन्तरं च चिच्छेद शिरांसि च महाबलः । बाहूनपि च संरब्धो रावणस्य रघूत्तमः ॥ 55
ततो घोरां महाशक्तिमादाय दशकन्धरः । विभीषणवधार्थाय चिक्षेप क्रोधविह्वलः ॥ 56
चिच्छेद राघवो बाणैस्तां शितैर्हेमभूषितैः । दशग्रीवशिरश्छेदात्तदा तेजो विनिर्गतम् ॥ 57
म्लानरूपो बभूवाथ छिन्नैः शीर्षैर्भयङ्करैः । एकेन मुख्यशिरसा बाहुभ्यां रावणो बभौ ॥ 58

Bleeding profusely, these heads fell down on the ground like palmyra fruits from the tree. **47.** In the chaos created by battle, neither day time nor night, neither their junction time nor the quarters could be perceived distinctly. Even the persons of Rama and Ravana engaged in battle could not be recognised. Now Rama began to think in wonder. **48.** "I have cut down hundred and one heads of Ravana; still I do not find Ravana dying." **49.** Then Rama, who was master of all missiles, began to think within himself in spite of the fact that he had all these missiles under his control. **50.** "Those missiles with which Rakshasas of great prowess have been killed in large numbers are now found ineffective in respect of Ravana."

Death of Ravana (51-76)

(51-52). When Rama was thus thinking anxiously, Vibheeshana who was standing near by said, "It is well-known that he has been granted boons by Brahma. His heads and hands if severed would come up again immediately. Such was the boon given to him by Brahma. **(53-54).** In his umbilicus, there is a certain mass of Amrita deposited. Burn it up with Agni missile. After that it will be possible to kill him." Hearing these words of Vibheeshana, Rama of great prowess attached the fire-missile to his bow and wounded Ravana in his umbilicus. **55.** After that, mighty Rama full of wrath began to cut-off Ravana's heads and arms. **56.** Now Ravana with a view to kill Vibheeshana, threw his mighty weapon called Shakti at him. **(57-58).** With his shining arrows, Rama cut that Shakti to pieces. As several of his heads had been cut, Ravana's prowess was in abeyance, and seeing his fallen heads, he became very

रावणस्तु पुनः क्रुद्धो नानाशस्त्रास्त्रवृष्टिभिः। ववर्ष रामं तं रामस्तथा बाणैर्ववर्ष च ॥ 59

ततो युद्धमभूद्घोरं तुमुलं लोमहर्षणम्। अथ संस्मारयामास मातली राघवं तदा ॥ 60

विसृज्यास्त्रं वधायास्य ब्राह्मं शीघ्रं रघूत्तम। विनाशकालः प्रथितो यः सुरैः सोऽद्य वर्तते ॥ 61

उत्तमाङ्गं न चैतस्य छेत्तव्यं राघव त्वया। नैव शीर्ष्णि प्रभो वध्यो वध्य एव हि मर्मणि ॥62

ततः संस्मारितो रामस्तेन वाक्येन मातलेः। जग्राह सशरं दीप्तं निःश्वसन्तमिवोरगम् ॥ 63

यस्य पार्श्वे तु पवनः फले भास्करपावकौ। शरीरमाकाशमयं गौरवे मेरुमन्दरौ ॥ 64

पर्वस्वपि च विन्यस्ता लोकपाला महौजसः। जाज्वल्यमानं वपुषां भातं भास्करवर्चसा ॥ 65

तमुग्रमस्त्रं लोकानां भयनाशनमद्भुतम्। अभिमन्त्र्य ततो रामस्तं महेषुं महाभुजः ॥ 66

वेदप्रोक्तेन विधिना सन्दधे कार्मुके बली ॥ 67

तस्मिन्सन्धीयमाने तु राघवेण शरोत्तमे। सर्वभूतानि वित्रेसुश्चचाल च वसुन्धरा ॥ 68

स रावणाय संक्रुद्धो भृशमानम्य कार्मुकम्। चिक्षेप परमायत्तस्तमस्त्रं मर्मघातिनम् ॥ 69

स वज्र इव दुर्धर्षो वज्रपाणिविसर्जितः। कृतान्त इव घोरास्यो न्यपतद्रावणोरसि ॥ 70

स निमग्नो महाघोरः शरीरान्तकरः परः। बिभेद हृदयं तूर्णं रावणस्य महात्मनः ॥ 71

much dejected. He was left with only one head and two arms. **59.** Next, incensed very much, Ravana sent showers of arrows and other weapons at Rama and Rama did the same in respect of him. **(60-61).** The fierce battle causing horripilations in onlookers continued for long. Then Matali the charioteer reminded Rama saying, "O Rama! Scion of the Raghu's line! Release Brahma missile for his death without delay. The pre-determined time for his death has now arrived.**62.** O Rama! Do not cut-off his head. He cannot be killed by severing his head. He has to be struck at vulnerable points in his body." **63.** Reminded thus by the words of Matali, Rama took an arrow that hissed like a serpent in its course. **(64-67).** That Brahma-missile had Vayu at its rear, Surya and Pavaka in its front, Akasa in its middle and Lokapalas on its sides. It was as weighty as the mountainsMeru and Mandara. Resplendent in itself, it shone like a sun now. Now Rama of very great prowess repeated the Mantras connected with this wonderful missile and attached it to his bow according to the directions given in the science of archery. **68.** When Rama attached that missile to his bow, all beings trembled and there was tremor on the earth. **69.** In a very wrathful mood, Rama pulled his bow to its maximum with all his power and sent that arrow at the vital part of Ravana. **70.** Like thunderbolt weapon released by Indra, that irresistible missile with a terrific end struck Ravana in his chest like the god of death himself. **71.** That missile

रावणस्याहरत्प्राणान्विवेश धरणीतले । स शरो रावणं हत्वा रामतूणीरमाविशत् ॥ 72

तस्य हस्तात्पपाताशु सशरं कार्मुकं महत् । गतासुर्भ्रमिवेगेन राक्षसेन्द्रोऽपतद्भुवि ॥ 73

तं दृष्ट्वा पतितं भूमौ हतशेषाश्च राक्षसाः । हतनाथा भयत्रस्ता दुद्रुवुः सर्वतोदिशम् ॥ 74

दशग्रीवस्य निधनं विजयं राघवस्य च । ततो विनेदुः संहृष्टा वानरा जितकाशिनः ॥ 75

वदन्तो रामविजयं रावणस्य च तद्वधम् ॥ 76

अथान्तरिक्षे व्यनदत्सौम्यस्त्रिदशदुन्दुभिः । पपात पुष्पवृष्टिश्च समन्ताद्राघवोपरि ॥ 77

तुष्टुवुर्मुनयः सिद्धाश्चारणाश्च दिवौकसः । अथान्तरिक्षे ननृतुः सर्वतोऽप्सरसो मुदा ॥ 78

रावणस्य च देहोत्थं ज्योतिरादित्यवत्स्फुरत् । प्रविवेश रघुश्रेष्ठं देवानां पश्यतां सताम् ॥ 79

देवा ऊचुरहो भाग्यं रावणस्य महात्मनः । वयं तु सात्त्विका देवा विष्णोः कारुण्यभाजनाः ॥ 80

भयदुःखादिभिर्व्याप्ताः संसारे परिवर्तिनः । अयं तु राक्षसः क्रूरो ब्रह्महातीव तामसः ॥ 81

परदाररतो विष्णुद्वेषी तापसहिंसकः । पश्यत्सु सर्वभूतेषु राममेव प्रविष्टवान् ॥ 82

capable of piercing any target went deep into the chest of Ravana and pierced his heart. **72.** After destroying the life-energies of Ravana, it spent its force only on piercing the earth. After that it came back to the quiver of Rama.

73. From the hands of Ravana his mighty bow along with its arrow fell down. Lifeless, he fell to the ground like an object caught in a whirlwind. **74.** On seeing him dead, all the surviving Rakshasas felt masterless, became panicky with fear and fled in all directions. **(75-76).** Now that the enemy had been conquered, the monkeys were filled with joy and began to talk loudly among themselves about Ravana's death and Rama's victory.

Ravana's salvation through confrontation (77-89)

(77-78). The sky was now filled with the delightful sound of the kettle-drums of the Devas from all sides; showers of flowers fell on Rama. The Munis, the Siddhas, the Charanas and the other inhabitants of the heavenly regions sang hymns of praise, and everywhere in the sky the Apsara damsels began to dance. **79.** All the Devas witnessed how from the body of Ravana, a brilliance equal to that of the sun emerged and entered into Rama. **(80-82).** The Devas said, "Look at the good fortune of the high-souled Ravana. Even we, virtuous persons like Devas, who are special objects of Mahavishnu's mercy, are immersed in Samsara characterised by fear and sorrow. But see how this Rakshasa who is noted for his cruelty, who abducts other people's women, who kills ascetics, who is antagonistic to Vishnu, who is characterised by intense Tamas—how even he has entered into Rama in the sight of all."

एवं ब्रुवत्सु देवेषु नारदः प्राह सुस्मितः । शृणुतात्र सुरा यूयं धर्मतत्त्वविचक्षणाः ॥ 83
रावणो राघवद्वेषादनिशं हृदि भावयन् । भृत्यैः सह सदा रामचरितं द्वेषसंयुतः ॥ 84
श्रुत्वा रामात्स्वनिधनं भयात्सर्वत्र राघवम् । पश्यन्ननुदिनं स्वप्ने राममेवानुपश्यति ॥ 85
क्रोधोऽपि रावणस्याशु गुरुबोधाधिकोऽभवत् । रामेण निहतश्चान्ते निर्धूताशेषकल्मषः ॥ 86
रामसायुज्यमेवाप रावणो मुक्तबन्धनः ॥ 87

पापिष्ठो वा दुरात्मा परधनपरदारेषु सक्तो यदि स्या-
न्नित्यं स्नेहाद्भयाद्वा रघुकुलतिलकं भावयन्सम्परेतः ।
भूत्वा शुद्धान्तरङ्गो भवशतजनितानेकदोषैर्विमुक्तः
सद्यो रामस्य विष्णोः सुरवरविनुतं याति वैकुण्ठमाद्यम् ॥ 88

हत्वा युद्धे दशास्यं त्रिभुवनविषमं वामहस्तेन चापं
भूमौ विष्टभ्य तिष्ठन्नितरकरधृतं भ्रामयन्बाणमेकम् ।
आरक्तोपान्तनेत्रः शरदलितवपुः सूर्यकोटिप्रकाशो
वीरश्रीबन्धुराङ्गस्त्रिदशपतिनुतः पातु मां वीररामः ॥ 89

इति श्रीमदध्यात्मरामायणे उमामहेश्वरसंवादे
युद्धकाण्डे एकादशः सर्गः ॥ ११ ॥

(83-87). To the Devas who were speaking in this way, Narada said with a smile, "O Devas who know the secret of Dharma! Listen. Ravana, on account of his antagonism to Rama, has always been talking about him with his servants, besides ever anxiously thinking about him. Fearing that he would meet with death at Rama's hand, he was in the habit of seeing the spectre of Rama everywhere. Every night, in his dreams, he was seeing Rama. This anger of Ravana towards Rama has served him in a better way than teachers and relatives. In the end, being killed by Rama, he has been rid of all his sins. Released from all bondage thereby, he has become one with Rama. **88.** Even if a person is sinful, evil-minded, addicted to other people's wealth and women, if he, be it out of love or fear, thinks of Rama, he becomes purified in mind and freed from the sins of numerous births. He thereby attains directly the eternal Vaikuntha, the highly coveted Status of Vishnu who has incarnated Himself as Rama. **89.** May heroic Rama protect me-- Rama who killed in battle Ravana incapable of being conquered by anyone in the three worlds, who with his left hand holds his bow resting firmly on the ground, who is whirling an arrow with his other hand, the ends of whose eyes are red-tinged, whose body is covered with wounds caused by arrows, who has the brilliance of numerous suns, whose form is beautified by the glory of victory, and who is the object of praise of all divinities."

द्वादशः सर्गः

श्रीमहादेव उवाच

रामो विभीषणं दृष्ट्वा हनूमन्तं तथाङ्गदम् । लक्ष्मणं कपिराजं च जाम्बवन्तं तथा परान् ॥ 1
परितुष्टेन मनसा सर्वानेवाब्रवीद्वचः । भवतां बाहुवीर्येण निहतो रावणो मया ॥ 2
कीर्तिः स्थास्यति वः पुण्या यावच्चन्द्रदिवाकरौ । कीर्तयिष्यन्ति भवतां कथां त्रैलोक्यपावनीम् ॥ 3
मयोपेतां कलिहरां यास्यन्ति परमां गतिम् ॥ 4
एतस्मिन्नन्तरे दृष्ट्वा रावणं पतितं भुवि ।
मन्दोदरीमुखाः सर्वाः स्त्रियो रावणपालिताः । पतिता रावणस्याग्रे शोचन्त्यः पर्यदेवयन् ॥ 5
विभीषणः शुशोचार्तः शोकेन महतावृतः । पतितो रावणस्याग्रे बहुधा पर्यदेवयत् ॥ 6
रामस्तु लक्ष्मणं प्राह बोधयस्व विभीषणम् । करोतु भ्रातृसंस्कारं किं विलम्बेन मानद ॥ 7
स्त्रियो मन्दोदरीमुख्याः पतिता विलपन्ति च । निवारयतु ताः सर्वा राक्षसी रावणप्रियाः ॥ 8
एवमुक्तोऽथ रामेण लक्ष्मणोऽगाद्विभीषणम् । उवाच मृतकोपान्ते पतितं मृतकोपमम् ॥ 9
शोकेन महताविष्टं सौमित्रिरिदमब्रवीत् । यं शोचसि त्वं दुःखेन कोऽयं तव विभीषण ॥ 10
त्वं वास्य कतमः सृष्टेः पुरेदानीमतः परम् । यद्वत्तोयौघपतिताः सिकता यान्ति तद्वशाः ॥ 11

Chapter 12

EVENTS AFTER RAVANA'S DEATH

Lakshmana's Sermon to Vibheeshana (1-28)

(1-2). Now Rama cast his joyous glance at Vibheeshana, Hanuman, Angada, Lakshmana, Sugreeva, Jambavan and others and said, "By the heroism you all have displayed, I have been able to kill Ravana. **(3-4).** Your holy fame will last so long as the sun and moon abide. By reciting these exploits of yours in relation to me, which can remove the sins of people and purify the world, men will attain the supreme goal."

5. In the meantime, seeing the fallen body of Ravana, Mandodari and other women who were under Ravana's protection, fell down before Ravana's body and began to bemoan his death. **6.** Vibheeshana, too, overcome with great sorrow,fell by Ravana's side and indulged in mourning in various ways. **7.** Thereupon Rama said to Lakshmana, "You enlighten Vibheeshana about his duties. Let him do the cremation of his brother. Why should it be delayed? **8.** Mandodari and other wives of Ravana are all mourning. Let Vibheeshana come forward and pacify them."

9. On being so instructed by Rama, Lakshmana went to the dead body of Ravana, by the side of which Vibheeshana was lying like another dead body. **(10-12).** Lakshmana said as follows to sorrow-stricken Vibheeshana, "O Vibheeshana! What is he to you—he for whom you are mourning? What was he before his body

संयुज्यन्ते वियुज्यन्ते तथा कालेन देहिनः ॥ 12

यथा धानासु वै धाना भवन्ति न भवन्ति च । एवं भूतेषु भूतानि प्रेरितानीशमायया ॥ 13

त्वं चेमे वयमन्ये च तुल्याः कालवशोद्भवाः ।

जन्ममृत्यू यदा यस्मात्तदा तस्माद्भविष्यतः । ईश्वरः सर्वभूतानि भूतैः सृजति हन्त्यजः ॥ 14

आत्मसृष्टैरस्वतन्त्रैर्निरपेक्षोऽपि बालवत् । देहेन देहिनो जीवा देहाद्देहोऽभिजायते ॥ 15

बीजादेव यथा बीजं देहान्य इव शाश्वतः । देहिदेहविभागोऽयमविवेककृतः पुरा ॥ 16

नानात्वं जन्म नाशश्च क्षयो वृद्धिः क्रियाफलम् । द्रष्टुराभान्त्यतद्धर्मा यथाग्नेर्दारुविक्रियाः ॥ 17

त इमे देहसंयोगादात्मना भान्त्यसद्ग्रहात् । प्रभा यथा तथा चान्यद्ध्यायतोऽसत्सदाग्रहात् ॥18

प्रसुप्तस्यानहम्भावात्तदा भाति न संसृतिः । जीवतोऽपि यथा तद्वद्विमुक्तस्यानहङ्कृतेः ॥ 19

was generated? What relation has he now after death and hereafter? Who after all are you to him? Just as in a flowing river, particles of sand and water come together for a time and are separated by the current, so are men joined and separated in this world by the flow of time. **13.** Among seeds sown, some sprout and produce other seeds, while some perish without sprouting. Their relationship is casual and uncertain. Just so are all relationships brought about by the force of the Lord's Maya between beings born of other beings. (Or, just as in a quantity of grains, some, on being fried, mix with others and then disunite, in the same way do creatures unite and disunite, impelled by the Maya of the Lord). **14.** You, he and all others are alike the creatures of Time. One's birth and death will occur as pre-determined in respect of time and place. **15.** The Lord of all, who is unborn and unmotivated, engages Himself in creation like a child. He plays with the help of these beings, who are not free but are under His control. He makes them the cause of generation and destruction among themselves. **16.** A body is always born of another body ensouled by a Jiva, just as a seed can come out of another similar seed. But the Jiva is eternal while the body is short-lived. This relationship between the body and the Jiva is not real but born of delusion and ignorance. **(17-18).** The various differentiating forms of birth, growth, death and enjoyment of fruits of Karma attributed to the the Seer (Self), are like the attribution to fire of the shape it assumes wholly due to the fuel that it burns. In contact with the fuel the fire takes various forms and shapes according to the form and shape of the fuel. But the fire in itself has no such forms. It only burns and shines. So also none of the attributes and experiences of the body really belong to the Self who is only the Witness. They appear to be that of the Self because of the connection of the Seer with the body arising out of ignorance. **(19-20).** A caravansarai is really an empty

तस्मान्मायामनोधर्मं जह्यहम्ममताभ्रमम् ।
रामभद्रे भगवति मनो देह्यात्मनीश्वरे । सर्वभूतात्मनि परे मायामानुषरूपिणि ॥ 20
बाह्येन्द्रियार्थसम्बन्धात्याजयित्वा मनः शनैः । तत्र दोषान्दर्शयित्वा रामानन्दे नियोजय ॥ 21
देहबुद्ध्या भवेद्भ्राता पिता माता सुहृत्प्रियः । विलक्षणं यदा देहाज्जानात्यात्मानमात्मना ॥ 22
तदा कः कस्य वा बन्धुर्भ्राता माता पिता सुहृत् । मिथ्याज्ञानवशाज्जाता दारागारादयः सदा ॥ 23
शब्दादयश्च विषया विविधाश्चैव सम्पदः । बलं कोशो भृत्यवर्गो राज्यं भूमिः सुतादयः ॥ 24
अज्ञानजत्वात्सर्वे ते क्षणसङ्गमभङ्गुराः । अथोत्तिष्ठ हृदा रामं भावयन् भक्तिभावितम् ॥
अनुवर्तस्व राज्यादि भुञ्जन्प्रारब्धमन्वहम् । भूतं भविष्यदभजन्वर्तमानमथाचरन् ॥ 26
विहरस्व यथान्यायं भवदोषैर्न लिप्यते । आज्ञापयति रामस्त्वां यद्भ्रातुः साम्परायिकम् ॥
तत्कुरुष्व यथाशास्त्रं रुदतीश्चापि योषितः । निवारय महाबुद्धे लङ्कां गच्छन्तु मा चिरम् ॥ 28

place, but it seems to be full when many people gather there temporarily. In the same way when unreal entities are firmly held as real, multiplicity seems to rule everywhere. Even when a man is alive, there is no experience of Samsara for him in deep sleep, as there is no sense of 'I' there. In the same way for the liberated one who is without the sense of 'I', the objects of worldly life do not shine. Therefore, know all this to be mental creation born of Maya and hence abandon the false sense of 'I and mine'. Fix your mind on Rama, who is none but the Lord who has taken a human form. He is the Supreme Being, the highest Self who, though transcendent, has assumed the form as the All. **21.** Releasing the mind little by little from its entanglement with external objects by recognising that such contacts are harmful, connect it with the bliss that is Rama. **(22-23).** It is due to the sense of identification with the body that ideas of relationships like that of brother, father, mother, friend, dear one etc. arise. With the power of discrimination, when one is able to differentiate the Self from the body, then who is one's relative, who is one's mother, father and friend? It is as a result of false knowledge that there are ideas like wife, home and other possessions. **(24-28).** Objects of sense life, various kinds of wealth, army, treasury, attendants, kingdom, landed property and sons and relatives are all born of ignorance. Therefore, they are all of momentary duration and are subject to destruction. Always contemplating in one's heart in a spirit of devotion and undergoing the predetermined enjoyments and sufferings born of one's own action (Prarabdha), perform your duties like govering the country. Now abandon your mood of sorrow and get up. Without thinking of the past and the future, concern yourself with the present only, and behave as it is proper. Thereby, you will not be affected by the evils of Samsara. Rama is ordering you to perform the funeral obsequies of your brother. O intelligent one! Perform all those rites according to scriptural dictates. Console

श्रुत्वा यथावद्वचनं लक्ष्मणस्य विभीषणः । त्यक्त्वा शोकं च मोहं च रामपार्श्वमुपागमत् ॥ 29
विमृश्य बुद्ध्या धर्मज्ञो धर्मार्थसहितं वचः । रामस्यैवानुवृत्त्यर्थमुत्तरं पर्यभाषत ॥ 30
नृशंसमनृतं क्रूरं त्यक्तधर्मव्रतं प्रभो । नार्होऽस्मि देव संस्कर्तुं परदाराभिमर्शिनम् ॥ 31
श्रुत्वा तद्वचनं प्रीतो रामो वचनमब्रवीत् । मरणान्तानि वैराणि निवृत्तं नः प्रयोजनम् ॥ 32
क्रियतामस्य संस्कारो ममाप्येष यथा तव । रामाज्ञां शिरसा धृत्वा शीघ्रमेव विभीषणः ॥ 33
सान्त्ववाक्यैर्महाबुद्धिं राज्ञीं मन्दोदरीं तदा । सान्त्वयामास धर्मात्मा धर्मबुद्धिर्विभीषणः ॥ 34
त्वरयामास धर्मज्ञः संस्कारार्थं स्वबान्धवान् । चित्यां निवेश्य विधिवत्पितृमेधविधानतः ॥ 35
आहिताग्नेर्यथा कार्यं रावणस्य विभीषणः । तथैव सर्वमकरोद्बन्धुभिः सह मन्त्रिभिः ॥ 36
ददौ च पावकं तस्य विधियुक्तं विभीषणः । स्नात्वा चैवार्द्रवस्त्रेण तिलान्दर्भाभिमिश्रितान् ॥
उदकेन च सम्मिश्रान्प्रदाय विधिपूर्वकम् । प्रदाय चोदकं तस्मै मूर्ध्ना चैनं प्रणम्य च ॥ 38
ताः स्त्रियोऽनुनयामास सान्त्वमुक्त्वा पुनः पुनः । गम्यतामिति ताः सर्वा विविशुर्नगरं तदा ॥ 39

all the weeping womenfolk. Do not delay any further to go to Lanka."

Cremation of Ravana (29-39)

29. Hearing this inspiring advice of Lakshmana, Vibheeshana abandoned sorrow and delusion and went to meet Rama. **30.** The righteous Vibheeshana, having pondered over the words of Lakshmana on right conduct, decided to obey Rama's instructions and said in reply. **31.** "O Lord! I am unfit to cremate one who was merciless, murderous, untruthful, unrighteous, immoral and lusting after others' wives." **(32-34).** Hearing his words, Rama was much pleased and said, "Enmity extends only up to death. We have accomplished our task (and we need not think further about the past). Perform his funeral rites. He is now as dear to me as he is to you." Complying with Rama's order, Vibheeshana the righteous now consoled the wise queen Mandodari by kind words. **(35-36).** A firm adherent of Dharma, he now hurried all his relatives to attend to the rites of cremation. He now made a funeral pyre according to scriptural injunctions, and then performed all those obsequial rites for Ravana along with his ministers and relatives according to the procedures to be adopted for one eligible for performing Agnihotra. **(37-39).** Vibheeshana lit the funeral fire according to injunctions and consigned Ravana's body to it. He then took his bath, and dressed in wet cloth, offered the departed one sesame seeds with water. He offered him water also separately and bent down his head in prostration. He then consoled all those women again and again, and persuaded them to go back to the city.

प्रविष्टासु च सर्वासु राक्षसीषु विभीषणः। रामपार्श्वमुपागत्य तदातिष्ठद्विनीतवत् ॥ 40
रामोऽपि सह सैन्येन ससुग्रीवः सलक्ष्मणः। हर्षं लेभे रिपून्हत्वा यथा वृत्रं शतक्रतुः ॥ 41
मातलिश्च तदा रामं परिक्रम्याभिवन्द्य च। अनुज्ञातश्च रामेण ययौ स्वर्गं विहायसा ॥ 42
ततो हृष्टमना रामो लक्ष्मणं चेदमब्रवीत्। विभीषणाय मे लङ्काराज्यं दत्तं पुरैव हि ॥ 43
इदानीमपि गत्वा त्वं लङ्कामध्ये विभीषणम्। अभिषेचय विप्रैश्च मन्त्रवद्विधिपूर्वकम् ॥ 44
इत्युक्तो लक्ष्मणस्तूर्णं जगाम सह वानरैः। लङ्कां सुवर्णकलशैः समुद्रजलसंयुतैः ॥ 45
अभिषेकं शुभं चक्रे राक्षसेन्द्रस्य धीमतः। ततः पौरजनैः सार्धं नानोपायनपाणिभिः ॥ 46
विभीषणः ससौमित्रिरुपायनपुरस्कृतः। दण्डप्रणाममकरोद्रामस्याक्लिष्टकर्मणः ॥ 47
रामो विभीषणं दृष्ट्वा प्राप्तराज्यं मुदान्वितः। कृतकृत्यमिवात्मानममन्यत सहानुजः ॥ 48
सुग्रीवं च समालिङ्ग्य रामो वाक्यमथाब्रवीत। सहायेन त्वया वीर जितो मे रावणो महान् ॥ 49
विभीषणोऽपि लङ्कायामभिषिक्तो मयानघ ॥ 50
ततः प्राह हनूमन्तं पार्श्वस्थं विनयान्वितम्। विभीषणस्यानुमतेर्गच्छ त्वं रावणालयम् ॥ 51
जानक्यै सर्वमाख्याहि रावणस्य वधादिकम्। जानक्याः प्रतिवाक्यं मे शीघ्रमेव निवेदय ॥ 52

Vibheeshana's Installation (40-50)

40. After all the Rakshasa women had gone back to the city, Vibheeshana in all humility went and stood before Rama. **41.** In the company of Lakshmana and Sugreeva and the army, Rama now rejoiced as Indra did after the destruction of Vritra. **42.** Matali, the heavenly charioteer, now circumambulated Rama and with his permission went back to the heavenly regions. **(43-44).** Rama then said to Lakshmana in a very joyous mood, "I have awarded even earlier this kingdom of Lanka to Vibheeshana. You go even now to the central part of Lanka and along with the Brahmanas administer the installation bath to Vibheeshana to the accompaniment of all Mantras and ceremonial rites." **(45-47).** Being so commanded, Lakshmana asked the monkeys to bring water from the ocean in golden vessels and with that performed the Rakshasa leader's ceremonial bath of installation. Immediately after, Vibheeshana along with Lakshmana, came to Rama with objects of presentation, followed by the citizens of Lanka also carrying presents. They all now made prostrations before Rama the mighty. **48.** Seeing Vibheeshana installed king, Rama and Lakshmana were very much pleased and felt satisfied that they had done a duty that they owed to themselves. **(49-50).** Rama now embraced Sugreeva and said, "O heroic one! With your help, I have been able to be victorious over the mighty Ravana. I have also been able to install Vibheeshana in Lanka."

Sita's Ordeal By Fire (51-85)

(51-52). Then he addressed Hanuman, who was standing by his side in all humility,

एवमाज्ञापितो धीमान् रामेण पवनात्मजः । प्रविवेश पुरीं लङ्कां पूज्यमानो निशाचरैः ॥ 53
प्रविश्य रावणगृहं शिंशपामूलमाश्रिताम् । ददर्श जानकीं तत्र कृशां दीनामनिन्दिताम् ॥ 54
राक्षसीभिः परिवृतां ध्यायन्तीं राममेव हि । विनयावनतो भूत्वा प्रणम्य पवनात्मजः ॥ 55
कृताञ्जलिपुटो भूत्वा प्रह्वो भक्त्याग्रतः स्थितः । तं दृष्ट्वा जानकी तूष्णीं स्थित्वा पूर्वस्मृतिं ययौ ॥
ज्ञात्वा तं रामदूतं सा हर्षात्सौम्यमुखी बभौ । स तां सौम्यमुखीं दृष्ट्वा तस्यै पवननन्दनः ॥ 57
रामस्य भाषितं सर्वमाख्यातुमुपचक्रमे ॥ 58
देवि रामः ससुग्रीवो विभीषणसहायवान् । कुशली वानराणां च सैन्यैश्च सहलक्ष्मणः ॥59
रावणं ससुतं हत्वा सबलं सह मन्त्रिभिः । त्वामाह कुशलं रामो राज्ये कृत्वा विभीषणम् ॥60
श्रुत्वा भर्तुः प्रियं वाक्यं हर्षगद्गदया गिरा ॥
किं ते प्रियं करोम्यद्य न पश्यामि जगत्त्रये । समं ते प्रियवाक्यस्य रत्नान्याभरणानि च ॥ 61
एवमुक्तस्तु वैदेह्या प्रत्युवाच प्लवङ्गमः । रत्नौघाद्विविधाद्वापि देवराज्याद्विशिष्यते ॥ 62
हतशत्रुं विजयिनं रामं पश्यामि सुस्थिरम् ॥ 63

with the words: "With Vibheeshana's permission, you go to Ravana's palace and inform Sita, the daughter of Janaka, of the destruction of Ravana, and bring to me her reply without delay." **53.** At this command of Rama, the intelligent Hanuman, the son of the Wind-god, entered into Lanka, welcomed by all the Rakshasas. **(54-56).** Going to Ravana's palace, he saw underneath the Simsapa tree the sorrow-stricken Sita surrounded by Rakshasa women and always engaged in the contemplation of Rama. In all humility Hanuman made a prostration to Sita. Then with joined palms he stood humbly before her with deep devotion. Seeing him, Sita for a while remained silent. Then old memories came to her. **(57-58).** She recognised him as Rama's messenger and her face at once brightened up with joy. On seeing Sita calm and collected, Hanuman now began to communicate to her the message he had brought from Rama. **(59-60).** He said, "O great lady! With the help of Sugreeva and the co-operation of Vibheeshana, Rama along with Lakshmana has crossed over to Lanka with an army of monkeys and destroyed Ravana along with his sons and all his forces. He has after that installed Vibheeshana as the king of Lanka. He has now sent me to you to convey this joyful news."

61. Hearing this gladdening news from her husband, Sita with her voice choked with the feeling of joy, replied, "What shall I give you now for bringing this joyous news? I think there is no jewel or ornament in the whole world that can be a fitting reward for your sweet words."**(62-63).** At these words of the daughter of Videha, the monkey leader said in reply, "That I am now able to see Rama victorious and established in power is a more precious reward for me than all collection of precious

तस्य तद्वचनं श्रुत्वा मैथिली प्राह मारुतिम् । सर्वे सौम्या गुणाः सौम्य त्वय्येव परिनिष्ठिताः ॥64
रामं द्रक्ष्यामि शीघ्रं मामाज्ञापयतु राघवः ॥ 65
तथेति तां नमस्कृत्य ययौ द्रष्टुं रघूत्तमम् । जानक्या भाषितं सर्वं रामस्याग्रे न्यवेदयत् ॥ 66
यन्निमित्तोऽयमारम्भः कर्मणां च फलोदयः ।
तां देवीं शोकसन्तप्तां द्रष्टुमर्हसि मैथिलीम् । एवमुक्तो हनुमता रामो ज्ञानवतां वरः ॥ 67
मायासीतां परित्यक्तुं जानकीमनले स्थिताम् । आदातुं मनसा ध्यात्वा रामः प्राह विभीषणम् ॥68
गच्छ राजन् जनकजामानयाशु ममान्तिकम् । स्नातां विरजवस्त्राढ्यां सर्वाभरणभूषिताम् ॥ 69
विभीषणोऽपि तच्छ्रुत्वा जगाम सहमारुतिः । राक्षसीभिः सुवृद्धाभिः स्नापयित्वा तु मैथिलीम् 70
सर्वाभरणसम्पन्नामारोप्य शिबिकोत्तमे । याष्टीकैर्बहुभिर्गुप्तां कञ्चुकोष्णीषिभिः शुभाम् 71
तां द्रष्टुमागताः सर्वे वानरा जनकात्मजाम् । तान्वारयन्तो बहवः सर्वतो वेत्रपाणयः ॥ 72
कोलाहलं प्रकुर्वन्तो रामपार्श्वमुपाययुः ॥ 73
दृष्ट्वा तां शिबिकारूढां दूरादथ रघूत्तमः । विभीषण किमर्थं ते वानरान्तारयन्ति हि ॥ 74
पश्यन्तु वानराः सर्वे मैथिलीं मातरं यथा । पादचारेण सा यातु जानकी मम सन्निधिम् ॥ 75

gems or even the abode of the gods." **(64-65).** Hearing those words of Hanuman, Sita said to him, "O giver of joy! All virtues reside in you. Now I am anxious to see Rama. May Rama be pleased to give permission for that without delay." **66.** He agreed to convey this message to Rama and departed making prostrations to her. Reaching Rama's presence, he narrated to him all that Sita wanted to convey through him. **67.** He said to Rama, "She for whose sake all these activities were undertaken and this victory won—that sorrow-stricken lady wants to meet you. Be pleased to permit her to do so."

68. When Hanuman said so, Rama, the wisest of men, resolved in his mind to do away with the Maya Sita and bring out the real Sita who was hiding in fire. With this in mind, he said to Vibheeshana: **69.** "O king! You now please go and bring Sita. Let her take bath, put on clean clothes and be adorned with all the ornaments. Bring her to my presence quickly." **(70-72).** Hearing the words of Rama, Vibheeshana along with Hanuman went into the city of Lanka. They got old Rakshasa women to bathe Sita and adorn her with all ornaments. Guarded by attendants wearing turbans and coats and with staffs in hand, handsome Sita was brought in a majestic palanquin. In their eagerness to have a look at her, the monkeys gathered all around. **73.** With bodyguards driving away the monkeys on all sides, and amidst the tumult produced thereby, Sita was brought before Rama.

(74-75). Seeing from a distance Sita com-

श्रुत्वा तद्रामवचनं शिबिकादवरुह्य सा । पादचारेण शनकैरागता रामसन्निधिम् । 76

रामोऽपि दृष्ट्वा तां मायासीतां कार्यार्थनिर्मिताम् । अवाच्यवादान्बहुशः प्राह तां रघुनन्दनः ॥ 77

अमृष्यमाणा सा सीता वचनं राघवोदितम् ।

लक्ष्मणं प्राह मे शीघ्रं प्रज्वालय हुताशनम् । विश्वासार्थं हि रामस्य लोकानां प्रत्ययाय च॥ 78

राघवस्य मतं ज्ञात्वा लक्ष्मणोऽपि तदैव हि । महा काष्ठचयं कृत्वा ज्वालयित्वा हुताशनम् ॥79

रामपार्श्वमुपागम्य तस्थौ तूष्णीमरिन्दमः । 80

ततः सीता परिक्रम्य राघवं भक्तिसंयुता । प्रणम्य देवताभ्यश्च ब्राह्मणेभ्यश्च मैथिली ॥ 81

पश्यतां सर्वलोकानां देवराक्षसयोषिताम् ।

बद्धाञ्जलिपुटा चेदमुवाचाग्निसमीपगा । यथा मे हृदयं नित्यं नापसर्पति राघवात् ॥ 82

तथा लोकस्य साक्षी मां सर्वतः पातु पावकः ॥ 83

एवमुक्त्वा तदा सीता परिक्रम्य हुताशनम् । विवेश ज्वलनं दीप्तं निर्भयेन हृदा सती ॥ 84

दृष्ट्वा ततो भूतगणाः ससिद्धाः सीतां महावह्निगतां भृशार्ताः ।

परस्परं प्राहुरहो स सीतां रामः श्रियं स्वां कथमत्यजज्ज्ञः ॥ 85

इति श्रीमदध्यात्मरामायणे उमामहेश्वरसंवादे

युद्धकाण्डे द्वादशः सर्गः ॥ १२ ॥

ing in a palanquin, Rama, the leader of the Raghus, said to Vibheeshana, "Why are you driving away the monkeys? Let them all have a look at Sita just as they see their mothers. So let her come walking to my presence." **76.** Hearing these words of Rama, Sita got down from the palanquin and slowly walked towards Rama. **77.** Seeing that magical Sita who was created for a definite purpose, Rama addressed her in words that were improper for him to have used. **78.** Being unable to bear those words of Rama, Sita said to Lakshmana, "Please make a pyre of fire for me in order that I may infuse confidence in Rama and satisfy the public opinion." **(79-80).** Lakshmana knew this to be in agreement with Rama's ideas and immediately collected the necessary fuel and made a raging fire. He then stood silently by the side of Rama.

(81-83). Then Sita, with a devoted heart, circumambulated Rama and in the presence of all including, Devas, Rakshasas and women, made salutations to the Devas and holy men, and approaching the fire, said as follows with palms held in salutation: "May the Fire-deity, who is the witness of everything in the world, protect me by showing in a way convincing to all that my heart has never wavered from its allegiance to Rama." **84.** With these words, Sita, the embodiment of chastity, circumambulated the fire and fearlessly entered into its raging flames. **85.** Seeing Sita enter into the raging fire, the Siddhas and other semi-divine beings exclaimed, expressing their grief, "Alas! How has Rama, an enlightened one, chosen to abandon Sita who is none but his inseparable Consort Sri?"

त्रयोदशः सर्गः

श्रीमहादेव उवाच

ततः शक्रः सहस्राक्षो यमश्च वरुणस्तथा । कुबेरश्च महातेजाः पिनाकी वृषवाहनः ॥ 1

ब्रह्मा ब्रह्मविदां श्रेष्ठो मुनिभिः सिद्धचारणैः । पितरो ऋषयः साध्या गन्धर्वाप्सरसोरगाः ॥ 2

एते चान्ये विमानाग्र्यैराजग्मुर्यत्र राघवः । अब्रुवन्परमात्मानं रामं प्राञ्जलयश्च ते ॥ 3

कर्ता त्वं सर्वलोकानां साक्षी विज्ञानविग्रहः । वसूनामष्टमोऽसि त्वं रुद्राणां शङ्करो भवान् ॥ 4

आदिकर्तासि लोकानां ब्रह्मा त्वं चतुराननः । अश्विनौ घ्राणभूतौ ते चक्षुषी चन्द्रभास्करौ ॥ 5

लोकानामादिरन्तोऽसि नित्य एकः सदोदितः । सदा शुद्धः सदा बुद्धः सदा मुक्तोऽगुणोऽद्वयः ॥

त्वन्मायासंवृतानां त्वं भासि मानुषविग्रहः । त्वन्नाम स्मरतां राम सदा भासि चिदात्मकः ॥ 7

रावणेन हृतं स्थानमस्माकं तेजसा सह । त्वयाद्य निहतो दुष्टः पुनः प्राप्तं पदं स्वकम् ॥ 8

एवं स्तुवत्सु देवेषु ब्रह्मा साक्षात्पितामहः । अब्रवीत्प्रणतो भूत्वा रामं सत्यपथे स्थितम् ॥ 9

Chapter 13

DEPARTURE TO AYODHYA

The Hymn of Brahma (1-18)

(1-3). Then there gathered at the place where Rama was, Divinities like Indra, Yama, Varuna, resplendent Kubera, Siva riding on the bull, Brahma the best of enlightened beings, the Munis, Siddhas, Charanas, Pitris, Rishis, Sadhyas, Gandharvas, Apsàras and many others. Saluting Rama, the Supreme Being, they said to him: **4.** "Thou art the creator of all the worlds. Thou, whose form is made of Pure Consciousness, art the witness of everything. Among the Vasus, Thou art the eighth, and among the Rudras, Thou art Sankara. **(5-6).** Thou art the real creator of the world. Brahma endowed with four faces, who is ordinarily called the creator, is only a manifestation of Thee and not different from Thee. The Aswini Devas are Thy nostrils and the moon and the sun are Thy eyes. Thou art the origin, the middle and end of the worlds. Thou art the one eternal Being without a second. Thou art ever awake and ever pure. Thou art Pure Consciousness and the source of all that is good and great. **7.** To those whose vision is hidden by Thy Maya, Thou appearest as a human being but to those who always remember Thy sacred name, Thou, O Rama, appearest as Pure Consciousness, ever shining. **8.** Ravana had deprived us of our status and our prowess. Thou having killed him, we have been restored to our positions."

9. While the Devas were thus speaking, Brahma the father of the worlds, made prostrations to Rama, the embodiment of

ब्रह्मोवाच

वन्दे देवं विष्णुमशेषस्थितिहेतुं त्वामध्यात्मज्ञानिभिरन्तर्हृदि भाव्यम् ।
हेयाहेयद्वन्द्वविहीनं परमेकं सत्तामात्रं सर्वहृदिस्थं दृशिरूपम् ॥ 10

प्राणापानौ निश्चयबुद्ध्या हृदि रुद्ध्वा छित्त्वा सर्वं संशयबन्धं विषयौघान् ।
पश्यन्तीशं यं गतमोहा यतयस्तं वन्दे रामं रत्नकिरीटं रविभासम् ॥ 11

मायातीतं माधवमाद्यं जगदादिं मानातीतं मोहविनाशं मुनिवन्द्यम् ।
योगिध्येयं योगविधानं परिपूर्णं वन्दे रामं रञ्जितलोकं रमणीयम् ॥ 12

भावाभावप्रत्ययहीनं भवमुख्यैर्योगासक्तैरर्चितपादाम्बुजयुग्मम् ।
नित्यं शुद्धं बुद्धमनन्तं प्रणवाख्यं वन्दे रामं वीरमशेषासुरदावम् ॥ 13

त्वं मे नाथो नाथितकार्याखिलकारी मानातीतो माधवरूपाऽखिलधारी ।
भक्त्या गम्यो भावितरूपो भवहारी योगाभ्यासैर्भावितचेतःसहचारी ॥ 14

त्वामाद्यन्तं लोकततीनां परमीशं लोकानां नो लौकिकमानैरधिगम्यम् ।
भक्तिश्रद्धाभावसमेतैर्भजनीयं वन्दे रामं सुन्दरमिन्दीवरनीलम् ॥ 15

Truth, and said: **10.** "I salute Thee, O Lord, who art all-pervading and the sustaining force behind all, who art meditated upon in their hearts by spiritually awakened ones, who art above the pairs of opposites differentiated as acceptable and rejectable, who art pure Existence and the Dweller in the hearts of all, and who art of the nature of pure witness-consciousness. **11.** I salute that Rama with gem-studded crown and with the radiance of the sun, whom undeluded ascetics perceive after having confined the Prana and Apana in their hearts and after cutting asunder with their firm determinative faculty (*niscaya-buddhi*).

12. I salute Rama, who transcends the Maya, who is the consort of Lakshmi, who is the original source of the universe, who was before all other beings, who is immeasurable, who is the dispeller of delusions, who is fit to be worshipped by Munis, who is the object of meditation for Yogis, who is the support for all Yogis, who is ever satisfied, who attracts all the worlds and who is the quintessence of all beauty. **13.** I salute Rama, who is above the concepts of being and non-being, whose lotus-feet are worshipped by Bhava and other Yogis, who is devoid of worldly attachments, who is indestructible, stainless, sentient, infinite, denoted by the Pranava 'Om' and heroic, and who is a conflagration to destroy the forces of ignorance. **14.** Thou art the one who accomplishest all that I pray for, who transcendest all measurements, who art the consort of Lakshmi, who art the support of everything, who could be approached by Bhakti, who assumest any form in which Thou art conceived, who art the destroyer of Samsara and who abidest in the hearts that are purified by Yoga. **15.** I salute Rama who

को वा ज्ञातुं त्वामतिमानं गतमानं मायासक्तो माधव शक्तो मुनिमान्यम् ।
वृन्दारण्ये वन्दितवृन्दारकवृन्दं वन्दे रामं भवमुखवन्द्यं सुखकन्दम् ॥ 16

नानाशास्त्रैर्वेदकदम्बैः प्रतिपाद्यं नित्यानन्दं निर्विषयज्ञानमनादिम् ।
मत्सेवार्थं मानुषभावं प्रतिपन्नं वन्दे रामं मरकतवर्णं मथुरेशम् ॥ 17

श्रद्धायुक्तो यः पठतीमं स्तवमाद्यं ब्राह्मं ब्रह्मज्ञानविधानं भुवि मर्त्यः ।
रामं श्यामं कामितकामप्रदमीशं ध्यात्वा ध्याता पातकजालैर्विगतः स्यात् ॥ 18

श्रुत्वा स्तुतिं लोकगुरोर्विभावसुः स्वाङ्के समादाय विदेहपुत्रिकाम् ।
विभ्राजमानां विमलारुणद्युतिं रक्ताम्बरां दिव्यविभूषणान्विताम् ॥ 19

प्रोवाच साक्षी जगतां रघूत्तमं प्रपन्नसर्वार्तिहरं हुताशनः ।
गृहाण देवीं रघुनाथ जानकीं पुरा त्वया मय्यवरोपितां वने ॥ 20

विधाय मायाजनकात्मजां हरे दशाननप्राणविनाशनाय च ।
हतो दशास्यः सह पुत्रबान्धवैर्निराकृतोऽनेन भरो भुवः प्रभो ।

is beautiful like a blue lotus, who is the origin and the end of the whole universe, who is transcendent and beyond the grasp of the means of knowledge available in the world, who is the regulator of all, and who is the one object fit to be worshipped with faith and devotion. **16.** I salute Rama, who transcends the bonds of all limits and all measurements, who is the object of worship by Munis, who will delight the Devas in Vrindavana in another incarnation, who is adored by Siva and other deities and who is the source of all joy. No man with attachment for the body can ever know Thee. **17.** I salute Rama, who is the object of discourse for all the Vedas and various kinds of Sastras, who is ever blissful, who is objectless awareness, who is eternal, who has assumed a human body for my sake, who is the Lord of Mathura and whose complexion is like that of emerald." **18.** Whoever recites with faith and devotion this unique and knowledge-generating hymn of Brahma addressed to Rama who is blue in complexion, who grants the prayers of all, and who is the Lord of all—that worshipper will be liberated from all sins.

Sita United with Rama (19-22)

(19-20). Pleased with the hymn of Brahma, Lord Agni, the deity of fire, now came out with Sita in his lap—Sita luminous like the light of the sun and dressed in a red cloth and adorned with divine ornaments. Then the Lord Agni, the witness of everything in the universe, said to Rama the redresser of the sorrows of all surrendered ones, as follows: "O Lord of the Raghus! The holy person of Sita whom you deposited in me in the forest, I am now restoring. Please accept her. **21.** O Lord Hari! In order to destroy Ravana, Thou didst create a

तिरोहिता सा प्रतिबिम्बरूपिणी कृता यदर्थं कृतकृत्यतां गता ॥ 21

ततोऽतिहृष्टां परिगृह्य जानकीं रामः प्रहृष्टः प्रतिपूज्य पावकम् ।
स्वाङ्के समावेश्य सदानपायिनीं श्रियं त्रिलोकीजननीं श्रियः पतिः ॥ 22

दृष्ट्वाथ रामं जनकात्मजायुतं श्रिया स्फुरन्तं सुरनायको मुदा ।
भक्त्या गिरा गद्गदया समेत्य कृताञ्जलिः स्तोतुमथोपचक्रमे ॥ 23

इन्द्र उवाच

भजेऽहं सदा राममिन्दीवराभं भवारण्यदावानलाभाभिधानम् ।
भवानीहृदा भावितानन्दरूपं भवाभावहेतुं भवादिप्रपन्नम् ॥ 24

सुरानीकदुःखौघनाशैकहेतुं नराकारदेहं निराकारमीड्यम् ।
परेशं परानन्दरूपं वरेण्यं हरिं राममीशं भजे भारनाशम् ॥ 25

प्रपन्नाखिलानन्ददोहं प्रपन्नं प्रपन्नार्तिनिःशेषनाशाभिधानम् ।
तपोयोगयोगीशभावाभिभाव्यं कपीशादिमित्रं भजे राममित्रम् ॥ 26

सदा भोगभाजां सुदूरे विभान्तं सदा योगभाजामदूरे विभान्तम् ।
चिदानन्दकन्दं सदा राघवेशं विदेहात्मजानन्दरूपं प्रपद्ये ॥ 27

magical Sita. Now Ravana has been destroyed along with all his sons and relatives. The world's burden has thus been relieved. So the double of Sita created by Maya, having fulfilled her function, has disappeared into me." **22.** Thereupon Rama, the Consort of Sri, accepted and seated Sita in his lap—Sita who was full of joy, who is inseparable from him, and who is Sri, the generator of all the three worlds.

Hymn of Indra (23-32)

23. Now Indra, the Lord of the Devas, seeing Rama resplendent with glory and united with Sita, came forward in great joy and saluting Rama with joined palms, began to recite a hymn in praise of him in a voice choked with feeling. **24.** Indra said: "I always adore Rama, whose complexion is like a blue lotus, who is like a fire to the forest of Samsara, whose blissful form is always adored by Parvati in her heart, who puts an end to the Jiva's involvement in Samsara, and in whom Siva and other deities take refuge. **25.** I adore Rama who is the chief redresser of the sorrows of the Devas, who though human in appearance is beyond all forms, who is worthy of praise, who is the transcendent Lord, who is supreme Bliss, who is the worshipful master of all, and who removes the burdens of the world. **26.** I adore Ramachandra, who generates joy in the minds of all surrendered ones, who has become propitious, whose name destroys the sorrows of all surrendered ones, who is fit to be contemplated upon by those endowed with austerity and concentration, and who is the friend and ally of the chief of monkeys. **27.** I seek shelter in Rama

महायोगमायाविशेषानुयुक्तो विभासीश लीलानराकारवृत्तिः ।
त्वदानन्दलीलाकथापूर्णकर्णाः सदानन्दरूपा भवन्तीह लोके ॥ 28
अहं मानपानाभिमत्तप्रमत्तो न वेदाखिलेशाभिमानाभिमानः ।
इदानीं भवत्पादपद्मप्रसादात् त्रिलोकाधिपत्याभिमानो विनष्टः ॥ 29
स्फुरद्रत्नकेयूरहाराभिरामं धराभारभूतासुरानीकदावम् ।
शरच्चन्द्रवक्त्रं लसत्पद्मनेत्रं दुरावारपारं भजे राघवेशम् ॥ 30
सुराधीशनीलाभ्रनीलाङ्गकान्तिं विराधादिरक्षोवधाल्लोकशान्तिम् ।
किरीटादिशोभं पुरारातिलाभं भजे रामचन्द्रं रघूणामधीशम् ॥ 31
लसच्चन्द्रकोटिप्रकाशादिपीठे समासीनमङ्के समाधाय सीताम् ।
स्फुरद्धेमवर्णां तडित्पुञ्जभासां भजे रामचन्द्रं निवृत्तार्तितन्द्रम् ॥ 32
ततः प्रोवाच भगवान्भवान्या सहितो भवः । रामं कमलपत्राक्षं विमानस्थो नभःस्थले ॥ 33
आगमिष्याम्ययोध्यायां द्रष्टुं त्वां राज्यसत्कृतम् । इदानीं पश्य पितरमस्य देहस्य राघवः ॥ 34

the chief of the Raghus, who is far away for those engrossed in worldly pleasures but near to those who are contemplatives, who is the source of all consciousness and joy, and whose forms give joy to Sita, the daughter of Videha. **28.** O Lord! Thou shinest in combination with Thy Yogamaya in a human body assumed for sport. Those whose ears are always hearing accounts of Thy sportive manifestations are filled with spiritual joy in this world. **29.** I did not know Thee in the proper light before, inebriated as I was with the pride of being the master of the worlds. Now, out of Thy grace, this pride in the lordship of all the worlds has been destroyed. **30.** I adore Rama who is bedecked with gem-studded armlets and with pearl-necklaces, who is like a forest fire to the world's burden of Asuras, who has got the face resembling the autumnal moon, whose eyes are like the petals of a lotus in bloom, and who is beyond the sea of Samsara which is difficult for Jivas to cross. **31.** I adore Ramachandra who is blue in complexion like Indraneela gem (Lapis Lazuli) and the blue lotus, who brought peace to the world by the destruction of Viradha and others, who is bedecked with a diadem and other ornaments and who is the cause of joy to Siva. **32.** I worship Ramachandra who is seated on a throne more brilliant than a crore of moons, who has got Sita seated in his lap—the golden-complexioned Sita who is brilliant like a flash of lightning—and who is free from all sorrow and weakness."

Events Preceding the Departure to Ayodhya (33-59)

33. After that, Siva in the company of Bhavani appeared in the sky in an aerial vehicle and said to the lotus-eyed Rama: **34.**

ततोऽपश्यद्विमानस्थं रामो दशरथं पुरः । ननाम शिरसा पादौ मुदा भक्त्या सहानुजः ॥ 35

आलिङ्ग्य मूर्ध्न्यवघ्राय रामं दशरथोऽब्रवीत् ।

तारितोऽस्मि त्वया वत्स संसाराद्दुःखसागरात् । इत्युक्त्वा पुनरालिङ्ग्य ययौ रामेण पूजितः ॥ 36

रामोऽपि देवराजं तं दृष्ट्वा प्राह कृताञ्जलिम् ।

मत्कृते निहतान्सङ्ख्ये वानरान्पतितान् भुवि । जीवयाशु सुधावृष्ट्या सहस्राक्ष ममाज्ञया ॥ 37

तथेत्यमृतवृष्ट्या तान् जीवयामास वानरान् ।

ये ये मृता मृधे पूर्वं ते ते सुप्तोत्थिता इव ।

पूर्ववद्बलिनो हृष्टा रामपार्श्वमुपाययुः । नोत्थिता राक्षसास्तत्र पीयूषस्पर्शनादपि ॥ 38

विभीषणस्तु साष्टाङ्गं प्रणिपत्याब्रवीद्वचः । देव मामनुगृह्णीष्व मयि भक्तिर्यदा तव ॥ 39

मङ्गलस्नानमद्य त्वं कुरु सीतासमन्वितः । अलंकृत्य सह भ्रात्रा श्वो गमिष्यामहे वयम् ॥40

विभीषणवचः श्रुत्वा प्रत्युवाच रघूत्तम। सुकुमारोऽतिभक्तो मे भरतो मामवेक्षते ॥ 41

जटावल्कलधारी स शब्दब्रह्मसमाहितः । कथं तेन विना स्नानमलङ्कारादिकं मम ॥ 42

"I shall come to meet Thee when Thou art received with honour in Ayodhya. Now please look at him, who is the generator of this body of Thine." **35.** Then Rama saw Dasaratha before him seated in an aerial vehicle. With great joy and devotion, Rama along with his brother Lakshmana, made prostrations to him. **36.** Dasaratha embraced Rama, kissed him on the crown of his head, and said, "O my dear son! On account of you, I have been rescued from the travails of the ocean of Samsara." Saying so, he embraced Rama once again. Rama thereupon worshipped him and Dasaratha disappeared from sight.

37. Rama now said to Indra the king of the Devas, who was standing before him with joined palms, "O thousand eyed one! On my orders please spray a shower of Amrita over these monkeys who have fallen dead on my account, and revive them soon." **38.** Agreeing to do so, Indra sent a shower of Amrita over the dead bodies, whereupon, the monkeys who had died in battle revived as if from sleep. Strong as before, they approached Rama in great joy. But the Rakshasas there did not become alive even by contact with Amrita.

(39-40). Now Vibheeshna made a full prostration to Rama and said, "If Thou art pleased with me, deign to bless me. Be pleased to bathe and be adorned along with Sita, and prepare to start tomorrow along with your brother." **(41-42).** At these words of Vibheeshana, Rama replied, "My brother Bharata, handsome and devoted, is awaiting my arrival. Dressed in tree-bark clothes and matted locks, he is immersed in meditation on Pranava. Without him there is no bath or decoration for me. **43.** Therefore, extend a reception to the monkeys headed by Sugreeva. If you host these mon-

अतः सुग्रीवमुख्यांस्त्वं पूजयाशु विशेषतः। पूजितेषु कपीन्द्रेषु पूजितोऽहं न संशयः ॥ 43
इत्युक्तो राघवेणाशु स्वर्णरत्नाम्बराणि च। ववर्ष राक्षसश्रेष्ठो यथाकामं यथारुचि ॥ 44
ततस्तान्पूजितान्दृष्ट्वा रामो रत्नैश्च यूथपान्। अभिनन्द्य यथान्यायं विससर्ज हरीश्वरान् ॥ 45
विभीषणसमानीतं पुष्पकं सूर्यवर्चसम्। आरुरोह ततो रामस्तद्विमानमनुत्तमम् ॥ 46
अङ्के निधाय वैदेहीं लज्जमानां यशस्विनीम्। लक्ष्मणेन सह भ्रात्रा विक्रान्तेन धनुष्मता ॥ 47
अब्रवीच्च विमानस्थः श्रीरामः सर्ववानरान्। सुग्रीवं हरिराजं च अङ्गदं च विभीषणम् ॥ 48
मित्रकार्यं कृतं सर्वं भवद्भिः सह वानरैः। अनुज्ञाता मया सर्वे यथेष्टं गन्तुमर्हथ ॥ 49
सुग्रीव प्रतियाह्याशु किष्किन्धां सर्वसैनिकैः। स्वराज्ये वस लङ्कायां मम भक्तो विभीषण ॥50
न त्वां धर्षयितुं शक्ताः सेन्द्रा अपि दिवौकसः। अयोध्यां गन्तुमिच्छामि राजधानीं पितुर्मम ॥ 51
एवमुक्तास्तु रामेण वानरास्ते महाबलाः। ऊचुः प्राञ्जलयः सर्वे राक्षसश्च विभीषणः ॥ 52
अयोध्यां गन्तुमिच्छामस्त्वया सह रघूत्तम। दृष्ट्वा त्वामभिषिक्तं तु कौसल्यामभिवाद्य च ॥53
पश्चाद् वृणीमहे राज्यमनुज्ञां देहि नः प्रभो। 54
रामस्तथेति सुग्रीव वानरैः सविभीषणः। पुष्पकं सहनूमांश्च शीघ्रमारोह साम्प्रतम् ॥ 55

keys, it is as good as honouring me." **44.** When Rama said so, Vibheeshana the chief of the Rakshasas, now presented to the monkeys according to their taste, an abundance of gold, gems and clothes. **45.** On seeing these leading monkeys treated liberally in this way, Rama thanked them all and permitted them to go to their respective places.

46. After that in the company of Vibheeshana, Rama got into the unique aerial vehicle Pushpaka, which was shining like the sun. **47.** The bashful Sita was seated in his lap, and his brother, the heroic Lakshmana, by his side. **48.** Seated in the aerial vehicle, Rama said to all the monkey and to Sugreeva, Angada and Vibheeshana: **49.** "Along with all these monkeys you have eminently fulfilled your duty towards a friend and ally. Now permitted by me, you are free to go to your respective places. **50.** O Sugreeva! Along with all your generals, you go to Kishkindha soon. And O Vibheeshana! You, who are my devotee, go and rule over your country Lanka. **51.** None including the Devas headed by Indra can overcome you. Now I desire to go to my father's capital, Ayodhya." **52.** All the monkey leaders and the Rakshasa Vibheeshana, who were thus thanked and commended by Rama, said to him with joined palms: **(53-54)** "O Rama, the greatest of the Raghus! We desire to go to Ayodhya and see your coronation and pay our respects to Kausalya. After that we shall go to our countries. O Lord! Be pleased to accord permission for this." **55.** Agreeing to this request, Rama said, "O Sugreeva! You along with Vibheeshana, Hanuman and the monkeys, get ready to start immediately and ascend

ततस्तु पुष्पकं दिव्यं सुग्रीवः सह सेनया । विभीषणश्च सामात्यः सर्वे चारुरुहुर्द्रुतम् ॥ 56
तेष्वारूढेषु सर्वेषु कौबेरं परमासनम् । राघवेणाभ्यनुज्ञातमुत्पपात विहायसा ॥ 57
बभौ तेन विमानेन हंसयुक्तेन भास्वता । प्रहृष्टश्च तदा रामश्चतुर्मुख इवापरः ॥ 58
ततो बभौ भास्करबिम्बतुल्यं कुबेरयानं तपसानुलब्धम् ।
रामेण शोभां नितरां प्रपेदे सीतासमेतेन सहानुजेन ॥ 59

इति श्रीमदध्यात्मरामायणे उमामहेश्वरसंवादे
युद्धकाण्डे त्रयोदशः सर्गः ॥ १३ ॥

the divine vehicle Pushpaka." **56.** Thereupon Sugreeva and Vibheeshana along with his ministers and all the monkey army got into that divine vehicle. **57.** When all of them had boarded it, that aerial vehicle of Kubera rose into the sky at Rama's order. **58.** Seated in that vehicle with the emblem of Hamsa, Rama, now filled with joy, looked like another Brahma himself. **59.** With Rama seated along with Sita and Lakshmana in it, this vehicle of sunlike brilliance originally obtained by Kubera by his Tapas, now shone in the sky all the more.

चतुर्दशः सर्गः
श्रीमहादेव उवाच

पातयित्वा ततश्चक्षुः सर्वतो रघुनन्दनः । अब्रवीन्मैथिलीं सीतां रामः शशिनिभाननाम् 1
त्रिकूटशिखराग्रस्थां पश्य लङ्कां महाप्रभाम् । एतां रणभुवं पश्य मांसकर्दमपङ्किलाम् ॥ 2
असुराणां प्लवङ्गानामत्र वैशसनं महत् । अत्र मे निहतः शेते रावणो राक्षसेश्वरः ॥ 3
कुम्भकर्णेन्द्रजिन्मुख्याः सर्वे चात्र निपातिताः । एष सेतुर्मया बद्धः सागरे सलिलाशये ॥ 4
एतच्च दृश्यते तीर्थं सागरस्य महात्मनः । 5
सेतुबन्धमितिख्यातं त्रैलोक्येन च पूजितम् । एतत्पवित्रं परमं दर्शनात्पातकापहम् ॥
अत्र रामेश्वरो देवो मया शम्भुः प्रतिष्ठितः ॥ 6

Chapter 14

RAMA'S RETURN JOURNEY TO AYODHYA

Description of Places as seen from above (1-14)

1. Now seated in the aerial vehicle, Rama looked all around and said to Sita of moon-like face. **2.** "Look at the shining Lanka at the top of the Trikuta mountain and see the battlefield near by, which is miry with the flesh and blood of the dead. **(3-4).** Here took place the fierce battle between the Asuras and the monkeys. This is the place where Ravana fell at my hand. All the other Rakshasa heroes like Kumbhakarna and Indrajit fell in this place. **(5-6).** See in the ocean the Setu

अत्र मां शरणं प्राप्तो मन्त्रिभिश्च विभीषणः । एषा सुग्रीवनगरी किष्किन्धा चित्रकानना ॥ 7
तत्र रामाज्ञया ताराप्रमुखा हरियोषितः । आनयामास सुग्रीवः सीतायाः प्रियकाम्यया ॥ 8
ताभिः सहोत्थितं शीघ्रं विमानं प्रेक्ष्य राघवः । प्राह चाद्रिमृष्यमूकं पश्य वाल्यत्र मे हतः ॥ 9
एषा पञ्चवटी नाम राक्षसा यत्र मे हताः । अगस्त्यस्य सुतीक्ष्णस्य पश्याश्रमपदे शुभे ॥ 10
एते ते तापसाः सर्वे दृश्यन्ते वरवर्णिनि । असौ शैलवरो देवि चित्रकूटः प्रकाशते ॥ 11
अत्र मां कैकेयीपुत्रः प्रसादयितुमागतः । भरद्वाजाश्रमं पश्य दृश्यते यमुनातटे ॥ 12
एषा भागीरथी गङ्गा दृश्यते लोकपावनी । एषा सा दृश्यते सीते सरयूयूपमालिनी ॥ 13
एषा सा दृश्यतेऽयोध्या प्रणामं कुरु भामिनि । 14
एवं क्रमेण सम्प्राप्तो भरद्वाजाश्रमं हरिः । पूर्णे चतुर्दशे वर्षे पञ्चम्यां रघुनन्दनः । 15
भरद्वाजं मुनिं दृष्ट्वा ववन्दे सानुजः प्रभुः । पप्रच्छ मुनिमासीनं विनयेन रघूत्तमः ॥ 16
शृणोषि कच्चिद्भरतः कुशल्यास्ते सहानुजः । सुभिक्षा वर्ततेऽयोध्या जीवन्ति च हि मातरः ॥17

(dam) that I constructed. This in future will be famous as the Setubandha in all the worlds—a holy place for people to visit and bathe. By doing so, they will be absolved from their sins. Here I installed Rameswara, the divine image of Siva. **7.** It is in this place that Vibheeshana with his ministers joined me. What you see there amidst beautiful forests is Sugreeva's city of Kishkindha."

8. As Sita was desirous of seeing the women folk of the monkeys, the aerial vehicle stopped there at Rama's behest, and Sugreeva soon brought Tara and other women for Sita to see. **9.** With these women also on board, the Pushpaka aerial vehicle quickly rose into the sky once more. Rama now said again pointing to Rishyamuka mountain, "See, here Vali was killed by me. **10.** Now see the famous place Panchavati where I destroyed a large Rakshasa force. Beyond that see the holy Ashramas of Agastya and Suteekshana. **(11-14)** O virtuous one! All those ascetics who then inhabited these places are still seen there. There you see the imposing mountain Chitrakuta. It was here that Bharata, the son of Kaikeyi, came to show his regard for me. You now see there Bharadwaja's Ashrama on the banks of Yamuna. And here is Ganga which purifies the whole world. O Sita! What you see there is river Sarayu with numerous sacrificial posts on its banks, and this that you see is Ayodhya. Make salutations to the city."

Hymn of Bharadwaja (15-38)

15. Travelling in this way Rama gradually reached the Ashrama of Bharadwaja on the fifth lunar day after fourteen years of absence. **16.** Rama along with Lakshmana saluted the sage Bharadwaja who was seated in the Ashrama and said to him in all humility: **17.** "Do you know whether my brother Bharata is getting on well? Is Ayodhya in a prosperous condi-

श्रुत्वा रामस्य वचनं भरद्वाजः प्रहृष्टधीः । प्राह सर्वे कुशलिनो भरतस्तु महामनाः ।
फलमूलकृताहारो जटावल्कलधारकः ॥ 18
पादुके सकलं न्यस्य राज्यं त्वां सुप्रतीक्षते । यद्यत्कृतं त्वया कर्म दण्डके रघुनन्दन ॥ 19
राक्षसानां विनाशं च सीताहरणपूर्वकम् । सर्वं ज्ञातं मया राम तपसा ते प्रसादतः ॥ 20
त्वं ब्रह्म परमं साक्षादादिमध्यान्तवर्जितः । त्वमग्रे सलिलं सृष्ट्वा तत्र सुप्तोऽसि भूतकृत् ॥21
नारायणोऽसि विश्वात्मन्नराणामन्तरात्मकः । त्वन्नाभिकमलोत्पन्नो ब्रह्मा लोकपितामहः ॥ 22
अतस्त्वं जगतामीशः सर्वलोकनमस्कृतः । त्वं विष्णुर्जानकी लक्ष्मीःशेषोऽयं लक्ष्मणाभिधः ॥
आत्मना सृजसीदं त्वमात्मन्येवात्ममायया । न सज्जसे नभोवत्त्वं चिच्छक्त्या सर्वसाक्षिकः ॥
बहिरन्तश्च भूतानां त्वमेव रघुनन्दन । पूर्णोऽपि मूढदृष्टीनां विच्छिन्न इव लक्ष्यसे ॥ 25
जगत्त्वं जगदाधारस्त्वमेव परिपालकः । त्वमेव सर्वभूतानां भोक्ता भोज्यं जगत्पते ॥ 26
दृश्यते श्रूयते यद्यत्स्मर्यते वा रघूत्तम । त्वमेव सर्वमखिलं त्वद्विनान्यन्न किञ्चन ॥ 27
माया सृजति लोकांश्च स्वगुणैरहमादिभिः ॥ 28
त्वच्छक्तिप्रेरिता राम तस्मात्त्वय्युपचर्यते । यथा चुम्बकसान्निध्याच्चलन्त्येवायआदयः ॥ 29

tion? Are all my mothers alive?" **(18-20).** Highly pleased to hear Rama's words, Bharadwaja replied, "All are doing well, and as for Bharata, he lives on fruits and roots and wears matted locks and tree-bark clothes. He rules the country dedicating his actions to Thy sandals and is awaiting Thy return. O Lord of the Raghus! By virtue of my Tapas and Thy grace, I have come to know about all Thy achievements in the Dandaka forest, consisting in the destruction of all the Rakshasas, putting forward Sita's abduction as the cause. **21.** Thou art verily the Supreme Brahman manifested, so that one could see Thee with the eyes. Thou art without beginning and end. In the beginning, Thou didst bring Water into existence. Thou, the cause of all, didst remain in slumber in the Water. **22.** Thou art Narayana because Thou art lying in Nara, water. Thou art Narayana also because Thou art the inner self of Naras or men. The grandsire of the world, Brahma, originated from Thy navel-lotus. **23.** Therefore, Thou art the Lord of the worlds, worshipped by all. Thou art Mahavishnu and Sita the daughter of Janaka, is Lakshmi. This personage, who is known as Lakshmana, is Adisesha. **24.** Thou createst this world out of Thyself, in Thyself, by Thy inherent power of Maya. Just like the sky, Thou art not attached or defiled by anything. With Thy power of knowledge, Thou art the witness of everything. **25.** Thou art pervading everything within and without. Thou art the Whole. Out of ignorance people see Thee in separation. **26.** Thou art the universe. Thou art also the support of the universe. Thou alone art the support of all beings. O Lord! Thou art both the enjoyer and the enjoyed. **27.** Whatever is seen, heard or remembered, all that is Thou Thyself. There is nothing else besides Thee. **(28-29).** For want of true knowledge of Thee, all

जडास्तथा त्वया दृष्टा माया सृजति वै जगत् ॥ 30
देहद्वयमदेहस्य तव विश्वं रिरक्षिषोः । विराट् स्थूलं शरीरं ते सूत्रं सूक्ष्ममुदाहृतम् ॥ 31
विराजः सम्भवन्त्येते अवताराः सहस्रशः । कार्यान्ते प्रविशन्त्येव विराजं रघुनन्दन ॥ 32
अवतारकथां लोके ये गायन्ति गृणन्ति च । अनन्यमनसो मुक्तिस्तेषामेव रघूत्तम ॥ 33
त्वं ब्रह्मणा पुरा भूमेर्भारहाराय राघव । प्रार्थितस्तपसा तुष्टस्त्वं जातोऽसि रघोः कुले ॥ 34
देवकार्यमशेषेण कृतं ते राम दुष्करम् । बहुवर्षसहस्राणि मानुषं देहमाश्रितः ॥ 35
कुर्वन्दुष्करकर्माणि लोकद्वयहिताय च । पापहारीणि भुवनं यशसा पूरयिष्यसि ॥ 36
प्रार्थयामि जगन्नाथ पवित्रं कुरु मे गृहम् । स्थित्वाद्य भुक्त्वा सबलाश्वो गमिष्यसि पत्तनम् ॥
तथेति राघवोऽतिष्ठत्तस्मिन्नाश्रम उत्तमे । ससैन्यः पूजितस्तेन सीतया लक्ष्मणेन च ॥ 38
ततो रामश्चिन्तयित्वा मुहूर्तं प्राह मारुतिम् । इतो गच्छ हनूमंस्त्वमयोध्यां प्रति सत्वरः ॥ 39
जानीहि कुशली कश्चिज्जनो नृपतिमन्दिरे । शृंगवेरपुरं गत्वा ब्रूहि मित्रं गुहं मम ॥ 40
जानकीलक्ष्मणोपेतमागतं मां निवेदय । 41

this is seen in separation. With the dawn of Thy knowledge, nothing is seen in separation. Maya with its products like 'I-sense,' creates this world at Thy will. Therefore, this creation is Thine alone indirectly. **30.** In the presence of a loadstone, iron and its products move. In the same way, by Thy look alone this insentient Maya is able to create. **31.** In Thy creative and protective aspect, Thou art said to be endowed with two bodies, the Virat or the Cosmic Whole as Thy gross body, and the Sutratma or the subtle Pervading Self known as Hiranyagarbha. **32.** Out of Virat Purusha, numerous Incarnations arise and after they fulfill their purpose, they dissolve into the Virat Purusha Himself. **33.** O Rama! In this world, whoever recites with attention and devotion the accounts of these Incarnations, they attain to Moksha. **34.** O Lord of the Raghus! Being requested by Brahma in days of old to relieve the burdens of the earth, Thou, who wert pleased with his austerities, incarnated Thyelf in the line of the Raghus. **(35-36).** O Rama! Thou hast achieved the purpose of the Devas in fullness. Incarnated as man, Thou hast performed actions impossible for any one to achieve. Famed all the world over for these achievements, the sin-destroying accounts about them will be the cause of the welfare of men both here and hereafter for thousands of years. **37.** O Lord of the worlds! Deign to purify my home. Today Thou with Thy forces can take Thy food and stay here. Tomorrow Thou canst proceed to Thy city." **38.** Rama agreed to this and stayed in that holy Ashrama for that night. He along with Sita, Lakshmana and the forces received the hospitality of the sage for the night.

Hanuman's Mission to Bharata (39-68)

(39-41). Thinking for a while, Rama called Hanuman, the son of the Wind-god, and said to him, "O Hanuman! You go

नन्दिग्रामं ततो गत्वा भ्रातरं भरतं मम । दृष्ट्वा ब्रूहि सभार्यस्य सभ्रातुः कुशलं मम ।
सीतापहरणादीनि रावणस्य वधादिकम् ॥ 42
ब्रूहि क्रमेण मे भ्रातुः सर्वं तत्र विचेष्टितम् ॥ 43
हत्वा शत्रुगणान्सर्वान्सभार्यः सहलक्ष्मणः । उपयाति समृद्धार्थः सह ऋक्षहरीश्वरैः ॥ 44
इत्युक्त्वा तत्र वृत्तान्तं भरतस्य विचेष्टितम् । सर्वं ज्ञात्वा पुनः शीघ्रमागच्छ मम सन्निधिम् ॥ 45
तथेति हनुमांस्तत्र मानुषं वपुरास्थितः । नन्दिग्रामं ययौ तूर्णं वायुवेगेन मारुतिः ।
गरुत्मानिव वेगेन जिघृक्षन् भुजगोत्तमम् ॥ 46
शृङ्गवेरपुरं प्राप्य गुहमासाद्य मारुतिः । उवाच मधुरं वाक्यं प्रहृष्टेनान्तरात्मना ॥ 47
रामो दाशरथिः श्रीमान्सखा ते सह सीतया । सलक्ष्मणस्त्वां धर्मात्मा क्षेमी कुशलमब्रवीत् ॥48
अनुज्ञातोऽद्य मुनिना भरद्वाजेन राघवः । आगमिष्यति तं देवं द्रक्ष्यसि त्वं रघूत्तमम् ॥ 49
एवमुक्त्वा महातेजाः सम्प्रहृष्टतनूरुहम् । उत्पपात महावेगो वायुवेगेन मारुतिः ॥ 50
सोऽपश्यद्रामतीर्थं च सरयूं च महानदीम् । तामतिक्रम्य हनुमान्नन्दिग्रामं ययौ मुदा ॥ 51
क्रोशमात्रे त्वयोध्यायाश्चीरकृष्णाजिनाम्बरम् । ददर्श भरतं दीनं कृशमाश्रमवासिनम् ॥ 52

quickly to Ayodhya and see whether every thing is going on well in the palace. Going to the city of Sringavera, inform my friend Guha that I have come along with Sita and Lakshmana. **(42-43).** After that you go to Nandigrama. See my brother Bharata and convey to him the news of my welfare as also of my wife and my brother. Inform him also about all that has happened—of the abduction of Sita and the destruction of Ravana. **(44-45).** Inform him that after destroying all the enemies and the complete fulfilment of my purposes, I am arriving along with my wife, Lakshmana and the leaders of the bears and monkeys. Learn also all the news about Bharata and his doings, and return to me quickly."

46. Agreeing to do so, Hanuman assumed a human body. Then with the lightning speed of a Garuda attacking a serpent, he quickly proceeded to Nandigrama. **47.** Reaching Sringavera city on the way, Hanuman addressed Guha as follows with a joyous heart: **48.** "Your friend, Rama the son of Dasaratha and an embodiment of Dharma, along with Sita and Lakshmana, is abiding in a happy condition. They convey their kind enquiries to you. **49.** Permitted by the sage Bharadwaja, Rama will soon arrive at your place and he will meet you." **50.** The resplendent Hanuman said so with great joy indicated by horripilations on his body. Then that mighty one leapt away at great speed.

51. Travelling with high velocity through the sky, Hanuman passed the lake of Parasurama and the river Sarayu and arrived at Nandigrama. **(52-55).** At Nandigrama, a Krosa (four miles) away from Ayodhya, he saw Bharata. He had put on a small piece of bark-cloth and a skin of black antelope. With his hair matted and dressed in tree-

मलपङ्कविदिग्धाङ्गं जटिलं वल्कलाम्बरम् । फलमूलकृताहारं रामचिन्तापरायणम् ॥ 53

पादुके ते पुरस्कृत्य शासयन्तं वसुन्धराम् । मन्त्रिभिःपौरमुख्यैश्चकाषायाम्बरधारिभिः ॥ 54

वृतदेहं मूर्तिमन्तं साक्षाद्धर्ममिव स्थितम् । उवाच प्राञ्जलिर्वाक्यं हनूमान्मारुतात्मजः ॥ 55

यं त्वं चिन्तयसे रामं तापसं दण्डके स्थितम् । अनुशोचसि काकुत्स्थः स त्वां कुशलमब्रवीत् ॥ 56

प्रियमाख्यामि ते देव शोकं त्यज सुदारुणम् । अस्मिन्मुहूर्ते भ्रात्रा त्वं रामेण सह सङ्गतः ॥ 57

समरे रावणं हत्वा रामः सीतामवाप्य च । उपयाति समृद्धार्थः ससीतः सहलक्ष्मणः ॥ 58

एवमुक्तो महातेजा भरतो हर्षमूर्च्छितः । पपात भुवि चास्वस्थः कैकेयीप्रियनन्दनः ॥ 59

आलिङ्ग्य भरतः शीघ्रं मारुतिं प्रियवादिनम् । आनन्दजैरश्रुजलैः सिषेच भरतः कपिम् ॥ 60

देवो वा मानुषो वा त्वमनुक्रोशादिहागतः । प्रियाख्यानस्य ते सौम्य ददामि ब्रुवतः प्रियम् ॥ 61

गवां शतसहस्रं च ग्रामाणां च शतं वरम् । सर्वाभरणसम्पन्ना मुग्धाः कन्यास्तु षोडश ॥ 62

एवमुक्त्वा पुनः प्राह भरतो मारुतात्मजम् । बहूनीमानि वर्षाणि गतस्य सुमहद्वनम् ॥ 63

शृणोम्यहं प्रीतिकरं मम नाथस्य कीर्तनम् ॥ 64

bark cloth, he was subsisting on roots and fruits, and constantly thinking of Rama. With Rama's sandals kept in front as a token of his presence, he was governing the country on Rama's behalf. He was surrounded by ministers and chief citizens, who were all dressed in ochre clothes. Seeing him, who looked like the embodiment of Dharma, Hanuman said with palms joined in salutation: **56.** "With a sorrowful heart you are thinking of Rama as living in the Dandaka forest as an ascetic—that Rama is now making enquiries about you. **57.** O noble one! I shall now tell you what is very dear to you. Abandon your intense sorrow. Soon would you be able to meet your brother Rama. **58.** Having killed Ravana and rescued Sita and thus achieved his purpose, Rama has reached the neighbourhood, along with Sita and Lakshmana."

59. This happy news filled the mind of the mighty Bharata with such intense delight that he swooned and fell on the ground. **60.** Reviving soon, Bharata embraced Hanuman who had brought him the joyful news, and literally drenched him with his tears of joy. **61.** He said, "You who have come here out of mercy—are you a Deva or a man? I shall grant a boon to you who have brought this joyous news to me. **62.** I shall give you as a reward a hundred thousand cows, a hundred villages and sixteen beautiful girls decorated with every kind of ornament." **(63-64).** Bharata continued, "It's long since my lord Rama has gone to live in the deep regions of the forest. It is only now I am getting some happy news about him. **65.** If a man lives for a hundred years, he will in the course of that have some joyous experiences—this common

कल्याणी बत गाथेयं लौकिकी प्रतिभाति मे । एति जीवन्तमानन्दो नरं वर्षशतादपि ॥ 65

राघवस्य हरीणां च कथमासीत्समागमः । तत्त्वमाख्याहि भद्रं ते विश्वसेयं वचस्तव ॥ 66

एवमुक्तोऽथ हनुमान् भरतेन महात्मना । आचचक्षेऽथ रामस्य चरितं कृत्स्नशः क्रमात् ॥67

श्रुत्वा तु परमानन्दं भरतो मारुतात्मजात् । आज्ञापयच्छत्रुहणं मुदा युक्तं मुदान्वितः ॥68

दैवतानि च यावन्ति नगरे रघुनन्दन । नानोपहारबलिभिः पूजयन्तु महाधियः ॥ 69

सूता वैतालिकाश्चैव वन्दिनः स्तुतिपाठकाः । वारमुख्याश्च शतशो निर्यान्त्वद्यैव सङ्घशः ।
राजदारास्तथामात्याः सेना हस्त्यश्वपत्तयः ॥ 70

ब्राह्मणाश्च तथा पौरा राजानो ये समागताः । निर्यान्तु राघवस्याद्य द्रष्टुं शशिनिभाननम् ॥ 71

भरतस्य वचः श्रुत्वा शत्रुघ्नपरिचोदिताः । अलञ्चक्रुश्च नगरीं मुक्तारत्नमयोज्ज्वलैः ॥ 72

तोरणैश्च पताकाभिर्विचित्राभिरनेकधा । अलङ्कुर्वन्ति वेश्मानि नानावलिविचक्षणाः ॥ 73

निर्यान्ति वृन्दशः सर्वे रामदर्शनलालसाः । हयानां शतसाहस्रं गजानामयुतं तथा ॥ 74

रथानां दशसाहस्रं स्वर्णसूत्रविभूषितम् । पारमेष्ठीन्युपादाय द्रव्याण्युच्चावचानि च ॥ 75

ततस्तु शिबिकारूढा निर्ययू राजयोषितः । भरतः पादुके न्यस्य शिरस्येव कृताञ्जलिः ॥ 76
शत्रुघ्नसहितो रामं पादचारेण निर्ययौ ॥ 77

saying seems to have become true with regard to me. **66.** How did Rama come to have an alliance with the monkeys? Tell me the truth about it. I shall believe your words." **67.** On being thus questioned by high-minded Bharata, Hanuman narrated the incidents of Rama's story one after another. **68.** With great joy he heard the narration of Hanuman and then jubilantly called Satrughna and said:

Bharata goes to meet Rama (69-100)

69. "O scion of Raghu's line! Let worship and offerings of every kind be done in every temple in the city without an exception. **70.** Let a large group consisting of panegyrists, bards, musicians and dancing girls proceed immediately. **71.** Let the royal ladies, ministers, the Brahmanas, the leading citizens and the tributary princes proceed to see the moon-like face of Rama." **(72-75)** Hearing Bharata's words, Satrughna ordered the city to be decorated with pearls and jewels, with buntings, flags and with all other kinds of decorations. Houses were decorated by people who were experts in that art. All who were eager to see Rama now started in a body. That group consisted of a hundred thousand horses, a thousand elephants and ten thousand chariots with golden decorations. The people following were all carrying objects fit for presentation to royalty. **76.** Following this group were the royal ladies in palanquins. **77.** Bharata walked on foot along with Satrughna, himself carrying the sandals of

तदैव दृश्यते दूराद्विमानं चन्द्रसन्निभम् । पुष्पकं सूर्यसङ्काशं मनसा ब्रह्मनिर्मितम् ॥ 78
एतस्मिन् भ्रातरौ वीरौ वैदेह्या रामलक्ष्मणौ ।
सुग्रीवश्च कपिश्रेष्ठो मन्त्रिभिश्च विभीषणः । दृश्यते पश्यत जना इत्याह पवनात्मजः ॥ 79
ततो हर्षसमुद्भूतो निःस्वनो दिवमस्पृशत् । स्त्रीबालयुववृद्धानां रामोऽयमिति कीर्तनात् ॥ 80
रथकुञ्जरवाजिस्था अवतीर्य महीं गताः । ददृशुस्ते विमानस्थं जनाः सोममिवाम्बरे ॥ 81
प्राञ्जलिर्भरतो भूत्वा प्रहृष्टो राघवोन्मुखः ॥ 82
ततो विमानाग्रगतं भरतो राघवं मुदा । ववन्दे प्रणतो रामं मेरुस्थमिव भास्करम् ॥ 83
ततो रामाभ्यनुज्ञातं विमानमपतद्भुवि ।
आरोपितो विमानं तद्भरतः सानुजस्तदा । राममासाद्य मुदितः पुनरेवाभ्यवादयत् ॥ 84
समुत्थाप्य चिराद्दृष्टं भरतं रघुनन्दनः । भ्रातरं स्वाङ्कमारोप्य मुदा तं परिषस्वजे ॥ 85
ततो लक्ष्मणमासाद्य वैदेहीं नाम कीर्तयन् । अभ्यवादयत प्रीतो भरतः प्रेमविह्वलः ॥ 86
सुग्रीवं जाम्बवन्तं च युवराजं तथाङ्गदम् । मैन्दद्विविदनीलांश्च ऋषभं चैव सस्वजे ॥
सुषेणं च नलं चैव गवाक्षं गन्धमादनम् । शरभं पनसं चैव भरतः परिषस्वजे ॥ 87
सर्वे ते मानुषं रूपं कृत्वा भरतमादृताः । पप्रच्छुः कुशलं सौम्याः प्रहृष्टाश्च प्लवङ्गमाः । 88

Rama on his head and with his hands joined in salutation.

78. At a distance he saw the aerial vehicle Pushpaka, built by Brahma by an act of will, shining like the sun and the moon. **79.** Now Hanuman said, "In that Pushpaka, you will see the heroic Rama and Lakshmana along with Sita as also Sugreeva, the king of the monkeys and Vibheeshana with his ministers." **80.** Then the sky was filled with the joyous exclamations of that concourse of men and women, young and old: "O here is our Rama! O here is our Rama!" **(81-82).** Those who were riding in chariots or on the backs of elephants and horses got down and walked. They saw Rama seated in the Pushpaka Vimana just like the moon in the sky. In great joy they all saluted him with joined palms. **83.** Next the joyous Bharata made prostrations to Rama seated in the Vimana just like the sun on the mountain Meru. **84.** Now, commanded by Rama, the aerial vehicle touched the earth. Bharata along with his brother Satrughna entered into it with great joy and made prostrations once again. **85.** Rama who was meeting his brother Bharata after a long time, seated him in his lap and embraced him in great joy. **86.** Next Bharata approached Lakshmana and Sita, and announcing his presence by name, saluted them. **87.** Bharata then embraced Sugreeva, Jambavan, the heir apparent Angada, Mainda, Dvivida, Neela, Rishabha, Sushena; Nala, Gavaksha, Gandhamadana, Sarabha and Panasa. **88.** All these monkeys, being capable of taking any form, assumed the appearance of men and received Bharata.

ततः सुग्रीवमालिङ्ग्य भरतः प्राह भक्तितः । त्वत्सहायेन रामस्य जयोऽभूद्रावणो हतः ॥ 89

त्वमस्माकं चतुर्णां तु भ्राता सुग्रीव पञ्चमः । शत्रुघ्नश्च तदा राममभिवाद्य सलक्ष्मणम् ॥ 90

सीतायाश्चरणौ पश्चाद्ववन्दे विनयान्वितः । रामो मातरमासाद्य विवर्णां शोकविह्वलाम् ॥ 91

जग्राह प्रणतः पादौ मनो मातुः प्रसादयन् ॥ 92

कैकेयीं च सुमित्रां च ननामेतरमातरौ । भरतः पादुके ते तु राघवस्य सुपूजिते ॥ 93

योजयामास रामस्य पादयोर्भक्तिसंयुतः । राज्यमेतन्न्यासभूतं मया निर्यातितं तव ॥ 94

अद्य मे सफलं जन्म फलितो मे मनोरथः । यत्पश्यामि समायातमयोध्यां त्वामहं प्रभो ॥ 95

कोष्ठागारं बलं कोशं कृतं दशगुणं मया । त्वत्तेजसा जगन्नाथ पालयस्व पुरं स्वकम् ॥ 96

इति ब्रुवाणं भरतं दृष्ट्वा सर्वे कपीश्वराः । मुमुचुर्नेत्रजं तोयं प्रशशंसुर्मुदान्विताः ॥ 97

ततो रामः प्रहृष्टात्मा भरतं स्वाङ्कगं मुदा । ययौ तेन विमानेन भरतस्याश्रमं तदा ॥ 98

अवरुह्य तदा रामो विमानाग्र्यान्महीतलम् ।

अब्रवीत्पुष्पकं देवो गच्छ वैश्रवणं वह । अनुगच्छानुजानामि कुबेरं धनपालकम् ॥ 99

Versed in good conduct, they made enquiries about Bharata's welfare in great joy. **(89-92).** Then Bharata said respectfully addressing Sugreeva, after embracing him, "With your help, Rama has been victorious and has destroyed Ravana. So, you, O Sugreeva, are a fifth brother to us four." Now in all humility, Satrughna made prostrations to Rama and Lakshmana and after that to Sita also. Then Rama went to his mother who had become lean and pale on account of sorrow. Producing great joy in her mind, he saluted her, touching her feet. **(93-95).** Rama then saluted his other mothers Kaikeyi and Sumitra. Bharata now put on Rama's feet that pair of sandels of his, which he had been worshipping with great devotion till now. He said, "The kingdom that you entrusted to me, I am now restoring to you herewith. O Lord! I have attained the highest fulfilment of my life in seeing you return to Ayodhya. My aspirations have been fulfilled. **96.** The granary, the army, the treasury, and other limbs of the State that you had entrusted to me have, by your grace, now grown tenfold. Now, O Lord, govern your kingdom." **97.** Hearing these words of Bharata, all the monkey leaders shed tears and in great joy praised Bharata. **98.** Then Rama in a mood of great joy seated Bharata in his lap and proceeded to Bharata's Ashrama in that aerial vehicle. **99.** Then Rama got down to the ground from that aerial vehicle and addressed it thus, "Now I give you permission to go. You can be at the service of Kubera, the son of Visravas and the lord of wealth."

रामो वसिष्ठस्य गुरोः पदाम्बुजं नत्वा यथा देवगुरोः शतक्रतुः ।
दत्त्वा महार्हासनमुत्तमं गुरो-रुपाविवेशाथ गुरोः समीपतः ॥ 100

इति श्रीमदध्यात्मरामायणे उमामहेश्वरसंवादे
युद्धकाण्डे चतुर्दशः सर्गः ॥ १४ ॥

100. Rama then saluted the Guru of his family, Vasishta, just as Indra salutes the Guru of the Devas. He offered an honoured seat to the Guru and sat by his side.

पञ्चदशः सर्गः

श्रीमहादेव उवाच

ततस्तु कैकयीपुत्रो भरतो भक्तिसंयुतः । शिरस्यञ्जलिमाधाय ज्येष्ठं भ्रातरमब्रवीत् ॥ 1
माता मे सत्कृता राम दत्तं राज्यं त्वया मम । ददामि तत्ते च पुनर्यथा त्वमददा मम ॥ 2
इत्युक्त्वा पादयोर्भक्त्या साष्टाङ्गं प्रणिपत्य च । बहुधा प्रार्थयामास कैकेय्या गुरुणा सह ॥ 3
तथेति प्रतिजग्राह भरताद्राज्यमीश्वरः । मायामाश्रित्य सकलां नरचेष्टामुपागतः ॥ 4
स्वाराज्यानुभवो यस्य सुखज्ञानैकरूपिणः । निरस्तातिशयानन्दरूपिणः परमात्मनः ॥ 5
मानुषेण तु राज्येन किं तस्य जगदीशितुः । यस्य भ्रूभङ्गमात्रेण त्रिलोकी नश्यति क्षणात् ॥ 6
यस्यानुग्रहमात्रेण भवन्त्याखण्डलश्रियः । लीलासृष्टमहासृष्टेः कियदेतद्रमापतेः ॥ 7

Chapter 15

RAMA'S CORONATION

Rama's entry into Ayodhya
(1-29)

1. Next Bharata, the son of Kaikeyi, spoke to his brother with great devotion joining his palms in salutation. **2.** He said, "O Rama! My mother Kaikeyi did a wrong to you. You bestowed the kingdom on me. In the same way I am giving it back to you." **3.** With these words, Bharata made a full prostration to Rama and along with his mother Kaikeyi, requested Rama many times to accept the kingdom. **4.** Rama, who was the Lord of all but followed all the ways of man, agreed to the proposal and received back the kingdom. **(5-7).** To him, the Supreme Soul and the Lord of all, who is ever immersed in His inherent Bliss-consciousness, whose Bliss transcends every other forms of joy—to Him, the Lord of all, of what account is the attainment of the worldly kingdom? He, by the movement of whose brows, all the three worlds get destoyed, He by whose blessing all the glory and wealth up to that of Indra are obtained, He who out of sport creates this world—for that Lord of Ramā,

तथापि भजतां नित्यं कामपूरविधित्सया । लीलामानुषदेहेन सर्वमप्यनुवर्तते ॥ 8

ततः शत्रुघ्नवचनान्निपुणः श्मश्रुकृन्तकः । सम्भाराश्चाभिषेकार्थमानीता राघवस्य हि ॥ 9

पूर्वं तु भरते स्नाते लक्ष्मणे च महात्मनि । सुग्रीवे वानरेन्द्रे च राक्षसेन्द्रे विभीषणे ॥ 10

विशोधितजटः स्नातश्चित्रमाल्यानुलेपनः । महार्हवसनोपेतस्तस्थौ तत्र श्रिया ज्वलन् ॥ 11

प्रतिकर्म च रामस्य लक्ष्मणश्च महामतिः । कारयामास भरतः सीताया राजयोषितः ॥ 12

महार्हवस्त्राभरणैरलञ्चक्रुः सुमध्यमाम् । ततो वानरपत्नीनां सर्वासामेव शोभना ॥ 13

अकारयत कौसल्या प्रहृष्टा पुत्रवत्सला ॥ 14

ततः स्यन्दनमादाय शत्रुघ्नवचनात्सुधीः ।

सुमन्त्रः सूर्यसंकाशं योजयित्वाग्रतः स्थितः । आरुरोह रथं रामः सत्यधर्मपरायणः ॥ 15

सुग्रीवो युवराजश्च हनूमांश्च विभीषणः । स्नात्वा दिव्याम्बरधरा दिव्याभरणभूषिताः । 16

राममन्वीयुरग्रे च रथाश्वगजवाहनाः । सुग्रीवपत्न्यः सीता च ययुर्यानैः पुरं महत् ॥ 17

वज्रपाणिर्यथा देवैर्हरिताश्वरथे स्थितः । प्रययौ रथमास्थाय तथा रामो महत्पुरम् ॥ 18

सारथ्यं भरतश्चक्रे रत्नदण्डं महाद्युतिः । श्वेतातपत्रं शत्रुघ्नो लक्ष्मणो व्यजनं दधे ॥

of what account is this worldly kingdom? **8.** Still in order to fulfil the aspirations of all those who worship Him, he has assumed this human form and has been following all these human ways.

9. Next, at the order of Satrughna, skilled barbers came and attended on Rama. All the ingredients for the coronation were also gathered. **(10-11).** After the removal of their hairs, Bharata, the high-souled Lakshmana, Sugreeva the king of the monkeys, and the Rakshasa Vibheeshana had their baths. Next with his matted locks shaven off, Rama finished his bath, and decorated with beautiful garlands and anointed with fragrant unguents and dressed in costly robes, stood there resplendent. **(12-13).** The high-souled Bharata himself attended to the decoration of Rama and Lakshmana. **14.** The royal women dressed and adorned the beautiful Sita. The good-natured and affectionate Kausalya attended in great joy to the decoration of the wives of the monkeys. **15.** By this time according to the orders of Satrughna, Sumantra had got ready a chariot shining like the sun. **(16-17).** Rama devoted to Truth and Dharma now sat in that chariot. Sugreeva, Angada, Hanuman, Vibheeshana and others, after bath and decoration with ornaments and costly dress, preceded and followed Rama in chariots and on the backs of horses and elephants. Sita and the wives of Sugreeva followed in palanquins. **18.** Just as Indra travels in his chariot to which are yoked green-coloured horses, Rama now travelled to the great city in his chariot. **19.** Then at a certain stage

चामरं च समीपस्थो न्यवीजयदरिन्दमः । शशिप्रकाशं त्वपरं जग्राहासुरनायकः ॥ 20

दिविजैः सिद्धसङ्घैश्च ऋषिभिर्दिव्यदर्शनैः । स्तूयमानस्य रामस्य शुश्रुवे मधुरध्वनिः ॥ 21

मानुषं रूपमास्थाय वानरा गजवाहनाः । भेरीशङ्खनिनादैश्च मृदङ्गपणवानकैः ॥ 22

प्रययौ राघवश्रेष्ठस्तां पुरीं समलङ्कृताम् ॥ 23

ददृशुस्ते समायान्तं राघवं पुरवासिनः ।

दूर्वादलश्यामतनुं महार्हकिरीटरत्नाभरणाञ्चिताङ्गम् ।
आरक्तकञ्जायतलोचनान्तं दृष्ट्वा ययुर्मोदमतीव पुण्याः ॥ 24

विचित्ररत्नाञ्चितसूत्रनद्धपीताम्बरं पीनभुजान्तरालम् ।
अनर्घ्यमुक्ताफलदिव्यहारैर्विरोचमान रघुनन्दनं प्रजाः ॥ 25

सुग्रीवमुख्यैर्हरिभिः प्रशान्तैर्निषेव्यमाणं रवितुल्यभासम् ।
कस्तूरिकाचन्दनलिप्तगात्रं निवीतकल्पद्रुमपुष्पमालम् ॥ 26

श्रुत्वा स्त्रियो राममुपागतं मुदा प्रहर्षवेगोत्कलितानननश्रियः ।
अपास्य सर्वं गृहकार्यमाहितं हर्म्याणि चैवारुरुहुः स्वलङ्कृताः ॥ 27

of the procession, majestic Bharata officiated as the charioteer, Satrughna held the white royal umbrella with golden handle and Lakshmana held the peacock-feathered fans. **20.** Standing near-by, Sugreeva waved the white chauri fan while Vibheeshana held another in his hand. **21.** In the sky was heard the sweet sound of praises the Devas, Siddhas and holy Rishis were singing in honour of Rama. **(22-23).** The monkeys in human form rode on elephants to the accompaniment of sounds of kettledrums, conchs, Mridanga, Panava and Anaka. Rama, the eldest of Raghu's line, now entered the beautifully decorated city of Ayodhya. **24.** The citizens rejoiced to see the arrival of Rama, who was of blue-complexion like a blade of Durva grass, who was decorated with an imposing diadem and jewels, and who had lotus-like eyes tinged slightly red. **25.** The citizens saw Rama, who wore a yellow cloth held in position by a golden belt studded with charming gems, and the interspace between whose powerful arms was adorned with priceless pearl necklaces. **26.** The citizens saw Rama, who was attended upon by famous and serene monkey leaders like Sugreeva, who was resplendent like the sun, on whose body was applied sandal paste mixed with Kasturi, and who was adorned with a garland made with the flowers of the Kalpaka tree. **27.** On hearing about Rama's arrival, the womenfolk, with their faces bright with enthusiasm, abandoned all their household work and took their positions, having decorated themselves well, on the high terraces of houses.

दृष्ट्वा हरिं सर्वदृगुत्सवाकृतिं पुष्पैः किरन्त्यः स्मितशोभिताननाः ।
दृग्भिः पुनर्नेत्रमनोरसायनं स्वानन्दमूर्तिं मनसाभिरेभिरे ॥ 28

रामः स्मितस्निग्धदृशा प्रजास्तथा पश्यन्प्रजानाथ इवापरः प्रभुः ।
शनैर्जगामाथ पितुः स्वलङ्कृतं गृहं महेन्द्रालयसन्निभं हरिः ॥ 29

प्रविश्य वेश्मान्तरसंस्थितो मुदा रामो ववन्दे चरणौ स्वमातुः ।
क्रमेण सर्वाः पितृयोषितः प्रभुर्ननाम भक्त्या रघुवंशकेतुः ॥ 30

ततो भरतमाहेदं रामः सत्यपराक्रमः । सर्वसम्पत्समायुक्तं मम मन्दिरमुत्तमम् ॥ 31

मित्राय वानरेन्द्राय सुग्रीवाय प्रदीयताम् । सर्वेभ्यः सुखवासार्थं मन्दिराणि प्रकल्पय ॥ 32

रामेणैवं समादिष्टो भरतश्च तथाकरोत् । उवाच च महातेजाः सुग्रीवं राघवानुजः ॥ 33

राघवस्याभिषेकार्थं चतुःसिन्धुजलं शुभम् । आनेतुं प्रेषयस्वाशु दूतांस्त्वरितविक्रमान् ॥ 34

प्रेषयामास सुग्रीवो जाम्बवन्तं मरुत्सुतम् । अङ्गदं च सुषेणं च ते गत्वा वायुवेगतः ॥ 35

जलपूर्णान् शातकुम्भकलशांश्च समानयन् ॥ 36

आनीतं तीर्थसलिलं शत्रुघ्नो मन्त्रिभिः सह । राघवस्याभिषेकार्थं वसिष्ठाय न्यवेदयत् ॥ 37

28. Producing great delight in the mind, they drank, as it were, with their eyes the form of Hari, which was a delight for the eyes to see. With smiling and bright faces, they showered flowers on him. **29.** Rama, who was none but the Supreme Hari, moved like another Brahma Himself, and with a smiling face cast his benevolent glances on his subjects. Moving forward with unhurried steps he entered the well-decorated palace of his father, which resembled the very abode of Indra.

Coronation of Rama (30-45)

30. Moving into the inner apartments of the palace, the lordly Rama made prostrations at the feet of his mother with great delight. Then he made prostrations also to the other wives of his father. **(31-32).** Then Rama, noted for his righteousness, addressing Bharata said, "Provide for the residence of my friend Sugreeva, the king of the monkeys, my great palace furnished with all luxuries. Next provide houses for the comfortable stay of all the others." **33.** On being so instructed, Bharata did accordingly. Bharata of majestic countenance said to Sugreeva: **34.** "For the ceremonial cornonation-bath of Rama, please despatch some fast messengers to fetch water from all the four oceans." **(35-36).** Sugreeva thereupon despatched Jambavan, Hanuman, Angada and Sushena on this errand. They travelled fast like wind and soon brought water from the oceans in golden pots.

37. Satrughna along with the ministers,

ततस्तु प्रयतो वृद्धो वसिष्ठो ब्राह्मणैः सह । रामं रत्नमये पीठे ससीतं संन्यवेशयत् ॥38
वसिष्ठो वामदेवश्च जावालिर्गौतमस्तथा । वाल्मीकिश्च तथा चक्रुः सर्वे रामाभिषेचनम् ॥39
कुशाग्रतुलसीयुक्तपुण्यगन्धजलैर्मुदा ।
अभ्यषिञ्चन् रघुश्रेष्ठं वासवं वसवो यथा । ऋत्विग्भिर्ब्राह्मणैः श्रेष्ठैः कन्याभिः सह मन्त्रिभिः ॥
सर्वौषधिरसैश्चैव दैवतैर्नभसि स्थितैः । चतुर्भिर्लोकपालैश्च स्तुवद्भिः सगणैस्तथा ॥ 41
छत्रं च तस्य जग्राह शत्रुघ्नः पाण्डुरं शुभम् । सुग्रीवराक्षसेन्द्रौ तौ दधतुः श्वेतचामरे ॥ 42
मालां च काञ्चनीं वायुर्ददौ वासवचोदितः । सर्वरत्नसमायुक्तं मणिकाञ्चनभूषितम् ॥ 43
ददौ हारं नरेन्द्राय स्वयं शक्रस्तु भक्तितः । प्रजगुर्देवगन्धर्वा ननृतुश्चाप्सरोगणाः ॥ 44
देवदुन्दुभयो नेदुः पुष्पवृष्टिः पपात खात् ॥ 45
नवदूर्वादलश्यामं पद्मपत्रायतेक्षणम् । रविकोटिप्रभायुक्तकिरीटेन विराजितम् ॥ 46

took the water thus brought to the royal priest Vasishtha. **(38-39).** Then the aged and devoted Vasishtha along with the other Brahmanas seated Rama on a golden pedestal studded with gems. The ceremonial bath was administered by a group of sages consisting of Vasishtha, Vamadeva, Jabali, Gautama and Valmiki. **(40-41).** They bathed Rama of Raghu's line, as the Vasus bathed Indra, with water fragrant with Tulasi, Kusa grass and flower essences and the juice of various kinds of herbs, while there stood in attendance Rishis, sacrificial priests, highminded Brahmanas, the ministers and virgins. From the sky above, the Devas and the Deities of the quarters and their attendants sang his praises and witnessed the ceremonial bath. **42.** Satrughna held over him the white royal umbrella, while Sugreeva and Vibheeshana held the Chowri fans in hands. **(43-45).** Prompted by Indra, the Wind-god presented a necklace of gold, while Indra himself came in person and presented to Rama, with great devotion, another necklace studded with all kinds of gems and golden embellishments. The Gandharvas sang and groups of Apsaras danced. The kettle-drums of Devas then sounded and showers of flowers poured down from the sky.

(46-50). There sat Rama, who was blue in complexion like fresh Durva grass, who had eyes large like lotus petals, who was adorned with a crown brilliant like a crore of suns, whose beauty excelled that of a crore of Cupids, who was dressed in yellow silk, decorated with divine ornaments and anointed with highly fragrant unguents, who was resplendent like a thousand suns, who was two-armed, and on whose left side was seated Sita of golden complexion and lotus-like arms and adorned with all ornaments. She was on his left lap, held by his left arm. Seeing this form of Rama more resplendent than anything else, Siva along with Uma and all

कोटिकन्दर्पलावण्यं पीताम्बरसमावृतम् । दिव्याभरणसम्पन्नं दिव्यचन्दनलेपनम् ॥ 47

अयुतादित्यसङ्काशं द्विभुजं रघुनन्दनम् । वामभागे समासीनां सीतां काञ्चनसन्निभाम् ॥ 48

सर्वाभरणसम्पन्नां वामाङ्के समुपस्थिताम् । रक्तोत्पलकराम्भोजां वामेनालिङ्ग्य संस्थितम् ॥

सर्वातिशयशोभाढ्यं दृष्ट्वा भक्तिसमन्वितः ।

उमया सहितो देवः शङ्करो रघुनन्दनम् । सर्वदेवगणैर्युक्तः स्तोतुं समुपचक्रमे ॥ 50

श्रीमहादेव उवाच

नमोऽस्तु रामाय सशक्तिकाय नीलोत्पलश्यामलकोमलाय ।
किरीटहाराङ्गदभूषणाय सिंहासनस्थाय महाप्रभाय ॥ 51

त्वमादिमध्यान्तविहीन एकः सृजस्यवस्यत्सि च लोकजातम् ।
स्वमायया तेन न लिप्यसे त्वं यत्स्वे सुखेऽजस्ररतोऽनवद्यः ॥ 52

लीलां विधत्से गुणसंवृतस्त्वं प्रपन्नभक्तानुविधानहेतोः ।
नानावतारैः सुरमानुषाद्यैः प्रतीयसे ज्ञानिभिरेव नित्यम् ॥ 53

स्वांशेन लोकं सकलं विधाय तं बिभर्षि च त्वं तदधः फणीश्वरः ।
उपर्यधो भान्वनिलोडुपौषधिप्रवर्षरूपोऽवसि नैकधा जगत् ॥ 54

त्वमिह देहभृतां शिखिरूपः पचसि भुक्तमशेषमजस्रम् ॥
पवनपञ्चकरूपसहायो जगदखण्डमनेन बिभर्षि ॥ 55

the Devas came forward in great devotion and addressed a hymn of praise to him.

Hymn of Siva (51-63)

51. Mahadeva said, "Salutation to Thee, the luminous Being in the company of Thy Sakti, who art handsome like a blue lotus, who art bedecked with a diadem, necklaces and armlets, and who art seated on a throne. **52.** O Lord of the worlds! Thou art the one Unitary Being without a beginning, middle and end. With Thy Maya, Thou dost create, protect and destroy this universe. But being ever immersed in Thy inherent Bliss, Thou art not affected by any of these actions. **53.** Assuming the Gunas of Prakriti, Thou, for the blessing of devotees who have taken shelter in Thee, manifestest as many incarnations among Devas, men and the like, and thus sportest in this world. Only the knowing ones ever understand this. **54.** Thou createst the whole of this universe through Brahma, who is only a part of Thyself. At the base of the universe, Thou bearest it in the form of Adisesha. Thou manifestest in this universe above and below in many forms as the sun, wind, moon, vegetation and clouds. **55.**

चन्द्रसूर्यशिखिमध्यगतं यत् तेज ईश चिदशेषतनूनाम् ।
प्राभवत्तनुभृतामिव धैर्यं शौर्यमायुरखिलं तव सत्त्वम् ॥ 56

त्वं विरिञ्चिशिवविष्णुविभेदात् कालकर्मशशिसूर्यविभागात् ।
वादिनां पृथगिवेश विभासि ब्रह्म निश्चितमनन्यदिहैकम् ॥ 57

मत्स्यादिरूपेण यथा त्वमेकः श्रुतो पुराणेषु च लोकसिद्धः ।
तथैव सर्वं सदसद्विभागस्त्वमेव नान्यद्भवतो विभाति ॥ 58

यद्यत्समुत्पन्नमनन्तसृष्टावुत्पत्स्यते यच्च भवच्च यच्च ।
न दृश्यते स्थावरजङ्गमादौ त्वया विनातः परतः परस्त्वम् ॥ 59

तत्त्वं न जानन्ति परात्मनस्ते जनाः समस्तास्तव माययातः ।
त्वद्भक्तसेवामलमानसानां विभाति तत्त्वं परमेकमैशम् ॥ 60

ब्रह्मादयस्ते न विदुः स्वरूपं चिदात्मतत्त्वं बहिरर्थभावाः ।
ततो बुधस्त्वामिदमेव रूपं भक्त्या भजन्मुक्तिमुपैत्यदुःखः ॥ 61

अहं भवन्नाम गृणन्कृतार्थो वसामि काश्यामनिशं भवान्या ।
मुमूर्षमाणस्य विमुक्तयेऽहं दिशामि मन्त्रं तव राम नाम ॥ 62

In the bodies of embodied beings, Thou art present as digestive fire, and manifesting in five forms, Thou digestest all things eaten. Thus dost Thou support this world. **56.** O Lord! Out of Thy prowess alone have come out all energies—energies manifest in the moon, sun and fire, the vitality in all living beings, as also the strength, courage and longevity found in them. **57.** O Lord! The Logicians speak of Thee in different ways as Brahma, Siva and Vishnu, and as Time, Karma, moon, sun etc. But this diversity posed by Logicians has no substance in it, as there is no existence other than Thee, the one Supreme Brahman. **58.** In the Vedas and in the Puranas, Thou, the only Existence, art spoken of as incarnating as fish, etc .In the same way, all that is considered cause and effect art Thyself. There is nothing separate from Thee. **59.** In this infinitely diverse creation, whatever existed before, whatever would exist hereafter and whatever exists now — all these moving and unmoving beings have no existence apart from Thee. Thou art therefore the transcendent Being. **60.** Because of Thy Maya, people do not understand Thy real nature. Only those whose minds have been purified by the service of Thy devotees, understand the supreme truth about Thee as the unitary Existence. **61.** As their minds are outwardgoing, all beings from Brahma down, do not understand Thy Supreme spiritual nature as the Truth of the Atman. So wise persons worship Thee in this form with devotion, and freed from all sorrow, attain to liberation. **62.** O Rama! I

इमं स्तवं नित्यमनन्यभक्त्या शृण्वन्ति गायन्ति लिखन्ति ये वै ।
ते सर्वसौख्यं परमं च लब्ध्वा भवत्पदं यान्तु भवप्रसादात् ॥ 63

इन्द्र उवाच

रक्षोऽधिपेनाखिलदेवसौख्यं हृतं च मे ब्रह्मवरेण देव ।
पुनश्च सर्वं भवतः प्रसादात् प्राप्तं हतो राक्षसदुष्टशत्रुः ॥ 64

देवा ऊचुः

हृता यज्ञभागा धरादेवदत्ता मुरारे खलेनादिदैत्येन विष्णो ।
हतोऽद्य त्वया नो वितानेषु भागाः पुरावद्भविष्यन्ति युष्मत्प्रसादात् ॥ 65

पितर ऊचुः

हतोऽद्य त्वया दुष्टदैत्यो महात्मन् गयादौ नरैर्दत्तपिण्डादिकाश्च ।
बलादत्ति हत्वा गृहीत्वा समस्तानिदानीं पुनर्लब्धसत्त्वा भवामः ॥ 66

यक्षा ऊचुः

सदा विष्टिकर्मण्यनेनाभियुक्ता वहामो दशास्यं बलाद्दुःखयुक्ताः ।
दुरात्मा हतो रावणो राघवेश त्वया ते वयं दुःखजाताद्विमुक्ताः ॥ 67

who have attained my objective by repeating Thy name, stay along with Bhavani always at Kasi, and in order to liberate the dying Jivas, impart to them the Mantra consisting of Thy name. **63.** Whoever with deep devotion hears, chants or writes down this hymn every day—may they, by Thy grace, attain to all happiness in this world, and afterwards reach Thy Supreme Status."

Hymns of Indra and Others (64-75)

64. Indra said, "On the strength of the boons given by Brahma, the Lord of the Rakshasas deprived me of all the glorious enjoyments of the realm of the Devas. O Lord! By Thy grace, all that has been restored to me after the destruction of that evil enemy of a Rakshasa."

65. The Devas said: "O Vishnu, the destroyer of Mura! The evil-minded Ravana had deprived us of our share of sacrificial offerings made by twice-born ones. He has now been destroyed by Thee. By Thy grace, we shall have our share of sacrificial offerings as before."

66. The Pitris said: "O great one! By Thy grace, this cruel Rakshasa has been destroyed. He had, by his power, deprived us of the rice-offerings which men used to give us at Gaya and other places. Now we are in a position to get them again."

67. The Yakshas said: "This Rakshasa used by his power to engage us always in servile work, making us carry him. O Lord of the Raghus! By the destruction of this Ravana, thou hast liberated us from innumerable woes arising from servile work."

गन्धर्वा ऊचुः

वयं सङ्गीतनिपुणा गायन्तस्ते कथामृतम् । आनन्दामृतसन्दोहयुक्ताः पूर्णाः स्थिताः पुरा ॥68

पश्चाद्दुरात्मना राम रावणेनाभिविद्रुताः । तमेव गायमानाश्च तदाराधनतत्पराः ॥ 69

स्थितास्त्वया परित्राता हतोऽयं दुष्टराक्षसः । एवं महोरगाः सिद्धाः किन्नरा मरुतस्तथा ॥ 70

वसवो मुनयो गावो गुह्यकाश्च पतत्रिणः । सप्रजापतयश्चैते तथा चाप्सरसां गणाः ॥ 71

सर्वे रामं समासाद्य दृष्ट्वा नेत्रमहोत्सवम् । स्तुत्वा पृथक् पृथक् सर्वे राघवेणाभिवन्दिताः ॥72

ययुः स्वं स्वं पदं सर्वे ब्रह्मरुद्रादयस्तथा । प्रशंसन्तो मुदा रामं गायन्तस्तस्य चेष्टितम् ॥ 73

ध्यायन्तस्त्वभिषेकार्द्रं सीतालक्ष्मणसंयुतम् । सिंहासनस्थं राजेन्द्रं ययुः सर्वे हृदि स्थितम् ॥ 74

खे वाद्येषु ध्वनत्सु प्रमुदितहृदयैर्देववृन्दैः स्तुवद्भि-
र्वर्षद्भिः पुष्पवृष्टिं दिवि मुनिनिकरैरीड्यमानः समन्तात् ।
रामः श्यामः प्रसन्नस्मितरुचिरमुखः सूर्यकोटिप्रकाशः
सीतासौमित्रिवातात्मजमुनिहरिभिः सेव्यमानो विभाति ॥ 75

इति श्रीमदध्यात्मरामायणे उमामहेश्वरसंवादे
युद्धकाण्डे पञ्चदशः सर्गः ॥ १५ ॥

(68-69). Gandharvas said: "We who are versed in music, used to sing accounts of Thee and thereby get immersed in a sea of Bliss and live self-satisfied. Afterwards, this evil-minded Ravana deprived us of our status and making us his servants forced us to sing his praise. **(70-72).** We who were in that condition have been saved by Thee from the oppression of that evil-minded Rakshasa." Thus the great serpents, Siddhas, Kinnaras, Maruts, Vasus, Rishis, Gavas, Guhyakas, the celestial birds, Prajapatis, Apsaras and all other heavenly beings approached Rama, feasted their eyes on his form, praised him individually and were in turn honoured by him. **(73-74)** All of them, including Brahma and Rudra, then returned to their respective stations, praising Rama in great joy, singing about his achievements, and meditating in their hearts on him seated on the throne with Sita and accompanied by Lakshmana.

75. Amidst the sounds of celestial musical instruments and showers of flowers from the sky and the chanting of hymns by the Devas and Munis, Rama, of blue complexion, with a smiling face, and accompanied by Sita, Lakshmana, Hanuman and the monkeys, shone with the brilliance of a crore of suns.

षोडशः सर्गः

श्रीमहादेव उवाच

रामेऽभिषिक्ते राजेन्द्रे सर्वलोकसुखावहे । वसुधा सस्यसम्पन्ना फलवन्तो महीरुहाः ॥ 1
गन्धहीनानि पुष्पाणि गन्धवन्ति चकाशिरे । सहस्रशतमश्वानां धेनूनां च गवां तथा ॥ 2
ददौ शतवृषान्पूर्वं द्विजेभ्यो रघुनन्दनः ।
त्रिंशत्कोटि सुवर्णस्य ब्राह्मणेभ्यो ददौ पुनः । वस्त्राभरणरत्नानि ब्राह्मणेभ्यो मुदा तथा ॥ 3
सूर्यकान्तिसमप्रख्यां सर्वरत्नमयीं स्रजम् । सुग्रीवाय ददौ प्रीत्या राघवो भक्तवत्सलः ॥ 4
अङ्गदाय ददौ दिव्ये ह्यङ्गदे रघुनन्दनः । 5
चन्द्रकोटिप्रतीकाशं मणिरत्नविभूषितम् । सीतायै प्रददौ हारं प्रीत्या रघुकुलोत्तमः ॥ 6
अवमुच्यात्मनः कण्ठाद्धारं जनकनन्दिनी । अवैक्षत हरीन्सर्वान् भर्तारं च मुहुर्मुहुः ॥ 7
रामस्तामाह वैदेहीमिङ्गितज्ञो विलोकयन् । वैदेहि यस्य तुष्टासि देहि तस्मै वरानने ॥ 8
हनूमते ददौ हारं पश्यतो राघवस्य च । तेन हारेण शुशुभे मारुतिर्गौरवेण च ॥ 9
रामोऽपि मारुतिं दृष्ट्वा कृताञ्जलिमुपस्थितम् । भक्त्या परमया तुष्ट इदं वचनमब्रवीत् ॥ 10
हनूमंस्ते प्रसन्नोऽस्मि वरं वरय काङ्क्षितम् । दास्यामि देवैरपि यद्दुर्लभं भुवनत्रये ॥ 11

Chapter 16

CONCLUSION OF RAMAYANA

Leave-taking of All Allies (1-23)

1. When Rama, the giver of joy to all the worlds, was crowned, the earth began to abound in vegetation and fruit-bearing trees. **(2-3).** At the time of Rama's coronation, flowers that are not generally fragrant began to emit sweet smell. Rama first presented innumerable bulls, horses and cows to holy men. Afterwards he also gave them huge quantities of gold, clothes and jewels. **(4-5).** He presented to the devoted Sugreeva a necklace of gems brilliant like the sun. To Angada he presented two armlets of superior make. **6.** Then he presented Sita with a necklace of pearls and gems having the brilliance of a crore of moons. **7.** Sita took the necklace from her neck, and holding it in her hand, looked repeatedly at all the monkeys, and at her husband to know his mind. **8.** Rama, understanding what was in Sita's mind, looked at her and said, "O Sita! You can present it to whomever you are pleased to give." **9.** In the presence of all, she presented that necklace to Hanuman, who stood there resplendent with that necklace on his neck and with his imposing countenance.

10. Seeing Hanuman standing by with palms joined in great devotion, Rama said with great joy: **11.** "O Hanuman! I am extremely pleased with you. You ask from

हनूमानपि तं प्राह नत्वा रामं प्रहृष्टधीः । त्वन्नाम स्मरतो राम न तृप्यति मनो मम ।
अतस्त्वन्नाम सततं स्मरन् स्थास्यामि भूतले । 12
यावत्स्थास्यति ते नाम लोके तावत्कलेवरम् । मम तिष्ठतु राजेन्द्र वरोऽयं मेऽभिकाङ्क्षितः ॥ 13
रामस्तथेति तं प्राह मुक्तस्तिष्ठ यथासुखम् । कल्पान्ते मम सायुज्यं प्राप्स्यसे नात्र संशयः ॥ 14
तमाह जानकी प्रीता यत्र कुत्रापि मारुते । स्थितं त्वामनुयास्यन्ति भोगाः सर्वे ममाज्ञया ॥15
इत्युक्तो मारुतिस्ताभ्यामीश्वराभ्यां प्रहृष्टधीः । आनन्दाश्रुपरीताक्षो भूयो भूयः प्रणम्य तौ ।
कृच्छ्राद्ययौ तपस्तप्तुं हिमवन्तं महामतिः ॥ 16
ततो गुहं समासाद्य रामः प्राञ्जलिमब्रवीत् । सखे गच्छ पुरं रम्यं शृङ्गवेरमनुत्तमम् ॥ 17
मामेव चिन्तयन्नित्यं भुङ्क्ष्व भोगान्निजार्जितान् । अन्ते ममैव सारूप्यं प्राप्स्यसे त्वं न संशयः ॥18
इत्युक्त्वा प्रददौ तस्मै दिव्यान्याभरणानि च । राज्यं च विपुलं दत्त्वा विज्ञानं च ददौ विभुः ॥
रामेणालिङ्गितो हृष्टो ययौ स्वभवनं गुहः ॥ 19
ये चान्ये वानराः श्रेष्ठा अयोध्यां समुपागताः । अमूल्याभरणैर्वस्त्रैः पूजयामास राघवः ॥ 20
सुग्रीवप्रमुखाः सर्वे वानराः सविभीषणाः । यथार्हं पूजितास्तेन रामेण परमात्मना ॥ 21
प्रहृष्टमनसः सर्वे जग्मुरेव यथागतम् । सुग्रीवप्रमुखाः सर्वे किष्किन्धां प्रययुर्मुदा ॥ 22

me what you desire. I shall grant you that, be it something that is difficult even for Devas to obtain." **(12-13).** With a heart elated with joy, Hanuman saluted Rama and replied, "O Rama! I am never satisfied with repeating Thy name. Therefore, I wish to remain always on this earth repeating Thy name. May this body of mine remain so long as Thy name is remembered in this world. O great King! This is the boon that I desire." **14.** Rama replied, "Liberated you will remain in this world till the end of the Kalpa. At the time of the world's dissolution, you will attain to oneness with Me. There is no doubt about it."

15. Now Sita said to him, "By my blessing all enjoyable things of life will follow you wherever you are." **16.** Blessed in this way by those divine beings, Hanuman joyously saluted both of them again and again, and reluctantly left their presence for the region of the Himalayas for performing austerities.

17. Next Rama turned to Guha who was standing there saluting with joined palms and said, "O friend! You now go to the beautiful city of Sringavera. **18.** Always think of me. Enjoy the fruits of the Karmas of your past. In the end, you will attain to the salvation of Sarupya (of being like me)." **19.** With these words, Rama presented him with superior ornaments, extensive kingdom, and knowledge of the spiritual truth. Then, embraced by Rama, Guha went to his kingdom with a joyous mind.

20. Next Rama made presentations of rare ornaments and clothes to all the leading monkeys who had accompanied him to Ayodhya. **(21-22).** Now all the visitors, including Sugreeva and Vibheeshana, after being thus honoured by the Supreme Being

विभीषणस्तु सम्प्राप्य राज्यं निहतकण्टकम् । रामेण पूजितः प्रीत्या ययौ लङ्कामनिन्दितः ॥23
राघवो राज्यमखिलं शशासाखिलवत्सलः । अनिच्छन्नपि रामेण यौवराज्येऽभिषेचितः ।
लक्ष्मणः परया भक्त्या रामसेवापरोऽभवत् । 24
रामस्तु परमात्मापि कर्माध्यक्षोऽपि निर्मलः । कर्तृत्वादिविहीनोऽपि निर्विकारोऽपि सर्वदा ॥25
स्वानन्देनापि तुष्टः सन् लोकानामुपदेशकृत् । अश्वमेधादियज्ञैश्च सर्वैर्विपुलदक्षिणैः ।
अयजत्परमानन्दो मानुषं वपुराश्रितः । 26
न पर्यदेवन्विधवा न च व्यालकृतं भयम् । न व्याधिजं भयं चासीद्रामे राज्यं प्रशासति ॥27
लोके दस्युभयं नासीदनर्थो नास्ति कश्चन । वृद्धेषु सत्सु बालानां नासीन्मृत्युभयं तथा ।
रामपूजापराः सर्वे सर्वे राघवचिन्तकाः । 28
ववर्षुर्जलदास्तोयं यथाकालं यथारुचि । प्रजाः स्वधर्मनिरता वर्णाश्रमगुणान्विताः ॥ 29
औरसानिव रामोऽपि जुगोप पितृवत्प्रजाः । सर्वलक्षणसंयुक्तः सर्वधर्मपरायणः ।
दशवर्षसहस्राणि रामो राज्यमुपास्त सः ॥ 30
इदं रहस्यं धनधान्यऋद्धिमत्दीर्घायुरारोग्यकरं सुपुण्यदम् ।
पवित्रमाध्यात्मिकसंज्ञितं पुरा रामायणं भाषितमादिशम्भुना ॥ 31

Rama, returned to their respective places in great joy. Sugreeva went to Kishkindha. **23.** And as for Vibheeshana, after receiving all honours from Rama, he returned to rule over the kingdom of Lanka, which was now free from all enemies.

Rama's Rule (24-30)

24. Rama, who was the object of everyone's love, now ruled the kingdom, and Lakshmana, though he never desired it, was installed as the heir apparent. He continued to serve Rama devotedly. **(25-26)** Rama in reality is the Supreme Being, the witness of all activities, free from all blemishes, devoid of agency and similar limitations, ever unchanging, and always immersed in his inherent Bliss. Still having taken up a human form and the role of a teacher, he performed innumerable Yagas including Aswamedha, in which he distributed an enormous quantity of wealth as Dakshina. **27.** During Rama's rule, women were never widowed and had not to mourn for that reason. There was no fear from serpents nor from diseases. **28.** The world never suffered from the depredations of thieves and no disaster overtook the people. There was never the unfortunate situation of old men surviving, while the young and the children died. All were devoted to the thought and worship of Rama. **29.** The clouds rained in season and according to necessity. The subjects were all devoted to Dharma and to the rules and regulations of Varna and Ashrama. **30.** Rama looked

श्रृणोति भक्त्या मनुजः समाहितो भक्त्या पठेद्वा परितुष्टमानसः ।
सर्वाः समाप्नोति मनोगताशिषो विमुच्यते पातककोटिभिः क्षणात् ॥ 32
रामाभिषेकं प्रयतः शृणोति यो धनाभिलाषी लभते महद्धनम् ।
पुत्राभिलाषी सुतमार्यसम्मतं प्राप्नोति रामायणमादितः पठन् ॥ 33
शृणोति योऽध्यात्मिकरामसंहितां प्राप्नोति राजा भुवमृद्धसम्पदम् ।
शत्रून्विजित्यारिभिरप्रधर्षितो व्यपेतदुःखो विजयी भवेन्नृपः ॥ 34
स्त्रियोऽपि शृण्वन्त्यधिरामसंहितां भवन्ति ता जीविसुताश्च पूजिताः ।
वन्ध्यापि पुत्रं लभते सुरूपिणं कथामिमां भक्तियुता शृणोति या ॥ 35
श्रद्धान्वितो यः शृणुयात्पठेन्नरो विजित्य कोपं च तथा विमत्सरः ।
दुर्गाणि सर्वाणि विजित्य निर्भयो भवेत्सुखी राघवभक्तिसंयुतः ॥ 36
सुराः समस्ता अपि यान्ति तुष्टतां विघ्नाः समस्ता अपयान्ति शृण्वताम् ।
अध्यात्मरामायणमादितो नृणां भवन्ति सर्वा अपि सम्पदः पराः ॥ 37
रजस्वला वा यदि रामतत्परा शृणोति रामायणमेतदादितः ।
पुत्रं प्रसूते ऋषभं चिरायुषं पतिव्रता लोकसुपूजिता भवेत् ॥ 38
पूजयित्वा तु ये भक्त्या नमस्कुर्वन्ति नित्यशः । सर्वैः पापैर्विनिर्मुक्ता विष्णोर्यान्ति परं पदम् ॥ 39

upon his subjects as his own children and they considered him as their father. They were all devoted to Dharma. In this way Rama ruled over the country for ten thousand years.

Greatness of Ramayana (431-45)

31. It was Siva who gave out this holy and esoteric text, which is called Adhyatma Ramayana (spiritual version of Ramayana), the study of which bestows prosperity, long life and health. **32.** Whoever studies or hears this with a mind steady, devoted and spiritually elevated, will attain to all objects that he has got in his mind and will be free from his numerous sins. **33.** Whoever hears or studies this Ramayana from the beginning to the coronation of Rama, will attain to great wealth if he desires wealth, gain a virtuous son approved by noble-minded persons if he be one seeking an issue. **34.** If a king hears this Ramayana, he will attain great wealth, extensive land and kingdom, freedom from all sorrows and victory over all his enemies. **35.** This Adhyatma Ramayana can be heard also by women who want to have long-lived sons and gain the respect of all. A woman considered barren will bear an excellent son, if she hears it with devotion. **36.** Whoever studies this with faith and is free from anger and jealousy, will overcome all difficulties. With devotion for Rama in his heart, he will be free from fears and blessed with all happiness. **37.** All Devas will be pleased if a man hears this Adhyatma Ramayana from the beginning. He will overcome every obstruction in his way. He will attain to great prosperity. **38.** A

अध्यात्मरामचरितं कृत्स्नं शृण्वन्ति भक्तितः । पठन्ति वा स्वयं वक्त्रात् तेषां रामः प्रसीदति ॥ 40
राम एव परं ब्रह्म तस्मिंस्तुष्टेऽखिलात्मनि । धर्मार्थकाममोक्षाणां यद्यदिच्छति तद्भवेत् ॥ 41
श्रोतव्यं नियमेनैतद्रामायणमखण्डितम् । आयुष्यमारोग्यकरं कल्पकोटयघनाशनम् ॥ 42
देवाश्च सर्वे तुष्यन्ति ग्रहाः सर्वे महर्षयः । रामायाणस्य श्रवणे तृप्यन्ति पितरस्तथा ॥ 43

अध्यात्मरामायणमेदद्भुतं वैराग्यविज्ञानयुतं पुरातनम् ।
पठन्ति शृण्वन्ति लिखन्ति ये नरास्तेषां भवेऽस्मिन्न पुनर्भवो भवेत् ॥ 44

आलोड्याखिलवेदराशिमसकृद्यत्तारकं ब्रह्म त-
द्रामो विष्णुरहस्यमूर्तिरिति यो विज्ञाय भूतेश्वरः ।
उद् धृत्याखिलसारसङ्ग्रहमिदं संक्षेपतः प्रस्फुटं
श्रीरामस्य निगूढतत्त्वमखिलं प्राह प्रियायै भवः ॥ 44

इति श्रीमदध्यात्मरामायणे उमामहेश्वरसंवादे
युद्धकाण्डे षोडशः सर्गः ॥ १६ ॥

समाप्तमिदं युद्धकाण्डम् ।

श्रीरामचन्द्रार्पणमस्तु ॥

woman who after her period hears this Ramayana from the beginning with devotion, will give birth to a noble and longlived son, and she will gain the respect of all the world **39.** Whoever worships the text of Adhyatma Ramayana (along with the study of it) and makes prostrations to it, will be free from all sins and will attain to the supreme Status of Vishnu. **40.** Rama's gracious blessings will be on one, who either himself reads or hears read the whole of this Ramayana with a heart full of devotion. **41.** When Rama, the Supreme Being, the soul of all, is pleased with a person, he attains to whatever he wishes of the four ends of life—Dharma, Artha, Kama and Moksha. **42.** To hear this Ramayana regularly without break, practising austerities, will be conducive to longevity, health and the destruction of the sins of innumerable lives. **43.** By hearing Ramayana, all Devas, planets, Maharshis and Pitris become pleased. **44.** Whoever studies, hears or writes down this ancient and wonderful Text called Adhyatma Ramayana, will obtain renunciation and spiritual enlightenment. They will have no more birth in this Samsara. **45.** This Text was given out by the Supreme Siva to His Consort Parvati, in very clear and unambiguous language, including in it all the most profound truths about Rama, after He had repeatedly thought over the whole of the Veda, and discovered that the Saving Mantra (Taraka Brahma) disclosed in it is Rama, the most esoteric aspect of Vishnu. He has briefly and in clear language stated this discovery of His in this Text.

Appendix

THE ADHYATMA AND THE VALMIKI RAMAYANAS : DIFFERENCES AND DEVIATIONS

It has already been stated in the Introduction that though Ramayana, the famous epic of Valmiki, and the Adhyatma Ramayana deal with the same topic, namely the Rama saga, they are planned from two different points of view—the former to depict Rama as an ideal man while admitting his divinity, and the latter to present him as the Supreme Being incarnate with the full remembrance of his divinity and the recognition of it by all wise men. Despite the unity of the topics the vast difference in their sizes, makes it incumbent for the latter to omit many elaborations, details of incidents, descriptions, conversation etc contained in the former. We are not concerned with all that, but only with certain striking additional features of the Adhyatma that make the spiritual implications of the Rama-incarnation explicit. We shall review the Texts, Kanda by Kanda, concentrating only on the important deviations.

BALA KANDA

1. Both the Texts accept in the beginning that Mahavishnu incarnated Himself in a human body as the son of King Dasaratha at the prayer of Brahma and the Devas for destroying Ravana. But Valmiki hardly alludes to this idea of incarnationhood afterwards until the end, but depicts Rama as a great man and as an exemplar of Dharma. He, however, credits Rama with many achievements impossible for a man and thus indirectly projects his Divinity. The Adhyatma on the other hand harps at every turn on Rama's Incarnationhood, though his character as a devoted adherent of Dharma is not neglected.

2. In the Valmiki, Rama is born as an ordinary human infant. But the Adhyatma presents him at birth as the four-handed Mahavishnu with all the divine emblems. His mother addresses a great hymn to Him, and Mahavishnu tells her of her antecedents and informs her that He has revealed His divine nature at birth itself, so that she may recognise His divinity even in the course of his life as a man. At the mother's request he transforms Himself into a human infant, so that His mother may practise devotion to him through parental love (Vatsalya-bhava).

3. Valmiki's Ramayana has twentyfour thousand verses while the Adhyatma has only 3653 verses.

4. In the Viswamitra episode, Vasishtha does not reveal Rama's divinity to Dasaratha in the Valmiki unlike in the Adhyatma, but advises him only in a general way to send him with Viswamitra.

5. In the Ahalya episode, according to Valmiki, she was converted into an invisible presence by her irate husband, Rishi Gautama, to do penance for her failing. Even before seeing Rama, the effect of the curse is exhausted, and she appears before Rama. It is Rama who does her obeisance as a great ascetic woman. According to the Adhyatma, she had been converted into a rock, and on Rama placing his feet on that rock, she gets her old form. She adores Rama and recites a grand hymn, exhalting him as the Supreme Being Himself.

6. In the encounter with Parasurama, the latter, after his discomfiture, addresses a highly philosophical hymn to Rama, revealing his divinity, according to the Adhyatma. It is not so in the Valmiki. Parasurama offers just a matter of fact farewell to Rama, offering his

submission, and just recognising him as the "Lord of all gods and the slayer of Madhu."

AYODHYA KANDA

1. In the Adhyatma, the section opens with a visit of Narada to Rama to remind him of the purpose of his incarnation, namely, the destruction of Ravana, which will be defeated if he continues to stay at Ayodhya. He chants a highly evocative hymn also. Rama tells him that he remembers his mission very well and that he will contrive to leave Ayodhya the very next day for the forest. All this is unknown to the Valmiki.

2. In the Adhyatma, the Manthara and Kaikeyi episode resulting in the banishment of Rama is accomplished by the Devas through Saraswati possessing the two women, at Rama's will. Valmiki represents it merely as the result of a court intrigue based on Dasaratha's domestic complications.

3. In the Adhyatma, Vasishtha visits Rama to announce the King's decision about his coronation and addresses a hymn to him expounding his Divinity. This is not given in the Valmiki. Only after Kaikeyi's obstruction of the coronation, Sumantra is sent to inform Rama of the King's decision to exile him.

4. In the Valmiki, to appease Lakshmana's wrath at the injustice of his father's decision, Rama only speaks to him briefly about Destiny and gives him some general advice. But in the Adhyatma this advice forms an elaborate philosophical discourse, the first of the Lakshmanopadesas of this Text.

5. In the Valmiki there is no lecture, as in the Adhyatma, on the Divinity of Rama by Vamadeva to appease the sorrow-stricken citizenry of Ayodhya on the announcement of the order for the exile of Rama to the forest.

6. In the Valmiki there is no philsophical discourse given by Lakshmana to Guha, as in the Adhyatma.

7. In the Valmiki, Rama is found indulging in a bitter lamentation over his misfortune to be an exile in the forest. This being a weakness, it has no place in the Adhyatma.

8. In the Valmiki,on Rama's arrival at Bharadwaja's Ashrma, he is only repectfully received by the sage, but he recites no hymn on Rama's divinity as in the Adhyatma. He only directs Rama to Chitrakuta as a fit place to stay in.

9. In the Valmiki, Rama's arrival at Valmiki's Ashrama is only just mentioned. In the Adhyatma it forms an elaborate section containing an evocative hymn addressed to Rama, and an account of Valmiki's evil past and his redemption by the power of Rama's name. All this is unknown to Valmiki's Ramayana.

10. In the Valmiki, Bharata is finally persuaded to return by Rama's most appealing persuasion. In the Adhyatma, however, when Bharata threatens fast unto death, Rama, by a sign of his eyes, requests Vasishtha to intervene, and Vasishtha, taking Bharata aside, reveals to him the Divinity of Rama, and informs him that the purpose of his coming to the forest is to achieve the destruction of Ravana, the object of his incarnation.

11. In the Adhyatma, Kaikeyi apologises to Rama at Chitrakuta, and recognising his divinity, asks him for spiritual counselling. Rama gives her a long devotional discourse. All this is unknown to Valmiki's Ramayana, where she makes a formal reconciliation with Rama, chiefly because her own son Bharata is mortally offended with her because of her conduct.

12. In the Valmiki, the great sage Atri receives Rama as a great and noble king, does hospitality, and introduces Sita to his wife Anasuya. But he shows no signs of recognition of Rama as the Divine incarnate, as in the Adhyatma.

ARANYA KANDA

1. The destruction of Viradha, the first incident in this Kanda, is described somewhat

differently in the two Ramayanas. Both state that he was a Gandharva become Rakshasa under a curse. In the Valmiki, as he could not be killed by weapons, he is buried in a deep pit. But in the Adhyatma, he is killed by weapons. He then regains his Gandharva form and praises Rama as the very Divinity in one of the most fervent hymns in the Text.

2. Much of the narrative in this Kanda consists of Rama's travel to the Ashramas of several famous sages, seeking advice for a suitable place of residence. Thus he visits the Ashrama of Sarabhanga, Sutikshna and Agastya. In Valmiki's account all these Rishis welcome Rama and receive him as a great ruler come to rid the forest occupied by Rishis, of the Rakshasas infesting them. But none of them addresses him as Divinity incarnate. For example, the sage Agastya receives him cordially with such words as: "........You are the king of all the worlds and a faithful adherent of Dharma and a great car-warrior too. You are a welcome guest who deserves to be shown all honour and deference." But in the Adhyatma all these sages receive Rama as Vishnu Incarnate and address highly fervent and in some cases, as in that of Agastya, highly philosophical hymns, which form one of the most attractive features of the Adhyatma Ramayana.

3. After settling down at Panchavati on Agastya's advice, Lakshmaṇa, according to the Adhyatma, asks Rama to instruct him on the means of attaining salvation. Rama then gives him an elaborate discourse on Jnana and Bhakti, conveying the quintessence of Vedanta. This is unknown to Valmiki's Text.

4. Before Ravana approaches Maricha to assume the shape of a golden deer and decoy Rama by his movements as the step preparatory to the abduction of Sita, Ravana, according to the Adhyatma Ramayana. soliloquises to the effect that Rama must be Vishnu incarnate come to destroy him, that destruction at Rama's hand is an easier way of gaining salvation than through spritual practices, and that by abducting Sita, he could provoke Rama to fight and kill him soon and thus enable him to attain salvation. Thus from the very start Ravana is introduced as one practising Vidvesha-Bhakti or devotion through confrontation. This attitude of Ravana is frequently alluded to in the Adhyatma with the progress of the narrative. This is a feature unknown to Valmiki, who depicts Ravana as really lusting after Sita and fighting to death for getting the prize of a Sita.

5. According to the Adhyatma, unknown to Lakshmana, Rama informs Sita that Ravana will be coming to abduct her, and that therefore he is handing her over to the Fire-deity Agni for safe custody till he takes her back again. In her place a double of Sita is left in the Ashrama, and it is this illusory Sita that Ravana abducts. This is unknown to the Valmiki, according to which it is the real Sita who is abudcted.

6. In the Valmiki, Ravana carries away Sita lifting her by her locks by one hand and holding her thighs with the other. But the Adhyatma, in spite of the fact that it is not the real Sita but her double that is being carried away, makes Ravana scoop the earth where Sita is standing, and take the whole of that scooped up earth away without touching Sita. This is done to safeguard Sita from the polluting touch of Ravana, and to show his diguised devotion to her.

7. According to the Adhyatma, Rama after killing Maricha and before meeting Lakshmana, soliloquizes that he will thereafter be lamenting bitterly over Sita's loss like any infatuated lover, just to make all believe that he is only a man. There are many places thereafter where Rama laments over Sita. All these according to Valmiki, however, are real lamentations, and they are elaborated in a touching manner with great poetic beauty.

8. In the Valmiki, Jatayu after meeting Rama and giving him some information about Sita, dies peacefully and attains to heaven. But in the Adhyatma, he appears in a divine form and recites a highly evocative hymn on the

Divinity of Rama in which Bhakti and Advaitic philosophy are blended.

9. Regarding the destruction of Kabandha, the accounts in both are mostly the same except that the Adhyatma puts a great hymn in praise of Rama in the mouth of regeneràted Kabandha, while in the Valmiki it is not there. On the other hand, he advises Rama to make friends with Sugreeva and gives details about the place when Sugreeva could be met. In both,Rama is asked to meet the woman ascetic Sabari in a nearby place at Pampa.

10. Sabari, an ascetic of low origin but possessed of great spiritual illumination, receives Rama with great respect. While in the Valmiki there is only a veiled reference to Rama's divinity in the talk of Sabari with him, in the Adhyatma, she praises him as the Supreme Being in a great hymn. Rama gives her a discourse on Bhakti and Jnana. According to the Adhyatma, it is Sabari who first tells Rama about Sugreeva and informs him that Sita is confined in Ravana's palace.

KISHKINDHA KANDA

1. After the destruction of Vali, his wife Tara's lament is given in both the Ramayanas. In the Valmiki, it is Hanuman who consoles her. Rama talks only very little to her. In the Adhyatma, however, Rama gives her an elaborate advice on the philosophy of Vedanta and the practice of devotion, besides consoling her.

2. In the Adhyatma, while Rama is staying at Mount Pravarshana after the coronation of Sugreeva, he gives an elaborate discourse to Lakshmana on the ritualistic worship of Mahavishnu (i.e. Himself), thus revealing his identity with the Supreme Being openly. This is absent in the Valmiki; but in its place there are elaborate descriptions of landscape and Nature's seasonal beauty as also piteous lamentations of Rama over the lost Sita, like that of any loving husband.

3. In the Adhyatma, Svayamprabha comes to meet Rama and offers him devoted worship and recites a hymn addressed to him, identifying him with the Supreme Being and displaying much philosophic wisdom and devotional fervour. After that, she goes to Badari on Rama's advice and attains Mukti there. All this is absent in the Valmiki. She shows great hospitality to the monkeys and continues to remain in her cave, performing Tapas. She does not meet Rama.

4. In the Adhyatma, Sampati gives an elaborate philosophical discourse to the monkeys who meet him, quoting what he has heard from sage Chandramas. This is absent in the Valmiki.

SUNDARA KANDA

1. In the Adhyatma, Ravana is depicted as sorrowing in mind that in spite of his having abducted Sita, Rama has not yet come to kill him. For, as has already been stated before, Ravana's sole object in abducting Sita, is to hasten his own death at Rama's hands, so that through the practice of devotion through confrontation, he may get liberation more quickly than through worship. In the midst of such anxious thought, one day he falls asleep at night and has a dream of an emissary of Rama coming as a small monkey to discover Sita, and of that monkey as hiding on the Simsapa tree to observe what is happening with Sita. Ravana thinks that this dream must be factual. He therefore feels that if he now goes to Sita and speaks harsh words to her, the monkey will hear it and report it to Rama, and Rama, on knowing the miserable condition of Sita, will hasten to come to her rescue. This is why he comes to Sita before daybreak with a retinue of women and makes advances to Sita and afterwards threatens to eat her up while Hanuman is watching from above on the Simsapa tree. Thus the Adhyatma tries to project Ravana as a covert devotee and not as one really meaning any offence to Sita. All this is unknown to the Valmiki, who depicts Ravana

as truly infatuated with Sita and longing to consort with her. This is made very plain in the Valmiki in a later context in the Yuddha Kanda when Ravana is asked by one of his lieutenants why he is not using force on Sita and consort with her. Ravana replies that once he did so in the past with an Apsara woman with whom he was infatuated, and he was cursed by Brahma that if he did so with another woman in future, his head would burst.

2. When Hanuman finally meets Ravana face to face, he gives the latter an elaborate advice on the philosophy of the Atman, the means of salvation, the conduct of righteousness etc. All this is absent in the Valmiki.

YUDDHA KANDA

1. On reaching the seashore Rama, in Valmiki, indulges in a bitter lamentation over Sita just like a passionate lover. The Adhyatma merely mentions that he lamented but immediately explains it away as an appearance only, attributed to him by ignorant men. It does not want to admit any human weakness in Rama, while Valmiki's effort is to show Rama as an embodiment of Dharma (Rightenousness) while being human. Valmiki's idea in such contexts as this, where he paints Rama with human imperfections, seems to be that when God becomes man, just as his body is subject to some of the human imperfections even amidst various excellences, so also is the case with his mind. He seems to think that Rama is the embodiment of Dharma, no doubt, but that does not mean that he need be free from all human weaknesses. He does not believe in giving an alibi for such weaknesses. A very clear and unambiguous expression of Valmiki in this respect will be described towards the end of the epic where Sita enters into fire. The Adhyatma on the other hand wants to highlight Rama's Divinity and explain away whatever human imperfections are found.

2. A conspicuous addition in the Adhyatma is Rama's installation of the Sivalinga Ramewara, before the construction of Setu (a bund or causeway), for the success of the enterprise, as also his declaration about the method and merits of pilgrimage to Ramaswara and Setubandha,for the information of the large number of pilgrims who, he forecastes, are bound to visit them in future. There is absolutely no mention about all this in the Valimiki, except of the construction of the Setu.

But, according to Valmiki, while Rama is returning from Lanka in the Pushpaka with Sita, among the places he shows to her, the Setubandha too finds a place, and he describes it as a future holy pilgrimage centre of great potency. He also says: "It was the place where the 'Great God', the mighty Lord, shed His grace on me." But whether this has any reference to installing Rameśwara is uncertain.

3. In the Adhyatma, when Vibheeshana comes and takes shelter under Rama, he recites a great philosophical and devotional hymn on Rama, on the same pattern as the hymns in other places. In the Valmiki it is not there.

4. In both the Valmiki and the Adhyatma, the Sea-deity Varuna submits to Rama only when threatened. But in the Valmiki, Rama observes fast and prayer for three days, after which only he threatens Varuṇa. The Adhyatma does not admit that Rama thus tried to please Varuna by becoming a votary for a time. Besides, when Varuna comes before Rama in submission, he recites a devotional hymn on Rama, according to the Adhyatma.

5. In the Adhyatma the spy Suka sermonises to Ravana, but in the Valmiki, he only gives an impressive report of Rama's strength which annoys Ravana. Besides, the Adhyatma gives a long account of the previous history of Suka which has no place in the Valmiki.

6. In the Valmiki, Malyavan only speaks to Ravana of the threatening portents seen, and strongly advises him to restore Sita but does not expatiate on Rama's divinity as in the Adhyatma.

7. In the description of the war there are many minor differences in details. Valmiki's being a more elaborate work, there are many more details and descriptions. We shall note here only a few deviations of significance. In the Valmiki, Meghanada binds and renders unconscious both Rama and Lakshmana with Naga (snake) missile. They are ultimately released from it and saved only by Garuda (the holy Eagle-mount of Viṣhnu) coming to the scene and destroying the snakes by directing his inherent power against the serpents, his natural antagonists. And Garuda addresses Rama as 'Comrade'. Further he tells him, "You should not be too curious to know how we happen to be friends. You will know about it when you have achieved your end in the war." This answer is very significant. In fact Rama being the incarnation of Vishnu, Garuda the mount of Vishnu, is only a humble servant of his. But Rama, according to Valmiki, is unconscious of his real identity until Brahma reveals it to him at the end. Garuda is now referring to this future revelation here. From this and the general treatment given earlier, according to the Valmiki, the incarnate Rama is not aware of his divinity till the end when Brahma imparts that knowledge to him.

In the Adhyatma this incident of Meghanada's victory over Rama and Lakshmana is described in an entirely different manner. It is with the Brahma missile and not the Naga that Meghananda binds Rama and Lakshmana and renders them unconscious. But Rama, being divine, recovers very soon, but not Lakshmana and others. To revive them Hanuman is sent to the Himalayas to get *Mrtasanjivani*, a herb that can revive one almost dead. Ravana comes to know of it and sends Kalanemi to obstruct Hanuman. This Kalanemi episode is given a very elaborate treatment in the Adhyatma, but there is not even a trace of it in the Valmiki. As the description of this event is different in the two Ramayana, the Adhyatma makes no mention of Garuda's visit and conversation with Rama.

8. In both the Adhyatma and in the Valmiki, Kumbhakarna chides Ravana. In Valmiki this chiding is only to the effect that he has been following wrong policies on the advice of cowardly and time-serving ministers and has thus brought himself to the present situation. But in the Adhyatma he speaks about Rama's divinity and advises Ravana to practise devotion in place of going to fight with Rama. This, of course, is not relished by Ravana.

9. In the Adhyatma there is a highly philosophic hymn by Narada addressed to Rama after the destruction of Kumbhakarna and before that of Indrajit. This is unknown to the Valmiki.

10. According to the Adhyatma, Lakshmana's special qualification for being deputed to confront and kill Indrajit, is that he has been observing fast and night vigil for the past twelve years. Indrajit could be killed only by such a person. There is no such reference in the Valmiki.

11. Indrajit kills a Maya Sita. Rama, failing to understand that it is an illusion created by black magic, falls into a depression and indulges in deep mourning, until Vibheeshana enlightens him about the illusory nature of the event. This has no place in the Adhyatma.

12. In the final fight between Rama and Ravana, there are several important differences between the Adhyatma and the Valmiki. In the Adhyatma, before the battle starts, Ravana begins a fire-rite for performing black magic on the advice of his Guru, Sukra, for gaining invincibility in battle. This rite is obstructed by the monkey forces. When they find that no amount of personal attack would distract Ravana from his concentration in the performance of the prescribed rite, they drag all the womenfolk of Ravana before him and begin to disrobe and insult them, especially, Ravana's chief queen Mandodari. Their cries and appeals make Ravana stop the rites and come out for battle. No such incident is described in the Valmiki.

13. After the above incident, there is, in the Adhyatma, an elaborate piece of advice given by Mandodari to Ravana on the Divinity of Rama, where she describes him as one among the list of incarnations. Ravana also admits his divinity, but adds that he has been following the course of confrontation with him in order to hasten his own slaughter at his hands and thus gain salvation early. All this is unknown to the Valmiki.

14. In the Adhyatma, Rama in the course of the fight cuts down the ten heads of Ravana, but they grow up again. Thus a hundred heads are cut, but still Ravana remains intact. Then Vibheeshana informs him that this was the effect of a boon given to him by Brahma. Further he is informed that Ravana has Amrita deposited in his umbelicus, and that until it is removed his puissance will not abate. Rama cuts his umbelicus with an arrow, and thereafter he is able to cut the heads and arms of Ravana. Ravana's power also decreases and he is killed with Brahma missile.

In the Valmiki the course of events is somewhat different. There is no mention of Amrita being deposited in the umbelicus of Ravana. When Rama stands perplexed to note that Ravana's power is unabating, the sage Agastya makes his appearance and advices Rama to recite the Mantra Aditya-hridaya for invoking the Sun-Diety. By doing so, the puissance of Rama is enhanced and victory comes to him soon. Finally he kills Ravana by splitting his chest with the Brahma missile.

15. According to the Adhyatma, on the death of Ravana, his spirit, having the luminosity of lightning, enters into Rama and attains salvation, to the utter astonishment of the Devas and the Rishis watching the course of the battle. To the astonished Devas, Narada gives the explanation of this apparently most cruel and violent tyrant of a Rakshasa gaining salvation. The explanation is that Ravana is a devotee at heart, practising what is known in devotional ideology as *Vidveṣa-bhakti* or devotion through confrontation. He knows that Rama is Mahavishnu and wants to get salvation easily by slaughter at his hands. Through the antagonism he developed towards Rama, he has constantly been thinking of him with an intensity of thought that even worshippers seldom have. Such concentration, being on the Lord, is enough to purify a man. And finally, by meeting death at Rama's hands, Ravana becomes eligible for immediate salvation. All these ideas have no place in Valmiki's Ramayana.

16. The sensational incident after Ravana's death, is Sita subjecting herself to ordeal by fire with the tacit approval of Rama. The main incident is the same in both the Ramayanas, but there are very significant variations in details and the context of events. In the Adhyatma, which wants to project Rama's divinity and explain away any expression of imperfection in him, the fire ordeal is only a ruse staged in order to replace the illusory or Maya Sita who has been substituted at Janasthana in the place of the real Sita, who has been entrusted by Rama to the care and custody of the Fire-deity. When the Maya Sita enters into the fire, the real Sita is brought out by the Fire-deity. But this is a secret known to Rama only and the whole event is given the appearance of a real ordeal.

In the Valmiki the ordeal is a real ordeal, as there is no place for Maya Sita in it. What is more, the ordeal becomes necessary, because Rama rejects Sita in very harsh terms, felt as extremely cruel by every one in that vast assembly. When Sita comes to meet Rama on being released from Ravana's palace, and stands before him, he speaks the following harsh words with a frown on his face: "Sita! I have done what a man should do to avenge the humiliation that has been heaped upon him. I have wrested you out of the enemy. Now know that I fought this tremendous war with the help of the heroic monkey forces, not for your sake, but to vindicate the honour of myself and the great royal family to which I belong. Your presence is unbearable to me as your conduct is suspect. Ravana would not have left you alone. You have been living in the Rakshasa's harem and have felt his obscene touch and his wicked gaze. I have therefore no use for you. You are free to go anywhere; all the ten directions are open to you. Or you may choose any one else and go to live with him—Lakshmana, Bharata, Sugreeva, Vibheeshana or anyone who appeals to you." These words are surprising and puzzling in the mouth of a Rama who was till now weeping and pining for Sita like an ardent lover from time to time. After Sita enters into the fire to prove her innocence and purity, the Devas, surprised at Rama's conduct, gather round him, and praying to him with folded hands and addressing him as the creator of the worlds, say: "How could you remain indifferent when Sita entered into the fire? How is it that you do not realise you are the first of the Deities, and that you existed when the worlds were naught and before they came into being? And yet you repudiate Sita like an ordinary mortal."

At this point, Valmiki, in consistency with his depiction of Rama's character, puts in his mouth a reply that would be surprising to many. He says, "I look upon myself as a man named Rama, born as Dasaratha's son. Be pleased to tell me my antecedents and why I am here." Then Brahma comes forward and reminds him that he is Narayana Himself, and then proceeds, to describe elaborately His divine majesties, attributes and cosmic functions. Finally he tells Him that in order to destroy Ravana he has assumed this human form and has now accomplished that purpose.

All this is absent in the Adhyatma. About Rama's harsh speech to Sita before the fire ordeal, the Adhyatma merely refers to it as something that should not have been said—*avācyam*. This seems to indicate that not only the Devas and others but even the author of the Adhyatma Ramayana, who everywhere projects the divinity of Rama, disapproves of this rank behaviour of Rama to Sita. The Deities like Brahma, Indra and others do come in the Adhyatma after Sita's entry into fire. They arrive only to witness her restoration by the Fire-deity, and then sing hymns of praise on Rama one after another.

This context explains Valmiki's conception of Rama as an incarnation. He refers to his divinity clearly when Mahavishnu promises to be born as man under the name of Rama, to destroy Ravana and also at the close of Ramayana proper, i.e. at the end of Yuddha Kanda. When born as man, he seems to have been unaware of his divinity, as he himself admits in the passage quoted above, and it requires Brahma to bring it back to his mind at the end of his mission of destroying Ravana. So also, all through his career, hardly any one, including the sages of Trikūta, Dandakaranya etc., seems to have recognised him as Divine. They all look upon him as a highly respected prince come to rid the settlements of the Rishis of the menance of Rakshasas. But the Adhyatma's attitude in this respect is quite the reverse. Rama at his very birth reveals himself as Mahavishnu, and all the sages like Viswamitra and, those whom he meets at Trikuta, Janasthana etc., were aware of his divinity. Even Ravana knows his divinity, and it is this knowledge that prompts him to cultivate antagonism to Rama as a means for easy salvation through *Vidveṣa-bhakti* or devotion through confrontation.

17. In the Valmiki there is no devotional hymn offered by sage Bharadwaja to Rama on his way to Ayodhya, as in the Adhyatma. In both the Texts, Rama stops at the sage's Ashrama and accepts his hospitality for the night. In addition, according to Valmiki, the sage offers a boon to Rama and Rama chooses the blessing that all the trees over a distance of the three Yojanas they have yet to traverse, may become fruit-laden and honey-yielding, so that his monkey followers may feast on them.